DO YOU WANT TO BE HAPPY AND WRITE?

Do You Want to Be Happy and Write?

Critical Essays on Michael Ondaatje

Edited by Robert Lecker

McGill-Queen's University Press
Montreal & Kingston • London • Chicago

© McGill-Queen's University Press 2023

ISBN 978-0-2280-1876-6 (cloth)
ISBN 978-0-2280-1903-9 (paper)
ISBN 978-0-2280-1996-1 (ePDF)
ISBN 978-0-2280-1997-8 (ePUB)

Legal deposit third quarter 2023
Bibliothèque nationale du Québec

Printed in Canada on acid-free paper that is 100% ancient forest free (100% post-consumer recycled), processed chlorine free

This book has been published with the help of a grant from the Canadian Federation for the Humanities and Social Sciences, through the Awards to Scholarly Publications Program, using funds provided by the Social Sciences and Humanities Research Council of Canada.

We acknowledge the support of the Canada Council for the Arts.
Nous remercions le Conseil des arts du Canada de son soutien.

Library and Archives Canada Cataloguing in Publication

Title: Do you want to be happy and write? : critical essays on Michael Ondaatje / edited by Robert Lecker.
Other titles: Critical essays on Michael Ondaatje
Names: Lecker, Robert, 1951– editor.
Description: Includes bibliographical references and index.
Identifiers: Canadiana (print) 20230218695 | Canadiana (ebook) 20230218709 | ISBN 9780228019039 (paper) | ISBN 9780228018766 (cloth) | ISBN 9780228019978 (ePUB) | ISBN 9780228019961 (ePDF)
Subjects: LCSH: Ondaatje, Michael, 1943—Criticism and interpretation. | LCGFT: Literary criticism.
Classification: LCC PS8529.N283 Z65 2023 | DDC C813/.54—dc23

This book was typeset in 10.5/13 Sabon.

Contents

Acknowledgments   ix

Introduction   3
Robert Lecker

POETRY

1 "dancing new / on this terrific ancient earth": Michael Ondaatje's Astonishing Poetics of Renewal   45
Di Brandt

2 Restlessness, Vertigo: Michael Ondaatje's Poetry   77
Karen Solie

3 Strange Familiars: Dogs in Michael Ondaatje's Early Poetry   100
Antje M. Rauwerda

4 The Scent of Paradise: Michael Ondaatje's "The Cinnamon Peeler"   118
Ulla Ratheiser

5 The Pivot: Michael Ondaatje's *Tin Roof*   130
Ian Rae

VISUALITY

6 "The illusion of the unexceptional": Michael Ondaatje as Editor   155
Allan Hepburn

7 Michael Ondaatje in the Cinema   174
Bart Testa

vi Contents

8 "Landscapes and stories flung into branches": The Photography
of Affect and Transnational Mobility in the Writings of
Michael Ondaatje 191
Lorraine York

INTERMEDIALITY

9 Creases and Broken Glass: Michael Ondaatje's Narrative and
Intermediality 211
Serena Fusco

10 Intermedial Aesthetics in *The Cat's Table* 228
Birgit Neumann

NOVELS AND NARRATIVES

11 Fascination and Liminality in Michael Ondaatje's *Coming
Through Slaughter* 247
Winfried Siemerling

12 "The animal out of the desert": The Nomadic Metaphysics of
Michael Ondaatje's *In the Skin of a Lion* 263
Jody Mason

13 Love, War, and the Other in Emmanuel Levinas, Jacques Derrida,
and Michael Ondaatje: *The English Patient* as the Dialogic Field 282
Kai-su Wu

14 Reconfiguring an East-West Dialectic of Trauma in Michael Ondaatje's
War Novels: *The English Patient*, *Anil's Ghost*, and *Warlight* 299
Justin M. Hewitson

15 Wartime Ghosts: War and the Liminal in *The English Patient*,
Anil's Ghost, and *Warlight* 317
Martin Löschnigg

ENDINGS

16 The Dead That Haunt *Anil's Ghost*: Subaltern Difference and
Postcolonial Melancholia 335
Mrinalini Chakravorty

17 Casualties of Love 355
Pico Iyer

18 Ondaatje's Late Style 366
Moez Surani

Contents   vii

19   "That eventual stranger": Toward Unrecognizability in *Warlight*   379
   Joel Deshaye

20   Teaching Ondaatje: Learning to Live   396
   Elias Schwieler

Works by Michael Ondaatje   413
Bibliography   417
Contributors   443
Index   447

Acknowledgments

I think of this book as a team effort from start to finish. My aim was to bring together a group of international writers and critics who would offer fresh insights into Michael Ondaatje's poetry and fiction. I was so lucky to be able to work with such an eclectic group of contributors. My sincere thanks to every one of them for producing excellent work while also respecting the inevitable deadlines and requests for information. I also want to express my appreciation to the team at McGill-Queen's University Press and especially to Editor-in-Chief Jonathan Crago, who was so helpful to me from the day I signed my contract right up to production time. Jonathan was both an anchor and an experienced editor who helped me understand more about the book and its shape and intentions. I am also grateful to Managing Editor Kathleen Fraser and Associate Managing Editor Lisa Aitken for seeing the book through production and for keeping everything on track. My very special thanks go to Sylvia Vance, copy-editor *par excellence*, who made sense of twenty-one voices that might have sounded much more cacophonous without her patience and profound expertise. In addition, I am grateful to Judy Dunlop for her incredibly detailed indexing and to Dorothy Turnbull for her eagle eye in the final stage of copy-editing prior to publication. Finally, I love the cover. Thank you to Jeremy John Parker, an amazing designer.

DO YOU WANT TO BE HAPPY AND WRITE?

Introduction

Robert Lecker

1

Near the beginning of Michael Ondaatje's *Tin Roof*, his long confessional poem set amidst the "pale blue waves" and the "black shore of volcanic rock" that mark the Hawaiian island of Maui, the speaker (he is a writer) pauses his account to picture "A man buying wine / Rainier beer at the store" (CP, 107). The quotidian image invokes a crucial poetic connection, for the name of the beer also reminds him of Rainer Maria Rilke and of all the solitude, joy, and pain that Rilke associated with the nature of poetic vision. A few lines later, the writer asks himself a central question, also inspired by Rilke: "Do you want / to be happy and write?" (CP, 105). This is not a question posed by some generic narrator. Ondaatje may at times distance himself from his speaker, but more often than not he invites us to see this poem as a portrait of himself, in crisis. In a reference to the *Duino Elegies*, Ondaatje writes, "Oh, Rilke, I want to sit down calm like you / or pace the castle" (CP, 122), just as Rilke did when he began to compose his elegies at Duino Castle in 1912. Ondaatje's fascination with Rilke is not new:

> I have circled your book for years
> like a wave combing
> the green hair of the sea
> kept it with me, your name
> a password in the alley.
> I always wanted poetry to be that
> but this solitude brings no wisdom

just two day old food in the fridge,
certain habits you would not approve of. (CP, 122)

Elsewhere in *Tin Roof*, Ondaatje refers to Rilke's "lovely letters" (CP, 123) and to the advice he gave the young poet he corresponded with between 1903 and 1908. In the first of his *Letters to a Young Poet*, Rilke advises Franz Xaver Kappus on how to write authentically:

Go inside yourself. Discover the motive that bids you write; examine whether it sends its roots down to the deepest places of your heart, confess to yourself whether you would have to die if writing were denied you. This before all: ask yourself in the quietest hour of your night: *must* I write? Dig down into yourself for a deep answer. And if this should be in the affirmative, if you may meet this solemn question with a strong and simple "*I must*," then build your life according to this necessity; your life must, right to its most unimportant and insignificant hour, become a token and a witness of this impulse.[1]

"Do you want to be happy and write?" is the question that arises as Ondaatje explores the complex motives that bind him to the poetic act. The question is existential, central, life-defining. It carries with it a sense of Rilke's proximity to the double-sided crisis that unfolds in Ondaatje's poem as he contemplates the dissolution of his marriage, his first encounters with a new lover, and his sense that he is split deeply enough to picture himself as an other: "he is joyous and breaking down. / The tug over the cliff" (CP, 107). In confronting his own depths, his own otherness, Ondaatje pays heed to one more aspect of Rilke's advice: "to go into yourself and to explore the depths whence your life wells forth; at its source you will find the answer to the question whether you *must* create."[2]

Ondaatje's career provides evidence of his response to this ongoing question. Yes, he *must* create, but the nature of that creation is constantly modified as he searches for the forms appropriate to his evolving sense of what it means to be a writer. As a confessional poem, *Tin Roof* exemplifies the kind of formal changes Ondaatje experimented with in the 1980s. As Ian Rae observes in his essay in this collection, "Ondaatje, by the 1980s, is an accomplished writer but unhappy, veering into the kind of 'terrible acute hatred / of his own privacy' that drives Ondaatje's father Mervyn to drink and an early death in 'Letters & Other Worlds.'" By 1982, with the publication of *Tin Roof*, "Ondaatje's domestic crisis causes him to spurn the modernist promise of aesthetic domination of the world through the word, represented for Ondaatje by the poetry of Wallace Stevens, and to move tentatively into the vulnerable and subjective territory of confessional verse" (132).

As many of the essays in this volume show, Ondaatje's power as a writer lies in his ability to undermine his own narratives, to cast shadow on the validity of the narrative act. This kind of self-referentiality is not strictly a feature of Ondaatje's interest in postmodernism, although he certainly aligned himself with many of the postmodern values first identified by Linda Hutcheon in her essay on Canadian historiographic metafiction, published in 1984 and still salient. Hutcheon notes that for the metafictional writer, both reader and author become engaged in "the processes involved in what in French is called the *énonciation*, the entire context of the production and reception of the text."[3] She emphasizes the way in which this departure from a mimetic model involves a shift in our conception of history: "What is perhaps most interesting about this emphasis on the complex situation of the *énonciation* is the way in which this kind of metafiction thematizes its own interaction both with the historical past and with the historically conditioned expectations of its readers."[4] Ondaatje's self-reflective writing process inevitably involves him in questions about the nature of history, ideology, and social order, for as Hutcheon says,

> in a very real sense history, while it had a real referent once upon a time, is only accessible to us in textualized form. Therefore the historiographic metafictionist who also deals with "events *already constituted*" but who "self-consciously signals their textual nature within his novel is perhaps in an even more difficult position than the historian: he is constrained by the demands of narrative fiction as much as by those of history's events. He must deal with literature's intertexts as well as history's documents."[5]

2

The essays collected here address many of those intertexts and historical narratives. Together, they form a conversation about the range of Michael Ondaatje's work, from his early poetry, published when he was a student at Bishop's University in the early 1960s to his later poetry and fiction, which reflect his broadening interest in moral and aesthetic questions related to the representation of war, genocide, diasporic consciousness, and transnational values. I also envisioned this collection both as a scholarly tribute and as a critical assessment of Ondaatje's eminent career.

Although this collection devotes considerable space to Ondaatje's later fiction, it also builds upon important critical commentary that laid the foundations for more recent critical inquiry. Central to this earlier commentary are the first collection of essays on Ondaatje's work – *Spider Blues* (1985), edited by Sam Solecki, later augmented by a special issue of *Essays on Canadian Writing* (1994), guest-edited by Karen E. Smythe; *Reconstructing the Fragments of Michael Ondaatje's Works*, edited by Jean-Michel Lacroix (1999); and Steven Tötösy de Zepetnek's *Comparative Cultural Studies and Michael Ondaatje's Writing* (2005). This volume is also indebted to a number of central studies that define many of the complex issues that distinguish Ondaatje's works. These include books by Dennis Lee (1977), Douglas Barbour (1993), Annick Hillger (2006), and Lee Spinks (2009). Some of the earliest commentary on Ondaatje remains crucial, including articles by Stephen Scobie (1972, 1978), Sheila Watson (1972), Frank Davey (1974), Sam Solecki (1978, 1983), Perry Nodelman (1980), T.D. MacLulich (1981). J.E. Chamberlin (1983), Smaro Kamboureli (1983), and Ann Wilson (1983). Any study of Michael Ondaatje's work also needs to acknowledge the formative influence of Coach House Press and its "patron saint," poet bpNichol, along with Stan Bevington and Victor Coleman, both of whom make appearances in the radical poetic manifesto that emerges in Ondaatje's "'the gate in his head.'" In editing this volume, I was also influenced by the only book-length biography of Ondaatje to appear to date, Ed Jewinski's readable and informative *Express Yourself Beautifully* (1994).

While the early influences and commentary on Michael Ondaatje's work was authored primarily by Canadian critics, the last two decades have been marked by a steady increase in international attention to his oeuvre, and particularly to his fiction. This collection emphasizes the transnational status of Ondaatje's art. It brings together a diverse range of international critics whose work demonstrates the extent to which Ondaatje's writing has long transcended its Canadian roots. They take the stage and direct us to the transcultural and transhistorical dimensions of Ondaatje's poetry and fiction.

Introduction 7

Does this widespread attention by international critics indicate that a fundamental shift has occurred in the way Ondaatje is viewed as an author? I believe that it signals a profound shift in his status; he now has dedicated readers all over the world. Ondaatje's importance as an author can be measured in several ways. There are the kinds of affirmation that are publicly canonical – for example, the fact that he was chosen as the winner of the Golden Man Booker Prize in 2018 (a special one-off prize awarded in commemoration of the 50th anniversary of the Booker Prize) or the fact that his 2007 novel, *Divisadero*, won the Governor-General's Award for that year. As one of the early (but unnamed) reviewers of this book noted, "while the era of evaluative criticism may be officially over, a volume like this exists because judgments – aesthetic, cultural, political, and historical – are being made." One of my judgments, as editor, is that Ondaatje's writing is unique. In his review of *Divisadero* included in this volume, Pico Iyer notes one of the characteristics that mark this uniqueness: "Part of the great delight of reading one of his books, therefore, comes in the sensation of a deeply curious traveler opening out his worn suitcase and letting all the odd pieces of information or memorable lines or exotic bric-a-brac he's collected tumble out" (360). In a review of *Divisadero* in *The New Yorker*, Louis Menand identifies another aspect of Ondaatje's work that makes it unique:

> There is a method of story writing that involves stripping the tale of every extraneous detail *plus one*, so that the nonextraneous bit becomes, in the reader's imagination, the piece that might explain everything. It's a formula for ambiguity. Kipling was expert at this; so was Hemingway. But ambiguity is virtually integral to literary expression – ambiguity, uncertainty, indeterminacy are ways that fictional texts mean what they mean. Ondaatje is doing something else. He is trying to change the medium.[6]

The same might be said about Ondaatje's poetry. Why is it different? Why does it deserve the kind of attention this collection gives it? One answer is provided by contributor Karen Solie: "In the simultaneity of the beautiful and awkward, the formed and shapeless, language, that third component, illuminates the difference between what is and could be. Between the clear and unclear the territory of difference expands. In it, both are true. A verb moves between them.

A lot of good poetry lives in this kind of zone. But few poets have found as many ways to inhabit it as Ondaatje" (79).

If international commentary on Ondaatje's work (predominantly his fiction) has increased so dramatically, it is because scholars understand that Ondaatje has changed the medium, as Menand says. But it is also because of the kinds of issues Ondaatje deals with in his fiction. Whereas the early poetry is about the self-reflexive artist and his vision of how poetry works, the later fiction demonstrates Ondaatje's widening interest in the construction of identity; the nature of memory and its relation to family origins and history; the contrast between Eastern and Western values and the southeast Asian diaspora; the role of the writer in depicting war, psychic trauma, and genocidal atrocities; the presentation of the human body as a site of contestation and struggle; the illumination of postcolonial consciousness in an increasingly transnational era; and the extent to which the contemporary writer is called upon to bear witness to the age. Few of these issues are discussed in early criticism of Ondaatje's work.

I want this collection to capture the kinds of transnational interests that have become increasingly apparent in Ondaatje's novels. I sought out international and domestic critics who spoke to those interests. But at the same time, as noted earlier, there is a bifurcation in the study of Ondaatje's oeuvre. His early novels and poetry are the subject of mainly Canadian scholarship. A collection that omitted that early commentary entirely would effectively erase the representation of that Ondaatje scholarship. By the same token, a collection that focused too much on the early scholarship would deprive the collection of some of the more recent criticism by international writers who often see Ondaatje's works from an entirely different perspective. In structuring the volume, I tried to achieve a balance that would represent both the early excellent scholarship devoted to the first few decades of Ondaatje's career as well as the more recent international scholarship, which tends to focus on the later fiction. This means, for example, that in addition to including one of the most informative analyses of *Coming Through Slaughter* (Winfried Siemerling's essay) or Ulla Ratheiser's postcolonial reading of "The Cinnamon Peeler," I also include new essays on some of the earlier poetry (Ian Rae's compelling reading of *Tin Roof*, Di Brandt's visceral and lyrical overview of Ondaatje's poetic trajectory, Karen Solie's transforming response to a renowned poet by a renowned poet).

Introduction 9

Younger readers may not be aware of the extent to which Ondaatje's early works completely disrupted the Canadian literary landscape. Ondaatje upended the narrative by publishing poetry and fiction that questioned the values and norms associated with late twentieth-century writing in Canada. This collection also functions to remind readers of his role in creating that inflection point. In their embrace of postmodern aesthetics and in their exploration of the role of the artist, those works stand as singular challenges to what was then a status quo predominantly associated with literary realism. While realism offers the false hope of representing things as if they could be identified, quantified, and known, Ondaatje embraced an epistemological aesthetic that ran counter to this myth of actuality. Instead, he pursued a completely different model of cognition, articulated in the closing lines of "'the gate in his head'":

And that is all this writing should be then.
The beautiful formed things caught at the wrong moment
so they are shapeless, awkward
moving to the clear. (*CP*, 40)

Although Ondaatje remains a private person, reluctantly caught in the spotlight of celebrity, he is in fact an international literary icon who has spent the better part of his career acclimatizing himself to that reality. Much of his early work represents his fascination with and repudiation of stardom. Fame beckons, but fame is repugnant. Ondaatje associates it with a repudiation of the writer's honesty; it compromises his ability to render perception without the interference of the outside world. It threatens his art. Yet his movement away from poetry and into a later career marked by the publication of several novels went hand in hand with a growing interest in public, rather than private, lives. If the early work was dominated by his self-referentiality, the later work engages with more communal questions focused on the nature of social justice, international conflict, historical migrations, and contemporary manifestations of the power of myth.

I still remember the shock I felt when I first opened *The Collected Works of Billy the Kid* to a photograph that contained no image. It would be up to me to imagine Billy. He had not been constructed for me in terms of the rounded characters I had been taught to value. Ondaatje was going to blow that concept up. And then Ondaatje hit me again with his postmodern representation of Buddy Bolden in

Coming Through Slaughter, startling to me in the way its author consciously identified with his suicidal and manic subject. In her essay for this volume, Di Brandt calls this Ondaatje's "deeply personal quest into his own hidden darkness" (67). Decades later, in one of many classes that I have taught on Ondaatje's work, I found myself directing students to the four pages of acknowledgments at the end of *Warlight*. There was some kind of elegiac narrative behind those credits that also revealed the extensive historical research underlying the novel, testimony to the way Ondaatje had moved from his self-perceptions as a poet to a much broader field of reference in the later part of his career. He seemed to be saying goodbye by anchoring himself in repeated references to history and the passing of time.

3

While I have taken the liberty of advancing my own response to the trajectory of Ondaatje's career, I have also tried to mingle that response with the voices comprising this collection. The essays brought together here represent the efforts of a diverse range of critics whose work demonstrates the extent to which Ondaatje's writing has long transcended its Canadian roots. One important editorial decision involving the architecture of this collection concerns the extent to which new material is balanced by previously published commentary. Seven of the essays are reprinted, some of them in revised and updated forms. It might be useful to indicate why I felt this material warranted its presence in this volume.

Mrinalini Chakravorty's "The Dead That Haunt *Anil's Ghost*: Subaltern Difference and Postcolonial Melancholia" is an exemplary analysis of the way in which Ondaatje treats the metaphor of trauma. Chakravorty argues that "the usual ways of memorializing individual deaths that denote a singular, subjective life – through details such as place of belonging, linguistic and familial ties, ethnicity, name, age, and occupation – become insufficient to explaining the losses incurred. Human rights, and human wrongs, the novel implies, can no longer be adduced on grounds that value the sentience and security of the individual, historically legible subject" (335). Chakravorty explores "preoccupations with violence in postcolonial literatures, especially when linked to real historical events, that seem to shore up dubious stereotypes about insurmountable civilizational differences that structure our globe" (336).

Pico Iyer's essay originally appeared in *The New York Review of Books*. He draws our attention to Ondaatje's consistent interest in history and historical artefacts: "In every one of his books, Ondaatje alights upon some new territory and begins, with patient attentiveness, to excavate its forgotten history and secret treasures; it's no coincidence that so many of his characters are archaeologists, researchers, archivists" (357). I admire the ways in which Iyer leads us toward the elements of Ondaatje's encounters with history and language that we might have missed. Through his essay, we enter Ondaatje's work in a new way, via the eyes of another acclaimed writer who has also contemplated the relationship between writing and human consciousness.

Jody Mason's "The animal out of the desert" provides a groundbreaking treatment of the nomad figure in Ondaatje's novels, particularly in *In the Skin of a Lion*. Mason argues that "Ondaatje's strategy of 'nomadic metaphysics' obscures the material history of, and therefore important differences among, specific migrations, routes of travel, and/or patterns of mobility that his novel identifies" (264). Mason's essay situates the novel in relation to nomadic tropes that are highly relevant to the discussion of diasporic literatures today.

Ulla Ratheiser's "The Scent of Paradise: Michael Ondaatje's 'The Cinnamon Peeler'" treats Ondaatje's celebrated poem from an entirely fresh perspective. While most commentators on the poem approach it in terms of questions of agency (who has power in the poem, and how does the representation of that power shift?), Ratheiser reads the poem as an expression of postcolonial desire. I see her contribution working in conversation with Mason's, since both essays explore the idea of migrant desire. As she says, "it is precisely the elusiveness of the concept that generates the attraction paradise acquires in the migrant context, where it is repeatedly seen to be taking the place of another, possibly even more unattainable, location – home" (119).

Winfried Siemerling's "Fascination and Liminality in Michael Ondaatje's *Coming Through Slaughter*" remains one of the most insightful essays on Ondaatje's first novel, if it can be called that, given its poetic form. Siemerling's approach to history joins in other conversations about the past that permeate this collection. He says that "Ondaatje often alerts readers to the malleability of historical dates and events in his fiction. This kind of historiographic metafiction, however, may very well ask some of the most pertinent questions with respect to history – for instance, how, and why, historical figures and events become relevant to us, and what we consequently make of them" (248).

I cannot imagine a volume on Ondaatje that did not include a commentary on his work in film, and Bart Testa is the authority in this regard. Testa originally wrote an essay on Ondaatje's work in film for an issue of *Essays on Canadian Writing* that appeared in 1994. I found it to be the only essay that treated all of Ondaatje's activities as a filmmaker up to that point. For the current volume, Testa has revised the earlier essay to take account of more recent developments in Ondaatje's involvement with film, particularly in connection with the production and release of *The English Patient*, directed by Anthony Minghella, and with Ondaatje's only work of nonfiction, *The Conversations: Walter Murch and the Art of Editing Film*, a book also discussed in these pages by Allan Hepburn, Pico Iyer, and Lorraine York. Iyer notes that "Murch is the kind of craftsman – intelligent, highly idiosyncratic, and a little craggy – who might almost be an Ondaatje character (not least because his painter father came from Toronto) and Ondaatje professes himself fascinated, in a fascinating introduction, by the man's 'precise techniques'" (363).

Kai-su Wu's "Love, War, and the Other in Emmanuel Levinas, Jacques Derrida, and Michael Ondaatje's *The English Patient* as the Dialogic Field" was originally part of a much longer essay that considered the role of art and aesthetics in the work of Derrida and Levinas. I was attracted to Wu's analysis because it demonstrates, as does Justin Hewitson's, that Ondaatje's novels are particularly open to philosophical critique. I have seen no other studies that so fully incorporate philosophical dialectics into the interpretation of Ondaatje's work. Levinas's concept of the human face is deeply appropriate when considering a work like *The English Patient*, for the central figure in that novel is defined in every way by his visage. Wu's essay shows us how to read that visage and how it becomes an emblem of agency (or the absence of agency) in itself.

To provide a basic structure, I have divided the volume into five sections that do not always conform to neat dividing lines in terms of their subject matter. The first section focuses on Ondaatje's poetry, from his earliest publications in *The Dainty Monsters* (1967), to the four long poems comprising *Secular Love* (1984), and to his last published collection of poetry, *Handwriting* (1998). While some of these essays provide responses to the arc of Ondaatje's poetry over his career (Brandt, Solie), others (Rae, Ratheiser, Rauwerda) are devoted to specific poems or notable features of Ondaatje's work or writing habits, such as his preoccupation with dogs (what do they all mean to him?).

There are many ways of encountering Ondaatje's experiential aesthetics. Brandt notes the transformation from his early work ("the way every scene of violence came streaked with a vivid inner scream, lit up with horror, inscribed with hallucinatory madness" [47]) and later collections such as *Secular Love*, in which Ondaatje "launches on the terrifying and lonely journey into himself and back out again into the world that becomes this book" (63). His ability to say yes and no at the same time creates much of the tension and ambiguity in Ondaatje's poetry and fiction. In her meditation on Ondaatje's poetry, Karen Solie observes that various sets of "triangulations" lie at the centre of his work: "in Ondaatje's poetry the circulation of solitude, curiosity, and language is so necessary that one suspects if any should go, the others would follow." This "three-point circuit" arcs "through distance, across lack"; it explains a fundamental dynamic at the centre of Ondaatje's early and later verse – "lover, beloved, and that which comes between them." In following this triangulation, Solie also tracks the poet as he descends into "an unknown level of interiority" that reflects his "forensic hermeticism," the isolation of a writer who inhabits "some sub-basement of the self" (78). In this world, language is always met by suspicion and silence. As Solie says, "the risk of collapse into stasis is alive from Ondaatje's early poems" (82).

Several of those early poems are discussed by Antje Rauwerda, who draws our attention to Ondaatje's preoccupation with dogs. For Rauwerda, "dogs provide perspective, a means of expressing sexual desire, an embodied mongrel hybridity, and the confluence of human and animal, alongside the confluence of conscious and unconscious insight" (100). In other words, dogs – and particularly mongrels – symbolize the mingling of worlds: "Ondaatje's dogs encode a 'double gesture' themselves, in which they embody what it is to be fully at home while at the same time embodying an inscrutable foreignness" (102). They provide a means of accessing otherness; they point to both Ondaatje's and the reader's inevitable hybridity, or "mongrel blood lines" (109).

One could say that many of Ondaatje's most powerful poems focus on his search for those blood lines. *Running in the Family* is an extended account – in poetry and prose – of Ondaatje's return to the country of his birth. Brandt speaks about the "hard work" that Ondaatje engaged in by "coming to terms with the shameful, shocking, and ultimately heart-breaking legacy of his father's madness," an effort that prepared him for "the painful revisionary journey inward and forward" (64) that marks his later work. "The Cinnamon Peeler," one of his best-known and most controversial poems (first published in 1981), was included in *Running*. I say the poem is controversial because it gives rise to charged questions about agency and domination. Who has power in this poem? Is it the speaker, who imagines himself to be a cinnamon peeler, using his eroticized scent to control the woman he loves (or dreams of loving)? Or does he cede power to her, his creation? But since it is he who has imagined her, can she ever have any agency of her own? Brandt calls it "a poem about the marks we do leave on each other in love and marriage, which scar and also transform and uplift" us (70).

Ulla Ratheiser offers yet another approach to this polyvocal expression of fetishization and desire. She interprets "The Cinnamon Peeler" as an expression of the "ambivalent colonial criticism inherent in the poem." She identifies "varied notions of paradisiacal places" in order to demonstrate that the imagined cinnamon peeler's idea of paradise is questionable in the way it reframes notions of diaspora: "In Ondaatje's poem, the persona's conquering of the female body weaves timelessness and universality into the narrative of colonizing paradise, while the relocation of the landscape to Asia mimics and criticizes the actual physical colonization that determined centuries of Asian experiences" (127).

Critics often bypass the publishing proximity of *Running in the Family* and *Tin Roof*; both appeared in 1982. One work records Ondaatje's return to his birthplace, his family, the myths and stories associated with his childhood, the healing power of return; the other is a confessional poem about the poet's breakdown, the end of his marriage, his acute sense of dislocation, his deeply felt insecurity about his ability to write at all. In what was arguably his most productive year as a writer, Ondaatje was still asking, "Do you want / to be happy and write?" (CP, 105). In his extended analysis of *Tin Roof*, Ian Rae shows that one way Ondaatje answers that question is to explore plural forms of writing, as if those forms offered multiple expressive possibilities but also multiple escape routes to a

Introduction 15

poet who was reluctant to pin himself down. As Rae says, the poem demonstrates that Ondaatje is more interested in exploring "recurring motivic connections between poems" rather than "continuous narrative or stylistic consistency across poems" (144).

The second section of this collection is organized around visual elements in Ondaatje's work. Sometimes, this interest in visuality is a product of Ondaatje's editorial practice and tells us a great deal about how he understands the process of constructing his poems and novels. In a wide-ranging consideration of Ondaatje's role as an editor and film director, Allan Hepburn shows that "the technique of building narrative out of visual material" (160) informs Ondaatje's narratives: "More specifically, putting a scene in one place rather than another can change the meaning of the story. The reader sees different patterns according to the sequencing of material" (161). Characters and scenes in Ondaatje's work are often assembled through an editorial process that employs filmic editorial methods. Hepburn draws our attention to the influence of Walter Murch, as recorded in Ondaatje's dialogue with the director in *The Conversations* (2002), which "provide a vocabulary for describing what happens between the first draft of a novel and its finished form" (156). Lorraine York also emphasizes Murch's influence. She considers *The Conversations* "not only as a source commentary on Ondaatje's abiding fascination with cinema but as a primary document in Ondaatje's oeuvre that, like the memoir and novel," is "caught up in the affects and politics of moving photography" (202). Ondaatje's interest in international cinematic culture "echoes his own experiences – both felt and narrated – of transnational mobility" (203). For this reason, York argues, "Ondaatje's photographic writings are crucially related to the feeling – the everyday tactility – of bodies and communities in motion" (205). Pico Iyer also comments on the affinities between Murch's work as a filmmaker and Ondaatje's work as a writer: "As they talk, what Ondaatje is really exploring is the art of splicing together a narrative: how to shuffle the order of scenes so as to intensify the tension; how to save a scene in the fifty-third minute by making a small change in the seventh; how, most importantly, to use radical jump cuts to create a natural sense of flow" (363–4).

In his exploration of visual elements in Ondaatje's work, Bart Testa considers Anthony Minghella's award-winning adaptation of *The English Patient*. He argues that the film's success rests, in large part, on the director's ability to turn Ondaatje's multifocal narrative into a more unifocal story: "Minghella has meticulously smoothed Ondaatje's multivocal system of narration to adapt the novel to the regime of classical film form and its protocols of narration" (181). In doing so, Minghella creates "a dominant plot" that "does not intend to be in any way of narrative form a real adaptation of Ondaatje's novel" (183).

The third section extends the consideration of visual elements in Ondaatje's work by focusing on his attraction to forms that "remediate" music, painting, and photography to show how the influx of other media catalyzes what Serena Fusco calls "previous hidden (or less visible) literary potentialities" that reveal how Ondaatje treats historical presence and agency as a function of art and medial objects. For Fusco, "the historical dimension of a medial occurrence in Ondaatje is always accompanied by a reflection on history" (212). These intermedial excursions undermine "fixed boundaries" while highlighting what Birgit Neumann calls "heterogeneity, plurality, and difference" (228). In her treatment of *Running in the Family, The English Patient, and The Cat's Table*, Neumann discusses how Ondaatje "takes up Euro- and American-centric visual practices, often implicated in colonialism, to explore their epistemic and affective potential, that is, their power to shape ways of knowing, being, and belonging" (229–30). Further, "Ondaatje's engagement with visuality and vision dismantles the seemingly neutral Western gaze" (230). Fusco references Emmanuel Levinas's assertion that these ex-centric "modes of seeing" break with what Levinas called the "synoptic and totalizing objectifying virtues of vision" (232) in his *Totality and Infinity*. Levinas's conception of the other also appears in Kai-su Wu's essay on *The English Patient*, as previously noted.

Six essays on Ondaatje's fiction make up the fourth section, which takes us from Ondaatje's experiments with narrative as a liminal form in early fiction such as *Coming Through Slaughter* to other forms of liminality in his later novels (Löschnigg). Winfried Siemerling demonstrates that Ondaatje's attraction to historical figures is often linked to the process of self-discovery. In *The Collected Works of Billy the Kid*, the narrating consciousness "enters a liminal state of simultaneous discoveries of self and other" (248–9). Similarly, in *Coming Through Slaughter*, the account of Bolden's self-destructiveness "threatens to pull the narrating consciousness ... through the picture frame into its self-destructive ban" (250).

In his discussion of representations of war in *The English Patient*, *Anil's Ghost*, and *Warlight*, Martin Löschnigg shows that while representations of actual combat are not present in the novels, war is always "on the margins and in the centre at the same time, decisively shaping the lives and memories of the characters." War creates "transitional spaces that they negotiate, and liminal experiences and moral complexities that they work through" (317). Löschnigg encourages us to think about the multiple ways in which Ondaatje treats war as a metaphor for the creative process. In his view, it "functions as a thematic crystallization point for an art that explores the interstices between history and fiction and the real and the imaginary" (317–18). This treatment of war metaphors in Ondaatje's fiction can be linked to many aspects of his writing. For example, his preoccupation with the editorial process, as discussed by Hepburn, could also be seen as a kind of war on the page, as a form of violence done to language itself, a war about the nature of words. If that is true, then editing and war are both metaphors tied to the shifting nature of identity. Editing is existential; it is a form of self-making.

As Löschnigg argues, Ondaatje's rejection of rootedness and facticity is reflected in his use of intermedial and liminal motifs; it also appears as an aspect of what Jody Mason calls his "nomadic metaphysics" – a term that describes Ondaatje's "interest in the routes of travel and a concomitant dismissal of the fixity of rooted identity" (263), particularly as it appears in *In the Skin of a Lion*. Two of the essays in this section explore how Ondaatje's works can be interpreted through the lens of Eastern and Western philosophies. Justin Hewitson illustrates that Ondaatje "weaves Indian and Western epistemes to produce nuanced psycho-spiritual and geopolitical views of violence and trauma" (304). At the same time, his work can be read through Levinas's ideas about alterity and otherness, which provide a fertile context for considering the importance of "the calling of the face" in *The English Patient* (Wu, 286). Although Ondaatje's novels may communicate "the social origins of conflict driven by power-hungry individuals manipulating national or religious beliefs to foment collective ideological passion" (Hewitson, 303), that does not necessarily mean that they interrogate their own power dynamics or their own objectification of others.

A final section called "Endings" considers the later period in Ondaatje's career. In its treatment of war motifs, Löschnigg's essay provides a segue into closure, since he is also concerned with endings and "the persistence of trauma" in Ondaatje's fiction (317). Mrinalini Chakravorty also discusses the representation of violence in *Anil's Ghost*, which figures trauma through paradoxes "that arise in postcolonial nations dealing with spectres of death moored to a particular place and real events" (336). Pico Iyer's discussion of *Divisadero* meditates on the representation of war in Ondaatje's fiction. He notes that "the question ... that always haunts these elliptical and delicate works is how much their very beauty takes us away from the war and scenes of great pain they describe and to what extent, in courting art, they leave real life behind" (356). Iyer suggests that for Ondaatje, there is a style of representing beauty and a style of representing violence and pain. What distinguishes his prose is the ability to move between what he calls "eruptions" of pain and beauty. For Iyer, the tension in Ondaatje's work has much to do with "the interplay between the hurts that arise from those eruptions and the impulse to take care of those hurts, to tend to them with a surgeon's professionalism" (357).

Ondaatje's preoccupation with trauma and the "denunciation of dominant regimes" may characterize what Moez Surani calls his "middle period" as a novelist, but it does not describe his "late period" in which trauma is associated with a divorce from one's past. For Surani, "It's a perceived state of being outside – a being outside imparted by trauma" (373) and "trauma-induced soul-searching" (374). Two concluding essays focus on *Warlight*. Joel Deshaye explores the novel's thematic and formal engagement with the concept of *schwer*, of difficulty, both as a key to private and public identities and as a means of illuminating the metaphorical and literal journeys of protagonists. Similarly, Elias Schwieler finds in Ondaatje an author who repeatedly returns to a cluster of archetypes that define his creative world: journey, recollection, memory, story, history, orphanhood, family ties, loss, love, secrets, and forgiveness.

4

Ondaatje's central characters often represent different configurations of the artist. And in one way or another, each of those characters meditates repeatedly on the nature and value of the creative process. Do you want to be happy and write? Are writing and happiness compatible, or is the process of creation so fraught with doubt and uncertainty that unhappiness itself becomes a central creative force? The question returns us to Rilke, meditating on the nature of inspiration in the *Duino Elegies*, which, like *Tin Roof*, is itself a confessional narrative about the status of the poet. Rae notes that *Tin Roof*, which is "a poetic account of the dissolution of the poet's first marriage to the painter Kim Ondaatje" (131), was partially inspired by a copy of Rilke's poetry that Kim gave to Ondaatje as a wedding present in 1964.[7] In 1985, Ondaatje became co-editor of *Brick* magazine with his second wife, Linda Spalding. He continued to edit the journal until 2017. Every issue contains this statement by Rilke on the masthead: "Works of art are of an infinite loneliness and with nothing to be so little reached as with criticism. Only love can grasp and hold and fairly judge them."[8]

Ondaatje's debt to Rilke, his compulsion to "go into yourself," lies at the heart of his oeuvre. Sometimes, this interior voyage results in a confessional voice that is directly related to the practice of writing, to what Di Brandt calls "an increasing sense of transparency in relation to his own personal life and vision" (49). We witness this kind of self-referential transparency in *Tin Roof*:

> I am too often busy with things
> I wish to get away from, and I want
> the line to move slowly now, slow
> -ly, like a careful drunk across the street (CP, 122)

At other times, Ondaatje invokes Rilke as a guide in his attempt to understand whether it is ever possible for the poet to be in the world or whether, anonymous and voiceless, the poet is ultimately absorbed into the universe, without leaving a trace. In one of the poems in "Rock Bottom," entitled "(the space in which we have dissolved – does it taste of us?)," Ondaatje pays tribute to Rilke's lines in the second of the *Duino Elegies*:

> O smile, where do you run,
> eyes turned to the sky ...
> new, warm, receding wave
> of the heart's own sea?
> O sorrow:
> all these things are what we are.
> Is there any taste of us in that
> eternity into which we merge?

Do angels reclaim only perfect light,
or does some hint of what we were remain?
Do our faces linger, if only in that
slight way a mother's face reflects
her unborn child?
They cannot see it in their swirling
return to self! (How could they see it?)[9]

In his desire to join the world, to enter "infinite space," the poet confronts the limitations of his own imaginative being. Looking outward leaves him looking in. There are few alternatives to this preoccupation with the perceiving self. The tendency to turn inward manifests itself in several ways. In "Social Call," which is probably Ondaatje's earliest published poem (it appeared in Bishop's University student magazine *The Mitre* in 1962), we meet a narrator who "drained a vein" in a suicidal attempt to gain some kind of insight that would allow him to "understand success," as if Ondaatje was already imagining the conditions of celebrity he had not yet achieved. (Incidentally, Ondaatje's first experiment in fiction, which also appeared in *The Mitre*, was titled "In Search of Happiness.") What he sees are those who have made it, "those who burst their freedom / in my face."[10] Freedom is aligned with violence, but the problem is that this violence cannot be divorced from romantic self-consciousness:

I still could feel the warm air
rising off scarred water;
I still could sense the shiver
caused by blackening suns in winter[11]

In so many of Ondaatje's poems, and throughout his career, he returns again and again to the torturing question of what it means to write. Here he is in "Rock Bottom," from *Secular Love*:

I have beaten my head with stones
pieces of fence
tried to tear out my eyes
these are not exaggerations
they were acts when words failed
the way surgeons
hammer hearts gone still (CP, 131)

Introduction 21

How can poetry operate when words fail? To what extent can poetry exist without feeling, as a kind of clinical act? How does the poet understand himself as a being tied to history and place, or can he transcend those forces in his pursuit of a momentary vision? Can any kind of truth be achieved through the medium of language, or is language always inadequate and suspect, a cold and distant lover? And if language inevitably fails, if the writer's own conception of himself is suspect, what can his work say about morals, or laws, or genocidal conflict? If the writer's very imagination is suspect, do the renditions of his inevitable failure take precedence over the worlds he creates? Can celebrity thrive as a function of failure? Is the primary narrative in Ondaatje's poetry and fiction the narrative of self-doubt? Ondaatje performs his feelings of inadequacy as a writer. One (anonymous) reviewer of this collection's initial manuscript expressed the power of this inadequacy as a shaping force in Ondaatje's work: "Ondaatje's vision is stoic, death haunted, godless, tragic from start to finish. There are moments of happiness, but he never forgets Beckett's mantra that ends with 'Fail better.' Or to paraphrase [Leonard] Cohen, 'There ain't no cure for history.'"

His central characters embody a displaced version of this performative narrative of self-hatred and self-doubt. Ondaatje is suspicious of every word he writes. His manuscripts are filled with obliterated lines, inserted words, cryptic notes to himself – all expressions of a writer who feels that he will never get it right, that language doesn't work, but who recognizes that it is the only tool he possesses in his quest to find truths that he already knows will prove false. Or as he describes the writer in his poem "Burning Hills":

He has written slowly and carefully
with great love and great coldness.
When he finishes he will go back
hunting for the lies that are obvious. (CP, 42)

When he was a student at Queen's University, in 1966, Ondaatje published several poems in *New Wave Canada*, edited by Raymond Souster. In "Henri Rousseau and Friends," Ondaatje portrays the artificiality of Rousseau's jungle animals. Ondaatje is drawn to the "inversion" that makes them so exact, so symmetrical, so perfect. Their "greatness" has been achieved precisely because they transcend the laws of nature. Rousseau's canvas gives the apes and parrot and snake "complete liberation" through their idealized, "platonic forms." But there is a problem with this perfect textbook world, framed and frozen in time. The animals have become celebrities, as has Rousseau. They hang impotent on the walls of New York philanthropists. They have become the static currency of a material order. It is an early poem that captures Ondaatje's concerns about how his own identity as an artist is represented in his work. And it implicitly interrogates the authenticity of Rousseau, whose success ultimately depended on his distortion of the real.

Do you want to be happy and write? That is also the question informing Ondaatje's first and only extended work of literary criticism, his 1970 study of Leonard Cohen. If literary criticism is a form of internal projection (Eli Mandel once told me he thought criticism was poetry in disguise), then what Ondaatje has to say about Cohen at this formative moment in his career says a good deal about Ondaatje himself. I imagine that this assertion would not be well received by Ondaatje, who begins his commentary by observing that "nothing is more irritating than to have your work translated by your life" (LC, 3). Yet in discussing the evolution of Cohen's career, that is exactly what Ondaatje does. What he admires in Cohen's writing could equally apply to his own work in the years to come. For Ondaatje, Cohen's universe is populated by "Christ figures, martyrs, saints" who move in "a delicate virgin world where rape, murder, political intrigue, crucifixions are seen with a sheen around them. Beauty is all, and violence is one of the sources of beauty – for knife wounds are seen as caresses" (LC, 14). (A side thought: Ondaatje's literary landscapes are often informed by sonic landscapes, musical allusions working in the background. Could Ondaatje's reference to "rape, murder" be a subtle allusion to the Rolling Stones' "Gimme Shelter," released the same year Ondaatje was writing his study of Cohen? Was Ondaatje's study of Cohen a means of seeking shelter in Cohen's work, which also focused on rape and murder? I am reminded of Ondaatje's description of Cohen's literary landscape as a place where "rape, murder, political intrigue, crucifixions are seen with a sheen around them" [LC, 14].)

Like Cohen, Ondaatje eventually "dropped his wide-ranging view of the world and turned to two specific themes or subjects: himself as an artist, and his love life" (LC, 15). When he says that Cohen "cleverly incorporated the prostitution of personality that comes with success into his raw material" (LC, 4), could the same statement not be made about his own craft? Similarly, when Ondaatje discusses Cohen's first novel, *The Favourite Game*, he speaks of its central character, Breavman, in words that might well describe the writer depicted in poems like "'the gate in his head,'" "White Dwarfs," or *Tin Roof*: "Breavman is a writer studying various episodes in his life. He watches himself take part in a play. We have already noticed this image of the poet watching himself; it becomes one of the most important characteristics in this novel." In other words, "Breavman is studying his own portrait while making it, and the stress is on the fact that the portrait is unfinished" (LC, 24).

The subtle invocation of the *Künstlerroman* and of *Portrait of the Artist* reinforces one's sense that, through Cohen, Ondaatje is channelling his own creative performativity. Although Ondaatje understands that Cohen creates narrators who are ostensibly removed from his authorial identity, he observes that this separation is not very convincing. While "he studies himself as the supposedly objective narrator, placing himself as 'he' in the landscape with other characters," in fact "the book is an autobiography of Breavman as a thinly disguised Leonard Cohen": "Breavman, then, is studying his own portrait while making it" (LC, 24). As that portrait emerges, even in his early career, we see another feature of the artist that Ondaatje shares with Cohen, who has "already turned inward and has started to use his mind and body as guinea pig of his age." In other words, "no matter what the topic is, Cohen is at the centre of the story. His ego takes over and he writes a million autobiographies, real or imagined." Along with Stanley Spencer, Ondaatje notes, Cohen believed that "the most unexpected thing I ever came across was myself" (LC, 7–8). Ondaatje's reflection on Cohen ("this image of the poet watching himself" [LC, 24]) is a self-reflection. He believed that Cohen was driven by "the need movie stars have of participation in menial tragedies in order to strengthen their dramatic importance" and equally by the belief that "his mind is always more dramatic than the world outside," because "in his mind he is always the hero" (LC, 9, 10).

Ondaatje published *The Collected Works of Billy the Kid* in the same year as his study of Cohen, a synchronicity that suggests that the self-referential qualities of one work would naturally be found in the other. In some ways, *Billy* illustrates Ondaatje's attraction to Cohen's early method. Ondaatje points to Cohen's tendency to create scenes rendered in ways that are "intentionally flamboyant and naïve." In Cohen's world, as in *Billy*, "death is sensual, the violence almost erotic. Nature cannot destroy these shreds but feasts and grows on them" (LC, 8). Although William Bonney (a.k.a. Billy the Kid) is a widely mythologized outlaw figure – very public in his criminality – Ondaatje internalizes him, makes him a cypher for the artist who must at all costs retain control. Ondaatje's identification with Billy is established, as many have noted, by his presence in the book in the photograph he includes of himself as a young boy in cowboy garb. Ondaatje's long poem is self-consciously experimental, juggling literary forms and narrative voices, always aware of the writer's presence in the story as it is being constructed. Billy the Kid becomes the subject of a "collected works," an anthological title reminding us that the book is a composite of poetic experiments in which the ostensible subject of the work – Billy – is often fused with the author as an equally self-conscious subject, meditating upon the formal and technical qualities of what he is writing: "Not a story about me through their eyes then. Find the beginning, the slight silver key to unlock it, to dig it out. Here then is a maze to begin, be in" (CW, 20). Di Brandt asks whether, in this early long poem, Ondaatje was "trying to find a violent enough, macabre enough story to underscore the crazy, hallucinatory mental states he was then interested in exploring" (50). Brandt's question pinpoints the way in which Ondaatje's poetry so often signs his work through extremes – the monstrous, the mute, the deformed, the insane, the criminal, the suicidal, the asymmetrical, the ex-centric, the socially deviant – all features of the heroes he loves most in "White Dwarfs":

Why do I love most
among my heroes those
who sail to that perfect edge
where there is no social fuel (CP, 47)

As Ondaatje's career developed, he became increasingly preoccupied with what it means to inhabit "the dung pile of the front-line writer" (CW, 35). Inspired by Cohen, he took on the persona of "the pop-saint who is important not for what he says but for the way he says it and the fact that he delivers these statements with the right kind of music" in order to realize his own "private cells of anarchy" (CW, 61). Ondaatje's characters – most of whom are fashioned as artists or quasi-artists – confront their author's doubts about the kind of moral

Introduction

and aesthetic responsibilities attached to literary stardom. In this context, it is useful to remember that for the first decade of his career as a writer, Ondaatje only published poetry. As a poet, he did not command an international audience. Even *Coming Through Slaughter*, published in 1976, could be defined more as a long poem than as a novel, while *Running in the Family*, appearing in 1982, is a poetic autobiography. His first novel, *In the Skin of a Lion* (1987), did not appear until he had been publishing for twenty years. In retrospect, that novel now seems like a prototypical *Künstlerroman*, with Patrick Lewis as an artist in the making – a searcher, a worker, a lover.

The status of the artist – his place in the creative process – is explored in many of the poems Ondaatje published over more than two decades, from *The Dainty Monsters* (1967) to *The Cinnamon Peeler: Selected Poems* (1989). The poems appearing during this period are characterized by their preoccupation with the poet's interiority, by the conditions that define his home, his family, his local landscape, his circle of friends. In these poems, Ondaatje often creates social worlds reminiscent of those he described in his study of Leonard Cohen, where "the mythologizing of friends and the way Cohen sees beauty (gardens, potency, and art) grow out of death and violence. The result is a jarring blend of beauty and blood" (CW, 9). The lens is always turned inwards, always turned back upon the writer interrogating his circumstances and what it means to give them voice. In what she describes as her "visceral reading of Ondaatje's poetics" (59), Brandt notes that he is "primarily interested in landscape only insofar as it can be used to reveal inner states of being" (57). In "The Respect of Landscapes," the speaker meditates on his ability to enter new landscapes and realizes that he can only do that if, Rousseau-like, he pursues the artificial, by taking on "the egoism / of cigarette cartonned birds, / and becoming like them the centre" (DM, 50). His desire to "translate" those landscapes makes him and his consciousness the poem's focal point.

In "The Martinique," the poet finds himself listening to music, "the clarinet's staggering weave" working its spell on him, "waking the snakes in my head." Ondaatje has said that if he could begin his career again, it would be as a musician, not as a writer. As if the jazz player could find some form of release that the writer is perpetually denied. The poet reflects upon himself "sitting in this cool smokeless room," his writing modulated by "each change of rhythm," each beat "shaping black liquid on this paper" (DM, 28).

In "King Kong Meets Wallace Stevens," he contrasts two photographs – one of King Kong ("staggering / lost in New York streets again" with a mind that is "nowhere") and one of Stevens ("portly, benign, a white brush cut / striped tie"). Although the stark contrast between Kong and Stevens seems irreconcilable, Ondaatje uses the poem to illustrate his own aesthetic – one that wants to encapsulate both of the poem's central figures, however impossible achieving such a fusion might be. Like Stevens, he will become the writer who "is thinking chaos is thinking fences" (CP, 39) in a single breath, as if the act of thought is never pure enough unless it is subjected to violence. Or perhaps it would be more accurate to say that the poem questions whether the creative process can ever be rational, for beneath the costume of his businessman's suit, Stevens's primordial identity is revealed: "the dark thick hands, the naked brain," and "the bellow of locked blood." Ondaatje places himself in the middle of the poem's aesthetic tensions, drawing attention to his own alignment with the chaos, monstrosity, and recklessness associated with Kong: "(Is it significant that I eat bananas as I write this?)" (CP, 39).

By identifying himself directly with the writer in the poem, Ondaatje implicitly asks what it means to write. In "White Dwarfs," the aesthetic conundrum raised in "Kong Meets Wallace Stevens" (can the poet embody both chaos and control?) is translated into a problem with the nature of language itself: can the poet use language to give voice to what is real, or is that reality destroyed by any attempt to give it voice? The poet tells us directly about his fears. He enacts what Solie calls his "fear of wordlessness" and "the end of metaphor" (83):

There is my fear
of no words   of
falling without words
over and over   of mouthing the silence (CP, 47–8)

Ondaatje is already anticipating the pull toward self-destruction that becomes such a prominent motif in *Tin Roof*:

I wanted poetry to be walnuts
in their green cases
but now it is the sea
and we let it drown us,

Introduction

and we fly to it released
by giant catapults
of pain loneliness deceit and vanity (CP, 121)

A mantra begins to emerge: poetry is about the problem of its writing, about the problem of it being what it is. The more the nature of writing is interrogated, the more Ondaatje realizes that it will not deliver him from pain, or loneliness, or deceit, or vanity. "Do you want to be happy and write?" In its repeated attempts to answer this question, Ondaatje's poetry often becomes prescriptive, as if the poet needs to remind himself about the aesthetic values he is embracing. In "Spider Blues," he tells us that "I admire the spider, his control classic":

A kind of writer I suppose,
He thinks a path and travels
the emptiness that was there (TTK, 62)

Ondaatje understands that the spider anticipates celebrity and the troubled relationship between the performer and his audience: "Spiders like poets are obsessed with power." Their "murderous art" becomes a mouth "to catch audiences" who love the calculating writer and the homicidal aesthetics that have seduced them. Those audiences are like the fly, tempted by the seductive power of the spider who will ultimately destroy them:

And spider comes to fly, says
Love me I can kill you, love me
my intelligence has run rings around you (TTK, 62–3)

Ever self-conscious of his role as an artist, Ondaatje reminds us, through the spider, of the love/hate relationship that exists between celebrity and audience:

And the spider in his loathing
crucifies his victims in his spit
making them the art he cannot be. (TTK, 63)

This problematized relationship between author and audience is symptomatic of the quality of Ondaatje's sense of himself as a writer always operating on the edge of celebrity. On one hand, his work focuses on the power of a writer who loathes both his audience and his staged performances, who treats his readers with contempt and turns his back on them in a futile attempt to guard the very privacy he has exploited in his self-reflective and confessional poems. On the other hand, there is an aspect of fear embodied in Ondaatje's self-representations, as if he is reluctant to engage in publicity, even though he understands that such publicity is the source of his fame and power. This desire for an audience that is simultaneously intimate and distanced is an example of what Lorraine York calls "reluctant celebrity." In words that might well describe Ondaatje, York observes that reluctant celebrity "registers ambivalence at the very site of celebrity subjectivity – at, but not crossing, the threshold of withdrawal."[12] She adds that reluctant celebrity encompasses "feelings, acts, and relations that can be at once complicit and uncomfortable, desiring and recoiling."[13] Or as Ondaatje says in his study of Cohen, certain celebrities (he names Norman Mailer and Bob Dylan) are "public artists," and as a result they "rely heavily on their ability to be cynical about their egos or pop sainthood while at the same time continuing to build it up. This paradoxical manner provides a built-in self-defence to their privacy: they can con the media men who are their loudspeakers, yet keep their integrity and appear sincere to their audiences" (LC, 4).

Reluctant celebrity might explain why so much of Ondaatje's early work is focused on a private, rather than a public, imagining of fame. For the artist whose primary subject is himself, celebrity can be both a catalyzing and a paralyzing force. In "Heron Rex," originally published in 1973, Ondaatje captures the tortured essence of creators who have stepped into the public, the "Mad kings" who live on the peripheries between stardom and self-destruction, those who are "proud of their heritage of suicides" (CP, 36). The poem provides an anaphoric inventory of the attributes of the poet, culminating in the realization – often present in Ondaatje's work – that the desire for artistic perfection drives the poet's creative energies while those same energies drive him mad. Ondaatje sees himself as part of a community of creators who understand the price of celebrity. He speaks as the "representative" of this sacrificial order:

There are ways of going
physically mad, physically

mad when you perfect the mind
where you sacrifice yourself for the race
when you are the representative when you allow
yourself to be paraded in the cages
celebrity a razor in the body (CP, 36)

Ondaatje seldom allows the reader to forget that he is present in his poems, struggling with their form, always distrusting his method, plagued by the sense that he will never be able to get to the essence he wants to articulate. "Burning Hills" presents us with the figure of the solitary poet who "came to write again" in an isolated cabin reminiscent of the "small cabin" in *Tin Roof*. There, waiting for some kind of inspiration, "he would come and sit / for four months and not write a word down" (CP, 42), as if the "time machine" he inhabits will allow him to enter history – memories associated with his teenage youth, his sexual awakenings, "handmade orgasms," the "complex tension" involved in thinking about "pieces of history" (CP, 43).

Although Ondaatje's perspective in this poem broadens to include a past, it is a past comprised of the "layers of civilization" involving his youth – "old photographs he didn't look at anymore" (CP, 43). He cannot edit out the past completely, for there is one photograph he cannot ignore. In it, he poses with his teenage friends, "trying against the glare to look 21 and confident." Now he knows that he was never innocent, that the apple he was eating in the photo is actually "wretched," an open wound that is "fresh and white" (CP, 44).

5

How to get back to the essence of the past? How to regain that moment of innocence Ondaatje both records and repudiates? As in so many of his most powerful poems, Ondaatje seeks to answer these questions through the act of writing itself. He searches for the words that will capture pure experience, just a moment in which language could be trusted, however briefly. This is why, in "Burning Hills," he writes "with great love and great coldness" (CP, 44). In Ondaatje's poetry, such purity can never be found. As Brandt says, he is "writing himself into spiralling isolation" (59). His self-distrust is profound.

By the mid-1970s, Ondaatje's preoccupation with the nature and responsibilities of the artist takes on a new urgency. The publication of *Coming Through Slaughter* in 1976 marks a definitive turning point. It demonstrates Ondaatje's shift toward fiction in his poetic renderings of the life and times of Buddy Bolden, the legendary New Orleans jazz cornetist. While Ondaatje's poetry remains focused on himself, his family, his poetic desires, *Slaughter* broadens the canvas in its portrayal of the Storyville district Bolden inhabited. Yet at several points in the narrative, we hear Ondaatje's voice intruding, directly associating the narration of the story with his own aims and objectives regarding the construction of the tale as it unfolds. As Brandt says, the book represents Ondaatje's "deeply personal quest into his own hidden darkness" (67).

While hesitation about making direct associations between the author and his narrator usually leads critics to avoid comparing Bolden and Ondaatje, it is precisely that kind of association that distinguishes the novel. When the book opens with the words "His geography," one senses that the terrain to be explored has as much to do with the author's interior landscape as it does with the streets of New Orleans that Ondaatje is cruising in search of Buddy Bolden and the remnants of his life. As Ed Jewinski notes, "Ondaatje felt the novel should be a statement about an artist, not a true history of a man."[14] Drawing on an interview with Ondaatje by Mark Witten, Jewinski points to the way in which *Slaughter* functions as a self-referential form: "Ondaatje's novel shoves the reader into moments of baffling fictional confession. Bolden's plight is Ondaatje's own. Ondaatje admits this, though he has altered Bolden's inner experiences to create what he calls (records Witten) 'a parable of the 20th-century artist. Everybody at one point writes *A Portrait of the Artist*. Their version of it.'"[15] Through Bolden, Ondaatje projects his own vision of the alienated artist who plunges into the madness and eroticism he associates with the creative act. As Fusco notes: "A man who needs certainties but profoundly loathes them, Ondaatje's Bolden undertakes a painful identity journey, attempting to reconcile himself with his audience. During this journey, he changes: from social animal, popular because of his music, to considering celebrity an oppressive lie and, finally, to a strenuous, dangerous, ultimately failed attempt at a self-centredness that recognizes and accepts something profound and obscure" (215).

In Bolden's erratic behaviour, in his pursuit of the perfect note, in the orgasmic parade performance that finally drives him insane,

Ondaatje creates another portrait of the artist who is always asking whether he can be happy and write. Ondaatje is metaphorically part of the parade, conscious of how he is creating the scene and its wild momentum. He draws our attention to his own performative role as writer. No sooner is the parade scene over than we hear him evaluating his rendering of it: "What I wanted" (CS, 131). Siemerling notes that by "seeing his own face in the picture of the other," the narrator of *Slaughter* "seems to have gone into the picture, through the surface into the world of the other" (255). For Siemerling, photography in Ondaatje represents the remnants of what Walter Benjamin called the "aura," which creates a "dialectic of proximity and distance" that "challenges our senses" through the creation of opposites that "seem to coalesce" (249–50). Siemerling asks: "Is this moment, then, a total identification with the extreme artist Bolden? Or, inversely, a recognition that would make it possible to let go of the fascination and resist a temptation that is ultimately self-destructive?" (255). Fusco also argues that Ondaatje uses photography "to stretch the limits and possibilities of both historical narrative and narrative in general" (217). As York puts it, Ondaatje's "camera-obsessed writings" are "kinetic and affective" (196). Ondaatje openly associates himself with Bolden. He repeatedly draws attention to his photographic presence in the narrative, commenting on how he takes "fast bad photographs into the sun." One of those photographs is revealing: "The photograph moves and becomes a mirror. When I read he stood in front of mirrors and attacked himself, there was the shock of memory. For I had done that. Stood, and with a razor-blade cut into cheeks and forehead, shaved hair" (CS, 108).

In other direct parallels between the author and his subject, Ondaatje remarks that he "Did not want to pose in your accent but think in your brain and body" and that "When he went mad he was the same age as I am now" (CS, 133) or that, like Bolden, he too might have gone mad "by playing too hard and too often drunk too wild too crazy" (CS, 134). The words evoke Ondaatje's poem, "Claude Glass," in which he describes himself "Dancing and falling across coffee tables, / asking his son Are *you* the bastard / who keeps telling me I'm drunk?" as he finds himself "continually going through gates / into the dark fields / and collapsing" (CP, 95). One of those gates must be "'the gate in his head,'" to invoke the title of one of Ondaatje's finest poems.

Throughout the novel, Ondaatje repeatedly emphasizes his identification with Bolden's self-destructive impulses ("Scratch of suicide at the side of my brain" [CS, 89]). Ondaatje draws attention to Nora Bass's passion for the drawings of Audubon and his attraction to "psychologically neurotic creatures," like the Purple Gallinule, "which seemed to lean over the water, its eyes closed, with thoughts of self-destruction" (CS, 25), much like the poet in *Tin Roof* or the mad birds in "Heron Rex." In another comment on Bolden, fictionally attributed to his bandmember Frank Lewis, Ondaatje could easily be correcting the public perception of his own writing: "But there was a discipline. It's just that we didn't understand it. We thought he was formless, but I think now he was tormented by order, what was outside it. He tore apart the plot – see his music was immediately on top of his own life. Echoing" (CS, 37).

In writing about Bolden's breakdown, Ondaatje anticipates the existential crisis that unfolds in *Tin Roof* or the self-interrogatory stance of the self-afflicted poet in "Burning Hills," who sits alone in his small cabin, silent, hunting for the lies that are the symptom of his art. And then there is the poet/artist/musician in *Coming Through Slaughter*:

Here. Where I am anonymous and alone in a white room with no history and no parading. So I can make something unknown in the shape of this room. Where I am King of Corners. And Robin who drained my body of its fame when I wanted to find that fear of certainties I had when I first began to play, back when I was unaware that reputation made the room narrower and narrower, till you were crawling on your own back, full of your own echoes, till you were drinking in only your own recycled air. (CS, 86)

At one point in *Coming Through Slaughter*, Ondaatje comments that Bolden's "later crack-up" could be interpreted as "a morality tale of a talent that had debauched itself" (CS, 13). Could the same statement serve as a description of *Tin Roof* and of its solitary poet inhabitant who meditates on his potential demise? The question returns me to Rilke's eighth letter to his young poet, where he ponders the nature of solitude:

Introduction   33

A man who was taken from his study, almost without preparation and transition, and placed upon the height of a great mountain range, would be bound to feel something similar: an uncertainty without parallel, an abandonment to the unutterable would almost annihilate him. He would imagine himself to be falling or fancy himself flung outwards into space or exploded into a thousand pieces: what a monstrous lie his brain would have to invent in order to retrieve and explain the condition of his senses.[16]

For Ondaatje, there is something about the forms of poetry that allow no escape route. Is there a single poem in any of his early books that offers a vision of freedom and release beyond that provided by alcohol or fame or violence or sexuality? I don't think so. In order to break out of this self-reflexive prison Ondaatje had to break with poetry itself.

6

In her essay, Lorraine York cites a 1988 comment by Steven Heighton that identifies an increasing impulse attached to Ondaatje's performance of celebrity. Heighton points to Ondaatje's "desire to make his art more accessible, more communal," for it is the "dynamic elements of other artforms that make such communalization possible."[17] I take this movement toward the "communal" as another way of describing Ondaatje's slow turn toward fiction in the 1980s. The experience of returning to Sri Lanka and the completion of *Running in the Family* allowed him to understand his own Asian roots and the idea of otherness in a new way that was tied to his own identity. Looking back from the perspective of Sri Lanka, how did he conceive of his arrival in Canada as an immigrant in 1962, and what did that immigrant experience signify? How could that signification be captured on the page? In seeking to portray the texture of inhabiting a new country from a diasporic perspective, Ondaatje turned to fiction. The first result of this shift was *In the Skin of a Lion*. Ondaatje began to explore the metaphor of facelessness itself by depicting the lives of immigrants who often remained metaphorically faceless in the communities they came to inhabit. What did it mean to inhabit an identity that defied identification, that moved among borders, that was invisible to its surrounding culture? What did it mean to be defined by invisibility, to remain unknown in the culture you now called home? These were the questions informing *The English Patient*, Ondaatje's most celebrated novel.

After the novel won the Booker Prize in 1992, Ondaatje's life as a writer fundamentally changed. He achieved the celebrity that he had been exploring through characters who faithfully broke the rules: the escaped convict in *the man with seven toes*, the silent ghosts who haunt the "ether peripheries" in "White Dwarfs," the "sane assassin" who is Ondaatje's Billy the Kid, the mad musician embodied in Buddy Bolden, the arsonist Patrick Lewis. When Anthony Minghella's film adaptation of *The English Patient* won nine Academy Awards in 1997, Ondaatje's international success prompted him to turn with even greater commitment toward the novel. After the publication of his selected poems in *The Cinnamon Peeler*, Ondaatje did not publish another book of poetry for close to a decade, when *Handwriting* appeared in 1998.

In considering the novels, the central question of whether the writer can be happy and write remains relevant, but it expands to include whether the writer can be happy and right. Ondaatje's novels begin to grapple with moral issues and to struggle with the extent to which the writer can engineer effective forms of ideological critique.

In the Skin of a Lion focuses on the marginalized immigrants who contributed to the building of Toronto in the early decades of the twentieth century. While the plot is driven by the search for the missing entertainment tycoon Ambrose Small, accounts of the construction of the Bloor Street Viaduct, and Patrick Lewis's plans to blow up the R.C. Harris water filtration plant, it is also energized by Ondaatje's passion for historical detail. Like all of his later fiction, it is the product of wide-ranging research and an illustration of the extent to which he has moved away from the figure of the lone poet or the lone performer at the centre of the work. It also demonstrates Ondaatje's interest in building a contemporary narrative on a historical and mythological base. The title of the novel comes from *The Epic of Gilgamesh*. As Gordon Gamlin writes:

> *In the Skin of a Lion* revises Toronto's civic history. While official accounts mention chiefly the town's city planners and corporations, Ondaatje allots less narrative space to such functionaries and their visions and concentrates on those who

built the city and their stories instead. His "study of the New World" (79) does not focus on the controlling centre but turns to the workers at the periphery. Their diversity is rendered best through oral narratives which defy conventional monomorphic presentations. In search of a narrative model, *In the Skin of a Lion* reverts to oral narrative strategies and to the beginnings of storytelling. The work finds structural and thematic underpinnings in the Gilgamesh epic from which its title and much of its characterization stems.[18]

In her essay on the novel, Jody Mason draws attention to Ondaatje's interest in "the trope of nomadism." She argues that by "Linking a series of the novel's mobile figures together and suggesting their equivalence as nomadic migrants, *In the Skin of a Lion* dissolves the distinction between native and foreign workers" (263). In this way, Ondaatje seeks to resist essentialist notions about "the fixity of rooted identity" and to show that the "'nomadic metaphysics'" informing the novel actually "obscures the material history of, and therefore important differences among, specific migrations, routes of travel, and/or patterns of mobility that his novel identifies" (264). Ondaatje's "resistance to realism" complicates his desire to depict migrants as real; in fact, Mason argues, these "marginal, mobile figures" are ironically used to resist the literary realism that might recognize their existence apart from "the controlling boundaries of the nation-state" (265) that have defined them as other. Mason's analysis of nomadic metaphysics also helps us to understand Ondaatje's deprivileging of women as viable nomadic beings: "If ... the novel's privileged form of mobility is that of the nomad, female characters are clearly excluded from inclusion in this trope." In "rendering all of his female characters similarly immobile," Mason adds, "Ondaatje further elides the differential access to movement that exists within gender categories and across ethnicity and class" (278).

One question explored in this volume concerns the evolution of Ondaatje's writing over a career that spans some sixty years. How have his preoccupations and his style changed? In his essay on Ondaatje's "late style," for example, Moez Surani identifies three phases in Ondaatje's career: early, self-referential works that "dramatize personal rebellions against the corrosive power of the mainstream" in which "single friendships are prized and psychic loneliness supercharges into eros" (366, *The Collected Works of*

Billy the Kid and *Coming Through Slaughter*); a middle period that focuses on "a gallery of characters whose rebellions are explicitly politicized" and who enact "a critical attitude toward nations and nationalism" (366, *In the Skin of a Lion*, *The English Patient*, and *Anil's Ghost*); and the "late style," centred on "literal or emotional orphans who cope with unresolved pain and walk out into the world with an essentially ascetic disposition" (366–7, *Divisadero*, *The Cat's Table*, and *Warlight*). These late narratives are focused on protagonists who are each "coping with trauma" (367).

In a comment that is reminiscent of York's view of "reluctant celebrity," Surani observes that in their relationships these characters "mimic a familiar dance: that of contemporary celebrities who toggle between being proximate – when they are relatable, familiar, and connected – and out of reach. Like celebrity, too, what is being restricted and what exists in a state of scarcity in these intimate relationships is access" (369). Because such access is restricted, Ondaatje ultimately could not create fictions that melded "political heft and community ethos" rather than the "desire-fuelled volatility" (374) marking his later novels. Those works are "backward-looking," according to Surani, populated as they are by "an inward antagonist characterized by an inability to fully know another person and forge durable intimacy" (374–5). He says that this ultimate preoccupation with self makes it impossible for Ondaatje to sustain the political activism associated with the fiction of his middle period, when he created characters who fought "against the unjust activity of nations and their economic systems: class barriers, the limits and coercion of borders, and a country's ability to forget the cruelty it has authored" (375). In some ways, then, Surani reinforces the view, held by a number of contributors to this volume, that Ondaatje's self-conscious literary form is never finally able to escape doubts about the authenticity of that form. In other words, the issue of representation in Ondaatje's work is always about the problem of self-representation. What does this work say I am? How does it say who I am?

Several of the essays on *The English Patient* and *Anil's Ghost* testify to the qualities Surani associates with the "middle period" of Ondaatje's writing. Kai-su Wu draws on Emmanuel Levinas's philosophy of the other as a means of understanding the kind of radical departures from conventional notions of identity that mark the presentation of characters in *The English Patient* as

Introduction 37

they confront the experience of war: "For Levinas, holding on to being is an essential logic on the battlefield and in the ontological grasp of human existence." Levinas's "notion of passivity" is not the same as indifference; "it should be regarded as a gesture of non-assimilative responsiveness to the thematization, or the institutionalization, of violence" (293). Wu writes that "Ondaatje's delineation of rationality, nationality, and humanism in *The English Patient* adds up to a large-scale expression of reservations about the role of Western humanism at the mercy of its own perilous focus on the self's one-way communication with the other" (296), represented most powerfully by the ever-present face of the English patient, a "transcendental being of alterity" (286).

In his discussion of Ondaatje's war novels – *The English Patient*, *Anil's Ghost*, and *Warlight* – Justin Hewitson departs from the view, held by some readers, that these novels struggle "to reconcile postcolonial perspectives with his circumspect portrayal of the hegemonic forces fracturing the world view and identity of different characters" (299). Instead, Hewitson argues, the war novels "embrace an East-West dialectic, navigating Western colonial attitudes threaded with Indian Tantric and Buddhist theories of cyclical suffering (karma), responsibility, and detached compassion to interrogate ideological attitudes toward war trauma" (299–300). When read from this perspective, the war novels can be seen as "an extended transcultural dialogue about cyclical violence and trauma, intimating that compassion and detachment transform suffering into peace" (300).

The turn toward the final four essays in this volume is eschatological. These essays deal with endings, mourning, memory, trauma – the final outcome of decisions made. Mrinalini Chakravorty considers the ways in which the depiction of violence in *Anil's Ghost* reveals "paradoxes that arise in postcolonial nations dealing with spectres of death moored to a particular place and real events." Chakravorty is concerned with how the "prism of death" in the novel challenges Western responses to violence in postcolonial nations by forcing readers to interrogate "how we as humans understand our finitude, understand our entanglements with the deaths of others, and ascribe meaning to death itself" (336). She introduces the fertile concept of "postcolonial crypts." The reconstruction of Sailor, the novel shows, is not a singular or unique event. Rather, it is a confrontation with death writ large – as a proximate and shared condition that works through an illogic of substitution. Death here is not an exceptional, irreplaceable, and unshareable ontological experience unique to the individual. It is best understood as an endlessly reproducible event that enfolds all who come within its purview. Reading *Anil's Ghost* is hence like entering an open crypt where the book itself serves as a repository for death's relational and recursive form. (339)

As a site of collective mourning, the text binds its readers to a shared vision of "violent death as a staple of the postcolony" (336) and bonds them to it. The postcolonial crypt "figures death as an omnipresence that signifies collective trauma" (339). In creating this "phantasmatic transmission of trauma," Ondaatje succeeds in animating what Chakravorty calls "the need to dwell in loss, or to be melancholic, as the new ethical obligation in reconciling ourselves to the deaths of others" (346).

In light of Chakravorty's comments, it might seem that Ondaatje's later novels would continue to interrogate what she calls "the sovereignty of the Western self adopted by human rights discourse and rooted in the false notion of the sovereignty of the nation-state's borders by implying that humanity is saliently interconnected on the basis of mutual attachments and responsibility" (352). But Ondaatje does not rigorously pursue this kind of critique in *Divisadero* (2007), *The Cat's Table* (2011), or *Warlight* (2018). As Surani observes, "The late period returns to an inward antagonist characterized by an inability to fully know another person and forge durable intimacy. The stakes have cooled and narrowed" (375). In some ways, Surani argues, the later novels return us to the kind of privacy and intimacy associated with Ondaatje's early poetry:

Without political import, the plea for a sentimental mindset is a request for us to encounter the world around us with feeling before intellect, with a sense that the activity of the world is sacred, not oppressive or ever coolly banal, and that the processes of sympathy, consolation, and pity are what is most needed. These, of course, are laudable processes, and these three books model how they play out. But, crucially, these feelings lack something essential. The critical, the combative, the radical. (376)

Introduction 39

Other contributors to this volume describe the evolution of Ondaatje's fiction in different terms. Joel Deshaye treats *Warlight* as an example of detective fiction; it is "a spy novel and a mystery" about how the central character, Nathaniel, navigates his sense of public and private identity, a search that is difficult. He calls it *schwer*. For Deshaye, the effects of war are personal. Nathaniel is "traumatized by war and its losses," and as a result, "he does not know himself or he does not recognize himself" (380). He embodies a movement away from publicity, from celebrity: "he wants something that he recognizes and that offers safety: parental figures and a safer house" (384). The emphasis on this private world, on the desire for domesticity and refuge, is reminiscent of the family focus that marks Ondaatje's early poetry. One thinks of poems such as "Light," "Letters & Other Worlds," "Bearhug," "Claude Glass," or these lines from "The Concessions":

We are new and ancient here
talking through midnight's
tired arms,
letting go the newness.
I am home.
Old farmhouse, a defunct red truck
under the trees
conversation all evening
and I have nothing more to say
but this is a magic night.
Our bodies betray us, long for sleep.
Still – talk about the bear, the cause
of theatre, the first time we all met. (CP, 176)

There is a poignancy here, a vulnerability, a version of what Surani calls "feeling before intellect" (376). That openness, Ondaatje's willingness to let us into this private world, is part of what makes his poetry so seductive because that world is beautiful in its loneliness, its desire, its aesthetic edge. I am reminded of Karen Solie's comments on Ondaatje's sense of isolation and injury as signatures of selfhood: "Pain is a kind of solitude, an edge where there is no social fuel. The soul lingers at that threshold" (94).

The last essay included in this collection carries a particular import for me, as editor. It has to do with teaching Michael Ondaatje's novels and poetry over more years than I care to count. I am referring to the essay by Elias Schwieler, who has graciously allowed me to quote from some of our correspondence about his contribution to this book. In that exchange, I made an observation that (unknowingly) would result in the title of this book. I encouraged Elias to consider the pedagogical implications of Ondaatje's work:

> Even in Ondaatje's early poetry, like *The Collected Works of Billy the Kid*, there is an emphasis on aesthetics and education: how do you learn to be the perfect killer? How do you perfect the art of killing? Ondaatje is obsessed with the idea of HOW to make art, what art IS, and whether what HE is creating is credible or phony. (As the narrator in *Tin Roof* asks himself: "Do you want to be happy and write?")

That is the question I posed at the beginning of this introduction, and it is the question I ask my students to consider in relation to all of Ondaatje's work. I was fortunate to find in Elias a kindred spirit in terms of my pedagogical interest in what it means to talk about Ondaatje in a classroom, how one translates his concerns to young people who have had little or no exposure to his writing but who are there to find out – something, perhaps something about how they understand the nature of art.

In his essay, Schwieler offers an existential exploration of what it means to engage in this kind of pedagogical sharing. On one level, he sets out "to explore teaching and its relation to knowledge, colonialism, and postcolonialism so as to question our role and function as teachers in relation to our students" (396). On another level, he conveys his developing sense of how the sharing of Ondaatje's work creates what he calls a "democratic epistemology" that emerges from a recognition of "the uncertainty and ambiguity of art and how this uncertainty and ambiguity can teach us something about learning to live" (396–7). He considers the ways in which *Warlight* embodies the concept of *schwer*, of difficulty, in the sense that, among other meanings, the word characterizes "what is at stake in teaching and learning literature" (397). Schwieler's essay captures how students entering Ondaatje's world are drawn into *schwer*, which, like the English patient's copy of Herodotus's *The Histories*, becomes "an exploration of what has been in order to learn what is and what might be" (399). For this reason, there is a clear parallel between the

Introduction 41

experiences of Ondaatje's characters and the experiences of those who study his work because "the protagonists' journeys (metaphorical and literal) are journeys of learning. They turn to memory in order to find the truth of their lives, a truth that by its very nature slips away, 'mercurial'" (402). Schwieler affirms that for him, as a teacher, "encountering the *schwer*, the difficult and radically different," is a means of entering art: "Art is, precisely, this missing history, a history beyond recovery, and this is, likewise, the other story so often told in Ondaatje's work" (409).

A history "beyond recovery." A truth that "slips away." A "mercurial" presence. The words bring me back to *Tin Roof* and the disappearing poet in the cabin at its centre:

> The cabin
>   its tin roof
> a wind run radio
> catches the noise of the world.
> He focuses on the gecko
> almost transparent body
> how he feels now
> everything passing through him like light.
> In certain mirrors
> he cannot see himself at all.
> He is joyous and breaking down.
> The tug over the cliff.
> What protects him
> is the warmth in the sleeve
>
> that is all, really (CP, 108)

NOTES

1 Rilke, *Letters to a Young Poet* [2002], 12.
2 Ibid., 13.
3 Hutcheon, "Canadian Historiographic Metafiction," 228.
4 Ibid., 231.
5 Ibid., 232.
6 Menand, "The Aesthete," 92.
7 Jewinski, *Michael Ondaatje*, 111.

8 Rilke, *Letters to a Young Poet* [2002], 17.

9 https://rilkepoetry.com/duino-elegies/second-duino-elegy.

10 Ondaatje, "Social Call," 30.

11 Ibid.

12 York, *Reluctant Celebrity*, 5.

13 Ibid., 11.

14 Jewinski, *Michael Ondaatje*, 100.

15 Ibid.

16 Rilke, *Letters to a Young Poet* [2002], 37.

17 Heighton, "'Approaching that Perfect Edge,'" 223–43.

18 Gamlin, "Michael Ondaatje's *In the Skin of a Lion* and the Oral Narrative," 68–77.

Poetry

1

"dancing new / on this terrific ancient earth": Michael Ondaatje's Astonishing Poetics of Renewal

Di Brandt

The man we know as Michael Ondaatje, his mature poetry tells us, is a family man, a homebody, a cozy local community and close friends attending-garage-sales-in his-neighbour's-front-yards kind of guy. His poems are strewn with affectionate, committed relational family terms: "my wife," "my son," "my father," "my daughter," "my uncle." His idea of romance is deeply inflected with (fairly conventional) notions of long-term marital commitment, loyalty, and domesticity. His idea of parenting and being a father is unusually gentle, generous, collaborative, and dialogic. His contemporary idea of friendship, both professional and personal, is affectionate and close-up yet casual and flexible, allowing for movement and change. The poet's idea of work is locally and relationally embedded. Ondaatje's aspiration as an artist is not to escape or change the world around him or to stand aloof and apart, as in our inherited modernist tropes. He is not interested in the currently fashionable escape fantasy of global catastrophe. His hope for art is something much more homey, stable, and humble. The poet's aspiration is to document our ordinary, social human and interspecies experience with laughter, sorrow, and deep, unironic appreciation.

Ondaatje's poetic vision includes in its affectionate embrace the "labour of hands" that sustains our modern lives of convenience, the painstaking labour of agriculture and construction and the daily kitchen. His relationship to the green world, the world of trees and rivers and dogs and wild animals, is close-up, playful, and humorous and never forgets the "red river" of blood that connects us all in the bodily sense to each other, through generation, the politics of the garden, and the hunt. Ondaatje's poetic relationship to the past performs attitudes of reverence, remembrance, and ancestral homage but does not forget the violent facts of territorial conquest and the intercultural complexities of rank and transnational and transpersonal accommodation under political duress. He does not overlook or turn away from the long shadow cast by political violence, of privilege and threat, interpersonal dysfunction, and emotional scarring, often carried out across many generations, before finding consolation and resolve. The poet embraces the loving close-up while also taking the long view; he looks the wounded in the face while simultaneously cultivating a rare compassion for both victims and perpetrators. He is able to trace the scars others have made on the skin of those he cares about with forgiveness, with blessings on the present, and warm, open hope for a shared and kinder future. Ondaatje's vision is wide-angled, comprehensive, globally inflected but locally rooted and demanding in its emotional and interpersonal reach.

Yet his poetry is also, at the same time, soft. It's easy on us, his lovers/readers, delicious, delicate in its sensuality and sense of grace. The poet is a family man, a homebody but also a generous man, a public man, a traveller, a visionary, and an international leader. He's also a fun guy, the party guy next door. He invites us, he brings us along, to the many colourful parties he hosts and attends, his drunken ecstasies, and his sober awakenings. He shares with us the home movies projected on a white sheet in the garden above the rhubarb and burdock beside the duck pond, the album of family photographs viewed alone late at night on his white porch in the rain, coffee cup in hand, its embedded pleasures and heartbreaks and losses from another place and time. Michael Ondaatje the poet is alert to the quirky, trickster possibilities of the comic and the macabre, the ordinary (sur)real. The weasel running by in the night wears the blood of the duck it's just caught like a scarf. The kitchen in his drunken hours seems clear and wavering under the river water he has invited into it in his dream-like state. He is never far from the dark undertow of loss, and grief, and worries about the uncertain future. But he never lets the darkness sink him. He navigates the complex, whimpering, heaving world he has inherited with courage, vulnerability, perceptiveness, levity, and hope. The poet's aspiration is, ultimately, to sing, to celebrate, to cast his lot with the lit-up company of those who are "dancing new on this / terrific ancient earth,"

Ondaatje's Astonishing Poetics of Renewal

perhaps to nothing more than the simple music of a red accordion played by "a woman with black hair" at a local garden party, her left foot resting on a stump (*S*, 112).

You might not know any of this reading Ondaatje's early poetry of the 1960s and 1970s when this extraordinary restorative poetic vision was just beginning to find its feet. In those days, the poet's appreciation of the grotesque and the macabre was often front and centre, more often than not fuelled by shocking fictional or fictionalized accounts of inhumane violence, sadism of various sorts, rape, murder, mayhem, with possibly racist and misogynist implications at play. It was all very startling, dramatic, and attention-getting in the violent, shocking headline manner we've come to expect in the daily news, say, or blockbuster films. The early poet presented himself as a sort of unflinching white-bread middle-class male North American, able to traverse the foundational legends and imaginative habits of the modern globalized nation-state, particularly in its darker aspects, with glib irony, impersonal toughness, and glee. (But even then you could see strands of desperation, contradiction, remorse, grief, revision, and emergent tenderness glistening in the pulse of every scene, ready to leaf up and unfurl, given half a chance. There were intriguing hints of a more colourful transnational multiculturalism scattered here and there.)

The first critical responses to Michael Ondaatje's poetry, of the 1970s and 1980s, make for startling reading now. Academic readers were keen to exonerate and support this early complicated vision but often did so by metaphorically championing the inhumane violence in the poems as troubled (or gleeful) analogues for artmaking, or the act of literary reading, or the general state of the world.[1] Critics generally tended to overlook the emotional torque and multicultural perspectives the poems also enacted, the way every scene of violence came streaked with a vivid inner scream, lit up with horror, inscribed with hallucinatory madness, which suggested at the very least other approaches, other reality zones at play. Or if they saw it, they tended to either accept the desperate inner emotional/psychological dimension as fated and inevitable, or, more often, they dismissed it as the poet's fondness for exaggeration, his "Byronic romanticism," as one critic called it.[2] Christian Bök's critique of the violence inherent in many of these readings and Lorraine York's feminist affirmation of Ondaatje's evolving poetics in the direction of greater relational gentleness in the early 1990s signalled a welcome change in direction in the reception of Ondaatje's poetry, more in tune with the poet's own radically evolving oeuvre. Ondaatje's poetry changed gradually after those first decades of publishing shocking, macabre works. Alongside poems of violence, we began to see more socially nuanced, mature poems commenting on landscape, domestic relationships, the animal world, and the machinic. The critical responses became more socially engaged, more historically based, and more gender-conscious. These were the years when Canadian literature was finding a global market and becoming more transnationally inflected. Ondaatje's writing was front and centre in these developments, and soon his poetry also began to show a more internationalist, multicultural, and feminist side. We began to think of him as a South Asian mixed-race new immigrant, a Sri Lankan-British-Canadian, with Dutch, Sinhalese, Tamil, and Portuguese roots. His poetry acquired deeper personal aspects, and it began to enact imaginative revisionary strategies for understanding his complex cultural and family legacy and his relationships with other people, particularly women and children. There were new affiliations with ancient Buddhist and Hindu literatures, introducing a whole new complex transnational, intercultural trajectory that could not have been foreseen in the early writing.

We are able to look back on Ondaatje's early shocking poetry with new eyes in light of these numerous developments and the surprising change we see toward more wholesome, community-minded, intimate, and interpersonally sensitive poetics in the later works. So, with an eye to a retrospective, revisionary reading from Ondaatje's more mature, happier poetry back to the earlier more macabre, shocking work, highlighting the deliberate choices made by the poet in the direction of transformation and healing at key moments, here is a brief walkthrough of Ondaatje's radical evolutionary poetics, from the violent, grotesque, macabre, funny, dramatic, parodic early long poem *The Collected Works of Billy the Kid* and the commentary it has elicited all the way to – it couldn't be more different, could it? – the meditative, reverent gestures of homage to revered South Asian ancestral traditions and their gifts to the present of *Handwriting*.

I note parenthetically that the personal portrait of Michael Ondaatje, the man, offered here is not personal in the sense of extra-literary or biographical but, rather, gleaned directly from his poetry and information the poet has given in public readings and interviews about his writing and life. Some of Ondaatje's poetic works are more obviously fictionalized or mythologized than others. The fact that there have been such extraordinary changes in the poet's vision over the years of the oeuvre being looked at here, from the 1960s to 1998, with an increasing sense of transparency in relation to his own personal life and vision, particularly in the later volume *Secular Love*, means there have been opposite critical approaches taken in reading the different texts, resulting in very divergent portraits of Ondaatje as a poet and as a man. These are not differences we can reconcile or resolve, given the way they are inscribed in the oeuvre and the archive of critical responses to it. But what we can do is to note the changes in the oeuvre over time, the transformation points in the poet's evolving life vision, and the resemblances and crossovers between different texts and interview comments made. There's an astonishing trajectory of personal change, revision, remaking evident in the oeuvre over time, and it's this drama of regenerative transformation and courageous reinvention of the man that is being tracked and celebrated here.

THE COLLECTED WORKS OF BILLY THE KID

This innovative long poem was widely celebrated in Canada when it was published, receiving the Governor-General's Award for Poetry and becoming a national bestseller. Its somewhat cartoonish, gun-popping story was a favourite among poststructuralist critics, who were particularly interested in Ondaatje's deployment of pastiche and bricolage, his inventive use of cinematic effects to enact shifting points of view, and the bringing together of "high" and "low" forms of storytelling and poetic expression in a new kind of multi-genre long poem. Rereading *The Collected Works* now, we can see that the weight of the narrative, despite its fragmented camera angles, is mostly on the close-up, visceral, blood and guts drama of the killings in and around Billy's hard life, the convulsions of the shot victims as they're expiring, the fast-paced dangerous drama of frontier life. And inventively, on Billy's troubling schizophrenic state, hallucinating bizarre scenes that wrack his brain and spirit in torturous, hellish fashion. The many unbearable scenes are made poetically palatable (barely) in the images, musical rhythms, and complex cinematic effects of the storytelling. And in unexpected moments of humour, which jerk us uncomfortably from horror to nervous laughter and back again: "HAW HAW HAW" (CW, 57).

Was Ondaatje's intention to question American frontier outlaw legend by drawing attention to the psychic and physical costs of the killings involved? Was he anticipating the harsh imminent increase of violence and proliferation of clever special effects in blockbuster film practice we now see all around us and wanting to find a way to hitch contemporary English poetics to its profitable wagons? Was the book intended comically while performing imaginative exorcisms of violent fantasies as the poet moved into the social commitments of his North American adult life? Was he trying to find a violent enough, macabre enough story to underscore the crazy, hallucinatory mental states he was then interested in exploring? Whatever the case, we can see, looking back, that Ondaatje's version of the story is set mostly in barnyards filled with squawking chickens and red dirt and the nearby trail, punctuated with the intimate contact of rider and horse: "body split at the edge of their necks / neck sweat eating at my jeans / moving across the world on horses" (CW, 11). "Some morals are physical," the poet narrator reflects in the ventriloquized voice of Billy. The world of the text is real, is flesh and blood, is materially bounded, is barnyard and horses and chickens and sex and hunger and death, not something abstract, vague, unfocused, provisional, and shifting, as the poststructuralist construct would have it.

In other words, for Ondaatje the frontier legend offers the opportunity to aggressively touch earth, to touch ground, to feel again the materiality of the body in the world. To remember the intimate connection of human and animal, the irrevocable blood connection between us. For urban audiences in the present, the staged bullfight and the rodeo offer a safe carnivalesque echo of the old contest between man and beast, whose ascendancy, at least in the present era, was long ago decided in favour of man. Ondaatje delights, like the rodeo, in occasional comic reversals of the conquest of human over animal we've come to take for granted: for dramatic tension and perhaps to remind us of how tenuous our human victory over nature really is. It's a point we are all remembering anew in our lives in the present era of global pandemic and climate change challenges.

Just at the murderous climax of a shooting or capture, we find absurd, mock-heroic images and exclamations like these: "Get away from me yer stupid chicken" (CW, 15) and "I rolled off the horse's back like a soft shell-less egg wrapped in thin white silk and I splashed onto the dust blind and white but the chain held my legs to the horse and I was dragged picking up dust on my wet skin as I travelled in between his four trotting legs at last thank the fucking Christ, in the shade" (CW, 78). Not to mention those packs of hungry dogs sniffing at the corners of every scene, tragedy and humour inexorably mixed at the extreme edge of existence: "this breaking where red things wade" (CW, 95). Several books later, we found out that Ondaatje spent his early childhood years on a large chicken farm in the lush treed mountains of northern Sri Lanka, managed by his schizophrenic, alcoholic father, so the barnyard interest and outside eye, from a less mechanized place, and interest in states of hallucinatory madness are experientially earned ("Final Days / Father Tongue" [RF, 192]). In "Travels in Ceylon," we also found out that his father was once involved in a frightening, hallucinatory, suicidal scene involving a frightening pack of hungry, snapping dogs (RF, 147–55). So the nightmarish nature of *The Collected Works* had in fact tangible, visceral roots and real life implications for the poet, whose meaning wasn't clear to readers (or maybe even the author himself) at the time.

It's easy enough to understand Ondaatje's interest in playing with a famous North American frontier legend, a sophisticated literary game of "cowboys and Indians," the legacy of Buffalo Bill's Wild West Show, that inspired children's games around the world for a century. But nevertheless, it's hard, now, to get past those "3 Indians" prominently listed in the catalogue of the "killed" and, then again, "5 Indians in self defence (behind a very safe rock)" that launches Billy's story (CW, 6). They are brushed aside brutally, casually, and never talked about again in the book or mentioned much in the extensive commentary about the book. Stephen Scobie has written insightfully about the historical facts behind the legend of Billy the Kid and the ways Ondaatje has altered it for his own artistic purposes. Christopher M. Sterba, more recently, comments on the multi-ethnic confrontations at the American-Mexican border that feature prominently in the legend of Billy the Kid and tangentially in Ondaatje's version.[3] American Indians, or Canadian Indigenous peoples, are not featured much in any of Ondaatje's subsequent books either, despite the poet's later awakening to his own complex mixed-race heritage rooted in another land, although we could argue that his evolving poetics increasingly reflects values more in synch with contemporary Indigenous poetics than the postmodern.

As Billy's adventures unfold, we are presented with some unbearable scenes of Billy hallucinating, psychotic episodes that plunge him into extreme sensation: "I was drowned, locked inside my skin sensitive as an hour old animal, could feel everything, I could hear everything on my skin, as I sat, like a great opaque ostrich egg on the barebacked horse." The scenes are gussied up with bizarre imagery and violent sexual jokes, "there I was, my cock standing out of my head," et cetera (CW, 77), which have perhaps served to deflect critics' attention from Billy's developing schizophrenia. Many of the early postculturalist critics tried to make a case for the insubstantiality and unreliability of historiography and memory and perception in this text. But there are still the bodies of the dead, the "necklaces of blood," and the hallucinatory catalogues of the insane to come to terms with, the real, earthly geographies of violent conquest and the enslavements of human and animal. Marilena Zacheos of the University of Nicosia, Cyprus, offers a recent updated, transnationally inflected reading of the book, suggesting that we can now recognize in Billy's suffering in the American frontier situation an oblique reflection of Ondaatje's personal inheritance of family madness and social suffering and the recurring inter-ethnic political violence of Sri Lanka's ancient and recent past.[4] Robert McGill proposes another interesting allegorical reading, suggesting that Ondaatje's Billy the Kid was an oblique stand-in, at the time of the book's writing, for the traumatized young American soldiers coming back from Viet Nam, looked at from a distancing camera/media angle in neighbouring Canada.[5]

THERE'S A TRICK WITH A KNIFE I'M LEARNING TO DO

These shorter poems, selected from earlier collections from 1963 to 1978, with a few new ones added, are roughly contemporaneous with *The Collected Works of Billy the Kid* and reflect many of the same poetic interests and motifs in briefer, lyrical fashion. I'm setting aside in this overview previous poetry collections like *the man with seven toes*, another disturbing text, and poems not included in *There's a Trick*, from *The Dainty Monsters*, *Rat Jelly*, and *Pig Glass*.[6] Again we encounter disturbing, slightly mythologized, exotic figures harbouring explosive personal violence and hallucinatory disorientation, interspersed with flashes of naughty humour to make

Ondaatje's Astonishing Poetics of Renewal

them palatable, and vivid bizarre sequences delighting in the macabre. There is also a growing strand of more personally inflected, family and community-oriented interest happening in these poems that opens into motifs of gentleness, community, and even forgiveness for absences and failures in the poet himself as well as others. How could the same person have written both of these kinds of poems in roughly the same period of his life?

There's first of all the cover image: the armless knife-thrower hurling knives with his socked feet around the terrified figure of the completely unprotected thinly dressed woman with her back against a wall. An archival photograph, from another era, of an old circus trick, with a freak twist, adding the frisson of disability to the scene. Did Ondaatje pick the cover? We can assume he had some say in it as a self-professed, very hands-on publisher of poetry.[7] Perhaps Ondaatje means to interrogate a cultural tradition that put disabled people on show, that once regularly threw knives around women for "entertainment." That's the impression we get from the poem "War Machine," halfway through the volume, in which the speaker withdraws unhappily from the dinner conversations he has been part of, recognizing them suddenly as crackling with "non-fiction whips." Not having an effective comeback or protection against their malign influence – only the small, close-up company of "wife kids dogs couple of friends" – he retreats into desperate self-reflection:

Perhaps
wd like to live mute
all day long
not talk

just listen to the loathing (TTK, 48)

But the very next poem, "Rat Jelly," covers all that over with a macabre, immature, naughty boy joke in the voice of a jolly chef who has found a live rat in the jelly and serves it in a pie, with its "steamy dirty hair and still alive." The poem wants us to jump back in disgust: "(caught him last sunday / thinking of the fridge, thinking of you" [TTK, 49]): just in case you considered yourself above the social immaturity and "loathing" of freak shows and the inane conversations of "War Machine," well, you're not. You're caught in the same net.

Again, in this collection, there are the disconcerting but instructive close-up images of small creatures: flies, dogs, bats, bees, scorpions, snakes, crows. In poem after poem they appear to us at eye level, at brain level, where they are easily the size of the human and maybe the more powerful of the two. It's a motif we'll come back to again and again in Ondaatje's poetry. And there is the terrifying mythologized portrait of the rapist "Peter," whose sudden eruption into sexualized violence is anchored in a backstory of desperation, abandonment, unremitting humiliation, and finally rage. This poem has been much admired and written about, although perhaps not always in the way Ondaatje intended. He himself does not, did not ever really identify with the cool, detached attitude toward violence his characters sometimes exhibit, it seems; his focus is on the horror. Finishing the poem, we know, coincided with an acute appendicitis attack, famously memorialized in the poem "Signature."[8] The latter poem details his hospital ordeal, ending with the exclamation, "O world, I shall be buried all over Ontario," an image that reminds us, among other things, of Margaret Atwood's portrait of nineteenth-century English immigrant Susannah Moodie, planting her deceased son in the new land "like a flag."[9] How do you land in a new land? The necessary burial of human remains we're intimately connected to by blood and/or emotion is one of the ways.

The hapless Peter in Ondaatje's poem by that name acts out his hot rage, perversely, on the one person who showed him a semblance of friendship and play in the castle grounds, the vulnerable and innocent – and curiously unprotected – king's daughter Tara. The assault and rape are graphically, nauseatingly described, but so is Tara's suffering and, by extension, Peter's own displaced suffering. Afterward, he lies there "breathing at her neck / his face wet from her tears / that glued him to her pain" (*TTK*, 32). Where's the king, where's Prospero, who should have been looking out for her, and for him, adopted and enslaved as he is on the castle grounds? Where are the mothers, and the king's men, who should have together prevented these tragic events from happening? To the extent that Ondaatje the poet identified with Peter, he surely meant it in the most ironic sense: as warning, as limit, as taboo. As in: *There be monsters if you sail over that particular edge, don't ever, ever go there*, even if you know something – especially if you know something – about what fuels that slide. The poem needs a sequel to limit the malevolent power of

Ondaatje's Astonishing Poetics of Renewal 55

this frightening figure and poem. A sequel that begins with standing by the wounded crime victim, Tara, and continues with a cautious, reflective recuperation of the lost sensitivities of this enraged man, beyond their temporary perverted recuperation through violence. Or at the very least with carefully erected protections against the possibility of relapse and proliferation, all the terrifying internal undertow of this scene.

Hasn't Michael Ondaatje the poet been writing the sequel ever since? Think of the beautiful love poem "To a Sad Daughter," which appeared a decade and a half later in *Secular Love*. The mythical absent dad-king and bereft children have been replaced here by a loving, kind, good-humoured, live-in, flesh-and-blood dad, munching Alpen for breakfast with his sixteen-year-old daughter, marvelling at the feisty teenager she has become, dazzled by the forsythia in bloom outside the window. The poem is poised on that tender liminal moment, streaked with loss and grief for the parent and all bravado and adventure for the adolescent, when parents must begin to give up their protectiveness over their growing-up children and let them go into the world, carefully, slowly, with sensitivity and gentleness, as we hope, to minimize the potential and inevitable woundings on the way. This dad is alarmed by his daughter's attraction to public fictions of fierce, masked, combative hockey players, but he gives her a beautiful, generous, open blessing anyway, a wish for an adventure-filled life, wherever it takes her, with these tender caveats, these loving parental talismans to take with her: "Remember the afternoon's / yellow suburban annunciation" and

Your goalie
in his frightening mask
dreams perhaps
of gentleness (*S*, 97)

It's a beautiful, wholesome, mature, tender, caring, protective, generous parental giveaway. And so much less overbearing than its 1921 model, Yeats's "A Prayer for My Daughter." (See Lorraine York's essay on the poem for an articulate explication of Ondaatje's struggle to revise the paternalistic stance of Yeats and patriarchal fathering generally.) There is much more transformative work to be done to get from the nightmare vision of "Peter" to the loving vision of *Secular Love*. Still, the emergent practice of cultivating greater gentleness comes into view right here in *There's a Trick*, alongside the poems of monstrosity with their inarticulate heart's cry.

"Letters & Other Worlds" represents the first major turning point in Ondaatje's poetry toward a more loving vision. There's a key here, a gloss, albeit an oblique one, to the hallucinatory craziness of Billy the Kid and the temptation to rage and violence in "Peter." Unlike his emotionally devastated, hallucinatory, alcoholic father, Ondaatje has managed to evade the lurking spectre of the world failing him:

> There is my fear
> of no words   of
> falling without words
> over and over   of
> mouthing the silence
>   ("White Dwarfs," TTK, 68)

The poet accomplishes this feat with courage and imagination and will. Forgiveness is a word and concept not much in vogue nowadays. But there is in fact a large, moving gesture of forgiveness here, forgiveness for his father's failure to be a father to him, forgiveness for his failure to be a functioning man, forgiveness for his intensely troubling emotional legacy to his family in the ongoing:

> My father's body was a globe of fear
> His body was a town we never knew
> He hid that he had been where we were going
> His letters were a room he seldom lived in
> In them the logic of his love could grow
>   ("Letters & Other Worlds," TTK, 44)

Forgiveness through the deliberately chosen and developed practice of empathy, reaching across the empty spaces and losses between them to reconnect with love: it's one way to transform a dysfunctional trajectory, if you can figure out how to accomplish it.

"Walking to Bellrock," a poem published in this same period, offers a casual and slightly spooky portrait of two friends navigating a river, on foot, stumbling around on slippery rocks right *in* the river, for three hours, on their quirky way to town. What did they look like, half submerged in the water, what did they talk about, what did their feet miss in the slime under the water, what did they

Ondaatje's Astonishing Poetics of Renewal

see across the fields along their way, the poem asks, offering occasional sharp glimpses of the same, in random vivid images: "just our heads decapitated / glide on the dark glass" (*TTK*, 82). The poem is almost perverse in its casualness, insisting there is "no metaphor," "no history or philosophy" here, only the "heat of the water, the coldness of the rain," the quirky companionship of the friends, following the pre-ordained "stupid fucking plot to town" (*TTK*, 81–3). Try as he might, though, the poet cannot evade metaphor or plot in the poem despite his imagist aspirations; the resonances and echoes pile up and ripple out beyond his control. But his images never lose their visceral, material, flesh-and-blood reality, despite their inevitable rippling in all directions.

Again, we see a preoccupation with the small, usually overlooked, lowly creatures in the surrounding landscape: "Turtle, watersnake, clam." Sam Solecki suggests in his monograph *Ragas of Longing* that the small animals in the poet's iconography, generally speaking, represent the threat of impending "chaos"[10] or, alternatively, "the rediscovery of the instinctual world within the self."[11] In fact, Solecki writes, "I think it is safe to say that ... Ondaatje is primarily interested in landscape only in so far as it can be used to reveal inner states of being."[12] Solecki's fine evolutionary reading of Ondaatje's poetics has influenced my own approach to the oeuvre in certain ways, but I disagree with this statement. As I'm trying to show, Ondaatje cares deeply about landscape as landscape and small animals as small animals. "I am fond of these foolish things," he writes in a later poem in *Secular Love*, referring to frogs lurking on deadly highways in the Ontario countryside, welcoming him home, driving by in the night. It's true, he goes on to metaphorize the little "foolhardy" frogs:

One of them is my youth
still jumping into rivers
take care and beware of him
("When you drive the Queensborough roads at midnight")
(*S*, 121)

But he surely means this in the sense of imaginatively identifying with them, the actual little frogs, rather than appropriation or dismissal of their separate, real lives.

"Breaking Green," another poem of this period, offers a potentially innocent scene of ground-clearing somewhere in rural Ontario.

There's nothing innocent about it in Ondaatje's portrait. The removal machine tears violently at the tree roots, efficiently levelling the gentle hill where it stood. In contrast to the bright green machine, the earth is dark and rich with the smell of subterranean life. There's a bright-eyed snake. The machine moves over it, but the snake is too quick and slithers easily from its blade. The poet and his companion laugh to see this lucky escape, but the driver of the machine is furious and jerks the machine's blade back onto the snake's back. Repeatedly unsuccessful, he eventually alights from his seat, grabs the snake and smashes it by hand against the blade. The poet offers this brief eloquent lament: "He blocked our looks at it. / The death was his" (*TTK*, 51). It's the kind of poem that has critic Carl Watts lamenting Ondaatje's "aesthetics of efficiency" in the early Ontario poems, the close-up focus on snakes and momentary human feelings for it no match for the creeping industrialism that is demolishing the living landscape for economic development.[13] But what's most interesting about the scene is the contrast between the cold efficiency of the machine (and its officious name "Euclid") and the hot fury of its driver, whose conquest over the landscape is not complete in his mind without the death of the snake, which he accomplishes after all with his bare hands, the machine being too clumsy for its slithering quickness. Perhaps Ondaatje means to observe, ironically, that the primeval faceoff between man and beast may have been reduced to miniscule sizes for us in the industrialized world now, but the threat and irrational fear of the wild, with its occasional blood and guts engagement with us, remains, for all our machinic efficiencies, undiminished. Perhaps he means to imply that the most dangerous ferocity lies not in the wild but in the modern appetite for violent conquest over every living thing, a latent rage threatening to boil up when this narrative of conquest is threatened even a little. In this sense, it's the poet's identification with both the snake and the anger of the man that's most significant in the poem: a heartfelt meeting of opposites, a momentary poetic truce between traditional warring enemies, held out as flimsy but eloquent, spiritually compelling hedge (we might say) against catastrophic overdevelopment in our machinic era.

"Burning Hills," another important poem in this series, depicts the poet in a writing retreat in a lonely cabin near Kingston, Ontario, accompanied by the familiar bullfrogs, and the terror of the blank page. Most poets write poems like this at some point, about sitting alone in a room writing poems: the self-reflexive gesture of the solitary figure, the hand drawing itself on to the page, in the absence of ministering angels and muses. What distinguishes this iteration is the contrast between the generic, unfamiliar landscape outside the cabin window and the very specific, dated, commercially manufactured things he has brought with him, the "Shell Vapona Strip" to catch flies, the "Hilroy writing pad" and "yellow Bic pen." Ginger ale, cigarettes. What brand? He doesn't say. The smokes belong to the more generically represented "nature" ledger in this particular catalogue. The poet has also brought a few inspirational and recreational texts along, among them a postcard of Rousseau's "The Dream."[14] What I'm interested in, in this visceral reading of Ondaatje's poetics, is the irreducible materiality of the flycatcher and the pen and paper. These are the physical media that tether him to time and place while in his poet's mind he roams through a tangle of memories: glimpses of early adolescent sex, the easy camaraderie of teenage friends, forgotten details like a half-eaten apple and the white and black keys of the first girlfriend's family's piano on which she played music for him. The remembered objects reappear with unexpected imagist solidity, akin to the present materiality of the yellow Bic pen and Hilroy writing pad. Again, Ondaatje's focus is not on the insubstantiality of memory and history (as some critics have argued) but on precisely the opposite: its sensory solidity that can be magically recalled, with visceral recognition and substantial affect, through the attraction of poetic resonance, from wherever they are stored in us over time.

The smaller machinic haunting here is reminiscent of "Breaking Green" in the deadly insect-killing device of the Vapona Strip and the burning hills outside the cabin window, set alight, we assume, for more ground-clearing purposes. By the time he's smoked five cigarettes and finished the first draft of the poem, the poet observes, he's burned several hills. That is to say, the poet is not above the burden we've placed on nature in our modern time, but neither is he wholly identified with the voracious industry that makes it so. He is able to withdraw into simplicity, for the purposes of reflection and possible change, in the direction of greater appreciation for gentler, smaller, more organic joys, apples, friendship, sex, music, art. He makes that choice. Despite its restorative and transformational promises, however, the writer's retreat holds great hazard for this poet (and maybe for every poet). Is he writing himself into spiralling isolation, away from the friends who had sharp words for him before he came, "strict as lightning / unclothing the bark of a tree, a shaved hook" (*TTK*, 58)? Is he beginning to do what his own father did, filling the space between himself and the world with eloquent words without being able to soften the intervening sharpness? The poet's admitted "coldness" in the writing process is a hedge against that possibility, a limit set to the empathy he can afford for the memory of his father, a limit also to his own solipsistic temptations in the present.

The poet's coldness (accompanied by much love, as he also observes) is perhaps also aimed outwardly at the admitted necessary violence of life on this planet. Ondaatje is not an idealist. He never forgets the economy of the barnyard, the politics of hunger and desire and territory and the hunt in his poetic explorations, that "necklace of blood" around our necks. The imaginative and emotional limits he sets for himself in the discipline of learning greater love are not about denying the reality of violence as a major factor in the making of our world but, rather, about learning to undo the post-traumatic stresses that distorted his own family history and that disabled otherwise loving people from healthy functioning. The coldness is the poet's meditative antidote to the mental and emotional habit of "hot," alcohol-fuelled, out-of-control rage that makes up the most dangerous, undesirable, volatile strand of his inheritance. Such recuperation can help set limits around the necessary violence of our lives for the purposes of survival: a very important lesson for us in our new era of global climate change.

I turn now to "Bearhug," what must surely be the sweetest little love poem in Canadian literature, addressed to the poet's young son Griffin. Note its warm embrace, its apology, its animal heat, the simultaneous strength and humility in the intimate, tender paternal voice. The minor dark notes in the poem are not so much ominous reminders of lurking threats[15] as they are reassurances of the power of love over danger, powerful enough at least to keep away fear so we can get restful sleep through the night. A classic lullaby gesture for the restless world. For all those readers still tempted by the macabre seductions of the earlier poems of derangement and violence, despite the clear redirections being enacted in his middle and later works, let me propose "Bearhug" as the mature poet Michael Ondaatje's signature poetic expression. It's hard to understand how the hard-edged, macho, jocular voice of *The Collected Works* could be transformed all the way to the lullaby tenderness of "Bearhug," but that is the astonishing trajectory being tracked here. It's not an

Ondaatje's Astonishing Poetics of Renewal   61

imperceptible slide: it's a gradually developing reversal, inversion, conversion, re-invention, of dramatic and deeply significant dimensions, of the sort the whole world is crying for, in every corner, now. There are few analogues to the tender masculine gesture of this poem to a child in our literature, in any literature. The equally tender (and cosmically inflected) lullaby, "Oh Little Bear" – also featuring a bear! – in Tomson Highway's more recent collection of songs is another such, related, signature exception.

Ondaatje worked hard in those years at revising the violent and sometimes misogynist tendencies in his poetry. "Somewhere in those fields," he muses on another long country walk, "they are shaping new kinds of women" (*TTK*, "Early Morning, Kingston to Gananoque," 5). He even penned an oblique apology for the misrepresentation of women in a previous work (as generously there for men with no subjectivity of their own) in the poem "Sallie Chisum / Last Words on Billy the Kid" (*TTK*, 68), in which he gives her the "last word" (*TTK*, 98–9). So new kinds of men were being made in those years too! It is already hard to remember now how rigidly defined and differentiated gender roles were before that time and how uninformed we all were about how to incorporate personal vulnerability with generosity and strength into our changing sense of self. We are just now coming to understand the implications of those world-historical changes and Ondaatje's inspiring contribution to that task during the globally influential women's movement that forms much of the context of his revisionary work at this time.

The collection ends with "Light," a love poem to Ondaatje's quirky, colourful, artistic, and sometimes crazy extended family of origin in Sri Lanka. The poem is a miniature study for the more extensive family portrait to come in the memoir *Running in the Family*. "Light" is dedicated to the poet's mother Doris Gratiaen and performs a lyrical elegy to her memory. I would have liked to see her described doing something independent, something for herself, and not just serving others (in this case serving her brother in their shared youth, an image that speaks volumes about gender expectations in that era). Nevertheless, it is a loving portrait, reaching across time and space and certain abandonments and crazinesses, across the pain of leaving them behind in another country, a testament to the "magnet in the blood" (the image he used to describe his deep sense of connection to his young son Griffin), the magical power of love in the sense of extensive affiliative relationship over

62 Di Brandt

every kind of scar and loss. We are used to a very shallow, narrow sense of "family" in North America now and nervous about "blood" as the determining factor in social affiliation, as opposed to, say, neighbourhood or office or nation. For Ondaatje, these are not oppositional notions, nor choices to be made. We are both deeply intergenerational beings bound together by historical circumstance and family ties and by more lateral, social engagements and obligations in the present. We are the children of mothers and fathers, history and ideas, the communities that sustain us, and the food we eat, the ground beneath our feet.

This collection was followed by two poetic prose books. *Coming Through Slaughter* is a tribute to Buddy Bolden, the reputed inventor of jazz in New Orleans at the beginning of the century. The memoir *Running in the Family* takes us to Sri Lanka (which the poet remembers as Ceylon), on a luminous childhood and ancestral roots tour, in search of traces of his long-lost father and the troubled legacy he left behind; the book is ultimately an elegy to his memory. These journeys are deeply significant to the evolving poetics of renewal in Michael Ondaatje's poetic oeuvre, and while they fall slightly outside the attentions of this essay in terms of genre, I shall refer to them tangentially in commenting on the poetry collection *Secular Love* that followed.

SECULAR LOVE

And so we come to this extraordinary book of love, of falling newly in love, of leaving a broken marriage, of swimming through near drowning on the "edge of the sea," of "breaking down" and feeling almost transparent, "everything passing through him like light" (*S*, 25, 28). Miraculously, in that terrifying journey, the poet also finds a new way of being in the world, a new life that involves an increase in gentleness and appreciation and a much greater satisfaction in relationships and life in general. Isn't this, after all, what poetry should be, what the poet has taught us: "The beautiful formed things caught at the wrong moment / so they are shapeless, awkward, moving to the clear" ("'the gate in his head,'" *TTK*, 64)? Pointing us all along, we can see now, toward the promise of this new time, this season of celebration, of renewal, of gathering in.

Secular Love is arranged as a trilogy, resembling the three movements of Dante's *Divine Comedy*, down, inward, then up, then outward to celebration, with a preliminary fourth movement to set up the journey. Each movement begins with a quirky epigraph that serves, in typical Ondaatjean manner, as a light-hearted, off-kilter introduction and simultaneous apology, or perhaps warning: please, come in, but know the poems to come are not for the faint of heart. The book as a whole also bears an epigraph, a passage from a novel by Peter Handke (*The Left-Handed Woman*), in which a filmgoer is speaking with an actor and challenging him to become more emotionally expressive in his roles on screen – advice Ondaatje struggles to take up as he launches on the terrifying and lonely journey into himself and back out again into the world that becomes this book.

The preliminary short movement is called "Claude Glass," referring to a popular seventeenth-century European painterly device also known as a black mirror. The painter viewed the vista he or she was hoping to paint backwards, over a shoulder, through the black mirror, which offered simplified tones and colours to aid in the work of representation of landscape on canvas. The jumbled, madcap poem that follows takes us drunkenly, stumbling more or less backwards, through an alcohol-infused night of partying, running out into the darkness and inviting the nearby river to enter the house and submerge the now sleeping life in it with cleanliness and clarity.

The surrounding landscape of rural Ontario features the kinds of small animals and nocturnal sounds we've come to expect in Ondaatje's poetry, transformed here into something rich and strange, everything vividly alive and humming – and also delicious!

> ducks are nothing but landscape
> just voices breaking as they nightmare.
> The weasel wears their blood
> home like a scarf,
> cows drain over the horizon
> and the dark
> vegetables hum onward underground
>
> but the mouth
> wants plum (CL, 15)

The intense liveliness of everything, then the turn to the comforts of the kitchen, Billy the Kid's "necklace of blood" worn as a beautiful night scarf by the weasel – and visible also as a faint red thread under the dribbling chin of the crimson plum's eater, marvellous.

"Claude Glass" also begins with a drunken party and alcohol-infused dream. Here, the dream is not about the past and does not initiate a journey back in time as that one did. It's rather a startling, terrifying, starkly warning dream about the present, about the poet's current family, whom he may lose "if he closes his eyes" and stops playing "the sentinel" against the dark, where the deluge of his waylaid desire and anger lurks. It's the "hour of magic" (*S*, 14), and the sequence ends with him swimming brilliantly up and out of his alcoholic stupor, and suddenly, "With absolute clarity / he knows where he is" (*S*, 19). Something heart-breaking and life changing is about to happen. As we enter this new transformative journey with the poet, we can better see how Ondaatje's journey into the past in *Running in the Family*, and the hard work he accomplished there in coming to terms with the shameful, shocking, and ultimately heart-breaking legacy of his father's madness, and the madcap social circumstances that surrounded and contributed to it in ambience of privilege and lavish love, prepared him for the painful revisionary journey inward and forward he must undergo now.

And before that, we remember Ondaatje's prior empathetic exploration of the experiences of another man whose love and brilliant achievement was mixed with madness and violence, leading to a tragic end: Buddy Bolden, the reputed inventor of jazz in early twentieth-century New Orleans, who spent his last years in an insane asylum. Ondaatje could have ended that story in the richly sensual, synaesthesic portrait he made of Bolden's life and music in *Coming Through Slaughter* on the triumphant note of Bolden's brilliant breakout jazz moment during a public parade through the city. But he chose to follow him into the asylum, to step right into his madness, to understand the man along the whole trajectory of his being. That act of imaginative generosity and courage, we can see looking back, set the stage for Ondaatje's own personal and family transformations as documented and enacted in *Running in the Family* and *Secular Love*. It is surely not accidental that Ondaatje's oblique references to the desperations of the post-slavery moment for newly emancipated Blacks in New Orleans should hold also an echo of his own complex emancipation or at least movement away from a mixed heritage of plantation owners and lowly servants on another continent to the middle-class milieu of modern Canada. If he were writing these stories now, we can imagine Ondaatje foregrounding class and race in that complex and racialized inheritance more directly in the context of the rich contemporary discourses on these subjects pervasive in Canada at present, though we can also appreciate what a long reach it was for the poet to "arrive" in postmodern anglo-inflected North America and Ontario of the 1960s and 1970s and the accommodations required to get by, as it might have been for him, then.

The first movement of the main trilogy of *Secular Love*, the Inferno in Dante's model, is *Tin Roof*. We are back in the solitary room of the writer but this time in a small borrowed cabin on the Pacific Rim on the "edge of the sea" (*S*, 24, 25). The poet arrives "drowning." The ocean waves outside his window "touch the black shore of volcanic rock / and fall to pieces." "In certain mirrors," he writes, "he cannot see himself at all." He is breaking down, but he is also, strangely, "joyous." His life is coming apart, but he senses light ahead. There is the dangerous "tug over the cliff" (*S*, 28). There are echoes of the terrifying image of his naked father in the train tunnel on the verge of suicide. The poet listens to the ceramic wind chimes, which become, riding the wind off the Pacific, "bells of the sea" (*S*, 30). He delights in the "tiny leather toes" of the unknown little sea creatures hugging the window glass in the night. He takes note of the ceremonial bamboo pipe in the cabin,

that drips
every ten seconds
to a shallow bowl (*S*, 26)

turning the poet's study into a kind of temple, a space of soulful meditation. He reaches for beer, cold showers, breakfast. He leaps violently into the sea. And then there she is, the "long legged / woman from Kansas" (*S*, 38), who will accompany him into his new, transformed life. Right now she is here only for a brief hour, unnamed, in a surprise romantic interlude, a fortuitous erotic encounter, and then she is gone. (How did they meet? Where did they meet? Who is she? We would have liked to know more!) The poet has already fallen back into the awesome, oceanic silence.

The poet reaches for Rilke, composing long notes of homage to the literary master, who also spent much of his life in lonely solitude, dreaming about love. He murmurs Rilke's life mantra, "'to live by the heart and nothing else'" (*S*, 43). The bird whistles "*duino/ duino*" (*S*, 31). The movement ends with an eloquent lament:

I wanted poetry to be walnuts
in their green cases
but now it is the sea
and we let it drown us,
and we fly to it released
by giant catapults
of pain loneliness deceit and vanity (*S*, 43)

One has to have a very stout heart, a very disciplined "buddha mind," also an easily delighted imagination and a musical spirit, to be able to weather such flying, such thrown-ness, such frank admission peering into the black mirror, to perceive the truth of the inner life and to follow the unexpected new directions of its deepest undersea desires all the way back into language and song, through the painful necessities of radical midlife change. Such a venture entails huge personal risk, involving a complete about-face from the disembodied, cynical, violent, ironic subjectivity of Ondaatje's hard-boiled frontier characters in *The Collected Works of Billy the Kid* and from the early critics who championed that stance, from the displaced fragmented outlook of early cubism and the dry alienation of Eliot's *Waste Land*, from the neatly ordered rows of modern suburbia, to something, yes, more akin to *jazz*: a joyful unruly fluidity bubbling up from the bottom of the sea, the pit of the belly, the groin, from the disregarded, discarded subjectivities of the oppressed, the misunderstood, the lost part of the self in us, all the way up through the heart into the brain and into song. It is not work without peril, as the many references to Ondaatje's own sense of near mortality in his poems demonstrates, for example, in the dramatic line "This last year I was sure I was going to die" that opens the *Tin Roof* movement of *Secular Love* (*S*, 23); there are many other such lines scattered through the early parts of the oeuvre.

The poet casts about for role models, muses, guides in this challenging work, calling up Humphrey Bogart, Frank Sinatra, Burt Lancaster, and Tony Curtis, before settling finally on Rilke and also Phyllis Webb, to whom the sequence is dedicated. "I want the long lines my friend spoke of," he writes (*S*, 42), invoking Webb's marvellous poetic mantra, "Poetics against the Angel of Death," with its quirky meditation on strong poetic metre as a hedge against suicide. But Bolden's musical breakthrough into jazz, with its attendant risks of madness, in the previous work *Coming Through Slaughter*, is surely Ondaatje's greatest inspiration in this new journey, this deeply personal quest into his own hidden darknesses. Bolden's breakdown, painstakingly dramatized at the end of *Coming Through Slaughter*, might have turned into emotional break*through* with more empathetic support of the sort Ondaatje the poet seeks out here, of the sort Bolden was able to offer himself, in a rare moment, to the deeply troubled "mattress whores" on Canal Street shortly before his own breakdown (CS, 116–17). Alas, the tragedy of Bolden, with its dark backstory of slavery, is of a scope that will take more than one generation of intense creative effort to heal, just as the tragedy of Ondaatje's own cultural and family legacy has been spread over several generations and only now finding release. These are some of the ways Ondaatje's poetry, read developmentally as I'm trying to do here, offers a hopeful recipe for responding to the world's traumatic legacies in the contemporary context. That's what "secular love" means, to him, in its widest sense.

The second movement, the Purgatorio of *Secular Love*, is called, ominously, "Rock Bottom" – as if all that hadn't been challenging enough, that drowning under the *Tin Roof* on the edge of the sea, that floundering on a balcony overlooking the "city of suicides" (*S*, 38). The movement is set in two parts and begins gently, if also somewhat terrifyingly, with the experience of falling deeply, unexpectedly, powerfully in love, "with all the hunger / I didn't know I had" (*S*, 48). It's a bittersweet experience because of the pressure it puts on the opening future, his faltering marriage at home, the vulnerability of the children he may have to leave. The poet feels morally confused:

The lines I read
about 'cowardice' and 'loyalty'
I don't know
if this is drowning
or coming up for air ("Saturday," *S*, 52)

The liminal moment of a marriage coming apart and a new life being born in the midst of it, as we know, can be devastating, if also life-saving and life-renewing. Part one is filled with poems of insomnia, rage, fantasy and desire, adultery and betrayal, the detailed preparations of loss. Part two gives us poems of lonely nights and mornings in derelict cafés and bars, all his belongings locked up somewhere, poems of disorientation, of bewilderment. "Who are these words for," he asks, even the poems failing to offer consolation or promise (*S*, 71). There are half-hearted stabs at humour, mostly lame, and naked moments of trepidation, regret, sorrow, desire ... and also small glimpses of returning joy. There is one very funny moment of ironic self-reflection in the "period poem" that begins "We. Were. Talking. About. The. Aeniad." The poem goes on to describe a quirky conversation among friends, discussing together the problematic macho legacy of the lone silent rugged hero of epic fame. The speaker blurts out that he hates Aeneas. "F." says, "Yeah. He. Keeps. All. His. / Troubles. To. Himself." "S" turns to the speaker and ripostes, "I. Don't. Know. Why. You. Should. / Dislike. Him. Then" (*S*, 58). It's a marvellous moment of self-recognition, apology, setting up for the transformations in the offing, all told in the context of a joke, a mixing of radically different social codes to absurd effect. The mock heroic moment offers a powerful critique of the lone rugged male warrior archetype and its inappropriate hold over many men's (and sometimes women's) emotional lives, even in the domestic and amorous realms. Cultural and environmental theorist Philip Slater has observed that the great "disconnector" virtues of courage and perseverance and dutifulness are detrimental to the cultivation of softer, more relational and affiliative virtues like pleasure, feeling, emotional vulnerability, and expressiveness, and he bets firmly on the latter as more conducive to helping us to develop what he calls "simple communities" to help us solve the environmental crisis.[16] Here Ondaatje the poet labours, we might say, to disarm so as to be able to let in these more receptive, feminine virtues, for the sake of the animals he so loves, for the sake of simple community, for himself and his newfound aching need for intimacy and love.

The poet's new understanding of relationship coming into view here is less certain than what he'd understood in the past. He gives himself to this new experience, its lively, urgent provisional pulsing, anyway, not knowing the outcome:

Whether we pass
through each other
like pure arrows
or fade into rumour
I write down now
a fiction of your arm (*S*, 72)

Crucially, he lets go of possessiveness over the past and future, over the "other," welcoming in the plenitude of the present, its full presence:

We've each had our stomachs
kissed by strangers
to the other

and as for me
I bless everyone
who kissed you here (*S*, 81)

Separation and divorce and changes in relationships have become common now, and the language of starting over, of provisionality, of accepting multiple narratives, of negotiating multiple loyalties in the domestic realm has also become much more common. In the early 1980s, Ondaatje had to invent much of it from scratch, and his version is a rich contribution to this new social narrative that has become in a broad sense our new, more creative and flexible, more gracious shared social space. Some critics called his move to more personally transparent writing in *Secular Love* a turn to the "confessional." But perhaps it could, more accurately, be called a turn to "life writing," a term that was promoted in the women's movement, particularly, to denote a kind of autobiographical writing that involves self-invention, as opposed to recording the experiences of a stable, already recognized sense of self.[17]

My favourite movement in *Secular Love* is the third and final, his Paradiso, delicately titled "Skin Boat." There is a new sense of the domestic coming into being here, a warmer, smaller, more intimate, more loving sphere than the poet's known in the past. There are poems of tenderness, frank sensuality, simple gratitude, of happy times in humble circumstances. "I am home," the poet declares at the beginning of "The Concessions," a four-part sequence celebrating the rural Ontario landscape and community to which he is welcoming his new lover. The poem delights in ordinary local, domestic things like "Elmira coffee cake" and "the Wawanosh concessions." In another breath he invokes the "peace" and "comfort" and "friendship" these new lovers and the local community so generously offer each other. Such notions and diction have been unfashionable in the jagged, dramatically inclined postmodern, but how can we argue with their beneficence, their miraculous worth after the poet's desperate soul-searching, navigating his way without reassurances through the terrors of breaking down under a tin roof and hitting "rock bottom" before finding solid ground and a renewed life?

Two of Ondaatje's lightly mythologized Sri Lanka poems from *Running in the Family* reappear in this movement, "Women Like You" and "The Cinnamon Peeler." The poems allow Ondaatje to import some of the rich flavours of traditional Sri Lankan culture and art encountered in his journey there back into his modern life in Canada. Such journeys to revisit a lost homeland, to say goodbye a second time to the life remembered but no longer available, and to retrieve valuable heirlooms where possible can be greatly beneficial to the hard work of successful emigration to a new land, to enacting a successful rerooting, and we see this happening in the poet's newfound sense of "home" in Ontario in "Skin Boat." The poem "Women Like You" quotes a luminous poetic fragment from the graffiti at Sigiriya Rock, a tourist site the poet visited with his family in Sri Lanka, alongside mysterious ancient paintings of beautiful women dressed in ceremonial colours, preparing lavish dishes of food for a feast. No one seems to know how long the paintings have been there or what sort of feast is being held, whether religious or civic or both. They become merged, in Ondaatje's poem, with a lyrical love poem to the woman in North America he's falling in love with in the present, extending that sense of the grace exemplified in the Sigiriya art across space and time, a valuable gift of inheritance to offer to his new lover.

The second poem, "The Cinnamon Peeler," is often anthologized and is the title poem of one of Ondaatje's later selected poetry collections. The poem is unforgettable for its sharp fragrances, its gorgeous sensuality, its unforgettably sexy last line: "Smell me." The woman he's courting invites him to take possession of her through this most visceral of the senses, through his delicious cinnamon smell, which she will wear like a "scar." All this is spoken in the voice of the male lover. It's his fantasy of how she might freely bind herself to him. On the other hand, taken in its highest senses, it's a poem about the marks we do leave on each other in love and marriage, which scar and also transform and uplift and beautify us. I find reading it in the context of "Skin Boat" helps in this regard, with its new cautions in the realm of love:

I write about you
as if I own you
which I do not.
As you can say of nothing
this is mine. (*S*, 78)

Where in *Running in the Family* the poet invoked the tragic dimensions of *King Lear* to express the immensity of grief he feels over the unfathomable legacy and tragic loss of his father to inner despair and alcohol, the poems here invoke, rather, the simple country entertainments of *A Winter's Tale* and the wild, predatory bear turned trickster, lumbering oafishly across the stage in the middle of this developing tragedy. This unexpected moment elicits our sudden, unexpected laughter and initiates the transformation of the story and its characters into pastoral romance, a richly performed scene of simple, local, communal happiness.

"The Concessions," where "the bear" appears and reappears in conversations, thus deftly offers tribute to the local Ontario countryside, the poet's home region (where the animal was no doubt recently seen in a theatre performance at the nearby Stratford Shakespeare Festival). There is also a delightful echo here of the wild boars in the "Wilpattu" chapter in *Running in the Family*, where the poet and his family suddenly realized the dangers of having stayed overnight in a guest house on the edge of the lethal jungle, filled with predatory lions and other large wild animals. His missing soap, as they are packing up to leave the compound, was attributed by the servants of the house to theft by roaming wild boars, and as they leave the compound the poet imagines them, comedically, "scrubbing their armpits in the rain" before lumbering off "in Pears fragrance to a dinner of Manikappolu garbage" (RF, 143). Back in rural southwestern Ontario, the wildlife is so much smaller but no less ubiquitous in its reminder of the nonhuman otherness of the terrain, if now (sadly) lacking in larger game.

The poem remembers a talented community of influential artists born and bred here. "Let me tell you, I love them more and more," the poet declares to his new lover, sharing his community with her, and with us:

These country hearts, a county conspiracy.
Their determined self-portraits

Where alone one picks
Up the pencil, begins with nothing
But these blank pages. (*S*, 112)

Here the artist has become dreamer, magician, healer, summoning up beautiful entertainments out of the void but in the most ordinary of circumstances, surrounded by family and friends and trees and rivers and the humble halls of neighbouring towns. There is an intentional smallness here, a new sense of locality, of humility and generosity to nearby others. Looked at another way, we see grandeur. In his emotional reach, and the breathtaking span of his spiritual evolution over the course of these volumes, Ondaatje the poet begins to resemble English literary master William Shakespeare, who similarly remade himself over and over, moving from hard-hearted early plays like *The Taming of the Shrew* and *Macbeth*, through the heartbreaking tragedies of Hamlet and Lear, to the rich, sweet intimacy of *Romeo and Juliet* and *Antony and Cleopatra*, and arriving, finally, in the simple, humble, grateful, magical homeyness of *The Winter's Tale* and *The Tempest*.

HANDWRITING

Fourteen years after the publication of *Secular Love* and several years into the novelistic phase of Ondaatje's writing career, this slim volume of poems appeared. It's such a different book from anything that came before that it took another radical readjustment for readers steeped in his previous work to catch up to it. Certainly that was true in 1998, and I think it is still true now. After rooting us back into the consolations and "county conspiracies" of southwestern Ontario and his new-found domestic happiness in *Secular Love*, the writer Ondaatje found new international acclaim in the publications of the much celebrated novels *In the Skin of a Lion*, set in Toronto during the building of the Don Valley Viaduct in the early 1900s, and *The English Patient*, set in an abandoned villa in Tuscany in the 1940s, with flashbacks to life on the Allied military front in northern Africa. Ondaatje was by this time being claimed as an English writer, an American writer, a Sri Lankan writer, a South Asian writer, with a global readership and attending transnational critical commentary to match. And the advent of fiction gave the socially minded critics much "new historicist" ground to play in.

Ondaatje's Astonishing Poetics of Renewal

And then, suddenly, here's our poet again, taking us unexpectedly on an exotic far journey, this time into the ancient sacred literatures and royal legends of the ancient Sri Lankan past! The poems echo these texts, but minimally so, in mere gestures, simple lines, echoes, letting the white space around the words carry the eloquence of the traditions merely hinted at in the words. We are forced into attitudes of mindfulness, reverence, the deep listening that is as attuned to silence as to sound, and the adoption of imaginative trajectories hearkening back to Sinhalese, Tamil, and Sanskrit traditions. Among the assumptions found along these trajectories, we might highlight communalism and a deep sense of connection to ancestors, nature, the cosmos, and the Divine: all of these interests squarely contradicting the theorized, intentionally superficial abstractions of the poststructuralists.

The collection slyly answers to gaps in previous works. The poems are dedicated to the memory of Rosalin Perera, Ondaatje's childhood amah; a gorgeous tender love poem in the middle of the collection is devoted to her. The middle section of the book is luminously titled "The Nine Sentiments: *(Historical Illustrations on Rock and Book and Leaf)*." The nine sentiments in Indian love poetry, a footnote explains, are "romantic / erotic, humorous, pathetic, angry, heroic, fearful, disgustful, amazed, and peaceful. Corresponding to these are the aesthetic emotional experiences, which are called rasas, or flavours" (HW, 78). "What we lost," he writes in another poem (in the preceding section):

> The interior love poem
> the deeper levels of the self
> landscapes of daily life
>
> ...
> The art of the drum. The art of eye-painting.
> How to cut an arrow. Gestures between loves.
>
> ...
> Nine finger and eye gestures
> To signal key emotions. ("Buried 2, iv," HW, 24)

For those many of us wary of the "domestic" for various historical reasons, these are valuable reminders from a bygone era, instructions for how to imbue the personal and the domestic with elaborate communally mediated ceremony and artful teachings of beautiful conversational expression.

Cultural theorist Eve Kasofsky Sedgwick has tracked the downgrading of the domestic in English literature in the modern period and along with it the value of deep feeling, which became increasingly denigrated as the merely "sentimental."[18] This downgrading of feeling in the English imaginary perhaps explains the curious dearth of critical commentary on the deep emotional aspects of Ondaatje's poetry and his heroic efforts to cultivate emotional maturity and more harmonious experience throughout the oeuvre. Sedgwick points out how harmful the downgrading of emotional understanding and expression has been, splitting us off from the deep wells of our real emotions and preventing us from developing emotional intelligence and deriving spiritual power from those (now often underground) sources. She argues passionately that we must find ways to get our real expressive emotional lives back. Ondaatje would surely agree; it's his main poetic project.

A tragic bass line thrums through the poems in *Handwriting* in glimpses of recurring ancient wars, kings sneaking into each other's castles for unspeakable scenes of massacre, mothers hiding their young children from danger, young women swallowing poison to avoid capture and enslavement, and "torture." The larger historical and ongoing fact of war, its ever-present possibility of recurring, continues to haunt Ondaatje, despite the courageous healing work he's done to mitigate the effects and impulses of personal and political violence in his personal and family inheritance. How are the personal and the political, the micro and the macro dimensions of our lives in the human and earthly realms related to each other? Ondaatje asks the question here and in many of the novels of this period, though I'm not sure he answers it anywhere as luminously as he's asked it here. We need another poetry collection! Scattered among the darker images in *Handwriting*, there are also many happy images of ancient "poets as famous as kings" ("Buried 2, viii," HW, 29), of beautiful women tiptoeing through the night unadorned for secret love trysts. There is the delightful discovery that the graceful intricate Sinhalese and Tamil alphabets have their origin in the curved instruments used to make marks on rock and leaf. There are the delicious rolling rhythms of a lost mother-tongue: "*tharu piri ahasa* the sky lovely with its stars" (HW, 29). There are breathtaking lines repeating ancient sacred understandings of the interconnection of everything: "The sea is in the leaves / The waves are in the palms" ("House on a Red Cliff," HW, 67). The poet's interest, his gift to us here, is to weave together the wide, disparate components of life scattered across time and space into a shining whole. The rocks and leaves are not mute or separate from the human but are singing and are inscribed with alphabetic writing and carved into gods, a woman's beauty is imbued with starlight, the treasures and losses and bygone sorrows of history are interwoven.

It's a grand vision but with great tenderness at its heart, shining with tears for the memory of the poet's beloved, and now deceased, amah Rosalin and for his own tender child self, so sweetly touched by her early presence and so bereft, both then and again now, by her loss. There is tenderness also for the anticipated moment, hopefully still far away, when the poet will break through the "thin border of the fence" at the far end of his life, still "Leaping and bowing" (HW, 75). The project of poetry, that is to say, is not to contain or conquer or complete the changing, phenomenal world in which we live, or even to protect our lives in an ultimate sense, but, rather, to assuage life's horrors and dance with its delights, to carry appreciation for the beauty of our lives to their limit: and even beyond that, opening out into the nothing, the everything, the source of all life that we can call, despite the secular mindset of our times, the Divine.

NOTES

1 See, for example, Solecki's *Spider Blues.*
2 Marshall, "Layering: The Shorter Poems of Michael Ondaatje," 90.
3 See Sterba, "'¿Quién es? ¿Quién es?,'" 721–49.
4 Zacheos, "Michael Ondaatje's Sri Lanka in *The Collected Works of Billy the Kid.*"
5 McGill, "Michael Ondaatje's *The Collected Works of Billy the Kid* and 1960s America."
6 See Solecki, *Ragas of Longing,* and Spinks, *Michael Ondaatje,* for detailed commentaries on these texts.
7 Solecki, *Ragas of Longing,* 55.
8 Ibid., 11.
9 Atwood, "Peter," 30–1.
10 Solecki, *Ragas of Longing,* 22.
11 Ibid., 68.
12 Ibid.
13 See Watts, "Ondaatje's Aestherics of Efficiency," 77–92.

14 See Scobie, in Solecki, *Ragas of Longing*, 96–8, and McDaniel for critical commentary on their implications for the poem.
15 Solecki, haunted by Ondaatje's earlier nightmarish poetry, tries to make this argument in *Ragas of Longing*, 131–2.
16 See Slater, *Earthwalk*, particularly the closing chapters, "Watermelon Seeds and the Ways of Change" and "The Broken Circuit," 181–209.
17 See, for example, the numerous essays theorizing "life writing" in the feminine in *Tessera: Autograph(e)*.
18 Sedgwick, *Touching Feeling: Affect, Pedagogy, Performativity*.

2

Restlessness, Vertigo:
Michael Ondaatje's Poetry

Karen Solie

1

In October 2002, in John Berger's home in the hamlet of Quincy, in Mieussy, France, he and Michael Ondaatje clearly engage less in an interview than in a conversation evolving over many years of friendship. There are gestures, laughter, pauses for thought. A fly buzzes around, bothering no one. They speak of the influence of film, painting, and music, of the private, secret space in which art is created and in which it is received. When Ondaatje says that he requires somewhere "excessively private" in order to write, Berger asks if this means withdrawing into the self.

Not withdrawing so much as descending – trying to descend to a level I haven't gone before. If I began to write something I already knew, it would be a problem for me. So I need to accept the given of what I know, then write something I don't know. A process of discovery rather than clarification.

You need oxygen for that descent – is the oxygen language, or something else?

Maybe it's curiosity.

While his novels begin with something "like a tone in music," Ondaatje says, and "you go toward that tone," when Berger asks if writing the poems is the same, Ondaatje responds "I think it's more to do with language. The source is language."

Curiosity appears a first principle of living creatures. In *The Philosophy of Curiosity*, Ilhan Inan contends that human curiosity is also "language laden," that "novel curiosity requires linguistic creativity." Inan's claim that curiosity cannot exist without language to articulate it, that "the broader the language is, the broader the scope of our curiosity,"[1] is a question for the philosophers, but in Ondaatje's poetry the circulation of solitude, curiosity, and language is so necessary that one suspects that if any should go the others would follow. They are the triangulation by which the work gets made, work re-oriented in the solitude of the reader's mind, in a geometry informed by their own desire. "We forget that this is a miracle," writes Guy Davenport, "a metaphysical unlikelihood."[2]

Davenport is writing on Anne Carson's *Eros the Bittersweet*. Carson, in her reading of Sappho, emphasizes this triangulation as a live force rather than a stable form, "a three-point circuit" arcing through distance, across lack. In the "three structural components – lover, beloved, and that which comes between them" – can be seen the self in its solitude, that which draws the curiosity, the language that is both a means and a limit to pursuing it.

They are three points of transformation on a circuit of possible relationship, electrified by desire so that they touch not touching. Conjoined they are held apart. The third component plays a paradoxical role for it both connects and separates, marking that two are not one, irradiating the absence whose absence is demanded by eros. When the circuit-points connect, perception leaps. And something becomes visible, on the triangular path where volts are moving, that would not be possible without the three-part structure. The difference between what is and could be is visible.[3]

The solitude of excessive privacy and curiosity's search for knowledge outside the self may initially appear somewhat at odds. Descending with what one knows to an unknown level of interiority is an image of forensic hermeticism, the writer in some sub-basement of the self, highlighting passages in boxes of files under a desk lamp's pitiless bulb. Clarification rather than discovery. But Ondaatje's poetry has always been restless, feeling its way through its skills: "when you / don't see the feet you concentrate on the feet" ("Walking to Bellrock" [CP, 57]). It is a poetry interested in limits, where, as Peter Handke writes, "The utmost need to communicate comes together with the ultimate speechlessness."[4] Although the principle of an excluded middle does not really apply, Sam Solecki has offered that Ondaatje, "Not content to raise just the usual issue about the limitations of language as a representational medium," is more concerned with poetry's ability to "do justice to the existential complexity of reality because of the inevitable tendency of the mind to see pattern and clarity where life offers only flux and ambiguity."[5] Yes. But ambiguity is also poetry's wheelhouse. Coleridge's "best words in the best order" is what allows ambiguity to arise, two or more distinctly felt possibilities simultaneously in play.[6] Even when contradictory, our intuition recognizes their simultaneity as true to experience. In Ondaatje's "'the gate in his head,'" the mind "pouring chaos / in nets onto the page" is reoriented in the "blurred photograph of a gull." / ... "The stunning white bird / an unclear stir."

And this is all that writing should be then.
The beautiful formed things caught at the wrong moment
so they are shapeless, awkward
moving to the clear. (CP, 40)

In the simultaneity of the beautiful and awkward, the formed and shapeless, language, that third component, illuminates the difference between what is and what could be. Between the clear and unclear the territory of difference expands. In it, both are true. A verb moves between them. A lot of good poetry lives in this kind of zone. But few poets have found as many ways to inhabit it as Ondaatje has.

The early multi-genre works *the man with seven toes* (conceived as performance) and *The Collected Works of Billy the Kid* carry their lamps up to what Ondaatje's poem "White Dwarfs" calls the "perfect edge / where there is no social fuel" (CP, 47). Madness, the unintelligible, blow through them from the other side like a wind full of sand. We feel the tension of material holding itself together in the structures of the poems, their language, and in the bodies of characters. Teju Cole, in his essay on the painter Caravaggio, quotes Julia Kristeva: "Corpses show me what I permanently thrust aside in order to live." Cole adds, "The smell of death, the smell of the fact" infiltrates, "threatens one's identity."[7] Corpses accumulate in *Billy the Kid*, and in *the man with seven toes* Potter and Mrs X flee the Indigenous camp inland to the "civilization" of English settlement with death and madness tearing at them, "clothes rotted, flesh / burned purple, split in streaks / dress and skin stank and flapped" (*tmst*, 33). The violence that makes the difference between life and death illuminates their proximity, which expands into a territory where known things start to break down.

However harrowing our sojourn here, there is great pleasure in the writing. The joy of exercising language is always present; the clarity, beauty, and, yes, humour of the writing make the horror of what's expressed in it even worse. That is, better. According to Wallace Stevens, "One reads poetry with one's nerves."[8] He says, "The reading of a poem should be an experience," and "Its writing must be all the more so."[9] When Potter says "lost my knife. Threw the thing at a dog / and it ran away. The blade in its head. / Sometimes I don't believe what's going on" (*tmst*, 27), we are likewise incredulous, but we also feel the incredulity in the writing itself, as though it has come suddenly upon a thing it can't unsee. What Ondaatje has written about Margaret Avison's poems – that they enact "discovery during the actual writing of the poem" – might refer also to his own.[10] But the cause of this headlong effect is carefully judged movement. A short poem from *Billy* comes to mind:

> You know hunters
> are the gentlest
> anywhere in the world
>
> they halt caterpillars
> from path dangers
> lift a drowning moth from a bowl
> remarkable in peace
>
> in the same way assassins
> come to chaos neutral (CW, 43)

This is like the speaker of "Burning Hills," who "has written slowly and carefully / with great love and great coldness. When he finishes he will go back / hunting for the lies that are obvious" (CP, 44). Like Stevens in "King Kong Meets Wallace Stevens," he is "thinking chaos is thinking fences" (CP, 39). He is thinking about the holes in those fences, what escapes, what creeps through. How far one might track an idea before words lose themselves in a wilderness of abstraction – virtue, beauty, error, meaning, something, everything, nothing.

Even when at home in the domestic and most recognizably lyric, Ondaatje's poems tend to live in this uncertain place. Here is an odd

Michael Ondaatje's Poetry

case, from "The Diverse Causes," which appears in his first collection, *The Dainty Monsters*:

Three clouds and a tree
reflect themselves on a toaster.
The kitchen window hangs scarred,
shattered by winter hunters.

We are in a cell of civilized magic.
Stravinsky roars at breakfast,
our milk is powdered.

[...]

I turn a page
careful not to break the rhythms
of your sleeping head on my hip,
watch the moving under your eyelid
that turns like fire,
and we have love and the god outside
until ice starts to limp
in brown hidden waterfalls,
or my daughter burns the lake
by reflecting her red shoes in it. (DM, 22–3)

How on earth is that powdered milk both thoroughly domestic and an occult substance patiently anticipating its reconstitution? It has something to do with the integration of the imaginatively lyrical and utterly frank that occurs throughout his poetry. Despite the work's accessibility – or maybe because of it – one often doesn't see what's coming.

The final image leads us to a verge, the house and its civilized comforts (though there is that shotgunned window frame) suddenly at a great distance. The house looks like a doll house from where we end up, where some unknown consequences of diverse causes are about to play out – the daughter grown large and powerful, the god lower-cased, ice limping inside the hidden brown waterfalls, the lake subject to her will. I'm reminded of Stevens again, his "A Rabbit as King of the Ghosts," which is among other things a child's poem: "You become a self that fills the four corners of night. And the little green cat is a bug in the grass."[11] In both poems, a trans-formation of scale and potential illuminates a consciousness that exceeds its physical boundaries. In Ondaatje's, this happens in part in the prepositions – until, in, or, by – that speak imminence, hidden-ness, possibility, volition. So at home entering the poem, we have to feel our unnerved way out of it. In these often-neglected wild bits of language where things act on each other are relationships in excess of their context. From the fragile comforts of the domestic scene (again, that shot-up window!) we're swept to the perimeter. As W.S. Merwin reminds us, "poetry covers the ground at a speed that prose very seldom can ... Sometimes it's just incredible."[12]

2

Solitude is a writer's necessity, vanity, ritual. "Any attempt to try to do something worthwhile is ritualistic," says Derek Walcott, who speaks of writing as "a withdrawal into some kind of silence that cuts out everything around you." What one finds there, he says, "is really not a renewal of your identity but actually a renewal of your anonymity."[13] And it's not without its peril. The risk of collapse into stasis is alive from Ondaatje's early poems. Philoctetes in "The Goodnight," abandoned and bitter, is "a man who roared on an island for ten years" (CP, 17). In "Philoctetes on the Island," he kills "to fool myself alive," to avoid the self-destruction that would see him "heaving round the wood in my lung" (CP, 18). The condition that might allow one to write "with great love and great coldness" may also flirt with a destructive isolation. "The inadequacy of writ-ing is similar to that of connecting to another person," writes Yiyun Li.[14] A danger of solitude is that it will collapse around this inade-quacy into an ever-tightening circle, around that wood in the lung, the end of thinking. But in the myth, at least, Philoctetes moves on.

Not so the speaker's father in "Letters & Other Worlds," whose "body was a globe of fear," who retreated to a room with two bot-tles of gin and "came to death with his mind drowning." And while he composed letters "of the most complete empathy,"

> [...] he himself edged
> into the terrible acute hatred
> of his own privacy
> till he balanced and fell

the length of his body
the blood entering
the empty reservoir of bones
the blood searching in his head without metaphor.

When in the marvelous and frightening line "he died in minutes of a new equilibrium" (CP, 28–30), it is a final balance he dies of. Balance not a verb but a noun. The end of metaphor.

A fear of wordlessness recurs in the poetry, of falling from the multiple and partial into the unvaried and total. Although the edge-land is often where the action is, it also induces vertigo. And as Ondaatje confesses to Colum McCann in an interview about the writing of *In the Skin of a Lion*, "I have a terrible fear of vertigo."[15] Triangulation, of course, is also a method for steadying oneself relative to points in the landscape and a process of navigation.

Self-destruction may be total, but completion may be likewise. From where they end up, it's hard to see the difference. In "Birds for Janet – The Heron," the bird, in the perfect solitude of a hermit, is found through the path of his suicide, "walking to the centre of the lake" (DM, 13). Achieving perfection seems to have a lot in common with reaching the end of one's abilities. As in "Heron Rex," "There are ways of going / physically mad, physically / mad when you perfect the mind," when you perfect the posture of "balancing on that one goddamn leg" (CP, 36). And where does one go from the "perfect white between the words" Dashiell Hammett occupies in his success? ("White Dwarfs" [CP, 48]). At the conclusion of "Late Movies with Skyler," the speaker remembers how "In the movies of my childhood the heroes / after skilled swordplay and moral victories / leave with absolutely nothing / to do for the rest of their lives" (CP, 69). Being left with nothing is not even the problem. It's being left with nothing *to do*. Setting aside the question of whether perfection is possible or not, it's a terrible ideal. And "What about Burt Lancaster / limping away at the end of *Trapeze?*" (S, 40): Mike Ribble has quit the circus. Gina runs after him. The love triangle is resolved. The movie ends.

As Berger has written, the compulsion to language lies in that "*potentially* it is complete, it has the potential of holding with words the totality of human experience – everything that has occurred and everything that may occur. It even allows space for the unspeakable."[16] In this way it is like mathematics in its relationship to

84   Karen Solie

quanta. But like the relationship of desire to lack, the potential of language exists in its incompleteness. Robert Creeley, somewhat tongue-in-cheek, suggests that nothing can follow from the exhaustion of possibilities available to the artist in a particular endeavour that "is altogether successful."[17]

Running in the Family is a document of the multiple and partial, of how memory, curiosity, invention, and history converge to trouble any search for the truth. Much has been written about the ways in which Ondaatje combines autobiography and fiction to record his return to Sri Lanka, his efforts to resolve familial mysteries. In the acknowledgments, he confesses that "While all these names may give an air of authenticity [...] the book is not a history but a portrait or 'gesture' [...] in Sri Lanka a well-told lie is worth a thousand facts" (RF, 206). One might remember Aristotle's characterization of poetry as creating its own practical landscape: "It is Homer especially who has taught the other poets how to tell lies as they should be told."[18]

The book contains several poems that reappear in *Secular Love*, as well as passages of lyrical beauty that certainly create what Derrida would call an experience of the poetic that can't be reduced to the poem, as "It sees itself, the response, dictated to be poetic, by being poetic." Whether fact or fiction, found or invented, prose or poetry, the answer is always yes, "absolutely one and the other [...] neither one nor the other."[19] I'm not making a case for *Running in the Family* as a collection of poetry, but it is a gate of sorts, a passage from the earlier poems to the work of *Secular Love* and Ondaatje's latest collection, *Handwriting*.

Near the beginning of *Running in the Family* is "not so much a dream as an image that repeats itself": "I see my own straining body which stands shaped like a star and realise gradually I am part of a human pyramid [...] we are approaching the door which being twenty feet high we will be able to pass through only if the pyramid turns sideways. Without discussing it the whole family ignores the opening and walks slowly through the pale pink rose-coloured walls into the next room" (RF, 27). Walls are forever being walked through in this book – peacocks step through windows, snakes emerge from drains, people escape by unusual means, fact passes into fiction and fiction into memory, and "memory invades the present in those who are old, the way gardens invade houses here" (RF, 112). If, as Cole writes, a door "is a site of potential, imbued with transitional energies,"[20] all these ad hoc thresholds expand the territory of transition, rewild the effort of equilibrium. Balance acquires a larger range of motion. The speaker in search of family truths finds that "No story is ever told just once [...] we will return to it an hour later and retell the story with additions and this time a few judgements thrown in. In this way history is organized" (RF, 26). Yet "truth disappears with history" (RF, 53). Truth, also, is restless, both before and behind us. As in the final lines of Fanny Howe's "Now I Get It," "Your own life ahead follows you / Like a scientist posing as a shepherd."[21]

Published two years after *Running in the Family*, *Secular Love* finds a new capaciousness in the lyric. But in these transitional energies is renewed precarity. "Claude Glass" recalls "Letters & Other Worlds," though the speaker says, "He is not a lost drunk / like his father" (S, 14). Nevertheless, parties find him "continually going through gates / into the dark fields / and collapsing," searching for insight but finding unconsciousness. The alcohol promising to relieve inertia ends up pouring more into him. There's a manic edge to his descriptions of "the hour of magic," "the hour for sudden journeying," as he tries to hold his life together. In spite of a relatively quiet syntax, reasonable lines that break reasonably, one is left with the sensation of a scary carousel whose vivid details blur. A weasel wears the blood of a murdered duck "home like a scarf," "pictures fly without targets." As a party ramps up, lines break on prepositions and verbs and the room begins to slide. When "His anger / and desire" form a closing circle, "With absolute clarity / he knows where he is" (S, 13, 19). When you are alone, Thomas Merton writes, "it sometimes becomes difficult to see how you are going to get rid of yourself."[22] When the river, invited, enters the house, we suspect something is about to be borne away.

Indeed, as the speaker in *Tin Roof* says, "We go to the stark places of the earth and find moral questions everywhere" (CP, 109). His recognition that solitude "is not an absolute, / it is just a resting place" (CP, 117) echoes Mark 6:31. Yet, as Merton asks, "Is it right or wrong for me to be alone? When I have no solitude, I am convinced I need it. When I am alone, I am convinced I have found the situation I need. Then I wonder if my need for it is enough to imply a right to it."[23] For the speaker, who addresses Rilke as a mentor in solitude, the admission that it

brings no wisdom
just two day old food in the fridge,
certain habits you would not approve of

does feel, in the section's quieter exploratory register, both "joyous" and a "breaking down" (CP, 108). "Claude Glass" is in the third person singular, a displacement. But in this section the first person begins, tentatively, to return. In his new lover, in a liberation of desire, is found an outbound path for his curiosity.

In a letter from Rome dated 14 May 1904, Rilke advises Franz Kappus that "you should not let yourself be confused in your solitude by the fact that there is something in you that wants to move out of it. This very wish, if you use it calmly and prudently and like a tool, will help you spread out your solitude over a great distance."[24] I hear this ringing up ahead in the poems of *Handwriting*. The question in *Tin Roof*, however parenthetical, "(Do you want / to be happy and write?)" may be met by Rilke's speculation in the ninth of the *Duino Elegies*: "Are we here, perhaps, for saying: house, / bridge, fountain, gate, jug, fruit-tree, window – ."[25] The love of Ondaatje's speaker for the "stark / luxury of this place" is expressed in a similar attention to its facts of " – no armchairs, a fridge of beer and mangoes / / Precipitation" (CP, 107). Rephrased a few pages on as a longing affirmation, the question begins to understand that, as in Rilke, salvation lies in noticing, and saying. And as in Rilke, nothing is that simple. Though the sea may represent for Ondaatje's speaker a generative immersion in language, the isolation of "pain loneliness deceit vanity" (CP, 123) experienced since the dissolution of his marriage still lies both behind and before him.

The poems of the first part of "Rock Bottom" are spoken out of a loneliness that denies even the respite of unconsciousness. In his insomnia, the speaker confesses to acts of self-harm when words fail that recall Philoctetes' wood in the lung (S, 55). Floating in the debris cloud of separation, he wants "the roulette of a lightning bolt / to resolve all" (S, 71), but the poems have already begun to move outward into play, empathy, desire, community. He is refreshed in teaching Neruda, "reading his lovely old / curiosity about all things," envying the poet's "slide through complexity" (S, 78). As he begins to map his new world, his solitude is nourished by complexity.

In "Her House," he recognizes that "When I first met her I saw nothing but her, and now, as she becomes familiar, I recognise the

Michael Ondaatje's Poetry 87

small customs" (*S*, 87). Familiarity, even as it closes physical distance, promotes ease and understanding, opens awareness of the other's irreducible complexity – privacies of thought, histories of beloved objects, habits formed in another life – a gap illuminated by the activity of relation. "Aren't lovers / always arriving at boundaries, each of the other"?[26] The poems in this final section, "Skin Boat," feel acutely the distances between the self and others. Yet the speaker seems more oriented against the vertiginous gravity of isolation. "To a Sad Daughter" he offers advice on thresholds – "Want everything. If you break / break going out not in" (*S*, 97) – even as he aches with loss as she explores her own world. It's advice he takes himself in "All along the Mazinaw": "Those things we don't know we love / we love harder" (*S*, 99). The poems develop a more mobile and inquisitive relationship to community.

I've referred to the speaker of *Secular Love* as consistent through the poems. In an interview with Solecki, Ondaatje says he was tempted to subtitle the collection "a novel," and it does read that way to me. Meanwhile, "7 or 8 Things I Know about Her / A Stolen Biography," a series of brief prose sections, reads rather like a short story. There are no hard edges here. Weather and animals invade the house. Most differentiations are a matter of degree. The verb-status of balance and triangulation depends, like the acrobats and high-wire acts that appear more frequently in *Handwriting*, on how skills translate a leap of faith. The stilt-walkers of "To Anuradhapura," with "their minimal arms / and 'lying legs' ... become gods" (*HW*, 17). But it's less about mystery than learned skill; their effort appears effortless. They represent the wonder of achievement and the human desire for play, for the entirely voluntary, the necessity of that which exceeds necessity. "The poetic, let us say it," Derrida writes, "would be that which you desire to learn, from and of the other and under dictation, by heart, *imparare a memoria*."[27] As in "A Dog in San Francisco" in the final section of *Secular Love*, "Heart and skills, there's nothing else" (*S*, 104). In *Handwriting*, more than in any of Ondaatje's collections, is the fear of wordlessness countered by this collaboration.

3

Given the intrinsic nature of curiosity, it's curious how few studies have been made of it. As Inan states, "The Ancient Greek idea that all philosophy starts with wonder deserves more serious attention than it has received by philosophers. Wonder, if taken to mean astonishment, admiration, and awe, does not provide the required impetus to do philosophy; only when such attitudes motivate us to be aware of our ignorance that leads into curiosity do we get the motivation to inquire into the unknown."[28] Like *Running in the Family*, *Handwriting* explores its speaker's relationship to Sri Lanka by following its curiosity into the abundance of lived experience inside names, objects, places, dates – experience documented, imagined, or both. Truth appears and disappears like the eyes of animals in the underbrush. Knowledge is partial and the writing, by implication, forever unfinished.

Although we write poems using our knowledge and our skills, says Merwin, the unknown is both a source and destination: "The arrogance would be the assumption that what you know has some kind of final value and you can depend upon it, and it will get rid of a whole world which you will never know, which really informs it. Both of these worlds, in my view, are without meaning ... but the sense of the world of relation comes from them nonetheless."[29] Meaning is an ongoing activity of relation, and individuality, as Carson has said, "resides in the way links are made."[30] It also expresses itself in a feeling for what to exclude. In a conversation with Cole, alongside Miles Davis's famous line about listening to what can be left out, Ondaatje references Donald Richie's study of Japanese aesthetics that explores its "net of associations composed of listings or jottings, connected intuitively, that fills in a background and renders the subject visible."[31] This mode resists the imposition of a linear structure actually antithetical to experience, and when he read Richie, Ondaatje says, he thought thank God, as "I really do believe that one makes something out of details."[32] Richie's study also notes a concern with process over product, with self-construction over self-expression.[33] This is the mode of *Handwriting*. And it's a mode in which readers participate with our own intuition, making connections, listening at the gaps.

The first poem, "A Gentleman Compares His Virtue to a Piece of Jade," playfully references the gentleman of Confucian philosophy who, in the *Analects*, among many qualities, cautions, observances, and actions, has nine concerns: clarity of vision, acuity of hearing, warmth of expression, a respective bearing, in his words sincere, in service reverent, and, when in doubt, he wants to ask questions. The jade he esteems is that which, having been unearthed in raw form,

Michael Ondaatje's Poetry   89

acquires value over time by a process of refinement. The poem's details – which feel as though they emerge in real time – speak to the refinements of skill, ritual, art, language that attempt to give mystery physical presence. And like objects chosen for a shrine, the sacred and the secular inflect each other with their contexts:

Bamboo tubes cut in 17th-century Japan
we used as poem holders.

We tied bells onto falcons.

A silted water garden in Mihintale.
The letter M. The word "thereby." (HW, 3)

Whether it's Federico Tesio, who "graced us with the Breeding the Racehorse," or that "The Buddha's foot shifted at the moment of death," images of transformation feel at once vulnerable and persistent. But among manifestations of faith secular and sacred appear also images of war. The poem introduces violent conflict as embedded in place and people, alive in them, even as faith, art, and wonder are simultaneously alive, balanced "in the darkness above us" like "That tightrope-walker from Kurungala / the generator shut down by insurgents" (HW, 3, 5).

Its engine noise having just quit, the lights gone out – this is absence we can hear and feel. *Handwriting* is among other things a book of silences, of absent presences. Silence nests in its title – a solitary activity, a mark of the individual, and a means to communicate over distance, across time. "It's a long way from one life to another. Why write at all," asks Li, "if not for that distance."[34] Silence is structural in the poems, felt in the breaks amid short stanzas, heard between lines, read in the structures of the lines themselves. It expands into the pauses initiated by punctuation, expands around the clarity of the phrases. Never does the disappearance of something feel more imminent than when it is intensely present. Even though I've been calling this structural element silence, I could as easily call it distance, or time, which is for Berger "the very basic theme" of poetry.[35] Lacking the awareness of the passage of time, poetry, like a room, "risks becoming inanimate. Or, to be more accurate, its silence risks becoming inanimate."[36] The poems create an experience of the "lived durée" that is "not a question of length but of depth or density."[37] In lived time, silences are also structural. As Maria Stepanova observes, "lacunae and gaps are the constant companions of survival."[38] The poems attend to these gaps, to time passing inside them. Lines and sentences possess the tensile strength of someone listening hard. Stanzas create a feeling of perimeter, of edge, of standing at their doors.

The final image above is Dionne Brand's, from *The Blue Clerk*. In it she writes that poetry – using time, *as* time – "can make you see the xylem between the then and the after, or the now and the after."[39] It can also "expose the heterogeneous qualities of a life, or of life, in an age in which all efforts both corporate and State, seem to homogenize."[40] In *Handwriting*, what official records neglect or overwrite are inscribed in practices and in place:

> Monks from the north came
> down our streams floating – that was
> the year no one ate river fish.

> There was no book of the forest,
> no book of the sea, but these
> are the places people died. (HW, 6)

In the long poem "Buried," stone and bronze gods are consigned to the earth to protect them from centuries of conflict, the "massacre and race" (HW, 8) above ground. The passive "To be buried in times of war" transitions into the active and urgent "To bury, surrounded by flares," "carrying the faith of a temple," and "Hiding / the gestures of the Buddha" (HW, 7). We witness events as they arrive, then find ourselves again in the position of the listener as the past tense returns. Layers of time are exposed. The poem creates a simultaneity of event and duration – ancient ruins and armed men hiding in jungles, war's modern degradations and roots spreading slowly across the face of the Buddha, statues unearthed after centuries "into heatwave, insect noise, bathers splashing in tanks" (HW, 9). This simultaneity seems embodied in the "black lake where water disappears / below mud and rises again," whose colour in the eight Rasas represents terror. But also there are saffron robes of monks seven centuries ago, "and at this hour the sky / almost saffron" (HW, 10), a colour representing courage in the face of terror.

Michael Ondaatje's Poetry   91

When the first-person finally appears, it is "shaking from fever" with "water in my bones," as if history's black lake has invaded the speaker in solitude "buried / in the darkness of a room." Vertigo shimmers in fever's uncanny rearrangements of surroundings. And, here at the end of the poem, is the vertigo of looking through storeys of time rising and receding. "Lightning over that drowned valley" reminds the speaker of "Thomas Merton who died of electricity" (HW, 13), prompting the speculation, "But if I had to perish twice?" (HW, 7–13). In the eighth century, Li Po wrote to his friend Du Fu: "Thank you for letting me read your new poems. It was like being alive twice." It might seem for someone whose world is doubled in attention that the vertigo of loss is doubled likewise.

What rises in the floods of history can take a personal toll. Curiosity is not without its hazards. Alberto Manguel notes that "The tension between the curiosity that leads to discovery and the curiosity that leads to perdition threads its way throughout our endeavors."[41] In "Buried 2," the acquisitive curiosity that leads to conquest – that leads kings to visualize water gardens in forests, to assert

ownership of trees,

boundary lines – the fruit
and where it fell (HW, 26)

– is of the variety that sets out, as Hume wrote, to conform "our ideas of objects to their real existence" as opposed to the open-ended curiosity interested in "discovery of proportions of ideas."[42] And it is contrasted in the poem to what is flattened beneath it – libraries, local knowledges, rituals of art and observance that die with the people "whose bodies / could not be found." In the disputed forests:

The Ola leaf on which to compose
our stanzas of faith

Indigo for eyelids, aerograms

The mid-rib of a coconut palm
to knit a fence (HW, 26)

92 Karen Solie

Acts and objects speak to lived experiences more clearly, writes Jacques Ranciére, "than any chronicle of their endeavours; a household object, a piece of fabric, a piece of pottery, a stele, a pattern painted on a chest or a contract between two people we know nothing about."[43] A plenitude resonates between discrete images. As how, between four Sinhalese phrases and their English translations that are the poem's final entry – between "*Hora gamanak yana ganiyak*" and "A woman who journeys to a tryst" – a bit of untranslatability lies, a bit of excess is liberated (HW, 21, 29).

"The Nine Sentiments" continues to tease out the particulars of the previous poem, its "Nine finger and eye gestures / to signal key emotions," its "small boats of solitude" (HW, 24). Desire is experienced in specificities: "The brush of sandalwood along the collarbone," the silk of a dress whose green represents love. Desire, like the devil, is in the details. It, like faith, arcs across distance and time to the other whose being is in excess of what is known. Of the Nine Sentiments of Tamil love poetry as indicated in the collection's notes – "romantic/erotic, humorous, pathetic, angry, heroic, fearful, disgusted, amazed, and peaceful" (HW, 78) – humour in this section is prominent, expressed in the pleasure and play of language. There is "sidelong coquetry / at the Columbo Apothecary." Also:

Aliganaya – "the embrace
during an intoxicated walk"
or "sudden arousal
while driving over speed bumps" (HW, 35)

There are "gold / ragas of longing" (HW, 35) that correspond to the yellow that signifies wonder. Desire, like laughter, is both extra and necessary. Laughter at desire's state of perpetual wonder, its infinite variation, escapes the habitual and persists counter to destruction and chaos. "Comedy," as Robert Hass writes, "is on the side of Eros," and laughter "in the service of an imagination of life that has some power to hold at bay, or at least mitigate, the power in us of the imaginations of violent triumph and destruction."[44]

Still,

The king's elephants

Michael Ondaatje's Poetry 93

have left for war
crossing the rivers. (HW, 36)

Still, "His guards loiter in the dark corridors" (HW, 36). But a charged awareness of details of body and surrounding is supplemented by a pleasure in the delicate attentions of language:

the Bhramarah bee is drunk
from the south pasture

this insect that has
the letter "r" twice
in its name (HW, 37)

It's delicious. As is the single line of the following sixth sentiment, "Five poems without mentioning the river prawn" (HW, 38), that puts that prawn retroactively in each of the preceding poems. It becomes the "uncaught prawn hiding" by the feet of the women mid-river in the next sentiment, among "laughter when husbands are away" (HW, 39).

But desire, like curiosity, can also manifest dangerously as greed, conquest, madness. Where there is desire "Where is the forest / not cut down / for profit or literature" asks "The Ninth Sentiment." And where there is desire there is also loss. In fear, a falcon may become a coward. Desire is loneliness and trouble, and "Where is there a room / without the damn god of love?" (HW, 43). Where indeed. Some consolation may lie in three ways literature resists destruction and despair. "The first," Hass writes, "is by imagining peace. The second is through laughter. The third is through witness. There are probably others."[45]

If one can speak of epiphanies in this book, they are of the kind Cole characterizes as "not only revelation or insight," but "the reassembly of self through the senses [...] an engagement with the things that quicken the heart, through the faculties of the body, the things that catch the heart off guard and blow it open."[46] They lie in physical gestures like that of the seventy-year-old lady on Air Lanka Flight 5 who braids her hair, "curls it into a bun, like my mother's" (HW, 47). The speaker's reassembly embraces, in "Wells," the lost word for water, *vatura*, in the welling up of the memory of his ayah Rosalin Perera, of whom he has no other evidence but the book itself, dedicated to her (*HW*, 50). Water, again, flows through this section. I remember *Secular Love*'s "Claude Glass," the speaker driving to the river party pulling branches through the car window. And that while Merton wrote "When the poet puts his foot in that ever-moving river, poetry itself is born out of the flashing water," he also said, "No one can come near the river unless he walks on his own feet. He cannot come there carried in a vehicle."[47] In *Handwriting*, Ondaatje's speaker has arrived on his own feet.

Like water, the soul is a symbol of passage. It is a word for the unknown in others and in ourselves, the experience of selfhood felt in excess of physical being that others recognize in us,

> the way someone you know
> might lean forward
> and mark the place
> where your soul is
> -- always, they say,
> near to a wound. (*HW*, 51)

"No poem without accident," writes Derrida, "no poem that does not open itself like a wound, but no poem that is not also just as wounding."[48] Many readers have noted the presence of wounds, scars, in Ondaatje's work. They are a mark of change, a word for pain written on the body. Pain is a kind of solitude, an edge where there is no social fuel. The soul lingers at that threshold.

"Death at Kataragama" returns to a room like that of the speaker's earlier fever, a room of no change, just "A constant fall of leaf around me in this time of no rain like the continual habit of death" (*HW*, 55). In a "brutal aloneness" (*HW*, 56) in which words drift away, the speaker imagines his soul migrating into the body of a woodpecker, a water buffalo, a creature to bear it from inertia toward, as in Rilke, "that openness / that is so deep in the animal's vision" ("The Eighth Elegy"). Animals are mystery in the familiar, their territory further beyond the fence than we can go, outside language as we know it. Berger writes of a customs checkpoint, a hare crossing the road ahead. "And although it was running slowly," he notices "it ran for its life."[49] In Czeslow Milosz's "Encounter," "a hare ran across the road. / One of us pointed to it with his hand." That neither the hare nor the one who pointed to it are still alive prompts the speaker to ask, "O my love, where are they, where are they going / [...] I ask not out of sorrow, but in wonder."[50] They, like Ondaatje's animals, illuminate a distance, a difference, an excess that can only be addressed in the attention to it. A gesture in the direction of a disappearance.

From here, *Handwriting* travels outward into story, into the mystery of the future that is also the mystery of the past. In "The Great Tree" blossoms the plum whose flowering at the end of winter symbolizes persistence and hope. The poet Yang Weizhem is here, "whose father built a library," and

Zou Fulei, almost unknown,
who made the best plum flower painting
of any period. (*HW*, 58)

His "One branch lifted into the wind" evokes Ondaatje's own style in this collection, the poet Weizhem's solitude of concentration assured by a removable staircase pulled away (*HW*, 58–9). The staircase, facilitator of passage, appears elsewhere in the collection, though between storeys of past and future it seems largely hidden away. In "The Story," perhaps only

For his first forty days a child
is given dreams of previous lives
[...] before we bury the maps. (*HW*, 60)

The child in the womb listening to his father's prediction becomes a protagonist in a story he can no longer remember. The poem unfolds a narrative of bravery, love, war, and skill, illuminating gaps in time, in knowledge, that our curiosity plays in. We leave the characters suspended between the high windows and the darkness of the night, as we all are suspended, and "We do not know what happened" (*HW*, 60, 66). The story, the reading, forever incomplete.

Handwriting's final poems offer a way to think about inhabiting the vertiginous territory of balance between our solitude and that of others, between language and where it fails, between what we know and the unknowable. Where, as in "Step,"

The ending disappears,
replacing itself

> with something abstract
> as air, a view. (*HW*, 69)

Against "something abstract" is held the ruin of a lotus pavilion, where

> desire became devotional
> so it held up your house,
> your lover's house, the house of your god. (*HW*, 71)

Ondaatje has written that in Gabriel Garcia Marquez's work "Meditation/contemplation/solitude is achieved through various interests: making gold fishes, translating the manuscript, working on the heritage of mercury. But these acts are also the end results of solitude and contemplation. They are not symbolic but are the thought."[51] In devotion, desire becomes a skill passed on through what it makes. Attention to the made attends to the making, is itself a creative act, resisting the inertia of the chaos, as in "Last Ink," "circling your winter boat." In the boat is writing, the image of a mountainside, "Life on an ancient leaf / or a crowded 5th-century seal," the memory of "When you first saw her" (*HW*, 72–3). And, as Berger writes, details of lived lives are not only significant to matters of art and spirit. "How easy it is to lose sight of what is historically invisible – as if people lived only history and nothing else! Popular ingenuity is often invisible. Occasionally, when gathered into political action, it becomes visible."[52]

In the "Night of the Plum and Moon" (*HW*, 72) in plum's persistence illuminated by that symbol of enlightenment and the ineffable, the poem evokes the Buddhist simile of the moon-pointing finger. The simile cautions against the presumption that meaning lies in either the finger pointing, in the word, or in the idea that what it points to can be wholly understood. We might recall Merwin's belief that both of these worlds are without meaning except in their relation. We might recall Milosz's hare. The simile invites contradictions, writes Chien-Hsing Ho, but also a permeability.[53] What's important is that the mind follows the gesture across distance and considers what is illuminated by the arc of it. From

> Our altering love, our moonless faith.
> Last ink in the pen.
> My body on this hard bed,

Michael Ondaatje's Poetry 97

Ondaatje's speaker finds

The moment in the heart
where I roam restless, searching

for the thin border of the fence
to break through or leap.

Leaping and bowing. (*HW*, 74–5)

"The general is where solidarity begins," writes Cole, "but the specific is where our lives come into proper view."[54] *Handwriting*, a personal contemplation, is also a profoundly ethical book. Its observance of detail and deep study of place, its imaginative engagement with the dimensions of others' lives, enacts the sensitivity that Cole says "can function as a reminder, as an intensifier, of what we have always owed each other."[55] The predominance of the third-person plural, multiple rather than general, reminds me a bit of the play of *Elimination Dance*: participants eventually excluded by virtue of outrageously specific experiences end up gathered, one imagines, on the other side in a new awareness of variety. Even taking into account the formal experiment and visceral intensity of *Billy the Kid* and *the man with seven toes*, the candour and expansiveness of *Secular Love*, *Handwriting* reads to me as Ondaatje's riskiest collection. Its attentions are restless and incisive, its act of witness highly relevant. The language and the poetic structures, while beautiful, liberate complex implications that require active reading. In its title, Solecki discerns the mother in *Running in the Family* whose handwriting radically changes at thirty, as if she had "lost the use of a habitual style and forced herself to cope with a new dark unknown alphabet" (*RF*, 150). Similarly, he says, the shift in Ondaatje's style from *Secular Love* to *Handwriting* "is as dramatic as that between early and late Montale or Merwin."[56] It could be true at the same time (as Ondaatje has said of *Billy the Kid*) that it is the style in which this particular book demanded to be written.

Ondaatje is fond of a quote from Berger's novel *G* that appears as an epigraph to *In the Skin of a Lion*: "Never again will a single story be told as though it were the only one." And no one way even to tell a single story. In form, style, perspective, genre, exploring

98   Karen Solie

vertiginous landscapes lit variously by the forces that animate them, Ondaatje's poetry refuses to settle down. His poetry is among his best writing, and *Handwriting* one of his finest books.

NOTES

With thanks to Stan Dragland.

1 Inan, *The Philosophy of Curiosity*, 183.
2 Davenport, "Eros the Bittersweet, by Anne Carson," 189.
3 Carson, *Eros the Bittersweet*, 16–17.
4 Handke, *A Sorrow beyond Dreams*, 67.
5 Solecki, "Nets and Chaos: The Poetry of Michael Ondaatje," 36–48.
6 Coleridge, *Coleridge's Table Talk*, 46.
7 Cole, *Black Paper*, 199.
8 Stevens, *Collected Poetry and Prose*, 919.
9 Ibid., 909.
10 Ondaatje, "Introduction," *The Long Poem Anthology*, 11.
11 Stevens, *Collected Poetry and Prose*, 190.
12 Merwin, "Fact Has Two Faces: An Interview with W.S. Merwin," 46.
13 Walcott, "The Art of Poetry No. 37," n.p.
14 Yiyun, *Dear Friend, from My Life I Write to You in Your Life*, 81.
15 Ondaatje and McCann, "Without a Map."
16 Berger, *and our faces, my heart, brief as photos*, 95.
17 Creeley, "A Sense of Measure," 487.
18 Aristotle, *Poetics*, 1,460a.
19 Derrida, "Che cos'è la poesia?," 223.
20 Cole, *Black Paper*, 218.
21 Howe, "Now I Get It," 214.
22 Merton, *A Search for Solitude*, 40.
23 Ibid.
24 Rilke, *Letters to a Young Poet* [1986], 23.
25 Rilke, "The Duino Elegies." Translated by A.S. Kline, https://www.poetry-intranslation.com.
26 Ibid.
27 Derrida, "Che cos'è la poesia?," 227.
28 Inan, *The Philosophy of Curiosity*, 182.
29 Merwin, "Fact Has Two Faces," 49.
30 Carson, *Eros the Bittersweet*, 204.
31 Ondaatje, conversation with Cole, interviewed by Tonny Vorm.

Michael Ondaatje's Poetry 99

32 Ibid.

33 Richie, *A Tractate on Japanese Aesthetics*, 15.

34 Yiyun, *Dear Friend, from My Life I Write to You in Your Life*, 20.

35 Berger and Demirel, *What Time Is It?*, 92.

36 Ibid., 18.

37 Berger, *and our faces, my heart, brief as photos*, 35.

38 Stepanova, *In Memory of Memory*, 78.

39 Brand, *The Blue Clerk*, 112.

40 Ibid., 110.

41 Manguel, *Curiosity*, 33.

42 Hume, "Of Curiosity, or the Love of Truth," *A Treatise of Human Nature*.

43 Quoted in Stepanova, *In Memory of Memory*, 43.

44 Hass, *What Light Can Do*, 88–9.

45 Ibid., 80.

46 Cole, *Black Paper*, 191.

47 Merton, "Message to Poets," 176.

48 Derrida, "Che cos'è la poesia?," 233.

49 Berger, *and our faces, my heart, brief as photos*, 6.

50 Milosz, "Encounter," 3.

51 Ondaatje, "Garcia Marquez and the Bus to Aracataca," 27.

52 Berger, *and our faces, my heart, brief as photos*, 63.

53 Chien, "The Finger Pointing toward the Moon," 164.

54 Cole, *Black Paper*, 149.

55 Ibid., 205.

56 Solecki, *Ragas of Longing*, 165.

3

Strange Familiars:
Dogs in Michael Ondaatje's Early Poetry

Antje M. Rauwerda

Michael Ondaatje's early poetry is rampant with animals, wild and domestic. *The Dainty Monsters* – which features, among other creatures, dragons, cows, crows, groundhogs, and cats – alerts us to what Douglas Barbour calls "a modern bestiary" in its very title,[1] but subsequent collections too are rife with goats and birds (*the man with seven toes*), rats, iguanas, herons, and spiders (*Rat Jelly*), with more cats, chickens, horses, and rats (*The Collected Works of Billy the Kid*), with more crows (*Pig Glass*), with geckos, more herons, ospreys, and more loons (*Secular Love*), and with bears, hawks, more crows, frogs, and even more loons (*The Cinnamon Peeler*). All manner of fauna populates Ondaatje's poetry, but none is mentioned more frequently and, this essay argues, none bears more significance in the effort to contextualize human identity than the dog. I am defining Ondaatje's early poems as those published before 1991.

In Ondaatje's early poetry, dogs provide perspective, a means of expressing sexual desire, an embodied mongrel hybridity, and the confluence of human and animal, often alongside the confluence of conscious and unconscious insight. They are the foil to the humans Ondaatje represents. If, as Eluned Summers-Bremner observes, Ondaatje's poetics is "a continual restaging of the mobility of dwelling; a sustained re-encounter with nature's – and human nature's – strangeness," then Ondaatje's dogs are a continual investigation of how dwelling might be rooted and how strangeness might be rendered familiar.[2] Dogs are paradoxical insider-outsiders; they are the untamed in the domestic, the far-flung world emplaced at the hearth.

Ondaatje is not unusual in using canine presence to examine the boundaries of human identity and experience, nor is he unusual for his frequent representations of beloved canines. Eighteenth-century wit Alexander Pope doted on his dogs, and he wrote poems for dog collars that argued for humans being doglike themselves: "I am his Highness's dog at Kew / Pray tell me sir, whose dog are you?"[3] William Hogarth painted his pug Trump so often that he was himself satirized for it in a work called "Pug the Painter" by Paul Sandby.[4] The nineteenth century saw dogs ever more imbricated in the emotional fabric of human life. Keridiana Chez argues that in Victorian literature, dogs are frequently "intimately implicated in the making of the human."[5] Indeed, their othering helps "demarcate" human boundaries.[6] However, it can also be "accompanied by a joining, an attachment, an assimilation – a *togethering* as it were – an intimate merger of self and other."[7] In these respects, Ondaatje is also not unusual: dogs provide differentiation (what makes humans human) and facilitate the exploration of an otherness that can coexist with the self. In Ondaatje, what is unusual is the extent to which this last is nuanced: dogs represent the "intimate merger of self and other," as Chez would have it, but retain an obdurate unknowability. What motivates Ondaatje's dogs? Ondaatje typically lets this remain a mystery. These animals do not simply reflect human affect. Humans, rather, grapple with emotions that are fragile and partial compared to those expressed by the wiser, more knowing dogs. Ondaatje's dogs do not reveal their full selves to the humans around them, despite their embeddedness at the heart of human life. Humans are laid bare in front of the onlooking canines; the dogs are more reserved, circumspect.

Ondaatje's dogs ultimately represent a paradoxical double position: they are animals (outsiders to the human world) and yet live as insiders, right at the heart of human domiciles. They suggest both wild freedom *and* contained domesticity. They are a kind of Ondaatjean ideal, living beyond the limits of nation or other constrained identities, while also clearly having a place at the hearth, the most centred and rooted part of the home. Christopher McVey observes that

Many read in Ondaatje's writing a longing to fly beyond the nets of nationality, language, and religion in order to reach, like James Joyce's Stephen Dedalus, some level of autonomy from the national and historical worlds of which one is a part. Yet I argue that Ondaatje's work frequently incorporates a countervailing desire to return, to reclaim, and to bear witness to the historical and national worlds from which his characters emerge. More specifically, this ambivalence registers itself through bodily wounding and trauma. These bodies – mongrel, interstitial, and frequently wounded – encode what I term a "double gesture." They function as troubled sites between the past and the present, bearing that past forward but inevitably occluding or frustrating the present's ability to decipher that past.[8]

There are numerous insights in McVey's analysis that have an analog in Ondaatje's use of dogs. First, Ondaatje's dogs are a device that allows him to explore the possibility of existing in a domestic space while simultaneously flying "beyond the nets of nationality, language." Second, although not wounded, Ondaatje's dogs are also not wholly human, so they occupy the kind of fissured positioning McVey associates with wounding or trauma (they are also sometimes explicitly "mongrel" or hybrid). Third, McVey creates the notion of a "double gesture" in which figures bear the past into the present but also obscure that past. I would argue that Ondaatje's dogs encode a "double gesture" themselves, in which they embody what it is to be fully at home while at the same time embodying an inscrutable foreignness.

The "double gesture" of Ondaatje's dogs, to thus borrow and riff on McVey's terminology, allows insight into human affect while also clarifying how obscure human emotions are to humans themselves. In this respect, Ondaatje's exploration of what dogs experience can be seen as more about what humans would experience were they able to be like dogs. Indeed, Ondaatje's writing about animals in general is often inflected by the human desire to be like that other creature, if just for a moment, in order to learn something about themselves.

My reading of this human desire to experience as if an animal differs from readings by, for instance, Lee Spinks. In his analysis of "Birds for Janet – The Heron" in *The Dainty Monsters*, Spinks sees "tension between the irrefragable alterity of the natural world and an instrumental vision of nature determined to see that world in man's technological image."[9] Spinks perceives a dualism that it is tempting to see in Ondaatje's work, between animals as other and

Dogs in Michael Ondaatje's Early Poetry   103

humans as self. I would contend, rather, that animals, and certainly dogs, invite us to consider an unsettled *human* alterity in relation to the animal's ease of being and fullness of self. My reading of "Birds for Janet – a Heron" suggests that the bird has human characteristics rather than bird-like ones. Its feathers are "fingers," it rests a "hairless ankle" on a "starved knee," and, absurdly, given this long-legged wading bird's ability to fly, it apparently "suicides" where its footprints lead to the lake's water and disappear.[10] The heron is clearly being represented as though expressive of something about humans, even something about the speaker and his own hairless ankles, his own desire to walk into the lake's oblivion. "Best herons are not beautiful / but handsome," the poem concludes, seemingly with a flirtatious wink to "Janet" from a masculine poet/speaker who would like Janet to think of him as handsome too. Spinks reads the human character grafted onto the description of the heron as insufficiency: Ondaatje does not capture what the heron truly is. For Spinks, Ondaatje's heron represents "its imprisonment within an anthropomorphic perspective"; the poem is trying to catch the heron's essence, and "poetic language makes rudimentary sense of this creature but misses what is essential to its nature."[11] I would argue instead that Ondaatje's speaker was never actually trying to scientifically document or capture in full the heron's nature but, rather, to understand something about himself in imagining himself as a heron. In this way, the heron and other animals, notably dogs, in the "modern bestiary" are an exploration of what it might feel like (for a human like the speaker) to be one of the beasts.[12]

On the one hand, "animals can play a highly significant symbolic role in stabilizing the psyche."[13] On the other, animals can represent the human mind's frailty, as in the rat caught in a biscuit tin / "rat fyt in my head" metaphor in *The Collected Works of Billy the Kid* (cw, 38). Psychiatrists Vamik Volkan and Salman Akhtar consider that in a less industrialized setting (as one might find, perhaps, in the Ceylon of Ondaatje's early childhood or the Ontario of his university years),

Animals of all varieties – cows, buffaloes, horses, donkeys, cats, dogs, camels, monkeys, snakes, spiders, butterflies, and even elephants, bears and tigers – can form a part of one's everyday existence. They become receptacles of projected fantasies, containers of unexpressed personal emotions, carriers of phallic exhibitionism, providers of maternal soothing, targets of dark eroticism, and brotherly companions in the journey of life.[14]

Volkan and Akhtar's matter-of-fact listing of the roles animals can play reads almost as a checklist for the functions of animals in Ondaatje's poems. The ways in which animals can bear our projected fantasies and more frankly express sexuality ("phallic exhibitionism") or be "brotherly companions" seem very true of Ondaatje's dogs in particular. Ondaatje's dogs can be a "safety valve" or emotional "surrogate,"[15] but in his poems, human relationships with dogs can also be associated "with emotional self-indulgence ... (irrational, excessive, uncontrollable)."[16]

Dogs are seemingly ubiquitous in these early collections. They "are everywhere" (CW, 72). They are present in iterations of family history, the "fragments" recollected in a storm (so markedly different from Wordsworth's "emotion recollected in tranquility") with "the dogs restless on the porch" ("Light" [CP, 4]). When a group has gathered to move a friend's outhouse, the dog is suddenly interested, the humans suddenly engaged: "everybody screaming to keep the dog away" (CP, 53). Dogs rank more highly than human friends: "Love wife kids dogs couple of friends" ("War Machine" [TTK, 48]). Note how the dogs come after the kids but before the friends. In "Loop," a dying dog is explicitly kin: "Departing family" (TTK, 53).

The dogs in "Loop" are even ubiquitous across time and cosmos. The one-eyed dog dies but "transient as shit – will fade / to reappear somewhere else." The dog is both transient in its physical body and permanent in its essence, omnipresent:

And magic in his act of loss.
The missing eye travels up
in a bird's mouth, and into the sky.
Departing family. It is only the loss of flesh
no more than his hot spurt across a tree.

The dog's fleshly body is as temporary as a stream of urine, but the missing eye travels up to the firmament (rather like Belinda's lock of hair in Pope's "The Rape of the Lock"), and you will forever catch glimpses of this dog, everywhere: "He is the one you see at Drive-Ins / tearing silent into garbage / while societies unfold in his sky"

(*TTK*, 53). Solecki argues that the dog is more important for what he represents than for what he is as a dog: "In the pull between Loop as dog and Loop as symbol, we sense the second is stronger."[17] Solecki continues, suggesting that this dog is nudged "from realism to romance or what Ondaatje calls myth. He becomes less a particular dog than the embodiment and personification of a way of being in the world."[18] This analysis suggests a maneuver useful in reading all of Ondaatje's animals: nudge them toward the romantic. We are to remember that they are on one level animals, but on another they are myths that allow us to investigate alternate ways of being in the world.

Unlike other beasts that live in the out-of-doors, peacocks, loons, horses, cows, and their kin, dogs live in the home. They are at the centre of the house itself, in the middle of family life. Whatever alternate ways of being they magic into our lives, they do so from the position of domestic familiars. In "Late Movies with Skyler," the speaker and Skyler watch movies in the middle of the night; their interaction is easy, close, and companionable. The dog is also right there with them: "The darkness / breathes to the pace of a dog's snoring" (*CP*, 69). Indeed, the dog's snoring is the engine that makes the darkness breathe. It is the life, the energizing force, at the heart of the warm relationship Ondaatje describes. "Birth of Sound" gives us a family home at night, with dogs again centring and anchoring the domestic world:

At night the most private of a dog's long body groan.
It comes with his last stretch
In the dark corridor outside our room.
The children turn.
A window tries to split with cold
the other dog hoofing the carpet for lice.
We're all alone. (*CP*, 32)

The dogs are outside the adults' bedroom and on the carpet scratching. In the night while everyone else is sleeping they are in the main parts of the house, the significant hallways, the open rooms. They are at the centre of things. The last line "We're all alone" is manifestly ambiguous: each person is alone? Each person and each dog is alone? Or, and this is my preferred reading, all the creatures in the house are together, dogs and humans, but the household is like an island, alone amidst the rest of the world. In these instances, the dogs are not actually watching the humans, though in other poems they are spectators.

Dogs are "the unheralded voyeurs of this world" in "Postcard from Piccadilly Street," in which the spaniel "shudders / walks out of the room" when the humans are physically intimate, for "she's had her fill of children now" (TTK, 39). The lines are humorous: the dog has herself matured past interest in procreation and so absents herself from the youthful follies of the humans. They also highlight the pervasiveness of the canine spectator.

We are invited to consider, repeatedly, a canine perspective on human activity as it shapes our perception of people. In "Four Eyes," the speaker is "Naked" with a lover and sees a picture of her, "a photograph of you with posing dog":

> This moment I broke to record,
> walking round the house
> to look for paper.
> Returning
> I saw you, in your gaze,
> still netted the picture, the dog.
> The music continuing
> You were still being unfurled
> shaped by the scene. (TTK, 17)

In these lines, the male lover sees his female partner, sees her in a picture with a dog, and sees her looking at the dog in the picture. In his eyes, she is shaped by both the immediate tableau of his watching her considering the picture and her own consideration of herself in relation to the dog in the picture. The figure with the most agency in this scenario is the dog, posing in the photo, shaping the woman both past and present.

In "Claude Glass," an outdoor screening of a film is interrupted by a dog passing through the projector beam: "and the dog walks under the hover of the swing / beam of projection bursting in his left eye" (S, 17). This is similar to a moment in *The Collected Works of Billy the Kid*: "the outline of houses / Garrett running from a door / – all seen sliding round / the screen of a horse's eye" (CW, 94). Both dog and horse catch the human world in their eyes. In their eyes we see the human world more clearly, as one sees a projector beam more clearly when it is trained upon a screen. However, the dog's eye

Dogs in Michael Ondaatje's Early Poetry 107

bursts with the projection, refracting light back out and projecting a new meaning of its own.

One meaning projected outwards is sexual, Ondaatje's dogs more frankly embodying, desiring, and pursuing their sexual passions. *Secular Love* opens with the Elvis Presleyian dedication "Rock Bottom is for any hound dog's sake." "Rock Bottom" itself begins with the question "Will this be ... unblemished art and truth"? Will it be, the speaker asks,

> What I know of passion
> having written of it
> seen my dog shiver
> with love and disappear
> crazy into the trees
>
> I want (*S*, 47)

The speaker takes his cue from his dog. The dog's passion represents the "unblemished art and truth" that the speaker would like to record in reference to his own love. The speaker is trying to be as honest, trying to get to the clarity of "I want," a clarity that his dog has accessed much more readily. In "The Strange Case," Ondaatje writes,

> My dog's assumed my alter ego.
> Has taken over – walks the house
> phallus hanging wealthy and raw
> in front of guests, nuzzling
> head up skirts
> while I direct my mandarin mood. (*TTK*, 40)

The speaker's mood is polished and complex, though sexually interested. While it is the dog that nuzzles his head up women's skirts and walks around the house with his sex exposed, the seemingly more civilized human speaker would like to do such things himself. The dog's frankness is preferable to the speaker's artifice.

In Ondaatje's poems, the imposition of human artifice is the worst thing that can happen to a canine bloodline. At the very nadir are the purebreds and inbreds of *The Collected Works of Billy the Kid*. Henry the Bassett Hound is the product of "'fat noblemen whose hounds were too fast for them when they went hunting. So they got the worst and slowest of each batch and bred them with the worst and slowest of every other batch and kept doing this until they got the slowest kind of hound they could think of. Looks pretty messy to me,' I said" (CW, 59). It's the humans who look bad out of this, the French noblemen too fat to keep up with their dogs, designing a monster to suit their own grotesque corpulence. But the story that follows that of Henry clarifies a connection between the psychological instability of humans and our need to shape dogs to suit us. It concerns a man named Livingstone, "mad, apparently," who set out to "breed a race of mad dogs," to breed, in other words, dogs that were as mad as he was himself (CW, 60). Livingstone breeds the most insane with the most insane, producing dogs "Whose eyes bulged like marbles; some were blind, their eyes had split ... They didn't snarl, just hissed through the teeth – gaps left in them for they were falling out" (CW, 61). The dogs eventually devour the man, which seems appropriate, meeting his atrocious agenda with what retribution they are able. They start to eat each other, and many die. The remaining dogs are shot. The problem with Henry, and with Livingstone's dogs, is that humans tried to shape them to suit a human agenda. This, in the magical-mytho-romance of Ondaatje's poetry, is aberrant, the most severe inversion of order. The animals, the dogs, are to be exemplars and models for humans, not the other way around.

These rapacious, murdering "mad dogs" are unusual in Ondaatje's poetic corpus for the unmythologized, unvarnished nature of the crimes they commit. Consider, by way of contrast, *The Cat's Table* (a novel that features dogs far more than it does cats). Here dogs also kill a man, but the circumstances are rife with superstition, uncertainty, and mystery. The illness of Hector de Silva is attributed to a curse that makes his beloved Sealyham Terrier first contract rabies and second bite him (CT, 62–5). De Silva takes *The Oronsay*, travelling to the English doctors who might be able to cure him. En route, a small white dog is smuggled on board in a kind of retaliatory mischief by the female passengers who were not *supposed* to go ashore at Aden but did anyway, in disguise (CT, 101–5). Once on board, this second dog escapes and, seemingly fulfilling the curse, runs into the first class cabin of de Silva to bite him in the neck, thereby finishing the already dying man off (CT, 106). The second dog is seemingly connected to the first, and both act surprisingly, motivated seemingly by the curse under which de Silva had been placed. Both dogs, the terrier and the white mongrel, seem fictive, or dreamt, or not-quite real. Both are transformed by some kind of magic that makes them other than themselves.

In Ondaatje's early poetry, dogs can similarly model magical transformations and transmogrifications; at their best they are transient both in terms of corporeal form and spatial location. In "Uswetakeiyawa" (named after a beach village north of Colombo, Sri Lanka), car headlights at night reveal

 the dogs
who lean out of the night
strolling the road
with eyes of sapphire
and hideous body

 so mongrelled
they seem to have woken
to find themselves tricked
into outrageous transformations
...
This is the dream journey
we travel most nights
returning from Colombo. (CP, 63)

The dogs embody Sri Lanka itself, with their sapphire eyes (Sri Lankan sapphires being among the most famous and sought after in the world). However, the dogs are in the midst of change. They are walking along the road, moving, transient. They are "mongrelled," of chaotically mixed bloodlines. McVey argues that "Ondaatje is interested in ... the recovery of personal identity and origin, even if that origin is hybrid, mongrel."[19] These Sri Lankan dogs shadow out of the darkness into the ambiguating beam of headlights, revealing Ondaatje's own hybridity, his Sri Lankan past transformed by years in the UK and then, more permanently, in Canada so that he too is mongrelled, hybrid. The Uswetakeiyawa dogs wake to find themselves changing even more and ever more outrageously. The dogs are representations of the humans' own journey on that metaphorical road, humans' own transience, their own mongrel blood lines, and their own ongoing, outrageous transformations.

Part mythological beast, part emblem of hybridity and transience, part awake and part asleep, the Uswetakeiyawa dogs exist in a zone that is itself part dream. In Ondaatje's poems, dog dreams give access to experiences that outstrip what seems to be domesticity or that connect the domestic to something more cosmopolitan, exotic, adventurous. In "Biography," for instance, "The dog scatters her body in sleep." In her waking life, she is "tacked to humility all day," "children ride her," and "pull hind legs." She is constrained in domesticity: tacked, ridden, pulled (perhaps like the human parent of those same children). In her dreams, the dog's biography is freedom, passion, appetite: "she / tore bulls apart, loosed / heads of partridges, / dreamt blood" (*TTK*, 12). The dog's dreams teach the human how to escape in dreams of his own.

In "Insomnia," the human speaker dreams as a dog having a heart attack, from which potentially fatal experience he wakes with a comical "hello":

> The dog sleepwalks
> into the cupboard
> into the garden and heart attacks
> hello
> I've had a dog dream
> wake up and cannot find
> my long ears (*S*, 54)

The speaker wakes from the dream and mocks himself, quipping about the absence of his hound-dog ears. However, the dream dog's heart attack is an expression of the human speaker's "devastation" – other parts of the poem show him breaking windows, beating his head with stones, shattering a glass tumbler into his own hand. The dog dream allows expression of how severe, how lethal, his own upset is. A shard of glass remains trapped in his finger. The lines "glass / on its voyage out / to the heart" make it sound like the heart attack in the dog dream was a premonition of a human heart attack still to come (*S*, 55).

Things bleed together: meaning accretes in a dream-like fashion. "Country Night," for instance, tells us "We have all dreamed of finding the lost dog," posing it as an existential desire in all of us, to find the lost one and bring them back home, to fold the errant back into the bosom of family (*TTK*, 73). "Buying the Dog" (in

Dogs in Michael Ondaatje's Early Poetry   111

Trick this occurs three pages *after* "Country Night") gives us the dog bought, carefully transported home, only to run away, becoming, perhaps, lost:

> Carefully
> the dog puts his feet
> like thin white sticks out of the car and
> takes off JESUS
> like a dolphin
> over the fields for all we know
> he won't be coming back – (TTK, 76)

This dog dolphining away is "Country Night"'s lost dog, or it *could* be. As we reach for meaning, the poems together feel like something we have dreamt about dogs. Read "Country Night" in light of "Buying the Dog," and it feels like the lost dogs, the errant, the wanderers, the exiles, the hound dogs (the canine characters not unlike the human Ondaatje himself) are shaping our dreams.

Dog dreams occupy a fluid, multi-dimensioned liminal space between human and animal-savant as well as between conscious and subconscious experience. In his poems involving rivers and dogs, Ondaatje creates explicit images of fluidity and motion, the transit between what is immediate reality and what is ephemeral (myth, memory, aspiration). In the poems about rivers without dogs, the task is more simply for the human to be human, to feel themselves in the water, making a journey. One can contrast the two types of river poem.

"Walking to Bellrock," for instance, has no dogs. It chronicles a journey in a river: "Two figures in deep water ... are walking / as if half sunk in a grey road" (CP, 56). One wants to read this through the classics, to think of Lethe and ferrymen, but Ondaatje insists "There is no metaphor here ... there is no history or philosophy or metaphor with us / The problem is the toughness of the Adidas shoe." He insists we read this river walk as simply about two men walking in a river "following the easy fucking stupid plot to town" (CP, 57). He wants us to think about slippery rocks and how there wasn't profound conversation, just movement.

Conversely, "Inner Tube" takes place on a "warm July river" and features both "a dog / learning to swim near me" and a "blue heron" whose flight makes it look like one of them, heron or man, must be "upside down":

slowly paddling
towards an estuary between the trees

there's a dog
learning to swim near me
friends on shore

my head
dips
back to the eyebrow
I'm the prow
on an ancient vessel,
this afternoon
I'm going down to Peru
soul between my teeth. (*S*, 49)

We think, at first, it is the man paddling, but the subsequent stanza ("there's a dog" etc.) suggests that this could also be the dog. Whose friends are on shore? The dog's or the man's? The two, dog and man, have become one fluid consciousness on the river. Out of this fluid and mingled canine-human identity comes the dream: "I'm the prow / on an ancient vessel ... going down to Peru." There is a confluence of dog and man both literally in the river and in the dream they perhaps share. "Walking to Bellrock" had neither metaphors nor dreams. It is apparently the dog in "Inner Tube" that allows that poem's speaker to drift into an imaginary world.

"Escarpment" (a poem without dogs) summarizes a human approach to rivers: "He loves too, as she knows, the body of rivers. Provide him with a river or a creek and he will walk along it. Will step off and sink to his waist, the sound of water and rock encasing him in solitude" (*S*, 125). To be human in a river is to experience oneself, alone, which may be to experience oneself more fully. However, to be a dog in the river, or human-as-dog, is to lose one's edges, to become more than oneself, to dream new autobiographies, histories, and identities. Returning to "Uswetakeiyawa,"

Once in the night we saw
something slip into the canal.
There was then the odour we did not recognize.
The smell of a dog losing its shape. (*CP*, 64)

Dogs in Michael Ondaatje's Early Poetry

The dog in the water loses its shape, transforms into something new. It escapes the boundaries of what it had been. It teaches humans to do the same.

The speaker in "Claude Glass" wakes out of a dream of the tropics to the river-like scene that is his home at night. It leads to the dog, which embodies both the stable hearth and the possibility of transformation:

> At 4 a.m. he wakes in the sheet
> that earlier held the tropics in its whiteness.
>
> The invited river flows through the house
> into the kitchen up
> stairs, he awakens and moves within it.
> In the dim light
> he sees the turkish carpet under water,
> low stools, glint
> of piano pedals, even a sleeping dog
> whose dreams may be of rain. (S, 18)

The speaker wakes, or dreams, and travels a river that runs through the kitchen and up the stairs, defying gravity. The speaker's movement (Is it swimming? Wading?) follows the current and finds in the flow "a sleeping dog" at the centre of the home and the centre of the dream itself. The dog may be dreaming a different dream (of rain), but both dreamers – man and dog – are together in the same watery element.

Out of this fluid scene, from the domesticity that should be firm but is mutable, the speaker escapes:

> This is the hour for sudden journeying.
>   Cervantes accepts
> a 17th Century invitation
> from the Chinese Emperor.
> Schools of Chinese-Spanish Linguistics!
> Rivers of the world meet! (S, 17)

The dog is at the hearth that holds the home and family together but also represents possibility, the dream of another life, another identity entirely, one that here is explosive with international travel and transformation.

Of Ondaatje's novel *Warlight*, Mike Marais argues that "To be open to other lives ... is to make oneself vulnerable to being affected by the stranger whom one has failed to understand."[20] Marais has humans principally in mind here, but his comment elucidates the dogs in this novel too. *Warlight*'s smuggled racing greyhounds are "immigrants ... with false identities" and forged papers (WL, 83). In the dark empty houses in which they meet, protagonist Nathaniel courts "Agnes," a girl using a false name, just as the dogs have false identities. He opens his heart to both the strangeness of the animals and that of the girl. In one of these encounters, Nathaniel has had to bring four of the greyhounds with him. He and Agnes are naked in the dark, but they play with the dogs, literally baring their hearts to the animals: "in the large semi-dark rooms of this borrowed house, we wrestled them to the ground, their long mouths warm against our bare hearts" (WL, 91). Here, and in Ondaatje's early poetry, dogs are, to return to my slanting of McVey's "double gesture," strangers in that we never fully know them and also, paradoxically, intimate familiars, as close as possible to the heart of human life. As such, they occupy two conflicting positions at once: the outsider and the family member (sometimes even the confidant: the dog is the only one to know the beloved's name in "Rock Bottom" [S, 72]). Dogs are calm, anchoring presences at the centre of the home and also dreaming visionaries that open the minds of the human near them to outrageous, incredible transformations.

Considering *Warlight* once more, Nathaniel's encounter with Agnes and the dogs explicitly expresses the paradoxical intimate otherness of dogs, bringing ideas from Ondaatje's early poems to fruition in this later novel:

> when they curled up to sleep we slept on the floor beside them
> as if all around us these animals were our longed-for life, our
> wished-for company, a wild unnecessary essential unforgotten
> human moment in London during those years. When I woke,
> a dog's thin sleeping face was beside me, breathing calmly into
> mine, busy with its dreams. It heard the change in my waking
> breath and opened its eyes. Then shifted position and placed
> its paw on my forehead gently, either as a gesture of careful
> compassion or superiority. It felt like wisdom. "Where are you
> from?" I asked it. "What country?" (WL, 92–3)

The dogs make it safe to sleep, they domesticate the space, yet they are "wild." The moment with dogs creates a consummately "human moment." The sleeping dog has its own "busy" dreams. Nathaniel is like a child next to this parental calmness, next to the "wisdom" the dog seems to impart when it places its paw on Nathaniel's forehead. Most of all, the dog is a stranger, an outsider, just as Nathaniel himself feels: "Where are you from? ... What country?"

Marais's work includes a reading of this novel's greyhounds and the fact that they are never given names. These are dogs introduced to the racing scene to create chaos (WL, 105). That these dogs are unnamed is significant. Marais argues that "to name the other person is to contain his or her otherness and so to master him or her" (WL, 92). Ondaatje's unnamed dogs are uncontained. Indeed, Ondaatje's poetic dogs are also very seldom given names. Mostly, the dogs in the poems I describe above are simply "the / a dog." They are, to follow Marais, unmastered, which is a significant deviation from the human-canine dynamic one might expect (one thinks, for instance, of RCA's emblem "His Master's Voice" and the dog listening to the gramophone). The rhetoric of mastery rings false: Ondaatje never engages a Hegelian master-slave paradigm in framing these animals. However, the rhetoric of strangeness of, as Marais would have it, our vulnerability in our failure to understand the stranger rings true. The "double gesture" of the dogs is ultimately embedded in the love we share with them, which makes us most vulnerable to what we don't understand. In that emotion in particular, dogs are self and other, known and unknowable. Dogs are a benison, and a mystery.

"Flirt and Wallace" may be named in the title of that poem, but primarily they are the unnamed "life force[s]" that embody our capacity to love all while not submitting to our control or comprehension.[21] In the body of this poem they are "The dog" and "The other dog." The first

> almost
> tore my son's left eye out
> with love, left a welt of passion
> across his cheek. (RJ, 36)

The violent almost-blinding of a child, one of the most monstrous acts a human parent could imagine, is here attributed to the dog's fervent love for the boy. The word "passion," which sounds consummately human and erotic, makes one think that all intimate relations, maybe especially those among human lovers, must have within them intense proximity combined with what can never be fully known about another living being. Here, as elsewhere, imagining what it is to be the dog reveals something about what it is to be human. Solecki sees in the naming of the dogs in this poem's title an "anthropomorphic gesture."[22] This reminds me of Spinks, who saw in Ondaatje's heron "imprisonment within an anthropomorphic perspective."[23] However, "The dog" Flirt (free of his name by line 1), and "The other dog" Wallace (free of his name by line 5) are anything but imprisoned by anthropomorphism. The human world does not constrain them.

The strange and savage otherness of these dogs is domesticated *by the speaker* when he describes the scrape mark teeth have left as a contained and mild-sounding "welt" on the boy's cheek. The word "welt" reads like the kind of lie parents tell themselves when they need reassuring that their child is not too badly hurt. The child did not lose an eye. Stitches are not required. It is just a "welt." We remember, however, that the dog bit the child in the face. Human words may try to neutralize the act, but its strangeness and how vulnerable we are to that strangeness remains.

This while the second dog is licking "the armpits" of the speaker's shirt "for the salt / the smell and taste / that identifies me from others" (*RJ*, 36). The strangeness and violence to which we are vulnerable is juxtaposed with the fact that the dogs know us and, seemingly, know us fully. They know us, implicitly, in all the ways that make us distinct from other humans. They know us better than other humans do. The poem's final stanza brings together the ways in which dogs are other and the intimacy with which they touch our lives as "selves":

> With teeth which carry broken birds
> with wet fur jaws that eat snow
> suck the juice from branches
> swallowing them all down
> leaving their mouths tasteless, extroverted,
> they graze our bodies with their love. (*RJ*, 36)

Their behaviours are inscrutable. The "extroverted" mouths taste and consume life fully, maybe more fully than humans can. The carrying of dead birds, eating of snow and branches are mysteries.

Dogs in Michael Ondaatje's Early Poetry 117

In the poem's last line, we are blessed by their gracing us with their contact ("grace," an almost homophone for "graze") in spite of the injury they can inflict (a "graze" that, like a "welt," could have been much worse) when "they graze our bodies with their love."

NOTES

1 Barbour "Controlling the Jungle," 111–13.
2 Summers-Bremner, "Reading Ondaatje's Poetry," 2.
3 Pope, "Dog Collars.".
4 [Sandby], *Pug the Painter Following the Example of Messrs Scumble Asphaltum & Varnish.*
5 Chez, *Victorian Dogs, Victorian Men*, 1-5.
6 Ibid., 14.
7 Ibid., 15.
8 McVey, "Reclaiming the Past," 141–2.
9 Spinks, *Michael Ondaatje*, 22.
10 Ondaatje, *The Dainty Monsters*, 12 13.
11 Spinks, *Michael Ondaatje*, 22.
12 Hobkirk writes about birds in Ondaatje's novel *The English Patient*, arguing that in this work "Birds cannot be birds ... all appear in different states than is natural" ("Villa San Girolamo," 145). This is an assertion midway between Spinks's (the essence of the heron is insufficiently captured) and my own (the point was always to suggest what it might be like for a human to be heron-esque) in that it suggests that Ondaatje represents birds but not really as themselves.
13 Volkan and Akhtar, "Immigration, National Identity, and Animals," 263.
14 Ibid., 262.
15 Chez, *Victorian Dogs, Victorian Men*, 5.
16 Ibid., 21.
17 Solecki, *Ragas of Longing*, 89.
18 Ibid., 90.
19 McVey, "Reclaiming the Past," 144.
20 Marais, "Uncertainty in the Time of the Stranger," 99.
21 Solecki, *Ragas of Longing*, 90.
22 Ibid., 89.
23 Spinks, *Michael Ondaatje*, 22.

4

The Scent of Paradise:
Michael Ondaatje's "The Cinnamon Peeler"

Ulla Ratheiser

On the surface, Michael Ondaatje's "The Cinnamon Peeler" is a love poem in which the lyric subject imagines how intimate relations with his beloved become traceable by the smell of cinnamon he leaves on her body. At the same time, however, the poem lends itself to a more dendritic reading that explores how our olfactory senses, memory, and desire intersect to help create a vision of an ideal elsewhere. As the following analysis will endeavour to demonstrate, Ondaatje utilizes the spice and its distinctive smell to create in the delineation of the beloved's body an ultimately desirable location that the perpetually wandering lyric subject can take possession of, even if it is only in an act of the imagination. Just as John Donne, in "To His Mistress Going to Bed," has his lyric subject compare his beloved to "Mahomet's paradise," his "kingdom, safest when with one man mann'd,"[1] Ondaatje employs the scented and marked female body as a projection of paradise, the most unreachable yet most sought-after place that his lyric subject, in turn, can govern. In doing so, Ondaatje builds on established constructions of access to and expulsion from paradise, which is also regulated by access to and expulsion from the consumption of a particular food. In toying with his reader's memory of the smell of cinnamon as well as the persona's imaginary reconstruction of it, he clearly positions his projection, first, in each reader's personal experiences but, secondly, in a specific geographical location – Sri Lanka. However, this specification is simultaneously unhinged through a shifting of temporal levels so as to bring his construction of an Edenic place in line with the habitual uncertainty that inhabits all notions of paradise.

Michael Ondaatje's "The Cinnamon Peeler" 119

It could be argued that it is precisely the elusiveness of the concept that generates the attraction paradise acquires in a migrant context, where it is repeatedly seen to be taking the place of another, possibly even more unattainable, location – home. "Home" is clearly a powerful motif in migrant literature, even though Rosemary Marangoly George, for one, proposes a revaluation of the concept in connection with diasporic writing. She argues that the "immigrant genre," surprisingly, "is often marked by a detached and unsentimental reading of the experience of 'homelessness,'"[2] while Iain Chambers observes that "the promise of a homecoming – completing the story, domesticating the detour – becomes an impossibility"[3] in migrant literature. But even though the possibility of a return remains elusive, "symbols of return or the invocations, often through the sacred, of the homeland or the home-idea"[4] assume a prominent position within the experience of diaspora. Precisely this elusiveness arguably holds one of the great potentials of "home" in the diasporic context, as Aamir Mufti and Ella Shohat, too, have suggested: "the idea of home appears locked within a fundamental ambivalence: 'home' – place or desire?"[5]

Ondaatje transmutes this ambivalence in conceptualizations of home into a projection of paradise, possibly the ultimate imaginary homeland (to refer to Salman Rushdie's idea of the imaginary recreation of the unattainable home)[6] even though, for more than two thousand years, the term has largely resonated with religious meaning. While paradise, in its Old Iranian version *pairidaēza*, originally referred to a wall surrounding a garden or orchard or an enclosed garden itself, its meaning has evolved over time to denote a place of unequalled pleasure and eventually, in the Greek translation of the Bible, to refer to the Garden of Eden:[7] "And the Lord God planted a garden eastward in Eden; and there he put the man whom he had formed" (Genesis 2:8).

Relevant in connection with Ondaatje's poem and how it creates an idea of paradise by relying on the powers of cinnamon is the strong link that exists between the various conceptions of paradise and food. Although the secular meaning already establishes this connection (through the magnificent garden and its produce), this association becomes particularly tangible in the religious inscription of paradise that is traceable in all Abrahamic religions. It is the breaking of a food taboo[8] that prompts the expulsion from paradise, despite the differing relevance of the concept in the Abrahamic religions.[9] By the same token, a possible return, which is especially important in the Christian and Muslim context, is linked to the consumption of food such as the Christians' eating of Christ's sacrificed body in the form of the host.[10] In Hinduism and Buddhism, too, there are concepts comparable to Abrahamic notions of paradise, although they tend to have a more fixed temporal limitation. What is inscribed in all these religious notions of paradise, however, is the difficulty of ever reaching it, as well as the ever-pending expulsion. Just as Marcel Proust was convinced that "les vrais paradis sont les paradis qu'on a perdus,"[11] the close connection between a return to a (projected) paradise and migrant literature becomes palpable.

One axis that traces yet another level on the multi-dimensional grid joining notions of paradise, migrant literature, and Ondaatje's "The Cinnamon Peeler" is how potently particular tastes and smells conjure up associations with home and an imagined paradisiacal locale. Jopi Nyman explores the relevance of food in a migrant context, in which notions of home, food, and memory become inextricably linked to processes of identification, "where the tropes of taste and food play a double role, stitching the group together but also separating it from the dominant."[12] At the same time, food becomes a powerful tool to connect with the past and traditions and as such aid the construction of a "home away from home."[13] Hence, when Seni Seneviratne writes, in her poem "Cinnamon Roots,"

> Cinnamon, sweet wood spice, once traded like gold,
> when I look for my roots I find you, yellowish brown
> like my winter skin, native of Sri Lanka, growing wild,
> in the jungles of the Kandy Highlands.[14]

she particularly highlights this dimension by establishing the close link between a (dislocated) self and the country of origin, manifest in the relation to the all-pervading smell, taste, and materiality of food, in this case cinnamon. Cinnamon, after all, is not only an essential ingredient in Sri Lankan cooking[15] but can also be read as metonymically representing Sri Lanka itself, powerfully signifying the contested historical position of the island.[16]

Cinnamon is one of the oldest spices[17] and is also mentioned repeatedly in the texts of the Bible (as in Exodus and Proverbs). It was an essential ingredient in Egyptian embalmment and was also well known to the Greeks and Romans, as Cosmas Indicopleustes, for example, illustrates in his Topography.[18] Geographically, it is inextricably intertwined with Sri Lanka, the "pearl in the Indian Ocean," the "tropical paradise,"[19] which was known as Cinnamon Island.[20] The spice's botanical name itself bears witness to this in referencing the colonial term for the island, Ceylon: *Cinnamonum verum* or *Cinnamon zeylanicum* is the finest and most desired form of cinnamon,[21] cultivated in Sri Lanka for many centuries,[22] and fundamentally connected to the colonial exploitation of the island. Thus, Florence Ratwatte identifies cinnamon as the "Holy Grail of foreign invaders" in that it became "the main article of trade for the great Dutch East India Company and over which long and costly wars were fought between Portugal and Holland."[23] A Dutch historian termed the spice the "rich bride Helen" for whom the Portuguese and the Dutch engaged in fierce and frequent battles.[24] With British colonization, cinnamon lost its centrality as a main export item, the emphasis now lying on coffee, tea, and gum production.[25] Nevertheless, so intertwined seem the fates of the island and the spice that one becomes unfathomable without the other; so mutually inscribed are their histories that one has come to denote the other.

Precisely these notions – religious and secular, spatial and temporal, historical and political, culinary and olfactory – are multiply exploited by Ondaatje in the "The Cinnamon Peeler." Ondaatje has his persona imagine that he is a cinnamon peeler. By adopting this profession, the persona believes, he would not only acquire the distinctive smell of cinnamon but also pass it on to his wife, thereby distinguishing her from other women and identifying her as his wife, who would bear his smell like his name.

In a first reading, the poem can be understood as a love poem exploring the various sensual and sensational aspects of physical love, expressed by a variety of images appealing to all the senses, although the olfactory, tactile, and visual prevail.[26] A second reading of the poem, however, reveals that the poem touches not only upon the lovers' relationship but also on an idea of a paradisiacal dreamland. In peeling off some of the poem's bark, one finds that "The Cinnamon Peeler" communicates multi-layered notions of a return to paradise, projected into complex conceptions of space and time. To explore these, it will prove worthwhile to follow some of the multidirectional associations the poem affords, just as the migrant might follow the various calls of paradise and of home.

One evocation clearly locates the poem in a particular space without ever naming it openly; by stating, "If I were a cinnamon peeler" (CP, 156–7) and later on referring to the monsoon, the persona prompts assumptions that his imagination places him in Sri Lanka, the "cinnamon island." As his projection illustrates, for him this would be a blissful place saturated with a multiplicity of smells – saffron, honey, tar – and demarcated exclusively by the body of his beloved. By referring to this dimension of Sri Lanka only, though, the poem deliberately excludes the island's particularly fraught political situation and violent past and present. Thus, the inherent – and tragic – irony that such an identification of Sri Lanka with paradise would support is neither sidestepped nor even ignored; after all, the temporal elusiveness of this imagined place rules out any anchoring in an actual temporal and/or spatial realm.

Despite its spatio-temporal elusiveness, Ondaatje's poem evokes powerful associations of home. The close connection between food and a sense of home, not only in a migrant context, has already been discussed.[27] Here the sense of home is created by the scent of cinnamon throughout the text. What we associate with certain smells is, of course, very much culture bound, although there seems to be a grain of universally shared and therefore easily *decipherable* olfactory quality in cinnamon that binds it inextricably to private experiences: while it is used in the Western world to spice cakes, puddings, and biscuits, in Sri Lankan cooking it features prominently in all kinds of curries, and in Greece, for example, it is used to give a particular scent to candles in church.[28] In other words, Ondaatje's poem appeals to a very specific understanding of cinnamon to conjure an emotionally charged environment. Cinnamon leaves its traces not only on the female body but also on the poem itself; thus, the spice as such becomes the strongest metaphor for the projected return by evoking a sense of coming home, albeit to an imagined paradisiacal place.

The poem's third layer opens a temporal perspective in that the implied return to paradise becomes a journey into an imagined past. It is above all through the time shift between the second and the third strophe that the poem's intention to invoke a paradisiacal (idealized?) past is made obvious: whereas in the opening passage the persona hypothesises about becoming or being a cinnamon peeler ("If I *were* a cinnamon peeler / I *would* ride your bed / and leave the yellow bark dust / on your pillow" [lines 1–4; emphasis added]), from the third strophe onwards his suggested metamorphosis is already

Michael Ondaatje's "The Cinnamon Peeler" 123

accomplished, with that strophe forming a kind of bridge: "You *will be known* among strangers / as the cinnamon peeler's wife" (lines 17–18; emphasis added). From the fourth strophe on, then, the lyric subject *was* the cinnamon peeler who marked his wife with his smell and talks about varieties of prenuptial lovemaking that would leave his presence unnoticed to the "keen nosed" mother. The return to paradise is thus not only a spatial process but also a temporal one – the paradise is to be found in (an elusive) past, retrieved in an act of nostalgic resuscitation.

This ties in with Ingrid Dämmrich's observation that "references to remote past or future paradises frequently function as signals that there is a 'different story' to be told that contrasts with the present, non-paradisiacal condition. In expressing nostalgia for a location or condition of former or future bliss, such narratives incorporate a critical stance toward the corruption and loss of innocence, freedom and bliss of the present age."[29]

This "different story" is purposely omitted by Ondaatje and can only be inferred through negative exclusion; indeed, the present situation of the persona and his beloved might be decidedly less drastic than the paradise association would have us assume; by employing the traditional trope, Ondaatje might just as well be exploiting "paradise ... as a privileged location for love."[30] But even though the lovers' present age might be less corrupt and less marked by a loss of innocence than Dämmrich's observation would suggest, depending on where the reader places them on an actual spatio-temporal level, what cannot be neglected is the powerful antithesis this blissful nostalgic place forms to the Sri Lanka of today.

An evocation in yet another direction is of special political relevance, since the persona as an outsider imagines his return to a culture and a profession that he has either long left behind or has never had. Thus, the aspiration to become a cinnamon peeler,[31] a very traditional profession reserved for members of a specific caste (like the Salagama caste)[32] in Sri Lanka, becomes synonymous with an attempt to gain access to a restricted culture and to occupy an exclusive position within it. The parallels suggested by this intrusion into a restricted area once again highlight the notions of paradise resonant throughout the poem.

In sketching the body of the beloved woman as this very paradise, "The Cinnamon Peeler" most powerfully evokes associations with a projected return to paradise, a paradise that is marked out by the particular smell of cinnamon, the Sri Lankan spice. Ondaatje thus constructs his paradise in two directions that might be seen as overlapping. On the one hand, he has the lyric subject re-enact the historical process of colonization of Sri Lanka, with the female body taking the place of the colonized island. On the other, through the temporal and spatial unhinging of the poem, as outlined above, the invasion of the female body can be read as an act of transcending the historical reference, anticipating the recreation and consequential conquest of paradise on a more universal level.

The persona tenderly invades the woman's body, marks her out, leaves her with his traces. He can thus be seen as creating his very own paradise in her body, a paradise that only emerges as a reality through his conquest and naming. Like a colonizer, he proceeds strategically in his sketching and invasion of paradise by first creating the defining walls of his Edenic place, fencing her off against the gaze and grasp of other men:

> Your breasts and shoulders would reek
> you could never walk through markets
> without the profession of my fingers
> floating over you. The blind would
> stumble certain of whom they approached. (lines 5–9)

At the very end he can be sure that his colonization has been successful when it emerges that her identity is bound up exclusively with his act of colonization and she proclaims, "I am the cinnamon / peeler's wife. Smell me" (lines 45–6). Consequently, "The Cinnamon Peeler" envisages not only a return to a (self-created) paradise, by possibly hinting at the manufactured reality of all paradises, but also a conquest of it. The colonizing act is enabled in that the woman is presented as a corporeal entity only, by means of which she can appear like an empty space turned into a specific location through the lyric subject's naming and mapping of her body.[33] The envisaged dreamland is rewritten[34] by the traces of cinnamon left on the female body. Like a cartographer, the persona maps the female body with his cinnamon smell. Lilijana Burcar speaks of the male gaze in Ondaatje's writing, which "turns the female body into a self-divorced, socially shaped and historically colonised territory": "She cannot escape being tampered with, mapped, and designated according to the culturally implanted expectations and desires of

Michael Ondaatje's "The Cinnamon Peeler"

gazing man. His perception and his language trap her in a fixed position that reduces her to her body and to her sex alone."[35] In a comparable act, the persona in "The Cinnamon Peeler" declares, as if mapping the valleys, mountains, rivers of his paradise:

> Here on the upper thigh
> at this smooth pasture
> neighbour to your hair
> or the crease
> that cuts your back. This ankle. (lines 12–16)

It is the "I" that "brings the colonized space into being," as Ashcroft, Griffiths, and Tiffin have noted.[36] In the case of "The Cinnamon Peeler," the lyric subject can succeed in his colonization because the woman appears radically decontextualized.[37] The woman is clearly deprived of a specific setting and individuality, manifested in the neglect of the female face, which is why the female body can be seen as forming a contrast to the probably over-contextualized land to which the persona wishes to return. Consequently, Ondaatje may be said to employ his imperialistic stance not to criticize colonialism but to perform a neocolonial act: the cinnamon peeler conquers the woman to establish his paradise, which, as Dämmrich has shown, is a frequently employed method in paradise literature:

> Originating in the strongly patriarchal society, the canonical literature of paradise reflects a predominantly male point of view. Men are portrayed as the questers, antagonists, and designers of their own paradisiacal bliss. Women are assigned stationary positions in either the non-paradisiacal reality abandoned by questers or paradisiacal spaces, where they frequently function as focal objects of the male quest. True paradisiacal bliss is often only achieved when the male questers have conquered or been given the desired female object. Identifying paradise in the body, face or eyes of the beloved is nearly exclusively a male preoccupation.[38]

That Ondaatje writes from and not necessarily against the tradition of these canonical texts also becomes apparent when one examines once more the connection between his poem and religious paradises. Already in the biblical love poem "Song of Solomon," the woman is compared to an enclosed garden, evoking associations with paradise; it is an association on which Ondaatje draws heavily, as the following lines from the Bible will help to illustrate.

> Thy lips, O my spouse, drop as the honeycomb: honey and milk are under thy tongue; and the smell of thy garments is like the smell of Lebanon.
> A garden inclosed is my sister, my spouse; a spring shut up, a fountain sealed.
> Thy plants are an orchard of pomegranates, with pleasant fruits; camphire, with spikenard,
> Spikenard and saffron; calamus and cinnamon, with all trees of frankincense; myrrh and aloes, with all the chief spices:
> A fountain of gardens, a well of living waters, and streams from Lebanon.
> Awake, O north wind; and come, thou south; blow upon my garden, that the spices thereof may flow out. Let my beloved come into his garden, and eat his pleasant fruits. (Song of Solomon, Cant. 4:11–16)

The analogies between Ondaatje's poem and the biblical text are considerable: both establish the woman as paradisiacal space, both spaces are also marked by distinctive smells, various luxurious spices in the one text and the one spice, cinnamon, in the other, which functions as a clear marker of the spatial dimension of this paradise, namely, Sri Lanka. But while the woman in "Song of Solomon" *is* the garden that harbours such riches as "saffron; calamus and cinnamon," Ondaatje's poem introduces the spice from the outside, through the hands of the persona who wants to return to paradise, the invader of paradise, as outlined above.

Precisely at this intersection of paradise construction, colonization, and the female body, the bouquet of meanings Ondaatje's poem has to offer can fully develop: by referencing a classic Western text (the Bible), "The Cinnamon Peeler" replicates colonization on a textual level while at the same time subverting it through the appropriation of space and (biblical) text. By reinventing and reshaping the paradisiacal landscape, he interlaces "unfamiliar or unpredictable features with familiar or predictable components of the canon," thus creating a "dynamic, ever-changing and challenging panorama of possible landscapes that both deconstructs and reconstructs the

Michael Ondaatje's "The Cinnamon Peeler" 127

canon."[39] "The Cinnamon Peeler" at once confirms and transcends the canonical constructions that in "Song of Solomon" sketch the woman as an enclosed garden and in John Donne's "To His Mistress Going to Bed" locate the (desired) female body in the (desirable) new colonies in the Americas:

Licence my roving hands, and let them go
Before, behind, between, above, below.
O, my America, my Newfoundland,
My kingdom, safest when with one man mann'd,
My mine of precious stones, my empery;
How am I blest in thus discovering thee![40]

In Ondaatje's poem, the persona's conquering of the female body weaves timelessness and universality into the narrative of colonizing paradise, while the relocation of the landscape to Asia mimics and criticizes the actual physical colonization that determined centuries of Asian experiences. And precisely by powerfully evoking Jean-Jacques Rousseau's observation concerning the relationship between smell, desire, and memory, Ondaatje draws the reader into his elaborate scenario. If the cinnamon his persona leaves on the female body helps him to project a paradise he can conquer, in an actual (or mimicked) colonial move, by the mere associations that the intensive spice evokes in the readers, they become his accomplices: to the extent to which the spice is multiply defined as marking the entry point to Eden as well as the expulsion from it and, at the same time, as forming the walls that enclose paradise, it will also help to create a very specific, emotionally defined (mental) space for the readers of Ondaatje's poem. They, too, are likely to have strong emotional associations with the smell; for them, too, it can conjure up memories and kindle desires, and yet, the very fact that cinnamon can produce these emotions in people with no connection to Sri Lanka helps to bring to the fore the seemingly ambivalent colonial criticism inherent in the poem. Not only the persona's but possibly also our own projection of paradise is ultimately an exploitative act – even though it might be based on consent – that relies on a multiplicity of cultural, religious, and personal encounters. Thus, by drawing on these varied notions of paradisiacal places and relying on long-established literary projections of these onto the female body, Ondaatje reinvests an age-old practice with new urgency to reframe contemporary yet age-old experiences of diaspora and the notions that have always sprung from them of an ideal place called paradise.

NOTES

Reprinted from *Projections of Paradise: Ideal Elsewheres in Migrant Postcolonial Literatures*, ed. Helga Ramsey-Kurz and Geetha Ganapathy-Doré (Amsterdam: Rodopi, 2011).

1 Donne, "To His Mistress Going to Bed," in *John Donne's Poetry*, 62.
2 George, *The Politics of Home*, 175.
3 Chambers, *Migrancy, Culture, Identity*, 5.
4 Mishra, *The Literature of the Indian Diaspora*, 212.
5 Mufti and Shohat, "Introduction," 1.
6 Rushdie, "Imaginary Homelands," 10.
7 Metcalf, *The World in So Many Words*, 125.
8 Food taboos can be traced in all cultures and are often religiously defined; see den Harto, "Taboos," 384–6.
9 In all three Abrahamic religions there is a paradisiacal garden from which Adam and Eve are expelled due to their eating from the fruit of the Tree of Knowledge. Not only is this exclusion from paradise rated differently (Judaism and Islam do not read Adam and Eve as sinful in contrast to common Christian interpretations), though, but also the standing paradise has within each religion is divergent: whereas it is a central concept in Christianity and Islam, it is less vital from a Jewish perspective. See Scafi, *Mapping Paradise*, 32–44.
10 Norman, "Religion and Food," 173.
11 "The only true paradise is the paradise we have lost"; Proust, *À la recherche du temps perdu*, 449.
12 Nyman, *Displacement, Memory, and Travel in Contemporary Migrant Writing*, 92, 94.
13 Ibid., 97.
14 Seneviratne, "Cinnamon Roots," in *Wild Cinnamon and Winter Skin*, 51, lines 1–5.
15 Seneviratne, *Exotic Tastes of Sri Lanka*, 6.
16 Conspicuously, in the writing of the Sri Lankan diaspora, cinnamon habitually becomes a prism through which experiences of dislocation, projections of return, and evaluations of present situations can be fractured and reassembled, to which, to name only a few, Shyam Selvadurai's

Michael Ondaatje's "The Cinnamon Peeler" 129

Cinnamon Garden, Seni Seneviratne's *Wild Cinnamon and Winter Skies*, and Ondaatje's "The Cinnamon Peeler" give evidence.

17 Küster, *Kleine Kulturgeschichte der Gewürze*, 288.

18 Woodward, "Herbs and Spices," 188.

19 Seneviratne, *Exotic Tastes of Sri Lanka*, 3.

20 Bicking, *Die Zimtwirtschaft auf Sri Lanka (Ceylon)*, 1.

21 Chinese cinnamon (*Cinnamonum aromaticum*), also known as cassia, has a similarly long history; it is, however, of lesser quality and cheaper in its production (Küster, *Kleine Kulturgeschichte der Gewürze*, 288–9; Bicking, *Die Zimtwirtschaft auf Sri Lanka (Ceylon)*, 3).

22 Küster, *Kleine Kulturgeschichte der Gewürze*, 288.

23 Ratwatte, "The Spice of Life," 1.

24 Quoted in Ratwatte, "The Spice of Life," 6.

25 Bicking, *Die Zimtwirtschaft auf Sri Lanka (Ceylon)*, 110–12.

26 This underlines the physical side of the love described.

27 See also Döring, Heide, and Mühleisen, "Introduction," 4.

28 For further usage around the world, see Ratwatte, "The Spice of Live," 6–7.

29 Dämmrich, *Enigmatic Bliss*, 69.

30 Ibid., 126.

31 Although the aspirations seem to be directed rather toward the side effects of the trade: namely, the smell that would then linger with the peeler and, as a consequence, with his wife.

32 See Ratwatte, "The Spice of Life," 2.

33 On the concepts of space and place, see Ashcroft, Griffiths, and Tiffin, *Key Concepts in Post-Colonial Studies*, 177–83.

34 Even though this might not have been Ondaatje's intention, as he states in an interview about some later poems that he didn't want to write a "sequence of autobiographical poems where [he] returned and rewrote Sri Lanka." Quoted in Jaggi, "With Michael Ondaatje (2000)," 252.

35 Interestingly enough, Burcar's analysis refers to Ondaatje's *The English Patient*. See her "Mapping the Woman's Body in Michael Ondaatje's *The English Patient*."

36 Ashcroft, Griffiths, and Tiffin, *Key Concepts in Post-colonial Studies*, 175.

37 Macdonald, *Representing Women*, 105–6.

38 Dämmrich, *Enigmatic Bliss*, 160.

39 Ibid., 48.

40 Donne, "To His Mistress Going to Bed," 62, lines 25–30.

5

The Pivot:
Michael Ondaatje's *Tin Roof*

Ian Rae

In the final section of Ondaatje's serial poem *Tin Roof*, the poet pays homage to Rainer Maria Rilke's *Duino Elegies* with a humorous anecdote about the Austrian poet's suspicious cook "who believes down to his turnip soup / that you speak the voice of the devil."[1] Ondaatje then claims, "I want the long lines my friend spoke of" (*S, 42*), but he rarely employs long lines in *Tin Roof*, unless by "long line" one means a shift toward the long poem, which was the topic of the influential *Long-liners Conference* in 1984, as well as the drift of Ondaatje's own work in this period as editor of *The Long Poem Anthology*. Ondaatje's homage to Rilke serves, instead, to disarm the reader with humour before Ondaatje asserts his talent for striking images and linked metaphors. In the subsequent passage, Ondaatje develops a simile and metaphor that, through nearly every noun and verb (circle, book, wave, hair, sea, name), elaborate on images and figures that structure earlier poems in the series:

> I have circled your book for years
> like a wave combing
> the green hair of the sea
> kept it with me, your name
> a password in the alley. (*S*, 42)

I, too, have circled Ondaatje's *Tin Roof* for years and wondered why more critics have not written about this gorgeous volume, first printed on Vancouver Island in 1982 as part of the Island Writing Series, edited by John Marshall and Daphne Marlatt. To my knowledge, no

Michael Ondaatje's *Tin Roof* 131

critic has ever assessed *Tin Roof* as a stand-alone work. Most critics devote a few pages to analyzing it as a section of a larger poetry collection, *Secular Love*, from 1984 (Barbour, Norris, Solecki) or as part of an overview of his works (Glickman, Hsu, Spinks). However, *Tin Roof*, so finely crafted in every respect, deserves better. Greenboathouse Press recognized this fact when they reissued *Tin Roof* in 2012 after embarking on "a rather epic adventure into the technical side of fine-press printing, which has made all other Greenboathouse Press projects seem like practice sessions for the real thing."[2]

In fairness to poetry scholars, it is not clear which critical methodology might enable one to write effectively about *Tin Roof*. To employ biographical criticism and treat *Tin Roof* as a poetic account of the dissolution of the poet's first marriage to the painter Kim Ondaatje, who gave him a copy of *Duino Elegies* as a wedding present in 1964,[3] and the beginning of his subsequent relationship with the novelist Linda Spalding would be to diminish the intricate figurative patterning of the serial poem. To employ formalist strategies to create a blueprint of Ondaatje's poetic machinery would trivialize the raw anguish of the poet in the midst of a personal breakdown that has him poised precariously on the verge of suicide. Canadian critics might employ the nationalist strategy of essaying the poem's "sense of place," which would account for the very localized quality of the descriptions of the titular cabin with its tin roof, but such a methodology would fit awkwardly with the poem's tropical setting on a volcanic island in the middle of the Pacific. Diasporic critical approaches might prove helpful in approaching this text, which Ondaatje positions as partway to Asia, culturally and geographically. In practice, however, diasporic critics prefer Ondaatje's full-fledged return to Asia in *Running in the Family*, a memoir about Ondaatje's family in Sri Lanka, and the novel *Anil's Ghost*, the story of a forensic anthropologist who returns to a war-torn Sri Lanka after fifteen years in the West (Cook, Pirbhai, Sanghera). Of necessity, then, I will resort to working partially with all these modalities because it seems that the alternative is critical silence. I will first consider some thinly veiled biographical details about the breakdown of Ondaatje's first marriage that are crucial to understanding the personal crisis dramatized in *Tin Roof*. I will then investigate what Jonathan Flatley calls the "affective mapping" of the speaker's personal crisis onto the cliffside setting of the poem and the figures he develops out of his geographical circumstances.[4] Finally, I will

132   Ian Rae

illustrate how Ondaatje's shift toward an Asian poetics helps the speaker to transcend the "to be, or not to be" question that threatens, increasingly, to drive him off a cliff.

The setting of *Tin Roof* is a small cabin of wood and glass in a remote part of Hawaii. Ondaatje "happens to love the stark / luxury of this place" (*S*, 27), and his attraction to a stripped-down material setting, wherein he will write poems to grapple with emotional chaos, should be familiar to readers of Ondaatje as well as to those of Leonard Cohen, the subject of Ondaatje's only book of criticism, *Leonard Cohen*. The cabin setting is not quite monastic – there is beer and television and "certain habits" of which Rilke would "not approve" (*S*, 42). Amidst all this general austerity, the poet nonetheless fulfills the ostensible goal of the writer's retreat by churning out lyrics about the geckoes clinging to the cabin's window and the "wild sea and her civilization" (*S*, 31). However, moral questions raised by the erotically charged visits of a new lover to the cabin disturb the idyll of solitary withdrawal. If aesthetic control in the face of personal, moral, and environmental disintegration gets the heroic treatment in Ondaatje's early publications, such as *Coming Through Slaughter* or "White Dwarfs," here it is treated with derision: "Ah you should be happy and write" (*S*, 37). Ondaatje, by the 1980s, is an accomplished writer but unhappy, veering into the kind of "terrible acute hatred / of his own privacy" that drives Ondaatje's father Mervyn to drink and an early death in "Letters & Other Worlds," from *Rat Jelly* (26). This time, however, the broken marriage, distant children, and carefully crafted missives from the edge are Ondaatje's own, a fact compounded by the poet's contemporaneous research toward *Running in the Family*. Ondaatje's domestic crisis causes him to spurn the modernist promise of aesthetic domination of the world through the word, represented for Ondaatje by the poetry of Wallace Stevens, and to move tentatively into the more vulnerable and subjective territory of confessional verse. However, given the early deaths by suicide of such accomplished mid-century confessional poets as Sylvia Plath and Anne Sexton, even Ondaatje's more guarded forays into confessional verse come charged with ominous implications.

The mortal stakes of the writer's retreat in *Tin Roof* are clear from the opening lyric, wherein the speaker stands "still for three days / for a piece of wisdom" that would bring peace to his divided heart (*S*, 23). He gazes at "cue cards / blazing in the sky" before hitting upon a "solution" that is not a solution: "This last year I was sure / I was

Michael Ondaatje's *Tin Roof* 133

going to die" (*S*, 23). He is not dead, but apparently the year is not over. As with Plath and Sexton, adultery lies at the heart of this existential crisis, and the tumultuous visits by the woman to the cabin seem to be driving the speaker toward the "solution." A fight between the new lovers turns the balcony into "an entrance / to a city of suicides," as the speaker, already weighted with the guilt of his failed marriage, asks:

And what were you
carrying? in your head
that night Miss
Souri? Miss Kansas?

while I put my hands
sweating
on the cold
window
on the edge
of the trough of this city? (*S*, 38–9)

The woman depicted here is not named but also is not hard to identify. She is the novelist Linda Spalding, who was born in Topeka, Kansas, before moving to Hawaii to work in public television, where Ondaatje met her in 1980.[5] Although *Tin Roof* depicts their relationship as a combination of fleeting passion and misery ("Miss Souri"), Spalding would move to Canada in the same year that *Tin Roof* was published. Two years later, Ondaatje dedicated *Secular Love*: "This book is for Linda" (*S*, n.p.). Spalding and Ondaatje married, and she became his collaborator on the editorial board of the literary magazine *Brick*, as well as publishing *Daughters of Captain Cook*, her first of several novels, in 1988. This happy ending is nowhere present in *Tin Roof*, where the enjambments and unstable anaphora of the passage above – "on the," "on the," "of the" – position the speaker as tottering over the edge.

Ondaatje's sensitive depictions of the island landscape at first seem to foreordain the lover's leap through images of natural violence:

and all day the tirade pale blue waves
touch the black shore of volcanic rock

and fall to pieces here (*S*, 24)

The waves of assonance (day, tirade, pale, waves) and consonance (black, volcanic, rock) in these lines create a sense of propulsion toward a shattering end. The anthropomorphic diction (tirade, touch) fuses the speaker's predicament with natural processes: "Waves leap to this cliff all day" while "[u]ntidy banana trees" tempt "the plunge / to black volcanic shore." One senses that geography will ultimately determine the story's outcome: "It is impossible to enter the sea here / except in a violent way" (*S*, 30). The prophetic overtones of the first lyric in the series make the suicide seem like less a question of "if" than of "when" and "how":

> How to arrive at this
> drowning
> on the edge of sea (*S*, 25)

The insistent conflation of the howling winds and the "blue wild silk" (*S*, 29) of the sea with the lovers' bed makes drowning seem the logical outcome of this tempestuous affair.

One might dismiss such ominous imagery as Romantic posturing, but both vernacular and literary notions of Romanticism are treated with suspicion in *Tin Roof* from the opening epigraph, which Ondaatje added to the *Secular Love* version, by the American novelist Elmore Leonard:

> She hesitated. "Are you being romantic now?"
> "I'm trying to tell you how I feel without exposing myself. You know what I mean?" (*S*, 21)

Initiating a new romantic relationship enthralls the speaker but makes him feel at risk. Although the speaker admires Rilke's resolve, in a letter cited on the final page of *Tin Roof*, "to live by the heart and nothing else" (*S*, 43), the speaker oscillates between the brooding avoidance of a past that troubles his sleep and the *carpe diem* impulse to wrest an erotic escape from world and time:

> This *flower* of wood
> in which we rose
> out of the blue sheets
> you thin as horizon

Michael Ondaatje's *Tin Roof*

reaching for lamp or book
my shirt

hungry
for everything about the other

here we steal places to stay
as we steal time

never too proud to beg,
even if we never
see the other's grin and star again (*S*, 34)

Although the speaker boasts that "there is nothing resigned / in this briefness," the same lyric concludes with a portrait of the lovers as "precarious in all our fury" (*S*, 34). The implacable "long waves" of the sea in the subsequent lyric represent the constant pressure of a larger narrative battering the coast of the lovers' island refuge (*S*, 35). Furthermore, the Byronic disregard for the moral codes of society ultimately strikes the speaker as dangerous, like the life-threatening feat at the centre of the plot of the film *Trapeze*:

So how do we discuss
the education of our children?
Teach them to be romantics
to veer towards the sentimental?
Toss them into the air like Tony Curtis
and make 'em do the triple somersault
through all these complexities
and commandments? (*S*, 41)

The Romantic valorization of the lyric "I" whose genius overrides commandments is, in *Tin Roof*, subverted by the repeated presentation of the man "[b]reaking down after logical rules" (*S*, 40). This breakdown confounds the bold self-assertions of the erotic passages. As Douglas Barbour observes, pronominal shifts between "I," "you," and "he" underscore the subject's emotional instability and caginess: "if love protects the subject *in* the text, the refusal of the confessional mode protects the subject *of* the text, as he slips once more into another pronominal presence, slips away from our regard even in the act of making moral pronouncements."[6] Finally, the Romantic promise of revelation in solitude also fails for the speaker from his vantage point on high: "this solitude brings no wisdom / just two day old food in the fridge" (*S*, 42).

The only Romantic convention Ondaatje does not challenge is the poet's profound communion with nature. As Barbour observes of *Secular Love*, the "tone keeps sliding from humour to anger to pain, with no single emotion allowed to dominate, as the man keeps struggling over and over again out of the house and into nature."[7] Yet the landscape in *Tin Roof* is both alien to the poet and mediated by modernity, his presence in it facilitated by cars, fridges, and radios, and his consciousness of the setting shaped by American film and television, as well as twentieth-century music. Here, Jonathan Flatley's theory of affective mapping in modern literature helps to make sense of the speaker's creative transformation of his emotional distress in the island setting. Flatley argues that some writers develop a distinctively modern response to the symptoms of melancholy, the latter being "sadness, grief, fear, affective withdrawal, loss of interest."[8] Flatley maintains that such melancholia can be converted from a depressive condition into "a way to be interested in the world" through a distinctively modern relationship to one's surroundings, a dynamic that resembles a form of mapping.[9] "Affective mapping," in this modern context, does not mean the kind of organic connection between artists, rustic folk, and nature that characterizes the works of Wordsworth and Thoreau. Dislocation is part of the modern condition, and Ondaatje's speaker is aware that he is a tourist and that solitude "is not an absolute, / it is just a resting place" (*S*, 37). At every turn, the landscape strikes the speaker as strange and exotic, but this estrangement offers him insight into his emotional predicament by removing him from his normal context. "My own emotional life must appear unfamiliar, not-mine, at least for a moment, if I am to see its relation to a historical context," Flatley argues.[10] This estranged perspective on the speaker's selfhood in *Tin Roof* sometimes slips into a distanced and cinematic third-person vantage point:[11]

In certain mirrors
he cannot see himself at all.
He is joyous and breaking down.
The tug over the cliff. (*S*, 28)

By momentarily losing himself, by reading his emotional life into his surroundings, and by reading his surroundings for clues ("cue cards") into his existential predicament, a reciprocal dynamic develops between self and surroundings that opens the door to a sense of communion with nature. Later, this communion will extend to artists, such as Rilke, who have combatted melancholia through similar investments of emotion into place.

According to Flatley, a key element that distinguishes creative melancholia from depressive incapacity is a particular attitude toward being, a kind of attunement (*Stimmung*) that is part of the melancholic mood.[12] Ondaatje employs this attunement to convert the tin roof of the Hawaiian cabin into a "wind run radio / [that] catches the noise of the world" (*S*, 28). The speaker listens closely to both the quiet sounds around the cabin and the clamour of the surf:

> On the porch
> thin ceramic
> chimes
>
>   ride wind
> off the Pacific
>
> bells of the sea
> [...]
> How we have moved
> from thin ceramic
>
> to such destruction (*S*, 30).

The speaker is also visually perspicacious and derives from the tiny feet of the geckoes a moral lesson about how to hang on in a precarious situation. Unlike the depressive, Ondaatje's speaker feels, smells, tastes, touches, and sees things with acute intensity as he maps the intersections between different scales of material and sensory experience.

The resulting map is made literal in one of the longest poems in *Tin Roof*:

> There are maps now whose portraits
> have nothing to do with surface

Remember the angels, floating compasses
- Portolan atlases so complex
we looked down and never knew
which was earth which was sea? (*S*, 36)

Affect inscribes the topography of Ondaatje's maps:

And beneath the sea
there are
these giant scratches
of pain
the markings of
some perfect animal
who has descended
burying itself
under the glossy
ballroom (*S*, 36)

Affective mapping, then, begins with attunement to one's surroundings, but it is ultimately about "the ways we become the subjects that we are by the structuring of our affective attachments."[13]

Still, the implications of the cliffside setting in the logic of the speaker's affective attachments produce ominous results. Cartography is traditionally the science of princes, a mode of colonial control and domination. Ondaatje's speaker, in contrast, sees in maps only a fated merger of the living with the landscape. The confusing Portolan atlases remind the speaker of:

The way birds the colour of prairie
confused by the sky
flew into the earth
(Remember those women
who claimed dead miners
the colour of the coal they drowned in) (*S*, 36)

This parenthetical passage is part of a linked series of images in which the suicidal speaker fantasizes about women mourning their dead. This image pattern connects the woman "who clutched my hair / like a shaken child" to the aforementioned green hair of the sea and the place of hair in "traditions of death" (*S*, 31):

Michael Ondaatje's *Tin Roof*   139

Remember
those women in movies
who wept into the hair
of their dead men? (*S*, 31)

Affective mapping, in the case of the hair motif, makes suicide seductive by enabling the speaker to fantasize about the women who will mourn his passing.

However, Flatley argues that affective mapping is redemptive, not destructive, precisely because of the community it builds:

> "Affective mapping" is the name I am giving to the aesthetic technology – in the older, more basic sense of a *techne* – that represents the historicity of one's affective experience. In mapping out one's affective life and its historicity, a political problem (such as racism or revolution) that may have been previously invisible, opaque, difficult, abstract, and above all depressing may be transformed into one that is interesting, that solicits and rewards one's attention. This transformation can take place, I argue, not only because the affective map gives one a new sense of one's relationship to broad historical forces but also inasmuch as it shows one how one's situation is experienced collectively by a community, a heretofore unarticulated community of melancholics.[14]

This theory particularly helps to make sense of the final poems in *Tin Roof*. Although the speaker makes a few passing references to radio and television over the course of the poem, the final two entries offer a barrage of musical, cinematic, and literary allusions to contextualize the speaker's condition, and thereby to build an affective community, even if the artists he names (Frank Sinatra, Burt Lancaster, Van Morrison, Rilke) seem unrelated. One passage is particularly telling in its reimagining of the ending of *Casablanca*:

I could write my suite of poems
for Bogart   drunk
six months after the departure at Casablanca.
I see him lying under the fan
at the Slavyansky Bazar Hotel
and soon he will see the truth
the stupidity of his gesture (*S*, 40)

By comparing the speaker's condition in his adulterous affair to that of Rick in *Casablanca*, wherein the character played by Humphrey Bogart helps the husband of his beloved Ilsa to escape capture, the speaker comes to the conclusion that choosing to forego true love makes one a "stupid fucker" (*S*, 40). The misnaming of Rick's American Café after a hotel in Anton Chekhov's "The Lady with the Little Dog" further expands this artistic community by alluding to another story about adultery.[15]

Ondaatje thus crowds the end of *Tin Roof* with lovelorn melancholics whose examples help to structure the speaker's subjectivity, while also creating a sense of community for the isolato. Tellingly, the second person address, "Oh Rilke," that begins Ondaatje's final poem undergoes a pronominal shift toward the first person plural in the last section:

I wanted poetry to be walnuts
in their green cases
but now it is the sea
and we let it drown us,
and we fly to it released
by giant catapults
of pain loneliness deceit and vanity (*S*, 43)

Affective mapping thereby converts the life-threatening sea, as material fact, into a life-sustaining creative force with the help of Ondaatje's knack for metaphor.

Ondaatje perhaps also uses the "tirade blue waves" to answer the famous question that Rilke poses in the "First Elegy":

Who, if I cried out, would hear me among the angelic
orders? and even if one of them pressed me
suddenly to his heart: I'd be consumed
in that overwhelming existence. For beauty is nothing
but the beginning of terror, which we can just barely endure,
and we stand in awe of it as it coolly disdains
to destroy us. Every angel is terrifying.[16]

Ondaatje answers Rilke's question by assembling a community of melancholics who hear Rilke's cry and answer with their own. That Ondaatje takes much of his inspiration for the form of the

Michael Ondaatje's *Tin Roof* 141

serial poem from the American poets Jack Spicer and Robin Blaser, who in turn looked to *Duino Elegies* as a model, cements this transnational community.[17]

Ondaatje begins his serial poem with the speaker not knowing "whether / seraph or bitch / flutters at [his] heart" (*S*, 23). However, the grappling with Rilke's angels helps to clarify the situation:

listen   in the end
the pivot from angel to witch
depends on small things
this animal, the question
are you happy?

No I am not happy
lucky though (*S*, 37)

If one judges by the Bogart analogy, the speaker ultimately chooses the happiness that his new lover brings him, with its raft of dire moral consequences, over the life that had left him unhappy.

And yet, Ondaatje subtly complicates the either/or questions that dramatize the speaker's decision-making. These complications work against any sense of narrative resolution that the final poem might seem to supply. For example, the reference to "Miss / Souri, Miss Kansas" cited above seems to refer to the speaker's American lover in *Tin Roof*. However, a seemingly humorous throwaway line earlier in the serial poem splits this identification of the two states with the one woman:

We go to the stark places of the earth
and find moral questions everywhere

Will John Wayne and Montgomery Clift
take their cattle to Missouri or Kansas? (*S*, 29)

By aligning this cinematic "moral question" with the speaker's own marital one, one might reconceive the speaker's address as a question posed simultaneously to his first wife "Miss / Souri" (Misery) and his new lover "Miss Kansas." This beauty contest would seem to construct an easy binary between former and new lover. Yet if Solecki is correct that readers should hear in "witch" the echo of "Wichita," the

142   Ian Rae

largest city in Kansas, then has the speaker made the right choice in favouring "Miss Kansas"?[18] Has he forsaken a "seraph" by allowing a "bitch" to flutter at his heart? Do all these derogatory and misogynistic terms, including the analogy between the women and cows, suggest that the speaker is too angry to love any woman? Is that why the speaker hurtles into the arms of men in the final poems?

A potential way out of all the either/or predicaments that the Western cultural references create arises through the Asian elements within the serial poem. For example, Hamlet's famous existential conundrum, "To be, or not to be – that is the question,"[19] echoes across the opening section of the fifth lyric in *Tin Roof*:

> To be lost
>
> A man buying wine
> Rainier beer at the store
> would he be satisfied with this?
> Cold showers, electric skillet,
> *Red River* on tv
> Oh he could be (5, 27)

What are the virtues of being lost? What would it be like to lose being? How would a suicidal poet write if he just forgot about *Hamlet*? The exact meaning of the existential question here is less important than the fact that the speaker feels a need to find a new way of being. Ondaatje emphasizes this need through the imperative verb in the first line, through a kind of medial alliteration across the first four lines (be, buying, beer, be), and through a more insistent use of internal and end rhyme in the final two lines (tv, he, be).

Solecki's portrait of Ondaatje's fraught mindset in this period, wherein Ondaatje begins to come to terms with his Asian upbringing in his writing, is helpful in tracing the nascent Asian elements that reframe the Western problems in *Tin Roof*:

> We have to imagine the ambiguity of his situation after his return from Sri Lanka in 1978. We have to picture a writer who, having established himself in one language and in a particularly dominant literary tradition, now wants to belong as well to another culture and literature. Having finally returned, though as a visitor, he now finds himself wanting to write not only about

the place that used to be his home but also from within it. But without access to either of the native languages, the best he can do is to forge a style *in English* that will evoke the now *foreign* language, poetry, and culture.[20]

Solecki illustrates how Ondaatje pursues these objectives in *Handwriting* by using Sinhala words and concepts and even presenting one bilingual poem.[21] Ondaatje also showcases this cross-cultural interest in *Anil's Ghost* by including a subplot about translators and ancient stone inscriptions.

However, Ondaatje's Hawaiian experience is an under-analyzed part of this diasporic journey, which included long trips to Sri Lanka (1978), China (1979), Sri Lanka (1980), and a "one-year post as creative writer at the University of Hawaii at Manoa."[22] Ondaatje maps some of this journey with place names in the acknowledgements to *Secular Love*: "Bellrock-Toronto-Honolulu-Colombo-Blyth-Collingwood-Madoc" (*S*, n.p.). The Ontario place names are the settings of Ondaatje's early poetry, while Colombo is the focus of the Sri Lankan books. Hawaii, in turn, offers an opportunity for the author to explore Pacific Rim aesthetics not explicitly tied to Sri Lanka, as Ondaatje's financier brother did by sponsoring the Sir Christopher Ondaatje South Asian Gallery at the Royal Ontario Museum, which opened in 2000. In the case of *Tin Roof*, set in a "tin bucket on the Pacific Rim," Japanese, Chinese, and Hawaiian aesthetics are more pertinent than South Asian ones (*S*, 24). Consider, for example, the play of translations around the word "hana." The word first appears as the name of the "Hana Road" that the speaker drives to reach the cabin. Hāna is the name of a small town and a forest reserve in one of the most remote areas on the island of Maui. The word, in Hawaiian, means "craft" or "work," so it seems an appropriate spot for a writer's retreat.[23] However, a different translation of "hana" appears later in *Tin Roof* and points to an East Asian influence on Ondaatje's craft:

> Cabin
>
> 'hana'
>
> this *flower* of wood (*S*, 34)

Here, Ondaatje translates "hana" into Japanese as "flower," an association he sustains across the text, from the "large orange flowers" that "lean half drunk / against the steps" to "the dogwood flower growing / like a woman's sex outside the window" in the final section (*S*, 30, 43). This multilingual translation practice shapes one of the clusters of association that fuel the serial poem through slippages and linkages between key images and words. That "Hana" becomes the name of an important character in *In the Skin of a Lion* and *The English Patient*, the daughter of Patrick's second lover Alice, should strike no one as a coincidence because Ondaatje's poetry has always informed his prose.[24] However, in *Tin Roof*, "hana" signals Ondaatje's wish to make a new (for him) kind of poetic craft flower, one that is decidedly Asian.

The acknowledgements in *Secular Love* illustrate how Ondaatje pursues this interest in other sections of the collection, as he states: "Two poems, 'The River Neighbour' and 'Pacific Letter,' are based on Rihaku-Tu Fu-Pound poems. They are not so much translations as re-locations into my landscape."[25] Ezra Pound's development of the Imagist aesthetic, with its distaste for abstract and discursive poetry and its emphasis on a succession of concrete images in free verse, out of translations of classical Japanese and Chinese poetry is too well known to rehearse here.[26] Ondaatje's MA thesis from Queen's University (Kingston, Ontario) in 1967 on "Mythology in the Poetry of Edwin Muir: A Study of the Making and Using of Mythology in Edwin Muir's Poetry" also focuses on a poet favoured by Pound, one whose poetry is "almost Imagist in its feeling" according to Russell Fraser and one that suggests a bridge between the Imagists and the mythopoeic aesthetics that informed Ondaatje's early writing.[27] Ondaatje's shift in the 1970s toward the variousness of the serial poem, which is organized by recurring motivic connections between poems instead of by continuous narrative or stylistic consistency across poems, shirks any obligations to a particular school and actively seeks to combine different ones.[28] Thus, in addition to Rilke, one can see clearly in *Tin Roof* the influence of the Imagist mantra "no ideas but in things," a phrase coined by William Carlos Williams that Ondaatje claims was instructive for him.[29]

More traditional Japanese and Chinese influences are also present. Consider, for example, the haiku tradition. In English translation, one normally thinks of the haiku as a syllabic poem written over three lines that introduces a striking image from everyday life in the first line (five syllables); before shifting toward a comparison, simile, or metaphor in the second line, also known as the pivot line (seven syllables); before introducing a related image that provokes thought without

Michael Ondaatje's *Tin Roof*   145

commentary in the third line (five syllables). In traditional practice, however, a haiku could emerge from one or more lines, and its main constraint was the limit of seventeen syllables. Originally, a haiku also introduced a longer poem, "hence *hokku* ('opening part')."[30] Many of the poems in *Tin Roof*, such as the passage about the wind chimes cited earlier, feature sections that open with a tight, imagistic, and almost syllabic organization, before relaxing into a more colloquial voice that breaks the rules of haiku and Imagism, as Ondaatje does in the wind chime poem when he concludes with the self-reflexive comment on the move from "thin ceramic" to "destruction" (*S*, 30). The metaphoric logic of the structure of haiku is also apparent in the wind chime poem, as the spare image of the cabin's chimes shifts out of its quotidian context in the fourth (pivot) line through the metaphoric use of the verb "ride," which pertains to sailing in the sense of riding the wind but which in Hawaii carries connotations of surfing. This metaphoric connection between land and ocean, as well as between human and natural spaces, transforms the landlocked chimes into the more grandiose "bells of the sea," thereby ranging from the microcosmic to the macrocosmic in a fashion typical of haiku.

The most crucial of the Asian influences in *Tin Roof* concerns the bamboo motif, introduced in the fifth poem, which begins:

Tell me
all you know
about bamboo

growing wild, green
growing up into soft arches
in the temple ground (*S*, 26)

The presence of bamboo in the Hawaiian landscape is important because its gives Ondaatje access to "the traditions" of bamboo in the Pacific Rim, which his teenage experience in England and his adulthood in Central Canada have not.[31] Importantly for the heartsick lover, one of these traditions is the use of bamboo in torture, the bamboo shaft "driven through the hands / through the heart."[32] This impaling motif recurs in the serial poem to frightening effect.

Yet another tradition of bamboo, the one that the speaker values "most of all" and that ultimately suggests an alternative to the aforementioned violent ends, relates to Buddhist meditation gardens:

146 Ian Rae

                this

        small bamboo pipe
        not quite horizontal
        that drips
        every ten seconds
        to a shallow bowl (*S*, 26)

The speaker's attentiveness to the bamboo in the garden draws him into the tranquil state of being he seeks, providing a momentary reprieve for the anguished soul, until the motif takes a drastic turn:

        I love this
        being here
        not a word
        just the faint
        fall of liquid
        the boom of an iron buddhist bell
        in the heart rapid
        as ceremonial bamboo (*S*, 26)

Note the syllabic organization of the first five lines in this citation, each line employing three syllables until the extra, falling syllable of "liquid" marks the drop of water. This tiny drop nonetheless has a resounding effect, like the body-shaking resonance of an iron bell, which Ondaatje mimics through the echoing alliterations of "boom," "buddhist," "bell," and "bamboo."

Dire as the bamboo-in-the-heart motif seems, with its cupid-like overtones of love as an affliction, the bamboo pipe in the garden nourishes a better "solution" than death for the speaker. While Western metaphysics attempts to draw a hard distinction between being and non-being, the four-fold logic of Buddhist metaphysics (*catuskoti*) adds two additional categories, one a combination of the first two propositions (being and non-being together) and one a negation of both of the first two propositions (neither being nor non-being).[33] We have already seen how Ondaatje's speaker seeks alternatives to hard binaries by sidestepping the question of whether he is happy or unhappy through the quip that he is "lucky," a solution that the serial poem negates through the portrait of Bogart, six months after Isla's departure, lamenting that he "used to be lucky"

(S, 40). The implication here is that the luck of the speaker in *Tin Roof* will run out if he does not pursue his lover and he will turn into a self-loathing drunk. Yet the moral consequences of pursuing the adulterous relationship catch the speaker in a double bind, as guilt and punishments await:

> Above the bed
> memory
> restless green bamboo
> the distant army
> assembles wooden spears (S, 32)

The only thing that protects the speaker is "the warmth in the sleeve" of the kimono he wears in the cabin, "that is all, really" (S, 28). The visually absent, but nonetheless felt, warmth inside the tubular sleeve becomes "all" to the speaker, becomes his "real." Whereas bamboo at first impales the adulterer's heart, the morphological correspondences between the shape of the bamboo and the shape of the green kimono's sleeve slowly transform the Asian signifiers into analogues of the heart and its arteries:

> Illicit pockets of
>
> the kimono
>
> Heart like a sleeve (S, 27)

The kimono, heart, and bamboo motifs converge in the image of the speaker's "heart clapping / like green bamboo" in one of the erotic scenes (S, 33). Thus the Asian heart, as it were, of this poem begins to enliven a more affirmative response to the sense of nothingness that plagues the speaker in the suicide sections of the poem.

Here the poetic precedent of the classical Chinese poet Tu Fu, mentioned by Ondaatje above, is instructive, as is the classical Chinese attitude toward nature and its "local biomes."[34] Gary Snyder says of the misty mountains and blurry distances of Chinese poetry (and I would add landscape painting):

> They are not really about landscapes or scenery. Space of distant hills becomes space of life; a condition the poet-critic Lu

148 Ian Rae

Chi called "calm transparency." Mountains and rivers were seen to be visible expression of cosmic principles; the cosmic principles go back into silence, non-being, emptiness; a Nothing that can produce the ten thousand things, and the ten thousand things will have that marvelous emptiness still at the center. So the poems are also "silent." Much is left unsaid, and the reverberation or mirroring – a flight of birds across the mind of the sky – leaves an afterimage to be savoured, and finally leaves no trace.[35]

From this altered perspective, the hollow of the bamboo and the emptiness of the kimono's sleeve ultimately become lifegiving. Likewise, the speaker's affective experience of breaking down and emptying out ultimately becomes the lifeblood of a new future and a poetics of *Not Needing All the Words*.[36]

Shou-Nan Hsu is also correct that the ethics of "interconnectedness" in *Secular Love* deserve greater critical attention because the poems are explicitly concerned with moral problems.[37] The ethics that emerge from Ondaatje's Asian influences in *Tin Roof*, and that exist alongside the more overt Western themes, can be clarified by Kenneth Rexroth's summary of Tu Fu's world view:

For Tu Fu, the realm of being and value is not bifurcated. The Good, the True, and the Beautiful are not Absolute, set over against an inchoate reality that always struggles, unsuccessfully, to approximate the pure value of the absolute. Reality is dense, all one being. Values are the way we see things. This is the essence of the Chinese world view, and it overrides even the most ethereal Buddhist philosophizing and distinguishes it from its Indian sources. There is nothing that is absolutely omnipotent, but there is nothing that is purely contingent either.[38]

Moving toward a final affirmation of life and craft at the end of *Tin Roof*, Ondaatje discretely merges the Asian traditions of bamboo and Western literary history in a passage that will return us to opening paragraph of this essay:

I want the long lines my friend spoke of
that bamboo which sways muttering
like wooden teeth in the slim volume I have
with its childlike drawing of Duino Castle. (*S*, 43)

Michael Ondaatje's *Tin Roof* 149

The puzzling reference to "long lines" in this passage can now be reinterpreted through the bamboo motif. The speaker has learned to model his poetic line on bamboo, not merely on its length but on its versatility and the way that it makes a generative virtue out of emptiness.

Intriguingly, the bamboo motif brings the poet's journey full circle back to Canada. Ondaatje dedicates *Tin Roof* to Phyllis Webb of Salt Spring Island, British Columbia, and critics usually cite Webb's *Naked Poems* as an influence on *Tin Roof*. Barbour hears "linguistic echoes" of *Naked Poems* in *Tin Roof*,[39] and Norris argues that the style of *Tin Roof* is "very reminiscent of Webb's *Naked Poems*, the ultimate example in Canadian poetry of evocative restraint."[40] However, Robert Lecker rightly observes that Ondaatje's variegated serial poem is not as committed to minimalism as *Naked Poems* and that Webb's "Poetics against the Angel of Death" is the more relevant intertext,[41] as the last half of Webb's "Poetics" illustrates:

> Last night I thought I would not wake again
> but now with this June morning I run ragged to elude
> the Great Iambic Pentameter
> who is the Hound of Heaven in our stress
> because I want to die
> writing Haiku
> or, better,
> long lines, clean and syllabic as knotted bamboo. Yes![42]

This passage seeds many of the key elements that flower in *Tin Roof*: the death wish, the grappling with angels, the shift toward an Asian poetics, the formal inspiration of bamboo, and the hard-won affirmation. Such intertextual and cross-cultural complexities in Ondaatje's poetics help to explain why, in my experience, *Tin Roof* has functioned as a "password in the alley" among poetry lovers for years.

NOTES

1 Ondaatje, *Tin Roof*. The 1982 edition of *Tin Roof* (Lantzville: Island Writing Series, 1982) is unpaginated. Although I argue that *Tin Roof*

deserves attention as a stand-alone work, I use the pagination from *Secular Love* in the hope that it will make quotations easier to find.

2 Dewinetz, "Tin Roof."

3 Jewinski, *Michael Ondaatje*, 111.

4 Flatley, *Affective Mapping*.

5 Jewinski, *Michael Ondaatje*, 107–8.

6 Barbour, *Michael Ondaatje*, 166.

7 Ibid., 163.

8 Flatley, *Affective Mapping*, 1.

9 Ibid., 2.

10 Ibid., 6.

11 Norris, "The Architecture of *Secular Love*: Michael Ondaatje's Journey into the Confessional," 47.

12 Flatley, *Affective Mapping*, 5.

13 Ibid., 4.

14 Ibid.

15 Sam Solecki, *Ragas of Longing*, 148.

16 Rilke, *Duino Elegies*.

17 Blaser, "Statement," 323.

18 Solecki, *Ragas of Longing*, 153.

19 Shakespeare, *Hamlet*.

20 Solecki, *Ragas of Longing*, 168.

21 Ibid., 168–9.

22 Jewinski, *Michael Ondaatje*, 107.

23 "The Meaning of Hana – True to Its Name in Any Language."

24 See the chapter on Ondaatje in Rae, *From Cohen to Carson*, 91–137.

25 Ondaatje, *Secular Love*, n.p.

26 See Weinberger, "Introduction," *The New Directions Anthology of Classical Chinese Poetry*, xvii–xxvii.

27 Fraser, "Edwin Muir's Other Eden," 78–92.

28 See Blaser, "The Fire," 235–46.

29 O'Meara, "The Company of Thieves," 40.

30 "Haiku," *Princeton Encyclopedia of Poetry and Poetics*, 493–4.

31 Ondaatje, *Tin Roof*, 26.

32 Ibid.

33 Gunaratne, "Understanding Nāgārjuna's Catuṣkoṭi," 213–34.

34 Snyder, "Hsieh's Shoes," 203.

35 Ibid., 204.

36 See Hillger's *Not Needing All the Words*.

37 Hsu, "From Sexual Love to Peace," 112.

Michael Ondaatje's *Tin Roof* 151

38 Rexroth, "Tu Fu," 199.
39 Barbour, *Michael Ondaatje*, 163, 230 (ft. 6).
40 Norris, "The Architecture of *Secular Love*," 47.
41 I am indebted to Robert Lecker's excellent editorial suggestions for this insight.
42 Webb, "Poetics against the Angel of Death," 145.

Visuality

6

"The illusion of the unexceptional": Michael Ondaatje as Editor

Allan Hepburn

Writers are necessarily editors of their own works, if not of others'. Editing fiction means moving material around, subtracting passages, adding sequences, repositioning scenes to create pace and intensity, deleting characters or inventing new ones. At its best, editing is an invisible art: the less noticeable the signs of craftsmanship, the more skilled the editing. "The skill of writing offers little to a viewer," remarks Lucien Segura, a celebrated French writer in Michael Ondaatje's *Divisadero* (D, 193). Segura means that, in the hands of a good editor, deletions and additions leave no visible trace in a text, although the edges between sections and temporalities may show as part of the writer's design, like seams in a garment or corners in a building. For Ondaatje, editing brings out "patterns" and "hidden structures" (TC, 10, 27). In *Divisadero*, Segura compares editing to hammering metal: "Sometimes truth is too buried for adults, it can be found only in hours of rewritings during the night, the way metal is beaten into fineness" (D, 230). The writer-editor creates a story through technique and effort, although that effort shows only in the overall quality of the finished product.

In Ondaatje's view, writing and editing happen simultaneously rather than sequentially. "I don't do research, and then write, and then edit," he acknowledges. "When I'm writing I also edit on the side."[1] By his own admission, Ondaatje spends roughly two years editing his novels after he has a complete draft, by which he means "shaping the content into a new form, till it is almost a newly discovered story" (TC, xviii). At "the fixing stage of a book," as he calls it, he might transform several characters into one or shift scenes back and forth.[2] Drafts of his novels at the Harry Ransom Center indicate that he accumulates material in notebooks, including handwritten paragraphs, photographs, *découpage*, and scraps of printed text from any number of sources. He circles words, highlights others, deletes abundantly, and moves sentences and sections around to test their effect against each other.[3] "Everything is collage," Anna says in *Divisadero* with reference to the randomness of experience (*D*, 16), and that statement applies to Ondaatje's method of writing as a constant process of editing.

To describe the craft of editing and what he aims to achieve by assembling disparate materials into a pattern, Ondaatje frequently resorts to cinematic analogies. "I find the editing of a manuscript to be like the editing of a film," he told Sam Solecki in 1974, "that's when you determine the work's shape, rhythmic structures, etc."[4] The juxtaposition and duration of shots control pace in film, just as the juxtaposition and duration of sequences regulate the pace of fiction. Having seen how Walter Murch edited the film version of *The English Patient*, Ondaatje surmises that the final stages of cinematic editing come "closest to the art of writing" (*TC*, xviii). The structure of a film, like the structure of a novel, depends on its formal design, visual patterns, and handling of time. By treating films as analogous to novels, Ondaatje assumes that both rely on montage, in which shots, sequences, and segments build into stories. Ondaatje's own involvement with filmmaking – his contribution to *The Sons of Captain Poetry* and *The Clinton Special*, his unfilmed script for Robert Kroetsch's *Badlands*, his lengthy discussions with Murch about the art of editing film in *The Conversations* – provides a vocabulary for describing what happens between the first draft of a novel and its finished form.

"BEATEN INTO FINENESS" – WRITING AS EDITING

Theories of editing literary works tend to be ad hoc. Sometimes editing occurs at the macro-level of structure; sometimes it pertains to the micro-level of syntax and metaphor. Wherever it happens, editing requires a certain ruthlessness. Within the restrictions of space and length, some materials simply have to go despite their quality. To actualize the potential of a literary work or bring out its voice, editors make radical changes to the chronology of a novel or slash sections that do not contribute to the central plot. They recommend

Michael Ondaatje as Editor 157

word changes for the sake of cadence or intelligibility. "Revising is part of writing," counsel William Strunk and E.B. White in their classic manual, *The Elements of Style*: "If the work merely needs shortening, a pencil is the most useful tool; but if it needs rearranging, or stirring up, scissors should be brought into play."[5] Certain fiction editors have attained legendary status. Ellen Seligman, Sonny Mehta, and Liz Calder – Ondaatje's editors in Canada, the US, and the UK – are the dedicatees of his novel *Warlight*. Whatever their influence on Ondaatje's writing, they are largely invisible agents in the production of his novels. Anonymity defines most editorial interventions. As Dean Irvine and Smaro Kamboureli point out, "the texts we read are the result of an elaborate and intensely collaborative process that involves such players as literary agents, anonymous readers of manuscripts, book designers, and copy editors, but our reading act tends to bypass what transpires during the editorial and production stages."[6]

Although principally known as a poet and novelist, Ondaatje has edited anthologies and literary journals throughout his career. From 1965 to 1967, while completing an MA at Queen's University, he co-edited the little magazine *Quarry*. From 1977 until 1990, he worked as an editor at Coach House Press. In 1985, when Linda Spalding took over editing the literary journal *Brick*, Ondaatje became a contributing editor, and the magazine shifted its focus from book reviews to a dialogue between Canadian and world literature. From time to time, he has published essays in *Brick*, including a brief, funny paragraph about unfulfilled careers, in which he wishes he had been "a pianist in the style of Fats Waller" or "an illustrator of adventure books."[7] In 1991, Spalding and Ondaatje co-edited *The Brick Reader*, a selection of works previously published in the magazine. An anthology of essays called *Lost Classics*, pulled from *Brick* and edited by the four people then on the masthead – Ondaatje, Michael Redhill, Esta Spalding, and Linda Spalding – revives remarkable books that have been unjustly neglected. For his contribution, Ondaatje makes a pitch for Tissa Abeysekara's *Bringing Tony Home* because it reminds him of Sri Lanka and brings him "close to [his] lost self."[8]

Many of Ondaatje's editorial interventions fall under the category of selecting previously published works and arranging them into anthologies. In 1971, he chose the Canadian poems for *The Broken Ark*, republished as *A Book of Beasts* in 1979, with illustrations by

Tony Urquhart. In 1977, he assembled an anthology of short stories by four writers under the title *Personal Fictions: Stories by Munro, Wiebe, Thomas, and Blaise*. Other edited books followed: *The Long Poem Anthology, From Ink Lake, Brushes with Greatness*, and a selection of bpNichol's poetry called *An H in the Heart*. Among the short stories collected in *From Ink Lake*, he includes a section lifted from a memoir by Inuit writer Alice French and Hugh MacLennan's description of the 1917 Halifax harbour explosion. He calls these selections "outriders"[9] because they mix research with invention, a generic blending in which accuracy yields to the higher demands of representational truth.

As an editor, Ondaatje favours technique and process, or what he calls "the movement of the mind and language."[10] In poetry, he has a fondness for works that show "a process of knowledge, of discovery during the actual writing of the poem."[11] His own novels demonstrate a predilection for riffs, dreams, close-ups, careful miking of sound effects, and the relation of small details to a large structure. He likes to play with scale, from the minute to the panoramic. He refers to *The English Patient*, for instance, as an "intimate epic."[11] Intimacy is not a common characteristic of epics, which usually deal with odysseys, war, the conquest of civilizations, or the building of cities. Yet in *The English Patient* Ondaatje makes the epic intimate by putting a love story in the foreground and a panoramic story about desert warfare and the bombing of Hiroshima and Nagasaki in the background. In this case, editing means creating juxtapositions and edges to bring diverse narratives into stark relief.[13]

Writing is improvisation; editing is improvement. Like Fats Waller, Ondaatje takes his inspiration from the moment. By his own admission, he never writes a novel according to a plan. He claims that he would die of boredom if he had to follow a five-year blueprint for a work of fiction: "As a writer you have the licence to surprise yourself, veer off the path. You can always go back and remove mistakes, erase subplots that don't work. Nothing is written in stone, so why limit yourself to a preplanned story?" (*TC*, 219). In first drafts, he focuses on blocking and gestures rather than on finding the right words: "I write as if it were a rehearsal, I attempt to try out everything, though of course a subliminal editing is taking place" (*TC*, 37). Although writing and editing happen at the same time, they differ in the degree of critical distance taken from the text. Editorial objectivity allows the writer to see defects and correct them or, on the contrary, to see virtues and enhance them through revision. In a comment on Elizabeth Bishop's villanelle called "One Art," Ondaatje observes that "all the subtleties of nuance and precision of form were achieved during the editing" (*TC*, 136).[14] Like bone structure under skin, editing strengthens the "invisible specifics" that lie beneath the surface of a work yet shape its contours, size, appearance, and form (*TC*, xv).

At Coach House Press, Ondaatje refined his idea of the writer-editor. In 1967, Coach House published the deluxe first edition of his poems, entitled *The Dainty Monsters*, in a print-run of three hundred. Like his books that followed – *the man with seven toes*, *Rat Jelly*, and *Secular Love* – *The Dainty Monsters* is visually stunning, with an aesthetic closer to a handcrafted artwork than a commercially produced book. Known for its literary activism and enterprise in the 1970s and 1980s, Coach House published boxes of disassembled concrete poetry and a poem by George Bowering in the shape of a baseball pennant. Dabbling in "borderblurring" across fiction, poetry, drama, photography, and graphic media, Coach House developed a reputation as "a centre where all these categories interpenetrate and cross-fertilize."[15] For example, photographs, a telephone directory, and autobiographical fiction come together on the pages of David Young's *Incognito*, just one of the many books that Ondaatje helped to shape at Coach House. In his own poetry books, border blurring aims at the *dérèglement de tous les sens* through intermediality, whereby pictures, words, sounds, and music all meet and mix on the page.

An intuitive skill as much as it is an acquired one, editing poems means sharpening images and connecting units of text according to the inner logic of metaphors. Sometimes poems have to be rearranged to bring out latent meanings. The same can be said of novels. "I'm always preoccupied over what should be left in and what should be left out," Ondaatje admits: "I love restructuring things."[16] Yet when Solecki asks him point-blank how he goes about editing, he deflects the question and talks about every good poem being "like a well-made machine."[17] In editing, no single method fits every situation, which may account for Ondaatje's hesitation about describing how he works as an editor. Editing concentrates on particulars, right down to words and punctuation. In a conversation with W.S. Merwin, Ondaatje speculates on the role of punctuation in poetry and whether omitting it creates "freedom," especially interpretive freedom.[18] The point of editing, ultimately, is to create defined segments, with starts and stops in sounds and images, which allow the material to assume its own voice and become distinct in shape and meaning.

SEGMENTS, SEQUENCES, STORIES

When Ondaatje talks about editing, he regularly draws analogies from cinema. He describes *The Collected Works of Billy the Kid* as "the film I couldn't afford to shoot, in the form of a book."[19] In an interview with Catherine Bush in 1990, while he was still a fellow at the Canadian Centre for Film, Ondaatje compared the limitations of novelistic form to cinematic editing. He claims that "the subliminal and fluid cutting of film still hasn't been allowed into the novel except on the periphery,"[20] although his own novels go some distance to bucking that tradition. In film, he particularly admires shifting perspectives and exploiting a repertory of shots to advance the story. As Ondaatje told Maya Jaggi about his filmmaking efforts, "I loved the craft of film, specifically the editing process: how you can shift a scene from one point to another."[21] Ultimately, editing leads to the "discovery of the story and the form" (*TC*, 38). Arranging material provides access to the story, which, in Ondaatje's novels, means creating segments, sequences, and scenes that produce the story.

The technique of building narrative out of visual material informs all of Ondaatje's fictional narratives. He usually begins writing, he claims, with "some fragment that concerns me or that I'm curious about. It's often an image ... Gradually, as I stay with that image and that situation, a story will possibly emerge."[22] The repetition of images across time and narrative creates structure. In *Divisadero*, for example, a blue table appears intermittently and suggests visual continuity across disparate plotlines. Anna paints a table blue in Coop's cabin (*D*, 30). Lucien Segura writes his novels at a blue table (*D*, 93). Segura recovers the blue table from Marie-Neige's farmhouse (*D*, 239). The recurrence of the blue table implies a story that does not abide by the conventions of time or place. There are blue tables in California; there are blue tables in France. The blue tables may be part of a meaningful pattern or sheer coincidence, but they are all visually arresting. In this regard, narrative functions as a kind of "formlessness in which everything has a purpose" (*D*, 78).

Cinema is rarely far from Ondaatje's mind when he is reading, writing, or revising. When he first read Robert Kroetsch's *Badlands*,

Michael Ondaatje as Editor

161

he visualized scenes shot by shot, like a movie. In Ondaatje's opinion, Kroetsch's novel is "one of the few pure movies in our literature."[23] His script for *Badlands* traverses different temporalities – an expedition taken by four men through the Alberta hoodoos in 1916 versus a contemporary car trip taken by two women – by juxtaposing shots.[24] A dissolve allows the story to switch from past to present.[25] Movement is suddenly interrupted mid-stream, as in the instruction to "[c]ut as the dog splashes into the water."[26] The shot of the splashing dog disperses the continuity of the story by not showing the outcome of the situation or even the men's reactions to the dog jumping overboard. Does the dog reach shore? Does the sudden cut cause surprise or confusion? Is there a textual equivalent for such abrupt cuts?

With film in mind, Ondaatje talks about editing in terms of "architecture," "pattern," or "structure," which can be achieved by recourse to "repeating and building images."[27] More specifically, putting a scene in one place rather than another can change the meaning of the story. The reader sees different patterns according to the sequencing of material. To make this point, Ondaatje resorts to a comparison between what a spectator sees and where a story lies: when watching the replay of a horse race, a viewer does not pay attention to the winner, a story with a foregone conclusion, but to the horse in fourth place saving itself as best it can.[28] So, too, during revisions the writer looks for the stories buried within scenes and brings out their significance. Literary editors, like their cinematic counterparts, decide on the duration of segments; they reposition scenes in order to enhance the story that is not immediately apparent (*TC*, 32). "I think you can do on the page almost anything that film does," Ondaatje states: "The novel, and writing, is more advanced in terms of possibility. A film becomes most versatile in the editing process, in the sharpening of scenes."[29] Editing is the phase "when you decide on the film's structure. You remake the whole film,"[30] and the same holds true for editing fiction. You direct the eye of the reader by the placement of one image against another in a film, just as you direct the mind of the reader by the placement of one passage against another in a novel.

Ondaatje learned a great deal about the craft of editing from Walter Murch, whose credentials prior to editing *The English Patient* included *American Graffiti*, *The Conversation*, *The Godfather* (all three parts), *Apocalypse Now*, and *The Unbearable Lightness of*

Being. In *The Conversations*, Ondaatje and Murch discuss the intricacies of editing – namely, how to remove entire scenes, heighten tension, avoid bottlenecks in the plot, fiddle with something at minute seven to save a scene at minute fifty-three, or "disguise the fact that an essential scene was never shot" (TC, xv). When he re-edited and lengthened *Apocalypse Now* for re-release, Murch arranged material "elliptically" to suggest that a key moment has happened but, owing to its never having been filmed, does not appear on screen: "The audience will see the results of the missing scene rather than the scene itself" (TC, 76, 77). In *Divisadero*, Ondaatje applies Murch's lesson about omitted but essential scenes. "Not knowing something essential makes you more involved," Marie-Neige tells Lucien apropos of novel plots (D, 208). One vector of *Divisadero* ends when Coop and Claire pull up at their father's house years after all the characters have gone their separate ways. Yet the reunion of the family members never occurs. The story freezes on the frame of Coop and Claire's arrival, then cuts to another storyline altogether. Although the essential scene of reunion with the father is not represented, the promise of reunion resonates in the novel as a counterweight to Anna's complete break with her family. What remains elliptical within a narrative can still bear decisively on the story.

In conversation with Murch, Ondaatje puts forward the possibility that stories have an ulterior but not an anterior existence to sound, speech, music, character, shots, and sequences. One version of a story does not prevail over or prohibit others. In the best storytelling, the patterning of material is loose enough to intimate that alternative versions of a story are possible through other combinations: "there's a complete story *behind* the selection of material – it's back there in the distance. That's similar to the kind of thickness that a novel gives off. We are not held hostage by just one certain story, or if we are, we know it is just one opinion" (TC, 160). A different edit of the material, with a shift in emphasis on images and point of view, can reconfigure the story into something entirely new. Everything depends on the arrangement and structure that the editor gives to the material at hand.

The analogy between editing film and editing text has implications for scale (cutaways that zoom in on details) and visuality (the story implicit within an image). In their focus on images, Ondaatje's novels often contrast stillness and motion – the photograph of a worker dashing across the Bloor Street Viaduct on opening day while officials stand still behind him in *In the Skin of a Lion* or the immobility of the burnt aviator lying in a bed while a nurse reads to him in the opening pages of *The English Patient*. For *The Clinton Special*, Ondaatje wanted an effect of immobility, in which "each shot would almost be a static photograph."[31] In cinema, he sees opportunities for creating effects of stillness and surprise, like the sudden cut to black as soon as the last words are spoken in Ingmar Bergman's *After the Rehearsal*: "It's harsh and, in an odd way, bracing, strangely moving, because we've been pushed unexpectedly away from the usual time allotted for an emotion. I've always wanted to end a book that way" (*TC*, 222–3). The more abrupt or unexpected the cut, the more it disturbs the continuity of the story and complicates viewers' reactions.

The majority of Ondaatje's novels have segments and sections rather than chapters. In general, he writes novels as if he were storyboarding a film. Stories emerge from the interplay of sections, some of them quite disparate, with radical shifts in place or temporality figured by white spaces on the page. *In the Skin of a Lion* includes three "books" that divide into seven sections bearing provocative titles – "Little Seeds," "The Bridge," "The Searcher," "Palace of Purification," "Remorse," "Caravaggio," and "Maritime Theatre" – all designating buildings, feelings, or people. These seven sections further subdivide into segments that are set off on the page with blank spaces, as in Ondaatje's poetry. *The English Patient*, which is perhaps the most conventional of Ondaatje's novels in terms of its formal arrangement, has ten chapters that bear both numbers and titles. In *Divisadero*, the narrative fractionalizes into smaller and smaller units, as the title itself predicts.[32] This narrative technique recalls Borges's "The Garden of Forking Paths" and Italo Calvino's *If on a Winter's Night a Traveller*, while also tapping into a grammar of cinematic editing, in which shots build into segments, sequences, and finally scenes to create a continuous narrative.

The three parts of *Divisadero* – "Anna, Claire, and Coop," "The Family in the Cart," and "The House in Dému" – trace an uncertain trajectory through time, with zigzags backward from mid-century to the First World War and forward to the Gulf War and the Iraq War. Sections inside these three parts also bear titles, like chapters in a novel by Balzac.[33] These titles raise questions about continuity. Do the characters in the first part have some relation to the family in the cart? (They do not. Moreover, Anna, Claire, and Coop are

164   Allan Hepburn

raised as siblings, but none of them is biologically related to the others.) After dispersing in the first part, will Anna, Claire, and Coop regroup at the house in Dému to bring the narrative full circle? (No, they scatter and never re-meet as a trio. Although Claire and Coop meet again by coincidence, Anna disappears permanently from their lives.) Anna even sheds her name, although she never discloses her new name. Instead of knitting together various threads, the story leaves loose ends and mysteries. Ondaatje's intention is never to resolve a story with a distribution of fates in the manner of Charles Dickens or Robert Louis Stevenson. He arranges sections into patterns in order to liberate other possible stories and to hint at the unfinishedness of all stories.

Divisadero begins with an italicized prelude, narrated from an indeterminate time and place by the woman formerly known as Anna: "*The raw truth of an incident never ends, and the story of Coop and the terrain of my sister's life are endless to me*" (D, 1). This segment returns after Anna's transformation into an archivist and historian. When it comes back, the sentence sheds its italics and undergoes a slight syntactical transformation: "For the raw truth of an episode never ends, just as the terrain of my sister's life and the story of my time with Coop are endless to me" (D, 267). The restatement creates a rhythm for the novel; it takes the measure of how far the story has developed and, being focalized through Anna on both occasions, how far she may be removed from the raw truth of whatever incident she has in mind. The second statement is an edited version of the first. With its causal "for" and ambiguous "just as," the later version adds more complexity to the problem of how a story spins off from a motivating incident, which is the difference between "the raw truth of an incident" and "the story." In the first version, the story appears to be about Coop; in the second version, the story is about Anna's time with Coop, which is not quite the same thing. A story has multiple permutations, each of them an approximation of the raw truth.

Many of Ondaatje's novels begin with an italicized prelude. In these passages, which are rarely longer than a page or two, visual intensity takes precedence over dialogue and description. The prelude to *In the Skin of a Lion* sketches a situation and a story: "*This is a story a young girl gathers in a car during the early hours of the morning*" (SL, 1). The final pages of the novel refer back to this opening to bring the story full circle. In *Running in the Family*, a

Michael Ondaatje as Editor

memoir with distinctly novelistic tendencies, the prelude ranges across temporalities to register the disorientation of a man awaking from a dream in Sri Lanka; there are references to *"daybreak,"* *"December,"* *"twenty-five years,"* *"in ten minutes,"* and *"the morning ... already ancient"* (RF, 17). In these preludes, names are withheld and the situation anonymized, as if the narrator, whoever that might be, wants to focus on an image or the germ of a story, not the setting or the characters, which is another way of saying that pictures prevail over plots, at least in this initial phase of the narrative.

In their appeal to images, these segments recall the empty square on the opening page of *The Collected Works of Billy the Kid,* which is supposed to be *"a picture of Billy made with the Perry shutter as quick as it can be worked"* (CW, 5). To a certain degree, these preludes function like establishing shots in a film. They sketch an atmosphere and cue a problem that the narrative will try to solve. Who is Billy the Kid? Does the man in the car tell his story to the young girl for the first time? Why has the unnamed man returned to Sri Lanka after twenty-five years? The prelude to *Anil's Ghost* is equally provocative. an anonymous woman crouches beside two bodies in an excavated grave in Guatemala. The woman's husband and brother both disappeared a year earlier. To convey visual equivalents for her grief, the narration cuts to close-ups of *"a serape or banana leaf,"* *"a naked footprint in the mud,"* and *"a petal"* (AG, 6). These visual imprints imply a story, although it takes the rest of the novel to work out how those images, supplemented by others, add up to a story about disappearance and grief. Initially, Ondaatje could not find a place for this particular passage in the novel. After setting it aside because it fit nowhere, he situated the passage prior to the novel proper to clarify Anil's profession and establish "her unspoken compassion and empathy for the woman waiting beside the grave site as she worked. I had rejected that moment too quickly. But when I found the right place for it, it solved a lot of problems" (TC, 41). In *Anil's Ghost,* the prelude uses images to establish an emotive problem – how does one grieve the disappeared? – and the novel works out the implications of that problem.

For Ondaatje, a story is an extrapolation from available evidence. It is not predetermined. In *Anil's Ghost,* Sarath, an archeologist, wants to write a book about a city that no longer exists, "to tell the story of that place" (AG, 29). Over time, stories disappear from official records, and palaeographers and archeologists reconstitute them. Palipana, an epigraphist and Sarath's mentor, locates "an illegal story, one banned by kings and states and priests, in the interlinear texts" (AG, 105). He can read between the lines because he has a comprehensive grasp of history and an intuition about the logic of stories. Palipana's capacity to see complete stories within epigraphs does not mitigate the difficulty of rescuing those stories from oblivion. Stories require clearing away of debris, the way archeologists sift earth to find bones. With patience and effort, the pattern of the story can be discerned among fragments and rubble. Or, as Ondaatje tells Murch, the contours of a story emerge from a much larger quantity of material. In other words, the story has to be edited into existence.

CONVERGENCE AND DIVERGENCE

In *The Conversations*, Murch describes two cinematic methods of editing that allow multiple points of view: divergent and convergent. Divergent plots, according to Murch, begin "with all the characters in the same time and space" (TC, 252) As long as all the characters are shown together at the beginning of a film, an audience will follow their divergent trajectories. If, midway through a film, an editor introduces another character with a different point of view, there is a danger that "the late introduction will seem awkward or intrusive" (TC, 253). The way around this dilemma is to show newly introduced characters in relation to one of the initial characters. A classic instance of a divergent plot, according to Murch's criteria, is *The Godfather*, in which all the principal players appear at the wedding in the opening sequence. Whether in a film or a novel, material has to be edited in such a way as to establish the relationship among characters before they are sent off in different directions.

By contrast, in a convergent plot, two or three stories "start separately and then flow together" (TC, 253). Murch offers the film version of *The English Patient* as an example. Unlike Ondaatje's novel, which begins with the burnt aviator and the nurse in a ruined Italian villa, the script for the film begins with the Wehrmacht shooting down a plane over the desert in North Africa, followed by a sequence about a nurse in a train caring for wounded soldiers. The film thus juxtaposes two different plotlines, one shot in sunlight over open desert, the other shot in cramped quarters on a train moving through darkness. The film aims to blend these two disparate stories

Michael Ondaatje as Editor

or, at the very least, make them converge. What looks like convergence is, in fact, the result of editorial intervention. As Murch states, "you reach a point where almost accidentally these two stories fuse" (TC, 254).

Ondaatje's novels consistently operate on the principle of convergence and divergence. In *In the Skin of a Lion*, Patrick Lewis has an affair with Clara; when she disappears, he searches for her. The novel stops just before the couple reunite. In other words, the plot diverges and ends just prior to the expected convergence of the separated lovers. In *Running in the Family*, a fortune-teller predicts that Ondaatje's mother will continue to see her children during her lifetime but never all of them at the same time: "This turned out to be true. Gillian stayed in Ceylon with me, Christopher and Janet went to England. I went to England, Christopher went to Canada, Gillian came to England, Janet went to America, Gillian returned to Ceylon" (RF, 172). In their comings and goings, the siblings occasionally cross paths. They diverge and converge, like electrons orbiting around a nucleus, without all of them being together again.

The pattern of convergence and divergence often, but not always, concentrates on families in Ondaatje's novels. In *Anil's Ghost*, Sarath and his brother Gamini do not follow their father's example and become lawyers. Instead, they pursue their separate passions and destinies. As a family, "they scattered" (AG, 221). Similarly, in *The Cat's Table* and *Warlight*, family members drift off in several directions, and their reunions are as much a matter of haphazardness as they are a matter of longing. In this regard, Ondaatje edits material to create effects of chance, discontinuity, and luck. He wants the story to emerge from surprising juxtapositions rather than from the brain of an omniscient narrator who forecasts the destinies of every character before anything happens to them.

Ondaatje works out his plots of convergence and divergence through the trope of disappearance. Sometimes characters disappear for long intervals and then re-emerge unexpectedly. They exit one story to enter another, sometimes by walking away from their past entirely, the way that Anna disappears from the lives of her father and Claire in *Divisadero* before surfacing in a completely different story in France. Of course, some characters who disappear never reappear. Throughout *Anil's Ghost*, characters regularly disappear, either for political or for emotional reasons. In Sri Lanka during the civil war, "people just started disappearing" (AG, 17). Anil, a forensic scientist who has worked in Guatemala, Congo, and the American southwest, returns to Sri Lanka to work on a UN-sponsored inquiry into politically motivated disappearances. People disappear from her personal life as well. Her friend and co-worker, Leaf, suddenly vanishes, although she and Anil reunite through postcards, phone calls, and a brief meeting in the middle of nowhere. Anil stabs her boyfriend, Cullis, in the arm before disappearing definitively from his life. Disappearance in Ondaatje's novels – Anna in *Divisadero*, Ambrose Small in *In the Skin of a Lion*, the parents in *Warlight* – is necessarily a divergence, although it may turn out to be a prelude to a future reunion. These disappearances are the novelistic equivalents of Murch's divergent and convergent plots, in which characters unite to disperse and vice versa.

Anil's Ghost dwells on the fraught meanings of dispersal and reintegration as plot elements, always with the ulterior question of why characters disappear.[34] Anil and Sarath perform various forensic tests on an anonymous, recently buried body, given the nickname Sailor, found alongside four much older bodies at an archeological dig. At their laboratory in Colombo, Sarath cuts the head off Sailor's burned cadaver to make it look like the other skeletons found at the archeological site. By decapitating Sailor, Sarath wants to disguise the aim of the investigation, which is to prove that the government is executing Sri Lankan civilians. An artist named Ananda uses the severed head to reconstruct Sailor's face, which humanizes the skeleton and leads to a positive identification of the victim as Ruwan Kumara. The body thus disintegrates and comes back together to prove a political point. In effect, Anil and Sarath edit Sailor into existence: they piece together his identity much as a literary editor pieces together parts of a novel or a film editor splices together shots. But Sailor's story does not end with reintegration. Back in Colombo, where Anil intends to denounce the Sri Lankan government, someone abducts the headless body while Anil sits in a cafeteria with an official. With Sarath's help, Anil briefly recovers Sailor's body to complete her report for the UN, but the novel ends with a general dispersal of the characters. Sarath is murdered. Anil precipitously leaves Sri Lanka. Sailor's fate remains undisclosed.

Throughout *Anil's Ghost*, the pattern of dispersal and convergence repeats in various registers. In a sequence that lies adjacent to the plot about Sailor, the narrator describes, in a tone of remote neutrality, the plundering of a cave filled with twenty-six statues of

Bodhisattvas in the Chinese province of Shanxi, their heads severed from their bodies, their hands broken off, their body parts sold to museums in the West. From this story, the archeologist extracts a message about the transitoriness of art: "*Art burns, dissolves*" (AG, 12). As a counterpoint to this act of vandalism, Ananda reconstructs a giant Buddha blown up by thieves in Sri Lanka. Through this painstaking act, Ananda reverses the effects of damage and destruction. Instead of dissolving, art resolves. The artist, always an editor as much as a creator, makes a story materialize from bits and pieces.

"The editor is the one who has time to deal with the whole jigsaw," Walter Murch claims in *The Conversations* (30). To this statement, Ondaatje would probably add the proviso that putting together the whole jigsaw is an editorial illusion. Editing a novel is like editing a film insofar as both concentrate on cautious assembly of a story rather than the imposition of a predetermined structure or story. Ondaatje's characters disappear for long stretches of time to allow recurrences and convergences to happen as if by accident. When characters cross paths, stories emerge. About *The English Patient* – the novel and the film – Ondaatje claims that separate "stories expanded to the point that they met."[15] As stories expand, the probability of their attaching to other stories magnifies, through coincidence of events or the intersection of characters.

In *The Cat's Table*, diverse characters converge on board the *Oronsay* during a twenty-one-day voyage from Colombo to Tilbury docks. Throughout the novel, various sequences marked by different temporalities are inserted into the narrative to show discrepancies between what the narrator knew during the journey and what he knows long after the fact. Sequences in the novel are edited to fracture temporality and defy chronology. On board the *Oronsay*, a group of strays and strangers dine together: a silent man with a scarf around his neck, a woman who compulsively reads detective novels, a wan young woman who is deaf in one ear and hard of hearing in the other, a garrulous musician, three rambunctious boys. The table is a point of convergence. Years later, the narrator, teasingly named Michael – the parallels with the belatedly named narrator in *Remembrance of Things Past* are unmistakable – looks back on this sea journey and claims that "we used to imagine complex plots and stories for ourselves" (CT, 147). These stories leave plenty of room for guesses and error. Miss Lasqueti, she who reads detective novels, is rumoured to have connections in Whitehall. A manacled prisoner, brought out in the dead of night for exercise on the deck, turns out to be the father of the wan young woman who sits at the cat's table. In its blending of plots, the novel recalls *Treasure Island*, R.K. Narayan's novels, and *White Jacket*, all of which are explicitly mentioned in *The Cat's Table*. The ship itself becomes a forcing house for stories: with nowhere to go, characters necessarily converge, and their stories become elaborate and unlikely coincidences. The arrangement of materials forbids the narrator and the reader from knowing too much about what is going on until jump cuts that extend to other temporalities fill in gaps and round out the whole story.

In *The Cat's Table*, characters come together and drift apart. Michael befriends the two other boys at the cat's table, Ramadhin and Cassius. Their destinies converge, in the former case intimately and permanently, in the latter case importantly yet temporarily. Michael marries Ramadhin's sister, although their marriage ends in divorce. Michael never sees Cassius again after their adventures on the *Oronsay*, although he visits a gallery where Cassius's paintings are displayed, as if art were as good a place as any for meeting again. Years after the sea journey, Michael crosses paths with his cousin Emily. She has married, travelled, divorced, settled on an island near Vancouver, and started a new relationship. Her life has diverged completely from Michael's, yet their shared past ties them to each other. He claims to have trouble letting go of Emily, "despite our disappearances and separations" (CT, 256). Whereas some characters' destinies are complicated, enmeshed, and convergent, others barely touch and then diverge almost as soon as they come together.

The passage of time sharpens the meaning and consequences of a story. For this reason, one of the most resonant and certainly one of the most consistent phrases in Ondaatje's works is "years later." As a temporal marker, the phrase propels characters into their future selves, as happens to Patrick in *In the Skin of a Lion*: "Years later at the Riverdale Library he will learn how the shining leaf-chafers destroy shrubbery" (SL, 9). Sudden temporal dislocations sow seeds of doubt, as in *Divisadero*: "Years later, if he had been able to look back, Coop might have attempted to discern or reconsider aspects of his or Claire's or Anna's character" (D, 23). Although the conditional clause hints at the erasure of Coop's memory during a violent assault, which the reader learns about subsequently, time does not slow down because of his memory loss. Years later, Coop might have

Michael Ondaatje as Editor

looked back and retold the story of his involvement with Claire and Anna, but that possibility is cancelled even as it is held forth. The narrators in Ondaatje's novels tease out stories through patterns of expectation and delay. They juxtapose unlikely segments that abide by a logic of images more than a logic of time. Temporal dislocations allow jagged edges to intrude between the present and the future. They also allow for alternative interpretations of characters and past events. In *Anil's Ghost*, Anil, when looking at certain pictures "years later" (AG, 202), remembers her childhood. In *The Cat's Table*, Michael tells his children about his adventures at sea "years later" (CT, 52). In all these instances, the phrase "years later" recalls the opening line of Gabriel Garcia Marquez's *One Hundred Years of Solitude*, in which temporality switches nimbly back and forth between the present and the past, when Colonel Aureliano Buendía faces the firing squad and remembers the distant afternoon when his father took him to look at the ice.[36] In Ondaatje's fiction, "years later" almost always marks an insertion of a sequence that discombobulates narrative linearity and creates patterns that recall the filmic technique of juxtaposing shots. Hopping forward to a future point frees narrative from any single plotline. It also widens the opportunities for convergences and divergences, where characters come together then scatter to the four winds.

"THE ILLUSION OF THE UNEXCEPTIONAL"

Ondaatje pokes fun at people who believe editing is "an unknown, mysterious skill – some smoke and mirrors, some touching up, some old black magic" (TC, xi). Instead of relying on hocus-pocus, writers painstakingly assemble narratives out of odds and ends, images and sections, while trusting that a complete story will emerge once revision ends. In *Divisadero*, Lucien Segura writes during the day and revises during the night: "He sat there weighing what was already written, half-dreamt during the day, until he fell on a scrap of a sentence, something uncommitted, that would open a door for him" (D, 220). The distance closes between the time of writing and the time of editing until the two activities are virtually indistinguishable. Segura writes as he edits and edits as he writes, and both activities plumb language for its unconscious, half-dreamt possibilities. When Segura returns to what he has already written, the hidden potential in a scrap of a sentence opens like a door.

Although Ondaatje dismisses "smoke and mirrors" ideas about editorial intervention, as an activity it does have a certain abracadabra: editing creates an illusion of effortlessness. In *Divisadero*, Coop becomes an expert poker player – not an illusionist per se but close enough. Among the first lessons that he learns about sitting at a table with a bunch of cardsharps is to "give the illusion of the unexceptional" (*D*, 50). His mentors teach him that a poker player should never show off. He should keep a low profile and hold onto his cards until the right moment. Although these recommendations pertain to poker, they embody Ondaatje's most valuable tips about editing. Pretend that nothing is really happening. Save your best tricks until an opportune moment. Make it all look unexceptional, as easy as easy can be.

NOTES

1 Ondaatje, "We Cannot Rely on Only One Voice," 7:18 7:38.
2 Ibid., 8:41–9:02.
3 Krause, "Archive of Michael Ondaatje, Author of *The English Patient*, Acquired."
4 Solecki, *Spider Blues*, 21.
5 Strunk and White, *The Elements of Style*, 72.
6 Irvine and Smaro, "Introduction," 5.
7 Ondaatje, "More Lost Careers," 57.
8 Ondaatje et al., *Lost Classics*, 160.
9 Ondaatje, "Introduction," xvi.
10 Ondaatje, "What Is in the Pot," *The Long Poem Anthology*, 12.
11 Ibid., 14.
12 Rose, "Michael Ondaatje and Anthony Minghella Interview on *The English Patient*," 14:38.
13 In *The Conversations*, Ondaatje and Murch discuss sound in terms of its "edges" (246). Murch draws an equivalent between cuts in film and line ends in poetry (268). This statement resonates with Ondaatje's claim that film editing demonstrates "the kind of craft that any careful writer uses as he or she edits a novel, or the craft a record producer counts on to shape an album with a hundred small details in the last stages" (xvi).
14 Ondaatje praises Bishop's poem for its conversational voice and taut form: "Somehow the structure allows her a wild freedom of travel: Bishop goes

Michael Ondaatje as Editor — 173

all over the world with this form that's as strict and musical as a tango." "How Poems Work," D14.

15 Dragland, "Coach House Poetry, 1965–96," 82.

16 Solecki, *Spider Blues*, 327.

17 Ibid.

18 Ondaatje, Solecki, and Spalding, "An Interview with W.S. Merwin," 19.

19 Solecki, *Spider Blues*, 20.

20 Bush, "Michael Ondaatje: An Interview," 94.

21 Jaggi, "Michael Ondaatje in Conversation with Maya Jaggi," 10.

22 Ondaatje, "We Cannot Rely," 4:53–5:23.

23 Solecki, *Spider Blues*, 329.

24 Ondaatje wrote this screenplay circa 1977. A complete typescript is held in the Robert Kroetsch fonds, University of Calgary, Archives and Special Collections, Box 42.4. An excerpt appeared in *Descant* in 1983 under the title "The William Dawe Badlands Expedition 1916."

25 Ondaatje, "The William Dawe Badlands Expedition 1916," 54.

26 Ibid., 56.

27 Solecki, *Spider Blues*, 322.

28 Ibid., 324.

29 Bush, "Michael Ondaatje," 95.

30 Solecki, *Spider Blues*, 16.

31 Ibid.

32 De Smyter, "'We Live Permanently in the Recurrence of Our Own Stories,'" 99.

33 A homage to French literature, *Divisadero* alludes to Victor Hugo (142, 193), Honoré de Balzac (13, 77, 221), Stendhal (77, 106), Alexandre Dumas (28, 200), and Colette (77). There are also references to *David Copperfield*, Herman Melville, and *The Octopus*. Like all of Ondaatje's novels, *Divisadero* is a digest of other books, in which anthologizing itself is a form of editing.

34 Freed, "Invisible Victims, Visible Absences," 28.

35 Ondaatje, "We Cannot Rely," 5:48–5:52.

36 "The book that really affected me in the last year was Marquez's *A Hundred Years of Solitude*," stated Ondaatje in 1974 (Solecki, *Spider Blues*, 25). Several critics have commented on Marquez's impact on Ondaatje's novels (Hutcheon 88–9; Barbour 137, 139). Ondaatje himself refers to this influence and quotes the opening line of *One Hundred Years of Solitude* in "García Márquez and the Bus to Aracataca" (21).

7

Michael Ondaatje in the Cinema

Bart Testa

Michael Ondaatje's achievements as a poet and novelist were recognized early in his career by a coterie of Canadian readers and critics, and his works drew appreciative commentaries. He published small-press poetry collections beginning in 1967 and reached a significant audience with *The Collected Works of Billy the Kid: Left-Handed Poems* (1970). His novels began to appear later in the decade with *Coming Through Slaughter* (1976). After this, his circle of readers and commentators expanded steadily, especially around *In the Skin of the Lion* (1987), his first book published by Knopf. Ondaatje's next novel, *The English Patient*, was a towering success, shared the 1992 Booker Prize, and gained the writer a fully international readership, which soon exploded after the novel was made into an Oscar-winning feature film in 1996.

Ondaatje also made some films of his own during the early 1970s, and although they do not significantly extend his accomplishment as an artist, two of them reveal the enthusiasms and commitments of an artist who, from the start, placed himself within his Toronto community of aspiring poets and dramatists. Although Ondaatje did not work in the cinema for long, making just three short films between 1970 and 1974 when his initial poetry collections were gaining momentum, *The Sons of Captain Poetry* (1970) and *The Clinton Special* (1974) are sensitive documentaries while *Carry on Crime and Punishment* (1972) is a whimsical five-minute silent comedy. An enthusiastic cinephile, Ondaatje has spoken in interviews and occasional public talks about films he admires, like John Boorman's *Point Blank* (1967), and about directors like Sergio Leone, but his urge to continue making movies was muted. There was talk of film

Michael Ondaatje in the Cinema   175

adaptations of *Coming Through Slaughter*, and he did prepare a screenplay of Robert Kroetsch's novel *Badlands*, but none of these projects advanced beyond that.[1] In 1990, during a residence at the Canadian Film Centre in Toronto, Ondaatje wrote the screenplay *Love Clinic* (1991), apparently his last cinematic effort. Then *The English Patient* drew the admiration of a British TV and film director, Anthony Minghella, and so began an odyssey that resulted in the film in 1996 and that also later occasioned Ondaatje's only work of non-fiction, *The Conversations: Walter Murch and the Art of Editing Film* (2002).

Ondaatje's filmmaking efforts during the 1970s might seem to be those of a writer who makes a film, or several, to expand his or her concerns into that medium. Susan Sontag, Norman Mailer, and David Mamet have made films as such sidebars to their writing. A few writers have made a lasting transition to film, notably Pier Paolo Pasolini and Alan Robbe-Grillet. If Ondaatje ever realizes projects comparable to the films of such writers, its foundations are not obvious in the films he made in the 1970s. These initial remarks may seem dismissive, but they are intended to counter a tendency to assume that a writer of Ondaatje's distinction might also excel in other forms of art. Alternately, one might also assume that Ondaatje's filmmaking served him as a writer. This is the more seductive hypothesis, since Ondaatje has used the devices of juxtaposition, polyphonous narration, and heterogeneous stylistics suggesting cinematic montage. However, we should take André Bazin seriously when he observes that cinematic techniques, like montage, used experimentally by writers, are rarely used by filmmakers who rely on continuity editing, which aligns them more closely with classic realist fiction.

Carry on Crime and Punishment is a narrative whimsy, a silent film with music. Two hoboes sneak up to a cottage and kidnap the family dog. A chase headed by the children of the house ensues, and it ends when the thieves are cornered on a dock and jump off. The hoboes are low comic types; one hobbles theatrically on crutches. Ondaatje deliberately regresses to filmmaking of a type familiar between 1896 and 1907. The best remembered of chase films like these is the British director Cecil Hepworth's *Rescued by Rover* (1905), the plot of which Ondaatje has inverted by having the children rescue the dog.

The Sons of Captain Poetry is a documentary on poet bpNichol. It is a remarkably full portrait given its brevity (thirty-five minutes).

The film has five distinct types of footage, three of which are conventional, two idiosyncratic. The lengthiest and most valuable are the long takes of Nichol performing his poems and speaking about his work. He was a compelling performer and a thoughtful and forthcoming commentator, and Ondaatje captures him well. Extending this material are shots of printed concrete poetry with Nichol's comments heard in a voice-over. The third type of material is used for transitions comprised of action shots: Nichol plays volleyball or visits Therafields, home of his therapy group. These three types of material are conventional in a documentary, and they elicit no comment, except that one notices Ondaatje's unobtrusive tact. The two idiosyncratic types of footage show Ondaatje devising passages, including a prefatory montage of cows over which he places an aural collage of commenting voices. In a second preface, a set of broken windows fills the screen like a grid, and Nichol passes through one of the windows, making his entrance; he is presented as if he were slipping through the grid of conventional language.

The Clinton Special is the most enduringly popular of Ondaatje's films; it is also suggestive of a theme prominent in his fiction: the plurivocality of history. There is a preface in *The Clinton Special*, again shots of cows, but soon members of the Theatre Passe Muraille company are shown preparing to leave for Clinton, Ontario. There they will research what would become, in 1972, a documentary drama called *The Farm Show*. Settling for a season in the southern Ontario farming community and living in an old farmhouse, the troupe acquainted themselves with the people of the community and often worked alongside them on their farms. Then they adapted stories, characters, and anecdotes they had gathered into a sequence of dramatic episodes. The troupe performed *The Farm Show* on tour the next year to popular acclaim.

Ondaatje includes generous samples of their performances during the troupe's return to Clinton, performing to an audience made up of the play's subjects. Although the film alludes to the research and composition that went into *The Farm Show*, Ondaatje does not present the material in sequence. Instead, for most of the film's seventy minutes, he crosscuts between preparation and bits from the play and the reactions of the Clinton people. Here the footage includes scenes from the show shot in real locations, scenes being performed on stage with members of the community in attendance, and interviews. Cinematographer Robert Fresco seeks

Michael Ondaatje in the Cinema   177

a subtly diverse qualities of image, which Ondaatje exploits while editing (which he does himself). Different types of film stocks and lenses, a diverse range of camera distances and sound tones come into play. Fresco controls these to produce a carefully composed gallery of portraits in which differences between actors and subjects are modulated deftly. Fresco's images conform very well to Ondaatje's general strategy, which is to mix and match spontaneous monologues of the members of the farming community with the scripted dialogues and monologues performed by the actors. The Clintonites also comment on the way the actors portrayed their real experiences and suggest the fiction has distorted them, making them seem more "folksy." A later segment, about Charlie Wilson, is wholly a filmically constructed portrait; some realities cannot be found in a natural state and represented mimetically. For one thing, Wilson is dead, and Ondaatje ensures that this is the first thing we learn about him. His only existence in the present consists of his neighbours' memories of him, their anecdotes and verbal characterizations. The camera records his shack and the places he regularly visited while neighbours sketch his biography, explain his bricoleur's approach to being a handyman, and describe his sad last days. This is how Wilson becomes a film character possessing considerable pathos, and Ondaatje's sensitive montage of these diverse sources conveys this quality remarkably well.

The Clinton Special distinguishes itself from both a National Film Board documentary and an American cinema vérité documentary. An NFB filmmaker would have told us what the play means in the social process. An American film would typically have focused on the struggle the actors underwent to create the play. Instead, Ondaatje's interest is the literary and performative give-and-take of the farming community and the playmaking, observant of the slippages between the locals' self-presentations and the dramatic representation of them by the actors. The fascination of the film arises from its portrayal of the rigorous proximity the theatre troupe sought and its revelation of the fundamental impossibility of their documentary theatre.

Between 1991's *Love Clinic* and the adaptation of *The English Patient* in 1996, Ondaatje was not involved with filmmaking. That was about to change. Before all that, there was the great success of the novel itself. But this was just a prelude to greater excitement four years later when *The English Patient* became a motion picture. Immediately after he read it, Anthony Minghella brought

The English Patient to producer Saul Zaentz, and the two began work on a screenplay. The director and producer were later to be thrust into the Hollywood spotlight when *The English Patient* won nine Oscars (of twelve nominations) and accumulated ticket sales mounting toward $228 million. Ondaatje meanwhile kept himself well away from that spotlight. The novel was mentioned by movie reviewers often but just in passing, likely unread by most of them. Afterwards, however, a second wave of critics scrutinized the film closely as an adaptation of the novel.[2]

Ondaatje's role in the scripting and filming of *The English Patient* was, at most, consultative. Minghella invited him to review his drafts, but Ondaatje quickly recognized that the film was departing from his novel, explaining, "The choices made here aren't so much about the politics of the moviemakers; they are about the technical limits of film."[3]

The English Patient secured Ondaatje a wider readership than he had ever known, but it was not the kind of sensational best-seller usually optioned by film producers. Minghella did not know Ondaatje before he read the book, nor was he himself well known. Minghella's first film, *Truly, Madly, Deeply* (1990), was a small tele-film made at the BBC. His second, *Mr. Wonderful* (1993), a first foray into Hollywood, was a failure. Zaentz nonetheless accepted the challenge that *The English Patient* posed. He and Minghella reshaped Ondaatje's complex book into a filmable, if still ambitious, script and then sought financing to mount what would have to be an expensive production. Not altogether left outside the project, Ondaatje spent time in Italy with the crew and cast and formed a warm friendship with Minghella,[4] but perhaps more important was the relationship he developed with Walter Murch, film and sound editor for *The English Patient*. Their occasional conversations so interested him that Ondaatje arranged to record five sessions over the course of a year, starting in July 2000 (*TC*, xii). He then edited and introduced the discussions, resulting in a three-hundred-page book, *The Conversations*. While Ondaatje is modest about his contribution, the widely read volume is an extraordinary product of encounters between a thoughtful cinephile and novelist and an unusually cultivated filmmaker.[5]

The English Patient's path to the screen faced obstacles worth noting. The novel held little appeal in Hollywood studios. Reflecting a widespread attitude, Peter Biskind calls it "a difficult and stubbornly uncinematic novel."[6] Had Minghella and Zaentz not been so determined, it would have never reached the screen. When it did, the success of the filmed *English Patient* was fantastic, but it was also short-lived. It is the kind of prestigious romance film that is embraced by a public that rarely goes to the movies, aside from a seasonal fix. Such a "quality" film attracts that big occasional audience, wins Oscars, and then quickly fades from view.[7]

The main obstacle in front of Zaentz, however, went beyond the book's difficult reputation to include Minghella's inexperience and Zaentz's casting choices.[8] The film was eventually produced not by a Hollywood studio but by Miramax.[9] Zaentz, at seventy-five, was a tough industry veteran who specialized in transforming literary properties into prestige films that won awards and made money. Usually, Zaentz hired foreign directors, like the Czech Miloš Forman, who made *One Flew over the Cuckoo's Nest* (1975) and *Amadeus* (1984) for him, and the Brazilian-Argentine Héctor Babenco, who directed *At Play in the Fields of the Lord* (1991). Zaentz ordinarily self-financed his films, but the $20-million loss he incurred with *At Play in the Fields of the Lord* forced him to shop *The English Patient* around to studios.[10] Zaentz finally attracted 20th Century Fox for a commitment of $20 million. Just weeks away, Fox pulled its support, and Zaentz scrambled to make a deal with Miramax.[11]

What kind of film is *The English Patient*? In his insightful study of the film and its academic critics, David L. Kranz declares that the film is not an example of "Hollywood realism."[12] Free of such conventions, Kranz claims, the film is attempting to be true to the book. Yet his analysis indicates that the film is, in fact, a late example of "classical cinema." There can be several answers to the question of what kind of film is *The English Patient*. These can deal with the film's themes, which Kranz seeks to align with the book, or the formal design of the film and the genre it aimed for. It is the latter that the following discussion will try to sketch.

The English Patient was made within the conventions of classical film form, which is often loosely associated with "Hollywood realism" but is actually the default form of narrative films made everywhere.[13] Among classical cinema conventions are those that concern the ordering of plot and story. The plot, which branches into narration, is what a film actually presents directly to the viewer. Story is what the viewer constructs and infers from plot information. Comprehending the film's narrative depends on the eventual

180 Bart Testa

alignment of plot and story for the viewer. In many classical films, plot and story seem indistinguishable.[14] However, classical cinema affords leeway in how plotting can veer away from straight story-telling and allows temporary narrative gaps, deferred exposition, parallel plotting, the negotiation of complex timeframes, and mixtures of types of narration. Classical films will strive to guide the viewer to recuperate all narrative elements into a coherent story governed by cause and effect, usually centred on a main protagonist. In other words, classical films achieve closure.

By the measure of classical film form, any comparison of Ondaatje's novel to Minghella's film must observe that the novel has an idiosyncratic narrative form and style of narration. It deploys an unusually complex narration and shows a relative disregard for cause-and-effect relations. And it even casts the identity of its protagonist in ambiguity, although he is the titular "English Patient." Critics tend to generalize these and other features of Ondaatje's novels as "fragmentary."[15] For instance, Ondaatje's plot units are often written discretely, in the sense that while reading them the reader does not tend to ask so much what's next or how they fit into the story but is directed to dwell in the frame set by the plot unit. The plot units are then fitted, often retroactively, into a mosaic story structure. Another salient feature of Ondaatje's narrative design is that he does not privilege just one or two characters as principals and the others as adjuncts. He decentres his narrative units and does so across multiple characters.[16]

All this deviates to a significant degree from classical film narratives, which establish the principal characters early; a protagonist stands out equipped with attributes and purposes that promise a realization of goals. Classical films add other characters as needed but as supports: as, for example, comic asides, or helpers to the protagonist, or for romantic subplots. A reader can, in contrast, traverse Ondaatje's whole novel and, while inferring it, never finally decide that the Patient, bedridden and burned beyond recognition, is the same man as Almásy, the dashing desert explorer-archeologist and protagonist. (Or, for that matter, a reader might decide Kip or Hana is the protagonist.) In the film, confirmation of the Patient's lead role occurs early and is confirmed nearly immediately in the initial sequences, which show the plane crash and Almásy's rescue by the Bedouins. The viewer's identification of the Patient is then

Michael Ondaatje in the Cinema

181

redundantly reinforced by his role as the main narrational channel for the many flashbacks to Almásy's adventures and his passionate romance with Katharine Clifton that led to the catastrophe that ruined him. A great deal of Ondaatje's plotting is rearranged in the film, then, to conform to classical conventions. Instead of ambiguity, the film sets up the final effect of the plotting: the burned Patient is almost the first thing shown, and flashbacks lead the viewer back along the chain of causes and effects in the very late sequence of events that led him to his end.

Another feature of the novel's style is that Ondaatje's mode of narration shifts from a reportorial objectivity to character-narration/focalization without much cueing of the reader. In contrast, the film deploys narration with much careful cueing: for example, the shifts from the present in the villa to the past in the desert and Cairo use a variety of dissolves and graphic matches and sound bridges,[17] shifting the viewer to the Patient's focalization, then transiting to a flashback. We do more than just infer that the Patient remembers events from that past; we experience his memory-transitions to past experiences. Such intimacy with the film's characters is carefully mediated by POV shots and dialogues. Intimacy with characters in the novel is rarer and comes upon the reader as a slight shock, as in the introduction of Kip, asleep in chapter 3, and the passage during which Hana, sitting by the villa's fountain, reminisces about her past. So, too, when Ondaatje shifts from apparent reportage of facts and histories, a predominant feature of his novel, to dialogues and then to an interiorized lyrical style, or to dramatization, as in the tense passage in which Kip defuses a big bomb, the transit effect is abrupt, a cut not a dissolve. Almost none of the controlling narrational shifts in the film have equivalents in the novel. Minghella has meticulously smoothed Ondaatje's multivocal system of narration to adapt the novel to the regime of classical film form and its protocols of narration.

There are many principal characters distributed across the novel, and when they are front and centre they are the narration's close interest, sometimes for whole chapters. When his narration veers away from one character to another, the shift seems absolute.[18] Commentators on Ondaatje sometimes sum up his style of narration as polyphony. While there are filmmakers who seek polyphony (like Paul Thomas Anderson), Minghella is not one of them.[19] Although there are forty time-shifts across the film, they are all carefully segmented into plot units held together by succession, and most are linked to one principal character: the Patient.

This rough comparison of some of the formal differences between the novel and the film provides some initial signals of the kind of film *The English Patient* is and how it shapes the novel's material into a classical narrative form, with the results that narrative clarity is secured, ambiguity cleared, and direct deliveries of emotional pay-offs are well prepared.

Minghella's excisions of the novel have frequently been subjected to critiques by academic critics. There are also expansions of scenes in the novel, however, that are just as prominent. To mention obvious story elements that are substantially enlarged, the affair between Almásy and Katharine is the most obvious. Despite its importance in the novel, Ondaatje describes it rather tersely. Minghella dramatizes the affair in a long sequential series of flashback episodes, forming it into the dominant plot. This is the main reason *The English Patient* is correctly described by its first reviewers as a romance film.

Other parts of the novel are shrunk to make room for the affair. Some are reduced by being dramatized: the relationship between Hana and Kip is an example. The novel only gradually brings them together. In the film, Kip's relationship with Hana begins in two quite drastic encounters, both of which Minghella invents. Their first meeting, in an early sequence, consists of Kip's rescue of a distraught Hana when she is about to step into a minefield. Later, there is a second "rescue" when Kip arrives at the villa while Hana plays a snatch of Bach on a tipped-over piano. He warns her off and then exposes a boobytrap in the piano. From this point on their encounters rise by quick steps to the point where they become lovers.[20]

Minghella does excise a good deal: much of the novel's cut portions concern the international group of archeologists that explored the desert in the 1930s until the Second World War closed down their work.[21] The film cuts this back to a remnant of the group's efforts in order to isolate and privilege Almásy and to get Katharine on stage as fast as possible.

The English Patient begins with its depiction of the plane crash setting the film's main enigma, then it introduces Hana on a troop train, and then it picks up with the Patient's rescue by the Bedouins. The events that led up to the crash will soon become the film's focused narrative gap until, near the end, the Patient's final long flashback closes it by relating his attempt to save the injured Katharine he left in the cave. When he returns to her, finding her dead, he carries her to the plane, which flies off only to be shot down by German gunners. This closure segment confirms that Almásy is the same man as the burned and bedridden Patient. There should be no doubt concerning the Patient by this point, but the compositional and emotional satisfaction of closure as manifested here is a key part of classical film form.

What has just been outlined is how a dominant plot, distributed through a series of lengthening flashbacks, leaves nothing dangling. The kind of film *The English Patient* is does not intend to be in any way of narrative form a real adaptation of Ondaatje's novel. The romance plot that centres *The English Patient* is so enlarged in emotional and erotic investment that it virtually eclipses other aspects of the film. The director simply delays firmly answering the question of the Patient by using subplots, which include Hana's relationship with Kip, Caravaggio's accusations, and all the comings and goings of these adjunct characters, as supporting delays.

In a further answer to the question what kind of movie *The English Patient* is, the enlargement of the Almásy-Katharine affair makes the film, by genre, a romance while the locale and period make it an exotic-adventure-romance, and comparisons that reviewers made to the films of David Lean, like *Lawrence of Arabia* (1962), *Doctor Zhivago* (1965), and *A Passage to India* (1984), are apt.[22]

With this in mind, Minghella's film has been subject to considerable criticism by academics who specialize in film-and-literature studies. One could regard this scrutiny as simply a category mistake or misplaced expectation of a middlebrow adaptation like Minghella's film. Ondaatje's *The English Patient* was never destined to see a film faithful to the text, something that the author himself recognized. Most critics begin by ritually admitting that problem by declaring their disregard for the so-called "fidelity" position on literary adaptations. But the demurring only goes so far. For example, Josef Pesch declares, "[A]ny writer of screenplays will treat the work of fiction on which his idea is based as a starting point for a new creation. If that starting point is a complex work of art, the transformation cannot but change, alter, adapt that work into something it is not, and this fact has long since been accepted in film studies."[23]

As equitable as this sounds, Pesch adds that this does not preclude comparison prising out "patterns of transformation and strategies

184   Bart Testa

of adaptation."[24] This still sounds neutral, but Pesch quickly shows that such comparisons always lead to evaluations. He particularly looks to the excisions that Minghella's made when filming *The English Patient*. For Pesch, as for many academic critics, the crucial absence from the film is the passage in which Kip hears news of the dropping of the atomic bombs on Japan on his crystal radio and then burns with fury.

In her *Theory of Adaptation*, Linda Hutcheon gives a clear account of how the issue of this particular excision has usually been framed. She writes that it "transfigured [the novel]." It is worth quoting her at length, for she includes Murch's explanation.

> For instance, in offering a different ending in the film version of Michael Ondaatje's *The English Patient*, Anthony Minghella ... removed the postcolonial politics of the Indian Kip's response to the bombing of Hiroshima, substituting instead another smaller bomb that kills his co-worker and friend. In other words, a personal crisis is made to replace a political one. As the movie's editor, Walter Murch articulated the decision: "The film [unlike the novel] was so much about these five individual people: the Patient, Hana, Kip, Katharine, Caravaggio – that to suddenly open up near the end and ask the audience to imagine the death of hundreds of thousands of unknown people ... It was too abstract. So, the bomb of Hiroshima became the bomb that killed Hardy, someone you knew."[25]

It is worth noting that the passage Hutcheon quotes comes from *The Conversations*, and she might have noted that Ondaatje himself prompts Murch's remark when he recalls, "I saw it late in the editing of *The English Patient*. The sequence – which had already been filmed – in which the characters respond to the news of Hiroshima was not going to work" (*TC*, 213). For Ondaatje, it seemed a compositional problem that the excision and substitution solved. For Murch, it is an emotional problem of how to manage the viewers' responses to the film. Neither of them appears to have taken it as the kind of serious thematic issue that Hutcheon casts as removal of postcolonial politics. Critics have associated those politics with Kip and want to identify them with Ondaatje's intended themes. What Murch and Ondaatje do not mention is that in the novel, Kip's explosive response to the news serves as the novel's extended climax and not the flashback of Almásy's return to Katharine in the cave that Minghella deployed as his closure device. In the novel, Kip angrily brandishes his rifle while delivering three fierce speeches, then breaks off with everyone in the villa, including Hana. He roars out of the place on his motorcycle for a headlong dash to the Italian south. This is to be his first step in getting home to India. Kip's fierce speeches in *The English Patient* run several paragraphs, but the most cited line is: "American. French. I don't care. When you start bombing the brown races of the world, you're an Englishman" (286). Kip's Hiroshima protest opens the reader's memory to a carefully developed storyline of the novel completely absent from the film: Kip's wartime career, beginning with the young Sikh's decision to fight with the English Army while his anti-colonialist brother rebels against the British and goes to jail. In England, Kip loses his proper name – Kirpal Singh – on his first day in the barracks. He courageously endures the brutalities of the Italian campaign as a sapper, an engineer, and bomb disarmer. All this is fully plotted before Kip ever arrives at the villa. In Ondaatje's novel, what Hutcheon regards as the postcolonial politics may seem latent, but, retroactively, it comes to the fore when Kip flares with articulate anger; he made the wrong choice in siding with the British against the Germans. In the film, the postcolonial theme appears only as a few scraps in some of Kip's conversations with the Patient.

It is seldom noted, though it is by Ondaatje, that Minghella actually wrote and shot the atom bomb passage. Only in the late editing phase, after much material was removed and many pieces moved around, did the filmmakers, and Ondaatje himself, notice that the passage would not work. It did not work because of the kind of film *The English Patient* strives to be: a romance-adventure. The excised atom bomb passage seemed an incongruity in the film that has given itself to the romance plotting. In its place, the filmmakers transposed two sequences. The first is a riveting scene of bomb disarming moved from earlier in the novel, the second an invented new scene, the one Murch mentions. Late in the film, Kip is defusing a very big bomb lodged under a bridge in the town near the villa. Over his head, a group of heedless, cheering American soldiers cross the bridge in their heavy vehicles. The vibrations threaten an explosion that will engulf everyone. The juxtaposition of American raucous celebration and the bomb lurking beneath suggests that victory will betray not just Kip but everyone, just as the atomic bomb that gave the US its

186   Bart Testa

victory in Asia opens a global trapdoor into a new terror-ridden atomic age. In the novel, the Hiroshima news betrays the colonial compact that Kip has made and faithfully followed at great danger to himself. The big bomb scene does carry meaning away from the postcolonial politics Ondaatje wove into his novel, and Minghella shrinks it to an easily missed synecdoche for the nuclear "age of anxiety." The invented scene is an emotional replacement for the atomic bomb passage. Everyone is celebrating VE Day, and, in the town square, Kip's partner and friend Hardy, drunkenly happy, climbs a statue and it explodes, killing him. Kip retreats in grief but soon emerges to bid goodbye to Hana.

Aside from Ondaatje's agreement with the substitution of the exploding statue for the Hiroshima bomb, the issue for academic critics is whether or not the excision was a violation. Pesch regards the atom bombs and Kip's fury as pivotal to the novel.[26] Hutcheon clearly likewise regards their excision as a "transfiguration."[27] According to Bandi, the novel "touched a nerve" in the US reviewers.[28] Pesch sees the excision of the bomb from the film as a case of self-censorship, though without offering any evidence. Pesch is likely correct that Minghella "decides to present nostalgia, romance and exoticism" and, "as a matter of choice ... avoiding a film that would have been more political."[29]

There is no reason that a novel like *The English Patient* could not be adapted to the screen and succeed in entertaining the postcolonial politics that Ondaajte's critics see as pivotal to his writing. There are commercial American films that certainly do so, like the likewise desert-set *Three Kings* (1999) by David O. Russell, but what is much less likely for a commercial film of its type is to combine such politics with so strong a commitment to romance as Minghella's adaptation of *The English Patient*. Bronwen Thomas's conclusion is at once on the mark and ambivalent when she writes, "The film adaptation of *The English Patient* relies for its success on the mirage of romanticism."[30]

NOTES

1   An earlier version of this essay was published in *Essays on Canadian Writing* 53 (1994): 154–66.

Michael Ondaatje in the Cinema 187

Ondaatje's published screenplay of *Badlands* appeared in *Descant* in 1983. He has discussed his scriptwriting and his affection for film with Solecki in "An Interview with Michael Ondaatje" (*Spider Blues*). Ondaatje's remarks on his own filmmaking appear in an interview with Scobie and Barbour ("A Conversation with Douglas Barbour and Stephen Scobie," 19–22). Freedman's *Globe and Mail* profile ("From Gunslingers to Jazz Musicians") includes his admiring remarks about Leone, and he draws connections between Leone's westerns and *The Collected Works of Billy the Kid: Left-Handed Poems*. This book was adapted as a theatre piece at the Stratford Festival in 1973. *Coming Through Slaughter* was adapted and presented at Theatre Passe Muraille in 1980 under Paul Thompson's direction. More recently, Ondaatje began a project with filmmaker Guy Maddin at the Art Gallery of Ontario, but scheduling conflicts intervened. In 2017, Canadian producer Robert Lantos announced plans to make a film of *In the Skin of a Lion* as a coproduction between Lantos's Serendipity Pictures and two British companies, Film 4 and Potboiler Productions (McNary, "Simon Beaufoy to Adapt 'In the Skin of a Lion' from 'English Patient' Author"). There has been no further word of the project since then.

2 Kranz reviews a wide sample of academic critiques of *The English Patient* ("*The English Patient*: Critics, Audiences, and the Quality of Fidelity," 99–110).

3 Kamiya, "Delirious in a Different Kind of Way." It is telling that when Ondaatje did at last participate actively in a film, in 1998, he teamed up with Toronto directors Bruce McDonald and Don McKellar to adapt his comic poem "Elimination Dance (an intermission)." Rather than attempting the kind of narrative movie *The English Patient* had become, "Elimination Dance" shows Ondaatje returning to the kind of experimentation akin to his stage adaptations during the 1970s and early 1980s.

4 See Ondaatje, "Remembering My Friend Anthony Minghella." Ondaatje also formed a friendship with the actor who played Caravaggio, Willem Dafoe. Later, Dafoe published an engaging interview with Ondaatje.

5 The encounters that made up *The Conversations* took place five years after *The English Patient*'s run. Murch was by then editing the redux edition of *Apocalypse Now* and restoring Orson Welles's *Touch of Evil* and the early sound films of Thomas Edison. Ondaatje was then touring to promote his next novel, *Anil's Ghost*, and teaching in New York. So *The English Patient* does not figure centrally in their widely ranging discussions. Murch's family comes from Toronto, although he was born and raised in New York. He had a privileged education in the US and abroad.

188   Bart Testa

His work was initially in sound editing, and his innovations earned him many awards, as well as a celebrity status rare for editors. His work on Francis Ford Coppola's *The Conversation* (1972), *The Godfather II* (1972), and *Apocalypse Now* (1979) was pathbreaking. His switch from analogue to digital editing during the post-production of *The English Patient* probably figured in his earning an Oscar. It was the first major film to go digital.

6 Biskind, *Down and Dirty Pictures*, 243.

7 This commonly happened to kindred films like *Legends of the Fall* (Edward Zwick 1994), *Out of Africa* (Sydney Pollock 1985), *Atonement* (Joe Wright 2007), and Minghella's own later *Cold Mountain* (2003). Some films of this type do endure, like *Lawrence of Arabia* (1962), but these are surprisingly rare. See Smith, "*The English Patient* – Is It Time to Revive the Epic Romance?" She discusses the common popular fading of such films and their fall, and, she reports, the BBC is mounting a fresh adaptation of *The English Patient* as a television series.

8 Zaentz recruited Ralph Fiennes, Juliette Binoche, Willem Dafoe, and Kristin Scott Thomas for leading roles. They all had estimable reputations, but every studio Zaentz approached wanted bigger Hollywood names. Ironically, *The English Patient* made Fiennes and Scott Thomas stars.

9 Although owned by Disney after 1993, Miramax remained semi-autonomous. Over the 1980s, the company had been the leading supporter of low-budget independent American films like *sex, lies, and videotape*. The company later added production to their previous business of acquiring completed films for distribution. Miramax was also unusually successful in mounting campaigns for Academy Awards.

10 He was able to pay his way as an independent producer because Zaentz was co-owner of Fantasy Records, which, among many leading jazz musicians, like Dave Brubeck, was the home of Creedence Clearwater Revival.

11 To make the deal, Miramax demanded steep deferments from the cast and crew. Deferments are agreed-upon postponed salaries, usually a percentage, during production. They are paid after completion or after a film's release. Although *The English Patient* was very profitable, most of the deferments demanded by Miramax were never paid back to the cast and crew. When the company offered to pay off Minghella in a side deal, he refused. This tale is sadly typical of the predatory behaviour of Harvey and Bob Weinstein, the brothers who owned Miramax. See Biskind, *Down and Dirty Pictures*, 274–5.

12 Kranz, "*The English Patient*," 99–110. Kranz's article falls into three parts: the first section surveys critiques of the film. The second is

Michael Ondaatje in the Cinema   189

viewer-response analysis based on interviews. The third seeks to show how Minghella attempted to be faithful to the book.

13 This discussion follows a standard account of story and plot and the conventions of classical narrative films. See Bordwell, *Narration in the Fiction Film*, 48–61 (on plot and story) and 156–204 (on classical narrative and narration). Bordwell has revisited these topics to deal with contemporary films in *The Way Hollywood Tells It*, see especially 19–71. He argues that classical film form is still the main structure in American narrative cinema.

14 However, even the most seemingly unadventurous films can involve complex negotiations between plot and story. See, for example, Thompson, "The Ordinary Film," 47–9.

15 Thomas, "Piecing Together a Mirage," 197–228.

16 See Sternberg, "A Firmament in the Midst of Waters," 133–4. Sternberg analyzes Ondaatje's variable narrational points-of-view and makes the claim that such a plurality and complex temporal shifts of the novel are not suited to the narrative unity of a film, or at least not the kind of classical film that *The English Patient* became. The film has more time shifts than such films ordinarily do, which is why it was sometimes referred to as a puzzle film. One salient feature of the puzzle is delayed exposition: the viewer may infer who the Patient is, but this is only confirmed late in the film. In another version of this analysis, Kranz sees the film's numerous flashbacks as equivalent to the novel's "multi-vocal" style, although that multiplicity is actually limited to two characters (*The English Patient*, 99–110). Kip, for example, is afforded no flashbacks, although Ondaatje gives his past many pages. In the film, almost all the flashbacks are assigned to the Patient, the exception being Caravaggio, for whom Minghella (and not Ondaatje) provides several. Ondaatje deftly analyzes this expansion of Caravaggio in *The Conversations*, xix–xxi.

17 Minghella enumerates a number of these transitions in his informative DVD commentary (2004).

18 Ondaatje developed this narrative format for *In the Skin of a Lion*, which appears as a suite of separate characters having separate experiences, and they only converge toward the end of the book.

19 Burns, "The Polyphonic Film," 189–212.

20 Minghella also privileges the couple by transposing episodes from the novel. At one point, Kip takes Hana to a nearby church and hoists her on ropes up into the cupola. The camera and Hana dance together high among the frescos, which she illuminates with a flare. The passage, the most lyrical in the film, is a transposition of an early scene in the novel set in the Sistine Chapel. The rider is an aged art scholar, however.

21 As evidenced in the novel, Ondaatje did a good deal of research into this international group and the hardships they faced in the course of the expeditions over the course of the 1930s. These men do appear briefly in the film, but Minghella begins the story as the war is already ramping up in 1939. Katharine arrives with her husband at their expedition's desert camp almost immediately.

A real person, Lady Dorothy Clayton (born Dorothy Mary Durrant) was an accomplished pilot, a sculptor, and an explorer. She met but never had an affair with the real Almásy. Although she did die in a small-plane crash, it was not in North Africa but in Britain in 1933. The real Ladislaus von Almsy was a Hungarian adventurer, archeologist, and explorer, who made several archeological discoveries. He did later assist the Germans in the North Africa campaign but on an official basis and mainly by transporting spies in and out of Cairo. Almásy is an example of Ondaatje choosing a peripheral real historical figure and elaborating a fiction around him or her. The device reaches back to *Coming Through Slaughter* and *In the Skin of a Lion* before its use in *The English Patient*.

22 Minghella confirms his attraction to the prestige literary romance-adventure genre by using the same template for *Cold Mountain* (2003), his other award-bearing success adapting a popular literary novel. Minghella did not have the opportunity for a varied career. He died at fifty-seven in 2008, having directed just seven films.

23 Pesch, "Dropping the Bomb," 229.

24 Ibid.

25 Hutcheon, *Theory of Adaptation*, 13.

26 Pesch explains the pivotal role of the atomic bomb, but he deals with the novel only. "Dropping the Bomb," 231.

27 Ibid. Pesch recalls the opinion some hold that the replacement scene corrects an error that Ondaatje himself made by including the atomic bomb in the novel. He directs us to Craig Seligman, writing in the *New Republic*, "that only a sentimentalist would feel comfortable lumping Japan with the 'brown races of the world.'"

28 Bandi, *Adapting Novels into Film*, 112.

29 Pesch, "Dropping the Bomb," 31.

30 Thomas, "Piecing Together a Mirage," 228.

8

"Landscapes and stories flung into branches": The Photography of Affect and Transnational Mobility in the Writings of Michael Ondaatje

Lorraine York

As the Michael Ondaatje of *Running in the Family* prepares to take leave of his elderly and frail Aunt Dolly, who has met with him to share family stories, Dolly suddenly points to a treasured 1928 photograph of a fancy-dress party that releases within her a fresh wave of memory and anecdote. This photograph "has moved tangible, palpable, into her brain," her nephew reflects, "the way memory invades the present in those who are old" (RF, 112). It is only one of many references, in Ondaatje's long career, to the felt mobility and elasticity of an art form that has been, for much of its history, commonly associated with fixity, stillness, and capture.

By that token, it is not surprising that in the late 1970s, the 1980s, and the 1990s, as Michael Ondaatje's career as a writer of prose grew and enlarged his already distinguished reputation as a poet, critics of his work became increasingly fascinated by his literary engagements with photography and film, which were manifold and explicit. Critics delved into the significance of the frontier photographs of L.A. Huffman in *The Collected Works of Billy the Kid* and, especially, the tiny inset photograph of a grinning Ondaatje as a young child fitted out in chaps, cowboy hat, and toy pistols. They debated the significance of the fictionalized character based on the early twentieth-century New Orleans photographer E.J. Bellocq. Much of that critical writing emphasized the camera's technical capacity to freeze and fix temporal flux.[1] T.D. MacLulich, for instance, read *The Collected Works of Billy the Kid* as a cautionary tale about "the dehumanizing consequences of photographic voyeurism" and the "emotional anaesthesia" promoted by a photographic medium of violent stasis.[2] Perry Nodelman distinguished between Billy's art of violent photographic seeing and that of the poet who "makes things live and move in words rather than simply to capture their image and stop them dead."[3] And my own very early work on Ondaatje and photography in the late 1980s was, I now perceive, equally fixated on fixity. "Ondaatje voices the conviction that the camera is an agent of fixity,"[4] I declared, rendering the camera's capacity to preserve and memorialize the other side of what I perceived to be a persistent postmodern paradox.

These photographic "takes" on Ondaatje's work now appear, with the benefit of hindsight, to have been imbued and shaped by the intellectual moment and milieu of the 1980s. Ondaatje's camera-obsessed writings came to the fore in North America just as the poststructuralist wave reached our shores and, with it, the conceptualizing of postmodernism that was so exciting to graduate students entering academia, as I was when I first wrote the words I've quoted above. Photographic fixity became associated, in critical writings on Ondaatje and photography, at this time, with what Wolfgang Hochbruck called "the clearly defined edges, the mind-frames of realism" that many of us (I now think hastily) understood to be postmodernism's restrictive, simplistic other.[5] Consequently, Hochbruck, to take one representative example, read the "bad" – that is, the "blurred, blotchy, incomprehensible"[6] photographs included in *Coming Through Slaughter*, such as the damaged photograph of Buddy Bolden's band – as a defiant postmodernist rejection of realism's apparently singular and fixed truth claims.

Similarly inspired by theorists of postmodernism, such as my own mentor Linda Hutcheon in her definitive works *A Poetics of Postmodernism* and *The Politics of Postmodernism*, I readily recognized how contemporary movements in photographic theory resonated with the postmodernist thinking of the time. As I noted back then, twentieth-century photographic theorists were reacting (like poststructuralist theorists) against nineteenth-century pictorialism, "striving in the 1970s to focus critical attention away from what the art object contained or represented, towards its constitutive processes, the processes of making meaning" through the use of "strategies (all of which find their equivalents in recent literary theory), such as unmasking, the subjectivity of the photograph, undermining conventional notions of photographic truth, and reevaluating the role of culture in a medium traditionally associated with nature."[7] I, and many of my colleagues who were similarly affected by the arrival of poststructuralist theory, found all of this tremendously exciting and generative, for reasons that remain valid today.

In retrospect, though, our enthusiasm may have led us to prematurely embrace dualities that potentially underestimated the capacity of art to be many things at once in a way that did not leave it riven or conflicted: static *and* kinetic, pictorial *and* processual, artifact *and* affect. In thinking of photography's own capacity, like Aunt Dolly's photograph, to move (even as it remains) "tangible, palpable," into our "brain[s]," I resolved this situation in my own mind by christening the photographic condition a "paradox" that would allow both fixity and flux to share space. Responding to Perry Nodelman's observation, then, that Billy's violent, fixated photographic seeing is remedied by the poet who is able to "makes things live and move in words,"[8] I suggested that in Ondaatje, poetry (and photography) can do both: satisfy the artistic impulse to capture and fix while retaining movement through memory work and concepts of character as multiple and fluid. But this photographic combination remained a paradox nevertheless: an ongoing problem and tension.

In this collection of critical essays looking back on a remarkable creative career spanning more than half a century, we can – and should – also cast a retrospective gaze at the critical frameworks those of us who have been along for the ride have used in reading Ondaatje over those decades and then see where we might productively shift and deepen our thinking. What if, in the current instance, an additional five decades of theorizing of the still-young medium of photography could open new alternatives to our habit of seeing stasis and movement in photography as "paradox" and "tension" – sites of strife, uneasiness, or frustration? Could Ondaatje's photographic writing also be understood in a key that brings forth affects of a more joyful sort? The key to opening up those alternatives, I argue, is to bring together arguments for photography as kinetic – not simply cinema's other, as the term "still photography" appears to insist – and for photography as an affective medium. In a phrase: photography as *moving feeling*, with an intentional double entendre growing out of the adjective "moving" to suggest both kinesis and affective power.

To begin with one of these threads, the renewed emphasis on photography as a kinetic art has been a welcome product of recent work on intermediality. As Serena Fusco has cogently summed up this transition, "While we may tend to associate images ... with 'stasis' – in both a spatial and a temporal sense – pictures are not necessarily to be regarded as static. Jan Baetens and Mieke Bal have, for instance, challenged the idea that photographs, including single snapshots, cannot be read narratively in a rigorous and convincing fashion."[9] As Fusco points out, Bal's work "questions the deeply ingrained idea that visual art forms such as painting, photography, and sculpture are essentially non-narrative because they are 'still.'"[10] Extending this line of thought, I would add that this narratological school of thought not only demonstrates that these media are narrative in nature but also, by implication, that they are not "still" either, as Fusco's enclosure of the word in quotation marks implies.

Critics of Ondaatje's work have, it is true, long recognized what Steven Heighton calls its "kinetic techniques"; writing in the late 1980s, Heighton argued that Ondaatje's poem "'the gate in his head,'" for instance, "indicates the kinetic potential of the two most static artforms: photography and literature" and "prefigures Ondaatje's later efforts to realize the latent power of words."[11] And while the focus of Heighton's analysis remains the verbal techniques of the later poetry and fiction that create and model this kinesis, his brief acknowledgment that even photography can be rendered in kinetic terms opens the door to a fuller examination of the photographic mode in Ondaatje's work.

Heighton also claimed that the literary kinesis that Ondaatje performs is tied to the writer's "desire to make his art more accessible, more communal," for it is the "dynamic elements of other artforms that make such communalization possible."[12] This is a tantalizing prospect, and it is one that Heighton does not fully pursue or establish, beyond the assumption, perhaps, that expressly kinetic arts like the cinema do tend to reach a broader audience. As I will suggest in the further stages of this essay, one way we could think about Ondaatje's kinetic notion of photography as attuned to the communal is through its specifically affective possibilities.

Indeed, it is the affective register of photography that, when combined with a recognition of its kinetic potential, can bring a new depth to our reading of Ondaatje's photographic art. Mirroring the so-called "affective turn" in cultural studies, photographic theory is currently having its own affective moment.[13] As Thy Phu and Elspeth H. Brown explain in the introduction to their paradigm-shifting collection *Feeling Photography*, mid-twentieth-century photographic theory experienced a backlash against feeling, of the sort that I had written about at the time as a redirection of "critical attention away from what the art object contained or represented, towards its constitutive processes."[14] For photography, that earlier emphasis on content and representation was perfectly summed up by nineteenth-century photographic pictorialism. This school of early photographers that included Oscar Gustave Rejlander and Henry Peach Robinson sought to legitimize the new medium by demonstrating its capacity to render experience in a painterly, composed fashion, at times even visually approximating compositions typical of contemporary realist paintings that clearly called forth an emotional response. Phu and Brown see Victor Burgin's *Thinking Photography* from 1982 as a key expression of the following century's turn away from the affective; not surprisingly, Burgin's book was also a central reference point in my postmodern analysis of Ondaatje's photographic writing. To "think photography," in Burgin's terms, was to analyze its structural, materialist role as a cultural production that was entwined with the workings of Althusserian ideology. And as Phu and Brown note, "emotions were unthinking, problematic interlopers in the materialist project of 'thinking' photography" that Burgin espoused.[15] In short, "feelings" became the "collateral damage"[16] sacrificed in a 1970s and 1980s photographic critical practice that sought systematization and disciplinary respect. Phu and Brown maintain that this sacrifice of "feelings" further entailed a sacrifice of the photographic experiences and practices of "women, queer subjects, and racialized groups"[17] to the project of "thinking photography."

Much contemporary affect theory conjoins the two conditions I have foregrounded – movement and affect – and so I look to this body of work to help me trace these two capacities of photography and photographic writing in a way that is mindful of their interconnections. Sara Ahmed, for example, in her many writings on affect, is consistently attuned to the ways in which affect allows, or does not allow, subjects to move through cultural space. If, as Ahmed observes in *The Promise of Happiness*, "Feelings are how objects create impressions in shared spaces of dwelling,"[18] then how one feels about those objects will affect the way in which one moves, or does not move, through those "shared spaces." Picking up the notion of "flow" from Mihàly Czíkszentmihályi as "the experience of an individual engaged with the world,"[19] Ahmed notes that "The idea of 'flow' to describe the relationship between happy persons and happy worlds is powerful."[20] It follows that unhappy subjects experience the inverse: the blockage of flow when one is "stressed by the very forms of life that enable some bodies to flow into space."[21] And in her more recent thinking about diversity work and complaint, Ahmed consistently refers to the disruption of the hegemonic "flow" of "happiness scripts" using spatial, kinetic metaphors: coming up against the brick wall in *Living a Feminist Life* or not/passing through the door in *What's the Use?*.

The readings of Ondaatje's writing that I will propose in the remainder of this paper entwine these notions of photography as kinetic and affective, keeping in mind a specific manifestation of mobility and feeling: the transnational. Again, Sara Ahmed's thought is instructive, for in *The Promise of Happiness*, one of her exemplary figures who are widely perceived to block the flow of happiness is "the melancholic migrant."[22] And it is the movement of the migrant that is the particular source of the perceived dissonance: "This nostalgic vision of a world of 'staying put' involves nostalgia for whiteness, for a community of white people happily living with other white people."[23] It follows, then, that "migration enters the narrative as an unhappiness cause, as what forces people who are 'unalike' to live together."[24] The photographic writing that Michael Ondaatje has created over the five decades and more of his career, I suggest, produces a rich understanding of how photography can move, can flow, as a "tangible, palpable" feeling, into the experience of diasporic mobility in ways that challenge the scripts of nostalgic sameness. For the sake of space, but with attention to a broad range of genres, I will concentrate on one memoir, one novel, one book of conversations, and one poem by Michael Ondaatje that span from the early 1980s to the early 2000s.

In *Running in the Family*, a memoir whose very title resonates with Ahmed's thinking about flow, movement, and the ways in which family structures can facilitate or impede it, Ondaatje creates a photographic seeing that joyfully and mournfully embraces movement. Like numerous other critics, I turn to the photograph that Ondaatje as narrator declares he has been "waiting for all my life" (*RF*, 161): the postcard-joke that Mervyn and Doris Ondaatje send to their friends and family on their honeymoon:

> My father and mother together. May 1932 ... My father's pupils droop to the south-west corner of his sockets. His jaw falls and resettles into a groan that is half-idiot, half shock ... My mother in white has twisted her lovely features and stuck out her jaw and upper lip so that her profile is in the posture of a monkey. The print is made into a postcard and sent through the mails to various friends. On the back my father has written "*What we think of married life.*" (RF, 161–2)

In this ekphrastic passage of description, we find the three intertwined threads of what I've called "moving photography": kinesis, affect, and mobility. First of all, the passage modulates from a view of the photograph as static, then as mobile, and finally as static once more: from the glimpse of the photograph in the album and its typical caption listing subjects and date ("My father and mother together. May 1932") to the unsettling mobility of their features ("droop," "falls," "twisted," "stuck out"). And then, it appears, we return in this passage once more to the static artifact: print made into postcard. But that stasis is, in turn, undercut, first by the transit of the image, "sent through the mail," and more profoundly by the migratory journey of Mervyn and Doris's son, now visiting Sri Lanka from Canada and being profoundly affected by the discovered image of his parents. The larger trajectory of the son's migration enters this photograph, in fact, for it is, remember, "the photograph I have been waiting for all my life," throughout, that is, the years of transnational movement, first to England and then to Canada and now back to Sri Lanka and back in Canada. As Joseph Cummins and Ashley Barnwell comment in appropriately kinetic terms,

> the importance of this photograph in energizing Ondaatje's leap from the generalities of public history to the specifics of personal, familial memory – in firing Ondaatje's diasporic imagination – cannot be overstated. The intergenerational impacts of colonialism are borne out in his inability to access that past via unbroken connections to people and place, but rather in having to recollect and piece together a family story upon return.[25]

This temporality and movement of diasporic memory are at once geophysical and affective, for the section ends with an amplification of how this photograph is mobile in its affective reach: "It is the only photograph I have found of the two of them together" (RF, 162), before that moment, at that moment, and since that moment.

It is not only the explicitly ekphrastic descriptions of photographs in *Running in the Family* that betray the traces of "moving photography." In another much-quoted scene, Ondaatje's narrator recounts a dream, though "not so much a dream as an image that repeats itself," like a moving photograph:

> I see my own straining body which stands shaped like a star and realize gradually I am part of a human pyramid. Below me are other bodies that I am standing on and above me are several more, though I am quite near the top. With cumbersome slowness we are walking from one end of the huge living room to the other. We are all chattering away like the crows and cranes ... A Mr. Hobday has asked my father if he has any Dutch antiques in the house. And he replies, "Well ... there is my mother." My grandmother lower down gives a roar of anger. But at this point we are approaching the door which being twenty feet high we will be able to pass through only if the pyramid turns sideways. Without discussing it, the whole family ignores the opening and walks slowly through the pale pink rose-coloured walls into the next room. (RF, 27)

This tableau vivant bears meaningfully upon the affects and movements of mobility, of "running in" – and perhaps also away from and back to – "the family." The pyramid, as others have noted, figures the generational structure of the family: a family tree that has picked itself up off the parchment and gone walking. It has a sonic dimension ("chattering," "roars") and, relatedly, a broadly affective one that encompasses both amusement (Mervyn Ondaatje's joke) and outrage (his mother's "roar of anger"). There is also, notably, the "straining body" of the narrator himself, straining, that is, to hold this mobile pyramid that is a family and its narratives together in the memoir we are reading. Elsewhere in *Running in the Family*, there is plentiful consideration of the affective pressures involved in writing a collective memoir, the pressures exerted upon the "straining body" of the writer from the various layers of the family pyramid. ("'You must get this book right,' my brother tells me, 'You can only write it once'" [RF, 201].)

But finally, and despite the strain of ethical responsibility and the "cumbersome slowness" of the collecting of family stories, the

Photography of Affect and Transnational Mobility in Ondaatje 199

human pyramid sallies forth. In this passage, it approaches a door that initially presents a challenge to the family's ability to pass. Here I recall Ahmed's use of the figure of the door, in *What's the Use?*, to signal those spaces in which subjects are either allowed to move freely or discouraged from moving freely through cultural space. Queer subjects and sexual harassment complainants in institutions such as the university are Ahmed's primary foci here, but the door can signal a wide range of experiences of blockage and passage. The capacity of the Ondaatje family pyramid to pass through space appears to be related to issues of ethnicity, and here Mervyn's joke about his mother as a "Dutch antique" registers more fully. As the narrator reflects elsewhere in the memoir about the waves of European colonists who arrived on Sri Lankan shores over the centuries, "my own ancestor arriving in 1600, a doctor who cured the residing governor's daughter with a strange herb and was rewarded with land, a foreign wife, and a new name which was a Dutch spelling of his own. Ondaatje" (RF, 64). Land, marriage, name: all instruments of passing through the door of immigration and social acceptability that were bestowed upon Ondaatje's ancestor by the Dutch colonial forces that would ascend to power in Sri Lanka over the course of that century; as Ahmed reflects, "doors are not just physical things that swing on hinges; they are also mechanisms that enable an opening and a closing."[26] (In this passage, though, the family does not have to negotiate the door, as it turns out, and, instead, they float majestically through the "pale pink rose-coloured walls," itself arguably a metaphor for privilege.)

As an instance of "moving photography," this dream-tableau figures the memoir itself as a mobile project; when Ondaatje's brother warns him that "You must get this book right," the narrator responds by undoing the assumption of static, ultimate narrative and its consequent pressures: "But the book again is incomplete. In the end all of your children move among the scattered acts and memories" (RF, 201), themselves scattered around the globe ("Magnetic fields would go crazy in the presence of more than three Ondaatjes" [RF, 172]), like the moving human pyramid. That mobility carries with it an affective cost: "all this was happening [Mervyn's last illness] while his first family was in England or Canada or Colombo totally unaware of what was happening to him. That would always be the curse on us, the guilt we would be left with" (RF, 199).

While *Running in the Family* clearly foregrounds the photograph as artifact, both ekphrastically and through the inclusion of actual photographic images in the text, *The English Patient* tends more toward the embedded kinds of photographic writing I have just described in *Running*'s human pyramid scene. Critics of the novel who have productively thought about the patterns of Caravaggesque darkness and light (Sarris, Fusco) have addressed this mode of Ondaatje's writing, and I would add to that valuable analysis that the ethical and affective dimensions of movement and migration are closely tied to modes of "tenebristic" seeing.[27]

One of the few specific invocations of the photograph in *The English Patient* is the episode that leads to Caravaggio's brutal torture: his nighttime foray into a villa to retrieve a photograph taken earlier that night at a party attended by German officers that he had infiltrated for the purpose of stealing sensitive papers. "I was caught jumping from a woman's window," he tells Hana. "That woman I told you about, who took the photograph" (*EP*, 54). Captured twice: once on a film that, as Caravaggio notes, would have been developed in a government lab and checked by the Gestapo, and, once again, as he landed on the ground under the woman's window. The window, it seems, functions as another "door" or portal of passage or arrest – perhaps also a lens. But there is another photographic "capture" in this scene that precedes Caravaggio's physical capture on the ground outside, below the window. As he searches the woman's room, Caravaggio realizes that she is in it, making love with the German general and, what's more, she has seen him because he has been caught in a flash of light from car headlights.

These echoing images of flash-photography imagistically connect Caravaggio to Kirpal Singh, the sapper for whom being caught in a flash of light would spell doom. Repeatedly we hear of the faraway flash of light that accompanies the accidental detonation of a bomb that sappers are seeking to defuse ("now and then the possible light from an explosion" [*EP*, 112]). And the photographic connection runs deeper, into the realm of the kinetic, for both men are associated with movement; Hana describes Caravaggio to the English patient as "a thief" who "believed in 'the movement of things,'" not a "collector" who assembles stolen items into a static archive. "Half the things he stole never came home" (*EP*, 169), Hana adds. Similarly, we hear of Kip that "He moves always in relation to things, beside walls, raised terrace hedges. He scans

Photography of Affect and Transnational Mobility in Ondaatje 201

the periphery" (*EP*, 218) in what is surely a professionally inculcated habit. The kinetic in *The English Patient*, though, has deeper implications that a consideration of moving photography can help to elucidate – implications that reach into the heart of colonial claiming. As Caravaggio rages, "The trouble with all of us is we are where we shouldn't be. What are we doing in Africa, in Italy? What is Kip doing dismantling bombs in orchards, for God's sake? What is he doing fighting English wars? ... The armies indoctrinate you and leave you here and they fuck off somewhere else to cause trouble, inky-dinky parlez-vous. We should all move out together" (*EP*, 122). Caravaggio's vision, of a world of toxic movement, and his embrace of being where one "should" be, is not at all Ahmed's "nostalgic vision of a world of 'staying put'" that "involves nostalgia for whiteness, for a community of white people happily living with other white people,"[28] for Caravaggio dreams of a large-scale movement of the emergent and diverse community of Villa San Girolamo into the larger world.

A camera obscura tableau in *The English Patient* provides a photographic equivalent of Caravaggio's dream. Hana, Kip, and Caravaggio become caught up in a game, a "contest" regularly played by the two lovers (*EP*, 224). The villa, enclosed in darkness at the end of the day, becomes, one night, the site of three separately moving actors, playing a game of hide and seek: "Then everything in the room seemed to be in movement but Caravaggio. He could hear it all around him, surprised he wasn't touched. The boy was in the room. Caravaggio walked over to the sofa and placed his hand down towards Hana. She was not there. As he straightened up, an arm went around his neck and pulled him back downwards in a grip." Hana, triumphant with her arm around Caravaggio's neck and her naked foot on Kip's, proclaims "Got you. *Got you*" (*EP*, 223). The game encapsulates all of the strands of moving photography that I have been describing here: stasis and movement and light and dark. Like the walking family pyramid in *Running in the Family*, it offers us a glimpse of relationality in motion. Caravaggio's dream, "We should all move out together," is here performed as photographic tableau, but the affective forces unleashed by the performance encompass both joy and the lingering effects of the deadly movement of wars. The contest is, on one hand, the prelude to Hana and Kip's lovemaking. But, on the other hand, it revives the traumatic memory of Caravaggio's loss of his thumbs, when he hears

Hana jokingly taunt Kip "Give up. *Confess*" (EP, 223). He silently flees the scene, a foreshadowing of Kip's traumatic final breaking away from the Eurocentric pyramid: "Wherever Hana is now, in the future, she is aware of *the line of movement* Kip's body followed out of her life" (EP, 282; emphasis added).

Scenes like the foregoing are plentiful in Ondaatje's oeuvre; one thinks of similar tableaus, for instance, in *In the Skin of a Lion*, when Patrick whirls around a room in which Clara sits, blindfolded – until she moves and he strikes her: another "trick" (SL, 79–81, 80) or contest that performs relationality, affect, and the complications of movement and subjectivity. It is not surprising, given this repeated linking of "dark room" and movement, that critics have long engaged with Ondaatje's fascination with film.[29] These discussions were enriched by the 2003 publication of *The Conversations: Walter Murch and the Art of Editing Film*, Ondaatje's recounting of a series of exchanges between him and the celebrated editor of *Apocalypse Now*, *The Godfather* trilogy, *The Talented Mr. Ripley*, and *The English Patient*, among many other films. For my present purposes, I situate *The Conversations* not only as a source commentary on Ondaatje's abiding fascination with cinema but as a primary document in Ondaatje's oeuvre that, like the memoir and novel I have already examined, is caught up in the affects and politics of moving photography.

These conversations are not concerned with erecting barriers between photographic fixity and cinematic movement. Within a minute, Walter Murch pays tribute to the affective influence upon him of both cinematic modes and doesn't seem to appreciably distinguish between them. First, he cites "the freeze frame at the end of his [François Truffaut's] *The 400 Blows*. It was electrifying," he recalled, "both dramatically and as a possibility of what you could do technically with cinema" (TC, 23). In the next breath, he praises "The use of slow motion in *The Seven Samurai*," particularly in a scene in which a thief holding a girl hostage comes out of the house, moving in slow time, grasping at the air, and then falling dead on the ground. So the freeze frame creates drama, movement (or as Mieke Bal might say, narrative) for Murch, and the slow motion movement renders the final fixity of death.

So too the literary source materials of some of the films Murch has edited; "The kind of novel that makes a good film," he tells Ondaatje, "has a certain motion – whether that's physical motion

Photography of Affect and Transnational Mobility in Ondaatje 203

across the screen or emotional motion, moving from one state to another. Or, one hopes, both" (TC, 127). Clearly, like many editors and directors, Murch does not consider the novel as a changeless ur-text to which the filmmaker owes precise fidelity. And his concept of "emotional motion" relays precisely the kind of intertwining of mobility and affect in photographic thinking and writing that has fascinated me in Ondaatje's writing.

But these are, after all, conversations, and the text beautifully threads the artistic practices of these two artists together as they meditate on the relationships between filmic and literary creativity. Ondaatje, for his part in conversation with Murch, engages with the mobility inherent in world cinematic culture in a way that echoes his own experiences – both felt and narrated – of transnational mobility. While Murch, as an American film editor, is clearly embedded in that geographically specific industry and its conditions of production, his influences, like those of so many North American editors and directors, are much broader. Often, Ondaatje, tellingly, leads Murch into a consideration of Asian film. Describing their second of five conversations, Ondaatje recalls that it "once again ranged across large areas and included many subjects – from the influence of Beethoven and Flaubert on film; to the editing techniques handed down to the West by Eisenstein as well as Kurosawa and other Asians" (TC, 87). This sweeping survey recalls the final sentence of *Running in the Family* and its compact summation of the East-West transnational crossings of the narrator: "During the monsoon, on my last morning, all this Beethoven and rain" (RF, 203).

In *The Conversations*, Ondaatje is fascinated by the relationship between Eastern and Western cinematic culture, traditions, and styles. He tells Murch that "Some years ago I was reading an article by Donald Richie, about the difference between Eastern and Western film, or art" and that Richie argued that Western cinema relies upon the master shot (a long shot that contains all the action from one camera angle that keeps all the characters visible), whereas in Japanese film, "you can pick a small fragment of the corner of a table and that particular fragment can be used to suggest the whole scene" (TC, 107). Murch, in response, argues that the master shot is predominant in Western film because of the privileging of three-dimensional figures in space in Western art (TC, 108). At other moments in their conversations, Ondaatje refuses the notion of a strict demarcation between Eastern and Western film, noting, for instance, that in both Hong Kong director Wong Kar-Wai's *In the Mood for Love* and Francis Ford Coppola's *The Conversation* (which Walter Murch edited), the narrative is assembled from large reams of available footage in a way that actually determines or changes the film's narrative: a process that Ondaatje finds reminiscent of novel-writing and of the multiple possible narrative avenues available to the novelist while writing (unless they are programmatic followers of outlines). Once again, dualities of East and West, in this instance, may drift into view, but they are not master narratives, and these filmic texts can contain both distinctive and common vocabularies.

But what I find most resonant in this discussion of Eastern and Western film is the vocabulary it provides for describing some of the trademarks of Ondaatje's style: the quick, often dizzying alternation of master shot (long narrative scene) and intensely focalized detail. Think, to choose only one example, of *The English Patient*'s long, rambling narrative of his affair with Katharine Clifton (itself divided up and scattered in a way suggestive of his end-of-life fragmented memory) and the moments where the focus is brought in tight: on the small indentation at Katharine's neck to which he obsessively, repeatedly returns. ("This is called the vascular sizood" [EP, 241], his colleague Madox finally tells him, in parting.) *The Conversations* suggests that this may not only be a feature of Ondaatje's cinematic style but an oscillation within that style, between Western and Eastern modes: photographic mobility as narrative method.

Cinema and mobility are perhaps most concretely connected in Ondaatje's oeuvre in the scene from *In the Skin of a Lion* in which the narrator describes the importance of cinema to newly arrived immigrants to Toronto. He offers the sweeping statement, "The event that will light the way for immigration in North America is the talking picture" (SL, 43), for it allowed immigrant audiences for whom English was not a first language to hear and practise the language. In one of their conversations, Murch vigorously agrees with Ondaatje's observation that the demographic shift to cities at the end of the nineteenth century created an audience for film: "Particularly in North America, there was a large immigrant urban audience from many different countries who had no common language: cinema provided that language" (TC, 92). Murch uses this historical confluence, though, to support an argument about the preeminence of American cinema that is, in its implications, imperialistic: "That providence

Photography of Affect and Transnational Mobility in Ondaatje   205

[of a language] is a cornerstone of American cinema. It's one of the reasons American cinema proved and is still proving to be so strong all over the world: the roots of American filmmaking were in finding the common denominator that unified people from different cultural backgrounds" (TC, 92). Ondaatje, at this point, changes the subject to Thomas Edison, but at another moment in *The Conversations*, he implicitly provides a response to this empire-building narrative of American cinema. While discussing with Murch the editor's choice to cut scenes at the moments actors vocalize fricative consonants like s, f, or th, he recalls that "When I came from Sri Lanka to England I was eleven years old and I had a problem distinguishing between the letters v and w. So I would say 'wideo' or 'wagabond.' For the first three years in England, I'd always have to think twice before I said a v word or a w word." He adds, "That's probably a more cultural kind of halt" (TC, 143). A halt – or as Ahmed would say, a door – that reminds readers that English-language cinema as linguistic pedagogy allows some bodies and not others to flow into cultural space.

My attention to the implication of photographic affect for transnational mobilities offers us a fresh way of thinking about how Michael Ondaatje's photographic writings are crucially related to the feeling – the everyday tactility – of bodies and communities in motion. A perfect summation of this "moving photography," and so my closing example, is Ondaatje's poem "Claude Glass" from *Secular Love* and its description of an increasingly wild party that discloses a domestic "pyramid" in danger of falling apart:

On the front lawn a sheet
tacked across a horizontal branch.
A projector starts a parade
of journeys, landscapes, relatives,
friends leaping out within pebbles of water
caught by the machine as if creating rain.

Later when wind frees the sheet
and it collapses like powder in the grass
pictures fly without target
and howl their colours over Southern Ontario
clothing burdock
rhubarb a floating duck

> Landscapes and stories
> flung into branches[30]

The photographic images, here rendered both as "caught" and "free[d]" whirl in a maelstrom of feeling and memory, the images of journeys (perhaps to Sri Lanka, perhaps elsewhere) now splaying across the Southern Ontario landscape, disobeying the tidy categories of geographical location. In their wild explosion into the Southern Ontario landscape, these photographic images figure the transnational mobilities of the family, as well as the narrator's increasingly precarious affective state and fear of a domestic world spinning beyond his control. In the writing of Michael Ondaatje, photography catches and frees the "journeys, landscapes, relatives / friends" of human story in all their affective colours.

NOTES

1 See MacLulich, Nodelman, Scobie, Solecki, York.
2 MacLulich, "Ondaatje's Mechanical Boy: Portrait of the Artist as Photographer," 109, 118.
3 Nodelman, "The Collected Photographs of Billy the Kid," *Canadian Literature* 87 (1980): 79.
4 York, *The Other Side of Dailiness*, 93.
5 Hochbruck, "The Intangible Image of Buddy Bolden," para 32.
6 Ibid.
7 York, *The Other Side of Dailiness*, 11.
8 Nodelman, "The Collected Photographs of Billy the Kid," 79.
9 Fusco, "'Black Space Is Time,'" 147.
10 Ibid.
11 Heighton, "'Approaching that Perfect Edge,'" para 8.
12 Ibid., para 33, 40.
13 See Clough, *The Affective Turn.*
14 York, *The Other Side of Dailiness*, 11.
15 Phu and Brown, *Feeling Photography*, 2.
16 Ibid., 3
17 Ibid., 7
18 Ahmed, *The Promise of Happiness*, 14.
19 Ibid., 11.
20 Ibid.

21 Ibid., 12

22 Ibid., 49, 121–59.

23 Ibid., 121.

24 Ibid., 122.

25 Cummins and Barnwell, "Michael Ondaatje's *Running in the Family* and the 'Familia-graphic Gaze,'" 11.

26 Ahmed, *What's the Use?*, 179.

27 See Sarris, "*In the Skin of a Lion*," 183–201.

28 Ahmed, "The Promise of Happiness," 121.

29 See Finkle, "From Page to Screen: Michael Ondaatje as Filmmaker," 167–85, and Testa, "He Did Not Work Here for Long," 154–66.

30 Ondaatje, "Claude Glass," 16–17.

Intermediality

9

Creases and Broken Glass:
Michael Ondaatje's Narrative and Intermediality

Serena Fusco

INTRODUCTION

By means of an analysis and contextualization of four works –
*Coming Through Slaughter, In the Skin of a Lion, The English
Patient, Divisadero* this essay discusses the importance of intermediality in Michael Ondaatje's fiction. Throughout Ondaatje's
oeuvre, literary fiction "remediates" (to use Jay David Bolter and
Richard Grusin's famous term) other media – especially if/when
those media channel art forms and artistic modes of expression.
Here, I turn my attention to how Ondaatje's literary fiction "remediates" music, painting, and, especially, photography and how
these three, within the broader framework of literary writing,
"remediate" each other.

An intermedial perspective entails considering how a medium/
channel *A* changes and shapes a medium/channel *B* while *not* fully
overlapping with it. I mostly rely on Irina Rajewsky's literary use
of the category of intermediality. Rajewsky explores how literature
generates "an illusion of another medium's specific practices" within
itself.[1] If by intermediality here I mostly refer to the "channeling"
of (the illusion of) another medium through literature, I propose to
explore "creases": in other words, places where the friction, of the
"imperfect overlap" of the media involved becomes visible. Relying
on recent discussions of narrative across media,[2] I pay attention to
how literary storytelling is filtered by channels provided by (a verbal rendition of) non-verbal media so that narrative fiction itself is
revealed as inseparable from the transmedial world around it.

On the one hand, such an approach considers the historical dimension of the intermedial contact(s), that is, the emergence, use, or stylistic peculiarity of a medium at a specific moment in time (like early jazz music or documentary photography) and how such manifestations inform literature. On the other hand, I wish to suggest that if an influx on the part of other media can transform and defamiliarize the literary medium, it can also bring about – as Ondaatje's case demonstrates – the emergence and blooming of previously hidden (or less visible) literary potentialities, thus engendering powers that are, so to speak, both intrinsic and extrinsic to literature.

Last but not least, the historical dimension of a medial occurrence in Ondaatje is always accompanied by a reflection on history. Ondaatje's work has repeatedly been analyzed in its relation to history.[3] While his writings are clearly germane to all the topical issues that have informed the debate on history since postmodernism – history as one possible narrative among many; a complex and articulated dialogue between history and fiction; history as always reconstructed/written a posteriori according to different ideological stances – history is never trivialized or oversimplified in Ondaatje. One issue that is consistently raised in his writing is what historical presence, and historical agency, mean or add up to, including the historical presence and agency of art and medial objects.

Strictly speaking, none of Ondaatje's works under consideration here is multimedial. Only in two cases, image-making – obtained by means of different technical apparatuses – is directly reproduced on the page. Three sonographs are printed in the initial pages of *Coming Through Slaughter*; a hand-drawing of a few lines is found toward the end of *The English Patient*. Despite not being literally multimedial, Ondaatje's art is a demonstration that literary fiction cannot be isolated from the broader media system(s) around it.

"PUT YOUR HAND THROUGH THIS WINDOW": *COMING THROUGH SLAUGHTER*

Perhaps the most widely used definition of *Coming Through Slaughter* in terms of genre is "fictional biography." It is centred on the figure of Charles "Buddy" Bolden, a New Orleans musician active at the turn of the twentieth century, nowadays considered one of the precursors of jazz and a key figure in the historical development of this musical genre. An obscure figure for several decades,

Bolden has been increasingly "seriously" researched since Ondaatje's book came out.[4] I see Ondaatje's choice of Bolden as a "theme" around which to build a "literary composition" as a kind of artistic analogue to Bolden's position in the history of jazz. Bolden's seminal role in the development of what will, over time, become known as "jazz" is nowadays widely recognized, although the degree, scope, and influence of his individual contributions are very hard to gauge exactly because information about him can only be reconstructed through the tales of those who came after him: "no mention of his music appeared in print until 1933, two years after his death, and some three decades after Bolden contributed to the revolutionary birth of a new style of American music. Hence any assessment of his importance must be drawn from scattered and often contradictory accounts, almost all of them documented, sometimes with mixed motives, long after the fact."[5]

The intermedial quality of *Coming Through Slaughter* is part and parcel with its very existence. As noted by Emily Petermann, the novel is intermedial in the sense that, by means of another medium – the verbal literary medium – it channels Bolden's playing, which no one can hear nowadays because no recordings of it exist: "He was never recorded. He stayed away while others moved into wax history, electronic history, those who said later that Bolden broke the path" (CS, 37). The fragmented yet theme-driven structure of the novel channels Bolden's (in Petermann's terms) "unheard jazz" across space and time.[6] Stylistically a very spare narrative, yet richly employing metaphors to convey associations of disparate elements, *Coming Through Slaughter* can be defined as cryptic, poetic, lyrical, fragmentary. In several passages, Ondaatje uses punctuation sparingly, with the exception of full stops. Accordingly, next to very short and even one-word sentences, one finds long sentences in need of syncopation, where the reader must decide where to draw a breath or place a beat. In Pierpaolo Marino's terms, there are "different rhythms and tempos at work" in the text.[7]

On the other hand, the medial forms evoked in *Coming Through Slaughter* are plural, and the interplay is not limited to jazz and writing. There is photography, drawing on paper, as well as various types of other recordings (interviews, for instance) and their transcriptions. In what follows, I shall limit my discussion to a three-term confrontation involving writing, music, and photography. A discussion of these three can perhaps illuminate Ondaatje's choice to make the relationship between Bolden and the character of the photographer E.J. Bellocq a key element of the novel's plot and structure and may provide a chance to read this relationship against the emergence, in the text, of a double(d) "I": on the one hand, Bolden's narrating voice; on the other hand, an anonymous "I" who is openly working on his/her own version of Bolden's story.

The first of the three parts of *Coming Through Slaughter* centres, to a good extent, on the search that follows Bolden's enigmatic two-year disappearance from New Orleans. Early in the text, following Webb – Bolden's friend, former roommate, and cop – we learn that Bolden, who at the time was a well-known New Orleans musician, has vanished, without leaving word with his wife Nora, his kids, or his band. While Webb looks for him, it is revealed that, unbeknownst to Webb, Bolden has found refuge in nearby Shell Beach, is living with pianist Jaelin Brewitt and his wife Robin, and has become Robin's lover. The possible reasons for Bolden's mysterious stay at the Brewitts' are mostly considered in Part Two. One reason may be his need to drain himself of fame, of publicity: "Robin who drained my body of its fame when I wanted to find that fear of certaintion I had when I first began to play, back when I was unaware that reputation made the room narrower and narrower" (CS, 86).

Looking for people who might point him in Buddy's direction, Webb finds Bellocq. This character is Ondaatje's openly fictional version of New Orleans photographer Ernest Joseph Bellocq (1873–1949), nowadays mostly known for his private archive of photographs taken in the brothels of Storyville, New Orleans's red light district. In *Coming Through Slaughter*, the only extant photograph of Bolden and the ensemble he played with – an actual and to date unattributed picture – is fictionally attributed to Bellocq.

In Part Two, Buddy's disappearance is also explained as a result of his friendship with Bellocq. The two men are constructed as polar opposites: Buddy is a social creature, living and especially performing among others; Bellocq is not only a loner but seems to live independently of others, "self-sufficient, complete as a perpetual motion machine" (CS, 56). Crucially, Bellocq's isolation from the world is "misinterpreted" by Buddy as something that can still have a meaning or an importance *for the world*: "Bellocq did not expect that. Or he could have easily explained the ironies. The mystic privacy one can be so proud of has no alphabet of noise or meaning to

Ondaatje's Narrative and Intermediality 215

the people outside ... Aware it was him who had tempted Buddy on. Buddy who had once been enviably public" (CS, 64).

For Bolden, Bellocq's photos are "like windows" (CS, 59). They seem to lure him with a way out of the "furnished," stuffy rooms of his celebrity, an escape from the often misleading expectations of the audience: "You'd play and people would grab you and grab you till you began to – you couldn't help it – believe you were doing something important. And all you were doing was stealing chickens, nailing things to the wall. Every time you stopped playing you became a lie. So I got so, with Bellocq, I didn't trust any of that ... any more. It was just playing games. We were furnished rooms and Bellocq was a window looking out" (CS, 59). A man who needs certainties but profoundly loathes them (CS, 78), Ondaatje's Bolden undertakes a painful identity journey, attempting to reconcile himself with his audience. During this journey, he changes: from social animal, popular because of his music, to considering celebrity an oppressive lie (CS, 59, 89) and, finally, to a strenuous, dangerous, ultimately failed attempt at a self-centredness that recognizes and accepts something profound and obscure. Bellocq's "silences" become spaces of (dangerous) possibility (CS, 91) for Bolden, interrupting Bolden's music and making him feel the need to look at the darkness in himself:

And then back to his conversations about everything except music, the friend who scorned all the giraffes of fame. I said, You don't think much of this music do you? Not yet, he said. Him watching me waste myself and wanting me to step back into my body as if into a black room and stumble against whatever was there. Unable then to be watched by others ...
And me in my vanity accusing him at first of being tone deaf! He was offering me black empty spaces. Revived himself with matches once an hour, wanted me to become blind to everything but the owned pain in myself. And so yes there is a need to come home Webb with that casual desert blackness. (CS, 91)

Bolden's first-person voice gradually emerges, ideally culminating – and simultaneously undoing itself – in the breathless scene of his mental breakdown (CS, 129–31), stylistically realized through an increasing fragmentation of syntax, an increase in parataxis, and, finally, passages that remove even parataxis and do without punctuation. Bolden's mental dissolution erupts when he seems to

216 Serena Fusco

have found in one (imaginary?) person the right audience that he has looked for all his life – a girl "mirroring [his] throat in her lonely tired dance" (CS, 130). Discussing *Coming Through Slaughter*, Marino writes: "Jazz music is ... mostly about interplay and interaction ... concerned with the redefinition of the self ... in dialogical terms; it is an art form which, being strongly rooted in concepts such as enunciation and performance, confers centrality to listening."[8] The text, though, as shown by the mental breakdown sequence (and more), is far from romanticizing listening per se. This non-idealized listening is perhaps another key for engaging the whole text. Besides Bolden, there is another "I" in the text: a nameless narrating "I," also a photographer-I, who sees himself in Bolden (when Bolden is) looking into mirrors (Ondaatje reprises the unconfirmed story of Bolden working at a shaving parlour during the day):

The place of his music is totally silent. There is so little noise that I easily hear the click of my camera as I take fast bad photographs into the sun aiming at the barber shop he probably worked in ... *The photograph moves and becomes a mirror.* When I read he stood in front of mirrors and attacked himself, there was the shock of memory. For I had done that. Stood, and with a razor-blade cut into cheeks and forehead, shaved hair. (CS, 133; emphasis added)

Both the mirror/photograph motif and the window/photograph motif are present in *Coming Through Slaughter*. In the passage above, the mirror is not only the channel that puts Bolden and the other "I" in communication; it is also a window, a channel elsewhere, a mobilized photograph that reveals, under the surface layer of a captured moment, another layer, a mo(ve)ment that can spin off in other directions. This spinning is not free from danger, as the violence suffusing the text makes clear:

Once they were sitting at the kitchen table opposite each other. To his right and to her left was a window. Furious at something he drew his right hand across his body and lashed out. Half way there at full speed he realised it was a window he would be hitting and braked. For a fraction of a second his open palm touched the glass, beginning simultaneously to draw back. The

Ondaatje's Narrative and Intermediality   217

window starred and crumpled slowly two floors down. His hand
miraculously uncut ... She was delighted by the performance.
Surprised he examined his fingers. (CS, 16)

The motif of glass, central in *Coming Through Slaughter*, subsumes
both windows and mirrors; glass as motif, especially broken glass,
will be reprised in *Divisadero*.

The mutual remediation of photography and music is crucial for
understanding the rereading of jazz history in *Coming Through
Slaughter* through the figure of Bolden. At the same time, this "triple" intermedial confrontation in *Coming Through Slaughter* has
some interesting historical *and* poetical implications. For Ondaatje's
Bellocq, the interest of photography seems to reside not in the final
result as something to be prized or displayed for the sake of it but,
instead, in a dynamic, ongoing, partly circular and partly linear
process. "The picture is just a figure against a wall" (CS, 54), yet
photographing is for Bellocq a way to coax out and capture the (submerged) memory of past moments when his subjects, the Storyville
whores, dared to expect a better future – such hopes obviously unrealized. Such stirring of bygone hopes may seem rather cruel, yet this
time pattern structures, in my opinion, the very intermedial framework of *Coming Through Slaughter*. Photography is what excavates
the past to locate a moment when one looked ahead into the future,
a moment of expectation, realized or unrealized, that has personal
as well as historical value. Ondaatje sets here another pattern that
will be recurring in his work, that is, the use of photography to
stretch the limits and possibilities of both historical narrative and
narrative in general.

Those dark spaces, those unrealized hopes, are the silent, painful
background Bolden is looking for. It may be suggested that *Coming
Through Slaughter* provides ground not only for a rethinking of jazz
history but even for thinking of history as (proto-)jazz, the music
Bolden played: "Certainly Bolden, even if he did not invent jazz, had
mastered the recipe for it .... [H]is insistence on marrying [ragtime]
syncopations to the blues ... captured the attention of his contemporaries and the later chroniclers of New Orleans jazz."[9] History here
transforms into something to be played over again for variations,
off-beat, making sound resound where silence should be and filling
expected loudness with silence.[10]

STRATEGIC (PROTO-PHOTOGRAPHIC) CARAVAGGISM: *IN THE SKIN OF A LION*

Another crossmedial reference in *Coming Through Slaughter* is to John James Audubon's (1785–1851) drawings of birds. The "animal" motif is recurrent in Ondaatje's works. In all the texts discussed here, an ever-present desire for intimacy (think, for instance, of Bolden's search for a "corresponding" audience) is accompanied by stories of violence. The animal motif can underscore an idea of violence as ascribable to a pre-civilization, pre-human status. At the same time, though, violence in Ondaatje is clearly "civilized": it is the violence of socioeconomic, gender, and racial inequality and the violence of war.

The search for agency in or against the darkest aspects of history and civilization informs and is informed by intermedial dialogues. *In the Skin of a Lion* openly follows the synesthetic path opened up by Ondaatje's earlier works. At the same time, it is perhaps the most intensely visual among the four works discussed here, especially in the sense of having consolidated a recognizably Ondaatjean/ Caravaggesque mode of seeing. Here, seeing is sensorily predicated on an entwinement of light and darkness, just as the novel lays out a complex, multilayered entwinement of light and darkness as symbolically charged themes. I should immediately clarify that *In the Skin of a Lion*'s intensely visual quality cannot be ascribed to the presence of one isolated, "pure" medium. Visuality is always already constructed as/in an intermedial situation, in the sense that several (visual) media contribute, by remediating each other, to an intense effect even "before" the de facto remediation by the written medium. And, as already apparent in *Coming Through Slaughter*, the presence of other media within writing is charged with meta-literary value. The media that are most relevant to my argument are painting and photography, and related to them is the substantially "mixed" medium of the theatre, one involving visual channels besides other ones.

In the Skin of a Lion expands the rather spare colour palette – one revolving around black, white, grey, brown, and red – already experimented with in *Coming Through Slaughter*. This passage depicts a group of tanners on Cypress Street in Toronto (presumably) during the 1920s:

Ondaatje's Narrative and Intermediality   219

Circular pools had been cut into the stone – into which the men leapt waist-deep within the reds and ochres and greens, leapt in embracing the skins of recently slaughtered animals ... And the men stepped out in colours up to their necks, pulling wet hides out after them so it appeared they had removed the skin from their own bodies ...

To stand during the five-minute break dressed in green talking to a man in yellow ... (SL, 130)

The colour-filled pictorialism of this scene has been seen by some as an exploitative aestheticization of the workers on Ondaatje's part.[11] The limits of art in confronting the working class are explicitly mentioned in the novel: "This is how Patrick would remember them later ... If he were an artist he would have painted them but that was false celebration. What did it mean in the end to look aesthetically plumaged on this October day in the east end of the city five hundred yards from Front Street? What would the painting tell?" (SL, 130). How are we to read this criticism of painting within the novel? Is it a way to point out the recurring ethical dilemma of making the workers into passive aesthetic objects through art? Or it is a way to point out the necessity of celebrating them through the powers of a different artistic medium from painting, such as literary writing?

One must keep in mind, though, that the pictorial style that is mostly "remediated" in the novel is Caravaggism.[12] *In the Skin of a Lion* is the first of two (possibly three) novels by Ondaatje that feature a character whose last name is Caravaggio. Darkened spaces and/or sudden illuminations by splashes of dramatic light abound in *In the Skin of a Lion*. Among numerous examples, one can think of the nocturnal scene of loggers skating on a frozen Ontario river at night, seen by Patrick, the novel's protagonist, when he was a boy: "Each man held in one hand a sheaf of cattails and the top of these were on fire. This is what lit the ice and had blinked through the trees" (SL, 21).

Next to the aforementioned bold strokes of red, green, and ochre, the novel (again, partly like *Coming Through Slaughter*) subsumes its own variety of colour under a visual black-white polarization that corresponds to the poles of absence versus the presence of light. *In the Skin of a Lion* is, in this respect, as much photographic as it is pictorial, if one regards photography as the medium that literally "writes with light," that intrinsically combines light and darkness in endless possible grey-scales. The abattoir and tannery workers that were awash in colour are elsewhere rendered as "fading to white," vanishing among clouds of steam during their visit to the bathhouse: "A chain was pulled that forced wet steam into the room so that their bodies were separated by whiteness ... tattoos and hard muscles fading into unborn photographs" (SL, 136).

The phrase "unborn photographs" evokes a photographic process and simultaneously marks it with absence. It may refer to an overexposure and hence obliteration of the photographic image; an image erasure during photo development (something remindful of how Bellocq, in *Coming Through Slaughter*, finally dissolves in acid the film with Bolden's photo); or even photographs *not* taken. "Unborn photographs" also connect to the historiographic (or historiographically metafictional)[13] discourse underlying Ondaatje's oeuvre. Darkness (as well as whiteness, the other pole, also signifying an obliteration in photographic terms) as a motif in *In the Skin of a Lion*, similarly to what will happen in *The English Patient*, is related to painting, photography, and *history*. Darkened zones of the past, but also of the present, are a necessary background for what is illuminated and may resurface at later moments: "Patrick would never see the great photographs of Hine, as he would never read the letters of Joseph Conrad. Official histories, news stories surround us daily, but the events of art reach us too late, travel languorously like messages in a bottle" (SL, 145–6). Here art appears to be imbued with historical value, but most of it seems to reside in its being experienced/recreated through a time lag. Yet it is precisely this time lag that makes it possible for art to travel through the dark waters of time and become not only a snapshot of a certain historical moment but, crucially, itself a historical agent.

This interplay of light and darkness is not only a feature of Caravaggio's pictorial art; it is an intrinsic, technical feature of the photographic medium. Caravaggio's paintings are "proto-photographic" in their depending on a calculated dosage of light for being seen and interpreted. In Ondaatje, this (proto-)photographic Caravaggism accompanies and sustains specific literary strategies. Characters recur and re-emerge across different novels: Hana and Patrick from *In the Skin of a Lion* to *The English Patient*; David Caravaggio journeys between these two novels and arrives in *Divisadero*, with a different name: "Patrick never believed that

Ondaatje's Narrative and Intermediality   221

characters lived only on the page. They altered when the author's eye was somewhere else. Outside the plot there was a great darkness, but there would of course be daylight elsewhere on earth. Each character had his own time zone, his own lamp" (SL, 143).

Throughout *In the Skin of a Lion*, already-intermedial "proto-photographic" Caravaggism has a function that is at least partly analogous to the already-intermedial combination of (proto-)jazz music and photography in *Coming Through Slaughter*: the possibility to reimage, possibly recreate, a darkened zone of history through art, a function always accompanied by an overlap of different media, which are in turn remediated by literary writing. I conclude this paragraph with a reference to the most synesthetic of media, theatre, also featuring prominently in *In the Skin of a Lion*: "Alice had once described a play to him in which several actresses shared the role of the heroine. After half an hour the powerful matriarch removed her large coat from which animal pelts dangled and she passed it, along with her strength, to one of the minor characters ... Each person had their moment when they assumed the skins of wild animals, when they took responsibility for the story" (SL, 157).

There is no printed reproduction of any works by Caravaggio or Lewis Hine in *In the Skin of a Lion*; however, Ondaatje's idiosyncratic writing style absorbs painting, photography, and theatre and remediates them. Within a "media system," each artistic medium exists next to other media, both artistic and not, and all media exist *in the world* and can contribute to history in the world by becoming themselves historical agents.

THE RAGGED SURFACE: *THE ENGLISH PATIENT*

Narrating the encounter in a ruined Tuscan villa at the end of the Second World War among four scarred people and their respective pasts, *The English Patient* expands Ondaatje's (proto-photographic) Caravaggism while involving, again, many other media, arts, and codes: sculpture and drawing; music and radio devices; and, of course, writing, both literature and history. *The English Patient* pushes Ondaatje's metafictional historiographical search in a radical direction: it looks into the possibility of a future after the catastrophe of the Second World War or, speaking more broadly, after any catastrophe, after the death of (a) civilization brought about by nuclear warfare. Ondaatje is, I believe, deliberately ambivalent when he writes of the atomic bombing of Japan as "a terrible event emerging out of the shortwave ... The death of a civilization" (EP, 286). Not only has the attacked civilization been destroyed, but the attacker's has too. This radical historical positioning is, once again, inseparable from the author's intermedial strategies.

The English Patient is an inter-sensorial narrative: taste, hearing, smell, sight, and touch are all explicitly evoked on/by the written page. Milena Marinkova sees Ondaatje's sensorium as overall orchestrated by the sense of touch and argues that Ondaatje is the proponent of a "haptic" aesthetics, one in which "the foundational character of tactile sensibility informs all the other senses just as the intersubjective nature of affect transcends the boundaries of the subject and the individual body."[14] Marinkova's use of the haptic as a diffused dimension undercutting Ondaatje's creative world can be related, in my view, to Giuliana Bruno's dynamic (Deleuzian) idea of *surface* as *texture*. This idea calls attention to

how mediatic transformations can be sited texturally on the surface. In proposing that we pay attention to the pleats and folds that constitute the fabrics of the visual, I wish in particular to pursue what Gilles Deleuze calls a "texturology": a philosophical and aesthetic conception of art in which its "matter is clothed, with 'clothed' signifying ... the very fabric or clothing, the texture enveloping" ... To make this textural shift involves tracing what we might call the enveloping "fashioning" of the image and weaving this across different media. This means emphasizing the etymological root of *medium*, which refers to a condition of "betweenness" and a quality of "becoming" as a connective, pervasive, or enveloping substance.[15]

While Ondaatje's texts are not screens, their multisensorial quality, their adaptation of stylistic features usually ascribed to other media, and especially their being spaces where different media merge and alternatively "envelop" each other make them dynamic and changing in a way similar to Bruno's textured surfaces, which she also calls "screen-membrane[s]."[16] The visual arts, as well as the printed page itself, become tactile, thick, at the border between bi- and three-dimensionality. I offer two examples here, both involving Kip's character. First, while advancing with his sapper unit in Tuscany, Kip finds comfort in imagining himself skin to skin with the Queen of

Sheba frescoed by Piero Della Francesca in Arezzo: "The young Sikh sapper put his cheek against the mud and thought of the Queen of Sheba's face, the texture of her skin" (*EP*, 70). Later in the novel, Kip steps into a larger-than-life Annunciation scene, a three-dimensional tableau in the Neapolitan church of San Giovanni a Carbonara. A memorable suspended moment ensues, with Kip falling asleep at the feet of the Madonna and Angel, his presence the uncertain materialization of a future in the midst of impending death: "The tableau now, with Kip at the feet of the two figures, suggests a debate over his fate. The raised terra-cotta arm a stay of execution, a promise of some great future for this sleeper, childlike, foreign-born" (*EP*, 280–1).

Kip is also associated with sound and music, with both the lethal risks and the life-saving quality of them. Kip is always humming to himself, always whistling (*EP*, 74). Sound and music are *both* harbingers of death *and* tools to survive a catastrophe. Kip is always wearing an earphone connected to a portable radio device (something remindful of the burned patient and his hearing aid) "so he can hear sounds from the rest of the world that might be important to him. He will come into the house to pass on whatever information he has picked up that he thinks might be interesting to them. One afternoon he announces that the bandleader Glenn Miller has died, his plane having crashed somewhere between England and France" (*EP*, 76). Kip also selects carefully what to listen to when he defuses a bomb. Kip is the one in the villa who first hears of the bombing of Hiroshima and Nagasaki, the news on the shortwave shattering his already precarious faith in the late-imperial civilization he is a part of: "I'll leave you the radio to swallow your history lesson. Don't move again, Caravaggio. All those speeches of civilization from kings and queens and presidents ... such voices of abstract order. Smell it. Listen to the radio and smell the celebration in it. In my country, when a father breaks justice in two, you kill the father" (*EP*, 285).

Most characters in *The English Patient* have been wounded or maimed, are scarred in body and/or psyche. Christopher McVey writes that "[t]he wounded or scarred bodies in Ondaatje's fiction are ... *forms or sites of writing at the same time they signify an erasure*, a figural scarring-over of history, both personal and communal."[17] Scars signal both the healing of the wound and its permanence, just like history, in its apparent suturing of ruptures, is ragged with scars that make any surface uneven. Another memorable intermedial rendition of this is the final scene of *The English Patient*. Hana and Kip, separated at the end of the war, are, years later, momentarily "brought together" in a superimposition of scenes. One can imagine the page becoming a screen with two sides. A dislodged glass on one side "becomes" a falling fork on the other: "And so Hana moves and her face turns and in a regret she lowers her hair. Her shoulder touches the edge of a cupboard and a glass dislodges. Kirpal's left hand swoops down and catches the dropped fork an inch from the floor and gently passes it into the fingers of his daughter" (EP, 301–2). Are these two "parts" of the scene simultaneous? Are they two successive moments, as a narrative logic would suggest? However we decide to read them, their juxtaposition creates a crease, a fold, on the apparently even surface of the page/screen – a fold that can unravel in (at least) two directions, as we shall soon see in *Divisadero*.

"AS CLOSE TO THEIR REFLECTIONS AS POSSIBLE": *DIVISADERO* (IN LIEU OF A CLOSURE)

The superimposition of two moments – a superimposition that reveals inevitable creases – becomes in *Divisadero* the lopsided superimposition of two (or even more) stories. The most evident peculiarity of this novel is a structural asymmetry. It is divided into three parts. Part One occupies a little less than two-thirds of the text. Part Two functions as a bridge: Anna, one of the novel's protagonists and narrators, researches the life of writer Lucien Segura, whose story is narrated in Part Three.

This merging of different stories is evoked through an image at the end of Part One: "Eventually we come to a ford where our river meets a road and covers it, or from another perspective, where the road has come upon the river and sunk below its surface, as if from a life lived to a life imagined ... They merge, the river and the road, like two lives, a tale told backwards and a tale told first" (D, 167). A merging of stories is also evoked at the end of Part Two, in the short section "Two Photographs." It consists of an ekphrasis of two photos, hung side by side on a wall of a house in Dému, France, where Anna is living and where Segura once lived. One is an image of Segura, another of Anna; Anna's photograph "has been blown up to be the same size as the other, so it is, in a way, a partner to

Ondaatje's Narrative and Intermediality   225

it" (*D*, 187). As I have argued elsewhere, I find this photographic blow-up highly significant, and I share Julia Breitbach's idea that it provides a metaliterary moment revealing the intention behind the novel.[18] Compared to other works by Ondaatje, *Divisadero* is probably the one most overtly concerned with relations involving "items" of different proportions, thus raising the issue of *scale*. Small things, details, obscured or peripheral elements can be enlarged and beget possibilities, becoming seeds of other stories. Characters and events echo each other, repeat themselves, creating (imperfect) correspondences and duplicates.[19]

This asymmetrical correspondence of elements whose reciprocal proportions are both crucial and problematic is yet another correlative of Ondaatje's synesthetic vision and intermedial literary technique. A dialogue with another being, a companion moving through darkness with you, the road and its "black hedges coax you on" (*D*, 136): this scenario parallels how literary narrative becomes a mirror for music, architecture, even the visual magic brought about by shattered glass:

> All my life I have loved travelling at night, with a companion, each of us discussing and sharing the known and familiar behaviour of the other. It's like a *villanelle*, this inclination of going back to events in our past, the way the villanelle's form refuses to move forward in linear development, circling instead at those familiar moments of emotion. Only the *rereading* counts, *Nabokov* said. So the strange form of that *belfry*, turning onto itself again and again, felt familiar to me. For we live with those retrievals from childhood that coalesce and echo throughout our lives, the way shattered pieces of glass in a *kaleidoscope* reappear in new forms and are *songlike* in their refrains and rhymes, making up a single *monologue*. We live permanently in the recurrence of our own *stories*, whatever story we *tell*.
> (*D*, 136; emphasis added)

With its double movement, circular *and* onward, this passage epitomizes both the intermedial encounter – arts become channels for other arts – and the narrative pull that subsumes it and ultimately, I believe, motivates it. Discussing the role of music in *Divisadero*, Robert Lecker has argued that the variety of its musical references – as well as the fact that most of them are concentrated in Part One so the novel rather abruptly turns "silent" – help us to understand how it tackles "grand polarities" and makes room for contradictions, including a "double narrative pull. One impulse behind the narrative is to connect us to the immediate, to locate the story in mimetic terms ... [A]nother impulse is to work against the immediate, to cast the characters and their experiences as part of an allegorical universe in which actions and choices are symbolic, metaphoric, transhistorical."[20] What this intermedial continuum/cycle emphasizes is the importance of stories and narratives as intermedially connected, a compound within which Ondaatje chooses literary writing and simultaneously makes it a cave of resonance for everything else. Like in *Coming Through Slaughter*, mirrors can become windows and vice versa. *Divisadero* is a many-faced mirror, whose faces display reflections that suggest the possibility of traversing: "Some birds in the almost-dark are flying as close to their reflections as possible" (*D*, 273). Or, as Claire, Anna's adopted twin sister, seems to imply, *Divisadero* is a map whose halves do not fold neatly (*D*, 164) yet whose separating crease is as important as the landscape it represents.

NOTES

1 Rajewsky explores how literature generates "an illusion of another medium's specific practices" in "Intermediality, Intertextuality, and Remediation," 55.

2 See, for example, Ryan and Thon, *Storyworlds across Media*.

3 On the subject of history in Ondaatje, see, among many possible references, Bachner, McVey, Petermann, Vadde.

4 See, for instance, Marquis, *In Search of Buddy Bolden, First Man of Jazz*, published in 1978.

5 Gioia, *The History of Jazz*, 33.

6 Petermann, "Unheard Jazz," 223–33.

7 Marino, "Crossing the Borders of Jazz, Language, and Identity," 225.

8 Ibid., 219.

9 Gioia, *The History of Jazz*, 34.

10 In "'He Had Pushed His Imagination into Buddy's Brain,'" Bachner has offered a very sound reading of what she sees as a fundamental "escape" from history in *Coming Through Slaughter* yet one made in the name of history: more precisely, in the name of a questionable (metafictional) historiographical identification with a character like Bolden, whose (relative)

historical obscurity actually sets off the author's creative, ultimately privileged appropriation. While not necessarily sharing Bachner's idea of Ondaatje's exploitative relation vis-à-vis less fortunate historical subjects, I find her reading acute, especially when she points out that the fame/privacy dichotomy at work in *Coming Through Slaughter* is, in many ways, more apparent than substantial. Bolden's "journey" through the history of jazz is far from linear, and it seems to consist of an alternation of limelight and obscurity. After his death, those who spoke about him, remembered him, or remembered others talking about him reconstructed *a posteriori* how he was well known *in his time* (see Gioia, 33–7).

11 See, for instance, Davey, *Post-national Arguments*.

12 See Ingelbien and Sarris.

13 The term is, of course, Linda Hutcheon's.

14 Marinkova, *Michael Ondaatje*, 4.

15 Bruno, *Surface*, 3–4, emphasis in the original.

16 Ibid., 5.

17 McVey, "Reclaiming the Past," 144, emphasis added.

18 Fusco, "Fading into Unborn Photographs," 107–21. See also Breitbach, *Analog Fictions for the Digital Age*, 185.

19 See de Smyter, "'We Live Permanently in the Recurrence of Our Own Stories,'" 99–119.

20 Lecker, "Music in Michael Ondaatje's *Divisadero*," 276, 278.

10

Intermedial Aesthetics in *The Cat's Table*

Birgit Neumann

INTRODUCTION: ENACTING SEE-CHANGES

Michael Ondaatje's multi-faceted oeuvre abounds with intermedial references to visual media, that is, to photography, paintings, and films. Works such as *Billy the Kid* (1970), *Running in the Family* (1982), *In the Skin of a Lion* (1987), *The English Patient* (1992), *Anil's Ghost* (2000), as well as *The Cat's Table* (2011) make full use of both the aesthetic and political potential of verbal-visual configurations to showcase the close links between visual representation, power, and identification. Deeply suspicious of fixed boundaries, Ondaatje mobilizes these interrelations to bring to the fore heterogeneity, plurality, and difference within seemingly self-contained entities and to complicate one-dimensional approaches to the world. Manifesting in a complex intermedial aesthetics – an aesthetics that is intricately connected to aisthēsis – the fusion of images and words appeals to our senses to subtly redirect our gaze to formerly disregarded experiences (cf. Neumann and Rippl) and to enact "see-changes."[1] Projecting one medium onto another, verbal-visual configurations provide imaginary extensions of the boundaries of human perception and invite readers to see the world from different, multiplied, and multiplying angles. This multiplicity of intertwined perspectives matters as it sustains, by means of a collaborative form, new, pluralized modes of social recognition and relationality.

I suggest approaching these verbal-visual configurations in Ondaatje's work from the perspective of intermediality research, which has been flourishing in the last decades. The majority of this research has been and remains dedicated to intermedial aesthetics in

Western literatures, focusing, for instance, on the semiotic capacities of texts to evoke images and paint with words. But in postcolonial and transcultural fiction, intermedial relations take on specific resonances and therefore require modes of scholarly attention that consider the socio-political force of images and seeing, that is, their power to organize collectivity in an uneven world (cf. Neumann; Neumann and Rippl). Postcolonial and transcultural fictions make much of the semiotic and material difference that the translation of images into narrative involves, activating it to negotiate various forms of cultural otherness and difference. How, these fictions ask, have images, paintings, and films contributed to making visible specific experiences, and how do they partake in processes of stigmatization that cast people of colour as the objectified and exoticized other vis-à-vis white subjectivity? While frequently offering politically relevant revisions of dominant visual regimes and performing acts of looking back at the colonizer, the negotiation of otherness in these texts is not always antagonistic. Rather, the interplay between words and images may also result in multi-layered configurations of in-betweenness, fusion, and hybridity, which dismantle facile dualisms of self and other. Many of Ondaatje's works harness the "unstable element of linkage" that intermediality relies on to gauge cross-cultural relationality in an asymmetrically entangled world.[2] Asserting a provocative interplay between difference and relation, transgressions between medial boundaries thus assume greater socio-political relevance as they metonymically energize encounters and exchange across cultural borders. Such configurations of exchange are frequently enabled by a rebuttal of hegemonic, seemingly neutral ways of seeing, and the exploration of the questions raised by Rob Nixon – "Who gets to see, and from where? When and how does such empowered seeing become normative?" – serves as a springboard to develop alternative, more equitable forms of seeing.[3]

A range of Ondaatje's texts – *Running in the Family*, *The English Patient*, as well as *The Cat's Table* are probably the most prominent examples – are committed to re-membering hegemonic visual traditions from an ex-centric perspective to reveal previously hidden experiences and to articulate "the claim for the right to look where none exists."[4] Time and again, Ondaatje takes up Euro- and American-centric visual practices, often implicated in colonialism, to explore their epistemic and affective potential, that is, their power to shape ways of knowing, being, and belonging. In this process, he energetically subjects these visual artefacts to the transformative and differential influence afforded through literary visuality: by translating visual practices into words, these artefacts become available for reinterpretation and are confronted with alternatives that displace singular interpretations and authoritarian views. It is in this way that the intermedial aesthetics that pervade many of Ondaatje's works contribute to what Jacques Rancière calls the "distribution of the sensible," understood "as the system of *a priori* forms determining what presents itself to sense experience."[5] By offering elaborate descriptions of visual works, Ondaatje's texts illustrate that and how images produce visibility, which renders concrete some experiences and subjectivities while invisibilizing others. His literary descriptions ask readers to take a second look and consider what lies outside the frame, possibly seeking to protect them "from the harm of political blindness or indifference."[6] Importantly, these re-visions are not only directed at making readers "see ... something *other*" but also at inducing them to "learn ... to see *otherwise*," as Kenaan puts it.[7] More specifically, Ondaatje's engagement with visuality and vision dismantles the seemingly neutral Western gaze. This detached, disengaged, and disengaging gaze, is, as Jacques Derrida has shown, closely connected to surveillance, control, and mastery. It helped to foster a link between "theoretical objectivity and technico-political possession,"[8] which underlies many Western epistemologies and intersects with colonial ideologies. It is one of the achievements of Ondaatje's works to powerfully replace the neutral gaze by affective and pluralized modes of seeing – frequently "world-imaginings from below,"[9] which create fluid notions of the I/eye that remain open to others (cf. Emery, 243).

A RITE OF PASSAGE

The Cat's Table, published in 2011, tells a story of passage. In the most literal sense, the novel recounts the ship-passage of Michael – Mynah as he is called on board the liner *Oronsay* – who, in the 1950s, leaves his Sri Lankan home behind to join his mother in England. Such passages from home to the former mother country are a common trope in many postcolonial texts, most pronouncedly in V.S. Naipaul's *The Enigma of Arrival* and George Lamming's *The Emigrants*. But in contrast to these texts, *The Cat's Table* is

Intermedial Aesthetics in *The Cat's Table*

not primarily interested in exploring the mother country, a place of illusion and disillusionment for the new colonial citizens, but in gauging the affordances of the passage, the travel itself. As a matter of fact, the narrative's plot, though offering occasional glimpses into the protagonist's past in Columbo and his future in England as well as in Canada, is almost entirely set on board the *Oronsay* and thus unfolds in a genuinely transgressive, fluid, and liminal space. If, as Edward Said has argued, colonial discourse has established the "primacy of the geographical element"[10] to promote stable oppositions between peripheries and centres, then Ondaatje's text powerfully fluidizes them. The ship's passage through the Indian Ocean, the Arabian Sea, the Red Sea, the Mediterranean, and the Atlantic yields shifting and interconnected cartographies that persistently cut across colonial borders and open up new contact zones.

It is the passage and the kind of fluidity that it implies that become the generative principle of *The Cat's Table*. Playing on the life-as-journey trope but imbuing it with the socio-political complexities related to acts of migration, the journey from Colombo to Tilbury morphs into "a rite of passage" (CT, 72). Almost completely beyond the control of parents, guardians, and schoolmasters, the unordered and unbordered space of the transoceanic liner offers the eleven-year-old Mynah an opportunity for self-invention: "On the *Oronsay* ... there was the chance to escape all order. And I reinvented myself in this seemingly imaginary world" (CT, 17). Together with two friends, the reckless Cassius and contemplative Ramadhin, he heedlessly plunges into the adult world, making discoveries that would indelibly change him. Retrospectively, he notes: "We were learning about adults simply by being in their midst." What they are learning about, is, first and foremost, the full range of misbehaviour: "adultery, drug-smoking, burglary and even murder are never very far away from the beady eyes of the juveniles."[11]

Passages in Ondaatje's work are never only a topical concern but also and more importantly a creative principle underlying the narrative's complex poetics. *The Cat's Table* is marked by what Tobias Döring in a different context calls "a poetics of passage, of cross-cultural connectedness," of exchange and change.[12] This poetics of passage materializes in the text's experimental play with genres, a play that is constitutive of many of Ondaatje's texts. The novel brings together a range of genres, most importantly travel writing, the adventure novel, the mystery novel, the *Bildungsroman*, and life-writing, to show that classifications are never simple or exclusive. *The Cat's Table* consistently blurs the boundaries between fact and fiction, and, though autobiographically inspired, the narrator, now living as an adult in Canada, emphasizes that he is not interested in providing a factual account of the events on the *Oronsay*. What interests him is the creative potential of storytelling, which allows for revisiting, revising, and rearranging the actual: "Three weeks of the sea journey, as I originally remembered it, were placid. It is only now, years later, having been prompted by my children to describe the voyage, that it becomes an adventure, when seen through their eyes" (CT, 72). The quote makes clear that the boundaries between fact and fiction, truth and invention, self and others, telling and seeing are porous. For Ondaatje, this porosity is not a weakness to be reckoned with but a productive force that allows for shifts in perspective and ethically relevant revisions, which fuse perception, memory, and imagination.

It is at this point that the novel's multi-faceted intermedial aesthetics comes into play. This aesthetics provides a rich resource for exploring the interactions between seeing, visuality, and subjectivity and for generating symbolic forms that accept ambiguity, conflict, and plurality as immanent in any configuration. The intermedial aesthetics comes in many forms, ranging from there references to visual media to elaborate ekphrastic descriptions, but two manifestations assume central importance: first, modes of seeing that, as Levinas has argued in a different context, break with the "synoptic and totalizing objectifying virtues of vision"[13] and give validity to ex-centric perspectives. Second, these ex-centric visions are the enabling force for enacting socio-politically relevant re-visions that grapple with the epistemic violence inherent to hegemonic forms of visuality and reorder the asymmetric distribution of visibility.

"ANGLES OF VISION" – SEEING FROM THE SIDE

Inspired by filmmaking and painting, Ondaatje's writing is highly attentive to the formative potential of perspective and related modes of seeing. *The Cat's Table* resonates with James Elkins's claim that there is nothing innocent about seeing: "Seeing is transformation not mechanism"; it is "fraught with power relations" and permeated with desire.[14] The centrality of seeing is highlighted from the beginning, namely, in a quote from Joseph Conrad's novella

"Youth" (1902), which serves as an epigraph: "And this is how I see the East ... I see it always from a small boat – not a light, not a stir, not a sound." In "Youth," Conrad, an expatriate like Ondaatje, recounts the story of Marlow's first journey to the East and the ways he "sees the East." *The Cat's Table* reverses the direction of the imperial travel and puts centre stage three Ceylonese boys, who, repeatedly being reminded of their non-Englishness, claim "a right to look."[15] These acts of looking are all about transformation – and the fact that the quote from "Youth" featured at the novel's beginning rests on significant rearrangements and is a compelling expression of this transformative potential.[16]

Transformation, in *The Cat's Table*, is achieved through a dynamic of repetition and difference rather than through a complete break with colonially inherited models. What connects Ondaatje with Conrad's modernism is an interest in perspective, an acute awareness of the centrality of locality, and a fascination with the transience of first sights. Interestingly, the ways of seeing that Ondaatje configures in *The Cat's Table* are just as locally grounded and circumscribed as those of Marlow, who sees the East from what he considers to be "a small boat."[17] Throughout the novel, Ondaatje takes great care to mark the position from which Mynah sees and describes the goings-on aboard the *Oronsay*, yielding a scopic particularity that defies claims of neutrality, objectivity, and authority enshrined in the central perspective and neutral gaze. The most prominent of these positions is the eponymous cat's table, at which Mynah, together with eight other passengers, is allocated. It is, according to one passenger, "the least privileged place," "[l]ocated far from the Captain's Table" (CT, 10). Although one might interpret that kind of marginality as indicative of the social positioning of the postcolonial subject[18] and hence as part of a more comprehensive, structural mechanism of exclusion, it is important to acknowledge that Ondaatje manipulates marginality in a way that teases out its productive, liberating, and enabling potentials. The cat's table indexes an epistemic and normative principle, a mode of seeing, rather than a fixed location: Mynah quite willingly endorses the ex-centric perspectives that it offers, understanding that the embedded vision from the side provides him with an opportunity to see beyond the ossified gestures of power and status. Retrospectively, he notes: "That was a small lesson I learned on the journey. What is interesting and important happens mostly in secret, in places where there is no power" (CT, 103). Small lessons rather than grand insights are what Mynah gleans from his observations and which become constitutive for his decentred, meandering, and fragmentary narrative. It is the prism of these ex-centric perspectives that affords the multiplying of vision and the redistribution of centrality, thus refracting those social structures that operate in the name of a privileged few. Cassius advises his friends "to interpret anything that took place around [them] with a quizzical or upsidedown perspective" (CT, 55). Throughout the novel, Mynah adopts such decentring, unstable, and quizzical ways of seeing, slowly but forcefully turning a socially imposed position of marginality into a chosen and transformative strategy.

Ex-centric seeing brings to attention protagonists and experiences that frequently remain invisible, unnoticed, and latent, lying beyond what Judith Butler calls "frames." Frames, according to Butler, structure modes of perception by distinguishing what is important from what is deemed, according to hegemonic orders, negligible and irrelevant. Allowing for a sense of focus, the importance of frames is thus not only hermeneutic but also socio-political in nature, regulating recognition and misrecognition in the public sphere. Frames are, as Butler puts it, "politically saturated," since in "organiz[ing] visual experience" they "generate specific ontologies of the subject."[19] Butler's arguments are unwavering reminders of the fact that production of visibility is intricately, and oftentimes precariously, connected to social status.

The Cat's Table is responsive to the centrality of frames, and it does much to break and expand them. It is the ex-centric, the dissident, the sick, and the physically challenged characters, frequently located at the many cat's tables of the world, that Mynah's narrative puts into focus: the enigmatic Perinetta Lasqueti, who carries "several life birds" in the padded pockets of a "pigeon jacket" (CT, 109); the half-deaf and almost mute girl Asuntha, who "appeared to be the most powerless passenger on the ship" (CT, 76); Asuntha's father, the Asian prisoner Niemeyer, who is to be tried in England; the acrobats of the Jankla Troupe, the entertainment group, and their headliner, the Hyderabad Mind; "the one-eyed Assistant Purser" (CT, 108); Larry Daniels, a botanist, who tends a garden of medicinal plants in the bottom of the ship; Mr Gunesekera, a tailor, who does not or cannot communicate; Mr Perera, an undercover Ceylonese serviceman overseeing Niemeyer, who is eventually found dead; and so on. All of them slip in and out of Mynah's narrative, whose loose, associative, and non-linear makeup offers a potent site for accommodating a plurality of characters on a more or less equal level and for reclaiming submerged experiences. Ex-centric seeing valorizes embodied subjectivity as the possibility for knowledge that is inevitably limited and that, in the course of the novel, is being revisited and revised, thus capturing change, the fluidity of time, and the unfinishedness of knowing. Just like Caravaggio's paintings, which have a constant presence in Ondaatje's novels, *The Cat's Table* too sheds light on the porous edges of scenes, "the lost corners" (CT, 350) to prevent ephemeral impressions from disappearing. Repeatedly, *The Cat's Table* presents scenes, frequently haphazardly perceived and sometimes remaining inconsequential and mysterious, in which frames change or multiply, widen or contract, momentarily remaking the distinction between the centre and the margin, the inside and the outside. It is in this way that ex-centric seeing turns into a dynamic principle that redistributes limited attention and puts social heterogeneity, including the kind of openness that it entails, on the agenda.

Importantly, though Mynah's ex-centric looks are deeply committed to renegotiating the boundaries between the visible and invisible, they also work in the opposite direction. That is to say that they also accept the right to a certain degree of "opacity."[20] According to Caribbean philosopher Glissant, this right defends the inscrutability of cultural others, in particular of people of colour, whom Western societies almost obsessively seek to render transparent and readable. Many of the characters that the narrative revolves around remain strangers to Mynah; it is chance encounters and fleeting contacts that connect them to him. Time and again, the exact motivation of certain behaviours and actions remain opaque, and there is more than one secret surrounding the characters that the narrative refuses to resolve. The principle that the narrator eventually learns from the filmmaker Luc Dardenne provides an apt characterization of the novel's own appreciation of opacity: "He spoke of how viewers of his films should not assume they understood everything about the characters ... We should not feel assured or certain about their motives, or look down on them" (CT, 285). Instead of dissolving the characters' opacity through already available preconceptions, instead of subjecting them to what Levinas calls "the imperialism of the same,"[21] the emerging narrative confirms the impossibility of transparent, totalizing accounts that purport omniscience. But the respect for opacity does not preclude relation. After all, as Mynah comes to realize, it has always been strangers, people he has met "at the various cat's tables of [his] life" (CT, 270) who have changed and affected him. The duality of openness and distance manifests in a pluralistic, searching, and differential narrative that strikes a balance between what Marianne Hirsch calls "the act of holding," which is caring and protective, and the act of "withholding" that refrains from "absorb[ing] the other."[22] Another way to put this is to say that the narrative reaches out to others, while being punctuated by intermittent reminders of their opacity and the limits of identification.

In *The Cat's Table*, situated seeing from the side or from mid-air comes to index a non-hegemonic, embodied, and affective epistemology that undoes the links between far-seeing, privilege, and superiority that is operative in Cartesian rationalism. Embodied vision, grounded in what Emery calls the "physicality of the eye,"[23] dislodges the absolute point of knowledge to grasp the world in a relational, clearly subjective, and affective way. It is such a partial "angle of vision" (CT, 182) that Mynah, in his late twenties, also finds in Cassius's paintings. Visiting his friend's gallery in London, Mynah realizes that the paintings were all about that night in El Suweis, a night in which the *Oronsay* passes through the Suez Canal: "The very sulphur lights above the night activity that I still remembered, or at least began to remember that Saturday afternoon" (CT, 180). Mynah gradually comprehends that it is the particular, childlike perspective enshrined in the paintings that facilitates recognition of a half-forgotten past: "What I was seeing now in the gallery was the exact angle of vision Cassius and I had that night, from the railing, looking down at the men working in those pods of light" (CT, 182). Points of view here once again manifest their affective agency; much like Proust's madeleines, they are imbued with a sensual intensity, which triggers slumbering memories and creates temporalities in which past and present coexist. It bespeaks the novel's fascination with the interrelations of the arts that Mynah immediately associates Cassius's paintings with the early photography of Jacques Henri Lartigue, who is frequently celebrated as an innovator of twentieth-century photography. Among the many innovations that Lartigue introduced were experiments with perspective – as noted by the narrator, he frequently photographed scenes from ground level – with movement and time. The Scottish writer William Boyd, a great admirer and curator of Lartigue's work, stresses the unique power of his photos in capturing the transient and credits the French photographer with turning "the snapshot into art." Fittingly, Boyd compares Lartigue's photos to "Proustian madeleines in the form of black-and-white silver-gelatin prints," a characterization that brings us back to Cassius's paintings. The intermedial reference to Lartigue, seemingly dropped in passing, thus creates a fascinatingly dense network that entangles every new works of art, real and imaginary. It identifies some of the stylistic specificities of Cassius's paintings and Mynah's narrative (and, by implication, Ondaatje's writing), all of which are marked by a snapshot aesthetic, which Boyd eloquently characterizes as the blinking of "the camera's eye: Time is stopped, time is frozen, the milli-second captured."[24] Simultaneously, the reference establishes mutually transformative relations between painting, photography, and narrative, which grants visions that always rely on others. Just as the paintings hinge on the narrative to unfold their world-making potential, the narrative reaches out to the potentiality of images to enhance its aesthetic power. It is this border-transgressive interplay, which persistently works against self-enclosed and self-enclosing perspectives, through which the narrative turns the either-or logic into one of both-and.

POSTCOLONIAL RE-VISIONS

The novel casts Mynah's visions as politically relevant re-visions, many of which take issue with racialized and orientalizing representations of the East, such as those analyzed by Edward Said in his study *Orientalism*. *The Cat's Table* enters into a critical dialogue with a number of texts that have contributed to the invention of a fantasy Orient, an "imaginary geography,"[25] which first and foremost helped the West to consolidate its own identity. Rudyard Kipling has a constant presence in the novel; the ship's captain quotes some of his racist poems, and tellingly, Mynah, who is covered in motor oil to assist the Baron C with breaking into a cabin, sees himself, in one of the novel's many mirror images, as a "wild boy, somebody from one of the *Jungle Book* stories" (CT, 115). Even Mynah's diasporic sense of self is steeped in colonial imagery. But it is the engagement with visual media, including the epistemology and ontology that they imply, which, in *The Cat's Table*, becomes a springboard for postcolonial critique. Firmly locating visual artefacts, their production and circulation within the broader context of transnational media cultures, the novel is attentive to the connection between images and power structures and acknowledges their epistemic force.

A couple of days before the *Oronsay*'s landing in Aden, the passengers are invited to attend a screening of a film, *The Four Feathers* (1939) directed by Zoltan Korda and produced by his brother Alexander (tellingly, the Korda brothers also produced a film adaptation of Kipling's *The Jungle Book*). In a central passage of the novel, the narrator, shifting between his perceptions now and then, provides an elaborate ekphrasis of the film, which makes full political use of this device:

> We were just days away from landing in Aden, so the choice of *The Four Feathers* was, I see now, somewhat tactless, as it attempted to compare the brutality of Arabia with a civilised though foolish England. We watched an Englishman having his face branded ... so that he could pass himself off as an Arab in an invented desert nation. An old general in the story referred to the Arabs as something like "the Gazarra tribe – irresponsible and violent." (*CT*, 118)

The quoted passages, together with a number of subsequent descriptions Mynah details, provide a fairly apt summary of the ideological inclinations of *Four Feathers*, which is based on a 1902 novel by A.E.W. Mason (a novel the protagonist would read years later during his education at Dulwich College). The film by the Hungarian-born director tells an imperial adventure story set during the British army's Sudan campaign of the 1890s and is deeply steeped in colonial stereotypes. More specifically, it depicts both North African Arabs as well as Islamic Black Africans as "brutal" and "warring savage," thus reinforcing, according to Dunn, "the already established image of Africans as uncivilized barbarians."[26] Repeatedly pitting these representations against the controlled, courageous, and self-assured British troops, *Four Feathers* works toward promoting and naturalizing Britain's imperial myths, illustrating "the force of the image in empire-building."[27]

Mynah's extensive description of the film recodes and dismantles the filmic manifestation of the colonial gaze and what Ondaatje terms "jingoism" (*CT*, 119), and in so doing, the "battle against semiotic

Intermedial Aesthetics in *The Cat's Table* 239

otherness" that ekphrasis always entails[28] turns into a battle against racialized otherness. The narrator punctuates his comments on *Four Feathers* with a colourful account of the chaos emerging during its screening. An upcoming storm, its "forks of lightening in the distance" (CT, 119), adds a "subplot" to the film and thoroughly distorts the film's linear plotline, usually working in the service of progress and imperial victory. Moreover, the film's screening in both the First and Tourist Classes produces unintended "contrapuntal noises" (CT, 120), which scramble the film's all too obvious ideological message. And finally, a performance by the Jankla Troupe, parodying some of the film's scenes during the break, introduces a sense of the carnivalesque afforded by postcolonial agency: "[J]ust as First Class was witnessing the brutal massacre of English troops, exultant cheers rose from our audience" (CT, 120). Following Homi Bhabha's line of argumentation in "How Newness Enters the World," such acts of re-vision amount not to a "negation" of the "original structure of reference" but to its "negotiation": the re-vision turns Korda's film into a disjunctive expression of "the transcultural, migrant experience"[29] while simultaneously acknowledging its ambivalent ties to the hegemonic and creating a shared time between then and now. The transformative and decolonizing act is also enabled by the translation from image into word, which produces difference but also a temporal and epistemic unfinishedness as it challenges readers "to dwell on the overlapping zone between the sayable and the seeable so as to shuttle back and forth between the two."[30] The final image of Mynah's account – the bursting storm blows the screen "over the ocean like a ghost, and the images continued to be shot out, targetless, over the sea" (CT, 121) – surely symbolizes a liberating loss. And yet, the reference to the ghost, which, in Jacques Derrida's hauntology, is turned into an ethically charged figure of remembrance,[31] is a gripping reminder of the continuing presence of the imperial past and the need to remember it in creative ways. In more ways than one, Ondaatje's postcolonial re-vision entails a politics of memory, suggesting that we need to live with colonial images, acknowledge their precarious effects, and change them from within rather than simply discard them. Remembering here becomes future-oriented as it makes room for cross-cultural exchange, without glossing over the tensions that this exchange inevitably generates.

As *The Cat's Table* consistently teases out the socio-political potential of form to enable relation, the very device of ekphrasis is subjected to change. It is well known that ekphrasis, in Western literary history, is closely tied to Homer's depiction of Achilles's shield in *The Iliad*, where it is mobilized to promote imperial ideals and heroic notions of masculinity.[32] Ondaatje's *The Cat's Table* rigorously undoes ekphrasis's investment in imperial politics and renders it available for documenting histories of exchange and migratory subjectivity. As the novel fuses references to circulating images with the memories, dreams, and desires of its diasporic narrator, ekphrasis can no longer be read referentially. References compete, collide, multiply, and reroute one another. Ekphrasis, in the novel, thus produces a surplus, an excess of meaning, that, bearing witness to the irreducibility of each image and the differential potential of intermediality, attests the transformability of form, which affords liberation from the bounds of the past and initiates re-form.

THE AFFORDANCE OF THE TEXT

In *The Politics of the Aesthetic*, Jacques Rancière stresses that works of art are susceptible to political appropriation, which aims at negating aesthetic polyvalency and at actualizing a stable interpretation:

> The politics of works of art ... plays itself out in the way in
> which new modes of narration or new forms of visibility
> established by artistic practices enter into politics' own field of
> aesthetic possibilities. It is necessary to reverse the way in which
> the problem is generally formulated. It is up to the various
> forms of politics to appropriate, for their own proper use, the
> modes of presentation of the means of establishing explanatory
> sequences produced by artistic practices rather than the other
> way around.[33]

What follows for Rancière from such potentially one-sided, politically motivated interpretations is the necessity of an open-ended process of renegotiation that restores plurality. It is one of the major achievements of Ondaatje's intermedial aesthetics to engage in such processes of renegotiation to reveal how meaning and the kind of visibility that supports it are created and to establish, in the realm of fiction, a site in which multiple meanings can co-exist.

In a chapter, tellingly entitled "Miss Lasqueti: A Second Portrait," Ondaatje delivers several extended ekphrases, which, in different

Intermedial Aesthetics in *The Cat's Table*

though interrelated ways, explore the connection between visuality, power, and gender. Here, the narrator recounts how, years after his passage on the *Oronsay*, he has received a package in the mail from Perinetta Lasqueti. The package contains photocopied drawings of several passengers as well as a letter addressed to Michael's cousin Emily, which the narrator-protagonist unscrupulously opens. Jointly, the chapter, the letter, and the mentioned drawings produce one of the novel's many *mise en abyme* configurations, in which frames multiply to create complex resonances between seemingly unrelated incidents. The letter takes us to the Tuscan villa Ortensia, located near Florence, where Miss Lasqueti, in her twenties, worked for Horace Johnson, an American collector of paintings, tapestries, and sculptures, with whom she eventually begins a love affair. Their love affair is all about the eroticism of seeing; it is sparked by acts of masquerade, portraiture, and the joint tracing of a drawing's lines. At the heart of Perinetta's symbolically charged account is a tapestry, *Verdura with Dog*, produced in Flanders around 1530, which shows "the dangerous and blissful powers of love – depicted usually by hunting scenes" (CT, 301), a description that foreshadows Perinetta's sorry fate. Rather than provide detailed information about the specific artworks, Ondaatje's ekphrasis is committed to exploring the effects and affects they may elicit in the here and now: how they move, fascinate, and establish relations. Horace's seven-year-old son Clive is viscerally drawn to the tapestry, and one day Perinetta observes how the child brushes "very tenderly the coat of the hound" (CT, 300), obviously trying to compensate for his loneliness. She is moved by this act of tender, haptic looking, which confuses the real and the imaginary: "The boy saw a dog he did not have" (CT, 301). But as she shares the incident with Horace, he shows little understanding for his son's all too sensual reaction, which fails to maintain the distance between the seer and seen that he considers central to achieving true vision. For him, "the truth, depth" of the "sentimental tableau" (CT, 303) lies in its relation to power, ownership, and status. Horace even punishes his son for seeing something that he doesn't, and as Perinetta, confronting her lover with his betrayal, tries to hurt him with a pair of scissors, he "divert[s] the act of anger" (CT, 313) and stabs the scissors into the side of her belly. The claim that looking activates "violence," "ambition," and "power"[34] here loses its metaphorical dimension. Perinetta's scar indeed shows that, as Steven Connor phrases it in

The Book of Skin, "something real ... has taken place,"[35] stressing that seeing unfolds worldly potential that renders subjects vulnerable to others.

It is worth noting that the differences in Clive's and Horace's visions roughly coincide with the distinction that Laura Marks draws between so-called optical and haptic visuality.[36] Whereas in optical visuality, "the relationship between viewer and image ... tends to be that of mastery," haptic visuality blurs the boundaries between seer and seen to give rise to an affective relationship: "Haptic visuality implies making oneself vulnerable to the image, reversing the relationship of mastery that characterizes optical viewing."[37] In haptic visuality, viewers succumb to the affective potential of images; they give up their distance and embrace their disturbing, non-signifying potential of images to make room for novel entanglements. However, Ondaatje's novel is not interested in perpetuating facile dualisms. The point of the extended ekphrasis is not to dismiss, in any straightforward manner, Horace's vision – as power-obsessed as it may be. After all, he is the one who invites us to consider whether "[o]ne hundred women with their cold and chapped hands" or a single "man who conceived the scene" (CT, 303) should be credited with the tapestry's making. Modes of production are never external, secondary factors but formative forces that shape the ways in which visual arts can be conceived in the first place. The critical intervention that *The Cat's Table* makes is directed toward the singular, authoritarian, and appropriative interpretation, the reification of meaning, that Horace seeks to promote. But the meaning of a work of art is never stable. Rather, meaning is, as Norman Bryson suggests, "an action carried out by an *I* in relation to what the work takes as *you.*"[38] In other words, it emerges from an eventful relation between the image and the viewer. Ultimately, Horace's outburst aims to cancel out the disturbing subjectivity of another viewer, who threatens to reveal the unbearable contingency and partiality of his own point of view. It is a significant accomplishment of *The Cat's Table* that, by means of its intermedial aesthetics, it provides a space in which the eventful polyvalency of the visual arts is restored and different ways of looking can coexist, even if in conflictual tension. Readers need to tolerate the ensuing frictions, that is, to grapple with the text's openness, which involves ongoing engagements with multiple points of view.

In her study *Poetics of the Iconotext,* Liliane Louvel eloquently notes that intermedial references to images may serve as the winking "eye of the text."[39] These references inscribe the image's otherness into the verbal texture and in so doing open up a space for the self-reflexive, playfully disruptive, and transgressive (CT, 46). *The Cat's Table* makes full use of intermediality's self-reflexive potential, throwing into relief some of the text's affordances as it seeks to accommodate the specific capacities of images and struggles with their disruptive effects. In many respects, the weaving of the tapestry, achieved collectively, also reflects on the structural make-up, the texture, of *The Cat's Table*. Complicating notions of singular authorship, the novel consists of a plurality of different threads, and it punctuates the narrator's memories with the voices of other characters, quotes from poems, novels, and songs, descriptions of paintings and films, as well as entries from an examination booklet so as to conflate identity and alterity, consistency and difference, singularity and plurality. Importantly, the complexly woven texture and the multiplicity of different perspectival threads leading in and through the text do not simply amount to a confirmation of the partiality of vision. Rather, they entail an ethics of openness against the temptation of self-enclosed perspectives. The intermedial structure, the non-reducible interplay between image and word, also "figures as the acceptance of the other" (CT, 187), which involves the acceptance to be challenged by different visions.

NOTES

1 Döring, *Caribbean-English Passages*, 144.
2 Bhabha, *The Location of Culture*, 227.
3 Nixon, *Slow Violence and the Environmentalism of the Poor*, 15.
4 Mirzoeff, *The Right to Look*, 24.
5 Rancière, *The Politics of Aesthetics*, 13.
6 Jacobs, "Introduction," 10.
7 Kenaan, *The Ethics of Visuality*, xix.
8 Derrida, "Violence and Metaphysics," 91.
9 Wenzel, "Planet vs. Globe," 19.
10 Said, *Culture and Imperialism*, 271.
11 Hensher, "*The Cat's Table* by Michael Ondaatje."
12 Döring, *Caribbean-English Passages*, 7.
13 Levinas, *Totality and Infinity*, 23.
14 Elkins, *The Object Stares Back*, 12, 31.

15 Mirzoeff, *The Right to Look*, 24.

16 Cf. Brittan, "Michael Ondaatje Tricks the Eye," 307.

17 Conrad, "Youth," 35.

18 Cf. Ganapthy-Doré, "A Postcolonial Passage to England: Michael Ondaatje's *The Cat's Table*," 101.

19 Butler, *Frames of War*, 1, 3.

20 Glissant, *Poetics of Relation*, 189.

21 Levinas, *Totality and Infinity*, 87.

22 Hirsch, "Marked by Memory," 88.

23 Emery, *Modernism, the Visual, and Caribbean Literature*, 18.

24 Boyd, "Snap Judgement."

25 Said, *Orientalism*, 55.

26 Dunn, "Lights ... Camera ... Africa," 166.

27 Ramaswamy, "Introduction," 2.

28 Döring, *Caribbean-English Passages*, 159.

29 Bhabha, *The Location of Culture*, 226.

30 Ramaswamy, "Maps, Mother/Goddesses, and Martyrdom in Modern India," 443.

31 Derrida, *Specters of Marx*.

32 Cf. Quint, *Epic and Empire*; Neumann and Rippl, *Verbal-Visual Configurations in Postcolonial Literature*, 200.

33 Rancière, *The Politics of Aesthetics*, 65.

34 Elkins, *The Object Stares Back*, 31,

35 Connor, *The Book of Skin*, 53.

36 See also Marinkova, *Michael Ondaatje*, 9.

37 Marks, *The Skin of the Film*, 185.

38 Bryson, "Introduction," 5.

39 Louvel, *Poetics of the Iconotext*, 60.

Novels and Narratives

11

Fascination and Liminality in Michael Ondaatje's *Coming Through Slaughter*

Winfried Siemerling

Michael Ondaatje's work often derives generative impulses from the crossing of boundaries, the "in-between," and the transfiguration of elements that are taken to the limit of their identity or recontextualized. Quite in keeping with this sense of exploratory transformation, his early long poem, *the man with seven toes*, turned also into a stage version (by Toronto's Theatre Passe Muraille), as did those two transgeneric collages in which Ondaatje delved into his own fascination with two American legends: *The Collected Works of Billy the Kid* (1970) and *Coming Through Slaughter* (1976), an evocation of the New Orleans (pre-record era) jazz musician Buddy Bolden. In both texts, Ondaatje also experiments with the encounter between two other usually generically constitutive elements, prose and verse, and the interaction between texts and visual elements such as frames and photographs.[1] Photography in particular is used here to investigate the relationship between a transfixing perception and the movement of the object; it also becomes the metaphorical vehicle for probing the liminal area "in-between" where the perceiving, narrating self meets the figure of the historical other who emerges in the text. The empty frame at the beginning of *The Collected Works of Billy the Kid* is repeated at the end and contains there, in a bottom corner, the small photograph of a child in cowboy outfit, identified by Ondaatje as a portrait of himself.[2] The two superimposed frames relate the lawless outsider to the fascinated artist, two realms of boundary transgression communicating like the poles of a large-scale metaphor. Yet together with historical otherness and the fascinated self, the very praxis of writing that perceives and co-constitutes history, the self, and the other is under scrutiny throughout *The Collected Works of Billy the Kid* and *Coming Through Slaughter*.

I still find useful a critical term that was offered by Linda Hutcheon a few years after the publication of these works. Her coinage "historiographic metafiction" describes highly self-conscious works that reflect on the writing of history and rely on historical intertexts.[3] The self-reflexivity of metafiction abounds with metaphorical equivalences for writing (such as photography or music) and with instances of *mise en abyme*, but what appears often as a formal play of the signifier opens upon what Edward Said has called the "worldly" – without forgetting the specificity of its own discursivity and materiality as writing. Ondaatje often alerts readers to the malleability of historical dates and events in his fiction.[4] This kind of historiographic metafiction, however, may very well ask some of the most pertinent questions with respect to history – for instance, how, and why, historical figures and events become relevant to us, and what we consequently make of them. Instead of historical veracity, in the following discussion of *Coming Through Slaughter* I will therefore focus on the forces of fascination and liminality in the encounter between self and (historical) other that is generative of both *The Collected Works of Billy the Kid* (which will serve as a reference point) and *Coming Through Slaughter*, two texts that negotiate, self-reflexively and often simultaneously, fascination and horror.

The Collected Works of Billy the Kid opens with a comment from the western photographer L.A. Huffman concerning a photograph he has taken of Billy. Huffman stresses his ability to ban moving objects on the plate. But while photography is commonly associated with representational wealth and detail, Ondaatje prefaces this remark with an absolutely empty frame. This void initiates a twofold discourse of the unknown that will pose questions not only about Billy the Kid but also about the process in which the "picture" of Billy will develop out of the white paper and, finally, about the evocative power his legend holds for a poetic imagination. Why is it that this imagination is attracted by a figure outside accepted norms and reason, by a legend full of blood and violence but also of precision and minute calculation of incident and movement? Fascinated consciousness enters a

Fascination and Liminality in *Coming Through Slaughter*   249

liminal state of simultaneous discoveries of self and other: "Here then is a maze to begin, be in" (CW, 20).

Similarly, *Coming Through Slaughter* begins with a silent, word-less frame, albeit containing the only known picture of Bolden and his band. Tellingly, however, Ondaatje has chosen a musician who never was recorded (although rumours of a lost Edison cylinder with his music persist). This factual silence, the gap, the absence, rather than the illusion of presence evoked by representation, is what Susan Sontag drew our attention to when she spoke of a photograph as "both a pseudo-presence and a token of absence." For her, photography was an "elegiac art."[5]

But is it? Walter Benjamin discovered in the photographed "human countenance" also the remnants of what he called the "aura."[6] Rather than an elegiac pastness, the aura of an object meant for him the experienced presence of a distance, "the unique phenomenon of a distance, however close it may be."[7] The phenomenological space-time of the aura suggests here the (often brief) experienced presence of a distant otherness through contemplation. Considering the aura as part of the cult value of a piece of art, however, Benjamin further insists that this otherness remains autonomous, while drawing the observing self outside of itself: "Unapproachability is indeed a major quality of the cult image. True to its nature, it remains 'distant, however close it may be.'"[8]

Such a quality seems to sustain the fascination so powerfully mediated by the only extant picture of Bolden in *Coming Through Slaughter*. If the threshold of otherness is crossed, the spell of fascination is broken. The Latin *fascinare*, as well as the Greek *baskainein* it derives from, designate the casting of a spell, the act of bewitching. And such a spell makes the narrator's senses stop at Bolden's picture and story, with both fascination and the recognition of significance. While for Benjamin the aura "withers in the age of mechanical reproduction," he suggests it is still emanating from faces in old portrait photographs.[9] And while Bolden's picture is mechanically (re)produced, its auratic fascination is increased by the fact that no other likeness exists of the musician.

Coming Through Slaughter is steeped in the aura's dialectic of proximity and distance signalled by Bolden's photograph. The picture challenges our senses and – the more we learn about it – our understanding. All opposites seem to coalesce. The outlines of the black musicians with their white shirts blend, particularly around Bolden, into the lighter background. The formal, static posture of the band belies the kinetic and sonic connotations that come with jazz. Like most pictures of musicians, the photograph evokes synesthetic expectations of sound – but remains silent. Not only are the book's metaphorical repertoires of jazz and photography prefaced here. Ondaatje's text also reveals the fascinating power that appears in the aura of the self-destructive artist Bolden, which threatens to pull the narrating consciousness, as it were, through the picture frame into its self-destructive ban. And with the narrator, we as readers become implicated in the question of the observer's position with respect to Bolden's world. The closer we let the picture and its stories come to us, the less certain becomes our own distanced observer status.

Let me offer a somewhat technical preface to this aspect. In a curious episode, a certain Antrim has a debate with a doctor over his right or left arm (CS, 142). Using here Billy the Kid's lesser-known historical name, Ondaatje obliquely references the motive of inverted photographs in *The Collected Works of Billy the Kid*. The picture of Bolden's band is similarly caught up in a historical debate concerning its possible physical reversal. It should have been easy, one might think, to determine whether the musicians of Bolden's band were left- or right-handed – at least in the thirties when one of Ondaatje's acknowledged sources, *Jazzmen*, was written or even in the forties and fifties when jazz research blossomed. But in his book on Bolden, Donald Marquis, who was able to ascertain the right-handedness of the bass player Johnson and of the guitarist Mumford,[10] leaves the question finally undecided and offers two photographs (a solution adopted as well, incidentally, in the New Orleans Museum of Jazz). Stephen Scobie, who alerts us to this discussion, reminds us also of the parallel with the "left handed poems" (subtitle) of *The Collected Works of Billy the Kid*: "Considering the fact that the legend of Billy the Kid's left-handedness originates with a reversed photograph, and that the original cover of *The Collected Works of Billy the Kid* featured a reverse image,[11] it would indeed be intriguing to think that Bolden also comes to us in a reversed negative."[12]

This question of certainty alerts us to the materiality of the signs conveying the Kid and Bolden, but it also concerns our own position: if the picture is reversed, we would find ourselves *behind* the correct version, as if we had stepped through a transparent negative, a permeable frame, or a window. Whether Ondaatje was aware of the ongoing debate about the picture or not (Marquis's book appeared after *Coming Through Slaughter*), the reversed finger positions of the clarinetists (on which the debate hinges) are there to puzzle, at least subliminally, any jazz-buff's eye (such as Ondaatje's). These reflections on the depth, the space, and the fascinating pull of the picture of Bolden's band take on particular weight when we begin to look at how the picture is thematized in the text.

* * *

Coming Through Slaughter leads us from a distanced, elegiac vision to a total identification with Bolden and from there to a further point that cannot be grasped necessarily as a dialectical sublation of the previous two perspectives. "His geography," the main text begins: "Float by in a car today and see the corner shops."

Readable both as elision of a speaking "I" and address to the reader, the sentence's ambivalence implicates us in an exploration that begins with absence. More precisely, we are invited to look at history as palimpsest: "The signs of their owners obliterated by brand names. Tassins's Food Store which he lived opposite for a time surrounded by DRINK COCA COLA IN BOTTLES, BARG'S, or LAURA LEE'S TAVERN, the signs speckled in the sun, TOM MOORE, YELLOWSTONE, JAX, COCA COLA, COCA COLA, primary yellows and reds muted now against the white horizontal sheet wood walls" (CS, 8).[13] Historical distance, however, vanishes as layers of Bolden's life surface in the course of Ondaatje's writing. At one extreme of this trajectory, the narrating consciousness experiences a moment of specular identity with Bolden. Bolden's breakdown in the middle of a parade in 1907 (after which he disappears into silence, consigned to an asylum until his death in 1931) occurs in the text at a moment when he pushes his art to a self-destructive extreme. The narrating imagination breaches the otherness of the other at this moment, which appears as . the culmination of an ineluctable fascination. Isolated on the bottom of that page, we read three words: "What I wanted" (CS, 131). This sentence fragment can be attributed to either the musician collapsing at the extreme limit of his art or a narrator who has come, with his imagined other, through this limit of consciousness at a moment of total identification. When we turn the page, however, we find only a cursory list of events in Bolden's life that partially resembles a hospital chart. A certain horror comes to the fore. The imagination seems to step back from the mirroring surface of the other, regaining a distance that had disappeared in a liminal identity. The clinically detached itemization of Bolden's life – which becomes the distanced account of the historical object Bolden – contrasts sharply with the prior moment of total identification.

The narrator now reasserts the complete absence of Bolden and his music. Instead, there is another sound: the click of the narrator's camera in the silence of the places where Bolden once lived (CS, 133). The sound evokes the enigmatic echolocation clicks of the dolphin sound sonographs that epigrammatically preface the text. Dolphins, we learn, use echolocation clicks for orientation. The relational aspect adumbrated metaphorically here is made much more explicit a few lines later; elegiac past and auratic present, but also the beginning of horror, coalesce when the disjunction of historical distance turns into the identity of coevals: "When he went mad he was the same age as I am now" (CS, 133). We are then offered two defining moments of the narrator's trajectory to the moment we have just witnessed. The moment of identity and recognition is summarized first when the photograph of the erstwhile distant other suddenly loses its fascinating aura and shockingly reflects a liminal self: "The photograph moves and becomes a mirror. When I read he stood in front of mirrors and attacked himself, there was a shock of memory. For I had done that. Stood, and with a razor-blade cut into cheeks and forehead, shaved hair. Defiling people we did not wish to be" (CS, 133). A moment later, we learn of the beginning of the narrator's fascination:

The thin sheaf of information. Why did my senses stop at you? There was the sentence "Buddy Bolden who became a legend when he went berserk in a parade ..." What was there in that, before I knew your nation your colour your age, that made me push my arm forward and spill through the front of your mirror and clutch myself? Did not want to pose in your accent but think in your brain and body, and you like a weatherbird arcing around in the middle of your life to exact opposites and burning your brains out. (CS, 134)

The narrator, of course, has just performed a similar movement, although in the opposite direction. After an intense fictional identification with a musician whose music is compared here with open-ended stories and thus appears as *mise en abyme* of the text we read, this narrator seems to arc away and withdraw into the safety of historical objectivity.

The text attributes Bolden's portrait to the photographer Bellocq, whose pictures of New Orleans sex workers one can see, for instance, in Al Rose's book on Storyville, the New Orleans red light district where Bolden used to play. Ondaatje also constructs a fictional friendship between Bolden and Bellocq, together with Bellocq's eventual suicide. When Bolden, who is seduced by the very silence and "black empty spaces" (CS, 91) in Bellocq's pictures that we ourselves encounter in the photograph, finally returns to New Orleans after his first disappearance, his wife Nora Bass puts part of the blame on the photographer: "Look at what he did to you" (CS, 127). The nameless narrator, more carefully balancing the give and take in the friendship between the musician and the photographer, nonetheless also attributes a decisive influence to Bellocq: "He had pushed his imagination into Buddy's brain ... They had talked for hours moving gradually off the edge of the social world" (CS, 64).

When Bellocq commits suicide by setting fire to his place, the walls he expects to hold him have gone up in flames. Bolden notes a similar disappearance of boundaries and surfaces in his pictures: "He was a photographer. Pictures. That were like ... windows ... We were furnished rooms and Bellocq was a window looking out" (CS, 59; first ellipsis in the original). In their unlikely friendship, Bellocq offers Bolden a space behind the mirror image of his musician's persona, just as his pictures are said to give the observer an opening to leave one's own furnished room behind. Attributing the picture of Bolden's band to this photographer, the text warns us as well that here is another potentially dangerous window, a fascinating surface that may, however, open toward an unexpected depth and induce a fall.

Windows, surfaces, and boundaries are usually not only approached but also breached in the text. The static surfaces of pictures open, windows and mirrors break, skin is cut, people and animals disappear below or emerge from water surfaces. When Bolden fights with his narcissistic other, Pickett, mirrors are broken and produce sharp weapons to cut the skin of the other, until the mirroring figures' struggle has them breaking through the barbershop front window to end up on tellingly named Liberty Street. Bellocq, on the other hand, finds death on the other side of the boundaries of his room.

What, then, happens to the narrating imagination that approaches the surface of Bolden's photograph, attracted by the fascination of its aura? The photograph first surfaces in the text itself during the detective Webb's search for his disappeared friend Bolden. Webb offers a parodic *mise en abyme* of the narrative quest in *Coming Through Slaughter*. Exemplifying the detective's search for control over the unknown, his character embodies (and self-critically questions) the narrative project to "cover" Bolden's disappearance.[14] The structural element of his search superimposes a semblance of linearity and novelistic causality on Ondaatje's album of silent-speaking sonographs. Yet with the image of the spider web evoked by the detective's name (as well as in Ondaatje's autotelic poem "Spider Blues"), he also likens the lines and network of his own writing to a deadly trap. "You're a cop Webb" (CS, 19), Nora Bass scolds the searcher in pursuit of Bolden. The aural ambiguity (cop Webb/cobweb [of writing]) points us to Ondaatje's own language, which, like the narrated searcher Webb, threatens to police, contain, and kill the fascinating other, Bolden.

Coming Through Slaughter, however, shows Bolden escaping containment time and again. Writing appears metafictionally as a tracing Webb/web that is motivated but ultimately also eluded by Bolden. One of Webb's first moves to "get a hold" of Bolden is his visit to the photographer Bellocq. In Ondaatje's passage, we witness a literal "re-production" of the musician. The enigmatic aura of the picture floats toward the detective (and us) from out of Bellocq's acid tray. The emergence of the photograph, however, signals remoteness in reality, all the more auratic because of a smile that seems directed at Webb personally:

Ten minutes later he bent over the sink with Bellocq, watching the paper weave in the acid tray. As if the search for his friend was finally ending ... The two of them watching the pink rectangle as it slowly began to grow black shapes, coming fast now. The sudden vertical lines which rose out of the pregnant white paper which were the outlines of the six men and their formally held instruments. The dark clothes coming first, leaving the space that was the shirt. Then the faces ... All serious except for the smile on Bolden. Watching their friend float into the page smiling at them, the friend who in reality had reversed the process and gone back into white, who in this bad film seemed to have already half-receded with that smile which may not have been a smile at all, which may have been his mad dignity. (CS, 52–3)

Like letters and words in the process of writing, the "sudden vertical lines" create figures on the page. Bolden's enigmatic smile, however, eludes the treacherous sense of grasped identity that the emerging black shapes (and Ondaatje's own writing) seem to promise. Webb, bent over the surface to which the image of his other rises "[a]s if" his quest is completed, seems to understand the inverted process by which the medium of acid dissolves as much of the plate as it leaves in order to create the illusion of presence.

Bolden himself has "reversed the process and gone back into white" – a reference to the inverse vectors of writing and historical reality. Bolden, however, will initially not only elude Webb but inversely hold great power over him. Webb seems to succeed when he finds Bolden outside of New Orleans and induces him to return to the surface of his public life. Already in this scene, however, the searching Webb, at the very moment of his seeming triumph, gazes at a bathwater surface where Bolden literally inverts the surfacing movement of his image in the acid tray: "Till Bolden went underwater away from the noise, opening his eyes to look up through the liquid blur at the vague figure of Webb gazing down at him gesturing, till he could hardly breathe, his heart furious wanting to leap out and Bolden still holding himself down not wishing to come up" (CS, 83). While Bolden in this instance does return to the surface, he finally eludes Webb and the pressures of fame and his own image after his final parade.

When Bolden disappears into silence, his photograph turns, as we have seen, into a mirror for the nameless "I" narrating this phenomenological journey. Seeing his own face in the picture of the other, this narrator seems to have gone into the picture, through the surface into the world of the other. Is this moment, then, a total identification with the extreme artist Bolden? Or, inversely, a recognition that would make it possible to let go of the fascination and resist a temptation that is ultimately self-destructive? If we imagine that the picture *was* reversed from the beginning, this otherness – seemingly outside – would have been, in fact, an interior self coming to the surface – an other self appearing from the room behind and inside the mirror. Both pictures, it seems, are possible.

* * *

At this point, more than twenty pages before the end, the text offers a strange sense of completion; the remainder of the text seems anticlimactic. This impression is furthered by the silent serenity of Ondaatje's Bolden in some of the final prose passages as he suffers insanity in the midst of the violence of the asylum. Interpretations have differed. Is it, as Sam Solecki has suggested, that the extremist artist Bolden "has found the peace he never possessed or could possess when sane"?[15] And that *Coming Through Slaughter* critiques a modern view of art that enshrines the suicidal madness of the artist as authentication of the sincerity of their enterprise?[16] In that case, the author Ondaatje distances that haunting demand through Bolden's image: "If Bolden's final commitment is to chaos, madness, and silence, Ondaatje's is to a controlled art that tries to understand Bolden's case – his own case – to make its contradictions intelligible without succumbing to them."[17] I will argue, however, that Ondaatje's text takes us to the very limit of control, alluding to its other side without ultimately excluding it. In its fascination with Bolden, the "ending" of *Coming Through Slaughter* comes indeed undecidedly close to the possibility of "chaos, madness, and [particularly] silence."

Readings that exteriorize the other and are "concerned with splitting off the self destructive Buddy Bolden from Ondaatje as articulate survivor"[18] have also been critiqued by Constance Rooke. "Imaginatively," she claims, "Ondaatje goes with Bolden all the way."[19] I agree, yet the question remains: Where does Bolden go, taking this imagination all the way? The text insists that Bolden has "gone back into white" (CS, 53). Rooke suggests a perfect grey: "in Bolden's final room, a scene only of apparent misery, grey becomes the colour of a perfect blend."[20] Similarly, she sees Bolden's music progress toward "the transcendence of the last parade (a perfect blend of self and other)" and considers his end triumphant; he finds "an all-inclusive other and so can destroy one version of the self to make another."[21]

Fascination and Liminality in *Coming Through Slaughter*   257

I would like to suggest that *Coming Through Slaughter* has several endings, endings that I find very hard to reconcile and that perhaps should not be reconciled. These endings "contain" Bolden as much as they may try to spew him back out into history. The "struggle for life" between "author and hero," of which Bakhtin speaks in his essay of that title, can be seen, in this perspective, to continue through the finishing line. Only the imagination of the final prose passages concerning Bolden's life in the asylum is marked by a peace that Rooke constructs as dialectical sublation. Even in these passages (that alternate with others in quite different moods), it is questionable if Bolden's serene withdrawal has really *encompassed* his earlier versions in an integrating movement toward completion – or closed them out. The collage of different text forms at the end retains the ideal of Bolden's music *before* "coming through Slaughter" (which, incidentally, turns out to be a village between New Orleans and the asylum). Like Galloway's guitar, which Bolden is shown to admire, the last pages could be said to have "swallowed moods *and* kept three or four going at the same time" (CS, 95; emphasis added). But the problem is whether one can swallow both the fascination and the horror that come with Bolden's fate. As in Ondaatje's earlier title, *Rat Jelly* (1973), there remains a certain violent indecision in that respect. The same paragraph in which we hear of Bolden being raped in the asylum speaks of his silence and the pain in his throat and yet entangles these moments in an entirely opposite mood. The possibility of vomiting, which Kristeva mentions in *The Powers of Horror* as a physical way of ejecting what is not wanted from the boundaries of the self, appears in the guise of a (seemingly) funny story: "Boot in my throat, the food has to climb over it and then go down and meet with all their pals in the stomach. Hi sausage. Hi cabbage. Did yuh see that ... boot. Yeah I nearly turned round'n went back on the plate. Who is this guy we're in anyway?" (CS, 139). The reader who can keep the whole paragraph down, including the rape at the beginning, cannot quite get rid of the horror that has been swallowed with it.

The Bolden of the text, in all his serenity, flexes his muscle, warning us that he is larger than any effort to comprehend and swallow him: "Laughing in my room. As you try to explain me I will spit you, yellow, out of my mouth" (CS, 140). We are not forced to believe his claim. The text itself, however, continues to pursue the question of control in the relationship between language and its object, Bolden, whom the text searches in need and fascination and seeks to distance in horror. Bolden's former colleague Cornish, for instance, would rather avoid the subject. Only in Bolden's safe absence, "when they began to realize that he would never come out then all the people he hardly knew, all the fools, [were] beginning to talk about him" (CS, 145). Bolden haunts Ondaatje's writing itself in this incriminating voice that it produces as fictive "transcription"; more dramatically and intriguingly, however, Ondaatje's metafictional searcher character Webb now seeks, without success, to vomit the very story he has helped to create by bringing Bolden back to New Orleans. The horror of Bolden's reality (or the reality of his horror) overwhelms Webb when he hears: "But he's not dead" (CS, 149). Webb cannot escape the knowledge conveyed by Bella Davenport's words, who "talked on not knowing he had brought Buddy home." Recognizing his role in Bolden's confinement, Webb is caught in a space he has created with his own words: "While he arched away ... his unknown flesh had taken over, and crashed fast down the stairs" (CS, 150). But he has swallowed the story that refuses to leave him: "I gotta throw up 'scuse me 'scuse me, but knowing there was nothing to come up at all." The "ugly" side of Bolden's story does not grant Webb the power to close or eject and exteriorize it, although part of it has breached his skin, the "sweat [that] had in those few minutes gone *through* his skin his shirt his java jacket and driven itself into the wall" (CS, 151; emphasis added).

As the stories about Bolden, with their haunting power of a ghost (in French, a *revenant*: one who returns), refuse to leave Webb and us in a "clean" ending we, like Ondaatje, are left with "stories to finish" (CS, 17). Instead, we are offered more stories and more choices, metafictionally primed by an earlier Bolden who muses about beginnings, endings, and control in the music of one of his contemporaries. While Robichaux "put his emotions into patterns which a listening crowd had to follow" (CS, 93), Bolden prefers motion without a teleological pattern of ending. "At each intersection people would hear just the fragment I happened to be playing and it would fade as I went further down Canal. They would not be there to hear the end of phrases, Robichaux's arches" (CS, 94). This sense of a fragmentary openness pertains also, I think, to *Coming Through Slaughter* itself. Ironically, Bolden's thoughts appear in an epistolary diary that is addressed to Webb, that searching figure that has moved very much like Ondaatje's writing toward Bolden. Webb

Fascination and Liminality in *Coming Through Slaughter* 259

himself had "circled ... taking his time ... entering the character of Bolden through every voice he spoke to." But these voices offer "stories [that] were like spokes on a rimless wheel ending in air. Buddy had lived a different life with every one of them" (CS, 63). The final passages of *Coming Through Slaughter* similarly continue to combine relatedness with an independence that points outward. Ondaatje expresses this open-endedness through Bolden's attitude toward audiences: "I wanted them to be able to come in where they pleased and leave when they pleased and somehow hear the germs of the start and all the possible endings at whatever point in the music I had reached then" (CS, 94).

Like the text's Webb/web, the reader has both found Bolden and been left behind with voices that offer different possible stories with their moods, beginnings, and endings but that do not add up to one single trajectory or a moral – be it one of debauched genius, of imagined serenity in madness, or of a successful distancing of self-destructive drives. To the very end, *Coming Through Slaughter* lets us listen to these voices it has encountered in its temptation by, its quest for, and its horror of the other. If there is any perfection in the very last fragment (before the credits and acknowledgments), it lies in the sense of incompleteness we are offered.

"I sit with this room. With the grey walls that darken into corner. And one window with teeth in it. Sit so still you can hear your hair rustle in your shirt. Look away from the window when clouds and other things go by. Thirty-one years old. There are no prizes" (CS, 156). Like Bolden's music, this passage shows us "all the possibilities in the middle of the story" (CS, 43) of the "discovery *self* makes of the *other*"[22] in *Coming Through Slaughter*. Nothing has been conquered. The very last words deny the *telos* of the quest. And we do not know who the speaker is. The age that indicates a point in a life's story is not attributed to either the narrating subject or the narrated object. This balance lingers hauntingly in the light of the earlier passage that equates the altered age of Bolden at the time of his breakdown both with the age of the narrator and with that of Michael Ondaatje two years before the publication of *Coming Through Slaughter* (CS, 133).[23] At this age, the Bolden addressed by the narrator is "like a weatherbird arcing round in the middle of your life" (CS, 134). This middle is not inherently different from the "right ending" suggested earlier, which "is an open door you can't see too far out of. It can mean exactly the opposite of what you are thinking" (CS, 94). The speaking "I" in this final passage remains similarly undecided between a mirrored identity of the self and a distanced outlook on the other.

The "I" neither has left this choice behind nor encompasses it. The "I" sits neither inside nor outside but *with* "this room"; it also sits with the grey walls that "darken into corner," undecidedly in the middle of encountering their limit. Most importantly, the "I" coexists with "one window with teeth in it" – a single opening that has, however, several possible associations at this point. The teeth imply a threat of cutting and swallowing and refer us to the literal imagination of Bolden's madness.

While the threatening element of the teeth would evoke Bolden's memory of having gone through the breaking window in his fight with Picket, we are also left with its aspect from the inside. The threat here simultaneously evokes the precise limit Bolden has approached earlier without getting cut when his hand inadvertently smashes a window:

> Furious at something he drew his right hand across his body and lashed out. Half way there at full speed he realized it was a window he would be hitting and braked. For a fraction of a second his open palm touched the glass, beginning simultaneously to draw back. The window starred and crumpled slowly two floors down. His hand miraculously uncut. It had acted exactly like a whip violating the target and still free, retreating from the outline of a star ... Surprised he examined his fingers. (CS, 16)

From this perspective, one possible reading of the final passage could see a writing hand withdraw from "the outline of a star" – from the star Bolden who, in Webb's mind, is "just an outline and music ... Something sharp" (CS, 51). In this case, the mirroring image has "starred and crumpled slowly," leaving the "I" to examine his writing fingers and his "hand miraculously uncut" by the threat of a suicidal imagination.

But this imagination, which could be attributed to Bolden or to the writing "I," has a keen sense of the independence of such a performance with respect to conscious control. When Bolden watches a woman cutting carrots, "the fingers have separated themselves from her body and move in a unity of their own that stops at the sleeve and bangle. As with all skills he watches for it to fail. If she

Fascination and Liminality in *Coming Through Slaughter*   261

thinks what she is doing she will lose control" (CS, 31). A minimal move of the hand can invert regularity and control. In the liminal space of the last paragraph, a similar minute shift in our perception, or of writing and the very syntax of a sentence, can make us perceive either an ending or a new, resurgent beginning: "Sit so still you can hear your hair rustle in your shirt." If we hear the "I" that the sentence omits, we hear factuality, silence, and maybe the sense of an ending. But the sentence without the "I," including us with a surprising, generalized "you," can also be read as being on the very limit of control. It depends on the linearity of our reading, on the unhesitating smoothness of its segmenting movement, to avoid "the same stress as with stars / the one altered move that will make them maniac" (CW, 41). Here, at the end of *Coming Through Slaughter*, the warning command to "Sit so still" cautions the mind not to react to the sound that may be synesthetically perceived in the sonograph of the star – in the trace and record of a breaking window (still "with teeth in it") that is itself silent like the photograph of the star Bolden and his band at the beginning. A photograph, we have been told, like a window, which has exerted an irresistible pull on the narrator's imagination. At the end, the fascination of that window and its star seems as powerful as ever.

NOTES

1 An earlier version of this essay was first published as "Fascination and Liminality in Michael Ondaatje's *Coming Through Slaughter*," *Over Here* (UK), 13, no. 2 (1993): 82–97. While these elements belong to a more general postmodern repertoire, one of the more specific explorations in this regard can be gleaned from Ondaatje's study of related elements in his *Leonard Cohen* (1970), published in the same year as *The Collected Works of Billy the Kid*.

2 Quoted in Mundwiler, *Michael Ondaatje*, 12.

3 See Hutcheon, "Canadian Historiographic Metafiction," 105–23; and "History and/as Intertext."

4 Such remarks can be found in the credits or acknowledgments sections of *The Collected Works of Billy the Kid*, *Coming Through Slaughter*, or *Running in the Family*, at the beginning of *In the Skin of a Lion*, or again in his Booker Prize–winning *The English Patient*. See, for instance, Heble, "Michael Ondaatje and the Problem of History."

5 Sontag, *On Photography*, 16, 15.
6 Benjamin, "The Work of Art in the Age of Mechanical Reproduction," 225–6.
7 Ibid., 222.
8 Ibid., 243, n. 5.
9 Ibid., 221.
10 Marquis, *In Search of Buddy Bolden*, 77.
11 The negative on the back cover was replaced, in subsequent printings, by reviewers' and critics' comments and by a picture of the author.
12 Scobie, "*Coming Through Slaughter*," 21, n. 2.
13 For a reading of these brand name references and of his geography as a signifier of race in the text, see Pennee, "'Something Invisible Finding a Form,'" 157–76; on the latter topic, see also Deshaye, "Parading the Underworld of New Orleans in Ondaatje's *Coming Through Slaughter*," 473–94, and "Racialized Rooms and Technologies of Stardom in Ondaatje's *Coming Through Slaughter*," 448–62.
14 Another sly reference here is Jack Webb's show *Dragnet*, which ran on NBC Radio from 1949 to 1957 and was an NBC television series from 1952 to 1959.
15 Solecki, "Making and Destroying," 263.
16 Ibid., 247.
17 Ibid., 264.
18 Ibid., 268.
19 Rooke, "Dog in a Grey Room," 269.
20 Ibid., 278.
21 Ibid., 279.
22 Todorov, *The Conquest of America*, 3.
23 Ondaatje was born in 1943 and worked several years on *Coming Through Slaughter* prior to its publication in 1976. The chart "Charles 'Buddy' Bolden" on page 132 of *Coming Through Slaughter* begins with the entry "Born 1876?," which makes Bolden thirty-one at the moment of his breakdown in 1907. The cataloguing data of the Anansi edition, however, lists Bolden as "ca. 1868–1931," an entry nicely followed by "– Fiction." Marquis dedicates his *In Search of Buddy Bolden* "To the memory of Charles 'Buddy' Bolden, September 6, 1877–November 4, 1931, who would probably wonder what all the fuss was about."

12

"The animal out of the desert":
The Nomadic Metaphysics of Michael Ondaatje's
In the Skin of a Lion

Jody Mason

In his poem "Loop," first published in the 1973 collection *Rat Jelly*, Michael Ondaatje demonstrates an early fascination with unfettered mobility and the untamed animal world. The speaker of "Loop" leaves behind "social animals" for a mythic dog, "transient as shit," who is "only a space filled / and blurred with passing." In "Loop," transience and velocity allow for metamorphosis, such that any particular animal is really a "nest of images" – a borderless montage that lacks individuation (*RJ*, 46). Ondaatje is clearly attracted to human mobility as well; from Buddy Bolden of *Coming Through Slaughter* to Mervyn Ondaatje's train-riding escapade in *Running in the Family*, his oeuvre is replete with elusive figures whose individual lives are difficult to apprehend. In the novels *In the Skin of a Lion* and *The English Patient*, Ondaatje's exploration of mobile figures moves toward an interest in the trope of nomadism. Linking a series of the novel's mobile figures together and suggesting their equivalence as nomadic migrants, *In the Skin of a Lion* dissolves the distinction between native and foreign workers.

Ondaatje thus attempts to resist the essentialist links between people and place that are prevalent in the kind of arborescent metaphors of belonging that poststructuralists like Gilles Deleuze and Félix Guattari critique. Instead of what Liisa Malkki calls "sedentarist metaphysics," *In the Skin of a Lion* subscribes to what Tim Cresswell refers to as "nomadic metaphysics" – an interest in the routes of travel and a concomitant dismissal of the fixity of rooted identity.[1]

Using theoretical critiques of both discourses of mobility and the trope of the nomad, I argue that Ondaatje's strategy of "nomadic metaphysics" obscures the material history of, and therefore important differences among, specific migrations, routes of travel, and/or patterns of mobility that his novel identifies. While I will complicate Ondaatje's romanticization of undifferentiated roving figures, I will first explore how the migrant figure in *In the Skin of a Lion* attempts to frustrate the power of controlling structures to monitor and restrict human mobility.

MIGRANT ROUTES

In conflating a series of migrant figures, *In the Skin of a Lion* emphasizes the apparent power of the migrant to move through what Deleuze and Guattari characterize as "espace lisse" – the smooth space – that is irreducible to and outside the mastery of the bourgeois state.[2] The figure of the migrant in the novel thus becomes a trope for that which lies outside official history, literary realism, state knowledge, the boundaries of the nation, and the control of capital.

Using migrant figures who are variously historical and fictional, *In the Skin of a Lion* explores narrative realism and the realist impulses of modern documentary art as controlling and limiting structures. Linda Hutcheon's well-known term "historiographic metafiction" (elaborated in *The Canadian Postmodern*) encapsulates the novel's ambivalent relationship to narrative realism. Hutcheon's theorization of the "ex-centric" figures of historiographic metafiction, for example, usefully points to the ways in which such figures emphasize the narrative qualities of historical "fact" and the simultaneous, if somewhat contradictory, need for a rewriting of historical narratives that erase marginal experiences. Indeed, *In the Skin of a Lion* demonstrates an interest in the migrant as a marginal figure who appears in a multitude of ever-changing factual and fictional guises. The novel does not give the reader the information with which to discern between factual and fictional figures, and some figures are a combination of both. Patrick is variously "an immigrant to the city" (SL, 53) and an incarnation of Gilgamesh who, mourning the death of his companion, Enkidu, dons the skin of a lion and wanders in the wilderness. Other important mobile figures are the sojourning Finnish bushworkers who appear in "Little Seeds" and whose

The Nomadic Metaphysics of *In the Skin of a Lion*   265

presence recurs via Cato in "Palace of Purification"; Ambrose Small, the elusive millionaire who does not wish to be found; Nicholas Temelcoff, the Macedonian immigrant who ends up running his own bakery in Toronto; and Caravaggio, the Italian-Canadian thief who cannot stay still for fear of arrest. Significantly, the migrant figures who constitute the thematic and structural centres of the novel are sometimes historical personages and sometimes not: the Finnish loggers and the politically radical Cato, Ambrose Small, and Temelcoff are all derived from textual records that Ondaatje used in the writing of the novel.[3]

If *In the Skin of a Lion* employs migrants – marginal, mobile figures – as part of its resistance to literary realism, the migrant figure also challenges homogenous national identity and the controlling boundaries of the nation-state. Using the irony of historiographic metafiction, Ondaatje asks how we know a nation's history (and, by extension, its culture and identity) and implies that the version we commonly tell ourselves is constructed from the point of view of men like the Toronto Commissioner of Public Works R.C. Harris – wealthy, powerful Anglo-Saxons. To right the historical record might be an impossible act, however, and this is an important aspect of the novel's treatment of migrant figures. Ondaatje's resistance to realism complicates the rendering visible of the historically invisible such that the reader's new knowledge of the migrant figure does not necessarily give her direct access to him. Patrick's knowledge of the Finnish loggers, for example, is mediated through an unreliable memory, the oral accounts of Cato's wife and daughter, and Cato's letters (all of which Ondaatje invents). In attempting to mentally recreate Cato's last moments through the architecture of his letters, Patrick is frustrated by the distance between them: "Patrick reads, aware that the smell of smoke is no longer on the porous paper. The words on the page form a rune – flint-hard and unemotional in the midst of the inferno of Cato's situation" (*SL*, 156). Rather than simply insisting on the reinsertion of migrants into the historical record, *In the Skin of a Lion* suggests that migrant figures explode the very epistemological and geographical borders with which a national history is commonly constructed.

The interests of capital, which are most obviously embodied in the novel's grand public works projects, are coterminous with the state's interest in monitoring the mobility of immigrant labourers and limiting the claims that such workers can make upon the state.

The Finnish loggers of Patrick's childhood, for example, form part of an economy that depends on the state's regulation of mobility. According to Deleuze and Guattari, the state's goal is to: "Fixer, sédentariser la force de travail, régler le mouvement du flux de travail, lui assigner des canaux et conduits, faire des corporations au sens d'organisme."[4] Accordingly, Deleuze and Guattari's concept of "le nomade" is meant to contest the state's desire to regulate the movement of workers. Using patterns to link migrant figures, *In the Skin of a Lion* similarly challenges the collaboration of the state and capital in the control of human mobility.

In making the assertion that *In the Skin of a Lion* uses pattern as an aspect of both form and content, I draw on the arguments of countless other critics and reviewers who have noticed Ondaatje's use of repetition. In particular, I am indebted to Julie Beddoes's claim that the novel's "most striking formal device is, perhaps, repetition."[5] Identifying Ondaatje's postmodern aesthetics of self-reflexive repetition, Beddoes asserts that these aesthetics "neutralize – or even oppose" the novel's "tentative thematizing of a radical class politics."[6] For Beddoes, this does not necessarily mean (as it does for Fredric Jameson) that the postmodern is ahistorical but that Ondaatje's postmodern tendency to emphasize the construction of "fact" through repetition also serves to render "equivalent those scenes that the book's thematics suggest should have quite different ethical value."[7] Susan Spearey's apprehension of migration and metamorphosis as recurrent structural and thematic elements of *In the Skin of a Lion* also influences my thinking about Ondaatje's use of repetition. Spearey describes Ondaatje's "synchronic method" as the linking of migrant characters through an obliteration of their "respective origins"; it is a method of spatialization that frustrates the possibility of both "linear progression" and "essential and predetermined character."[8] One might think of Spearey's formulation of synchronic method in relation to Cresswell's concept of "nomadic metaphysics," to which I referred earlier; if Ondaatje abandons the diachronic roots of migrant figures in favour of their synchronic (and analogous) routes of travel, then he is subscribing to a "nomadic metaphysics" that favours movement over location. Unlike Spearey, I find the synchronic quality of Ondaatje's "nomadic metaphysics" responsible for a host of conflations that obscure class, race, and gender differences more effectively than they, as she argues, resist essentialism. Arguing that the novel's various migrating characters

The Nomadic Metaphysics of *In the Skin of a Lion*　267

are linked together, Spearey misses the fact that the novel's "accounts of migration" are not all literally migrations. She compares, for example, millionaire Ambrose Small's "mysterious disappearance underground and subsequent calculated movements about the province" to both Nicholas Temelcoff's "harrowing passage from Macedonia to Canadian shores" and Patrick's "voyage from hinterland to metropolis."[9] These are clearly radically different itineraries involving dissimilar modes of travel and material privilege. Spearey is right to suggest that *In the Skin of a Lion* compares these migratory journeys, but the effect is not simply a resistance to foundational discourses of origin and determinism. If Ambrose Small is linked to Caravaggio by virtue of the fact that both are elusive figures who must plan their escape routes, then what of the difference between Small's self-indulgent game of hide-and-seek and Caravaggio's dangerous flight from prison?

Patrick is linked to the novel's various migrant characters through a process that emphasizes, to use Deleuze and Guattari's term, his rhizomatic quality. Like Patrick, the rhizome has "des entrées multiples" and, like a map, is "ouverte" and "connectable dans toutes ses dimensions."[10] Patrick is able to "devenir minoritaire" – to transform himself into other mobile characters in the novel – by virtue of "un médium et un sujet déterritorialisés" that are the elements of becoming as Deleuze and Guattari theorize it.[11] In other words, Patrick's specific subject position is unimportant to the process of becoming. One of the most compelling of the patterns in *In the Skin of a Lion* is the one that sews together Patrick and the enigmatic Finnish loggers who open the narrative. As a young boy, Patrick is fascinated with the sojourning loggers he sees skating on Depot Creek because they physically embody the resistant mobility of their working lives: "Their lanterns replaced with new rushes which let them go further past boundaries, speed! romance! one man waltzing with his fire" (SL, 22). For the young, impressionable Patrick, the mobility of the skating Finn represents a transgression of boundaries of all kinds.

Patrick is also linked to the loggers through the image of flame that recurs throughout the novel: the flaming sheaves of cattails in a nighttime skate on Depot Creek become the fire that cooks the tar in the dark Toronto morning of "The Bridge," the candles "for the bridge dead" (SL, 27), and the "temporary light" of the explosives Patrick uses to enter the water filtration plant in "Maritime

Theatre" (SL, 231). Each image of flame against blackness conjures the idea of literal or figurative illumination, which is appropriate given that Patrick's initial sighting of the Finns suggests that he will one day come to a greater knowledge of the world through them. Indeed, Patrick's later naming of the Finns is an integral part of his movement into political consciousness after Alice's death. He comes to know more about the sojourning loggers through Cato, who was Alice's lover and a radical Finnish union organizer in the logging camps of northern Ontario where many Finns were seasonal labourers. Cato's letters teach Patrick about the "union battles up north ... in the winter of 1921" and induce him to enter the sphere of political engagement that he had resisted in his conversations with Alice (SL, 157). Through Ondaatje via Patrick, the nameless Finns may gain some visibility in history, but it is important to note that the Finns are not developed characters in the novel; rather, they are expressions of Patrick's future self, metonyms of his eventual recognition of the need to take "responsibility for the story" (SL, 157). The patterns of movement and of light and darkness that link the Finns and Patrick together suggest their equivalence, but clearly this equivalence mostly serves to develop Patrick's character; that is, the Finns function primarily as catalyots for the illumination of Patrick's character. If likeness can suggest that migrant figures – or "ex-centrics," generally – cannot be unproblematically recuperated from the dim past into the light of the present, Patrick's centrality in the novel undermines the ironic effect of this suggestion. I am not objecting to what Hutcheon, in her rebuke of Fredric Jameson, calls the "mixing" and "tampering" with the "'facts' of received history"[12]; instead, following both Frank Davey and Smaro Kamboureli, I am pointing out that *In the Skin of a Lion* suggests equivalence while privileging the role of a single character – Patrick – who, owing to his place of birth, his Anglo heritage, and his privileged point of view, has greater agency than any of the other migrant characters in the novel.

While disingenuously implying equivalence, the novel's attention to Patrick's role effaces the Finns' specific history of radical politics and migration. As I have argued, the Finnish loggers represent for Patrick a potentially radical mobility, but it is also the collectivity of their skating that attracts him because "he could no more have skated along the darkness of a river than been the hero of one of these stories" (SL, 157). This collectivity is similarly represented

The Nomadic Metaphysics of *In the Skin of a Lion*   269

in Cato through his involvement in labour politics. Patrick has been a "searcher" (for Ambrose Small), a watcher, and a collector, but through the story of Cato and the memory of the loggers, he becomes aware of the need to act politically as a resistant, mobile figure. Thus, like the wandering Gilgamesh, he must assume the skin of a wild animal and avenge Cato's and Alice's deaths, which he does by travelling north and bombing a Muskoka resort. Yet, as Davey observes, Ondaatje favours Patrick's action as an individual over the collective action that Alice and Cato represent.[13] Given this observation, it is important to note that the historical figure upon whom Cato is based is not a single individual but, rather, two men named John Voutilainen and Viljo Rosvall. Radforth points out that these organizers for the Lumber Workers' Industrial Union of Canada (LWIUC) set off in 1929 for various Onion Lake camps to attempt to organize and extend a strike that had begun in Shabaqua, Ontario. Like Cato, they disappeared en route, and their bodies were eventually found five months later by a union-organized search party. Voutilainen's and Rosvall's deaths (like Cato's) were eventually judged "accidental drownings," but the LWIUC rejected this judgment.[14] The lacunae left by this verdict obviously intrigue Ondaatje, for he restages the murder as an execution perpetrated by men who say of Cato, "there have been union men before him and there will be union men after him" (*SL*, 156). Radforth is also clear that Finnish-Canadians played a central role in the radical politics of northern Ontario lumber camps, especially in the period between the World Wars. Two strong labour organizations developed in the 1920s, which were organized "almost exclusively" by Finnish-Canadian radicals – the International Workers' of the World–affiliated Lumber Workers' Industrial Union and the Communist Party of Canada–affiliated LWIUC.[15] Despite the historical evidence of a well-established culture of collective radical politics in the community of Finnish-Canadian bushworkers, Ondaatje chooses to reduce the evidence to Patrick's individualist, politically ambiguous actions. Moreover, Ondaatje's alignment of mobility and resistance to the state, which is figured in Patrick's bombing of a Muskoka resort and his later attempt to detonate the water filtration plant, is undermined in this negation of the transnational connectivity of Finnish labour radicalism.

Kamboureli reads the characterization of Temelcoff and Caravaggio as possible exceptions to Ondaatje's harmonization of difference through the figure of Patrick.[16] Yet the textual patterns that link Patrick to the Finnish loggers also define Patrick's relation to both the daredevil bridge-builder and Macedonian immigrant Nicholas Temelcoff and the Italian-Canadian thief Caravaggio. Ondaatje thematizes relations across space by linking Patrick and Temelcoff through their mutual qualities of spatial mastery. Davey points out that while Temelcoff has an intimately physical knowledge of the space of his work under the bridge, Patrick memorizes the geography of a room so well that he can negotiate it blindfolded.[17] This uncanny ability to master space also aligns Temelcoff and Patrick with Caravaggio, who "trained as a thief in unlit rooms, dismantling the legs of a kitchen table, unscrewing the backs of radios and the bottoms of toasters" (SL, 189). While Patrick comes to see his fate as imbricated in the lives of others, and while Ondaatje's aesthetic patterns (in this case, of spatial mastery in darkness) are meant to anticipate this realization, they also playfully conflate diverse journeys. As I have argued, Patrick's journey from passive observer to political actor draws on and effaces the particular history of Finnish migrant experiences. His journey is similarly inspired by the radicalism of the Macedonian community to which Alice introduces him and which she has presumably come to know through Temelcoff. Yet this Macedonian radicalism is part of a pattern within which the Finns and the Macedonians equally serve as metonyms of Patrick's journey into political consciousness. As a result, Macedonians and Finns become almost indistinguishable within the narrative, and yet their histories are quite different.

Moreover, the mobility that Patrick adopts as a political strategy is gleaned from the novel's migrant figures in a manner that fails to distinguish his movement from that of others. Patrick enacts his solitary, ill-defined political resistance through the mobility that he must assume as part of wearing the skin of the lion. Ondaatje represents this new mobility in a manner that explicitly calls attention to its evocation of the mobility that Patrick admires in Cato, the Finnish bushworkers, and Temelcoff. Patrick's route thus celebrates the covert, marginal, and resistant aspects of constant movement. For instance, his new mobility takes him out of the world of apprehension. When he travels north to plant his first bomb, for example, he moves in the darkness of a nighttime landscape, unseen or unnoticed by the rich whom he targets and positioned in the "no man's land" between train carriages (SL, 165). Though he walks through

The Nomadic Metaphysics of *In the Skin of a Lion*   271

light, it "has not attached itself to him" because he is "transparent, miniscule" (SL, 166). In the process of becoming minor, Deleuze and Guattari note that, like Patrick, the observable subject disappears:

> Le mouvement est dans un rapport essentiel avec l'imperceptible, il est par nature imperceptible. C'est que la perception ne peut saisir le mouvement que comme la translation d'un mobile ou le développement d'une forme. Les mouvements, et les devenirs, c'est-à-dire les purs rapports de vitesse et de lenteur, les purs affects, sont en dessous ou au-dessus du seuil de perception.[18]

Patrick's invisibility allows him to perpetrate his violence upon the "playground of the rich" (SL, 166). Yet if his movement draws on Cato's ability to "disappear under the surface" of "snow country," the Finns' transgression of boundaries on Depot Creek, and Temelcoff's ability to metamorphose out of history, it also, as noted above, confounds divergent kinds of mobility (SL, 155). Moreover, as Kamboureli argues, the anonymity of the Macedonian and other immigrant communities in the novel functions as a trope "that fulfills Patrick's own need for invisibility" without threatening his enjoyment of anonymity – a privilege that comes from his white skin.[19]

Despite the novel's insistence otherwise, Patrick's route is very different from that of the Finnish bushworkers. While Patrick is a migrant to the city of Toronto and, later, a roving anarchist of sorts, the Finnish loggers are transnational migrants who, as I argued earlier, have no claim to the land on which they work because they are a "collection of strangers" with no permanent home (SL, 7). As the work of Radforth and other historians demonstrates, the covertly resistant and romanticized mobility that Patrick eventually embodies has little in common with the history of Finnish migration to Canada. Varpu Lindstrom-Best's research shows that Finnish migrants came to Canada in large numbers during the first few decades of the twentieth century. Due to the seasonal nature of the early twentieth-century logging industry, most of the Finnish immigrants who found work in the bush camps of northern Ontario were unemployed for at least part of the year, when they would have to move to find other employment.[20] Although Radforth identifies the bushworkers' practice of "jumping" from camp to camp in search of better conditions and wages as an expression of agency, Finnish migrants to Canada in the early twentieth century were clearly subject to the whims of capital and the nation-state; the unemployment they experienced was a structural part of the Canadian economy and was not protected by the state in the form of insurance or other payment. Moreover, the relative control that Finns exercised over their transnational mobility in the early part of the century did not endure; the Canadian state halted immigration in the 1930s and subsequently targeted immigrant groups, especially those with ties to radical political groups, for deportation.[21] Therefore, in his synchronic representation of routes – in which mobility is a politically radical route that unites diverse characters – Ondaatje effaces important differences among kinds of travel and degrees of agency.

The romanticized, undifferentiated mobility that I have identified is an object of critique for many theorists of the relationships among culture, place, and movement. Cresswell argues that many postmodern (and, I would add, postcolonial) approaches to migration indulge in an "overly general celebration and romanticization" of human mobility."[22] Responding to the use by scholars such as James Clifford of "travel" as an all-encompassing metaphor to describe varieties of migration and tourism, Ien Ang invokes the term "traveler" to critique the ways in which nomadology "only serves to decontextualize and flatten out difference, as if 'we' were all in fundamentally similar ways always-already travelers in the same postmodern universe, the only difference residing in the different itineraries we undertake."[23] Jana Evans Braziel and Anita Mannur have interrogated the critical yield of tropes of travel in relation to diaspora studies, warning that an "explosion" in the use of the term "diaspora" to include "all movements, however privileged, and ... all dislocations, even symbolic ones" ignores the fact that "some forms of travel are tourism and every attempt to mark movements as necessarily disenfranchising becomes an imperialist gesture."[24] While careful differentiation on the basis of class, gender, and ethnicity is important, Caren Kaplan reminds us that "posing 'real' exiles against 'false' ones does not adequately address the subject positions that arise in the complex circulations of transnational cultures in postmodernity."[25] My reading of *In the Skin of a Lion* is therefore less concerned with sniffing out the "real" nomads/migrants from the "false" – with differentiating the immigrant characters in the novel from Canadian-born Patrick – than with critiquing the patterns of movement and mobility that suggest that all of the characters whom I have discussed have equal access to mobility.

The Nomadic Metaphysics of *In the Skin of a Lion*   273

TRAVELLING IN THE DESERT

Thus far, I have identified Ondaatje's novel as subscribing to a "nomadic metaphysics" – the tendency of postmodern thought to create a world of travel in which "nothing is certain or fixed."[26] Like the Finn who waltzes with fire as he speeds across the ice and thus indicates Ondaatje's fascination with velocity, Deleuze and Guattari's work is preoccupied with the potentially radical fluidity of movement that exceeds structures of control and domination. In their collaborative work *Mille plateaux*, Deleuze and Guattari employ the trope of *le nomade* to theorize their conception of fluid and mobile "rhizomatic" groups:

> Les meutes, les bandes sont des groupes du type rhizome, par opposition au type arborescent qui se concentre sur des organes de pouvoir. C'est pourquoi les bandes en général, même de brigandage, ou de mondanité, sont des métamorphoses d'une machine de guerre, laquelle diffère formellement de tout appareil d'État, ou équivalent, qui structure au contraire les sociétés centralisées.[27]

The essence of *la machine de guerre* that the nomad embodies is "*le trace d'une ligne de fuite créatrice, la composition d'un espace lisse et du mouvement des hommes dans cet espace.*"[28] As I noted earlier, this "espace lisse" conflicts with the interests of the state, which attempts to fix and regulate the space occupied by the nomad. This opposition between the interests of centralized structures like the state and those of amorphous, fluid, nomadic groups is, as I have argued, present in Ondaatje's use of migrant figures to challenge the boundaries of realism and the nation-state.

Deleuze and Guattari, however, distinguish between the fixed trajectory of the migrant and the constant mobility of the nomad; while "*le chemin sédentaire*" parcels out "*un espace fermé, en assignant à chacun sa part, et en réglant la communication des parts,*" the "*trajet nomade*" "*distribue les hommes (ou les bêtes) dans un espace ouvert, indéfini, non communiquant.*"[29] This distinction is important for theorizing Ondaatje's use of what I have called the migrant as a series of undifferentiated figures who move about in "espace ouvert" rather than having specific routes (and roots) of their own. Deleuze and Guattari's designation of "le nomade" for such a figure is therefore more germane to the terms of my argument than the term "migrant," which I have employed thus far.

Representations of nomadic movement permeate the form and content of *In the Skin of a Lion*; more specifically, the trope of the desert nomad appears in Ondaatje's deliberate blurring of the characters of Patrick and the thief whom he meets in prison, Caravaggio. Ondaatje thematizes his fusing of these characters and their resistant acts in the first scene in which they are presented together. Patrick, Caravaggio, and another prisoner named Buck are painting the roof of the Kingston Penitentiary "blue up to the sky so that after a while the three men working on it became uncertain of clear boundaries ... They would scratch their noses and realize they became partly invisible. If they painted long enough they would be eradicated, blue birds in a blue sky." Caravaggio recognizes the potentially subversive quality of their tedious task: "*Demarcation ... That is all we need to remember*" (SL, 179). Indeed, he is able to use the lack of demarcation as a means to escape the confining boundaries of the prison. This merging of lost demarcation and mobility is similarly evoked in Ondaatje's novel *The English Patient*; the English patient Almásy remarks that it is easy to "lose a sense of demarcation" in the desert, which is the geographic location of nomadism in the novel.[30] In a later scene in *In the Skin of a Lion* that recalls Caravaggio's escape from prison, Patrick is symbolically merged with Caravaggio when he becomes invisible in order to attack the water filtration plant: "Patrick is invisible except by touch, grease covering all unclothed skin, his face, his hands, his bare feet. *Demarcation*" (SL, 228). Patrick and Caravaggio thus inhabit a borderless space that is reminiscent of the "*espace lisse*" or the "*milieu sans horizon*" of the nomad – the "*steppe, désert ou mer*."[31] Furthermore, the militance of Patrick's underwater sabotage and the defiance of Caravaggio's transgressions of the law, both of which they effect through resisting demarcation, align them with the resistant qualities of the nomadic "*machine de guerre*." Deleuze and Guattari contend that this "*machine de guerre*" will engage in combat if it "*se heurte aux États et aux villes, comme aux forces (de striage) qui s'opposent à l'objet positif*."[32] Such "*forces de striage*" are certainly embodied in R.C. Harris, whose water filtration plant symbolizes the structured order of "the ideal city" (SL, 109).

The trope of the desert nomad that aligns Patrick and Caravaggio is more explicit in Ondaatje's method of conveying their respective capacities for mobility. In Caravaggio and Giannetta's violent

The Nomadic Metaphysics of *In the Skin of a Lion*

lovemaking/reunification scene, this trope becomes bestial: "She smells him, the animal out of the desert that has stumbled back home, back into oasis" (*SL*, 205). Deleuze and Guattari similarly see the desert beast and the nomad as analogous; they compare, for example, nomadic society to "*les meutes*" and "*les bandes*" of animals.[33] Moreover, as in the scenes that represent a lack of demarcation, this scene recalls the "espace lisse" of the nomad, which, like a desert, is "*un espace ouvert où les choses-flux se distribuent.*"[34] For example, the border between Caravaggio's and Giannetta's physical bodies and the boundaries of the room's objects are destabilized: "When she opens her eyes wide he sees glass and crockery and thin china plates tumbling down from shelf to shelf losing their order, their shades of blue and red merging, her fingers on his scar, her fingers on the thumping vein on his forehead" (*SL*, 205). Giannetta's eyes ("her eyes") open, but, in an unexpected narrative trick, it is Caravaggio ("he") who sees the chaos of the tumbling blue and red crockery, which both merges with and evokes the red of Caravaggio's scar and the blue of his "thumping" vein.

While Caravaggio's mobility is represented through the trope of the desert beast, Patrick is likened to a wandering desert inhabitant when he adopts his plan to resist the rich and those allied with the power and authority of the state. In Sandars's translation of *The Epic of Gilgamesh* (which Ondaatje used), Shamash the sun goddess comforts Enkidu, who is about to die, by telling him that when he is dead Gilgamesh will "let his hair grow long for your sake, he will wear a lion's pelt and wander through the desert."[35] This prophecy is, of course, mirrored in Ondaatje's epigraph, which is taken from Gilgamesh's speech over Enkidu's body: "The joyful will stoop with sorrow, and when you have gone to the earth I will let my hair grow long for your sake, I will wander through the wilderness in the skin of a lion." In the epic, Gilgamesh then proceeds to wander through the desert in search of everlasting life and eternal youth, which prove to be elusive. Like Odysseus, the epic hero then returns home and engraves his story on a stone. Though his quest also fails, Patrick does not return home; instead, the novel closes with a dream-like night scene in which Patrick has just awoken and is on the road between Toronto and Marmora. Unlike his epic counterpart, Patrick remains an elusive, mobile figure who is linked until the closing words with Caravaggio – the "animal out of the desert" – and other nomads in the novel.

As I have argued, this pattern of nomadism that links characters together has potentially radical implications; the novel favours the mobile qualities that enable characters to avoid being seen and apprehended by realist literary forms, by state structures, and by boundaries of all descriptions. While I have questioned the confounding of various types of mobility, however, one must also consider the particular trope of the nomad. Deleuze and Guattari clearly link this trope to a specific geography; while they locate "*la culture aborescente*" in the West and its fascination with agriculture and plant and animal breeding, the rhizomatic cultures of the East are associated with "*la steppe et le jardin (dans d'autres cas, le désert et l'oasis).*"[36] Caren Kaplan's critique of "poststructuralist deterritorializations" posits that tropes of the desert nomad and of desert space in general have been employed in both modern and postmodern thought in ways that solder them to colonial discourse. Kaplan identifies the ironic fact that the deterritorialization Deleuze and Guattari explore through the nomad or minority figure is always a colonizing act that "raids other spaces," such as the "margin" of the desert. Consequently, "deterritorialization is always reterritorialization, an increase of territory, an imperialization."[37] Moreover, Kaplan asserts that the Euro-American perspective that views the nomad as a "gypsy" or "immigrant" erases "temporal and spatial differentiations,"[38] an erasure of the kind I have been tracing in the "nomadic metaphysics" of *In the Skin of a Lion*.

Deleuze and Guattari seem aware, however, of the exoticist dangers and colonizing gestures that accompany the trope of the nomad. They ask,

> Car: comment faire pour que le thème d'une race ne tourne pas en racisme, en fascisme dominant et englobant, ou plus simplement en aristocratisme, ou bien une secte et folklore, en micro-fascismes? Et comment faire pour que le pôle Orient ne soit pas un fantasme, qui réactive autrement tous les fascismes, tous les folklores aussi, yoga, zen et karaté?[39]

They reply that they have attempted to ground their idea of the nomad in a singular race rather than a universal thinking subject but recognize that this geographic and temporal grounding will not necessarily avoid the dangers of racism and orientalism.[40] Indeed, *In the Skin of a Lion* is a good demonstration of the fact that the trope

The Nomadic Metaphysics of *In the Skin of a Lion*   277

of the nomad, despite Deleuze and Guattari's attempts to specify its material contexts, can be easily employed in a fashion that is less careful about geographic, cultural, and temporal distinctions.

While I agree with Kaplan that the trope of the nomad cannot be dissociated from specific histories of colonization and past and present struggles for decolonization, I nevertheless appreciate Deleuze and Guattari's attempts to conceive of a non-hierarchical epistemology. Deleuze and Guattari's thinking has been useful for considering, for example, women's diverse relationships to space and mobility. As Cresswell points out, the fluidity and lack of structure implied by the nomad metaphor can serve to deconstruct "the familiar dualisms of man / women; white / black; true / false," which are all "tethered to the geography of here and there."[41] Although the trope of the nomad is not, as I have discussed, without its attendant problems, it does point to the need for both a recognition of women's mobility and transnational feminist critical practices that can account for mobility – and location – in ways that are sensitive to differences of ethnicity, sexuality, and class. Significantly, however, there are some characters in *In the Skin of a Lion* who do not form a part of the patterns of movement and nomadism that I have identified. Although Ondaatje is subscribing to a "nomadic metaphysics" that privileges roving, unfixed subjects, his novel generally represents women as immobile. When Patrick blindfolds himself to show Clara his dexterity in darkness, for example, he is clearly responding to her impending journey toward Ambrose Small, over which he has no control. He thus "positions Clara on the bed and tells her not to move" and proceeds to dazzle her with his blind flight of unfettered mobility: "Then he takes off into the room – at first using his hands for security then ignoring them, just throwing his body within an inch of the window swooping his head down parallel to shelves while he rushes across the room in straight lines, in curves, as if he has the mechanism of a bat in his human blood" (SL, 80). Although Clara thinks Patrick is "magnificent" and "perfect" in his bat-like flight, she nonetheless resists his parceling out of space to her. She "moves off the bed," where he has told her to remain, and incurs physical pain because of her mobility: "Suddenly she is hit hard and her left hand jars against her skull, knocking her over" (SL, 80). Patrick is contrite but reminds her of his bidding: "You moved. I told you not to. You moved" (SL, 81). Although Clara is the only female character who is actually wounded as a consequence of her mobility, other women in the novel similarly serve to contrast male movement. Giannetta, for example, plays Penelope when she is found at home waiting for Caravaggio to arrive after having escaped from prison, and she is also represented as a still, sleeping figure while he practises his thief's trade. Just as Caravaggio somehow sees through Giannetta's eyes and thus appropriates her sexual experience in their violent lovemaking scene, so she must move vicariously through him. If, as I have argued, the novel's privileged form of mobility is that of the nomad, female characters are clearly excluded from this trope. Moreover, in rendering all of his female characters similarly immobile, Ondaatje further elides the differential access to movement that exists within gender categories and across ethnicity and class.

Through his depiction of nomadism in *In the Skin of a Lion*, Ondaatje fails to differentiate among diverse practices of mobility that are routed through transnational networks to exist in local contexts. Put somewhat differently, Patrick's prominence in the narrative and the narrative's reliance on colonizing tropes are symptoms of the novel's failure to grasp the complexity of transnational labour migration. While Ondaatje's "nomadic metaphysics" points to the important disaggregation of identity and place, the novel does not ultimately represent migration as a historically differentiated set of phenomena. The reader is thus left with a celebration of mobility that does not attend to the fact that labour migrants have not historically fared very well against the nation-state or the interests of capital in Canada.

NOTES

This essay was originally published in *Studies in Canadian Literature / Études en littérature Canadienne* 31, no. 2 (2006): 41–62.

1 Cresswell, "Introduction," 15–16.
2 Deleuze and Guattari, *A Thousand Plateaus*, 437. All further noted English translations are taken from Brian Massumi's 1987 translation of *Mille plateaux: A Thousand Plateaus*.
3 Ondaatje draws on Ian Radforth's study of northern Ontario bushworkers in the early twentieth century for his representation of Finnish migrants. The figure of Ambrose Small became known to Ondaatje through historical research; Small was originally the protagonist of the novel, but

The Nomadic Metaphysics of *In the Skin of a Lion* 279

Ondaatje began to "dislike him intensely" and thus shifted his focus to other characters (Turner, "In the Skin of Michael Ondaatje," 21). Nicholas Temelcoff is borrowed from the work of Lillian Petroff, whom Ondaatje acknowledges in *In the Skin of a Lion*. Petroff turned her doctoral work on Macedonian migration to Toronto into a book entitled *Sojourners and Settlers*, in which she recounts her 1975 interview with labourer Nicholas Temelcoff.

4 Deleuze and Guattari, *Capitalisme et schizophrénie*, 456. "Settling, sedentarizing labour-power, regulating the movement of the flow of labour, assigning it channels and conduits, [and] forming corporations in the sense of organizations" are the goals of the state (368).

5 Beddoes, "Which Side Is It On?, 207.

6 Ibid., 206.

7 Ibid., 207–8.

8 Spearey, "Mapping and Masking," 52.

9 Ibid., 47–8.

10 Deleuze and Guattari, *Capitalisme et schizophrénie*, 23, 20. Like Patrick, the rhizome has "multiple entryways" and is "open and connectable in all its dimensions" (12, 14).

11 Ibid., 357. Patrick is able to "become-minoritarian" – to transform himself into other mobile characters in the novel – by virtue of the "deterritorialized medium and subject" that are the elements of becoming as Deleuze and Guattari theorize it (292).

12 Hutcheon, "The Postmodern Problematizing of History," 367.

13 Davey, *Post-national Arguments*, 148.

14 Radforth, *Bushworkers and Bosses*, 124–5.

15 Ibid., 119–20.

16 Kamboureli, "The Culture of Celebrity and National Pedagogy," 51.

17 Davey, *Post-national Arguments*, 151.

18 Deleuze and Guattari, *Capitalisme et schizophrénie*, 344. "Movement has an essential relation to the imperceptible; it is by nature imperceptible. Perception can grasp movement only as the displacement of a moving body or the development of a form. Movements, becomings, in other words, pure relations of speed and slowness, pure affects, are below and above the threshold of perception" (280–1).

19 Kamboureli, "The Culture of Celebrity and National Pedagogy," 49.

20 Lindstrom-Best, *The Finns in Canada*, 26–7.

21 Radforth, *Bushworkers and Bosses*, 39. Ibid., 13.

22 Cresswell, "Introduction," 17–18.

23 Ang, "On Not Speaking Chinese," 4.

280   Jody Mason

24 Braziel and Mannur, "Nation, Migration, Globalization," 3.

25 Kaplan, *Questions of Travel*, 95.

26 Cresswell, "Introduction," 15.

27 Deleuze and Guattari, *Capitalisme et schizophrénie*, 443. "Packs, bands, are groups of the rhizome type, as opposed to the arborescent type that centers around organs of power. That is why bands in general, even those engaged in banditry or high society life, are metamorphoses of a war machine formally distinct from all State apparatuses or their equivalents, which are instead what structure centralized societies" (358).

28 Ibid., 526. "The essence of the war machine that the nomad embodies is the drawing of a creative line of flight, the composition of a smooth space and of the movement of people in that space" (422).

29 Ibid., 471–2. "While the 'sedentary road' parcels out 'closed space to people, assigning each person a share and regulating the communication between shares,' the 'nomadic trajectory' 'distributes people (or animals) in an open space, one that is indefinite and noncommunicating'" (380).

30 Ondaatje, *The English Patient* (Toronto: McClelland and Stewart, 1992), 18. The trope of the desert nomad in *In the Skin of a Lion* anticipates Ondaatje's later use of the nomad in *The English Patient*. In the latter, the moveable desert serves as a metaphor for Almásy's unstable position between life and death and, more significantly, his troubling of the boundaries between black and white skin and among the strong national identities of the postwar period. For conflicting interpretations of the nomad figure in *The English Patient*, see both Renger and Horta. While many postcolonial readings of *The English Patient* have accepted and even endorsed Ondaatje's use of the desert and the nomad figure, Horta's article begins the work of interrogating these tropes.

31 Deleuze and Guattari, *Capitalisme et schizophrénie*, 469. Patrick and Caravaggio thus inhabit a borderless space that is reminiscent of the "smooth space" or the "horizonless milieu" of the nomad – the "steppe, desert, or sea" (379).

32 Ibid., 519. Deleuze and Guattari contend that this "war machine" will engage in combat if it "collides with States and cities, as forces (of striation) opposing its positive object" (417).

33 Ibid., 443. Deleuze and Guattari similarly see the desert beast and the nomad as analogous; they compare, for example, nomadic society to "packs" and "bands" of animals (358).

34 Ibid., 447. Moreover, as in the scenes that represent a lack of demarcation, this scene recalls the "smooth space" of the nomad, which, like a desert, is "an open space throughout which things/flows are distributed" (361).

The Nomadic Metaphysics of *In the Skin of a Lion* 281

35 *The Epic of Gilgamesh*, 88.
36 Deleuze and Guattari, *Capitalisme et schizophrénie*, 28. Deleuze and Guattari clearly link this trope to a specific geography; while they locate "arborescent culture" in the West and its fascination with agriculture and plant and animal breeding, the rhizomatic cultures of the East are associated with "the steppe and the garden (or, in some cases, the desert and the oasis)" (15–18).
37 Kaplan, *Questions of Travel*, 89.
38 Ibid., 87–8.
39 Deleuze and Guattari, *Capitalisme et schizophrénie*, 470. "For what can be done to prevent the theme of a race from turning into a racism, a dominant and all-encompassing fascism, or into a sect and a folklore, micro-fascisms? And what can be done to prevent the Oriental pole from becoming a phantasy that reactivates all the fascisms in a different way, and also all the folklores, yoga, Zen, and karate?" (379).
40 Ibid., 469–70.
41 Cresswell, "Imagining the Nomad," 367.

13

Love, War, and the Other in Emmanuel Levinas, Jacques Derrida, and Michael Ondaatje: *The English Patient* as the Dialogic Field

Kai-su Wu

The strangeness of the Other, his irreducibility to the I, to my thoughts and my possessions, is precisely accomplished as a calling into question of my spontaneity, as ethics.

Emmanuel Levinas
Totality and Infinity

Among the critical works on Ondaatje's *The English Patient*, there are quite a few exemplary pieces that provide insights into the novel's varied themes of the human condition (Brittan, Carbajal, de Zepetnek, Hilger, Marinkova). Much of the commentary on the novel focuses on its backdrop, its leading characters' identity politics, and the polemics of Western culture. While de Zepetnek places emphasis on the claimed historical facts and factors behind the novel, Hilger leads the reader through the intertextual and interdisciplinary references connected to the novel's interweaving historical threads. Besides discussing the omnipresent *Histories* by Herodotus, Hilger discusses the history of Hungary and the Habsburg Empire. Brittan provides a unique commentary on the characters' fictional roles in the Second World War. Marinkova and Carbajal deal with Ondaatje's revisionist views of Western culture, one with its macropolitical totality, the other with its contentious humanism.

Another way of approaching the novel is to examine its presentation of otherness. Emmanuel Levinas's ethical thoughts provide a base upon which such a presentation can unfold. In his proximity to Levinas when it comes to the ethics of the other, Jacques

The English Patient as the Dialogic Field

Derrida proffers notions that complement the latter's comparative (and frequently misunderstood) portraits of politics and the death of the other.

Unlike Derrida, whose association with the literary field is consolidated through his copious production regarding varied genres of literature, Levinas's attitude toward literature is somehow ambiguous and even critical, at least during his earlier stage of writing. Nonetheless, he eventually comes to show a change in attitude. Seán Hand traces Levinas's transformation from contrasting "philosophical exegesis and criticism" with "artistic idolatry"[1] to acknowledging "how poetic language is able to generate signs beyond meaning, abandon the order present to vision and hold open transcendence" (74). Levinas eradicates his bias against the art after he savours Maurice Blanchot's literary and critical works, which he describes in these words:

> A discontinuous and contradictory language of scintillation. A language which can give sign above and beyond all signification ... But it is absolutely "in clear" both this side and beyond the inevitable conventions of languages. Though lying outside of the coded system of languages, it leads to it, like the metalanguages referred to in logistics, which "unlocks" the symbolism of writing.[2]

Levinas's later encounter with Paul Celan's poetry precipitates his demolition of the wall between philosophy and the artwork, a result of his reassessment of the "conventions of languages" that he used to attribute to works of art.

One way to untangle the complexity of Levinas's idea of alterity is via his accounts of the meaning of time in the death of the other. This is where Ondaatje and Derrida are drawn in. Thrown into the war, the leading characters in The English Patient are desperate for their own versions of redemption. For Ondaatje, their redemption lies in their encounter with otherness. Mourning, as the extreme form of this encounter, becomes the avenue that opens up the understanding of time related to the other's (imminent) demise. Mourning remains ethical because it is always already pre-mourning, carried out by the one who waits in patience. In the novel, mourning traverses two different worlds, occurring beside the bed in the villa San Girolamo and in the Cave of Swimmers, serving as a critical response to the war that cannibalizes beings in its synchronizing efforts of assimilation. The ethical elevation with the other, on the other hand, provides a diachronic register of time whose patience connotes a bearing of responsibility that will never belong to the Same.

LEVINAS AND THE ETHICS OF THE OTHER

Ethics always came first in the philosophy of Emmanuel Levinas, for whom the fundamental consideration was philosophy's thinking of the other. Confronted by what he saw as the ethical failure resulting from previous philosophers' emphasis on the subjectivity of human beings, Levinas was compelled to think beyond the existential being, and in this way he produced a mode of philosophy that debunks the self-righteous utopia of Western humanism. The gesture of thinking beyond self generates his varied inflective leitmotifs associated with the other.

Derrida, in his memorial text for Levinas, summarizes the latter's conception of the other as follows:

[T]he other is not reducible to its actual predicates, to what one might define or thematize about it, any more than the I is. It is naked, bared of every property, and this nudity is also its infinitely exposed vulnerability: its skin. This absence of determinable properties, of concrete predicates, of empirical visibility, is no doubt what gives to the face of the other a spectral aura.[3]

The other in the Levinasian sense is the other never perceived by the self as an ontological being. Irreducible to any intention coming from a perceiving subject and thereby unassimilated to the self, the other is beyond the self's territory. On the other hand, this very self is obliged to reach to the other by being unconditionally responsible to it. This self that is rendered ethical serves as an antithesis to any war instigators and supporters who reduce the other to something destroyable for the sake of their preservation of subjectivity.

For Levinas, existential thought has become a dead end for humanity, since it bypasses the consideration of the other in every ethical way and is thereby never humane enough. Existentialism without deliberating upon the "not-I" of the other may lead to the celebration of totality, which is politically rendered totalitarian through its extreme incarnation in the Nazi Party. Totality provides war with

The English Patient as the Dialogic Field   285

the reason to consume or calamitously eliminate the other, to be not responsible and responsive to the other, and to care only for selfish interests. War is, in short, abandonment of responsibility.

In "The Trace of the Other," Levinas explains the meaning of responsibility for the other by resorting to the idea of "patience," which coincidentally echoes the title of Ondaatje's novel:

> The departure without return, which does not go forth into the void, would also lose its absolute goodness if the work sought for its recompense in the immediacy of its triumph, if it impatiently awaited the triumph of its cause. The one-way movement would be inverted into a reciprocity. The work, confronting its departure and its end, would be absorbed again in calculations of deficits and compensations, in accountable operations. It would be subordinated to thought. The one-way action is possible only in patience, which, pushed to the limit, means for the agent to renounce being the contemporary of its outcome, to act without entering the promised land.[4]

"Patience" discussed here is in close proximity to Levinas's concept of responsibility. It is something gratuitous, asking no gratitude, no return, and no feedback. In the novel, Hana's attitude toward her English patient corresponds to the idea here. Her "absolute goodness" would not exist at all if it were based on value judgment and calculation. Levinas zooms in on the contingent manifestation of patience as always pointing to the future. It is what cannot be revealed at the moment it is executed or carried out by someone. Never present and incapable of being contemporary, patience awaits and abides by the promise of messianic time.

It would be a mistake if we were to understand Levinas's idea of patience as that which awaits in the sedate dimension of time or if we were to perceive Ondaatje's English patient as an object that simply receives when it comes to responsibility. Instead of merely representing a weak invalid in the story, the patient is a demonstration of alternative aspects that require an ethical rethinking of such notions as the above-mentioned "recompense" and "reciprocity" in an atrocity-ridden human world. And the idea of patience refers to the capability of not only accepting what is deferred in the past but envisioning what is to come. Ondaatje's delineation of care and love, Levinas's idea of face, and Derrida's idea of mourning share a tonal

Kai-su Wu

affinity and offer a way to think beyond the limit of *I*-dentity, beyond the *moi* that "must restrict itself" by waiting patiently instead of wasting itself in the wave of warfare that denies entry to lives going further. For them, ethics is a futuristic event that cannot be grasped in static now-ness. This radicality of ethics implies that only through recognition of the absolute other can the self escape the prison of false freedom cast as the true essence of humankind.

ENEMY, NATION, AND THE FACE OF THE OTHER

Both Levinas and Ondaatje employ the image of the face as a special field for discussion in their respective texts: the face as the (non-) representation of the other in the former and the face as an entity without identity in the latter. Mita Banerjee calls Almásy a "floating signifier. The emphasis is on the riddle his unidentifiable presence poses to the others."[5] Not dissimilarly, Michael L. Morgan clearly describes what the face exactly means: "Levinas employs the word 'face' with the greatest care. The face of the other person is not the appearance of that person; it is not a collection of features given to visual perception. It has no parts, no components. It is basic and, as he says, 'self signifying.'"[6] Banerjee and Morgan are two critics who emphasize the importance of the face as a kind of revelation or epiphany rather than a perceptible object. In *The English Patient*, Almásy's face is burned beyond recognition. In a sense, this face "has not parts, no components," its transcendental being of alterity invoking responsibility. Hana's, Caravaggio's, and Kip's respective relations with this face in the villa create a convergence of the ethical currents that have been unleashed by the summoning authority of the face that requires response from those who encounter it. However, the self, or the I, does not just respond to the calling of the face. It also seeks to construct the self through the process of approaching this face. Through the process, the possible relation with the other has been born.

In the second chapter of *The English Patient*, Hana refuses to have any mirrors in the villa, so she stores them away. Conscious of her own mental incompleteness, which is caused by her grief over the death of her beloved, Hana thinks a reflection of her physical wholeness in the mirror will only serve to create a depressing comparison with her deficient inside. The mirror has become for Hana a metaphor of reflecting and thus reaffirming a complete self. By caring for the other, she picks up the fragments of her traumatic self.

The English Patient as the Dialogic Field

On the other hand, the English patient, despite having known his own ravaged face, asks Hana to bring him a mirror. The patient's self-mirroring is not so much an attempt to examine the severity of his injuries as an attempt to search, symbolically speaking, for otherness through the image of his face, an attempt to ponder upon the interrelationship between humans.

This theme of looking at the alterity in the self reappears at the end of the following chapter of the novel when the English patient mentions one of Michelangelo Merisi da Caravaggio's most well-known paintings: *David with the Head of Goliath*. Instead of assuming the jubilant or satisfied expression of a victor, David in this painting, while holding the head of the giant, seems to squint at the face of Goliath with pity. While the model for the slain Goliath remains unanimously the artist in his middle age, there are at least two versions regarding the identification of the face of David: one refers to the painter's studio assistant-cum-lover; the other is Caravaggio at a much younger age. The patient opts for the latter and comments that it is "[y]outh judging age at the end of its outstretched hand. The judging of one's own mortality" (EP, 116).

The patient's connection of himself to Goliath in terms of mortality is cemented when he refers to the young Indian sapper Kirpal Singh, nicknamed Kip: "when I see him at the foot of my bed that Kip is my David" (EP, 116). The Anglicized Kip is trained as a bomb disposal specialist in the British military under Lord Suffolk, whom he respects as his life mentor. After a lethal bomb-defusing mission that kills Suffolk, the devastated Kip is transferred to another unit in Italy where he meets the three residents of the villa. The patient soon becomes his older friend as well as his connection to all that is related to the "English." Yet the comparison of the patient / Kip and Goliath / David pairing implies the forthcoming tension heightened by the nuclear bombing of Hiroshima. As a man of South Asian ethnic origin, Kip sticks to his belief that Westerners would by no means bomb their own race as they have done to Japan. Of course, when Kip storms into the room of the "Englishman" and points his rifle at the latter, he does not have the slightest intention of hurting him. Yet, for Kip, the patient represents the entire Euro-American warring communities that should be held accountable for the atrocity carried out by the Allies. The ending of the novel is not dissimilar to that of E.M. Forster's *A Passage to India*, in which the racial gap becomes impossible to be bridged within a short period of time.

Besides invoking the painting of *David with the Head of Goliath* to reflect upon the English patient's imminent death, Ondaatje also employs it to problematize the ideological dichotomy of friends and enemies. Such inquiry into the polarity of the two parties is properly conducted in Derrida's analysis of Carl Schmitt's *The Concept of the Political*. Schmitt maintains that all political activities and motivations are based upon the demarcation between friends and enemies. Identifying enemies is the prerequisite of the occupation of the political, which, in turn, is the foundation of the state. Briefly put, whenever there is war, there must be a separation into two parties. If there is no war in any form or manner, then there is no politics either. A world without politics is impossible to imagine for any country. Political enemies are thereby "created" and "constructed": "The invention of the enemy is where the urgency and the anguish are; this invention is what would have to be brought off, in sum, to repoliticize, to put an end to depoliticization."[7]

Derrida points out that Schmitt's attempt to reinvest the seemingly disappearing identification of the enemy to resuscitate the political aspects of the state allegedly marred by liberalism is paradoxically a simplification of the political, which ironically goes against the grain of Schmitt's own concept. For Schmitt, an enemy should be interpreted as one who shows "hostility," indicating that one is in an opposite position with a certain other without really bearing hatred against this other. And this justifies the claim Schmitt makes for the occlusion of the personal and private weight from the political scene. For Derrida, the clear separation of the concept of friends and enemies is out of the question. He notes that the image of enemy is produced for the sake of the political. Schmitt's gesture of demarcation leaves people stranded in the notion of homogeneity and totality that both Derrida and Levinas deem problematic.

In the novel, David Caravaggio, a Canadian thief and the namesake of the painter of *David with the Head of Goliath*, is, politically speaking, Almásy's enemy. Besides visiting his friend's daughter Hana, Caravaggio goes to the villa mainly to find out if the English patient is the one who helps General Rommel (a real historical figure: Erwin Rommel, the German Field Marshal) by escorting one of the most important German spies named Eppler across the deserts and into Cairo. Caravaggio asserts that the patient Hana is taking care of is the famous Hungarian Count Ladislaus de Almásy, an

The English Patient as the Dialogic Field 289

identity the patient refuses to admit until late in the novel. On the other hand, Caravaggio is at that time ordered to follow Almásy.

These two people, one for England and the other for Germany, are victims of the political. Although Caravaggio voices severe criticism against military operations and Almásy repels the notion of nations, they fail to hold off the ideological manipulation during the war – a Canadian man employed by England as an intelligence agent and a Hungarian desert explorer used by the German army to sketch maps of the deserts and guide spies through them. Caravaggio's relation with Almásy is predetermined by the political to be as enemies. However, after their encounter in the villa, Caravaggio gradually realizes that he bears no antipathy toward Almásy. He even considers the patient to be the most endearing person he has ever met. Even though their animadversion on the war and the nations could only be made by hindsight, the blurring line between friends and enemies precipitates the breaking of the impasse and registers the affective mobility of identity in transit: "[W]ho was the enemy? Who were the allies of this place?" (EP, 19).

It seems that Ondaatje follows a schema reminiscent of Michelangelo Merisi da Caravaggio's employment of the method of chiaroscuro in his paintings. The emphasis is never the light or darkness but the contrasting result of the two, which could be called the shadow of the third. As Almásy the patient stays in his limbo state, neither alive nor dead, he relates his dilemma woven in his kaleidoscopic affairs of lovers, traitors, enemies, and companions swamped in the bipartite nature of nationhood.

"Violence occurs when an irreducible alterity is reduced to sameness," comments Richard Cohen.[8] War is what brings nations, or, to be more specific, various ramifications of national supremacy, into opposition and conflict with one another. Ondaatje associates the ideology of totality with the idea of national supremacy, which caused the international catastrophe of the Second World War. His title character's aid to the German spy and criticism of the British army's refusal to help rescue Katharine Clifton might be seen as politically incorrect. Yet what Ondaatje intends to do is to reveal the fundamental similitude of these nations involved in the catastrophic activities of warfare. Ondaatje's dismissal of the boundary between the Allies and the Axis powers via Almásy contravenes the primary register of the Schmittian political. As in the author's other works such as *In the Skin of a Lion*, his characters favour a world view of cosmopolitan communities. Apropos of the notion of nations, Almásy regards it as the evil pitting people against one another. In his lamentation, he claims that his best friend Madox was sacrificed at the mercy of warring nations: Madox "heard the sermon in honour of war, pulled out his desert revolver and shot himself" (*EP*, 240).

Almásy's love of the desert is in complete opposition to this hatred: "The desert could not be claimed or owned ... All of us, even those with European homes and children in the distance, wished to remove the clothing of our countries ... Erase the family names! Erase nations! I was taught such things by the desert" (*EP*, 138–9). The political dimension of nationhood forces people to adopt a rhythm of oscillation between the roles of friend and enemy. In stark contrast to this ideological pitfall, the patient wishes for a world with no names and no nations, inveighing against any filiations with any *patrie* in these most frequently quoted words: "We were Germans, English, Hungarian, African – all of us insignificant to them. Gradually we became nationless. I came to hate nations. We are deformed by nation-states. Madox died because of nations" (*EP*, 138).

The crucial meaning of Ondaatje's image of the desert can be seen as an alternative for the people under the thralldom of nations. It also, as Alberto Fernández Carbajal cogently points out, "provides Ondaatje with the means of representing the affective crumbling of the colonial subject, the psychic fracture of Western rationalism and, in the meantime, also the belated discovery of new forms of accepting otherness." Carbajal terms this Ondaatje's "intimation of alternative non-European forms of humanism."[9]

MOURNING AND THE DEATH OF THE OTHER

Mourning obliges the self to reflect on the spectral aspects of both time and death. It is shown, for instance, in the revelation of the face of Hamlet's deceased father in the time that is out of joint. In other words, mourning concerns not merely death but time in its non-phenomenal original mode. It indicates that the self's asymmetrical relation with the other in another plane of height involves ethical thinking in which one no longer perceives death as nothingness and the end of time. Not dissimilar to Derrida's bringing together the two concepts of time and death, Levinas defines death as "a point

The *English Patient* as the Dialogic Field 291

from which time takes all its patience,"[10] and the death of the other, as claimed by him, is always the first death (43). To further explicate the nature of time, Levinas takes on the double meaning of the term "à- Dieu": time is

A patient awaiting. The patience and endurance of the beyond-measure, to-God [à-Dieu]; time as to-God. An awaiting without an awaited object, this would be a waiting for that which cannot be a term and which always refers from the Other to an Other [*de l'Autre à Autrui*]. The always of duration: a length [*longueur*] of time that is not the lengthiness [*longueur*] of the river that flows by. (115)

Levinas's concept of time, dissociated from the existentialist concern with an individual person's adopting (or abandoning) those projects that he is "able to" (*pouvoir*) grasp, is linked to the "situation of the face-to-face with the Other,"[11] a situation that entails the self's coming to grips with his/her disproportionate non-relation with the absolute infinite. In the meantime, it also denotes one's farewell to the other, who, alive or dead, withdraws from his life and leaves him a survivor abiding by his time that goes beyond measure. The notion of time, like that of death, escapes the phenomenon of intentionality. It is taken by Levinas as one key viewpoint from which the idea of overhauling the route of philosophy can be envisaged.

In Ondaatje's novel, the English patient, a man with no specific identity, is more than once referred to as a deathlike or spectral figure. He is "[Hana's] own ghost" (*EP*, 28). Attempting to persuade Hana out of her obsession for caring for the patient, Caravaggio tells her that "You've tied yourself to a corpse for some reason ... A twenty-year-old who throws herself out of the world to love a ghost" (*EP*, 45). This image of the patient as a corpse is overlaid at the outset of the novel when he is in proximity to experiencing a burial ritual by the Bedouin. His face is covered with "a mask of herbs," and his body is wrapped in linen. He is even described as a Jesus-like figure: Hana claims him as her "desperate saint," having "Hipbones of Christ" (*EP*, 3); the chemist of the Bedouin on the other hand is depicted as "an archangel" (*EP*, 9) as well as the "baptist" (*EP*, 10). Almost delineated as a Levinasian other, Almásy is a saint-like, sometimes perceived as a Jesus-like, figure to which Hana utterly dedicates herself. For Hana, Almásy embodies a responsibility always remaining to be borne. Far from only being responsible to this other, Hana responds to all the others represented by her English patient. While she is with him, Hana also memorializes her father Patrick, who died the same death as Almásy, burned by fire:

> Did her father struggle into his death or die calm? Did he lie the way the English patient reposes grandly on his cot? Was he nursed by a stranger? A man not of your own blood can break upon your emotions more than someone of your own blood. As if falling into the arms of a stranger you discover the mirror of your choice ... A novel is a mirror walking down a road. She had read that in one of the books the English patient recommended, and that was the way she remembered her father – whenever she collected the moments of him. (*EP*, 90–1)

The images of the two figures are overlapped here in Hana's recollection. In the beginning, Hana tries to avoid being devoured by her mourning of Patrick, since he is her "own blood." Only through the third, the spectre of the other, can Hana distance and later recover herself from the unbearable trauma. Almásy represents not only her deceased father and husband, and most of those seriously injured soldiers in the hospital, but her lost child as well, whose life she decides to stifle because "[t]he father was already dead. There was a war" (*EP*, 82). She cannot bear to see her child fall into the same fate.

The presentations of Patrick as the past, the English patient as the present, and the child as the future (though an aborted future) are merged together as one always overlaps another. Time is out of joint. All the lives that are destroyed by the war are seen on the face of Almásy, a face that demands or a face that, in Levinas's terms, demonstrates "authority." In other words, Almásy, a spectral image of the other superimposing the ghosts of her beloved, has always already been mourned by Hana, who foresees his death. Hana, like Almásy's mourning of Katharine Clifton, is haunted by a spectral memory that simultaneously concerns times behind and times ahead. The gesture of mourning indicates a coming to grips with the fact that while spectres belong to the past that come back to haunt us, they also abide by the futuristic time in patience.

Hana's reticent accusation of war is amplified by Levinas's reflection upon war-induced violence: "The true problem for us Westerners is not so much to refuse violence as to question ourselves about

The English Patient as the Dialogic Field   293

a struggle against violence which without blanching in non-resistance to evil, could avoid the institution of violence out of this very struggle."[12] To expose the polemic essence of "the war against war" that seeks to "perpetuate that which it is called to make disappear," Levinas sets the elongating sense of time in the war that continues indefinitely against the "patient" duration in the ethical:

> One has to reconsider the meaning of a certain weakness, and no longer see in patience only the reverse side of the ontological finitude of the human. But for that one has to be patient oneself without asking patience of the others – and for that one has to admit a difference between oneself and the others. (177)

For Levinas, holding on to being is an essential logic on the battlefield and in the ontological grasp of human existence. One's being patient, as is revealed in Levinas's stress on the ethical as a passive force, serves as an alternative to one's sticking to the logic and unfolds ethical provisions to keep the traumatic legacy of war in check. Levinas's notion of passivity does not indicate a state of indifference. Rather, it should be regarded as a gesture of non-assimilative responsiveness to the thematization, or the institutionalization, of violence. In this regard, patience, processing suffering in passivity, becomes a welded joint in Ondaatje and Levinas. Ondaatje's novel consists of a constellation of his characters' meandering reminiscences, in which the mourning in patience for the other speaks for itself in its undertone, and yet mightily so, against the war's dismantling of the work of the ethical.

There is another episode of ahead-of-time mourning and burial ritual in Ondaatje's novel. Before the war in the late thirties, Almásy falls in love with the wife of Geoffrey Clifton, an aerial photographer for British intelligence disguised as an explorer of the North African desert in Almásy's expedition. After discovering Katharine's extramarital affair with Almásy, Geoffrey decides to perish together with them by attempting an airplane crash. The suicidal mission ends up killing Geoffrey and fatally wounding Katharine. Bringing her to the Cave of Swimmers and sensing her imminent death, Almásy carries out an Egyptian "primitive burial ritual"[13] by applying "bright pigment," composed of "[h]erbs and stones and light and the ash of acacia" (EP, 260–1) to eternalize her soul, which mimics Herodotus's description of the immortalization of warriors in

Histories. Almásy mourns over Katharine before she dies. This event in Africa becomes the omnipresent haunting memory for Almásy in the villa San Girolamo in Italy.

If Almásy retained his cartographic penchant for naming while he was fervently infatuated with Katharine – "There was that small indentation at her throat we called the Bosphoros" (EP, 236) – he nonetheless gradually renounces it after realizing that the notion of ownership is precarious not only in the field of the political concerning one's sense of belonging but also in love affairs. While he used to claim body parts from Katharine – "This is my shoulder, he thinks, not her husband's, this is my shoulder" (EP, 156) – Almásy, now facing his dying beloved, becomes guilty and begins to feel contrite:

> Had I been her demon lover? Had I been Madox's demon friend? This country – had I charted it and turned it into a place of war? ... [Katharine's] body pressed against sacred colour. Only the eye blue removed, made anonymous, a naked map where nothing is depicted, no signature of lake, no dark cluster of mountain ... I believe in such cartography – to be marked by nature, not just to label ourselves on a map like the names of rich men and women on buildings. We are communal histories, communal books. We are not owned or monogamous in our taste or experience. All I desired was to walk upon such an earth that had no maps.
> (EP, 260–1)

Facing Katharine's death, Almásy undergoes a transformation of mindset in terms of proprietaries. Ondaatje specifically shows this metamorphosis of Almásy in the Cave of Swimmers. Symbolic of a womb-like space, the cave does not pertain to any modern Euro-American hierarchical classifications. Its pre-historical dimness refuses taxonomic illumination. The placement of Katharine in the "sacred" cave connotes an ultimate separation from the worldly and war-ravaged space. Delineating Almásy's sublimating ritualistic procedure of Katharine on her deathbed, with natural materials from the cave walls being applied on her skin, Ondaatje reinforces a constellation of superimposing images of Katharine's body and the natural landscape in the novel. Like the "mysterious Zerzura" (EP, 134) later to be found by the historical László Almásy, Katharine stands for the oasis that the fictional Almásy longs to recover in his desert life.

The English Patient as the Dialogic Field 295

The demonstration of Katharine in her last moments as a being that goes beyond her corporeality finds an echo in Levinas's analysis of eros and the feminine. Levinas begins his discussion of the term with the following statement: "In civilized life there are traces of this relationship with the other that one must investigate in its original form,"[14] followed immediately by a rhetorical question: "Does a situation exist where the alterity of the other appears in its purity?"[15] The above-cited sentences emphasize a fundamental cognition of the non-relation between the self and the other, with the words "original form" and "purity" referring to the metaphysical extension, rather than exclusion, of daily experiences. In this context, Levinas employs his notions of the feminine and eros not only to further explain his theory of the other but to challenge androcentrism. What distinguishes eros from the conventional ideal of love is that the former is construed on the premise that "[s]ex is not some specific difference. It is situated beside the logical division into genera and species."[16] Levinas traces the difference in sexes back to Plato, who holds the view that the partition of the originally unified human being into two sexes motivates one to search constantly for the complementary other. For Levinas, the Platonic binary denotes a final assimilation of the other in sameness. The feminine, the idea of the unassimilated, is not "an object that becomes ours or becomes us; to the contrary, it withdraws into its mystery ... The feminine in existence is an event different from that of spatial transcendence or of expression that go toward light. It is a flight before light."[17]

In *The English Patient*, the love affair between Katharine and Almásy has undergone a transformation from the mutual possession of the two to ritualistic manifestation of alterity and its cancellation of complementarity. It is a gesture of pointing toward a non-assimilative relation between lovers. The parting scenes thus become pivotal in the sense that in the process of mourning, Almásy realizes that separation is inevitable and that the obsession of "possessing, knowing, and grasping are synonyms of power"[18] when it comes to his affair with Katharine, which reflect his cartographic enterprise that is unintentionally complicit in the war. An attempt to comprehend – etymologically indicating forestalling in an act of seizing and taking – the other (lovers, friends, enemies) turns out to be the catastrophic undertone of the novel. Ondaatje's narrative deployment regarding the overlapping images of Katharine's body and deserts such as the one around the "mysterious Zerzura" seeks neither to feminize the landscape nor to objectify the feminine. Not dissimilar to Levinas, who asks not for an interpretation of the "mystery" of the feminine as something related to romantic courtship on the part of male,[19] Ondaatje suggests a sublimated erotic (non)relation in the Cave of Swimmers as a counterbalance to the all too glaring warlight (to borrow from the author's most recent novel) of gunfire and gunpowder, "a flight before light" and before comprehension. The mystery lies in "the plane of *eros*" that "allows us to see that the other *par excellence* is the feminine, through which a world behind the scenes prolongs the world"; it is not to be found in the domain of Platonic love, which resembles "a child of need" and "retains the features of destitution."[20]

Ondaatje's delineation of rationality, nationality, and humanism in *The English Patient* adds up to a large-scale expression of reservations about the part of Western humanism at the mercy of its own perilous focus on the self's one-way communication with the other. This delineation (and the critique it unfolds) can fruitfully be understood through consideration of Levinas's explication of what it means to be heteronomous. When Ondaatje describes the desert as nation-free and not able to be occupied, it is useful to be reminded of Levinas's manner of borrowing the idea of the infinite from René Descartes and his claims that there are certain entities that are ineffable and beyond the domain and demand of the self.

Levinas's notion of heteronomy is part of an attempt to propel the self into a tangential position in relation to the other. The self, instead of forsaking autonomy, empties out so as to be "experientially *ex nihilo*," as Simon Critchley puts it in his meditation on Levinas's thought in the context of making political decisions.[21] Critchley, in his enlightening critique of Levinas in "Five Problems in Levinas's View of Politics and a Sketch of a Solution to Them," indicates the fact that when it comes to the political dimension of ethics, the philosopher can never really deal with the shackles and chains that limit his Hebrew perspectives of thinking through certain political events. Yet Critchley suggests that if we understand the other's infinite authority over me and my decision not as the deprival of my subjectivity but as a beneficial boost to my being in the world in terms of occluding the pseudo-freedom of myself that inevitably sacrifices others' freedom, then the dilemma of Levinas's politics-ethics dualism might be resolved in their connection with the other:

The English Patient as the Dialogic Field   297

[W]hat we seem to have here is a relation between ethics and politics which is both non-foundational and non-arbitrary, that is, which leaves the decision open for invention whilst acknowledging that the decision comes from the other. If the "fact of reason" is the demand of the good that must be consistent with the principle of autonomy, then the "fact of the other" would be the demand of the good experienced as the heteronomous opening of autonomy which does not at all mean that autonomy is abandoned, it is simply rendered secondary.[22]

The shift from the "fact of reason" in the Age of Enlightenment to the "fact of the other" endorsed by Levinas and Derrida suggests an ethical turn that supports, rather than sabotages, the subjectivity of the self designated as taking up non-*Identity* and unconditionally admitting the non-diminishable nature of the other's alterity. The point of convergence of Ondaatje, Levinas, and Derrida, as far as the political dimension of ethics is concerned, bears the weight of what Zygmunt Bauman sees in Levinas's thought: "The moral self is a self always haunted by the suspicion that it is not moral enough."[23] The self's "state of being beholden to external influences" – influences that are wielded by the other whose face speaks of an externality that debunks the satisfactory state of existence of the self – is thus paradoxically the only solution to the varied ramifications of self-oriented righteousness and iniquity.

NOTES

The full version of this essay was originally published in *Concentric: Literary and Cultural Studies* 46, no. 1 (2020) and is reprinted with the permission of the journal.

1 Hand, *Emmanuel Levinas*, 65.
2 Levinas, "The Servant and Her Master," 156.
3 Derrida, *Adieu to Emmanuel Levinas*, 111.
4 Levinas, "The Trace of the Other," 394.
5 Banerjee, *The Chutneyfication of History*, 153.
6 Morgan, *Discovering Levinas*, 66.
7 Derrida, *Politics of Friendship*, 84.
8 Cohen, *Ethics, Exegesis and Philosophy*, 259.
9 Carbajal, *Compromise and Resistance in Postcolonial Writing*, 138.

10 Levinas, *God, Death and Time*, 7.
11 Levinas, *Time and the Other*, 79.
12 Levinas, *Otherwise Than Being*, 177.
13 Hilger, "Ondaatje's *The English Patient* and Rewriting History," 182.
14 Levinas, *Time and the Other*, 84.
15 Ibid., 85.
16 Ibid.
17 Ibid., 86–7.
18 Ibid.,, 90.
19 Levinas, *Existence and Existents*, 86.
20 Ibid.
21 Critchley, *Five Problems*, 100.
22 Ibid.
23 Bauman, *Postmodern Ethics*, 245.

14

Reconfiguring an East-West Dialectic of Trauma in Michael Ondaatje's War Novels: *The English Patient, Anil's Ghost,* and *Warlight*

Justin M. Hewitson

There is no life without trauma. There is no history without trauma.
Gabriele Schwab, "Words and Moods"[1]

Humanity's history of internecine violence has motivated our quest to minimize trauma. Postcolonial studies decode the systemic causes of violence to help individuals, but Eli Park Sorensen argues that the institutionalization of postcolonial theory gives it an "authoritative position of power" that sidelines the "specificity of the literary" for "certain political imperatives"[2] to support postcolonial optics. Works resisting this treatment are subjected to skepticism. Some critics of Michael Ondaatje's war novels *The English Patient, Anil's Ghost,* and *Warlight* have struggled to reconcile postcolonial perspectives with his circumspect portrayal of the hegemonic forces fracturing the world view and identity of different characters. W.M. Verhoeven, referencing the critical reception of *The English Patient*, notes that Ondaatje's extreme "signature generic indeterminacy and his self-reflexive narratology" overwhelm readers with a "lack of cohesion and resolution."[3] However, interlocutors claiming Ondaatje's novels lack "moral resolution" disregard their attempt to create a discourse problematizing the indeterminacy of "identity, self and language."[4] Ondaatje's detached representations of violence and suffering do not negate Western concerns. Rather, these novels embrace an East-West dialectic, navigating Western postcolonial attitudes threaded with Indian Tantric and Buddhist theories of cyclical suffering (karma), responsibility, and detached compassion to interrogate ideological attitudes toward war trauma. Ondaatje intersects his characteristically reflexive, apolitical descriptions of collective violence with his characters' intimate, although never fully realized, moments of detached connection with nature and spirit. By placing postcolonial strategies to isolate and identify the collective exogenous origins of violence under tension with Indian spirituality, tasking individuals to take absolute responsibility for suffering, his war novels reject solutions couched in the monocultural grammar of Eastern or Western epistemes. Read together, they become an extended transcultural dialogue about cyclical violence and trauma, intimating that compassion and detachment transform suffering into peace.

Ondaatje's multicultural background fuels his blending of Indian intuition and Western reason. Victoria Cook states that Ondaatje's "transnational identity" derives from this "polyglot mixture of Dutch, English, Sinhalese and Tamil"[5] public-school education in London and university studies in Canada. He lived in Sri Lanka surrounded by Buddhist and Tantric influences until he was eleven. Buddhism's canonical Pāli texts were transmitted to Sri Lanka in the third century BCE, with three-quarters of its Sinhala population following Indian forms of Buddhism. The remaining quarter are Hindus, generally practising the Shaivite branches of Tantra. Ondaatje's awareness of Indian Buddhism and Tantra appears in *Anil's Ghost*,[6] while *The English Patient* and *Warlight* refract India's spiritual traditions, art, and literature. Important scenes include excerpts from the writings of the Sri Lankan Indologist – Ananda K. Coomaraswamy – in *Anil's Ghost* to Rudyard Kipling's *Kim* in *The English Patient*.

Ondaatje's war novels eliminate peacetime norms and social structures, forcing protagonists to deal with the (in)direct trauma fracturing their world view and identities. The Moth character in *Warlight* explains to the siblings Nathaniel and Rachel how danger exists for "all of us" as they grow up exploring the rubble of Second World War London after the bombing ends. They realize "that nothing was safe anymore" when their mother disappears, leaving them to the care of strangers (WL, 31). *Anil's Ghost* takes place in Sri Lanka some six decades post–Second World War toward the end of the bloody twenty-six-year civil war between the Sinhala Buddhist government and Hindu Tamil Tigers. *The English Patient*, set mostly in Tuscany at the end of the Second World War, examines violence, passion, and trauma through Hana, a Canadian nurse caring for an unrecognizably burned man (the English patient), and Kip, the Indian Sapper. These works do not unequivocally privilege the Indian ideals of spiritual liberation – none of Ondaatje's protagonists achieves absolute peace. However, *Anil's Ghost* and *Warlight* conclude with scenes evoking Buddhist and Tantric detachment as Ananda and Nathaniel intuit karmic cycles while experiencing a compassionate (re)connection with the world, and *The English Patient*'s Hana is also drawn to Kip's spiritual tranquility.

Few studies have treated Ondaatje's inclusion of Indian themes in any of his novels as more than literary figuration or his notoriously ambivalent representations of war trauma.[7] To the best of my knowledge, this essay is the only transdisciplinary, East-West dialectical reading of all three. My first section, "Critical Indo-European Backgrounds to Ondaatje's War Novels," briefly prefigures Western and Indian approaches to violence and trauma. The second section, "Deconstructing Western Reason and Indian Intuition in Ondaatje's War Novels," (re)configures these threads into a metanarrative for Ondaatje's war novels.

CRITICAL INDO-EUROPEAN BACKGROUNDS TO ONDAATJE'S WAR NOVELS

International interventions targeting a reduction in mass violence identify relevant socio-political forces to punish or shame them and foster reconciliation between victims and perpetrators. Reconciliation is deemed critical to limiting future conflicts, but retribution and blame have not led to lasting peace. Kaushik Roy explains that the "strategic culture approach" developed at the close of the twentieth century deals with "cultural factors" to explain the "origins, conduct, and results of warfare." Paraphrasing Jeremy Black, he states that cultures determine how "societies understand loss and suffering at both the individual and collective levels of the soldier and the society."[8] Unfortunately, Western mediation favouring political or judicial strategies to treat harms misinterprets the needs of victims with other world views. Ondaatje therefore avoids structuring monocultural therapies but transfigures a transdisciplinary and intimately hybrid portrayal of trauma.

While Ondaatje's war novels do not unequivocally reify postcolonial or Indian spiritual therapies, the detached intuitions and aesthetics of India's contemplative traditions impact various protagonists' experiences of peace. Annick Hillger's postmodern analysis of Ondaatje's poem "Birch Bark" deconstructs the suppression of the body and its senses in the "age of reason" and how "aesthetic contemplation" liberates the "human body from the constraints of teleological thought" to treat the "often noted violence" in Ondaatje's texts.[9] She claims the poem re-evaluates "language as an epistemological tool" to provide readers with epistemes transcending the "logocentric tradition," opening us to new avenues of ontological exploration.[10] Likewise, Ondaatje's fiction fuses Western disciplines with India's spiritual epistemes because neither have resolved the cycles of violence. As the texts minimize issues of punishment and restitution, different characters' responses to and responsibility for their personal suffering configures an underlying cognitive narratology. These tropes parallel Tantra's practical alleviation of cyclical suffering when meditators experience how non-attachment frees consciousness to witness all mental desires and memories without being overwhelmed by passion. The Tantric philosopher P.R. Sarkar explains that every "particle of the universe is a modified form of [infinite] consciousness," so "the process of realizing any human desire is also 'the story of a journey' into consciousness itself."[11] Buddhism and Tantra consider mental transcendence as the meditator's cessation of compulsive identification with pleasurable or traumatic mental states.

My reading of Tantra's complex spiritual detachment in Ondaatje's novels can be clarified by the *Bhagavad Gita*'s ancient "epic Sanskrit" poetry on nonattachment and responsibility. Krishna, the avatar of *Brahman* (Cosmic Consciousness), tells Arjuna he must fight in a war "without being driven by desire."[12] Ithamar Theodor explains the common philosophical interpretation of the *Gita* that since action is inevitable, it is best to practise "*karma yoga*"[13] (desireless action)[14] to break the karmic chains of cause and effect. Krishna teaches that the "world is bound by action," except for actions born of "sacrifice" (actions devoid of egological identification), so Arjuna must act "without attachment" to his deeds. Because anger causes "delusion," a loss of "mindfulness," and therefore suffering, those "unyoked to hate and passions"[15] achieve peace. *Warlight* articulates this vision that "suffering [is] always a part of desire" (233).

According to Manoj Kumar Sinha, the first (pre)historical humanitarian approaches to war are found in India's *Ṛg Veda* and the *Laws of Manu*'s prescription that "combatants and noncombatants"[16] be separated, predating Western efforts by millennia. The 1948 Universal Declaration of Human Rights (UDHR) is modernity's overture to stopping war trauma by recognizing that the "inherent dignity and the equal and inalienable rights of all" are the basis of freedom, justice, and peace. And "disregard and contempt for human rights" has created barbarity outraging humanity, so our global dream is freedom of speech and belief without fear or want.[17] However, data from *Conflict Trends* 2019 research into global conflict suggests the UDHR's dream remains unrealized, with more than a hundred global conflicts that year.[18]

Ondaatje's novels communicate the social origins of conflict driven by power-hungry individuals manipulating national or religious beliefs to foment collective ideological passion. Eric A. Heinze observes that America's so-called "humanitarian intervention" into Iraq raised "well-founded fears" among interested academics that such altruistic arguments could "cloak exercises of hegemonic power."[19] Distrust in international justice arose decades earlier, following Japan's surrender to America and the subsequent human rights fiasco of the Tokyo Trials. Not a single member of the "five-general military commission" had legal training, yet they sentenced Japanese General Masaharu Homma to death. Homma stated, "I am being executed for the Bataan incident. What I want to know is: Who is responsible for the burning of 150,000 innocent civilians at Hiroshima – MacArthur or Truman?" By the time the Tokyo Trials began, there was outrage over the "legal underpinnings" of the Homma case. Newly appointed judges stated they would have "rejected the rationale of the earlier decisions."[20] In hindsight, those executed were part of what participating judge B.V.A. Röling described years later as a "huge scale theatrical production" with "more 'Hollywoodesque' things around than there should have been."[21]

DECONSTRUCTING WESTERN REASON AND INDIAN INTUITION IN ONDAATJE'S WAR NOVELS

When asked what inspires his novels, Ondaatje says he begins with a time and place or a specific image segueing into detailed research that introduces him to a "vast unknown landscape." Rereading *Anil's Ghost*, he discovered his awareness of "Sri Lankan habits and gestures."[22] His imagination and research become a "bricolage" of Indian and Western thought coalescing around trauma and the "uncertainty and doubt" of an "intimate and therefore trusted voice." He claims his texts are "light years" removed from "just political or public or thematic reasons for existence."[23] Although Ondaatje's writings incorporate political spectrums of violence, these social factors are viewed objectively, including Tantric and Buddhist perspectives to configure a transgressive dialectic. Ondaatje's consciousness of the depth of Eastern influences on his writing is relatively new. While Western discourse follows "order, logical progression" and "symmetry," he recently discovered that his novels follow or maybe "guess at aesthetics" coming "from the East."[24] Rather than propagating a vexing socio-political dissonance, he weaves Indian and Western epistemes to produce nuanced psycho-spiritual and geopolitical views of violence and trauma.

Political approaches to preventing genocide are necessary, but the macro effectiveness of modern political solutions remains undecided when *Realpolitik* and human psychology interfere with humanitarian ideals. *Anil's Ghost* addresses this: "In the shadows of war and politics there came to be surreal turns of cause and effect" as "it became evident that political enemies were secretly joined in financial arms deals. '*The reason for war was war*'" (AG, 41–2). It is also common for those who identify as victims to inflame the desire for retribution within their own circles. Mark A. Drumbl notes that 25 per cent of victims "have opinions on what should happen to their oppressors,"[25] with "revenge" driving "action against offenders."[26] Hana, the nurse in *The English Patient*, highlights this pattern in Tacitus's *Annals*: "The histories of Tiberius, Caligula, Claudius and Nero, while they were a power, were falsified through terror and after their death were written under afresh hatred (EP, 93)." Hsu Shou-Nan's deconstruction of Ondaatje's poem "Buried 2" states "people fight because of the desire for 'power and wealth' (25), and those who cannot possess these suffer from feelings of 'vengeance' and 'envy' (25), which are the seeds of future conflicts."[27] Therefore, Tantra and Buddhism establish each person's responsibility for overcoming the attachments that catalyze destructive historical cycles by seeking an elevated, detached view of existence.

Ondaatje's descriptions of gross violence are characteristically distanced, wide-angled cinematic visions of crumbling social structures before zooming into interiorized glimpses of his protagonists' trauma. Kathleen Fernando's account of the violence in *Anil's Ghost* frames how "violence in the narrative – its ubiquitous, primitive nature" suggests a "discourse of civilizational decay" and that foregrounding a "multiplicity of non-Western knowledges" is one of its primary themes. While some argue that the novel instantiates an "Orientalist gaze" and privileges a "discourse of violence,"[28] I propose violence dramatizes a universally relatable source of trauma for Ondaatje's readers. Gabriele Schwab's epigraph to my essay articulates this existential state: "There is no life without trauma. There is no history without trauma."[29] *Anil's Ghost* offers a distanced view of war, providing readers with pluralistic perspectives that reveal the recursive trajectories of violence and trauma.

War is not Ondaatje's only source of violence; passionate attachment generates "betrayals in war that are childlike compared with our human betrayals during peace" so that "a love story" is the "consuming of oneself and the past (*EP*, 97). Consuming the "past" symbolizes the suffering of karmic reactions. None of the sexes is innocent of aggression; women in *The English Patient* and *Anil's Ghost* physically assault their lovers in moments of obsession or fury. The English patient, Count László de Almásy, has an affair with Katharine Clifton that leaves him with "a list of wounds," including a plate broken over his head, "the blood rising up into the straw hair," a "fork" stuck into "the back of his shoulder," and other scratches and bites (*EP*, 153). Anil Tissera stabs her lover, Cullis, in the arm; "her right hand was still curled around the knife ... She wouldn't step back from her fury" (*AG*, 100). The archaeologist Palipana describes the power of emotional violence: "There has always been slaughter in passion" so that "even if you are a monk, like my brother, passion or slaughter will meet you someday" (*AG*, 102, 103). He articulates a postmodern and Indian interpretation of society and renunciation: "You cannot survive as a monk if society does not exist. You renounce society, but to do so you must first be a part of it, learn your decision from it." Reflecting Krishna's teachings that action is inevitable, he says that the "paradox of retreat" is that it does not guarantee safety, perhaps only equanimity. "My brother entered temple life. He escaped the world, and the world came after him. He was seventy when he was killed by someone, perhaps someone from the time when he was breaking free" (*AG*, 103). Even mediators engaged in short-term humanitarian projects confront risks.

Anil's Ghost's unsettling view of humanitarian interventions is supported by its nonjudgmental yet unflinching gaze at the powers creating or identifying victims. Susan F. Hirsch argues that official recognition for victims is frequently a critical goal "for those struggling to bring coherence to a damaged and wildly fluctuating sense of self," but victims differ on "what constitutes recognition" – will handshakes from dignitaries, press coverage, or memorials suffice? In some cases, yes. However, for many survivors any response fails their profound need for their "loss and self acknowledged."[30] *Anil's Ghost* accentuates the troubling disconnect between international humanitarian intervention and victims' needs. The novel's macro historical and economic perspective exposes how groups propagate violence and the dilemma of staying silent when confronting oppression. Sarath Diyasena, a Sri Lankan archaeologist, relates a history of the Sri Lankan conflict that speaks to humanity's universal culpability and the quandary of laying specific blame. He explains to Anil that the violence peaked in the late eighties, but "it was going on long before that. Every side was killing and hiding the evidence. *Every side*" (AG, 17). While *Anil's Ghost* tacitly recognizes that forensic accounts of violence are intrinsic to international justice and valued by victims, it also problematizes the role of humanitarian responses following human rights abuses.

Anil is an expatriate Sri Lankan trained in America as a forensic investigator tasked by the United Nations Center for Human Rights to uncover evidence of extrajudicial killings in Sri Lanka. Her mission is facilitated by Sarath and his brother Gamini, a trauma surgeon. After returning to the island, Anil doubts her forensic work can respond adequately to the history of Sri Lankan violence. She recalls her American teacher's statement on "human rights work in Kurdistan" that "*One village can speak for many villagers. One victim can speak for many victims.*" Yet even if she could give an identity to the skeleton of a government victim she names Sailor and uncover "the details of his murder, what then? He was a victim among thousands" (AG, 177). Her concerns reflect the text's postmodern appraisal of etic humanitarian interventions overseen by the very authorities being investigated. While Sarath drives Anil "into the high altitudes" of the mountains to visit a grave, he argues that Anil's humanitarian goals are undermined by her lack of an emic perspective into both the victims and possible perpetrators of violence: "'I'd believe your arguments more if you lived here,' he said. 'You can't just slip in, make a discovery and leave ... Or you'll be like one of those journalists who file reports about flies and scabs while

East-West Dialectic of Trauma in Ondaatje's War Novels 307

staying at the Galle Face Hotel. That false empathy and blame'" (AG, 44). The reality implicit in Sarath's denouncement is that such reports become consumer items composed to incite a visceral desire for justice or swift intervention, and this frequently generates more insidious forms of violence and repression.

Anil's Ghost's detached viewpoint further brings the pseudo-objectivity of etic mediators into view. Gamini doubts the justice of international interventions: "'I'm probably another example of trauma, you see ... And those armchair rebels living abroad with their ideas of justice ... They should come and visit me in surgery ... Mostly it's hideous mutilation.'" Yet the people "'setting off the bombs are who the Western press called freedom fighters ... And you want to investigate the *government?*'" (AG, 132). Early in the novel, the need for inclusive perspectives is symbolized by Sarath's mannerisms, which remind Anil of the "Asian Nod." The gesture's "almost circular movement [includes] the possibility of a no" (AG, 16). The round motion of the nod suggests that enough spatiotemporal distance allows any trajectory to transform into its opposite, serving as the text's self-referential nod toward the karmic cycles of suffering that reappear at its conclusion, as I examine later. Michael Barry notes that Ondaatje regularly employs an "aerial view,"[31] blurring the boundaries between perpetrators and victims to realize Ondaatje's vision that "we contain multitudes" and stories can reflect that.[32] As such, *Anil's Ghost* replicates a detached, often omniscient, vision of events contrasted with moments of violence that provoke outraged blame.

Anil's final report to the Sri Lankan officials starts with her detached status as a "foreign authority" offering an objective analysis of Sailor's murder, but it transforms into an emotional response when she self-identifies with the Sri Lankan victims: "'I think you murdered hundreds of us'" (AG, 271). Concerned for her safety, Sarath attempts to undermine the validity of her research. Anil's frustration compels her to respond that "'some government forces have possibly murdered innocent people'" and that he "'should believe in the truth of history.'" The novel's thematic concern with mediation is reinforced by Sarath's rebuttal that her status as an independent investigator is an illusion: "'This 'international authority' has been invited here by the government ... that means you do work for the government here'" (AG, 274). He continues that he "'believe[s] in a society that has peace, Miss Tissera. What you are proposing could result in chaos. Why do you not investigate the killing of government officers?'" Sarath also understands that "evidence of a certain kind of crime" often leads to other harms (AG, 275). His fears materialize after her evidence is confiscated, and she is raped in the same building where she gave testimony about human rights abuses: "'I really don't want your fucking help. But I can't walk. I was ... in there ...'" (AG, 182). Anil is explicitly transformed from a mediator into a victim because she becomes psychologically attached to the government's victims. On the other hand, Sarath is murdered for returning to the "intricacies of the public world, with its various truths" and for restoring Anil's evidence before she leaves (AG, 279). These tragedies are foreshadowed during that earlier drive up the mountain (reinstating the aerial view) after Sarath warns her to be careful of what she reveals. When she points out that she "*was* invited here,'" he says, "'International investigations don't mean a lot'" (AG, 44). Taken from a Western humanitarian point of view, one of the most distressing aspects of the crimes following Anil's speaking truth to power is the text's lack of answers. Anil is left haunted by Sarath's ghost, and no group is brought to justice. Perhaps this silence points to India's spiritual philosophy that passions – even for justice – introduce unwanted consequences in much the same way that humanitarian or political strategies exacerbate suffering by dividing people into perpetrators and victims over time.

The first of Ondaatje's war novels, *The English Patient*, delivers a broad account of how the powerful destroy peace. Caravaggio, Hana's older Canadian friend, proclaims that war is the behaviour of the "'compromised'" wealthy "'protect[ing] their belongings'" (EP, 122). The British and American armies use innocents, like the twenty-six-year-old Indian Kip, to risk their lives salvaging expensive villas because of their trust in Western civilization. Caravaggio declares that Kip's faith in the West is his "'First mistake'" and "'the trouble with all of us is we are where we shouldn't be ... The armies indoctrinate you and leave you here and they fuck off somewhere else to cause trouble'" (EP, 122). M.A. Bowers reasons the work shows that eliminating "the ideology imbued by one's nation" to transcend nationality is dangerous yet complying with "racially and imperialistically determined social conventions" is equally perilous; thus, "Almásy blames enforced national identities for warfare and a lack of personal freedom." Bowers continues that *The English Patient* stands against "Western nation-state politics" and their

East-West Dialectic of Trauma in Ondaatje's War Novels 309

conflicts as a reminder of how the Second World War created "growing anti-European and anti-colonial sentiment in Asia in the middle of the twentieth century."[33] The argument has merit vis-à-vis Kip's recollection of his brother's deep antipathy toward Europe: "'Asia is still not a free continent, and he [Kip's brother] is appalled at how we throw ourselves into English wars.'" But thematizing a vigorous anti-European view may go further than Ondaatje intends: Kip says, "'Japan is a part of Asia'" and the "'Sikhs have been brutalized by the Japanese in Malaya,'" yet his brother chooses to ignore that (*EP*, 217–18). These lines configure *The English Patient*'s unbiased transcultural dialectic on violence and trauma that I will show at the end of this essay extends to both *Anil's Ghost* and *Warlight*.

We have seen how disciplines mediating suffering face a vastly disputed reality, occluded by competing solutions and rationalizations of spiraling violence. *The English Patient* quotes the beginning of Tacitus's *Annals* to state that "many books open with an author's assurance of order," while "novels" begin with "hesitation or chaos" so that readers are "never fully in balance" (*EP*, 93). Lisa Pace Vetter notes that Ondaatje's writings "bridge past and present, East and West" to show that "conflict and violence are virtually inextricable from human affairs." Mixing "the personal and the political," Ondaatje's portrayal of humanity is "compelling to liberal pluralism" because his writings embrace the rationality of historical Western Enlightenment and Eastern "faith and tradition."[34] This position marks my final unravelling of the postcolonial and Indian threads in Ondaatje's dialectic on trauma. I do not propose that he explicitly reifies teleology over the political, but it is evident that certain protagonists' recovery aligns with the detached compassion of Buddhism and Tantra along with references to Indian literature and other religious iconography – particularly statues.

In *The English Patient*, the "Villa San Girolamo, built to protect inhabitants from the flesh of the devil, had the look of a besieged fortress, the limbs of most of the statues blown off during the first days of shelling." The war around the villa is a man-made evil, the "unexploded mines" (*EP*, 43) that beset Hana's movements in its gardens are bent on chaos and death. The damage wrought to the statues reflects Hana's traumatized psyche. She tells Caravaggio about aborting her child after its father was killed during the war: "'I was the one who destroyed it'" (*EP*, 85). These losses, compounded by her daily encounters with death, undermine her trust in society or ability to make human connections. "'Soldiers were coming in with just bits of their bodies, falling in love with me for an hour and then dying ... But I kept seeing the child whenever they died. Being washed away.'" (*EP*, 83). She is also psychologically battered by the anger of dying soldiers and her knowledge that the authorities coordinating these deaths do not care. "'Who would want to die like that? To die with that kind of anger'" (*EP*, 83). As war twists the natural order – the young dying to serve the old – she retreats into a neurotic disconnection from life: "'After that I stepped so far back no one could get near me ... Not with anyone's death'" (*EP*, 85). She discerns no wisdom among those guiding events – "'Every damn general should have had my job'" – and religiosity makes a mockery of violent death: "'Who the hell were we to be given this responsibility, expected to be wise as old priests ... I could never believe in all those services they gave for the dead. Their vulgar rhetoric ... How dare they talk like that about a human being dying'" (*EP*, 84). As Hana's gradual recovery intersects with her acts of nurture and Kip's compassionate concern, the novel configures an answer to these questions.

Although Hana cannot save the burned English patient, she nurtures a tenacious life back into the destroyed garden of the villa, treating the damage done to "the burned earth," despite a "lack of water," by throwing herself into restoring the garden so that "someday there would be a bower of limes, rooms of green light" (*EP*, 43). This growth amidst the destroyed statues and tortured soil invokes a cycle of neogenesis as a counterpoint to her losses. Her healing also intersects with her intimate relationship with Kip, a Sikh devotee who has left India to help the Allied forces clear explosives.

The Indian sapper confronts the extreme danger of his work with spiritual equanimity while defusing the bombs and mines left by the retreating German forces for the Allies. He also practises nonattachment while walking "up Italy" and fighting in battles "with eyes that tried to see everything except what was temporary and human" (*EP*, 218). Following brutal encounters fighting through "narrow streets everywhere that became sewers of blood so he would dream that if he lost balance, he would slip down those slopes on the red liquid and be flung off the cliff into the valley," he turns to the religious iconography scattered across the countryside. Religious symbols, such as a "grieving angel" and statues in a "captured church," become his guardians as he sleeps (*EP*, 110).

Kip's fearlessness and fullness of spirit contrast with Hana's morbid fearlessness and emptiness. She is drawn to her own death while helping him to defuse a bomb: "'I thought I was going to die. I wanted to die'" with "'someone like you, young as I am, I saw so many dying near me in the last year. I didn't feel scared. I certainly wasn't brave.'" If unable to reconcile these horrors with religious belief, she is comforted by Kip's serenity, wanting him to be a "still bed" so she can sleep without thought (*EP*, 103). In Kip's nightly embrace, she turns away from "the feuds of the world" to hold an "Indian goddess in her arms" (*EP*, 218). Hana's rejection of religious beliefs does not negate its influences. Kip describes Harimandir Sahib, the Golden Temple and holiest place for all Sikhs in Punjab, as a spiritual place, "'a haven in the flux of life, accessible to all,'" and a "'ship that crossed the ocean of ignorance'" (*EP*, 271). Tantra sees the ocean of ignorance as the human attachment to worldly passions rather than seeking to merge with the "highest state of reality" – the "infinite unqualified consciousness" that exists within all creation.[35] Even as Kip understands that Hana's "lack of a child and of faith" has left a "depth of darkness" in her, she, in turn, grasps that his spirituality enables him to "replace loss" with light. After a day spent "dismantling a bomb that might kill him at any moment," he would return "from the burial of a fellow sapper" lifted by his faith in "the various maps of fate" (karma) that would help him find "solution and light" where Hana "saw none" (*EP*, 272). Kip's spiritual vision helps him to accept intense psychophysical suffering, so Hana knows he will claim having a "good life," despite his brother's imprisonment, "his comrades blown up, and he risking himself daily in this war." He remains one of those not "destroyed by unfairness" (*EP*, 272). Despite Kip's spiritual equanimity, *The English Patient* offers a postcolonial interpolation when he reflects on his Indian identity while serving in a Western war.

Kip realizes that his sacrifices and heroism will not be recognized by the Europeans he serves, and Western readers rarely encounter brown-skinned heroes. "If he were a hero in a painting, he could claim a just sleep," but "he was the brownness of a rock." When "wise white fatherly men" successfully defused bombs, English novels ended with them as heroes, yet he will always be "the foreigner, the Sikh"; his "only human and personal contact was this enemy who had made the bomb and departed" (*EP*, 104–5). Likewise, *Anil's Ghost* records the West's failure to see that the violence is not over when Europeans go home. Gamini notes, "'The tired hero'" of "'American movies [and] English books gets on a plane and leaves ... He's going home. So the war, to all purposes, is over. That's enough reality for the West. It's probably the history of the last two hundred years of Western political writing'" (AG, 285). Ondaatje's war novels therefore acknowledge racial tensions to raise the issue of identification within an East-West framework.

Hana's reading of Rudyard Kipling's "*Kim*, with its delicate and holy sentences," to the English patient reconfigures Tantric soteriology and identity (EP, 94). She transports the dying man's imagination to the "sacred river" and Kim's meditation: "'In a minute – in another half second – he felt he would arrive at the solution of the tremendous puzzle'" (EP, 111). Ondaatje does not complete this passage from *Kim* – just as Kim's self-realization is left incomplete in Kipling's work. The unanswered question "Who is Kim – Kim – Kim?" is assuredly not about his physical identity but about the meditator's inquiry into consciousness. Ondaatje's awareness of our multiple identities, as I referenced earlier, compounds *The English Patient*'s reluctance to accept a single path to self-awareness, so the text cuts the direct quotation from Kipling just before Kim's encounter with a Yogi or "Hindu *bairagi* (holy man)." Observing Kim's spiritual struggle, he commiserates, "'I also have lost it ... It is one of the gates to the Way.'" The Way is the Tantric "'road to Enlightenment'" to the "'One'" to which "'we all travel.'"[36] From my reading, Ondaatje's configuration of Indian karma and detachment is fully realized at the conclusions of *Anil's Ghost* and *Warlight*, which expand *The English Patient*'s East-West dialectic.

At the end of *Warlight*, Nathaniel has spent his life working for the British intelligence trying to unravel his mother's clandestine work during the Second World War and her subsequent murder years later. "*Viola. Are you Viola?* I used to whisper to myself, slowly discovering who my mother was" (WL, 284). He finds an article written by a neighbour describing how the war helped the "survival" of "*Lathyrus maritimus*," the "almost extinct sea pea," also known as "'a happy vegetable of peace'" (WL, 283, 284). The pea's resurrection during the war parallels the vegetal life that will flourish in Hana's war-ravaged garden. *Warlight* uses the grammar of Indian karma to explain the life cycle as the opaque chain of actions and reactions that underpin life and suffering. Nathaniel is attracted to these "surprising liaisons, such *sutras* of cause and effect" (WL, 292). I emphasize *sutras* because this Sanskrit term for India's spiritual aphorisms has its etymology in *sūtra* – literally meaning thread – derived from the Sanskrit verbal root for sew. *Warlight* also invokes my earlier reference from *The English Patient* that "novels" begin with "hesitation or chaos" so that readers are "never fully in balance" (EP, 93). While Ondaatje conjures imbalance through violence, his characters' perspectives are threaded with Western reason and Indian intuition. Weaving these opposites unearths pathways to acceptance through detached responsibility: "We order our lives with barely held stories ... Gathering what was invisible and unspoken ... Sewing it altogether in order to survive, incomplete, ignored like the sea pea on those mined beaches during the war" (WL, 284–5). For Ondaatje, human life, shaped by past and future losses, remains incomplete. If his novels offer any hint of practical individual therapies, they are paradoxically encoded in a simultaneous detachment from – yet compassion for – the world and its suffering.

In their final respective scenes, *Warlight* and *Anil's Ghost* represent this heightened state as a caring touch that links protagonists to the natural and human world. Nathaniel recollects his mother's declaration that Handel's "breakdown" made him "'the ideal man' in that state, honourable, loving the world he could no longer be a part of, even if the world was a place of continual war" (WL, 283). He learns to live within nature's rhythms, eating when his Greyhound does. The dog comes to him in the evenings, lowering its "tired head" onto Nathaniel's hand, seeking "comfort, needing something warm and human for security, a faith in another." It comes to him, despite the man's "separateness and uncertainties," as if wishing to tell Nathaniel about its "haphazard life" and unknown past. While Nathaniel's job keeps him tracing the violence of the past, caring for the dog "who needs [his] hand" and taking pleasure in nature's surprise (the unexpected "blossoms" that suddenly appear in his garden) bring him peace in the present (WL, 283).

"Distance," the final chapter of *Anil's Ghost*, sees Ananda Udugama, who became a suicidal alcoholic following his wife's murder, perched 120 feet above the earth rebuilding a damaged Buddha statue. Ondaatje draws on Coomaraswamy's works to reference the Hindu mantras adopted by Buddhists during the completion of the Buddha's statue.[37] Just after he finishes the Buddha's stone face, Ananda enters a trancelike spiritual state and witnesses the cycles of karmic suffering. Like Nathaniel in *Warlight*, he is restored to the world by a compassionate touch. No longer able to "celebrate the greatness" of Buddhism, he understands his duty to remain an "artificer" or "become a demon." He comprehends that the "war" around him "was to do with demons, spectres of retaliation" (AG, 304). Buddhists view these "spectres of retaliation" as those who perpetuate suffering because of their attachment and identification with desires. J. Braarvig's discussion of hell in the 250–100 BCE Pāli Buddhist *Kathavatthu* identifies our absolute responsibility for our existence and suffering: "Any living being is totally responsible for his own fate, or rather state, since *we are all the result of what we ourselves have done*, and these worlds continue to exist because the beings in them continue to act."[38] Ananda's literal location high on the ladder restoring the Buddha's damaged eyes figuratively encapsulates his liminal state between heaven and earth, between action and detachment, and between suffering and transcendence. While the loss of his wife and the killings around him have destroyed his beliefs, his elevation and intense focus on the Buddha's eyes spontaneously establish a state of detachment – a reminder that authentic spirituality transcends belief, in accordance with the Buddha's instructions to his own disciple, also named Ananda, 2,300 years ago.

Ananda's work transforming the statue from sleeping stone into a waking "Buddha" is finished only after its eyes are completed. The eyes will "witness figures only from a great distance," compassionately observing the transitions of human history and nature (AG, 305). When Ananda's work is done, his awareness merges with that of the Buddha to see "all the fibres of natural history around him," to "witness the smallest approach of a bird, every flick of its wing, or a hundred-mile storm coming down off the mountains" (AG, 306). Ananda's consciousness expands into the human and natural world, "the smell of petrol and grenade. The crack of noise as a layer of rock on his arm exfoliated in the heat ... The great churning of weather above the earth." Even as the gravity of this "seduction" draws him outwards, he is reconnected to life by his assistant's concern in a "sweet touch from the world" (AG, 308). Ending on this dual note of detachment and compassion, *Anil's Ghost* reverses the suffering of its opening scene in which relatives conduct a "vigil for the dead," waiting to identify the remains of loved ones dug out of pits near the Buddha statues (AG, 5). Read together, both

Anil's Ghost and *Warlight* track the structure of novels laid out by Ondaatje, beginning with trauma and ending with a compassionate if detached acceptance of suffering.

While the postmodern world strives to remedy violence by confronting its collective causes and promoting restitution, India's ancient spiritual traditions offer individuals targeted psycho-spiritual disciplines to transform trauma into detachment. Both Tantra and Buddhism acknowledge that positive collective change is necessary; nevertheless, they prioritize the individual's responsibility to overcome socially constructed identities – whether as victims or perpetrators. The East-West fusion present in Ondaatje's war novels symbolizes this balancing of horizons. In this regard, Eric Wertheimer and Monica J. Casper argue that doing "intellectual work in the midst of great trouble" calls for a new humanities that respects "fact and heart even after the disciplines have diverged over arguments about society and imagination, propaganda and information, constructs and cold reality, representations and experience."[39] Ondaatje's dialectical refiguration of violence effectively instantiates a sorely needed non-judgmental portrayal of the psychosocial forces traumatizing individuals and groups. By "meld[ing] the scientific with the affective, the voices of narrated pain with the determined habits of repair and psychic healing, the archives and realms of theory with the visceral, lived experiences of practice,"[40] his writings explore how we confront suffering by weaving between Indian and Western humanitarian praxes. Negotiating a dynamic balance between Indian and Western thought, Ondaatje imbues his war novels with more openness but less systemic certainty. Following this thread, we can conclude that Ondaatje offers the delicate possibility that a history of war trauma does not necessarily circumscribe a future of suffering for those transformed by detached compassion.

NOTES

1 Schwab, "Words and Moods," 107–27.
2 Sorensen, *Postcolonial Studies and the Literary*, viii.
3 Verhoeven, "Playing Hide and Seek in Language," 21.
4 Ibid., 22.
5 Cook, "Exploring Transnational Identities in Ondaatje's *Anil's Ghost*," 6.

6 For an extensive treatment of the Buddhist and Tantric influences in *Anil's Ghost*, see Hewitson's "Mediating Suffering," 1–10. Ganz's "'The Reason for War Is War'" offers a Buddhist and Western reading of *Anil's Ghost* that argues truth is never singular.

7 See Goldman's "Representations of Buddhism in Ondaatje's *Anil's Ghost*," n.p.

8 Roy, *Hinduism and the Ethics of Warfare in South Asia*, 2, 3.

9 Hillger, *Not Needing All the Words*, 31.

10 Ibid., 3.

11 Hewitson, "Peterson vs. Žižek on the Evolution of Consciousness and Happiness," 69.

12 Davis, *The Bhagavad Gita*, 6, 18.

13 Theodor, *Exploring the Bhagavad Gita*, 42.

14 All Sanskrit translations are mine.

15 Flood and Martin, *The Bhagavad Gita*, 17, 19.

16 Sinha, "Hinduism and International Humanitarian Law," 291.

17 UN General Assembly, *Universal Declaration of Human Rights*, 217 [III] A.

18 Strand et al., "Trends in Armed Conflict, 1946–2019," 2.

19 Heinze, *Waging Humanitarian War*, viii.

20 Crowe, *War Crimes, Genocide, and Justice*, 199.

21 Ibid., 208.

22 Knopf and Ondaatje, "Michael Ondaatje: From Archives to Page," 78.

23 Halpé, "A Fox's Wedding: Sitting Down with Michael Ondaatje," 301.

24 Ibid., 300.

25 Drumbl, *Atrocity, Punishment, and International Law*, 42.

26 Hewitson, "Mediating Suffering," 5.

27 Shou-Nan, "Creating a Solid Foundation for Peace," 398, 399.

28 Fernando, "'Inhospitable Nation,'" 216.

29 Schwab, "Words and Moods," 42.

30 Hirsch. *In the Moment Of Greatest Calamity*, 44.

31 Barry, "Archaeology and Teleology in Ondaatje's Anil's Ghost," 138.

32 Knopf and Ondaatje, "Michael Ondaatje," 81.

33 Bowers, "Asia's Europes," 189.

34 Vetter, "Liberal Political Inquiries in the Novels of Michael Ondaatje," 27, 28.

35 Hewitson, "Tantric Metaseity in the *Rig Veda*'s 'Creation Hymn,'" 32.

36 Kipling, *Kim*, 229.

37 Hewitson, "Mediating Suffering," 8.

38 Braarvig, "The Buddhist Hell," 255.

39 Casper and Wertheimer, *Critical Trauma Studies*, 2.

40 Ibid.

15

Wartime Ghosts:
War and the Liminal in *The English Patient*,
Anil's Ghost, and *Warlight*

Martin Löschnigg

Wars constitute the backdrop to the plot in three of Michael Ondaatje's novels: the Second World War in both *The English Patient* and *Warlight* and the civil war in Sri Lanka in *Anil's Ghost*. A fourth, *Divisadero*, briefly sketches the experiences in the First World War of Lucien Segura, a fictitious French writer in whose life Anna, one of the main characters, becomes immersed. In the three novels first mentioned, war is on the margins and in the centre at the same time, decisively shaping the lives and memories of the characters. It creates transitional spaces that they negotiate and liminal experiences and moral complexities that they work through. Haunting and the persistence of trauma are conveyed by the motif that (at least for the characters) the war has never ended.

This essay will discuss the reverberations of war in *The English Patient*, *Anil's Ghost*, and *Warlight*, showing how in these novels the exigencies and ambivalences of war generate in-between worlds peopled by "wartime ghost[s]" (WL, 73). It will focus on the transformative power of war as depicted in the novels and on Ondaatje's exploring the impact of wartime experiences and memories, blurring the lines between the past and the present and the living and the dead. My specific contribution to the many existing scholarly discussions of *The English Patient* and *Anil's Ghost*, and to an emerging body of work on *Warlight*, is a comparative view of the war novels that highlights the way in which war functions as a thematic crystallization point for an art that explores the interstices between history and fiction and the real and the imaginary.

Ondaatje's texts are not war novels in a narrower sense, since they contain no representations of actual combat. Neither can the novels be regarded as being committed to an anti-war agenda. What they do illustrate, however, is how war breaches boundaries between combatant and civilian life, creating an ongoing mutual tension between the one and the other as it sweeps characters into its vortex. Ondaatje is interested in the dynamics of this process, a process that is captured by the image of a war machine in *The English Patient*: "The First Canadian Infantry Division worked its way up Italy, and the destroyed bodies were fed back to the field hospitals like mud passed back by tunnellers in the dark" (EP, 49). The war has created a "state of exception,"[1] the novel's characters being "embattled and war-weary exiles attempting to make sense of their lives in the absence of any supervening law or established social structure."[2] All that Hana has brought to the villa is "What she had taken from others in this war" (EP, 47), and it is from this utter reduction of her personality and struggling out of the vortex that she is beginning to define herself anew. In the same way, Anil Tissera has been drawn into the bewildering reality of the Sri Lankan civil war and an intimidating shadowland of uncertainties in which she and others are lost, trying to find answers to their questions. The same, although under very different auspices, applies to the world of *Warlight*, in which the first-person narrator attempts to come to terms with the (post)war activities of his parents, in particular his mother's work for Intelligence under the codename Viola, and his own life in the immediate postwar years.

In an interview, Ondaatje remarked on *Warlight* that "I wasn't setting out to write a war novel or a postwar novel; that became the landscape."[3] The liminal character of this storified "landscape of war and memory"[4] is visualized through the twilight that prevails in it. The world of *Warlight* is a shadowland that symbolizes the personal and historical secrets dominating the characters' lives in the novel's postwar setting. Nathaniel Williams's childhood memories of the "unlit roads" and "only partially lived in" (WL, 84, 82) parts of postwar London recall the twilight world of Eliot's "Prufrock," his trips along the dimly lit waterways of the Thames riverscape in part three of *The Waste Land*. Like the Tiresias of "The Fire Sermon," yet in a different sense, he, too, is "throbbing between

Wartime Ghosts

two lives"[5]: those of youth and early adulthood. The landscape in the early parts of *Warlight* reflects a spiritual exhaustion, rendering a narcotic dream world that spreads feelings of "apathy, moral or emotional anesthesia,"[6] yet which also proves a timeout world of adventure for the young protagonist: "We continued through the dark, quiet waters of the river, feeling we owned it, as far as the estuary. We passed industrial buildings, their lights muted, faint as stars, as if we were in a time capsule of the war years when blackouts and curfews had been in effect, when there was just warlight and only blind barges were allowed to move along this stretch of river" (WL, 81). The wartime dimmed lights and blackout have lingered in the form of the small orange lights on the bridges along the Thames, ghost lights that – like the cast of shadowy figures involved in espionage under codenames – point toward hidden realities. The novel's atmosphere is inspired by a "feeling of darkness that modulates across a range of registers,"[7] effectively conveying the otherworldly experience of wartime and postwar London.

The strangely timeless continuity of war as evoked in *Warlight* finds some correspondence in topographical warscapes that are as featureless as their representations on retouched maps, providing no orientation: along the Suffolk coastline during the Second World War, "All signposts, however inaccurate, were removed in preparation for a possible German invasion. The region became signless overnight ... Coastal towns were secretly removed from maps. Military zones officially disappeared" (WL, 137–8). In contrast, a life-sized replica of a German town is erected for training soldiers for street and house fighting (WL, 138). War suspends the conventional order of things, sometimes bringing forth "surreal turns of cause and effect" (AG, 42). It creates sites where the living and the dead connect and entry points to those sites: the forensic lab set up in a disused ship (the *Oronsay* of *The Cat's Table* in *Anil's Ghost*), guarded by "Cerberus" Dr Perera (AG, 25), the abandoned villa where the head of Sailor is restored in an act of retrieval and regeneration, and the derelict villa in *The English Patient*.

The de-limitation of spaces and blurring of topographical boundaries under the impact of war is an important aspect of *The English Patient*. In an interview, Ondaatje states that he had thought of the Villa San Girolamo as "an Eden, an escape, a little cul-de-sac during the war, and this was where healing began."[8] Indeed, the villa may appear as a sanctuary ("Everywhere else out there was a war" [*EP*, 174]), yet the war invades the precarious idyll that the characters attempt to create within it: "There seemed little demarcation between house and landscape, between damaged building and the burned and shelled remnants of the earth" (*EP*, 43). References to a garden and its restorative powers contrast with references to the Fall, anticipated by Almásy's fall from the sky, like Milton's Satan, in a burning plane. Thus, the painting of a garden in the villa "functions as an allegorical emblem that signals the loss of the true Garden"[9] – a reminder of mortality and of the fact that the villa is also the gate to a world of the shadows, soon to be entered by the Patient. However, the painting (like the many other works of art mentioned in the novel) also reminds one that art and war involve different modes of being and thinking: in war, a town will be thought of in terms of its strategic value rather than that of the artwork it contains.

Like the villa, the desert seemed to provide for Almásy a refuge from the onslaught of the mundane: "There is God only in the desert, he wanted to acknowledge that now. Outside of this there was just trade and power, money and war. Financial and military despots shaped the world" (*EP*, 250). However, the desert, too, lies open to being ravished by the war. Accordingly, as Spinks has claimed, Almásy "hates the war, not for reasons of political dissidence or humanitarian sympathy, but because it exposes the hollowness of his conviction that the desert cannot be claimed or owned."[10] The shifting topography of war, often expressed through images of light and darkness, is further highlighted, with metaphysical overtones, by a memorable episode in the novel: when sappers, including Kip, restore electricity to Naples, chances are that they will set off mines destroying large parts of the city: "Walls will crumble around him or he will walk through a city of light" (*EP*, 280).

Fluid topographies concur with fluid identities, conveyed through anonymity, code names, and pronominal shifts, with ethical and moral ambivalence, and, on the collective level, with changing allegiances. As the Allies support the partisans in the Northern Adriatic regions, "[o]rdinary people were now criminals of war. Some of us had been your allies, now we were the enemy. A shift of wind in London, some political whisper, so everything changed" (*WL*, 238). The mysterious people gathered at the house of Nathaniel's parents are "souls who, having at one time legally crossed some boundary during the war, were now suddenly told they could no longer cross

Wartime Ghosts

it during peace" (WL, 35). Ambivalences arise from the recruitment of "talent" (WL, 220), like that of Caravaggio, whose skills as a thief are "legitimized" (EP, 253) and "made ... official" (EP, 35) as part of the war effort. A Hermes figure, this god of thieves, messenger from a world beyond the villa, and escort of souls to the underworld thus becomes a projection site for the moral and ethical complexities created by war. The Patient himself found it "easy ... to slip across borders, not to belong to anyone, to any nation" when the desert, whose boundlessness taught him to "Erase the family name! Erase nations!" (EP, 139), became a theatre of war. Accordingly, what is conspicuously absent from his uniquely personalized copy of Herodotus "is his own name" (EP, 96). In contrast to Madox, whose sense of integrity received a devastating blow from the divisions caused by the war, this wily "Odysseus," as he terms himself, "understood the shifting and temporary vetoes of war" (EP, 241). Odysseus, of course, is prominent among mortal visitors to the underworld, trying to find answers to his questions and emerging with an expanded consciousness. In the same way, the shadowlands are formative for Nathaniel-Telemachus, whose family was one "with a habit for nicknames, which meant it was also a family of disguises" (WL, 6). The anonymity that rules his fatherless childhood world is liberating, since there are "fewer rules, less order"; however, it is almost like that of "the dogs with their fictional papers" (WL, 97–8) that he and the mysteriously named Darter ferry to the racecourses along the dimly lit canals in a parody of Charon ferrying the dead across the rivers of the underworld, as it were. Everything is elusive, like the signals intercepted by Viola "over the airwaves," and "unseen as well as familiar" (WL, 235), like Felon Marsh, aptly named secret agent and popular nature broadcaster at the same time. In a world still overshadowed by the war, identities must remain vague and shifting: "If you grow up with uncertainty you deal with people only on a daily basis, to be safer on an hourly basis. You do not concern yourself with what you must or should remember about them. You are on your own" (WL, 169).

Situated on the threshold between youth and adulthood, Nathaniel's experiences in postwar London make *Warlight* a *Bildungsroman*; as in *The Cat's Table*, initiation is symbolically rendered through voyages by water and takes place under highly unusual circumstances. Looking back from 1959, the now twenty-eight-year-old first-person narrator emphasizes that "I'd lost my youth, I was unmoored" (WL,

128). The blurry cityscape of the novel visualizes the transitional, as Nathaniel "was about to enter a borderless terrain between adolescence and adulthood" (WL, 65) and "wondrous doorways into the world" (WL, 99) were opening. The challenges he faces are experienced as enriching: "I had lived a mostly harboured life. Now, cut loose by my parents, I was consuming everything around me" (WL, 113). In the twilight world of his youth, conventional sensibilities had been subverted: "I suppose the war had further confused the way we read age or the hierarchies of class" (WL, 102). Nathaniel's anarchic London life is ended by an enemy attack and the reappearance of his mother Rose (Viola), as rendered in the last chapter of part one. "Where were we going? Into another life?" (WL, 118) is what he then asked himself, and indeed the chapter title, "Schwer" (from Robert Schumann's "Mein Herz ist schwer," op. 25, no. 15), denotes a change from the earlier lightness of being to the gravity of a life burdened by an obsession with the past and Rose's wartime activities. Liberating at first, the impact of the war has ultimately deprived Nathaniel of freedom, as is indicated by the determinism of his question: "Do we eventually become what we are originally meant to be?" (WL, 211).

In the shadow of war, trying to find oneself may involve disconcerting shifts between alienation and fulfillment. Confronted with Sri Lanka's civil war, Anil Tissera must face the burden of her heritage, which she has so far avoided by embracing foreignness: "she had ... lived abroad long enough to interpret Sri Lanka with a long-distance gaze" (AG, 11). As she becomes involved in the stories of the victims, however, the empathic unsettlement she undergoes will again strengthen the connection. In the case of Hana in *The English Patient*, self-abnegation turns into a precarious realization of self through an almost mystic sense of devotion: "Coming out of what had happened to her during the war, she drew her own few rules to herself. She would not be ordered again or carry out duties for the greater good. She would care only for the burned patient" (EP, 14).

"Wars don't end. They never remain in the past" (WL, 212) and "Wars are never over" (WL, 248), says Felon Marsh in *Warlight*, contradicting the idea that wars neatly divide time into a before and after, that they end peace and are again followed by it, and that therefore a defining characteristic of wartime is that it is temporary. As Mary L. Dudziak emphasizes, "war spills beyond tidy time boundaries," even if how we remember wars "remains encapsulated

Wartime Ghosts

between certain dates."[11] In Ondaatje's novels, too, war is not confined in time – on the contrary, wartime appears to be normal time. In *Warlight*, the narrator's job with the government enables him to trace some of his mother's activities during the war and during the "unauthorised and still violent war" that had continued after the armistice in ethnically contested regions of Europe and the Middle East, a war led by "guerrilla groups and Partisan fighters" carrying out "retaliations and acts of revenge" (*WL*, 131). These continuing hostilities destabilize the post in postwar, illustrating that "World War II was fuzzier around the edges than we usually imagine."[12] The lingering effects of the war are manifold, manifested not least in the still-evident destructions caused by the Blitz as described in *Warlight*. Regarding *The English Patient*, Spinks argues that the novel, "like the world it describes, is poised uncertainly between two worlds and two visions of international (dis)order"; this division, he goes on, is "symbolized" by the dropping of the atomic bomb, "an event that marks the transition from full-scale military conflict to the beginning of the Cold War."[13] The *English Patient*, like *Anil's Ghost* and *Warlight*, may envision processes of healing (the latter through Nathaniel's narrative act), yet there is also at times the impression of a "perpetual interwar,"[14] with the characters caught between the remembrance of wartime experiences and anticipatory mourning as the war is continuing around them or its effects are still palpable.

In *The English Patient*, temporal and spatial fuzziness correlate as the Allied push is shifting the frontline: "The war is not over everywhere," Hana learns. "The war is over. This war is over. The war here" (*EP*, 41). The moving forward that may bring the war's end is countered by a sinister stasis interlocking the microcosm of the villa with the macrocosm that is still a theatre of war: the devastation caused by the retreating Germans and the mines they have left behind represent war's "last vices" (*EP*, 29). In the villa, Kip has been checking a room for fuses, the dormant ghosts of the war; having been safely cleared, it "has now finally emerged from the war, is no longer a zone or territory" (*EP*, 224). His flight from the villa is rendered in terms of an attempt to turn back the time: "He was travelling against the direction of the invasion, as if rewinding the spool of war, the route no longer tense with military" (*EP*, 290). On a different level, the novel also emphasizes the historical continuity of war in the area: "The last medieval war was fought in Italy in 1943 and 1944. Fortress towns on great promontories which had been battled over since the end of the eighth century had the armies of new kings flung carelessly against them. Around the outcrops of rocks were the traffic of stretchers, butchered vineyards, where, if you dug deep beneath the tank ruts, you found blood-axe and spear" (EP, 69). The hills of Tuscany and Umbria "hold the remnants of war societies, small moraines left by a vast glacier" (EP, 92), while at Arezzo "soldiers would come upon their contemporary faces in the Piero della Francesca frescoes" (EP, 70).

Wartime, it seems, has suspended chronological time, collapsing the past and the present, as is also indicated by the "tableau" of the villa that assembles the characters "in private movement, momentarily lit up, flung ironically against this war" (EP, 278). Such a disruption of linear chronology is closely linked to the allegorical and apocalyptic elements and motifs in *The English Patient* as analyzed by Marlene Goldman. Drawing on Walter Benjamin's interpretation of Paul Klee's *Angelus Novus* as the Angel of History (an angel looking aghast at the piling up of catastrophes, while rushing away from the past with its back toward the future), Goldman claims that Ondaatje's "novel aligns catastrophe with the breaking of the bonds between past and present."[15] This rupture, symbolically rendered in the novel through the destruction of bridges, prevents a constructive narrativizing of past events, evoking instead an allegorical interpretation of history as heading toward an apocalypse.

In particular, the sense of being transfixed in time and the delimitation of spaces applies to "an unofficial war" (AG, 17), like that among the Sri Lankans, characterized by a permanent state of latent violence and intermittent outbreaks of hostilities, like a "Hundred Years' War with modern weaponry" (AG, 43). As the narrator repeatedly states in *Anil's Ghost*, such a war acquires a dynamic of its own: "*The reason for war was war*"; "the main purpose of war had become war" (AG, 43, 98). In the face of pervasive terror, "Death, loss, was 'unfinished,' so you could not walk through it" (AG, 56). "Walk through" echoes the work through of trauma theory, and indeed Ondaatje's novels show how traumatic experience "is not locatable in the simple violent or original event in an individual's past, but rather in the way that its very unassimilated nature – the way it was precisely not known in the first instance – returns to haunt the survivor later on."[16] Representing war as a totalizing event, the novels capture the intensity of experiences that cannot be relegated to the past but will resurface in the present, informing the way in which the characters understand the world and themselves. For Spinks, *The English Patient* illustrates the "idea that literature can reflect the structure of a traumatic experience by bearing witness to an event repeatedly relived in and through its forgetting."[17] It does so through textual "absences" pointing to "unrealized or abruptly cancelled potentiality: a mode of historical possibility or feeling that can find no authentic expression in its own contemporary world."[18] In *Warlight*, Nathaniel desperately tries to illuminate the present by reaching back into the past. However, his life has been yoked to the dimness of war and will ultimately remain unknowable, the persistence of his own wartime preventing the formation of reliable memories. The very failure of recapturing the past, however, bears witness to its profound impact and its continuing hold, like a ghost, on the writer's present.

Spectrality is a central motif in the novels here discussed, the "ghostly haunt" giving "notification" of the interminable demands of the past on the present.[19] As an example of life writing, *Warlight* in particular explores "the traces and elisions of the past," using "the vocabulary of interacting with 'ghosts.'"[20] Quite literally, Nathaniel is one day pursued by a "wartime ghost" (WL, 73), an unknown man associated with his mother's mysterious past, whose own ghosts will eventually catch up with her in the shape of her assassin. However, the assassination also carries with it a sense of exorcism and of an "ending of feuds, of a war. Perhaps allowing a redeeming." Indeed, the assassin is described as "running like a harrier over the fields as if she were my mother's soul leaving her body" (WL, 260). Will she and her son find closure, or will she live on as a ghost? For Nathaniel, there has been "So much left unburied at the end of a war" (WL, 253), while he feels that viable links into the past like the Darter have in fact "kept placing obstacles on the road back to our past, that wouldn't allow me to reach it" (WL, 270). The companions of his youth, ghostlike figures even then, have finally turned ephemeral, yet they are still occupying their very own nooks and crannies in the narrator's consciousness, straddling the boundaries between past and present: "Our heroes do not usually, after a certain age, teach or guide us anymore. They chose instead to protect the last territory where they find themselves" (WL, 269).

References to the spectres of the recent past are frequent in *The English Patient*: Hana, says the ghostlike Caravaggio, "throws herself out of the world to love a ghost," the burned patient, a "man with no face" (*EP*, 45), yet he is also aware that her devotion may in fact be a way of exorcising the ghosts of war: "Maybe this is the way to come out of a war, he thinks. A burned man to care for" (*EP*, 33). Hana's own fear when she tended to the wounded of the Italian campaign was that such faceless "ghosts" might materialize as people she knows or loves: "She feared the day she would remove blood from a patient's face and discover her father or someone who had served her food across a counter on Danforth Avenue" (*EP*, 50). Of her father, who has been killed in the war, she thinks as "a hungry ghost," yet the remembrance that this ghost demands of her is of a man "liking those around him to be confident, even raucous" (*EP*, 91). Like the Egyptian god Anubis evoked by Almásy (*EP*, 258), Hana, who "know[s] death," has conducted the dying to the other world, as it were, her indictment of their suffering carrying strong mythological overtones: "Every damn general should have had my job. Every damn general. It should have been a prerequisite for any river crossing. Who the hell were we to be given this responsibility, expected to be wise as old priests, to know how to lead people towards something no one wanted and to make them feel comfortable" (*EP*, 84). Like Hana, her "warrior saint" (*EP*, 209, 217) Kip, too, has been to the world of wartime ghosts, notably when he witnessed the emaciated Neapolitans liberated from the caves in which they had hid from the Germans and in which they had been locked for weeks: "The procession of them back into the city hospitals was one of ghosts" (*EP*, 275).

While shadowy ghost figures and the temporal and ontological disjunctions caused by wartime spectres play a significant role in *The English Patient* and *Warlight*, the notion of haunting, as already indicated by the title, assumes central importance in *Anil's Ghost*. Here, ghostliness is played out on a political level beside the ontological (the ghosts are reflections of the real rather than illusions, as Sarath will be for Ananda and Anil [*AG*, 305]); it pertains also to the collectivity of events and the colonial heritage of a ravished country.

As Michael O'Riley reminds us, the "spectre of colonialism" appears, among others, in the form of "civil warfare."[21] *Anil's Ghost* deals with trauma caused by the legacies of colonialism, addressing collective forms of trauma frequently neglected by trauma theory[22] as well as redressing trauma theory's "ethnocentric blindness."[23] The novel renders gloomy depictions of a haunted country, a country that has been turned into a "postcolonial crypt"[24] or "*death-world.*"[25] In

Wartime Ghosts 327

Sri Lanka, "the darkest Greek tragedies were innocent compared with what was happening here. Heads on stakes. Skeletons dug out of a cocoa pit in Matale. At university Anil had translated lines from Archilochus – *In the hospitality of war we left them their dead to remember us by*. But here there was no such gesture to the families of the dead, not even the information of who the enemy was" (AG, 11). The lines from the ancient warrior-poet Archilochos of Paros are profoundly ironic, since in this formulation the gift of the dead bodies that may enable mourning and thus, eventually, healing will at the same time keep alive the memory of their killers and thus bear the seeds of future violence. The narrator's addition in *Anil's Ghost* reduces the ambiguity: there are no bodies that will enable mourners to bury them and come to terms with their grief; through their absence, they will continue to haunt their families, as will the faceless spectres of their enemies. Accordingly, a *"vigil for the dead"* is one for *"half-revealed forms"* only (AG, 5), and the war around the characters is "to do with demons, spectres of retaliation" (AG, 304). Feeling like being "on a boat of demons," Sarath's doctor brother Gamini, another acherontic conductor of the dead, sees himself as "a perfect participant in the war" (AG, 224).

For Anil, the forensic specialist, the dead body is a key to the past and to the (imagined) narrative of the live person. Margaret Herrick has described Anil's journey to Sri Lanka in terms of a *katabasis*, a descent into the underworld that causes her to abandon the position of distanced witness in favour of a "realization of shared vulnerability."[26] Herrick argues that Anil's task is to "enter this underworld, to descend into the world of the dead, partly so that others ... might be able to leave it."[27] The way victims disappear in the civil war makes them exist in a kind of limbo, overshadowing the world of the living as ghosts. Reclaiming the bodies, and thus rendering them concrete, Anil helps to "settle the dead in the world of the dead,"[28] turning spectres into dead persons who can be mourned. She can thus help to overcome the "scarring psychosis in the country" of "unfinished" death and loss that cannot be "walk[ed] through" (AG, 56).

The dead bodies serve as a "conduit into the past"[29] – that of the life the dead had shared with their mourners. By rendering concrete the abstraction of death, and by providing specificity to its universality, they will finally help to release the ghosts hanging about the world of the living. This is illustrated by the "ceremony of nature" that can be observed in burial sites on the island, as stones have been placed on the interred bodies: "Years after a body was buried there would be a small shift on the surface of the earth. Then a falling of that stone into the space left by decayed flesh, as if signaling the departure of a spirit" (AG, 20).

Mythologically, this transformation is ensured by guiding figures as represented and alluded to in Ondaatje's novels, including deities like Anubis, the jackal-headed "opener of the ways" (EP, 258). As the dogs of war have been unleashed around the characters, the novels feature images of dogs or dog-like creatures that are associated with twilight and transformation, foremost among them the dogs in *Warlight*. Also, there is the "old mongrel, older than the war" (EP, 61) that comes to visit the Villa San Girolamo, a messenger from the underworld for the dying Patient, and its counterpart, the "ancient dog frozen in white ash" (EP, 278) in the National Archeological Museum in Naples, killed (and literally encased in the world of the dead) during the destruction of Pompei and Herculaneum. "All through the war I saw no dog," says Hermes-Caravaggio, and as he picks up the dog, the narrator surmises that the Patient must have had the impression "that the dog ... had turned into a man," Anubis-like. The dog- or jackal-headed gods are "creatures who guide you into the after-life," Almásy tells Katharine, "as my early ghost accompanied you, those years before we met" (EP, 258). In the ghostly surroundings of the cave, Almásy will finally become such a figure for her, embalming her with colours from the cave paintings, as it were (EP, 248), as the god Anubis is often shown to embalm corpses in Egyptian depictions. Being "linked to jackals," the god is also envisaged by Almásy's "jackal with one eye that looks back and one that regards the path you consider taking" (EP, 259). Like Klee's angel as viewed by Benjamin, the jackal is poised between the past and the future, and like the angel it points to the finality of death: "In his jaws are pieces of the past he delivers to you, and when all of that time is fully discovered it will prove to have been already known" (EP, 259). Similarly, Kip will have to bury the "black body" of the mummy-like Patient that he feels "sits on the petrol tank facing him ... facing the past over his shoulder" in his flight from the villa. The villa, like the Englishman's empire and its wars, shall "never be rebuilt," and its ghosts must be laid at rest in the past (EP, 294).

Ghostliness and its ontological and chronological liminalities are re-enacted by the text of Ondaatje's novels, itself a ghost in the sense of Maurice Blanchot's proposition that the work's demands on the reader result from the nullification (or death) of the author in the "space of literature." Ondaatje's narrative technique conveys the liminal through its shifts between the past and the present, fiction and truth, poetry and the documentary. War crystallizes the fusion of the real and the invented, the commonplace and the outrageous, as the "most precisely recorded moments of history lay adjacent to the extreme actions of nature or civilization" (AG, 55). *Anil's Ghost* is witness writing that "confirms the impossibility of an all-inclusive narrative" as it undermines the notion of a "secure perspective" and an "all-seeing and all-knowing subject."[30] The novel, like the others discussed here, renounces the aesthetic illusion created by realist representation, emphasizing instead the disruptions caused by war's violence through the intensity of suggestive images.

Ondaatje's "powerful narrative images," writes Douglas Barbour, create a "sense of permanence" that is, however, "illusory," as the "carefully casual *bricolage* of disassociated moments, the accumulation of narrative fragments, never quite solidifies into a plot, never quite denies us the traditional pleasures of narrative movement."[31] Modernist fragmentation is clearly a means of capturing the disruptive forces of war and the loss of the "power of language and logic" by "those who were slammed and stained by violence" (AG, 55). McVey even suggests that Ondaatje's texts "might be read as surrogate deformed, wounded, or mongrel bodies, their tissues woven together into forms that bear witness to the traumatic pasts that have shaped them."[32] The duality of tangible images and narrative fragmentation corresponds to the way in which, according to trauma theory, unassimilated events are continuously relived as a "double telling ... between the story of the unbearable nature of an event and the story of the unbearable nature of its survival."[33] In this process, as in Ondaatje's narratives, "wholeness remains elusive," and "the narrative structure itself is seemingly marked by the explosive forces of war."[34]

Ondaatje's novels do not only tell stories of war by means of an aesthetics of fragmentation; however, they also reflect on the making of these stories. This metanarrative dimension is manifested in the way the novels investigate the connection between reading, writing, and violence. Alice Brittan has shown how *The English Patient* highlights the association of print and power, making the handwriting in the Patient's Herodotus or Hana's notes in the villa's books "attempts to arrest the violent dislocations of war."[35] Likewise, the wounded bodies in the novels are sites of inscription, paradoxically bearing the marks of a violence that aims at annihilation and erasure. The war-marked body therefore testifies to the fundamental problem of how to tell about war and how its narrativizing may bear within it the aestheticizing of chaos and destruction. Through its delimitation of space and disruption of linear chronology, modern war in particular resists the order-creating capacity of narrative, rejecting the teleological and causal pattern that may be imposed upon it in the narrative act.

Most explicitly, however, metanarrative is vested in acts of reconstructing the story, like the activities of the forensic investigator and the memoirist. "We were used to partial stories," says Nathaniel in *Warlight* (WL, 8); his parents kept silent about their wartime activities, providing only "wisps of stories" to which their children "hung on" (WL, 25). His attempt at finding out the truth about their wartime past is a "gathering together" of "unconfirmed fragments" (WL, 114), of the "detritus of a not yet fully censored war" (WL, 145). Nicknamed "Stitch" by his mother, he is now "sewing it all together in order to survive," knowing that "We order our lives with barely held stories" (WL, 284) and knowing "how to fill in a story from a grain of sand or a fragment of discovered truth" (WL, 276). In the act of writing, he is aware, his present and past selves will temporarily collapse: "You return to that earlier time armed with the present, and no matter how dark that world was, you do not leave it unlit. You take your adult self with you. It is not to be a reliving, but a rewitnessing" (WL, 114). Will it be that, however, and can the past be laid to rest by giving it narrative shape? Despite the light that further knowledge or the imagination might bring to it, Nathaniel remains in the dark as to his mother's wartime career. Indeed, he even feels that "the real story" has gone past him, "while I still existed only in the maze of my mother's life" (WL, 279).

Ondaatje's novels depict war as a comprehensive and self-reinforcing event that defies epic conventions of time, space, and pacing. Instead, war and its effects are distinguished by a lingering continuity. Emphasizing haunting and the ghostliness of wartime and the lives impacted by violence, Ondaatje foregrounds the "irresolvable tension between life and war."[36] He uses multiple narrative

Wartime Ghosts

perspectives and refractions in order to pinpoint questions of shifting spaces, times, and identities, signifying a negotiating of binaries and the re-defining of belonging and alienation in the wake of war. War thus functions as a crystallization point for an art that probes the in-between spaces of life. It creates a nexus of containment and fluidity that embeds the novels' objects, enabling and undermining the narratives' attempts at grasping hold of these objects at the same time.

NOTES

1 See Agamben, *The State of Exception.*
2 Spinks, *Michael Ondaatje,* 173.
3 Williams, "Digging up the Past," 30.
4 For the concepts of "landscapes of war" and "landscapes of memory," see Grace, *Landscapes of War and Memory.*
5 Eliot, "The Fire Sermon," *Collected Poems 1909–1962,* 71.
6 Sontag, *Regarding the Pain of Others,* 80.
7 Truett, "Michael Ondaatje, *Warlight,*" 396
8 Wachtel, "An Interview with Michael Ondaatje," 252.
9 Goldman, "'Powerful Joy,'" 905.
10 Spinks, *Michael Ondaatje,* 196.
11 Dudziak, *War Time: An Idea, Its History, Its Consequences,* 36, 6.
12 Ibid., 62.
13 Spinks, *Michael Ondaatje,* 171.
14 Saint-Amour, *Tense Future,* 303ff.
15 Goldman, "'Powerful Joy,'" 915.
16 Caruth, *Unclaimed Experience,* 4.
17 Spinks, *Michael Ondaatje,* 188.
18 Ibid., 183.
19 Gordon, *Ghostly Matters,* 179.
20 Kirss, "Seeing Ghosts: Theorizing Haunting in Literary Texts," 26.
21 O'Riley, *Postcolonial Haunting and Victimization,* 2.
22 See Kirss, "Seeing Ghosts," 22, and Herrick, "*Katabasis* and the Politics of Grief in Michael Ondaatje's *Anil's Ghost,*" 38.
23 Burrows, "The Heterotopic Spaces of Postcolonial Trauma in Michael Ondaatje's 'Anil's Ghost,'" 162.
24 Chakravorty, "The Dead That Haunt *Anil's Ghost,*" 550.
25 Mbembe, "Necropolitics," 40.

26 Herrick, "*Katabasis* and the Politics of Grief in Michael Ondaatje's *Anil's Ghost*," 35.
27 Ibid., 40.
28 Ibid.
29 McVey, "Reclaiming the Past: Michael Ondaatje and the Body of History," 141.
30 Marinkova, "'Perceiving [...] in one's own body' the Violence of History, Politics and Writing," 108.
31 Barbour, *Michael Ondaatje*, 209.
32 McVey, "Reclaiming the Past," 144.
33 Caruth, *Unclaimed Experience*, 187.
34 Goldman, "'Powerful Joy,'" 921, 904.
35 Brittan, "War and the Book," 202.
36 Truett, "Michael Ondaatje, *Warlight*," 398.

Endings

16

The Dead That Haunt *Anil's Ghost*: Subaltern Difference and Postcolonial Melancholia

Mrinalini Chakravorty

After all, Taormina, Ceylon, Africa, America – as far as we go, they are only the negation of all that we ourselves stand for and are ... Ceylon is an experience – but heavens, not a permanence.

D.H. Lawrence, 3 April 1922

The problem here is not the Tamil problem, it's the human problem.

Michael Ondaatje, *Anil's Ghost*

The human problem in Michael Ondaatje's *Anil's Ghost* concerns the tidal waves of wounded affected by the political violence in Sri Lanka.[1] The novel's account of the disinterred, disappeared, assassinated, and injured reflects an archive of death. "We seem to have too many bodies around," laments Sarath, one of the main figures in the book (AG, 274).[2] The sheer magnitude of human loss signals the impossibility of properly recognizing the full humanity of all the actors in this conflict, much less grieving their loss. The usual ways of memorializing individual deaths that denote a singular, subjective life – through details such as place of belonging, linguistic and familial ties, ethnicity, name, age, and occupation – become insufficient to explaining the losses incurred. Human rights, and human wrongs, the novel implies, can no longer be adduced on grounds that value the sentience and security of the individual, historically legible subject.[3] Rather, *Anil's Ghost* presents us with a "human problem" of a different order, one that parlays collective death in generalizable terms and, by extension, our common vulnerability to violence into a new subjective experience.

Mrinalini Chakravorty

* * *

This essay examines representations of violence in *Anil's Ghost* to probe paradoxes that arise in postcolonial nations dealing with spectres of death moored to a particular place and real events. Preoccupations with violence in postcolonial literatures, especially when linked to real historical events, seem to shore up dubious stereotypes about insurmountable civilizational differences that structure our globe. The risk is that Ondaatje's Sri Lanka, like D.H. Lawrence's Ceylon, will remain only a foil for the West's self-assurance and self-complacency, a vision of impermanence against which to measure Western stability. After all, Ondaatje's odes to Sri Lanka – *Running in the Family, Handwriting, Anil's Ghost* – are written from Canada. In *Anil's Ghost*, Sailor's murder in the midst of a tumultuous civil war and the murkiness of seeking its redress suggest that the novel endorses a stereotype of civilizational difference in which the generic fictionalization of mass deaths leads readers to affirm the meaninglessness of individual life in the postcolony. Yet this essay takes an alternate tack. How, I ask, does our entering into the scene of Sailor's death as readers realign our fidelities? I suggest that by foregrounding violent death as a staple of the postcolony, novels such as *Anil's Ghost* implicate us as readers in a host of assumptions entailed in seeing the postcolony as an archive of death.

The prism of death in *Anil's Ghost* makes a critical demand on readers of this text to relinquish settled notions of how we as humans understand our finitude, understand our entanglements with the deaths of others, and ascribe meaning to death itself. Rather than static signs for the real, fictions of death and violence provide volatile aesthetic scripts that conjoin historical circumstance with phantasmatic expressions to raise important questions about mourning, collective agency, and the subalternity of postcolonial societies. The figural reproducibility of violence in the novel's formal experiments, affective signatures, and deliberate transnational gestures reforms commonplace ideas about the worldwide deployment of human rights projects. Postcolonial fictions of human injury compel us to re-envision human subjectivity on the basis of a politics of collective human sentience that goes beyond the individuated forms of human sovereignty allowed by legal, juridical orders.

The stakes of contemplating this alternative humanity become apparent in the novel's evocation of political deaths in the form of

Subaltern Difference and Postcolonial Melancholia 337

what I call postcolonial crypts. The presence of collective crypts reforms the ethics of trauma so that it is no longer an experience limited to the singular individual human subject privileged by human rights discourses in the West. Instead, the figure of the dead subaltern, in this novel but also in the larger global literary imaginary, stands at the crossroads of life understood in terms of an imperfect balance between singular and collective experiences of trauma in the postcolony. This essay concludes by examining the role of postcolonial literature in figuring the postcolony's exceptional tie to subalternity as the basis of global difference. If subalternity is understood as the boundless demand for recognition made on behalf of a radical other, its larger affective signification in the context of globalized violence pits one vision of collective human sentience against the hegemonic concern for individual human subjects furthered by human rights discourses. As *Anil's Ghost* shows, fictions about subaltern difference depend on joining fictional inventiveness to psychic and social terrains in unforeseen ways. Ultimately, they encourage us to assess our deepest assumptions about the way social life is lived and should be approached in the global South.

APPROACHING THE UNHISTORICAL DEAD: THE SENTIENCE OF FORM

Anil's Ghost adopts a volatile aesthetics by pitting the novel's narrative structure against story and theme, a formal strategy that unsettles how the novel's stereotypic allusions to Sri Lanka as the place of undifferentiated, mass deaths may be understood. The novel advances the idea that no wounded or dead person can again be accorded whatever socially coherent subjective self they may have previously inhabited. The narrative shadows the arrival of the forensic expert Anil Tissera, a Sri Lankan native who, after a fifteen-year absence, returns to the country in the early 1990s as an advocate for a human rights centre in Geneva. Soon Anil, along with Sarath, a local archaeologist assigned by the government to work with her, unearths the remains of a recent killing in a government-protected burial site in Bandarawela. Their discovery of the skeleton, whom they name Sailor, drives the motor of the story. Anil's quest to identify Sailor to make an evidentiary case against the abuse of governmental power is underscored by her initial confidence in her arguments with the doubt-prone Sarath: "But we can prove this,

338 Mrinalini Chakravorty

don't you see? This is an opportunity, it's traceable. We found him in a place that only a government official could get into" (AG, 52). However, by making Anil's findings initially suspect and ultimately inconsequential, *Anil's Ghost* unsettles the edifice of crime and punishment and hence the entire apparatus of judiciary and legal redress for political deaths.[4]

If, as Ondaatje writes, "[i]n her work, Anil turned bodies into representatives of race, and age, and place," the certainty and usefulness of such a subject-reproducing task are cast in doubt by the form and arc of the narrative more suggestively than the novel's plot or theme. Aside from Anil's realization that for now her findings "would be reported, filed in Geneva, but no one could ever give meaning to it" (AG, 55), the novel repeatedly evacuates the importance of her report on Sailor through fragmentary interruptions that detail an overabundance of such deaths in the forms of episodic vignettes, reportage, or simple lists. An episode of politically motivated murder is related in a jarring segment that describes a government officer being yanked from his seat and pushed out of a fast train shuttling through a tunnel; the incident is left unanchored from the rest of the narrative (AG, 31–2). Ondaatje also inserts lists of the disappeared with names, dates, times of disappearance, and snippets of details ("The colour of a shirt. The sarong's pattern"):

Kumara Wijetunga, 17. 6th November 1989. At about 11:30 p.m. from his house.
Prabath Kumara, 16. 17th November 1989. At 3:20 a.m. from the home of a friend.
Kumara Arachchi, 16. 17th November 1989. At about midnight from his house.
Manelka da Silva, 17. 1st December 1989. While playing Cricket, Embilipitiya Central College playground (AG, 41)

The list, as Sophia A. McClennan and Joseph R. Slaughter note, reproduces a 1992 Amnesty International report on unresolved disappearances during the Sri Lankan civil war that was brought, to little effect, before the United Nations Commission on Human Rights in 2005.[5] Ondaatje's list names ten missing persons and marks the surfeit of the "unhistorical dead" as always in excess of Anil's attempts to historicize Sailor (AG, 55). The names of the disappeared appear across from an enigmatic description of the National Atlas of

Subaltern Difference and Postcolonial Melancholia 339

Sri Lanka, whose indexes of geologic life, flora, fauna, and weather of the island are markedly empty of human presence: "No depiction of human life," Ondaatje writes, before filling in this blank with the serialized names of those vanished by war (AG, 40). Anil's discovery of Sailor's identity, abruptly revealed later in the text ("He was Ruwan Kumara and he was a toddy tapper" [AG, 269]), floats as a similarly hollow echo of yet another of the uncountable dead the novel has already listed.

Stripping historical meaning from this one death, however, unleashes the figurative as well as affective replacements this novel produces as its vision of proximal yet universal death in Sri Lanka. Sailor's death, in its emptiness, is endlessly capacious – alluding to every other named and unnamed dead person, as well as to the risk his skeleton poses to all the main characters. Anil barely staves off her own political killing; her aide, Ananda, attempts suicide; Ananda's missing wife, Sirissa, appears posthumously in a surreal moment as Sailor's reconstructed face; and Sarath is murdered. Confronting Sailor, *Anil's Ghost* suggests, is a confrontation with death writ large – as a proximate and shared condition that works through an illogic of substitution. Death here is not an exceptional, irreplaceable, and unshareable ontological experience unique to the individual. It is best understood as an endlessly reproducible event that enfolds all who come within its purview. Reading *Anil's Ghost* is hence like entering an open crypt where the book itself serves as a repository for death's relational and recursive form.

THE POSTCOLONIAL CRYPT: NARRATING COLLECTIVE CULTURAL MELANCHOLIA

In *Anil's Ghost*, death is reflected by formal arrangements that allow alternative affective significations of its presence to emerge in the midst of Sri Lanka's political turmoil. The novel intercepts the historical scene of conflict, with its global inflections, to shift the anglophone reader's perception of the war's collective societal impact. Insofar as the novel figures death as an omnipresence that signifies collective trauma, rather than a peculiarly individual one, the novel comes to represent a postcolonial crypt. The story of Lakma, who, at the age of twelve, witnesses the massacre of her parents, illustrates how the novel sutures the terms of collective melancholia to formal, linguistic expression. The event of her parents' killing, we're told, leaves Lakma irremediably scarred – mute, prone to nightmares, regressing into "infancy" in her verbal and motor skills, and "scared of the evidence of anything human" (AG, 103–4). In this state, she accompanies her sole surviving relative, the glaucoma-stricken and disgraced archaeologist Palipana, into the Grove of Ascetics, their forested retreat away from the world. It is Palipana, Sarath's mentor, who aids in Anil's search for Sailor's identity by introducing Sarath and Anil to Ananda, one of the few remaining artists who can reconstruct a face for the skeleton. Yet we are told that Palipana's professional fall from grace comes from having "step[ped] into another reality," where the archaeologist "began to see as truth things that only could be guessed at" (AG, 81, 83). Within the novel, Palipana's skepticism toward "truth," his conviction that "in our world, truth is just opinion," stands counter to the certainty of Anil's claim that "[t]he truth shall set you free!" (AG, 102).

Palipana's presence serves as a counterincentive to the human rights narrative Anil seeks to valorize. Palipana's attempts to tell "an illegal story" so that the "unprovable truth emerged" are attuned to the cryptic "secret" in which the deaths of Sailor, Lakma's parents, Sarath, Sirissa, and the many other war dead are shrouded (AG, 105, 83, 8a). Unlike Anil, who wants to tell a juridically and scientifically coherent story about these deaths, Palipana engages the "interlinear texts" that "contain the darker proofs" of phantasm in which each death resonates with the next (AG, 105). Such a reckoning with multiple deaths frames the violence of war as a collective experience of melancholia. As a crucible for collective melancholia, the postcolony as an open crypt becomes the site where the case for human rights violations given in Anil's mantra – "One village can speak for many villages. One victim can speak for many victims" – is alternatively nuanced (AG, 176). The prospect of attaining closure through juridical redress that follows the disclosure of violent acts is replaced by the compulsion to continually and collectively acknowledge the losses signified by the dead. The former, which is Anil's way, reconciles loss with proper mourning whereby in a Freudian sense the lost object is recognized as dead so that the ego can find an ethical reason to move beyond it. The latter, represented by Lakma and Palipana, makes dwelling in loss, signalled by the melancholic's refusal to move past the traumatic event, the ethical impulse of narrative.

The generative relation between collective melancholia and linguistic expression that anchors *Anil's Ghost* may be understood

Subaltern Difference and Postcolonial Melancholia 341

by considering the formation of psychic crypts. In their work on mourning, melancholia, and the transmission of trauma, Nicolas Abraham and Maria Torok usefully theorize the workings of the intrapsychic crypt and the idea of the phantom. The "inexpressible mourning" of the melancholic, exhibited by Lakma and others in the novel, unfolds, they argue, as the result of "a secret tomb inside the subject" that keeps the lost object "buried alive in the crypt" as a form of psychic incorporation.[6] It is only when "[f]aced with the danger of seeing the crypt crumble ... [that] the ego begins the public display of the interminable process of mourning," which is melancholia (AG, 136). In these subjects, the crypt conceals the source of a trauma or loss by deliberately confusing any attempt to articulate the loss. The presence of a crypt depends on a linguistic subversion that purposefully leaves the traumatic experience of loss unintelligible, deferred to other inaccessible forms of signification. The crypt marks a precarious psychic threshold that may inadvertently, through narrative or linguistic slip, at any moment reveal a trauma it must keep hidden. Even as the crypt forestalls melancholia, the secret preserved within it marks a psychic threshold that can collapse momentarily into expressions of melancholic grief whose intelligibility is contingent on how the story being told is made sensible.[7]

Although for Abraham and Torok the crypt describes psychic processes of individual grief, Abraham's idea of the phantom extends beyond personal loss to describe the workings of collective trauma. The phantom illuminates the way in which postcolonial crypts function in my analysis on a narrative level and as a generalized symptom of a cultural condition. Unlike the crypt that entombs the loss of an object of love within the individual, the transmission of transgenerational, interpersonal, and cultural trauma depends not on what is lost to ourselves but on how we are affected by what is lost to others. Rather than the unfinished personal mourning of an individual subject, the phantom signifies "a diverse species of ghosts" that comprise the wounds buried or encrypted in others that nonetheless also affect those near them. Describing the phantom effect of crypts, Abraham writes, "What comes back to haunt are the tombs of others" (AG, 172). The phantasmatic transmission of trauma allows that loss enclosed in singular crypts is transferable and has a ripple effect. By this analysis, individual melancholia, motivated by a particular wound, can produce a collective cultural sense of being melancholic. The phantom in Abraham's account, passing as it does from one unconscious to

342   Mrinalini Chakravorty

another (for example, parent's to child's), ventriloquizes the loss felt by another and "stages" its presence in "words" (AG, 176).[8] This narrative dimension in which "phantomogenic words" hint at the presence of the "gaps left within us by the secrets of others" notably "place[s] the effects of the phantom in the social realm (AG, 176, 171, 176).

When Palipana dies, Lakma sculpts an epitaph on a rock wall at the edge of a lake. With this gesture, the novel situates Palipana's death in relation to the trauma of Lakma's personal loss, as well as to the web of losses the reader is compelled to interpret in engaging the various crypts and phantoms that haunt *Anil's Ghost*. The novel reveals:

> [Lakma] had already cut one of [Palipana's] phrases into the rock, one of the first things he had said to her, which she had held on to like a raft in her years of fear. She had chiseled it where the horizon of water was, so that, depending on tide and pull of the moon, the words in the rock would submerge or hang above their reflection or be revealed in both elements. (AG, 107)

The sentence that Lakma carves remains secret in the novel, a double encryption of the trauma (her parents' deaths) that brought Lakma into Palipana's care and his subsequent death that removes him from hers. Its very secrecy imbues the sentence with a phantasmatic quality. Encapsulating as it does Lakma's fears, Palipana's consolation, and his legacy, it is deliberately rendered on the "horizon." Partially obscured and partially legible (now "submerge[d]," now "re-vealed"), the sentence possesses the capacity to transmit its etched trauma as a form of consuming melancholic expression. For the silent Lakma "the great generous noise of her work" as she carves the rock is voice-giving, "as if she were speaking out aloud" (AG, 107).[9]

The novel suggests that the partial disclosure of the origins of trauma inscribed in this manner endures as a palliative gesture because it lingers on loss. Hence, in the last days of Palipana's life, Lakma focuses on "[j]ust the sentence. Not his name or the years of his living, just a gentle sentence once clutched by her, the imprint of it now carried by water around the lake" (AG, 107). Like other partial disclosures – Sailor's identity, Sirissa's disappearance, Sarath's political allegiances, Palipana's gesture that discredits his academic reputation, Anil's tenuous ties to her American friend Leaf and her rift with her lover Cullis – this sentence, despite its inscrutability, compels the reader to interpret it as part of the general landscape

Subaltern Difference and Postcolonial Melancholia 343

of loss evoked by the island. "The yard-long sentence still appears and disappears," Ondaatje writes. "It has already become an old legend" (AG, 107). As a sign of the crumbling postcolonial crypt, the sentence becomes part of the phantomogenic aspect of *Anil's Ghost*, making one person's death material to how we read other deaths in the novel. Instead of foreclosing melancholia through the juridical accounting of individual death, *Anil's Ghost* amplifies how the loss of any subject circulates indiscriminately in communion with other deaths in a collective melancholia. In other words, instead of circumventing or curing melancholia, as human rights discourse aims to do, the novel compels us to experience collective loss in a way that affirms the value of collective loss. The permanence ascribed to the secret epitaph in the narrative ensures that the circuits of loss it returns us to stay embedded in the novel's larger engagement with death as a culture-wide expression of melancholia.

Novels such as *Anil's Ghost* serve as postcolonial crypts by invoking the relational aspects of death that indicate the presence of collective cultural trauma. Unlike intra-psychic crypts that enclose loss to curtail melancholia, these texts function as phantom crypts that ventriloquize the loss of others. Encrypted stories of loss circulate recursively within the narrative to include those for whom this loss may not be primary. If, as Abraham notes, "[t]he phantom which returns to haunt bears witness to the existence of the dead buried within the other,"[10] the text of *Anil's Ghost* is a phantomogenic script that bears witness to a transmission of trauma perpetuated by the many dead who are part of a generic cultural circumstance. Whereas the solitary crypt hints at a melancholia as yet undisclosed, the presence of the phantasmatic postcolonial crypt reveals the pervasiveness of a cultural melancholia conditioned by myriad crypts that are everywhere collapsing and whose traumatic secrets are revealed, whether partially or wholly, in the stories the novel tells. Such stories encapsulate the characters whose losses are encrypted in them but are also transferred to readers involved in deciphering them.

ARTICULATING DISCOURSES:
HUMAN RIGHTS AND SUBALTERNITY

Anil's Ghost is among few exemplary works that refuse any easy narrative closures where escape from one stereotype – death – is figured through recourse to other stereotypes of romantic love, migration to a pristine West, prelapsarian fantasies of the past, or the emergence of a liberal model of economic, social, or political development. Instead, *Anil's Ghost* forces us to reckon anew with the terms of death as a culture-defining stereotype. To do so requires us to consider that there is no singular story of love or survival or progress here and to ask: What do we make of a book in which an entire society is shown locked in the grip of death? What does it matter that such death, instead of being cast as a solitary ontological experience, evokes a collective cultural one?

If cultural stereotypes gain fictional currency by repeatedly ascribing an attribute to a particular culture or place or people in generalized and static terms, Ondaatje's novel participates in such a flattening. Its preoccupation with death, however, provokes questions about the values and liabilities that adhere to the stereotype in the first place. Sri Lanka's appearance as a subaltern place entangled in "brutal human violence" is, for example, intimately tied to Anil's itinerary there as a human rights advocate (AG, 55).[11] The novel evinces a deep skepticism about Anil's fact-finding mission, describing her as an outsider, as someone who "had courted foreignness" and "felt completed abroad" (AG, 54).[12] Anil regards the victims of violence she encounters in a way that advances assumptions about their capacity to be human within a narrow framework of liberal rights discourse that privileges language and reason as the predominant aspects of humanity under threat. Her conviction – "that those who were slammed and stained by violence lost the power of language and logic. It was the way to abandon emotion, a last protection of the self " (AG, 55–6) – is the basis of the case she intends to make for Sailor. "Who was he," she wonders, "[t]his representative of all those lost voices?" (AG, 56). Yet Anil's inability to restore Sailor's voice draws attention to the limited conception of self or the restrictive "ethics of subject formation" through which concerns about human rights violations are routinely funnelled.[13] That such ideas about selfhood are culturally alien and fall short of addressing the troubles at hand is echoed by Sarath's blunt appraisal of Anil's work: "You know, I'd believe your arguments more if you lived here ... You can't just slip in here, make a discovery and leave" (AG, 44).

The notion of a generic, radarless violence is what propels Anil's conviction that fear may be the only binding feature of humanity on the island. Travelling undercover to a remote location in search of Sailor's past, Anil suddenly recalls the "[a]mygdala," the "nerve

Subaltern Difference and Postcolonial Melancholia 345

bundle which houses fear" that long ago in London had "sounded Sri Lankan" to her when she first heard it (AG, 134–5). Confronted with her inability to make logical sense of the war, Anil is newly convinced that fear pervades the most ordinary aspects of life in Sri Lanka: "She remembers the almond knot ... [I]t governs everything. How we behave and make decisions, how we seek out safe marriages, how we build houses that we make secure" (AG, 135). The novel omnisciently reinforces Anil's meditations with a line from Anne Carson's *Plainwater*: "I wanted to find one law to cover all of living. I found fear" (AG, 135). Notable here is that a universal law is discovered in lieu of a human rights narrative that would restore voice and, by extension, selfhood and dignity under the law to a single unidentifiable corpse. It seems that the arbitrary civilizational norms that govern Anil's attempts to humanize Sailor can only be tested by other equally risky postulates about the primal nature of existence in Sri Lanka – fear, archaic forms of violence, death – that tenuously unites the postcolony to a larger human community. The manner in which stereotypes of death and violence in the postcolony are evoked as the condition for making and unmaking the abridged form of humanity admitted under rights discourses sanctioned by the West remains, as the novel implies, largely tautological.[14]

If there is value to such a stereotype, then it is this: the stereotype marks dying as a collective, far-reaching, and global experience, rather than a single event internal to individuals. The story sediments the postcolony as a place of subaltern dispossession while impelling us toward a divergent paradigm for how we relate to loss. Ondaatje uses the word "pietà" to describe Gamini's transformed relationship to his brother Sarath on finding him murdered for his involvement in Anil's mission:

> There are pietàs of every kind. [Gamini] recalls the sexual pietà he saw once ... There were other pietàs. The story of Savitra, who wrestled her husband away from Death ... But this was a pietà between brothers. And all Gamini knew in his slowed, scrambled state was that this would be the end or it could be the beginning of a permanent conversation with Sarath ... So he was too, at this moment, within the contract of a pietà. (AG, 288)

A pietà in this case not only involves an intimacy with the dead formed through piety and pity, as the etymology of the word

346   Mrinalini Chakravorty

suggests, but also cements into permanence a contract with the dead. For Gamini, this entails "a permanent conversation" with the dead Sarath, despite their previous alienation from each other. Gamini's life, which goes on despite his brother's death, signals the extent to which violent loss in the novel is a part of diurnal life. As the opening of another of the novel's postcolonial crypts, this moment highlights the need to dwell in loss, or to be melancholic, as the new ethical obligation in reconciling ourselves to the deaths of others.

Anil's Ghost formally animates such an ethics by withholding a singular explanation that resolves the mystery of Sailor's death. Instead, the reader, like Anil, is left to choose between several moments that punctuate the story, each confounding conclusions proffered by others about the novel's investment in recounting the crisis in Sri Lanka. Both readers and characters, as Margaret Scanlan notes, are forced to engage in "imperfect" "acts of reconstruction," catching only fragmented and fleeting scenes of life in a world perpetually disrupted by violent deaths.[15] If the reader initially identifies with the main premise of Anil's work as a human rights advocate – "the central truism in her work was that you could not find a suspect until you found a victim" (AG, 176) – the various end points of the novel muddle the clarity of such logic. The irrationality of violence, the unpredictability of its intrusions, effects both affective and material transformations in this work. Anil's work as a disinterested "reader of the intricacies of dead bodies" is compromised by her increasing involvement in the affective dimension of social violence.[16] A dispassionate reader implicated within Anil's "positivist philosophy" thus has to contend with the illogical progression of her investigation.[17] Anil's embrace of the skeleton, her inability to distinguish Sailor from Sirissa, and the lack of evidence with which she brings her report on Sailor before the government commission are moments when the narrative of human rights she wishes to tell comes to a halt. Each of these is also a moment when Sailor's story ends:

> There had been hours when, locked in her investigations ... she too would need to reach forward and lift Sailor into her arms, to remind herself he was like her. Not just evidence, but someone with charms, and flaws. (AG, 170)

> The firelight set the face in movement. But what affected her – who felt she knew every physical aspect about Sailor, had been

Subaltern Difference and Postcolonial Melancholia 347

along-side him now in his posthumous life ... – was that this head was not just how someone possibly looked, it was a specific person ... There was a serenity in the face she did not see too often these days. There was no tension. A face comfortable with itself ... She could no longer look at the face, saw only Ananda's wife in every aspect of it. (AG, 184–5)

What I wish to report is that some government forces have possibly murdered innocent people ... The skeleton I had was evidence of a certain kind of crime. That is what is important here. *"One village can speak for many villages. One victim can speak for many victims."* (AG, 275)

If this novel is about Anil's conversion from visitor, voyeur, and witness of violence to intimate participant or, as Sarath says, her becoming "finally [one] of us," it is also about excesses of violence that cannot be represented through the sentience of an individual subject. Nor can violence be represented by the instrumental logic of individuated crime and punishment, by the corpse counting and juridical accounting insisted on by human rights discourses and institutions (AG, 272). In this respect, Sailor is and is not Sirissa, and his story, precisely because finding evidence for it remains untenable, only stands in for the stereotype of collective death in the postcolony.

MAPS OF GLOBAL INJURY:
A SUBALTERN AESTHETICS

Despite its critique of human rights interventions, *Anil's Ghost*'s account of Sri Lanka as the place for an endless devaluation of life adheres to an age-old stereotype – the island as a scene of barbarous horror where the reality of life remains indistinguishable from carnage; where all recognition (distinguishing perpetrators from victims, for example) fails. How are we to make sense of the seemingly insurmountable civilizational rupture that the novel's depiction of violence leaves intact? After all, besides Anil, who may be unduly swayed by the influence of a liberal West, there are others who attest to the many crypts strewn over the country. The answer lies in how the novel's absorption with death alters our ethical relation to subaltern death and to a violence that seemingly occurs elsewhere. If, as Sarath speculates in a section entitled "The Life Wheel," "parting or death or disappearance were simply the elimination of sight in the onlooker" (AG, 278), *Anil's Ghost* continually returns us as readers of global fiction to the thresholds of death elsewhere to alter our perception of it.

To understand how, it is helpful to return to the questions with which we began: What does it mean that the location of all manner of human injury and annihilation in the novel is aligned with Sri Lanka in particular and the postcolony in general? Does envisioning entire swaths of the globe as crypts, organized around dying bodies, repeat Conradian stereotypes of the postcolony as primeval and fatalistic stereotypes that cast the global South as the eternal unconscious of the mature, developed world? Or are such stereotypes ambivalently reinvented here to suggest a contestable global model of subalternity? If so, is this model of what Kwame Appiah calls postcolonial pessimism useful as a critique of transnationalization? What are its pitfalls?[18] "In many ways," Ondaatje says in response to a question about his portrait of Sri Lanka, "the book isn't just about Sri Lanka; it could be Guatemala or Bosnia or Ireland. Such stories are familiar in other parts of the world."[19] To the extent that *Anil's Ghost* is a story about subjectivities formed anew, in and through lives lived in what Achille Mbembe has so tragically termed "deathworlds," this is Ondaatje's invitation to expand the terrain of such biocultural zones to multiple locations across the globe.[20]

The novel's far-flung global scope seems to dilute the possibility that assigning culpability or criminality for Sri Lanka's violence along specific ethnic or linguistic, religious, or national categories (for example, Tamil or Sinhala, Hindu or Buddhist, citizen or foreigner) can be intelligibly made. Instead, Sri Lanka remains an abstract location where dying, because *"the reason for war was war,"* is tautologically grounded (AG, 43). Unable to make a forensic and scientifically sound case against the government for human rights violations, Anil departs Sri Lanka for the West with the certitude that she is leaving behind a place of massacre: "She knew she wouldn't be staying here much longer. There was no wish in her to be here anymore. There was blood everywhere. A casual sense of massacre" (AG, 283). So just as Ondaatje dismantles, through Anil's failure, the programmatic human rights discourses of selfhood that for the West focalize civil war, ethnic strife, and genocide as a problem of the East or others, he returns us once more to a world-dividing difference.

This difference between secure and insecure lives is world-dividing insofar as the novel separates the metropolitan West from

Subaltern Difference and Postcolonial Melancholia 349

subaltern locations. The geographic distinctiveness of the novel's setting on the island and the larger global circuits of its references also make this distinction transparent.[21] Although Anil's expert training in medicine occurs in London and the United States, her excavation of human remains – her confrontations with fields of unidentifiable human bodies – takes place in Colombo, northern Sri Lanka, Guatemala, and the borderlands of the American Southwest. The novel begins with a vignette of Anil's time in Guatemala, where forensic work at gravesites is motivated by a collective "vigil for the dead, for these half- revealed forms" that locals keep (AG, 7). In juxtaposing the various burial locations that conjoin the discovery of death with localized gestures of care and grief and a more disinterested forensic effort to rationalize its causes, *Anil's Ghost* reflects generic postcolonial crypts.[22] These crypts, as Sarath reminds us, are strewn all over and infirmly closed: "The country existed in a rocking, self-burying motion. The disappearance of schoolboys, the death of lawyers by torture, the abduction of bodies from the Hokandara mass grave. Murders in the Muthurajawela marsh" (AG, 157).

The idea that collective death in the postcolony can be conveyed only as a universal stereotype is vital to the novel's critique of liberal, rights-based assumptions about global violence, even as the stereotype takes on a life of its own. All narrative threads within the text converge on scenes of collective or shared death that essentially flatten the social terrain of the postcolonial nation. Hence, in another culminating moment, President Katugala's death literally disappears into the death of the subaltern, his assassin:

> The cutting action of the explosion shredded Katugala into pieces. The central question after the bombing concerned whether the President had been spirited away. Because the President could not be found.
> *Where was the President?*
> ... There was blood on the unbroken windows ...
> Some flesh, probably from the bomber, was found on the wall across the street.
> The right arm of Katugala rested by itself on the stomach of one of the dead policemen ...
> ... The body, what remained of it, was not found for a long time. (AG, 294–5)

The destruction of the president's body, along with the body of the suicide bomber, eradicates political distinctions between them, those divides of "degree" and "motive" that Talal Asad argues differentiate the modern state's perpetration of violence from acts of terrorism.[23] The president, we must remember, is one who "claimed no knowledge of organized campaigns on the island" and who, "to placate trading partners in the West," gave in to international pressure to allow Anil's humanitarian mission (AG, 16). The subaltern assassin meanwhile remains anonymous, figured only as "flesh" without gender, ethnicity, age, or any other sign of social being.

The "subaltern effect" of the postcolony in *Anil's Ghost* resides in its depictions of the precariousness of life in Sri Lanka.[24] The exemplary associations of subalternity with death signal how the postcolonial literary text serves as a mode of disclosure that demands a different way of apprehending and responding to how deathly violence is globally allocated and experienced. Such novels transpose violence against particular subalterns who are excised from history on to a more general reflection of violence incurred in postcolonial societies. Ondaatje's ancestral memoir, *Running in the Family*, which describes the decadence and decline of his extended Burgher clan in colonial Ceylon, for instance, begins by casting the continent of his birth with a foreboding sense of demise: "Asia. The name was a gasp from a dying mouth. An ancient word that had to be widespread, would never be used as a battle cry. The word sprawled. It had none of the clipped sound of Europe, America, Canada" (RF, 22). In the throes of a death rattle, the continental space of Asia becomes a flattened crypt juxtaposing the ruins of the colonial Ondaatje family with that of the colony. *Running*, by recounting Ondaatje's return to Sri Lanka as a journey into "jungles and gravestones," presages the nation's birth as a moment that conjoins the false grandeur of old to an infirm subaltern present (RF, 69).[25] The risk of seeing Sri Lanka's emergence from colonialism as devolution into a repressed subaltern state is manifold. It promotes an unexamined nostalgia for a colonial past. It also lends itself to the immense flattening of the heterogeneity of postcolonial space as a space of failure.

When *Anil's Ghost* and other such novels delineate entire nations of the global South as deathscapes, they deploy a questionable stereotype that functions only through the homogenization of social actors and cultural spaces. As a consequence, the decolonial space stands apart and compressed for the explicit burden of violence it bears,

Subaltern Difference and Postcolonial Melancholia   351

becoming allied with other such spaces across the globe.[26] Most importantly, subaltern spaces so imagined reflect human struggles of the most elemental order – over life and death – as the dominant metaphor of global dispossession. As a postcolonial crypt that serves as a repository for representing deathworlds elsewhere, *Anil's Ghost* suggests that a transnational reading public may approach such crypts and respond to subaltern demands for recognition only in the most generalized terms.

THE AFTERLIFE OF STEREOTYPES

Constituting the postcolony in stereotypes of death and violence is inherently paradoxical, and this is its unresolved problem. As the stereotype proliferates, it leads to new interrogations about the bases of its assumptions while renewing old biases. Ondaatje's Sri Lanka is a stereotype that makes several demands. It moves us toward a new affective understanding of death as a relational human experience, a need to rethink the protocols of global human rights work, and a different paradigm for processing collective cultural trauma.[27] However, it also stabilizes the idea of the postcolony as absolute subaltern terrain, a place of danger and deficit, one in which no one is protected and nothing but brute violence remains a constant.

To acknowledge this problem is to recognize that stereotypes of violence in postcolonial contexts are volatile and stalling. As readers we may, as Anil does, escape the violent borders of Sri Lanka that Ondaatje enlivens with relief, leaving behind spectres of unlawful death that seem hazardous and overwhelming even in fiction. Or we may, again like Anil, be haunted by our encounters with those who inhabit this other world, carrying forth a baggage that includes Sailor's illegally smuggled skeleton, Sarath's voice on a tape recorder, and the memories of Ananda, the artificer who sculpts Sailor and Sirissa back to life. We may, on the basis of reading *Anil's Ghost*, reform our ideas about death as a phenomenal as well as ontological experience, taking stock once more of how we relate to the deaths of others near and far. And we may contemplate a reform of our own interventions into hot spots of violence that seem far away but remain proximal.

Anil's Ghost takes us toward fathoming the problem of collective death as an ethical bind that moves beyond our conception of ourselves as individuated, nation-bound subjects governed exclusively by reason. As readers implicated in the novel's depiction of collective loss and mourning, we cannot fully separate ourselves (even if we live in the West) from deaths in the postcolony. Such a separation would accept the notion that the postcolony has no historical or current relation to the West, with its own crypt of brutalities committed all around the global South in the name of reason and juridical accounting. Insofar as the reader is implicated, the place of the postcolony is not simply bounded by the geographic borders insisted on by Western ideas of nation-statehood. *Anil's Ghost* tests the sovereignty of the Western self adopted by human rights discourse and rooted in the false notion of the sovereignty of the nation-state's borders by implying that humanity is saliently interconnected on the basis of mutual attachments and responsibility. When asked about the "sense of responsibility" he felt to "make [Sri Lanka's] plight better known," Ondaatje recounts an old myth: "I remember reading the Indian myth, 'The King and the Corpse.' It's a strange, nightmarish tale about a king who ends up with a body round his neck that he has to be responsible for ... The king keeps burying the body, but he wakes up the next morning and it's round his neck again."[28]

This is the burden of responsibility faced by contemporary novels that render the postcolony's exceptional ties to violence. Representing the postcolony as a crypt risks the propagation of unfounded fears in hopes of shoring up unforeseen attachments. The affective dimensions of living through death that postcolonial crypts in *Anil's Ghost* evoke, those moments of waking up with another's corpse around our necks, make our perceptions of reality, as of ourselves, contingent on our imaginative capacity to be in the place of others even in the extreme moment of their death. In some measure, this is a unique attribute of fiction but also particularly in this case of the contemporary postcolonial novel. To the extent that the novel implicates us in its governing stereotype, it offers us an aesthetic script, however unsettling, for measuring our response to and indeed our share in death in other worlds.

Subaltern Difference and Postcolonial Melancholia 353

NOTES

A longer version of this essay was originally published in PMLA 128.3 (2013) and is reprinted with the permission of The Modern Language Association.

1 Tambiah, Horowitz, Hoole, Bandarage, and Daniel write of excess war deaths in Sri Lanka. Chamberlain, reporting for the *Guardian*, put the unconfirmed death toll at 20,000; Pallister and Chamberlain estimated that 14,000 were wounded in the May 2009 conflict.

2 Tambiah discusses "mass violence" in Sri Lanka in 1958, 1977, 1981, and 1983 (13–15). Other examples are the Janatha Vimukthi Peramuna (JVP) insurrections against Tamil Eelam in the late 1980s and in 2009.

3 Spivak observes that Western-influenced "human rights culture" binds members of elite classes across the global North and South ("Righting Wrongs," 527).

4 Stanton unconvincingly argues that *Anil's Ghost* compels the need for international criminal justice systems; others persuasively assert that it undoes the juridical expectations of colonial intrigue fictions (Siddiqi, 197) to provoke ethical reflections on affect (Staels).

5 McClennan and Slaughter highlight literature's capacity to address human rights concerns (10–12).

6 Abraham and Torok, *The Shell and the Kernel: Renewals of Psychoanalysis*, 130. Secrecy over trauma defers melancholia, rendering crypts secure. Secrets are deflected on to afflictions such as eating disorders, unkemptness, filth, and coprolalia (Abraham and Torok, *The Shell*, 132). See also Freud's theory of the death drive (*Ego*, 37–62; *Civilization*, 75–82).

7 Encrypted secrets, obscured by misleading language, forestall melancholia. Crypts crumble when secrets buried in language are deciphered, and the dissolution of crypts exposes "the open wound" of the melancholic (Freud, "Mourning," 212).

8 Transgenerational phantoms exceed Freud's formulation of repression in which the repressed returns as a response to social prohibitions ("Repression").

9 For Burrows, "Lakma's aphasia" signals empathy, a key to the novel's depictions of trauma (174).

10 Abraham and Torok, *The Shell*, 175.

11 For Ratti, human rights, signification, and the law are interlinked in the novel. Mutua indicts culturally discriminatory metaphors of human rights law.

12 The novel endorses Anil's alliance with the West. "I live here," she affirms, "[i]n the West" (36).

354 Mrinalini Chakravorty

13 Ong, "Experiments with Freedom: Milieus of the Human," 237.

14 Anil's human rights inquiry derives from weapons deals the Sri Lankan government forges with unnamed Western powers. This implicates her scientific rationalization of violence as emanating from the West. Anil's example shows how culpability – hers, ours, the West's – depends on global geopolitics.

15 Scanlan, "Anil's Ghost and Terrorism's Time," 302–3.

16 Burrows, "The Heterotopic Spaces of Postcolonial Trauma in Michael Ondaatje's *Anil's Ghost*," 161.

17 Ibid., 167.

18 Appiah, *In My Father's House*, 155. Appiah links pessimism in postcolonial African novels to a "transnational rather than a national solidarity" publicizing the "suffering of victims" (ibid.).

19 Jaggi, "With Michael Ondaatje (2000)," 253.

20 Mbembe, "Life, Sovereignty, and Terror in the Fiction of Amos Tutuola," 1. Biopower is key to Foucault's formulation of modernity's tolerance for "life" (*History*, pt. 5, 133–60; "Society," 239–64). Agamben argues that the rule of "bare life" that sanctions the deaths of neglected populations is the corollary to modern security regimes. Mbembe defines modern subjectivity as contingent on death, not life

21 JanMohamed and Patterson discuss the deficit and excess of subjectivity that the threat of death confers in slavery.

22 On psychic crypts, see Abraham and Torok, *The Shell*, and *Wolf Man's Magic Word*.

23 Hosseini's *The Kite Runner* is a counterexample.

24 Spivak's term "subaltern subject-effect" illustrates the conundrum of historians seeking to "recover" subaltern consciousness, will, and presence from colonial archives premised on the eradication of subalterns ("Subaltern Studies," 204–5).

25 *Running* reconstructs family history from ledgers, photos, and memories to reveal the debauchery of the Ondaatjes. The idyll of colonial frolic is transformed after decolonization: family ties fray as societal violence rises.

26 Necropolitics concerns globalized violence (evidenced in plantation slavery, apartheid and neocolonial settlements, oil wars, and sectarianism) that shows death as intimate to modern sovereignty (Mbembe, "Necropolitics").

27 In *Precarious Life* and *Frames of War*, Butler describes the ethical stakes of refusing to participate in the deaths of others.

28 Jaggi, "With Michael Ondaatje (2000)," 251.

17

Casualties of Love

Pico Iyer

Michael Ondaatje's novels are all about putting the pieces together. Quite literally, because they proceed through a series of exquisitely shaped vignettes that the reader has to fit into a pattern in her head, but more deeply, too, because their structure invariably reflects their theme. Nearly always they are about attempting to suture things together, to heal a fracture – between one side of Toronto and another in his first major novel, *In the Skin of a Lion*; between (and within) four wounded travellers in an abandoned convent in *The English Patient*; between a visiting forensic anthropologist and two divided brothers amidst the debris of Sri Lanka's ongoing civil war in *Anil's Ghost*. How to turn the fragments into a living whole, if only for a moment, is the burden of these elaborate, questing anthologies of scenes.

The main characters in these books are themselves in pieces too, scarred fugitives found in spaces not their own, deeply alone and at a jagged angle to society. Ondaatje's first book-length narrative, *The Collected Works of Billy the Kid*, was so much a set of disparate frames as it followed its splintered subject across the West that it is now listed among the author's nine works of poetry and not his six books of fiction. His next big work, *Coming Through Slaughter*, in 1976, served up another riffing picaresque about a messed-up jazzman in New Orleans at the turn of the last century (the real cornet player Buddy Bolden) who, after cutting up his wife's lover in a jealous rage, ends up cut up himself, on the run, and slowly loses his mind as well as his art. One source of such concerns is revealed a little, perhaps, in Ondaatje's much-acclaimed memoir, *Running in the Family*, in which, not really a local and not quite a foreigner, he

356 Pico Iyer

returns to Sri Lanka, where he was born, to piece through the shards of his own family's extravagant and wildly self-destructive history.

These are poets' novels, in other words, the work of a highly meticulous craftsman who creates scenes of uncanny beauty and precision and pieces them together like jewels in a necklace. Born to mixed ancestry in colonial Ceylon, educated in England, and resident in Canada since 1962, while travelling widely, Ondaatje is harder to place than even such exile colleagues as Salman Rushdie or Kazuo Ishiguro, and there is a sense that he is always pushing across forms as well as continents to create a new kind of mongrel fiction that leaves old categories behind. Few reading experiences, to my mind, are so enveloping and delectable as making one's way through the slow, spacious pages of an Ondaatje novel, as pleasing to the senses as sipping white wine in the sunlight, and there is a different and deeper delight in going through a second time – "Only the rereading counts," he cites here from Nabokov – to see the secret stitching that links a reference to Dumas in northern California to one in southern France or rhymes the image of one woman's hair darkening in a shower to another. The question, though, that always haunts these elliptical and delicate works is how much their very beauty takes us away from the war and scenes of great pain they describe and to what extent, in courting art, they leave real life behind.

Divisadero, Ondaatje's latest epic of intimate moments, ravishing and intricate, begins on a ranch north of San Francisco in the 1970s, and within pages we are in the half-magical, aromatic world that Ondaatje has made his own. A teenage girl is guiding her horse through the madrone above the morning mist while the local bar down below goes up in flames. Another girl is playing "Begin the Beguine" on an old wind-up gramophone, reading *The Leopard* before making love and hanging Buddhist prayer-flags above her cabin as if to sanctify that love. A skilful cowherd is showing us how to hammer "sharpened sticks of redwood or cedar" from the inside out to heal a leak in a water tower and how to splint up a broken wrist with willow.

Four people live on the ranch, and all are deeply bruised and correspondingly skittish: the patriarch has lost his wife while she was giving birth to his only daughter, Anna, now sixteen, and in his grief he has adopted another girl, Claire, born the same week, who likewise had her mother die in giving birth to her. The cowhand, Coop,

Casualties of Love

was taken in when, at the age of four, he hid out in a crawl space while his entire family was killed by a hired hand. The story comes to us through Anna at this point, but we are quickly made to see that there are pieces of every character in every other and identity will always be a shifting and uncertain thing for them.

It is the particular distinction of an Ondaatje novel to mix richly atmospheric scenes of Keatsian tenderness with moments of explosive violence – this is, after all, a writer who devoted his first long book to an outlaw who blew away twenty men by the time he was twenty-one. And the interplay between the hurts that arise from those eruptions and the impulse to take care of those hurts, to tend to them with a surgeon's professionalism, gives his books their drama and their theme. In this case, one of the girls gets too close to Coop, her father discovers them during a freakish ice storm, violence breaks out on every side, and all four characters, already fragile, are scattered to different corners of the world, more traumatized than ever.

The novel that follows picks them up two decades later, running from their pasts and trying to hide out in other worlds and new pursuits, and it shuffles fluidly back and forth between Coop, gambling his way across the American West, and Anna, remaking her life in the Gers region of southwestern France and settling down in a forgotten manoir to piece together the story of a French writer, Lucien Segura, who himself had disappeared from the house and who "had a wound in his voice" that speaks to her. The startling and unexpected risk in the novel comes when, in its third part, it travels back, at length, into the life of Segura himself, at the beginning of the last century, as if to say that the losses and divisions of the present can begin to be healed by looking at a completely different story in the past and gradually coming to some resolution in our heads.

In every one of his books, Ondaatje alights upon some new territory and begins, with patient attentiveness, to excavate its forgotten history and secret treasures; it's no coincidence that so many of his characters are archaeologists, researchers, archivists. And his settings are nearly always marginal places, far from the city, that few writers have chosen to light up before (part of *Divisadero* is set in the little central Californian town of Santa Maria, forty-five minutes by car from where I write this, in my long-time home in Santa Barbara, and yet unvisited by almost everyone I know). In that context, it's no coincidence that California's Gold Rush is evoked in the second paragraph of the book, as Ondaatje tries to find the bounty in neglected people and scenes (as recently as the 1970s, he tells us, five thousand people were still panning full-time for gold in California's rivers).

When we read of Anna fleeing the conflagration of her life, therefore, hitching a ride in a refrigerated truck through the Central Valley of California, we learn that John Muir found a sea of flowers in the valley and that the local Maidu mythology sees the Great Central Plain as having been born from an ocean. We read of gunfighters and thieves and "anarchic outlaw girls" in the area's past, and we see how the Okie labourers we might have met in a Steinbeck account are now joined – in good Ondaatje fashion – by waves of other immigrants, speaking Tagalog, Spanish, Italian, Chinese, and Japanese. At the end of the drive we come to an abandoned town that, decades before, was settled only – remarkably – by Blacks.

In just two pages, in short, describing an escape from a bloody confrontation, Ondaatje takes us on a passage through wonders so absorbing that we feel as if we are stumbling upon an undiscovered world. At the same time, though, at the most dramatic moment of her life, we read almost nothing of Anna's fears, her feelings, as the narrative moves laterally, as it were, and through indirections. Most writers would either fill the drive with dialogue or emotion or cut to the next location; Ondaatje's way is to look out the window to notice bodies of water (which will chime with the ones he later describes in France), renegade pioneers (who take us back to the contemporary card sharps we have met in an earlier panel of the story), cities named for "sacrament" and "mercy" (Sacramento and Merced), as if to remind us of the qualities his characters most painfully need.

This "science of patterns," as he calls it in another book, means that his works both demand and teach the closest of attention. When people call Ondaatje a poetic novelist, they are referring in part, of course, to his rare gift for language and observation: a dog joining a woman in bed sinks its claws into her back "like tuning forks," and two lovers emerging shyly from an afternoon tryst look "like humbled dormice." There are peacocks in charm trees here and a thief who marks his place in a book with a sprig of absinthe leaves. A scene of a boy on a runaway horse during an eclipse is as astonishing and hallucinatory as any such passage I can remember reading.

Yet the deeper aspect of his poetic background is that he structures narratives with the interlaced complexity of a lyric poem. At

Casualties of Love

one point, when Coop is learning how to play cards professionally, a section is called, with quiet wit, "The Red and the Black." But we realize that the title is not entirely casual when, a little later, Claire enters a club in Tahoe, of all places, called the Stendhal. And then, near the end of the book, the French writer Segura thinks back to the nightly seductions of *Le Rouge et le noir*, and one sees a parallel story shadowing this one (sees, too, that this is Ondaatje's first book to take in all the sadnesses of old age and to be as much about fathers and daughters as about lovers).

In much the same way, certain words – "hesitate," "dangerous," "wound" – toll through the book like motifs in a piece of music, and after we've spent time in an "abandoned base" in the West, something stirs in us, perhaps, when we come to an "abandoned farm" in France, and the "abandoned land" that Segura comes upon, and an "abandoned boat," the "abandoned town" that Anna arrives at after her flight, even an "abandoned wife." Few novelists are so precise about the images and clues they scatter through their narratives – wheels and Balzac and images of men sinking under water recur here – and almost the only one I have read who begins to resemble Ondaatje is, in fact, his fellow Torontonian and poet Anne Michaels, who summons in the very title of her only novel, *Fugitive Pieces*, two central elements of the Ondaatje universe.

Because, like most distinctive novelists, he has so commanding a vision, one knows in advance to some extent what kind of characters (in every sense of the word) we will meet in an Ondaatje book. The other man's wife, the attractive thief, the wounded fugitive, the scarred nurse: all these figures appear again and again in his work. No writer seems more averse to the nine-to-five round or the conventional stuff of society; you will be no more likely to meet an investment banker in an Ondaatje novel than in the works of W.G. Sebald or Nabokov. (There is a San Francisco public defender here, a man of great integrity though haunted by wounds of his own, having served in Vietnam, but his very name, Aldo Vea, suggests that he is at least in part a tribute to Ondaatje's novelist friend, also in San Francisco, Alfredo Vea, who likewise served in Vietnam and is mentioned on the first page of Ondaatje's last book, *The Conversations*.)

In *Divisadero*, therefore, we meet gypsies and chancers and musicians and drop-outs of every kind, most of them experienced at keeping their distance yet always reaching toward other drifting strangers whose scars may reflect their own. There is lots of

Pico Iyer

domesticity in the texture of the book – the ceremonial preparation of meals, the collection of herbs from the garden, the rites of sensual love, dogs (as in all Ondaatje's works) everywhere – yet there are no real homes that last, and all his people are on the move, emotional gypsies. And though he is rightly famous for his scenes of tropical romance – there are women in this book called Aria and Lina and Marie-Neige – he always roots them amidst people with dirt on their shoes and "lived-in, overused" hands.

More than any writer I've read, Ondaatje is fascinated by craft and by the special lore and lingo of the various occupations he meets, the secret tricks of, in this case, the card sharp, the clock-maker, the peasant farmer. When Coop receives training in how to cheat at cards, for example, we read sentences that delight in his new vernacular: "He will place this riffle-stacked slug of cards beneath a crimp, about where the player on his right usually cuts the cards. If the man cuts at the crimp, there will be no need for Coop to hop or shift the deck secretly." When the action moves to France and the agricultural region of Gascony, we read how a woman "sprinkled chimney soot over the rows where she had planted cabbage, dragged lime and ammonia through the claylike soil, and used cow dung, where it was sandy and horse manure where it was chalk." Ondaatje descends into the work of his characters as deeply as into their land-scapes (and their histories).

Part of the great delight of reading one of his books, therefore, comes in the sensation of a deeply curious traveller opening out his worn suitcase and letting all the odd pieces of information or memorable lines or exotic bric-a-brac he's collected tumble out. We learn here how troubadours in medieval France imitated bird calls so effectively that they may have changed migratory patterns. We read that a laser scope can measure the vibrations in the glass of a window across the street. We encounter the neglected recordings of Thelonius Monk, the Sanskrit fables collected by the scholar Wendy Doniger, the fact that Victor Hugo inserted a fictional street in Paris for Jean Valjean to hide in in *Les Miserables*.

For some readers, this may all seem too much a part of the Ondaatje imagination and too far from the workaday world. When, for example, Coop falls in with the maverick gamblers of California and Nevada, one of them, called the Dauphin, beguiles the hours by talking of Lady Murasaki, while another teaches Coop distraction techniques by telling a story of Tolstoy. After the group has pulled

Casualties of Love 361

off a $300,000 scam in a Vegas casino, the gambler's sweetheart who accompanies Coop in the getaway car starts talking about, of all things, a radio interview with William Styron she once heard.

There are also moments when Ondaatje's imagination is so strong that the characters he graces with his interest come to seem almost interchangeable. It's hard to distinguish the Deadhead card sharp from the one who says, "My name is Edward Dorn. Like the poet"; the Berkeley researcher born to privilege in California comes to merge a little with the peasant girl in France who's only just learned how to read. There are six different romances in the book, and each of them is gorgeous and singular in its effects, but if you were to be presented with any scene from one of them blindfold, it might be hard to say whether it belonged to the writer or the gypsy.

Beyond that, Ondaatje suffers, through no fault of his own, from the rare predicament of a serious literary novelist who has seen one of his books turned into a hugely popular, Academy Award–sweeping movie. There are many scenes in this book – of a man swinging through the belfry of a medieval church in France, of a man wooing a woman by reading a book to her, of a character summoning her lover in a garden shower, and of people in abandoned houses taking on new identities – that may feel familiar only because they all rhyme with moments in Anthony Minghella's memorable film of *The English Patient*. In fact, of course, Minghella drew for his inspired reimaginings only on the imagination of Ondaatje, but it can feel as if Ondaatje is influenced by Minghella rather than only by himself.

And yet, at the same time, the very closeness of the characters to one another is part of what enables Ondaatje to attempt some remarkable gymnastics. When Anna, for example, settles in France, she comes across a gypsy (who – this being Ondaatje – sits in a chair in an empty field under the moon and plays the guitar in emulation of his hero Django Reinhardt). She is drawn to him because of his "hesitancy," his "shyness," as "though in the past he had been burned by something." On first reading, perhaps, we just savour the supple details of their courtship. But as we proceed, we realize that the "hesitant" links the gypsy to the writer Segura and his love, who are always described with that same word, that the "burned" is not random because fires run through this book, and that the gypsy's talk of his territorial father takes us back to a horse we met on the first page with the distinctive name of "Territorial." Those figures forgotten by history, Anna says – and she may be speaking for her maker – are "essential as underground rivers," and rivers will also run through the book as the writer tries to bring the meandering waterways of France together with the straight roads of the American West.

This knowledge of many worlds, and an eagerness to bring them together, begins to account for the unique flavour of this writer's work. When we read of a gambler said to have won his wife in a bet, it is as if a moment from *The Mahabharata* has suddenly come into the parched deserts of the New World, with their characters otherwise compounded of Bob Dylan and Cormac McCarthy. And his ability to fashion scenes that are at once exact and suggestive accounts not only for the sensual thrill of the books but also for their literary pleasures and the sense of several stories unfolding at once. At one point, in the gambling section of the book, the Gulf War breaks out in the background, on TV, and Ondaatje is the rare writer who decides to name the agents of destruction – "the Cobra helicopter, the Warthog, the Spectre, and its twin, the Spooky" – and to catalogue the "thermobaric fuel, volatile gasses, and finely powdered explosives" they drop. When you recall that these scenes are playing out on a screen in the back of a sealed and air-conditioned casino, where a group of misfits is taking on a band they call "the Born-Agains" – in a game of Texas Hold'Em, no less – while the "'eye in the sky'" takes in every deceit, you realize that the book is, among many other things, a parable of contemporary America.

The best way to see what Ondaatje is attempting in every novel he writes is to look at the occupations he highlights. In *Coming Through Slaughter*, he focused on a wildly improvising jazzman and an archival photographer; in *In The Skin of a Lion*, he placed bridge-builders at the centre; in *The English Patient*, he was concerned with map-makers, bomb-defusers, archaeologists, and nurses. In *Divisadero*, the two main characters are a historical researcher and a gambler. And this is no stray detail, I think, because the book takes a great gamble itself by attempting to do things with narrative that have seldom been done before (leaving two major stories up in the air in the hope that they can be imaginatively tied together by a third).

There is always a clear and unhurried spaciousness to Ondaatje's paragraphs, a weightedness that allows them to breathe, as it were, and to stretch their limbs; they surround you with their density and proceed with the deliberation and care of a work of contemplation,

Casualties of Love 363

although bringing their attention to things of the secular world, in this case horses and rivers and fields. Yet in *Divisadero*, it is clear that Ondaatje is seeing what he can do with the traditional novel to open it up: he refers to a "tune that seemed to have no scaffolding" and, a little later, to a "song that had all of its doors and windows open." He wants to settle things, you feel, without stifling them in the way of a conventional resolution.

"We thought he was formless," someone says of the broken-up musician in *Coming Through Slaughter*, thirty-one years ago, but "Now I can see he was tormented by order." And there is much in this novel that suggests that Ondaatje has been thinking hard about how to make sure he is giving us not just scenes but a forward-moving story and a whole that can be greater than the sum of its alluring parts. At one point, for instance, Claire links the main characters to a "three-paneled Japanese screen, each one self-sufficient, but revealing different qualities or tones when placed beside the others"; the word "adjacent" comes up at least three times, as if to suggest how, in bringing two of the characters together, we are implicitly evoking a third. In the same way, we are told very early in the book, "Everything was collage, even genetics" and then, a paragraph later, "Everything is collage."

To see what lies behind all this, it is most useful, I think, to turn to what was in fact Ondaatje's most recent book, in 2002, although it was not accorded the attention that most of his novels bring, the extended series of discussions with the celebrated film editor Walter Murch that was called *The Conversations*. Murch is the kind of craftsman – intelligent, highly idiosyncratic, and a little craggy – who might almost be an Ondaatje character (not least because his painter father came from Toronto), and Ondaatje professes himself fascinated, in a fascinating introduction, by the man's "precise techniques" and by the fact that he is interested in Beethoven, in astronomy, in bees, in seemingly everything (Murch was translating the Italian prose of Curzio Malaparte into English poetry at the time these conversations took place). Beyond that, of course, Murch is an accomplished master in his field, having been responsible for the piecing together and cutting of *The Godfather* movies, *Apocalypse Now*, a new version of *Touch of Evil* that he put together according to the unregarded notes of Orson Welles, as well as *The English Patient*. As they talk, what Ondaatje is really exploring is the art of splicing together a narrative: how to shuffle the order of scenes so as to intensify the tension; how to save a scene in the fifty-third minute by making a small change in the seventh; how, most importantly, to use radical jump cuts to create a natural sense of flow.

The Conversations becomes, therefore, an entirely unusual and intensely detailed investigation into the tricks of storytelling and how, for example, when the English patient in the movie tastes a plum, a bell sounds half a mile away to suggest that his past is coming back. "I am always striving for a clear density," Murch says (much as in *Divisadero* we read that Bach, another household god in Ondaatje's work, offers a "spare thicket" of notes). As Ondaatje discusses his own interest in "leaping poetry," the largely Spanish form in which subliminal connections between juxtaposed passages "reveal a surprising path or link between strangers," you begin to see that if *Running in the Family* is his traditional memoir, *The Conversations* is his typically oblique self-portrait.

As *Divisadero* draws toward its close, it becomes ever more apparent that Ondaatje is trying something new with narrative, quickened, perhaps, by his talks with the film editor (twenty years ago, in the context of *In the Skin of a Lion*, Leon Edel brilliantly described Ondaatje's writing as "verbal cinema"). Perspective shifts constantly in the book, from first person to third, from past to present, till at one climactic moment at the very end we move from one character to another, as in a cinematic dissolve, in the space of a single paragraph. "The right ending," as Ondaatje wrote in *Coming Through Slaughter*, "is an open door you can't see too far out of."

In its final section, the novel homes in on the writer figure, abandoning his family, remaking his life in his books, even visiting the front of World War I to study diphtheria, which he then catches (a virtuoso paragraph on the history of diphtheria follows). As we watch the character go back and forth between what he remembers and what he imagines, between his experiences and the use he makes of them in art, we are reminded that Ondaatje has always put his faith, more than anything, in the imagination and the way we have to step away from the world to make it whole again.

"Divisadero" refers to the street in San Francisco where Anna lives and comes, of course, from the Spanish word for "division." But it may also derive, Ondaatje tells us, from divisar, which means "to gaze from a distance." We heal our divisions by looking at them from the safety of far off. On the very first page of this book, after all, we have been told, by Nietzsche, that "We have art so that we

Casualties of Love

shall not be destroyed by the truth," and that sentence is repeated seven pages from the end. In *The English Patient*, amidst all the destruction of World War II, a central line informed us "There was no order but for the great maps of art."

This is a creed that not every reader will accept, and there will always be some for whom Ondaatje is too rarefied and aestheticized. But for those who hold, as we are told here, that "sometimes we enter art to hide within it," the very beauty of the scenes becomes their own justification, a salve and also a sanctuary. *The English Patient* gave us a captivating latticework of stories about privacy and dissolving borders and then almost crushed them with a sudden reference, at the end, to the bomb dropped on Hiroshima; *Divisadero* ends more quietly by bringing us back to reflections, to disappearances, to the ways in which a river might meet a road. In the process, it extends the liberating and original territory of that earlier triumph so transportingly that it's hard, on finishing, not to turn back to the opening page and start all over again.

NOTE

This piece was originally published in *The New York Review of Books* under the title "A New Kind of Mongrel Fiction" on 28 June 2007. It appears here courtesy of the author.

18

Ondaatje's Late Style

Moez Surani

I shall focus on great artists and how near the end of their lives their work and thought acquires a new idiom, what I shall be calling a late style.

Edward Said, *On Late Style*

Delineating Michael Ondaatje's fiction into early, middle, and late periods is fairly straightforward. Each of these stages shares similar themes, imagery, and lexicons. His early, self-referential fictions, *The Collected Works of Billy the Kid* (1970) and *Coming Through Slaughter* (1976), dramatize personal rebellions against the corrosive power of the mainstream: vitality and originality lie at society's margin. Ondaatje published with small presses and wrote portrayals of people whose intensity manifested in a transgressive spirit. These works evoke an acute sense of isolation in which single friendships are prized and psychic loneliness supercharges into eros.

His middle period – *In the Skin of a Lion* (1987), *The English Patient* (1992), and *Anil's Ghost* (2000) – broadens the spirit of transgression and shows a gallery of characters whose rebellions are explicitly politicized. These characters resist both a life of bourgeois capital accrual and the profanity of day-to-day monotony and conformity. Their main concerns are borne from a critical attitude toward nations and nationalism: Is their country virtuous? What are a country's historical truths? What are the personal costs of nationalism?

Ondaatje has published three novels in the past fifteen years: *Divisadero* (2007), *The Cat's Table* (2011), and *Warlight* (2018). They share voice and tone, and they repeat fairly precise preoccupations. Together, these three express his late style. Each of these novels is a coming-of-age story centred on literal or emotional orphans who cope with unresolved pain and walk out into the world with an essentially ascetic disposition – none of them seeks money, status, influence, or material rewards. They desire intimacy, safety, and knowledge about themselves and their own actions and the facts about each other's history of love and pain.

Due to the collective pivot embodied by Ondaatje's last three novels, it's worth considering the implications of these works that constitute a shift to a sentimental mode of fiction and, specifically, to narratives focused on characters coping with trauma.

Beginning on a farm in California, *Divisadero* opens with a fragile triangle: Anna, Claire who is adopted by Anna's father, and an orphan, Coop, who is taken in by Anna and Claire's father as a labourer. When their father finds that Anna and Coop are having an affair, he explodes. This violence forks the book into three paths: Coop becomes a gambler, Claire a lawyer in San Francisco, and Anna goes to France to research the life of poet-turned-novelist Lucien Segura. While in France, Anna also has an affair with Rafael, who, emotionally, is Segura's son. The name of the dead author whom Anna studies in France, Segura, translates as "secure." For her and her near-siblings, the world of safety and security has, like the author, passed on.

Through Anna's sacralizing eyes, everything is lightly blessed as she retreats to a child's bedroom in Segura's house to find herself: "This 'smallest possible space' is where Anna wishes to be now. The truth of her life comes out only in places like this" (*D*, 75). Characters are treated as rare and special, and scenes have a heightened tone, as if the recovery from her trauma imparts a generalized halo to all things. What's implied is that the enchantment of the sacred helps to assuage trauma and that this sacralizing imperative allows these characters to rejoin the potentially distressing and disturbing incidences of life.

When characters in *Divisadero* meet, the discussion is rarely about the future or the present but is a recounting of personal history. Intimacy and secrets are key words; they are portals to a desired but evasive inner truth. Characters meet, become close, but retain their fundamental secrets: "There are layers of compulsive secrecy in [Anna]. She knows there is a 'flock' of Anna's, and that the Anna beside this unnamed river of Rafael's is not the Anna giving a seminar at Berkeley ... is not the Anna in San Francisco"

(*D*, 88). This tension of not knowing animates these relationships and keeps these characters at a mystifying distance from each other: "In spite of everything that had existed between Coop and Anna for those two months on the Petaluma farm, they had remained mysterious to each other" (*D*, 89). *Divisadero* continues with a signature Ondaatje trait: the absence of a nuclear family. A difference, though, from his earlier work is how this absence plays out. Rather than deconstructing the concept of the bourgeois family to expose social repression or economic imperatives, the notion of family is so essential in *Divisadero* that its lack overshadows these characters well into adulthood, thereby reinstantiating the concept of the nuclear family.

Related to this is the omnipresence of a traumatic backstory. Throughout his oeuvre, Ondaatje writes sensitively about pain, but the pain in *Divisidero* is focused on trauma incurred in childhood and adolescence: Coop's family was killed by a hired hand who beat his family with a wooden board while a four-year-old Coop hid in the crawl space for several days (*D*, 10). Anna and Claire's foundational trauma is their absent parents (for Anna, her mother; for Claire, both her parents). Neglect and pain are formative in these characters, distinguishing them from an imagined though never depicted wholesome family. The violence between Coop and Anna's father is a second layer of trauma for them that adds urgency to the questions that are implicated: How to dispense with immense personal pain? How to overcome a protective sense of guardedness and achieve intimacy with another? Does this individuating pain split one off irrevocably from a socially oriented consciousness, and what, in turn, is the implication of this for the narrative and the interpretations it yields?

These questions are largely developed in the I-thou of their love affairs in which love and trauma dovetail to create an ontological state centred in diffidence and woundedness: "Anna, who keeps herself at a distance from those who show anger or violence, just as she is still fearful of true intimacy" (*D*, 75). In *Divisadero*, knowing someone is inextricably linked with knowing their trauma: "All your stories, Rafael, tell me was there nothing terrible?" (*D*, 90). That is, the stories Rafael tells Anna are of less importance than those believed to be left unsaid. Moreover, trauma imparts an imperative of historical depth and gives a sense that people accrue from a past; people are not self-made or self-created, but their

Ondaatje's Late Style 369

personalities result from a deterministic algebra of experiences. As Anna notes, "We have become unintelligible in our secrets, governed by our past selves" (*D*, 141).

In *Divisadero*, because the distance between two can only be bridged through an understanding of trauma, sex takes on a constricted function in the novel; it carries the intermittent charge of intimacy and, with this, of being known. This feeling of mutual presence between two is sufficiently rewarding that it overshadows words and physicality: "They were not kissing now. It was more intimate, their faces staring at each other, almost touching. A breath, no words to accompany this, only watching each other's naked response" (*D*, 127). Trauma and love both result in a reluctance to speak about the incident: Rafael tells Anna of "an earlier relationship that had silenced him completely, and how he had almost not emerged from that. He was in fact coming out of that privacy for the first time with her" (*D*, 73).

Because of the emphasis on silences and secrets, in *Divisadero* loving someone presents the opportunity to tell a story – not to look ahead to future plans or feel an intensified sense of presence but to answer the question about whether or not to gift the beloved with a narration of the past. The residue trauma leaves is the obstacle to this desire to narrate. As such, the characters in *Divisadero* toggle between being known and unknown to each other. As they flicker between a state of intimacy and mystery, these relationships mimic a familiar dance: that of contemporary celebrities who toggle between being proximate – when they are relatable, familiar, and connected – and out of reach. Like celebrity, too, what is being restricted and what exists in a state of scarcity in these intimate relationships is access. Moreover, the denial of access creates a distanced sense of mystery that mints the currency of interest and intrigue: "In spite of everything that existed between Coop and Anna for those two months on the Petaluma farm, they had remained mysterious to each other" (*D*, 89). It isn't the sense of union and corresponding feeling that prompts this memory but, rather, the mystery that prevails that echoes into Anna's present consciousness.

A counterpoint to the troubled couplings in the novel is the artistic intimacy Lucien Segura achieves with his friend Mary-Neige. In her physical absence, he centres his plots around permutations of her personality; he narrates her and recontextualizes her. These are the popular stories Segura sells once he turns from poetry to picaresque fictions: "She entered the story sometimes as a lover, sometimes as a sister. And in this way he spent most of his days with Mary-Neige as an ally in the court, or as a village girl who saves the hero without his being aware of it" (*D*, 263). And, conclusively, "she was within him now" (*D*, 267). While this intimacy is only achieved in the monologic domain of his art where her autonomy is subordinated to the naturalizing rhetoric of authorial creativity ("as he wrote he waited for her arrival, usually halfway through a book, long after a location and a plot had been established" [*D*, 263]), this does serve as the novel's rare sustained union.

Published four years later, *The Cat's Table* is the first-person account of a child's three-week trip from Sri Lanka to England aboard the *Oronsay* with six hundred other passengers. The cat's table, to which the narrator, Michael, is assigned, is for the ship's least privileged passengers. Michael maps the boat spatially and rhythmically, and he takes an inventory of those aboard. *The Cat's Table* has a hagiographic voice; the child narrator looks up at a world of seeming giants. Michael collects tall tales, and his narration is suffused with the excitement and deviousness of his youth: the children swim in the first-class deck's pool before sunrise, there is the silent menace of a prisoner aboard, and there's a stop in Aden where a curse is fulfilled. The novel's tone is saturated with the wonder of childhood as Michael ranges through the boat searching out secrets for the intensity and exclusivity they confer. As the ship goes to England, through the Suez Canal and across the Mediterranean, the forward-looking joy of the book is counterpointed with flash-forwards of the adult narrator looking backwards to gain understanding of his own life: so, enchantment going forward and a more rationally minded disenchanted perspective looking back.

Even as Michael is about to leave Sri Lanka on this one-way, life-altering trip, his family makes little mention of the assortment of incoming changes. Michael notes that the only indication he received was the departure date being casually marked on the calendar. Why, in a first-person coming-of-age story, doesn't the narrative want to interrogate such an important and emotionally potent observation? An answer to this exists in the genres that inform the story: while the narrator's name, his journey, and the profession he will go on to excel at all promise a metafictional account that showcases narrative candour and personal excavation, *The Cat's Table*'s admixture of the picaresque instills a countervailing outward focus and the

Ondaatje's Late Style

corresponding attitude of whimsical adventure. That is, by employing the picaresque, the dramatizing of the story takes precedence over the enlightening but anti-dramatic possibilities of more analytic prose. An upshot of this is that the date noted on Michael's calendar signalling the start of the voyage works as an image to give emotional colouring, not a decision to be plumbed. Likewise, the terse paragraph on the breakup of his parents' marriage gives emotional colour but yields scant particularity into their marriage or context. Michael moves on in his narration, the brief foray into the demise of the marriage giving only an overlay of psychological pain. In his commitment to the acquisition of colourful stories, the picaro moves on to an excited account of swimming. Anecdote and whimsy stand in place of – and repress – sober and sustained interior study.

As in *Divisadero*, light crime is important in *The Cat's Table*. Each day aboard the *Oronsay* Michael and his two friends, Cassius and Ramadhin, must do one forbidden thing. Later, Michael is recruited into a breaking and entering scheme aboard the ship in which he climbs through cabin windows and unlocks the door from the inside. The crimes are largely innocent and comic. A list of "crimes" the captain of the ship is responsible for is enumerated by Michael. These include rude language in front of children and the reciting of an inappropriate poem after dinner (CT, 207). These are no longer the subversive political crimes like those depicted in *In the Skin of a Lion* or crimes of a life force in extremis like in *Billy the Kid*. The crimes in *The Cat's Table* fall into two categories: the first is crime as the breaking of rules, which serves as signs of someone's individuation and self-regard. The second type of "crime" involves insufficient care for others, in particular women and minors. Michael's pinnacle for showing proper care for another is Ramadhin who, as a thirty-something, takes an excessively protective role over a fourteen-year-old he tutors, Heather Cave. Michael views Ramadhin's inappropriate style of care for Heather Cave as knightly behaviour, and he sees Ramadhin as "a sort of saint," "a human one, the saint of our clandestine family" (CT, 155). Michael's willed enchantment prevails over an unsavoury recognition, and Ramadhin retains an august place atop Michael's mental pedestal.

Also like *Divisadero*, memories of trauma suffuse the narrative: "Our worst executioner was the junior school master, Father Barnabus, who still stalks my memory with his weapon of choice, which was a long splintered bamboo cane. He never used words or reason. He just moved dangerously among us" (CT, 13). Again, this wisp of information gives emotional colouring, but it does not inspire Michael into deeper thought about the ramifications or processes this memory creates. Later, as a relationship with Massi is dwindling, she pushes Michael: "Your goddamn cautious heart. Who did you love that did this to you? ... Someone damaged you. Tell me what happened when you came to England ... Because something must have happened" (CT, 203–4). Michael, though, yields nothing to her, and likewise, the narrative is equally terse with the reader.

There is a helpful metafictive moment toward the end of *The Cat's Table*: "we should never feel ourselves wiser than [the characters]; we do not have more knowledge than the characters have about themselves. We should not feel assured or certain of their motives, or look down on them. I believe this. I recognize this as a first principle of art" (CT, 208). The ars poetica instilled here is an aspiration for radical verisimilitude whereby the characters are not verbal creations existing in a created text but autonomous, breathing humans whose lives extend beyond the provided signs. It is a plea for characters to remain inscrutable and immune to the process of being read and understood; this is an ars poetica dedicated to making characters that resist legibility. What, crucially, does this mean for the narrative? First, Ondaatje is subservient to these verbal constructions, and, if we dare to take this with the full sincerity the tone of the passage asks one to in order to show his full respect to the characters, Ondaatje himself must resist the notion that he knows them. Where in *Divisadero* the prevalence of trauma made characters largely unknowable to each other, now in *The Cat's Table*, in a further step, they are estranged from their author. In this way, they are treated as images who can be felt, pitied, and admired from an acknowledged distance but never known.

Trauma, and the cavity of self-knowledge Ondaatje invokes, dovetails with this approach to verisimilitude: realism through unprobed unknowns. Late in the book, as an adult, Michael reflects on the untraceable effects of trauma:

I once had a friend whose heart "moved" after a traumatic incident that he refused to recognize. ... And I wondered then, when he told me this, how many of us have a moved heart? ... Emily. Myself. Perhaps even Cassius. How have our emotions glanced off rather than directly faced others ever since, resulting in simple

Ondaatje's Late Style

unawareness or in some cases cold-blooded self-sufficiency that is damaging to us? Is that what has left us, still uncertain, at a Cat's Table, looking back, looking back, searching out those we journeyed with? (CT, 257–8)

Aesthetically, for these characters to pass as real they must be enigmatic. To be known would let the air out of this stringent approach to verisimilitude based on authorial detachment. Moreover, trauma in *The Cat's Table* performs an important role in the novel's desire to be lifelike: it layers these characters and gives a sense of distinctiveness and authenticity. That is, trauma and style blend to produce conspicuous lacunae in these characters, a coded sense of reticence, that buttress the desired verisimilitude.

An important quality in *The Cat's Table* is retaining one's sense of being wild. After the passage of time into adulthood, what Michael wants to know from Cassius is if he is still wild. But wild here is conflated with being *outré* and unreconciled to civil life. It's a perceived state of being outside – a being outside imparted by trauma. Asking if someone is wild is akin to asking if they are still linked to the past and thus still a member of the coterie of the traumatized. The person whose present self is most vividly in a state of bondage to the activities of their past self is Niemeyer, the prisoner who paces the boat in chains. Where the incontrovertible effects of his past – "he sinks again, not yet free of his lock whose small, subtle portal is hard for the key to find in this dark water" (CT, 260) – cause his drowning, the other characters remain above water, with their state of bondage to their past selves psychological.

Ondaatje's most recent book, *Warlight*, is a sombre story of two children: Nathaniel, who narrates, and Rachel. They are left in post–Second World War London with a man the children nickname the Moth. Their parents' cover story for having abandoned the children is that they are off to Singapore to work for Unilever. They are raised by the Moth and an ex-boxer nicknamed the Pimlico Darter. Nathaniel works in kitchens and has his first sexual experiences in the off-hours. The children eventually discover that their mother's absence is not due to Singapore or Unilever: she's working for British intelligence. The story is steeped in non-violent crime (like trespassing and smuggling), none of which blemishes the characters. They retain an amiable virtuousness, or, rather, this is the light Nathaniel sees them in.

In part two of *Warlight*, Nathaniel, an adult now, looks back and tries to understand his childhood years and his mother's wartime activities. Two crucial terms recur in this book: secrets and anarchy. Again, characters meet and become close but retain their essential secrets, as Nathaniel makes clear: "I realized I'd lost [my mother's] living voice. All the quick-witted intelligence she owned when young, all the secret life she'd stepped into and kept from us, now lost" (WL, 188). Displaying the second key term, anarchy, is a sure way to win Nathaniel's admiration. But in a post–Second World War historical fiction that gains gravity through the politics it implicates, what is the substance of the anarchy Nathaniel extols? Nathaniel's use of the term strips it of both its political heft and community ethos and connotes instead an individual's desire-fuelled volatility, a joie de vivre that amounts to a personal commitment to avoid repetition and routine.

As Edward Said demonstrates in *Orientalism*, it's worthwhile to look beyond the curated sense of history a novelist presents. So what occurs parallel to the explicitly invoked politics of *Warlight*? What's present in this book but unsaid or only alluded to? At the time of the novel Britain, of course, was the planet's major imperial power and had Crown colonies and protectorates – or, less euphemistically, subject territories – across the Caribbean, the Middle East, Africa, and Asia, including the country of Ondaatje's birth, Ceylon. The timeframe *Warlight* occupies coincides with the violent, decolonizing partition of India and Pakistan and the violence of partitioned Ireland. This is the wider context in which *Warlight*, a story about the son of a British intelligence officer, occurs. Nathaniel's mother and her peers are not simply living within this global power but are working through the foreign office to strengthen Britain's international interests. Are these the first of Ondaatje's characters who are patriots? And are these the first characters who live in the country they're born into and in alignment with their country? These are remarkable changes for Ondaatje's mostly dissident and exile-obsessed fictions.

Looking back through Ondaatje's fictions, his writing begins in aggression, ages into broad political critique personalized through wide-ranging narratives, and concludes with three coming-of-age narratives and their trauma-induced soul-searching with the corresponding backward-looking tendency. In the latest novels, he expresses an ideal of comportment that respects both confidentiality

Ondaatje's Late Style

and a flickering openheartedness that permits only intermittent intimacy. No longer is there a denunciation of dominant regimes.

When considering the tensions vitalizing Ondaatje's work, it's worthwhile to look at the antagonists the protagonists vie against. In his early works, combustible protagonists Billy the Kid and Buddy Bolden, each housing intensities of force and self-destruction, are their own antagonists. His middle period sees his characters fight against the unjust activity of nations and their economic systems: class barriers, the limits and coercion of borders, and a country's ability to forget the cruelty it has authored. The late period returns to an inward antagonist characterized by an inability to fully know another person and forge durable intimacy. The stakes have cooled and narrowed. The green light seen from the dock, which Ondaatje's late-style characters reach for, is one's own youth and one's compromised ability to be open. But in this late period there's also something deeper happening. There's a more all-encompassing foe.

In *Tin Roof*, a poem from his poetry collection *The Cinnamon Peeler*, Ondaatje writes:

So how do we discuss
the education of our children?
Teach them to be romantics
to veer towards the sentimental? (*CP*, 121)

Given the emotional colouring and the ideas embodied in these late-stage novels, it's worth unpacking what is implied by the sentimental. The sentimental novel often bases itself in the distress of orphans and the suffering of those who have been excluded from society's care. As they seek to arouse sympathy, pity, and consolation, sentimental fictions have the potential to be both politically radical and prescient. They democratize care: a fiction that persuasively illustrated the plight of a woman in Victorian England or an enslaved person in America inspired a shift in public consciousness and gave energy to the belief that all people were worthy of being treated with dignity.

The Cat's Table acknowledges its allegiance to sentimental values in its observations on the pernicious implications of class differences: "[O]ur table's status on the *Oronsay* continued to be minimal, while those at the Captain's Table were constantly toasting one another's significance. That was a small lesson I learned on the journey. What

376   Moez Surani

is interesting and important happens mostly in secret, in places where these is no power. Nothing much of lasting value happens at the head table" (CT, 75).

This underdeveloped understanding of power, however, is a fig leaf. What matters is not anything gained from this impression but, rather, the intention of the passage, which aligns this work with the sentimental mandate: that it's noble and needed to analyze how power distorts people and relationships.

So why has a writer as talented and lauded as Ondaatje used these eleven years to triple down on the sentimental strain in his work and emphasize the need for a sentimental mindset? And are his subjects – a Californian family, or a boy who moves to England, or Nathaniel in the Second World War – politically radical subjects? And if not, what does this mean? Stripped of systemic critique, a sentimental story would simply be a gym to exercise one's sympathetic capacity. It's a place to feel and practise pity and consolation. Without political import, the plea for a sentimental mindset is a request for us to encounter the world around us with feeling before intellect, with a sense that the activity of the world is sacred, not oppressive or ever coolly banal, and that the processes of sympathy, consolation, and pity are what is most needed. These, of course, are laudable processes, and these three books model how they play out. But, crucially, these feelings lack something essential. The critical, the combative, the radical.

A sentimental mindset also has profound epistemological implications: it asserts that truths are known through feelings. These three books repeatedly bump up against this limited approach to knowing: "Who was Coop, really? We never knew what his parents were like" (D, 16). Then later, at a dance, Coop retains his inscrutability: "He kept his distance, laughing silently to himself, barely speaking. Who is Coop really?" (D, 21). Rafael has the same question as he becomes infatuated with Anna: "Who is she? This woman who has led him into a medicine closet of a room where most of her possessions exist" (D, 76). Michael in *The Cat's Table* also confesses a wish for knowledge: "Writing this, I do not want it to end until I can understand it better, in a way that would calm me even now, all these years later. For instance, how far did the intimacy go? I don't know" (CT, 116). Thinking of his romance with Massi and friendship with Ramadhin, Michael acknowledges, "But what did we really know, even of one another?" (CT, 146). The narrator of *Warlight* finds

Ondaatje's Late Style 377

himself in a similar quandary and wishes he could better know his context: "There are times these years later, as I write all this down, when I feel as if I do so by candlelight. As if I cannot see what is taking place in the dark beyond the movement of this pencil. These feel like moments without context" (WL, 107). Nathaniel also wishes he could better know those near him: "Sam Malakite remained a mystery to me. No one really understands another's life or death." He even laments not fully knowing his dog: "As if he might wish to tell me about his haphazard life, a past I do not know. All the unrevealed needfulness that must be in him" (WL, 283). Nathaniel repeatedly reports his frustrations with what he doesn't know, and he himself spots the cause of this frustration: "I had already been too sentimental" (WL, 125). When one can only know through what one feels, the world is indeed quite mysterious. With this limit, an understanding of one's context is impoverished, which in turn weakens one's ability to distinguish a grievance from an injustice.

For an art form as capacious as the novel, a sentimental fiction without any actionable political inspiration would be a remarkably constricted mode of human representation. It subjugates context and justice to precise shades of personal feeling, and, in prioritizing what's most fragile in a person, it exiles irony, vulgarity, critical thinking, and anything fun or absurd. For the late-stage Ondaatje, these are costs worth paying. Why is this so? Ondaatje has certainly revelled in these traits before and used them to empower and vitalize his literary output. What does it mean to be focused on survival at the end of a vaunted career?

The answer these books indicate is that they do fulfill the mandate of the sentimental novel: they do democratize care but to a subject population whose identity is not readily seen. What is democratized is a care and empathy for characters who have experienced trauma. As Christa Schönfelder writes, trauma texts "call for a critical reflection on how to respond to the wound of another, how to listen to another's pain, how to receive and react to stories of suffering."[1] The representation of lives impacted by personal trauma is the political valence of these sentimental fictions.

In Ondaatje's pictorial mode of verisimilitude whereby the author is aloof from the characters, personal trauma is the presence that doesn't wish to be present but also doesn't wish to be dispensed with. Thus, the characters are oscillating presences, reticent, largely averse to the social, and they find some comfort and solace in intimate encounters. This works to create a sense of promising potency, hushed confidentiality, mysterious pain, and a comprehensive split from an imagined mainstream. Trauma here is both individuating and negating. It taunts with promise of intriguing human layering, but it is also a smotherer of personal revelation and, more generally, thoughts oriented toward the future.

What's modelled by these characters is a mannered form of life in which the totalizing effect of trauma is counterweighted by an equally totalizing outlook of enchantment. As if a willed recovery of an innocence lost, they maintain an enchanted state, largely in one-on-one situations and on the social margins where they can instantiate this imperiled sense of magic in their life.

Ondaatje's belief in these characters is such that authorial analysis, interpretation, or intervention would be either unseemly or unethical. The beguiling paradox of these three books expresses the aesthetic and substance of Ondaatje's late style: that fictional trauma necessitates a mimetic representational approach while those represented are engaged in unconscious acts of personal enchantment. As such, Ondaatje's commitment to mimesis results in him occupying the role of the documenter, viewing them from an objective, external position, all while presenting subjects with formative subjective catastrophes.

NOTE

1   Schönfelder, *Wounds and Words*, 24.

19

"That eventual stranger":
Toward Unrecognizability in *Warlight*

Joel Deshaye

Repeatedly in *Warlight*, Michael Ondaatje's characters refer to *schwer*, a German word attributed to the composer Gustav Mahler in his commentary on his own music's notation. It is a word that Nathaniel, the narrator of *Warlight*, initially defines in sentence fragments: "Meaning 'difficult.' 'Heavy.'" (WL, 31, 170). Given the theme of difficulty, readers will wonder what is supposed to be "difficult" and for whom. Because both Ondaatje and his characters can be construed as making statements about difficulty, I will consider both possibilities, starting with the characters.[1] The novel focuses on Nathaniel's attempt to discover what happened to his parents and to learn more about his mother in particular. His search for them and their stories occurs mainly in Britain's secret national archives because his mother had disappeared to work in the spy agency at Bletchley Park during the Second World War (WL, 152), and she was later murdered, possibly by a double agent (WL, 260). In this novel of espionage, the exposure of secrets is one of the main difficulties for the characters, and so one of my interests in this essay is the value of secrecy to their identities. Secrecy itself, not only its exposure, creates difficulty for Nathaniel as he tries to figure out who he is and who his parents were. The difficulties of secrecy and exposure are associated with Ondaatje's career-long interest in celebrity, a topic that is oddly prominent in detective fiction – as with detectives such as Sherlock Holmes and Hercule Poirot who are famous in their own stories.

This chapter also has three connected arguments related to our difficulties as readers of a text that Ondaatje has thematized as difficult. First, Ondaatje marks *Warlight* as detective fiction but unconventionally refuses to allow Nathaniel to solve the murder of his mother, while nevertheless calling upon us to attempt to solve it. Second, in spite of the lack of fact-based narrative closure – a well-known *schwer* or difficulty for readers too – Nathaniel appears to achieve emotional closure after the loss of his parents, but this closure depends on symbolic measures that he takes to reinforce his own privacy and safety. Third, his feeling safe because of symbols is akin to cognitive dissonance, leading me to question both the tone of affirmation at the end of the novel and Nathaniel's knowledge of himself. I don't think he realizes that he is traumatized by war and its losses; he does not know himself or he does not recognize himself (in that shared epistemological and ontological sense of "recognition"), and this unrecognizability is a result of avoiding publicity (exposure) and maintaining privacy (secrecy). Nathaniel personifies a movement "towards unrecognizability" from publicity of one type or another.

Although Nathaniel is personally compared to Sherlock Holmes (WL, 104, 143) and does indeed serve as the novel's detective, he is not the (oddly) public figure that his mother Rose is (WL, 222, 237), and his movement toward unrecognizability is a coping strategy for avoiding the risks of exposure that Rose tolerated as a spy. Despite my own self-awareness of Ondaatje's ability to manipulate me as a reader of genre, later in this essay I am going to try to solve the mystery of the murder of Nathaniel's mother, Rose, because such an exercise will deepen the exploration of Ondaatje's representations of privacy and publicity. I am not sure that readers have sufficiently recognized that Ondaatje is a writer of genre fiction, from the Western to war fiction and beyond, but in *Warlight* he repeatedly marks the text as a spy novel and a mystery, most obviously when he invokes Sherlock Holmes (WL, 95, 104, 132, 143, 189). It is war fiction too, in a combination not unlike earlier books such as *The English Patient* and *Anil's Ghost*, but Ondaatje himself has minimized the war fiction.[2] The genres of mystery and espionage, which need no differentiation for the purposes of this chapter, are obviously suited to his ruminations on secrecy. With a complexity and conceptual overlap that stymies any reader who searches for a simple explanation, *Warlight* returns again and again to the anonymity, strangerhood, pseudonyms, recognizability, and celebrity of its characters. Some of them are eventually revealed as spies, and,

Toward Unrecognizability in *Warlight* 381

fascinatingly, some of those very characters, like Rose, even have a degree of celebrity on radio and television. The preoccupation with stardom is consistent with a long history of that theme in Ondaatje's work, perhaps especially in the main characters of *The Collected Works of Billy the Kid* and *Coming Through Slaughter* and in many individual poems. Ondaatje's representations of celebrity, and his experience of it as a prize-winning author, have already been established in the scholarship (York; Roberts; Deshaye, *The Metaphor of Celebrity*), so the theme probably needs no recapitulation here. Two of Ondaatje's later novels began to shift the emphasis more dramatically away from celebrity: *The English Patient* with its unrecognizable burn victim and *Anil's Ghost* with its unrecognizable disinterred corpse.[3] I see *Warlight* as a continuation of this shift. The word "recognition" comes in part from the Latin word *recognitio*, meaning "an act of perceiving that some thing, person, etc., is the same as one previously known" (OED). It is about knowledge and identity; it is epistemological and ontological, and so detective fiction, with all of its mysterious strangers, is an appropriate culmination (thus far) of Ondaatje's preoccupation.[4] Of course, *Warlight* also reflects *Coming Through Slaughter*, which is more conventionally a detective fiction; it features a former police officer, Webb, in search of the famous jazz cornetist Buddy Bolden, who had disappeared. *Warlight* positions Nathaniel not in the streets, nightclubs, and brothels of detective fiction but in the archives, creating a character who is a more obvious parallel to the reader than the detective usually is.

As Ondaatje appears to shift his interests toward unrecognizability, thereby invoking a lack of knowledge about identity that can be seen in the many references to strangers in *Warlight*, it also makes sense to contextualize the shift from the perspective of a reader of detective fiction because of the dynamics of privacy and publicity in this genre and because its readers are invited to try to expose the murderer even before the detective can. Lee Spinks invokes reading when he describes the titular character of *The English Patient*: "Anonymous, initially unreadable and consistently enigmatic, he is a constant hermeneutic lure and temptation ... a metaphor for the types of libidinal investment at stake in the process of reading itself."[5] Reading a mystery demands attention, demands close reading – demands "knowledge and imagination,"[6] and the "lure and temptation" are toward a solution that entails various invasions of privacy. Characters in a mystery have their private lives and untold desires laid bare by the detective. For Nathaniel, however, his search for answers about his mother's life has the added complication of her role in espionage and its infrastructure of dissembling. Ondaatje had imagined the gunslinger Billy the Kid and later Buddy Bolden as public figures in media and performance, and now in contrast Rose's privacy is secreted away in the highly classified documents of a secure government facility. *Warlight* is structurally less demanding on its readers than those earlier books, but as a mystery it is more difficult; readers even have the special challenge of a mystery that Nathaniel cannot solve. We might read Nathaniel's failure as detective *and as a reader* as the motivation for his memoir – the failed reader becoming the writer and maybe even recognizing, unconsciously, that Nathaniel is less able to interpret his own life than he is to fictionalize it.

Nathaniel surely recognizes that some measure of privacy is necessary to his security because Rose has veiled his life in secrecy. By arrangement of his mother because of his father's absence and her own imminent departure, Nathaniel meets The Moth and The Darter, whose pseudonyms imply "mother" or "mum" and "dad."[7] Because he knows or at least intuits their roles, he seems to know who they are – they're here for mum and dad – but also can't recognize *what* they might be. As a boy, he also infers that they are criminals because he has no idea that his mother is a spy (WL, 6), but when he and his sister are kidnapped in the short chapter entitled "Schwer" and The Moth is murdered by other spies (WL, 115–18) (a foreshadowing), his mother returns and saves them, meanwhile letting slip some of the details. If Rachel is not safe, Rose says to Arthur McCash, presumably her handler, "I will publicly turn against all of you, none of you will be safe" (WL, 116). She equates publicity with danger. Safety is secrecy, is privacy – a theme that I have explored at length elsewhere (see my *Metaphor*). Although Lorraine York's *Literary Celebrity in Canada* predates *Warlight*, it offers a conceptual explanation that remains relevant here: celebrity "signals the meeting and exchange of the public and private realms, and such a condition is itself productive of uneasiness."[8] This term, "uneasiness," recurs throughout York's study, as in "the uneasy balance" that she ascribes to Ondaatje's private work of writing that leads into his "world of public appearances."[9] She later attributes the paradox of "secretive fame" to Ondaatje,[10] an "uneasy" situation to be sure. In the context of Rose's deadly threat with the weapon of publicity, uneasiness might well be an understatement.

In his study of *Warlight*, Mike Marais does not cite York on uneasiness but proposes a related concept: uncertainty. Marais explains that in this novel "uncertainty is a necessary consequence of the limits and limitations of one's understanding and a manifestation of one's respect for the strangeness of the other person."[11] Referring to Nathaniel, Marais states: "*Warlight* is finally a record of his openness to and constant alteration by strangers."[12] Indeed, strangers provoke an uncertainty that affects the hospitality of characters, their openness to others. Marais believes that in the case of the narrator, Nathaniel, the uncertainty opens him up. I too see signs that Nathaniel is "happy" and at "peace" (WL, 284) at the end of the novel, but I am not as certain as Marais that the novel is an affirmation, partly because there are signs that Nathaniel is an unreliable narrator, not necessarily a liar or a delusional raconteur but someone who trusts the wrong people and sometimes misleads himself. There is also the possibility that Nathaniel's new ease could be the result of having protected himself in a home with a walled garden and an employer whose grounds are secure. (He is an archivist, not a spy, so his work for the agency does not entail the same risks that his mother's did.) For me, Nathaniel's uncertainty leads to insularity, to separation.

Whatever sense of happiness and peacefulness there is in *Warlight* might well have spatial limitations related to privacy and publicity. When Rachel dismisses *schwer* and places it in gestural quotation marks, she does so "after reading about [the effects of epilepsy on memory] in the library." She did not experience one of her traumatic "fits" (WL, 51) there; coincidentally or not, it is a safe space for her. Although a library is usually a public space (except sometimes the archives), it is also a private space for silent reading, so privacy and safety are associated. Rachel's easy dismissal of Nathaniel's concern for the safety of his family would later prove reckless when The Moth dies notably in or near "the lobby" of a theatre, a comparably public space that furnished safety for Rachel only because she and The Darter hid "behind a painted stage landscape" (WL, 118). Her earlier dismissal is partly a result of her confidence, her *lack* of uncertainty.[13] Although Nathaniel too has learned to accept the uncertainty that resulted from the disappearance of his parents during the war and their replacement by pseudonymous guardians, including The Moth and The Darter, he eventually learns through archival work that uncertainty should sometimes provoke caution. He therefore buys a home from the Malakites with a walled garden that reassures him of a modicum of safety, even though he has discovered that his mother was murdered by spies in her own home after attempting to retire or distance herself from the same agency. Uncertain and of course fearful, Nathaniel and others seek safety and find comfort in private spaces.[14]

The walled garden in *Warlight* symbolically represents safety, renewal, and, partly because it is the final section of the novel, Nathaniel's closure in his archival search for his lost parents. Closure is a spatial metaphor that usually refers to the resolution in the conflict of a plot.[15] It is about certainty, about knowing what a problem is and how to fix it. In *The Difficult*, Stan Dragland identifies a lack of closure as a feature of difficulty, of *schwer*: "Sans neat conclusion, something is left over. Something remains to think about ... But if the pondering brings no conclusion? Maybe the film (poem, story, novel) stays open."[16] Here Dragland echoes other Canadian creative writers. Quoting Christina Baillie, Dragland reminds us that "*the search for meaning [is] not over, never over.*"[17] Quoting Erín Moure to set up a contrast with "the difficult," Dragland relates that "[t]he accessible, by not questioning reading and language, ends up simply leading us to comfort."[18] Indeed "comfort" is exactly what Nathaniel says that he is seeking by purchasing a house with a walled garden (WL, 125) from parental figures such as the Malakites (whose family name might refer to malachite, a green mineral associated with renewal and healing).[19] He has had enough difficulty, enough openness. Against the odds, he wants something that he recognizes and that offers safety: parental figures and a safer house.

Although Nathaniel seems to achieve *emotional* closure by coming to terms with his mother's murder and replacing her symbolically with figures such as The Darter's lover Olive Lawrence and even his own lover Agnes (later also known as Sophie), he never receives a *factual or informational* closure on the disappearance of his father, who left for Singapore on business (so it was claimed) and was never heard from again.[20] His ending is open and uncertain in that sense, but when Nathaniel eventually learns how Rose died – shot twice at her own home – he writes: "This is, I now tell myself, how it happened ... Quick and fatal ... That is what I think now" (WL, 260).

He writes a closure into his own plot. As a detective, he has become desperate, and he almost admits that he could be manipulating the facts. Detective fiction is usually fixated on a closure resulting from the disclosure of uncovered facts, but Arthur Conan Doyle's Sherlock Holmes saga, Ondaatje's apparent model, has "remarkably little finality: it is provisional, suggestive, incomplete." Fans of Sherlock Holmes did not want his series to end, and Doyle complied for a long time.[21] It was a case of a writer resisting closure to give readers what they wanted: not so much "the accessible" as more of their hero. I think that, in *Warlight*, Ondaatje's refusal to disclose certain facts withholds factual closure from his readers; instead, he allows emotional closure for his main character.

Appropriately, before I move to the second half of this chapter and attempt to solve the murder, I want to gesture at a provisional closure to this chapter. In other words, here I synthesize what I have written so far. We have seen that Ondaatje's preoccupation with stardom is equally a preoccupation with related positions on the spectrum of privacy and publicity, from the most intimate to the most exposed, and the mystery genre and its game of secrecy management are ideal for illustrating these themes. In a mystery, a secret made public, even a little public, is a matter of life and death: *schwer*, difficulty. The movement of such a secret is from inside (privacy) to outside (publicity). Thus, Ondaatje's privacy-and-publicity–related concepts are concretized partly in representations of spaces.

Nathaniel survives the novel; the walled garden also represents not only privacy but, admittedly, the questionable success of privacy in a novel in which anonymity is repeatedly proposed as the best defence against social and political dangers such as assassination and revenge. He imagines that when the "young woman" who assassinates Rose is about to fire, she first confirms Rose's identity by demanding if she is the agent known as Viola: "Viola? Are you Viola?" (WL, 260; see also 130). The murder is accomplished partly because of the recognition of the target and possibly because of a connection to the target. The murderer's identity is not revealed, but I began to suspect that it is Olive Lawrence, who had been a surrogate member of the family, partnered briefly with The Darter, when the children were young.[22] Later, I thought about this possibility more and more. Indeed, Olive is the first person mentioned on the next page (WL, 263, after the section break), and she was mentioned immediately after Rachel dismissed her brother's concern for their safety as "just '*schwer*'" (WL, 51). The placements of these references might be only coincidences, or they might be classic misdirections (another spatial metaphor) of the mystery genre, but the genre calls on readers to be suspicious. When Nathaniel eventually tries to catch up with The Darter, in the social sense of catching up (WL, 269–73), his old guardian seems suspiciously uncomfortable, as if he had known that Olive was a foreign agent or double agent and that he was responsible for introducing her to the family.[23] Intriguingly, as Nathaniel reflects on writing his memoir, he comments that Olive was "a possible version of [his] mother" (WL, 60), and in fact they *are* the only characters in the novel to have names that refer to plants and, as such, could be grown in walled gardens in England's climate or in the greenhouse where the murder takes place.

Why might it matter if Rose is killed by a sort of mirror image or doppelgänger? I can offer various answers. The murder is perhaps a symbolic suicide that generates new life in the destroyer, an example of what Christian Bök calls Ondaatje's "motif of creative self-destructiveness."[24] Bök understands this "motif" alongside Ondaatje's motif of privacy and social isolation.[25] Rose and Olive are not the only anonymous or pseudonymous characters in this novel in which almost everyone has a nickname or a code name, but they are the ones whose actions indicate what Nathaniel calls, in Olive, "a state of separateness from all the others" (WL, 59). In their "separateness," they are figuratively walled off, as if in a walled garden. As figures of secrecy, they are protected, except from others, such as doubles or double agents, who have similar affordances of secrecy and can fight fire with fire.

In a key scene, Rose is not only walled off but ironically framed, not at all captured or exposed except by photography: "There's a photograph I have of my mother in which her features are barely revealed ... her blond hair covers her face ... [t]his almost anonymous person, balanced awkwardly, holding on to her own safety. Already incognito" (WL, 16).[26] In a study of Ondaatje's 1982 memoir *Running in the Family*, Lee-Von Kim suggests that "family photographs advance claims of affiliation: for Ondaatje [and other postcolonial writers], recollecting and looking at these pictures facilitates their efforts in reconstructing familial relations."[27] If the same explanation can shed light on the meaning of Rose's photograph for Nathaniel, it dramatizes his difficulty "in reconstructing

Toward Unrecognizability in *Warlight* 387

familial relations" because he realizes that he doesn't even know his mother – doesn't recognize her. After the war, their reconnection was only partial: Rose eventually returned to live at her childhood home, White Paint. Nathaniel claims: "Her anonymity was secure ... The unknown Viola was soon forgotten" (WL, 130). One identity is "forgotten," but the new one's "anonymity" effectively means a lack of identity. Rose's murder by her double (agent) implies their serial disposability as soldiers of secrecy.[28] They do not appear to be recognized, in the sense of being acknowledged and valued, by the agency that manipulates its employees in the service of the nation. I am not certain that Nathaniel ever realizes that his mother's job was so existentially damaging.

Marais suggests, however, that Nathaniel learns more about his life and about living than it might appear, partly because he seems to gain an almost panoptic clear-sightedness. As a memoirist, he has become both intimate with and critically distant from his mother:

> Even though the locus of Nathaniel's writing is the walled garden, he is thus no longer autonomous and sealed off from the outside world. In fact, his writing has connected him to other lives. On both an aesthetic and existential level, he has discovered what the novel describes as the lost-roof technique "where a high perspective, as from a belfry or cloister roof, allows you to see over walls into usually hidden distances, as if into other lives" (204). As I have intimated, this responsivity to other lives is also an openness to the past, which Nathaniel no longer treats as an enemy against which he must barricade himself.[29]

This explanation rings true, but Nathaniel's "lost-roof technique" is one of those understated details that are often quite complex in Ondaatje's fiction. First, the roof-climbing motif links Nathaniel to Marsh Felon, the thatcher whose romantic relationship with Rose is far more prominent in the novel than her relationship with her disappeared husband. Second, Nathaniel's version of roof climbing was recreational, not professional, but the word "technique" also invokes the ancient Greek concept of *techne* and its eventually resulting technology; alongside "a high perspective" and "hidden distance," it has a subtle parallel in Rose's radio work, which she conducted "as that supposed fire watcher on the roof of the Grosvenor House Hotel" (WL, 152; see also 24–5).[30] To be clear: the parallel is that roof climbing and rooftop radio transmission both raise communications into a space that is usually unseen – the air – but that also enables seeing. The irony is that Rose's coded wartime communications might also have enabled her enemies to "see" her figuratively.

Here then the details of Rose's own celebrity become relevant. Rose's code name, Viola, was actually her call sign as a radio operator: "in the fourth year of the war [she] began broadcasting over the airwaves into Europe. Her radio signature, Viola, became known widely on the airwaves. My mother had found her way into the larger world, somewhat the way that young thatcher [Marsh Felon] had done" (WL, 222). She was said to have had "a signature style on the airwaves" (WL, 237); it was an ironic degree of celebrity (in the sense of situational irony) in the electronic media that served secret messages.[31] Ironically again (in the sense of dramatic irony), her radio work might have somehow led her murderer to her or given the murderer a way of identifying her for the purpose of confirming the deadly mission. Insofar as radio is a parallel between Rose and her son, the parallel suggests that he does have *some* reason to "barricade himself" and be "sealed off," though such safety might come at a cost to further "responsivity," as Marais puts it. Celebrity and publicity remain a risk, and secrecy and privacy might yet offer an imperfect safety that Nathaniel uses to write his memoir.

Although the details of this theme of risky publicity can be very fine, Ondaatje also makes it as prominent as he can. The very title *Warlight* invokes the possibility of an exposure that is not only personally destructive but also a risk of mass injury.[32] When London was bombed during the Blitz, Nathaniel tells of a bomb that "probably" missed its target and hit a social district: "Nearly a hundred had been killed. It was a night with what our grandmother called 'a bomber's moon' – the city, towns, and villages in blackout but the land below clear in the moonlight" (WL, 21). Closer to the end of the book, Nathaniel reveals that The Darter had transported nitroglycerine through the city of London at night, admittedly not a mission that he would be likely to attempt if he too were a double agent, "even during the Blitz, when there was just warlight, the river dark save for one dimmed orange light on the bridges to mark the working arch for water traffic" (WL, 265). These lights and their attendant risks of exposure might not seem to have much bearing on privacy and publicity, but Nathaniel recounts an occasion when he played chess with his mother in the "thin glass shell" (WL, 168) of her greenhouse, during a thunderstorm no less.[33] He uses a martial metaphor to describe their game: "In a quarter second of lightning I saw her fall briefly into the wrong trench of the battle" (WL, 169). This more symbolic warlight relates to other examples, as when Nathaniel also remarks on how "my sister ... could make it look as if she were scurrying to evade a searchlight" (WL, 39). Similarly, "Rachel's later theatrical life" as an actor taught her "skill with limelight and fictional thunder [that] allowed her to clarify for herself what was true and what was false, safe and unsafe" (WL, 62).[34] Here the distant echo of "searchlight" in "limelight" elicits a comparison of threats of war to those of celebrity; York once wrote of Ondaatje's *Coming Through Slaughter* that it is "Ondaatje's definitive treatment of fame the destroyer,"[35] a "treatment" that he applies again in *Warlight* but with new implications for the scale of the destruction, as if celebrity could do damage globally.[36]

Again, I am not sure that Nathaniel ever realizes what he seems to be telegraphing subliminally. Instead of recognizing that celebrity is damaging, he suggests that it could be protective, only not to the degree that he might have wished:

Not even literary or artistic fame protects worldly things around us. The pond that [John] Constable painted dried up and was buried by Hampstead Heath. A thin tributary of the River Effra near Herne Hill, described by [John] Ruskin as a "tadpole-haunted ditch," whose water he sketched beautifully, exists now possibly only in an archive drawing. The ancient Tyburn [once a stream in London] disappeared and was lost, even to geographers and historians. In much the same way I believed my carefully recorded buildings along Lower Richmond Road were dangerously temporary, in the way great buildings had been lost during the war, in the way we lose mothers and fathers. (WL, 33–4)

I quoted this passage at some length because it brings me to a final theme of *Warlight* that must be considered alongside privacy, strangerhood, publicity, and *schwer*: Nathaniel's obsession with geography, especially with maps, which is an extension of the space-related developments of this chapter.[37] The novel is replete with examples (7, 9, 14, 124, 132–3, 137, 138, 141, 221, 224, 231, 249). The bodies of water listed in the example above demonstrate how features of the natural landscape can be covered up by urban development; in turn, wartime terraforming and attacks such as the Blitz can remake or ruin urban developments. In both cases, anything "carefully recorded" can be "dangerously temporary," but maps then become clues for historical geography and for the reconstruction of information and knowledge (if not places themselves). Marais explains that "maps are throughout the novel associated with a security that stems from the eradication of uncertainty" (WL, 96). For Nathaniel, they stabilize a life that was destabilized by the dynamics of espionage, of secrecy management and exposure.

Nathaniel writes that misleading signs in the area in which he grew up meant that people were often lost; "as a boy in London I was obsessively drawing maps of our neighbourhood in order to feel secure" (WL, 137). The word "order" here recalls the theme of chaos and order that Sam Solecki has considered in Ondaatje's poetry,[38] and of course it relates to the garden that symbolizes order in so much British and North American literature.[39] When Nathaniel is talking with Mrs Malakite about the house with the walled garden that he would buy from her husband after her death, "together [they] created a map of the garden, copying it down from her memory." In spite of her dementia, "[h]er knowledge was detailed, clearly accurate" (WL, 124), in other words, ordered. In his mother's papers in the government's secret archives, he also finds an incomplete map that he "copied onto a transparency and began projecting ... onto various maps" in the obscure map room of the archives. Able now to recognize and locate one of her hideouts during the war, and able now to know her better yet, he infers that "[t]he hand-drawn map suggested intimacy" (WL, 224). At the same time, as Alfred Korzybski famously stated, the map is not the territory, and it shows even less of Rose than she herself did when she was "incognito" in her photograph. Its cinematic "project[ion]" suggests a superimposition of publicity over the "intimacy." A palimpsest, intimacy is overlaid and remade.[40]

Images projected in light are also involved in the strangest of twists at the conclusion of the novel. The final section, "A Walled Garden," begins with Olive, who has written a book that has been adapted as a television documentary (WL, 264–5). The subject matter appears to be rock climbing and the science of environments that are accessible through the sport. Nathaniel writes: "In the brief time that I knew her, I believed Olive Lawrence was on my side" (WL, 265). His readers might be mistaken if we, in turn, believe him with the same confidence that he felt in having accurately mapped out his walled garden from an old woman's failing memory. He does not admit it, but he implies his own doubts when he mentions an only "brief time" with Olive and his having only "believed" her to be trustworthy. After seeing her on television and reading her book, he learns much more about her, but it is all so carefully scripted.

Nathaniel's own theory of his mother's murder is that the assassin had evaded the trap of the creaky floor of her house, "that landmine of noises which would signal any intruder entering her territory ... But that eventual stranger she expected never stepped indoors" (WL, 255). I've borrowed the main title of this essay from this phrase, "that eventual stranger," which is conceivably referring to Nathaniel. I think it's actually referring to Olive, who steps into the greenhouse, which is not quite "indoors." In contrast, Marais claims that Nathaniel "waits ... for the arrival of the stranger he will become, and who is unknowable from the perspective of what he presently is. At the end of the novel, he waits for a new beginning."[41] I want to believe this explanation because it is existentially hopeful. Marais had also asserted that "[t]he novel ends with Nathaniel in the Malakite house without any plans for the future,"[42] but the final paragraphs of the novel are in fact set at his mother's house, White Paint, with its characteristically creaky floor. And Nathaniel does not seem to "wait" because, after cleaning and ironing his mother's clothes, he put them away, "walked loudly along the ... floor, closed the doors, and left" (WL, 285) with Mr Malakite. Nathaniel *had* "stepped indoors" (into the house proper) to deal with Rose's belongings, so he does not seem to be "that eventual stranger," whose identity is never revealed to us with certainty and who might well be Olive, hiding in plain sight on television, glassed in by the screen and possibly vulnerable to justice if Nathaniel could only read his life more closely: as a mystery.

Nathaniel is not a perfect explainer like Sherlock Holmes or Hercule Poirot. He asks a great many questions throughout the novel but doesn't – unless I missed it – treat the murder of his mother as a question that he *could* answer. Rose dies in her greenhouse, as glassed in as Olive, in a fragile zone of exposure to the outside world, not to its climate but to its dangerous visibility. We could even read the novel, as with so many other novels of espionage, as an allegory of our contemporary world of surveillance, in which our attempts to be anonymous are about as effective as goldfish hiding in a fishbowl.

As a mystery, *Warlight* can sustain many theories, but I feel strongly that Ondaatje's figurations of space are not merely descriptive. They are clues to the dynamics of privacy and publicity in the novel; they help to demonstrate how privacy and publicity and the uneasy, uncertain, difficult relationship between them also matters to people's safety and security. When Nathaniel learns, years too late, that Mr Malakite had died, he toasts him "alone in a restaurant" with one of Mr Malakite's remembered phrases: "Only in open fields" (WL, 141). Openness is a trait that Nathaniel admires but to which he is temperamentally unsuited. He and his family members are perpetually unknown to each other, disguised, private. They fled from publicity because it was a threat: that conflation of wartime "searchlight" and big-time "limelight." Nathaniel is also, to some extent, unknown to himself. He admits to a lack of self-knowledge, although the admission itself is an example of it: "I am still uncertain whether the period that followed disfigured or energized my life" (WL, 8). I agree entirely with Marais when he states, "It is therefore striking that the narrating I of Ondaatje's novel should postulate a lack of progression in terms of knowledge between himself and his former self."[43] Relatedly, when Nathaniel confesses that he knew that understanding his mother had to involve loving her, he produces an understatement: "This was difficult" (WL, 170). As readers of *Warlight*, we might have a similar experience of trying to understand him and recognize who he is.

NOTES

1 The character who first mentions *schwer* is known initially as The Moth and is later the first of two prominent characters who are murdered in the cloak and dagger of the plot. Although The Moth uses the word *schwer* to comment on a serious situation – when Nathaniel's sister Rachel mysteriously disappears and reappears and then refuses to explain – he also downplays it "with his fingers" in "inverted commas" (32). Similarly, Rachel, who loved The Moth, "tossed away" the risk that she faced as a person with epilepsy as "just '*schwer*,'" again in "quotation marks" (50). Because difficulty is associated with "quotation marks" and "inverted

commas" and therefore narratorial self-consciousness, Ondaatje has signalled that it is relevant to our reading of *Warlight* too.

2   Asked by Deborah Dundas in the *Toronto Star* whether *Warlight* is a "war story," Ondaatje replied, "I didn't want it to be a book about the Second World War, or a war novel. It was much more a domestic situation in a way" (quoted in Dundas 2019). The private dimensions of the "domestic situation" will be more meaningful later in this chapter.

3   Notably, when The Moth is murdered, his body too is "unrecognizable" (118).

4   In terms of epistemology and ontology in *Intrigue: Espionage and Culture*, Hepburn states: "Ideology produces spies, but spies, like most people, temper ideology with private motives. Intrigue occurs where psychological and ideological commitments overlap and mask each other. The spy embodies ambiguous allegiances, some declared, some concealed. The spy therefore stands as a cipher for conflicts waged among national, international, familial, human, humanitarian, ethical, and romantic identities. A marionette in the theater of competing interests, the spy improvises roles by drawing on one or more of these identities at any given time. Acting a part, the twentieth-century fictional spy tells us that authenticity may be irrelevant to commitment or character. Indeed, a spy's identity is often an illusion," xiv.

5   Spinks, *Michael Ondaatje*, 178.

6   Glazzard, *The Case of Sherlock Holmes*, 5.

7   I thank Erin Cadigan for this observation, which emerged in my Canadian Literature: Making It New course at Memorial University in the winter of 2022, a course title that I inherited from the department, not one I would have chosen because of its American associations with the poet Ezra Pound.

8   York, *Literary Celebrity in Canada*, 4.

9   Ibid., 124.

10 Ibid., 125.

11 Marais, "Uncertainty and the Time of the Stranger," 94.

12 Ibid., 93.

13 I am reminded of when, years ago, I read on a literature department's website – I can't remember which – that the main benefit of studying literature is a tolerance of uncertainty.

14 For more on Ondaatje's representations and negotiations of private and public spaces, see my essay "Racialized Rooms and Technologies of Stardom in Ondaatje's *Coming Through Slaughter*," 1–15.

15 One exception is in stories of labyrinths in which stress is closed in and relief is outside (Mikkonen, "The 'Narrative Is Travel' Metaphor," 298).

394 Joel Deshaye

Another twist on the conventional idea of closure is in Kurnick's *Empty Houses: Theatrical Failure and the Novel*, which states "that the narratological category of closure derives from a spatial metaphor: closure in this sense refers not to what happens to individual characters but to the more elementary fact of their co-presence, their shared containment in the space of the work" (20). Kurnick's *Empty Houses* is relevant to my chapter for various reasons. It is about how the limitations of theatre changed the modern novel, and in *Warlight* Rachel is a stage actor who is also one of the people whom Nathaniel tries to understand by writing his novelistic memoir. It is also relevant because of all the empty houses that Nathaniel and his girlfriend Agnes (also known as Sophie) learn about through her brother, a real estate agent, and then have sex in. Kurnick's focus is "the novel of interiority" (4), which could well describe *Warlight*. Much more could be done to apply *Empty Houses* to *Warlight*.

16 Dragland, *The Difficult*, 1. Dragland mentions Ondaatje many times in *The Difficult* but only in passing and not in relation to *Warlight*. Ondaatje and Dragland were involved sequentially in *Brick* magazine and had editorial collaborations. See Betts and the "About Us" page of the *Brick* website, "What Is Brick?"

17 Ibid., quoted in 57, emphasis in Dragland.

18 Ibid., quoted in 29.

19 This insight, for me, is owed to Emily Benson from the class that I mentioned in a previous footnote.

20 I don't mean to suggest that facts and emotions are mutually exclusive; they simply have different aesthetic and philosophical connotations, such as objectivity for facts and subjectivity for emotions.

21 Ibid., 230–1.

22 I thank Pittman for this suggestion from the class that I mentioned in a previous footnote.

23 One of Dragland's slightly earlier books, *Strangers & Others*, mentions Ondaatje's *Running in the Family* and implies that strangerhood, for Ondaatje, is connected to foreignness (66).

24 Bök, "Destructive Creation," 120.

25 Ibid., 111–14, 117.

26 For an in-depth consideration of metaphors of narrative framing and (un)framing in Ondaatje's writing, see Rae's *From Cohen to Carson*.

27 Kim, "Scenes of Af/filiation: Family Photographs in Postcolonial Life Writing," 403.

28 On the topic of seriality, Joseph and Menon notice that, at White Paint, Rose finds herself in "a small repeating universe" with figures from her

past ("Memory Anchored by Place Attachment and Cognitive Maps in Michael Ondaatje's *Warlight* and *The Cat's Table*," 4; Ondaatje 254).

29 Marais, "Uncertainty and the Time of the Stranger," 99.

30 For much more on this lineage from *techne* to contemporary technology (if radio can still be called contemporary), see Roochnik's *Of Art and Wisdom*.

31 Another unexpected, in fact anachronistic, use of radio is in *Coming Through Slaughter* (Deshaye, "Racialized," 3) when a radio appears ten or fifteen years earlier than it should have.

32 Marais surveys "the novel's extended light metaphor" (95) with a set of examples that focus on shadows. Hepburn uses the "light metaphor" to comment on spies, who "flicker and vanish" (xiv).

33 The scene is reminiscent of Ondaatje's poem "Rainy Night Talk" in his long poem *Tin Roof*, which was included in *Secular Love*.

34 On truth, Nathaniel immediately follows up: "I loved the truth I learned from strangers" (63).

35 York, *Literary Celebrity in Canada*, 140.

36 Celebrity obviously does do damage globally, if we think of how it has energized populism in international politics, with the effect, as one example among many, of hampering evidence-based decisions such as those that would help to minimize fossil-fuel consumption and the climate crisis.

37 Ondaatje's literary mapping of historical locations has led to visual displays of his maps in some of the scholarship on his work – for example, a parade route from *Coming Through Slaughter* (Deshaye, "Parading the Underworld of New Orleans in Ondaatje's *Coming Through Slaughter*," 486).

38 Solecki, *Ragas of Longing*, 140.

39 See Harrison (73) for one example.

40 Regarding Ondaatje's more specifically cultural context, in *Writing Sri Lanka: Literature, Resistance, and the Politics of Place*, Salgado states: "Place is now a palimpsest, land and territory subject to simultaneous inscription and erasure as the migrant writer moves across multiple sites of belonging, writing betwixt and between cultural narratives and histories in a process of subject constitution" (128).

41 Marais, "Uncertainty and the Time of the Stranger," 105.

42 Ibid.

43 Ibid., 94.

20

Teaching Ondaatje:
Learning to Live

Elias Schwieler

> What for others are deviations are, for me, the data which determine
> my course. – On the differentials of time (which, for others, disturb the
> main lines of the inquiry), I base my reckoning.
>
> Walter Benjamin, *The Arcades Project*,
> "On the Theory of Knowledge, Theory of Progress"

In 2008, my essay "Reading *The English Patient*: Teaching and Difference" was published in the anthology *Neither East Nor West: Postcolonial Essays on Literature, Culture and Religion*. The essay is built loosely around my experience of teaching *The English Patient* to freshman students and the questions raised when teaching the novel. Addressing these questions led me to reflect on postcolonialism, the act of reading, and the practice of teaching, taking Ondaatje's novel *The English Patient* as an example of a text that problematizes teaching from a postcolonial perspective. By invoking Michel Foucault's notion of heterotopia, Carl Schmitt's friend-enemy distinction, and Edward Said's thoughts on Orientalism, I try, in the essay, to explore teaching and its relation to knowledge, colonialism, and postcolonialism so as to question our role and function as teachers in relation to our students. My somewhat vague conclusion, put forth in the essay, of how to teach not only *The English Patient* but what should permeate every teaching event, is to emphasize the radical difference that belongs to what I, in the essay, call democratic epistemology. This call does not urge every teacher to embrace and celebrate diversity and the sameness of equality in a dogmatic and programmatic manner; on the contrary, it is a call, rather, to recognize the uniqueness of each and every teaching situation, as well as the uniqueness of each of us involved (students, teachers) in the act of creating a place that transcends the search for objective knowledge and the rationalization of art. This might occur, not in order to denounce objectivity, knowledge, and rationality in favour of some lofty idea of the supremacy of certain values or opinions, but to recognize the uncertainty and ambiguity of art and how this uncertainty and ambiguity can teach us something about learning to live.[1] It goes without saying that this is hard and difficult to achieve in teaching.

In the present paper, my aim is to continue my exploration of the difficulty just described, specifically addressing Ondaatje's novel *Warlight*, and how it came to provide the basis for this essay by drawing on my experiences from teaching it in a freshman class in English literature on the theme "Learning to Live" at the University of Calgary. Difficult, *schwer*, is a keyword in Ondaatje's *Warlight*. As I will try to show, the word is also fitting to characterize what is at stake in teaching and learning literature. Moreover, and by chance, *schwer* is part of my family name, the name to which I am heir and which belongs properly to me and represents me formally and juridically and which, as such, makes me responsible. I am answerable to the name I bear when called upon; my name is my designation; it signifies, objectively, the truth of who I am and my place in society; my name gives me, to put it differently, my official identity. At least, this is the formal law of naming. Thus, the topic of the present essay is in a sense the act of naming and the name as such. The essay sets out to explore the *Schwerigkeit*, the difficulty, of the name, such as Schw(iel)er – signifying the difficulty for me, as a teacher, learner, and scholar to name by recollecting and reconstructing and so to stitch together what is to be learned by me teaching Ondaatje – the name Ondaatje here functioning as a metonymy for his work, or at least the part of his work with which I am most familiar.

In Ondaatje's work, the name often plays a prominent role; I'm thinking of the namelessness of the desert in *The English Patient*, the desert that nevertheless contains so many names, the nameless wind, unnamed because it killed the king's son, and, of course, the uncertainty pertaining to the name of the English patient, Almásy. Or in *The Cat's Table*, the adopted name of the prisoner on the ship *Oronsay*, Neimeyer – a name that, etymologically, denies the law, as a name taken, one could perhaps say stolen, by the prisoner,

Asuntha's father. The name Niemeyer reflects the man who appropriated it, and it so denies the law of naming itself, since according to the law the name is not properly his, it does not belong to him, it is illegitimate, he has no right to it. Or Anil, in *Anil's Ghost*, who bargained with her brother to procure his second name, the name of their grandfather. The name thus upsets not only patronymic inheritance but also the gendering of names. Interestingly, we never get to know Anil's two given names; she is known to us only by a name that is not properly hers but taken, bought, and so acquired against the law of the name. Taking this name, moreover, in a sense contradicts her forensic investigations in search of the identity of the dead and murdered. Or, in *Warlight*, the nicknames Stitch for Nathaniel and The Moth for Walter, signifying behaviour and personality traits, reflecting who they are informally, living on the margin of society, in secret or at least in the shadows, hiding their clandestine and at times illegal activities. Also, in *Warlight*, Nathaniel's first love, Agnes, named after a street, Agnes Street, whose real name the reader never gets to know conclusively, although she is later referred to as Sophie.

These names, all of them, are not symbols but rather broken symbols, which point to the palimpsestic and catachrestic character of the names. The quintessence of names, as they are presented to us in Ondaatje's work, is that they are signs appropriating their meaning and identity from their difference from other signs. The name, in Ondaatje, has the same function as story; that is, it aims to fill a lack and so explain an origin, which, however, was never there to begin with: stories begin when history ends. The names and the stories are often parentless, as they are born out of a desire to know, to make sense out of that otherness that haunts many of the characters in Ondaatje's novels. One could even say that otherness and being other is the ontological foundation of the characters' search for a place to belong. Still, they often find themselves exiled, parentless, marginalized, and without known origin. This is what drives the storytelling so that the stories (making up Ondaatje's work) that create the characters also create the characters' stories – stories, histories upon other stories and histories, one story translating and transforming another, one history substituting and supplementing another. We find ourselves in a profoundly heterotopic world, in which the characters are learning to live without a clear and stable lineage, history, or chronology. So, how, then, can we approach

Ondaatje's heterotopia[2] in the practice of teaching? Addressing this question includes situating teaching literature as an activity and practice concerned with knowledge and art, that is, as concerned with aesthetics. But, as we will see, Ondaatje's work suggests something other than an aesthetics as the accumulated knowledge of art. Instead, his work stages what could be called an antiaesthetics or perhaps a heterotopical aesthetics. It is this kind of aesthetics that I will base my thoughts on so as to develop the notion of democratic epistemology. Moreover, when teaching *Warlight*, democratic epistemology should, so I hypothesized, be founded on a sincere aspiration to give each student in the class a voice, and each voice should carry equal weight in terms of its importance for creating the heterotopical space in which we together in class come to learn of and through the other, the unknown and unfamiliar.

In Ondaatje's work, history, the flow of time, narrative, story, words, and signs often create or imply unfamiliar and unexplored names and places. They are also themes that can be gathered together in Foucault's notion of heterotopia – another topos, composed of the two words topic (with synonyms such as: theme, subject, matter, issue, concern, focus) and place (which carries synonyms such as: home, dwelling, location, site, situation, house). These two signs, within the word topos, write themselves over and against each other, creating a palimpsest of marks for a topos yet to be found; it is a history, like the English patient's copy of Herodotus's *The Histories*, which he has written over, marked, and signed, as an exploration of what has been, in order to learn what is and what might be. Thus, the search for a place to dwell and to learn gave me the opportunity to explore a teaching event that has as its topos "learning to live." This topic, however, is *schwer*; it is, indeed, heterotopic. It involves looking back, recollecting, gathering pieces of memory in order to stitch together a narrative, a story, out of the lives affected and portrayed in Ondaatje's novels, as well as the lives of us engaged in reading them. To attempt a comparison, we recognize this movement, this search, in Proust's great novel *In Search of Lost Time* (À la recherche du temps perdu). Just as in Proust, as Gilles Deleuze points out in his study *Proust and Signs*, the search applies the means of recollection and memory, not in the direction of the past but in the direction of the future, as does the movement of teaching as well as learning Ondaatje. Reading, in itself, combines the past and the future into a present that is, as we will see, both different from and a repetition of the past, striving toward the future. This characteristic of reading is staged in Ondaatje's work in a way that makes it an almost natural and integral part of teaching it.

In the following, I will repeatedly refer to Deleuze's reading of Proust, since his reading provides me with some crucial points to compare with what I see as important aspects of Ondaatje's work and how his texts can be approached in teaching literature. Of course, this means confronting two not wholly compatible lines of thought, that of Deleuze reading Proust and that of me, and the class, reading Ondaatje. There is a difference, needless to say, between Proust and Ondaatje; they do not translate each other seamlessly. However, they share similarities that will be of value to illuminate what is at stake in teaching Ondaatje's work. In fact, the notion of difference, as I point out in the essay on teaching *The English Patient* and that Deleuze also highlights in his reading of Proust, is of particular importance.

A topos as heteroptopia, in Ondaatje, is in Deleuze's words "the localized essence of time," "*the very being of the past in itself,*"[3] which is only set before us as that which eludes memory and history: Topos only happens as heterotopia (if it happens) as a maybe, that is, as art. Not art as mimesis but rather as the "as if," *als ob*, in Kant.[4] However, what *might* have happened is the essential, which implies a difference from, but at the same time an intensifying of, reality. What is more, the uncertainty implied in words like might, maybe, perhaps, possibly, and the "as if" also contains a fundamental doubt. It involves a doubt as the uncertainty of not knowing, that other place, which cannot be known but only presented through the medium that hides it, making it increasingly secret (like a name taken, stolen, without history and without legal status) to cover up and conceal a history that cannot be known. These are the heterotopic stories in Ondaatje's work, made up by the characters in order to know their past; it is their last resort after they have exhausted their rational research in archives, their reading of letters, examining dead bodies and historical sites, and scrutinizing the memories of themselves and others. In Ondaatje's texts, there is another history told, another story created to fill in the gap in time and space until reality blends in with imagination. In Ondaatje, the rational search for a self, or an identity, or a history to explain and shed light on the unknown seldom succeeds completely; there is always a supplement of difference, of an other time and place, which could be called the heterotopia of art. What is at stake is the protagonists' search for themselves, their desire to learn who they are and why they are who they are; they are learning to live by retelling and recounting what happened and what might have happened. They are, in a sense, apprentices on a journey of self-discovery. Similarly, in class, we struggled to find ourselves in relation to Ondaatje's novel *Warlight*, telling each other stories of the past, trying to figure out what it means for the one telling the story, as well as for us listening, that is, what it means to learn how to live. This, then, I contend, is part of what is at stake in teaching and learning literature and Ondaatje in particular. It is not perhaps what happens in the classroom that always takes precedence but what happens in other spaces and at other times, when we as students of Ondaatje's work learn to live by rethinking, remembering, relocating our thoughts about what learning to live might mean. Ondaatje's work provides us with signs to interpret and decipher to guide our journey and so search for what it means to live. This is, in fact, also what happened, in class and outside of class, when we discussed and compared the stories we shared and related them to Ondaatje's novel, where I, as a teacher, was only one of many contributing to the search for what it means to learn how to live. In the process, we accidentally stumbled on signs, signs that we pursued together, creating another story.

Signs are the sparks of Ondaatje's stories, signs are the clues to what might have happened; they are found in archives, letters, conversations, memories, in the confined space of a ship, and in dead bodies, there to be interpreted and deciphered so as to complete lost histories or solve mysteries or puzzles haunting the characters' thoughts. In other words, Ondaatje's work poses a challenge, for us and the characters in his novels, to learn. As Deleuze states at the outset of his work on Proust: "Learning is essentially concerned with signs. Signs are the object of a temporal apprenticeship, not of an abstract knowledge. To learn is first of all to consider a substance, an object, a being as if it emitted signs to be deciphered, interpreted."[5] This, I would like to argue, is true also of Ondaatje's work. In his novels, we are consistently encountering characters who are in search of how to live by interpreting signs, both present and absent, that is, signs of absence and signs of presence. The characters set out to learn from the signs that they are exposed to, trying to come to terms with them and understand them in a rational manner; these signs nevertheless remain insufficient to explain the past until they are gathered into the works of art that Ondaatje's texts constitute. Their trajectory is thus toward the future, although they, like Marcel in *In Search of Lost Time*, search for signs lost or hidden in time. Learning, in Ondaatje's work, is similarly an activity projected toward the future and of what is to come, or as Deleuze says of Proust, it is a question of "a temporal apprenticeship."

There are certain themes that recur in Ondaatje's work – for example, the journey, remembering a bygone time, the mystery, the uncertainty of identity, the search for missing bits and pieces in a character's history, or histories of other characters related, in some way or other, to the protagonist. His work could be said to revolve around lost time but lost in a way different from that in Proust's work. In Ondaatje's work, what is lost was often never there to begin with; it is a search for reasons why certain things happened, unknown to and not experienced by the protagonists themselves. By recounting the past and letting the imagination fill in the gaps in the history told, the protagonists try to stitch together (not uncover, discover, or recover) a history that helped to shape who the protagonists have turned out to be. "Memory and imagination," Deleuze writes, "relieve and correct each other; each, taking a step, impels the other to take a supplementary step."[6] This is true also of history and story in Ondaatje, where history relieves and corrects the story being told, while the story, in its turn, relieves and corrects history, where there is no record of events; in this way, both story and history move along step by step, supplementing each other. This is the difference and repetition that Deleuze suggests are the two powers of essence. Difference and repetition, I would like to add, are also the two powers of heterotopia, as well as of the name.

Thus, the protagonists' journeys (metaphorical and literal) are journeys of learning. They turn to memory in order to find the truth of their lives, a truth that by its very nature slips away, "mercurial," as Ondaatje puts it in *Warlight* (WL, 256). These memories necessarily install a difference in the characters' stories but also a simultaneous repetition of the past. Difference and repetition are, moreover, what constitute learning and what teaching attempts to facilitate. Difference and repetition, here, should not be understood as instructional technicalities or parts of a "learning theory" but rather as a way to approach teaching existentially, relating to what I have chosen to call democratic epistemology.[7] As I suggest in the essay on *The English Patient*, "knowledge is something always to

Teaching Ondaatje 403

come, never a determined category. Responsible knowledge is first and foremost a critical questioning of its own limits, responsible teaching is a critical questioning of the teaching position, its use of knowledge and power, and with what means this power and knowledge [are] used." Thus, teaching and learning, joined in one and the same process, constitute a "heterotopical site of crisis."[8] Crisis here should not be taken in a negative sense as disaster or catastrophe but, rather, as a pedagogical situation in which teachers and students, collectively, prepare for questioning (before any decision has been made) the foundation and modalities that make up the signs of, for example, the theme "learning to live." To further explore this kind of questioning I will in what follows turn, specifically, to Ondaatje's *Warlight*.

Warlight, very briefly, is the story of Nathaniel and his search for the truth about his mother and the meaning of the events that he experienced in his childhood and youth, shortly after the end of the Second World War. As in much of Ondaatje's work, the novel stages a tension between rational thought and imaginative or speculative thinking. The confrontation of these two modalities of thinking leads, through learning or apprenticeship, to what Deleuze calls "pure thinking," which is a form of thinking that comes to us by creating or contemplating art. In *Warlight*, it is the characters in the novel that stage the confrontation between the rational and the imaginative, while pure thinking is left as a possibility for the reader of the novel. A consequence of this is that the novel takes on an allegorical character. Beyond the plot and the events related in the novel, there is another story hiding, namely, the apprenticeship of art. But it is an apprenticeship conducted in a half-light. Thus, warlight, besides referring to the dimmed lights in London during air raids, signifies the obscure character of the memories that make up the basis of the protagonist Nathaniel's story.

Not only does remembering bring back a version of the past, but it also, as we will see, affects Nathaniel's present. As he tells the reader: "There are times these years later, as I write all this down, when I feel as if I do so by candlelight. As if I cannot see what is taking place in the dark beyond the movement of this pencil. These feel like moments without context" (WL, 32). His story, and the memories he relives, overshadow the present and become the only flickering light of his reality. The space he in these moments dwells in is inhabited only by the vague and haunted memories of people out of the

404 Elias Schwieler

past – a truly heterotopic space. These moments and this space are also part of his learning, of learning about himself through the past and part of learning to live. In his story, setting down on paper how he feels like he is writing in candlelight leads him to a specific memory from his childhood of how he used to draw detailed maps of his neighbourhood. This in turn leads him to once again return to reflect on his present situation:

> Some evenings, in the darkness of my walled garden during an October gale, I sense the walls shudder as they steer the east coast wind into the air above me, and I feel nothing can invade or break a solitude I've found in this warmer darkness. As if I am protected from the past, where there's still a fear of recalling The Moth's face lit by a gas fire while I asked question after question, trying to force an unknown door ajar. Or where I rustle awake a lover from my teenage years. Even if that time is a seldom visited place. (WL, 33)

Darkness and solitude, he writes, work on him as if they protected him from the past, a past that, for the teenage boy he is recollecting, was a time permeated with uncertainty and insecurity, as when he kept searching for answers from the people who populated what he then called home. The answers were most often withheld, and he finds himself, as an adult, forced to take up the search for possible answers and to write down what he finds. His fear of remembering does not prevent him from going back in memory in search for clues of what he might have forgotten or piecing memories together to discern what was lost or left unanswered. Interestingly, the last sentence in the passage merges time and space, as time is referred to as a place. The past is a place called back in an instant when he sees himself, or rather another version of himself, familiar yet strangely different, as if he were looking at himself in a mirror, the reflection being him but still not him.

To put the situation Nathaniel finds himself in differently, learning from the past is difficult, *schwer*, since it means entering a heterotopic space, where the past is repeating itself while it, at the same time, is radically different. As noted, such difference and repetition almost unintentionally, as if by accident, inform teaching and learning Ondaatje's work and *Warlight* in particular. In the novel, this goes for recollecting other people as well, and Nathaniel comes to reflect on this when he says:

Teaching Ondaatje 405

Is this how we discover the truth, evolve? By gathering together such unconfirmed fragments? Not only of my mother, but of Agnes, Rachel, Mr. Nkoma (and where is he now?). Will all of them who have remained incomplete and lost to me become clear and evident when I look back? Otherwise how do we survive that forty miles of bad terrain during adolescence that we crossed without any truthful awareness of ourselves? (WL, 114)

To learn to live, first of all, means asking these questions, even though there might never be a final truth to discover that would answer them. It means relating to and interpreting the signs that present themselves to us. This might be the drive that keeps us living on, that is, the promise of revelation when we do not have "any truthful awareness of ourselves." To learn is also to learn to survive, and for us to survive it is necessary to learn, to decipher the signs confronting us in the shape of memories, conversations, encounters, whether with people or in books or documents. It is worth repeating what Deleuze suggests about learning in relation to Proust's work: "Learning is essentially concerned with signs. Signs are the object of a temporal apprenticeship, not of an abstract knowledge. To learn is first of all to consider a substance, an object, a being as if it emitted signs to be deciphered, interpreted."[9] Nathaniel's search is, just like Marcel's in Proust, a "temporal apprenticeship," although the time regained in *Warlight* is not one of clarity and joy coming with the insight into the aesthetic superiority of art over reality but of a partial revelation, "incomplete," and made up of "unconfirmed fragments." Or as Nathaniel notes at the very end of the novel: "We order our lives with barely held stories. As if we have been lost in a confusing landscape, gathering what was invisible and unspoken – Rachel, the Wren, and I, a Stitch – sewing it all together in order to survive, incomplete, ignored like the sea pea on those mined beaches during the war" (WL, 284). Nathaniel here compares himself to the sea pea flower, which survived by being left untouched by humans because surrounded by danger. He also refers to his nickname, Stitch, signifying how he tries to patch together unfinished stories and fragments of truth, "invisible and unspoken," into a final revelation and understanding.

However, Nathaniel's search, his temporal apprenticeship, remains incomplete, even though his search was necessary for him to survive.

As Deleuze states: "There is always the violence of a sign that forces us into the search, that robs us of peace. The truth is not to be found by affinity, nor by goodwill, but is betrayed by involuntary signs."[10] If we relate this statement to *Warlight*, what is the sign that betrays the truth? There is one salient example I would like to highlight, namely, the sign on the wall in The Darter's flat, betraying the fact that The Darter is married to Agnes/Sophie and that Agnes's child, Pearl, is Nathaniel's daughter.

First of all, to trace the relationships between Nathaniel, Agnes, and The Darter (or Norman Marshall) reveals an almost Freudian scene. The scene, briefly, plays out in the following way: as teenagers, Nathaniel and Agnes become romantically involved; Nathaniel introduces The Darter to Agnes as his father (which he is not); at seventeen, Agnes becomes pregnant with Nathaniel's child, but their relationship is already over and Nathaniel does not know of the pregnancy; The Darter ends up marrying Agnes; in effect, Nathaniel's substitute father becomes the substitute father of his daughter, Pearl; and Agnes is identified as Sophie, which (possibly) is her real name. It is possible, too (which Nathaniel hints at), that The Darter has revealed to Agnes/Sophie that he is not Nathaniel's real father, but the scene remains, to say the least, complex.

Thus, when Nathaniel, as an adult, goes to visit The Darter as part of his project to stitch together the past, he has no knowledge of The Darter's marriage to Agnes/Sophie and that her child is in fact his daughter. As Nathaniel notes of The Darter ("my wild, unreliable hero from the past, my teacher" [WL, 272]): "He had a family now: a wife named Sophie, he said, and a daughter. This surprised me. I tried to guess which of his paramours had ensnared him or had been ensnared by him. Surely not the argumentative Russian. In any case, that afternoon he was alone in the flat and I did not meet Sophie" (WL, 270). And when Nathaniel tries to question The Darter about the past, The Darter avoids answering, remaining vague about most things they talk about. It is not until Nathaniel is about to leave, standing in the hallway, that he notices what he had not been searching for:

> There had been a closed door ahead of me as I stepped from The Darter's bathroom. Beside it, on the wall, was a framed piece of cloth with an embroidered blue sentence.

Teaching Ondaatje 407

I used often to lie awake
through the whole night,
and wish for a large pearl.

Below it, stitched with thread of a different colour, was a birth-
date, with the month and the year. (WL, 274–5)

These involuntary signs, stitched into cloth, hanging on the wall in
The Darter's home, were not part of his search – that is, his research
into the history of his childhood and his mother's secrets. They were
not to be found in archives or letters or in conversations with people from his past. These signs were meant to remain hidden; they
were not intended for him. Thus, it is not by a conscious and rational search that the truth is revealed to Nathaniel (for it is not he
who reveals it) but a chance happening, unplanned for and indeed
schwer. To repeat, it is an event that Deleuze calls "the localized
essence of time," "*the very being of the past in itself*,"[11] a heterotopia whereby the past becomes stitched onto the present, in a specific
place, causing a complete refraction of time and space, a radical
difference rupturing space and time.

For Nathaniel, the past, the present, and the place where he finds
himself are no longer the same after this event. Because what can be
more disrupting than being faced with the utterly unexpected, an
event that one cannot search for, research, plan, predict, or calculate
in advance? One can only account for it after it has occurred, only
learn from it after the fact, which makes this singular moment when
the sign betrays the truth similar to art. At least, this is what Deleuze
suggests in his reading of Proust. In contrast to this after-thought
that the unexpected calls for stands rational thought, or intelligence,
as Deleuze terms it, as employed in both science and philosophy,
which presupposes what is to be explored and anticipates the outcome. Intelligence, in other words, is put to use *before* the event. It is
a totalizing movement of our faculties that is incapable of accounting for the unexpected, the heterotopic space-time, which opens up
to that which is hidden in plain sight – such as a stitched sentence on
a piece of cloth mounted on a wall.

This event is in all essential aspects the conclusion of Ondaatje's
novel. Nathaniel's temporal apprenticeship has with this event
in some ways come to its completion, but it is a completion that

has undone the dream of full disclosure, a totalizing telos, with a conclusion that sums up the past into structured, categorized, and transparent knowledge. This is the case, since the truth revealed to Nathaniel opens up toward the inexplorable and the limitation of rational search, including both narrative rationalization and scientific explanation. Nathaniel learns that the unexpected and incalculable remain hidden behind and are covered over by the scientific search to discover and uncover and so recover the past. It is not so much the literal meaning of the embroidered sentence but how it reveals a hidden history, untold and kept secret. This embroidered sign can be compared to what Deleuze says about the hieroglyph[12] in Proust: "The hieroglyph is everywhere; its double symbol is the accident of the encounter and the necessity of thought: 'fortuitous and inevitable.'"[13] Indeed, Nathaniel encounters the sign by accident, which in turn forces him to rethink his search. Thus, it is not by way of *logos* as rational thinking and argumentative logic that Nathaniel gets to know the truth but by way of what Deleuze calls "antilogos." For Nathaniel, just as for Proust, antilogos is a questioning of "the great themes inherited from the Greeks: *philos, sophia, dialogue, logos, phone.*"[14] The hieroglyph on the wall in The Darter's flat, the embroidered sentence, is both letter and picture, both literal and metaphorical, a decoration and a reminder – in other words, a trace of a story not to be told. It is a deviation from the path of inquiry that ruptures the plotted course while at the same time it imposes an alternative chronology onto the history that Nathaniel has been attempting to record.

To relate this to another of Ondaatje's novels, the forensic and archeological stance in *Anil's Ghost*, set in Sri Lanka, explicitly points to the will to knowledge, as well as to the notion of discovery with its colonial baggage of mapping the unknown and the othering of the unfamiliar. However, this stance often runs up against the "unfinished" process of knowing and so, as I would like to suggest, of teaching and learning. Again, it is a question of interpreting signs, a hermeneutical activity to uncover and discover in order to recover what is lost or hidden. This is, moreover, contrasted with Indigenous ways of knowing in the novel. In *Anil's Ghost*, Palipana's straying from the strict rules of scientific methodology into imaginative thought, and also his way of knowing the traditions and history of Sri Lanka, present us with an alternative view of what knowledge is and another way of engaging with what is considered knowledge.

Palipana, interestingly, is characterized as a somewhat traditional, strict, and inflexible teacher when dealing with his research assistants, while he is portrayed as an extremely empathic and sensitive pedagogue when taking care of his traumatized niece Lakma.[15]

To return to *Warlight*, Nathaniel has to learn to live with the revelation of a truth that he cannot pursue further. It means finding and positioning himself against a history that is closed to him, that he is not allowed to know about – he is caught in the absence and emptiness of not knowing. Hence the need to supplement this inaccessible history with stories, that is, what *might* have happened and what *could* be the way things played out, "some version of the truth" (WL, 278), as he says. So, the decipherer of signs and hieroglyphics must apply his creativity and imaginative powers to learn what cannot be learned, which is the remainder left in all signs and hieroglyphs, as well as in works of art. "The Egyptologist, in all things," writes Deleuze, "is the man who undergoes an initiation – the apprentice."[16] Nathaniel and the story he tells involve two initiations: the first is the narration recounting his childhood and youth, the second is the initiation into the accidental but necessary signs and hieroglyphs that disclose truths that in part remain hidden and withdraw with every attempt to decipher them. Nathaniel has to accept the dimmed half-light, the warlight, upsetting the dichotomy of light and dark as symbolizing blindness and insight, ignorance and knowledge, and to endure the ambiguity of creative thinking, in which not knowing is the only truth to be reckoned with. "I did not know what to do," says Nathaniel when he realizes what the embroidered sentence means, "[h]ers had been the story I never followed" (WL, 275). He is thus forced to imagine, make up stories, perhaps to make up for not knowing: "I imagine the two of them," Nathaniel says of The Darter and Agnes, "with what? Envy? Relief? Guilt that I had not known what I was responsible for till now?" (WL, 276). Encountering the *schwer*, the difficult and radically different, he must enter the heterotopic space-time of art to mirror the story he never followed. He must learn to live again by learning how to think about a past that he didn't experience and a future that can never be his. Art is, precisely, this missing history, a history beyond recovery, and this is, likewise, the other story so often told in Ondaatje's work.

Teaching literature often boils down to this: how to teach what is not there, not even between the lines, but absolutely secret. We (students, teachers) must in a sense go through Nathaniel's journey and take up the same apprenticeship he did, meaning to search, research, read, talk, discuss, and use our intelligence (rational thinking and logic), ponder the aesthetics of objects, to prepare for the most difficult, the *schwer*, namely, that we might encounter and be struck by the unexpected and the inexplicable as antilogos and a heterotopical aesthetics. We must continuously struggle to name that which has no name, and, just like many of the names in Ondaatje's work, it will always be an illegitimate name, telling a different story. Such histories and those names can, however, let us learn how to ask some guiding questions that might be the beginning of learning to live, together.[17] This, furthermore, was also how a democratic epistemology started to develop in class to inform us of how to engage with the other, the unfamiliar, the different, and also difference as such, in that unique space in which teaching and learning take place. And this, finally, is what teaching Ondaatje's work has begun to teach me.

NOTES

1 In the fall of 2021, I had the chance to teach Ondaatje once again, this time at the University of Calgary, and my choice of text fell on the novel *Warlight*. The theme of the course was "Learning to Live," and it was through this theme that I and my students read Ondaatje's novel. I wanted, in teaching this course, to put into practice what I had suggested in my essay on teaching Ondaatje's *The English Patient*. Thus, I attempted to practise what I call democratic epistemology in my teaching. This meant that I wanted us to prepare for those unexpected insights that can come through genuine trust and collaboration without presupposing any final truths about the text. And I believe that what we achieved in our reading was to negotiate and merge rational and logical knowledge with that other knowledge that can only come to us unexpectedly and that is what teaches us to take one step on the path toward learning to live. I want to thank all my students in ENGL 251 05 and 10 for creating that truly heterotopic space in which we found the trust and courage to let the signs of *Warlight* betray themselves to us. This essay is built on the reading *Warlight* that we created together. Thank you all!

2 Heterotopia is Foucault's name for that which disrupts the order of culture, society, language, disciplines, even a classroom. It is a space in which if not the unimaginable and unthinkable, then at least the

Teaching Ondaatje   411

unimagined and unthought take place, a place in which we find ourselves faced with the radically other, similar and familiar, but at the same time utterly strange and foreign. For Foucault's most extended analysis of heterotopia, see his "Different Spaces."

3 Deleuze, *Proust and Signs*, 61.

4 For a discussion of "as if" as a philosophical and theoretical notion, see chapter 6 of my book *Aporias of Translation: Literature, Philosophy, Education*, in which I discuss how the "as if" fictionalizes discourse and problematizes the search for truth.

5 Deleuze, *Proust and Signs*, 4.

6 Ibid., 68.

7 Democratic epistemology should be read against such notions as cognitive and social justice, which have been introduced and theorized in response to the actualization of the growing heterogeneity of higher education and the diversification of knowledge.

8 Schwieler, "Reading *The English Patient*," 177.

9 Deleuze, *Proust and Signs*, 4.

10 Ibid., 15.

11 Ibid., 61.

12 A fitting definition of the hieroglyph is given by Orly Goldwasser in *From Icon to Metaphor*, 1: "Hieroglyphs are the crossroads par excellence of word and picture; words which do not describe pictures, but are *made* of pictures. The reader is carried relentlessly from literal meanings to various transposed meanings, and back to the literal. The final meaning of a word might be entangled with associations conjured up by the pictorial during the process, while echoes of ambiguities hover above. As in verbal metaphor, 'graphic rhetoric' may conceive and create new beings and may represent something that does not have a 'name'."

13 Deleuze, *Proust and Signs*, 102.

14 Ibid., 108.

15 This difference in Palipana's pedagogical attitude highlights the importance of care for learning. If the teacher is not engaged emotionally in the students' learning, they are left to their own devices when it comes to finding significant pedagogical experiences that might develop and deepen their knowledge. This is as true for research students as it is for children in lower grades. In his essay "The Call of Pedagogy as the Call of Contact," Max van Manen describes critical pedagogical experiences in the following manner: "We recognize pedagogical experiences because we have received the attentive care and worries of a mother, a father, a teacher, a grandparent, or some other adult who at various times played a formative

412   Elias Schwieler

part in our young lives. Without the pedagogical support from these adults, we simply could not and would not be alive today, or, for better or worse, we would not be who we are" (9). These pedagogical experiences, founded in attentiveness and care, have, as van Manen suggests, far-reaching existential implications. The example of this that Ondaatje gives us of Palipana and Lakma in *Anil's Ghost* highlights the existential force of education, seen as formative critical moments making up pedagogical experiences. Importantly, in *Anil's Ghost* as well as in *Warlight*, it is not in formal educational situations that these pedagogical experiences occur but in or growing out of situations of existential crisis. When it comes to *Warlight*, the absence of a mother and father capable of providing caring support and guidance is one of the principal forces behind Nathaniel's urge to stitch together the fragmented past into a more coherent reality. van Manen's statement that without such guidance "we simply could not and would not be alive today, or, for better or worse, we would not be who we are" applies equally well to both Nathaniel and his sister Rachel in *Warlight*. For an extended discussion of critical pedagogical moments and experiences, see van Manen, *The Tact of Teaching*.

16 Deleuze, *Proust and Signs*, 92.

17 Two examples of student comments that attest to what I wanted to achieve in the course Learning to Live, which included Ondaatje's *Warlight*, were the following: "I appreciate how well you listened to all of us and provided a safe space for us all to participate" and "[The course] was a different experience not only from high school, but other university courses too. You treated us with respect and allowed us the freedom to express our thoughts without judgement. In other classes, I've had condescending professors who treated us like our voices were not worth sharing. Thank you for treating us with respect, truly." Of lesser importance, at least to me, is if I came across as a "good teacher" or not. The significance of these comments is that at least these two students appreciated a learning environment based on mutual respect, the feeling of being heard in a safe space, and the freedom to learn. It is my belief that Ondaatje's *Warlight*, and his work more generally, lends itself extremely well to developing such a learning environment – a space that, I would like to think, contributes to developing democratic epistemology in the classroom and beyond.

Works by Michael Ondaatje

(AG)
Anil's Ghost. London: Bloomsbury, 2000. New York: Knopf, 2000. New York: Vintage, 2000. Toronto: McClelland and Stewart, 2000. Toronto: Vintage, 2001. 311p.

(CT)
The Cat's Table. Toronto: McClelland and Stewart, 2011. New York: Knopf, 2011. New York & Toronto: Vintage, 2011. 269p.

(CP)
The Cinnamon Peeler: Selected Poems. Toronto: McClelland and Stewart, 1989 and 1992. 194p.

(CW)
The Collected Works of Billy the Kid. Toronto: Anansi, 1970 and 1979. New York: W.W. Norton, 1970 and 1979. London: Penguin Books, 1970. 105p.

(CS)
Coming Through Slaughter. Toronto: House of Anansi Press, 1976. 156p.

(TC)
The Conversations: Walter Murch and the Art of Editing Film. Toronto & New York: Vintage, 2002. New York: Alfred A. Knopf, 2002. 339p.

Works by Michael Ondaatje

(DM)
The Dainty Monsters. Toronto: Coach House Press, 1967. 77p.

(D)
Divisadero. Toronto: McClelland and Stewart, 2007. New York: Knopf, 2007. New York & Toronto: Vintage, 2008. 273p.

(ED)
Elimination Dance. Ilderton, ON: Nairn Coldstream, 1978.

(EP)
The English Patient. Toronto: McClelland and Stewart, 1992. New York: Vintage, 1993 and 1996. 307p.

(HW)
Handwriting. Toronto: McClelland and Stewart, 1998. New York: Knopf, 1999. 78p.

(SL)
In the Skin of a Lion. Toronto: McClelland and Stewart, 1987. New York: Penguin, 1987 and 1988. New York: Vintage, 1997. 243p.

(LC)
Leonard Cohen. Toronto: McClelland and Stewart, 1970. 64p.

(LP)
The Long Poem Anthology. Toronto: Coach House Press, 1979. 343p.

(tmst)
the man with seven toes. Toronto: Coach House Press, 1969.

(RJ)
Rat Jelly. Toronto: Coach House Press, 1973. 71p.

(RF)
Running in the Family. Toronto: McClelland and Stewart, 1982. New York: Norton, 1982. General Publishing Paperback Edition, 1994. 207p.

Works by Michael Ondaatje

(s)

Secular Love. Toronto: Coach House Press, 1984. New York: Norton, 1984. 126p.

(TS)

The Story. Drawings by David Bolduc. Toronto: House of Anansi, 2005.

(TTK)

There's a Trick with a Knife I'm Learning to Do. Toronto: McClelland and Stewart, 1979. New York: W.W. Norton, 1979. 107p.

(WL)

Warlight. Toronto: McClelland and Stewart, 2018. New York: Knopf, 2018. London: Jonathan Cape, 2018. 289p.

Bibliography

Abeysekara, Ananda. *The Politics of Postsecular Religion: Mourning Secular Futures.* New York: Columbia University Press, 2008.

Abraham, Nicolas. "Notes on the Phantom: A Complement to Freud's Metapsychology." In *The Shell and the Kernel: Renewals of Psychoanalysis.* Vol. 1, 170–6. Edited and translated by Nicholas T. Rand. Chicago: University of Chicago Press, 1994.

– *The Wolf Man's Magic Word: A Cryptonymy.* Translated by Nicholas T. Rand. Minneapolis: University of Minnesota Press, 2005.

Abraham, Nicolas, and Maria Torok. *The Shell and the Kernel: Renewals of Psychoanalysis.* Vol. 1. Edited and translated by Nicholas T. Rand. Chicago: University of Chicago Press, 1994.

Agamben, Giorgio. *Homo Sacer: Sovereign Power and Bare Life.* Translated by Daniel Heller- Roazen. Stanford: Stanford University Press, 1995.

– *The State of Exception.* Translated by Kevin Attell. Chicago: University of Chicago Press, 2005.

Ahmed, Sara. *Living a Feminist Life.* Durham: Duke University Press, 2017.

– *The Promise of Happiness.* Durham: Duke University Press, 2010.

– *What's the Use?* Durham: Duke University Press, 2019.

Ang, Ien. "On Not Speaking Chinese: Postmodern Ethnicity and the Politics of Diaspora." *New Formations* 24 (1994): 1–18.

Appiah, Kwame Anthony. *In My Father's House: Africa in the Philosophy of Culture.* Oxford: Oxford University Press, 1992.

Aristotle. *Poetics.* The Perseus Catalog. www.perseus.tufts.edu.

Asad, Talal. *On Suicide Bombing.* New York: Columbia University Press, 2007.

Ashcroft, Bill, Gareth Griffiths, and Helen Tiffin. *Key Concepts in Post-colonial Studies*. London: Routledge, 1998.

– "Diaspora." In *The Post-Colonial Studies Reader*, 2nd ed., edited by Bill Ashcroft, Gareth Griffiths, and Helen Tiffin, 425–7. London: Routledge, 2006.

Atwood, Margaret. "Death of a Young Son by Drowning." *The Journals of Susanna Moodie*, 30–1. Toronto: Oxford University Press, 1969.

Bachner, Sally. "'He Had Pushed His Imagination into Buddy's Brain', or, How to Escape History in *Coming Through Slaughter*." *Rethinking History* 9, nos. 2/3 (2005): 197–220.

Bakhtin, Mikhail. "Author and Hero in Aesthetic Activity." In *Art and Answerability: Early Philosophical Essays by M.M. Bakhtin*, edited by Michael Holquist and Vadim Liapunov, 4–256. Translated by Vadim Liapunov. Austin: University of Texas Press, 1990.

Bandarage, Asoka. *The Separatist Conflict in Sri Lanka: Terrorism, Ethnicity, Political Economy*. London: Routledge, 2009.

Bandi, Raghu Ram. *Adapting Novels into Film: Three Case Studies*. New Delhi: Prestige Books, 2009.

Banerjee, Mita. *The Chutneyfication of History: Salman Rushdie, Michael Ondaatje, Bharati Mukherjee, and the Postcolonial Debate*. Heidelberg: C. Winter, 2002.

Barbour, Douglas. "Controlling the Jungle: A Review of *Dainty Monsters*." In *Spider Blues: Essays on Michael Ondaatje*, edited by Sam Solecki, 111–13. Montreal: Véhicule, 1985.

– *Michael Ondaatje*. New York: Twayne, 1993.

Barry, Michael. "Archaeology and Teleology in Ondaatje's *Anil's Ghost*." *Critique: Studies in Contemporary Fiction* 56, no. 2 (2015): 138–54.

Bauman, Zygmunt. *Postmodern Ethics*. Malden: Blackwell, 1993.

Bazin, André. "For an Impure Cinema: In Defense of Adaptataion." In *What Is Cinema?* Translated by Timothy Barnard. Montreal: Caboose Books, 2009.

Beddoes, Julie. "Which Side Is It On? Form, Class, and Politics in *In the Skin of a Lion*." *Essays on Canadian Writing* 53 (1994): 204–15.

Benjamin, Walter. "The Work of Art in the Age of Mechanical Reproduction." In *Illuminations*, edited by Hannah Arendt, 217–51. Translated by Harry Zohn. New York: Schocken, 1969.

Berger, John. *and our faces, my heart, brief as photos*. London: Bloomsbury, 2005.

Berger, John, and Selçhuk Demirel. *What Time Is It?* Kendal: Notting Hill Editions, 2019.

Bibliography   419

Berger, John, with Michael Ondaatje. Conversation 4, Episode 7. Lannan Podcasts. October 2002.

Bethell, Kathleen I. "Reading Billy: Memory, Time, and Subjectivity in *The Collected Works of Billy the Kid*." *Studies in Canadian Literature/ Études en Littérature Canadienne* 28, no. 1 (2003): 71–89.

Betts, Gregory. "Stanley Louis Dragland." *The Canadian Encyclopedia*. 15 November 2009. www.thecanadianencyclopedia.ca.

Bhabha, Homi K. *The Location of Culture*. New York: Routledge, 1994.

Bicking, Barbara. *Die Zimtwirtschaft auf Sri Lanka (Ceylon). Anbau und Vermarktung, historische Bindung und aktuelle Perspektiven eines traditionsgebundenen Produktes*. Mainz: Geographisches Institut der Johannes Gutenberg-Universität, 1986.

Biskind, Peter. *Down and Dirty Pictures: Miramax, Sundance, and the Rise of Independent Film*. New York: Simon and Schuster, 2004.

Bjerring, Nancy E. "Deconstructing the 'Desert of Facts': Detection and Antidetection in *Coming Through Slaughter*." *English Studies in Canada* 16, no. 3 (1990): 325–8.

Blanchot, Maurice. *The Space of Literature*. Translated by Ann Smock. Lincoln: University of Nebraska Press, 1982.

Blaser, Robin. "Statement." In *The New Long Poem Anthology*, 2nd ed., edited by Sharon Thesen, 323. Vancouver: Talonbooks, 2001.

– "The Fire." In *The Poetics of the New American Poetry*, edited by Donald Allen and Warren Tallman, 235–46. New York: Grove, 1973.

Bök, Christian. "Destructive Creation: The Politicization of Violence in the Works of Michael Ondaatje." *Canadian Literature* 132 (1992): 109–24.

Bordwell, David. *Narration in the Fiction Film*. Madison: University of Wisconsin Press, 1985.

– *The Way Hollywood Tells It: Story and Style in Modern Movies*. Berkeley: University of California Press, 2006.

Bowers, Maggie Ann. "Asia's Europes: Anti-Colonial Attitudes in the Novels of Ondaatje and Shamsie." *Journal of Postcolonial Writing* 51, no. 2 (2015): 184–95.

Boyd, William. "Snap Judgement: How Photographer Jacques Henri Lartigue Captured the Moment." *Guardian*, 27 May 2016.

Braarvig, Jens. "The Buddhist Hell: An Early Instance of the Idea?" *Numen* 56, no. 2/3 (2009): 254–81.

Brand, Dionne. *The Blue Clerk*. Durham: Duke University Press, 2018.

Braziel, Jana Evans, and Anita Mannur. "Nation, Migration, Globalization: Points of Contention in Diaspora Studies." In *Theorizing*

Bibliography

Diaspora, edited by Braziel and Mannur, 1–22. Oxford: Blackwell, 2003.

Breitbach, Julia. *Analog Fictions for the Digital Age: Literary Realism and Photographic Discourses in Novels after 2000*. Rochester: Camden House, 2012.

Brittan, Alice. "Michael Ondaatje Tricks the Eye." In *Modernism, Postcolonialism, and Globalism: Anglophone Literature, 1950 to the Present*, edited by Richard Begam and Michael Valdez, 297–314. Oxford: Oxford University Press, 2019.

– "War and the Book: The Diarist, the Cryptographer, and *The English Patient*." In *The History of the Book and the Idea of Literature*. Cooordinated by Seth Lerer and Leah Price. Special issue, PMLA 121, no. 1 (2006): 200–13.

Bruno, Giuliana. *Surface: Matters of Aesthetics, Materiality, and Media*. Chicago: University of Chicago Press, 2014.

Bryson, Norman. "Introduction: Art and Intersubjectivity." In *Looking In: The Art of Viewing*, edited by Mieke Bal and Norman Bryson, 1–39. London: Routledge, 2001.

Burcar, Lilijana. "Mapping the Woman's Body in Michael Ondaatje's *The English Patient*." *Canadian Literature and Culture*. http://www. postcolonialweb.org /canada/literature/ondaatje/burcar/burcar1.html (accessed 13 May 2022).

Burgin, Victor, ed. *Thinking Photography*. Toronto: Macmillan, 1982.

Burns, John. "The Polyphonic Film." *New Review of Film and Television Studies* 6, no. 2 (2008): 189–212.

Burrows, Victoria. "The Heterotopic Spaces of Postcolonial Trauma in Michael Ondaatje's *Anil's Ghost*." *Studies in the Novel* 40, nos 1–2 (2008): 161–77.

Bush, Catherine. "Michael Ondaatje: An Interview." *Conjunctions* 15 (1990): 87–98.

Butler, Judith. *Frames of War: When Is Life Grievable?* London/New York: Verso, 2010.

– *Precarious Life: The Powers of Mourning and Violence*. London: Verso, 2004.

Carbajal, Alberto Fernández. *Compromise and Resistance in Postcolonial Writing: E.M. Forster's Legacy*. Basingstoke: Palgrave Macmillan, 2014.

Carson, Anne. *Eros the Bittersweet: An Essay*. Princeton: Princeton University Press, 1986.

Caruth, Cathy. *Unclaimed Experience: Trauma, Narrative, and History*. Baltimore: Johns Hopkins University Press, 1996.

Bibliography

Casablanca. Director Michael Curtiz. Warner Bros., 1942.

Casper, Monica J., and Eric Wertheimer, eds. *Critical Trauma Studies: Understanding Violence, Conflict, and Memory in Everyday Life.* New York: NYU Press, 2016.

Chakravorty, Mrinalini. "The Dead That Haunt Anil's Ghost: Subaltern Difference and Postcolonial Melancholia." *PMLA* 128, no. 3 (2013): 542–58.

Chakravorty, Mrinalini, and Leila Neti. "The Human Recycled: Insecurity in the Transnational Moment." *Differences: A Journal of Feminist Cultural Studies* 20, nos 2–3 (2009): 194–223.

Chambers, Iain. *Migrancy, Culture, Identity.* London: Routledge, 1994.

Chez, Keridiana. *Victorian Dogs, Victorian Men.* Columbus: Ohio State University Press, 2016.

Clifford, James. "Traveling Cultures." In *Cultural Studies*, edited by Lawrence Grossberg, Cary Nelson, and Paula Treichler, 96–116. London: Routledge, 1992.

Clough, Patricia Ticineto, ed. *The Affective Turn: Theorizing the Social.* Durham: Duke University Press, 2007.

Cohen, Leonard. *Stranger Music: Selected Poems and Songs.* 1993. Toronto: McClelland and Stewart, 1994

Cohen, Richard A. *Ethics, Exegesis, and Philosophy: Interpretation after Levinas.* Cambridge: Cambridge University Press, 2001.

Cole, Teju. *Black Paper.* Chicago: University of Chicago Press, 2021.

Coleridge, Samuel Taylor. *Coleridge's Table Talk.* Edited by J. Potter Briscoe. London: Gay and Bird, 1809.

Connor, Steven. *The Book of Skin.* Ithaca: Cornell University Press, 2004.

Conrad, Joseph. "Youth." In *Youth, Heart of Darkness, The End of the Tethe*, edited by Owen Knowles, 11–42. Cambridge: Cambridge University Press, 2010.

Cook, Victoria. "Exploring Transnational Identities in Ondaatje's *Anil's Ghost.*" In *Comparative Cultural Studies and Michael Ondaatje's Writing*, edited by Steven Tötösy de Zepetnek, 6–15. West Lafayette: Purdue University Press, 2005.

Creeley, Robert. "A Sense of Measure." In *The Collected Essays of Robert Creeley*, 486–8. Berkeley: University of California Press, 1989.

Cresswell, Tim. "Imagining the Nomad: Mobility and the Postmodern Primitive." In *Space and Social Theory*, edited by Georges Benko and Ulf Strotsmayer, 360–79. Oxford: Blackwell, 1997.

– "Introduction: Theorizing Place." In *Mobilizing Place, Placing Mobility:*

Theories of Representation in a Globalized World, edited by Ginette Verstraete and Tim Cresswell, 11–31. Amsterdam: Rodopi, 2002.

Critchley, Simon. "Five Problems in Levinas' View of Politics and a Sketch of a Solution to Them." In *Levinas, Law, Politics*, edited by Marinos Diamantides, 93–105. London: Routledge-Cavendish, 2007.

Crowe, David. *War Crimes, Genocide, and Justice: A Global History*. New York: Palgrave Macmillan, 2014.

Cultural Studies and Ondaatje's Writing. Edited by Steven Tötösy de Zepetnek, 6–15. West Lafayette: Purdue University Press, 2005.

Cummins, Joseph, and Ashley Barnwell. "Michael Ondaatje's *Running in the Family* and the "Familia-graphic Gaze." *Journal of Postcolonial Writing*, 58, no. 3 (2022): 388–401.

Dafoe, Willem. "Michael Ondaatje." *Bomb* 58 (1997): 14–19.

Dämmrich, Ingrid G. *Enigmatic Bliss: The Paradise Motif in Literature*. New York: Peter Lang, 1997.

Daniel, E. Valentine. *Charred Lullabies: Chapters in an Anthropography of Violence*. Princeton: Princeton University Press, 1996.

Davenport, Guy. "Eros the Bittersweet, by Anne Carson." *Grand Street* 6, no. 3 (Spring, 1987): 184–91.

Davey, Frank. *Post-national Arguments: The Politics of the Anglo-Canadian Novel Since 1967*. Toronto: University of Toronto Press, 1993.

Davis, Colin. *Levinas: An Introduction*. Cambridge: Polity Press, 1996.

Davis, R.H. *The Bhagavad Gita: A Biography*. Princeton: Princeton University Press, 2014.

De Smyter, Sofie. "'We Live Permanently in the Recurrence of Our Own Stories': Michael Ondaatje's *Divisadero*." *Studies in Canadian Literature / Études en littérature canadienne* 34, no. 1 (2009), 99–119.

Deleuze, Gilles. *Proust and Signs: The Complete Text*. Translated by Richard Howard. Minneapolis: University of Minnesota Press, 2000.

Deleuze, Gilles, and Félix Guattari. *Capitalisme et schizophrénie. Mille plateaux*. Paris: Les Éditions de Minuit, 1980.

– *A Thousand Plateaus. Capitalism and Schizophrenia*. Translated by Brian Massumi. Minneapolis: University of Minnesota Press, 1987.

den Harto, Adel P. "Taboos." In *Encyclopaedia of Food and Culture*, edited by Solomon H. Katz and William Woys Weaver, 384–6. New York: Charles Scribner's Sons, 2003.

Derrickson, Teresa. "Will the 'Un-truth' Set You Free? A Critical Look at Global Human Rights Discourse in Michael Ondaatje's *Anil's Ghost*." *Literature Interpretation Theory* 15 (2004): 131–52.

Bibliography 423

Derrida, Jacques. *Adieu to Emmanuel Levinas*. Translated by Pascale-AnneBrault and Michael Naas. Stanford: Stanford University Press 1999.

Derrida, Jacques. "Che cos'è la poesia?" In *A Derrida Reader: Behind the Blinds*, edited by Peggy Kamuf, 219–36. New York: Columbia University Press, 1991.

– *The Gift of Death*. Translated by David Wills. Chicago: University of Chicago Press, 1995.

– *Politics of Friendship*. Translated by George Collins. London: Verso, 1997.

– *Specters of Marx: The State of the Debt, the Work of Mourning, and the New International*. Translated by Peggy Kamuf. New York: Routledge, 2006.

– "Violence and Metaphysics: An Essay on the Thought of Emmanuel Levinas." In *Writing and Difference*, 79–153. Translated by Alan Bass. London: Routledge and Kegan Paul, 1978.

Deshaye, Joel. *The Metaphor of Celebrity: Canadian Poetry and the Public, 1955–1980*. Toronto: University of Toronto Press, 2013.

– "Parading the Underworld of New Orleans in Ondaatje's *Coming Through Slaughter*." *American Review of Canadian Studies* 38, no. 4 (2008): 473–94.

– "Racialized Rooms and Technologies of Stardom in Ondaatje's *Coming Through Slaughter*." *The Journal of Commonwealth Literature* 37, no. 2 (2016): 1–15.

Devi, Mahasweta. *Breast Stories*. Translated by Gayatri Chakravorty Spivak. Kolkata: Seagull, 1997.

– *Imaginary Maps*. Translated by Gayatri Chakravorty Spivak. New York: Routledge, 1995.

Donne, John. "To His Mistress Going to Bed." In *John Donne's Poetry*, 2nd ed., edited by Arthur L. Clements, 61–2. New York: W.W. Norton, 1992.

Döring, Tobias. *Caribbean-English Passages: Intertextuality in a Postcolonial Tradition*. New York/London: Routledge, 2002.

Döring, Tobias, Markus Heide, and Susanne Mühleisen. "Introduction." In *Eating Culture: The Poetics and Politics of Food*, edited by Tobias Döring, Markus Heide, and Susanne Mühleisen, 1–16. Heidelberg: Winter 2003.

Dragland, Stan. "Coach House Poetry, 1965–96." *Open Letter: A Canadian Journal of Writing and Theory* 9, no. 8 (1997), 78–91.

– *The Difficult*. St John's: Pedlar Press, 2019.

424   Bibliography

– *Strangers & Others: Newfoundland Essays*. St John's: Pedlar Press, 2015.

Drumbl, Mark A. *Atrocity, Punishment, and International Law*. New York: Cambridge University Press, 2007.

Dudziak, Mary L. *War Time: An Idea, Its History, Its Consequences*. New York: Oxford University Press, 2012.

Dundas, Deborah. "Q&A: Michael Ondaatje on His Latest Novel, *Warlight*." Interview with Michael Ondaatje. *Toronto Star*, 4 May 2018.

Dunn, Kevin. "Lights ... Camera ... Africa: Images of Africa and Africans in Western Popular Films of the 1930s." *African Studies Review* 39, no. 1 (1996): 149–75.

Eliot, T.S. *Collected Poems 1909–1962*. London: Faber and Faber, 1963.

Elkins, James. *The Object Stares Back: On the Nature of Seeing*. 1996. San Diego: Harcourt Brace, 1997.

Emery, Mary Lou. *Modernism, the Visual, and Caribbean Literature*. Cambridge: Cambridge University Press, 2007.

The Epic of Gilgamesh. Translated by N.K. Sanders. London: Penguin, 1962.

Fernando, Kathleen. "'Inhospitable Nation': Violence, Maternal Desire, and Healing in Michael Ondaatje's *Anil's Ghost*." *South Asian Review* 37, no. 1 (2016): 215–32.

Finkle, Derek. "From Page to Screen: Michael Ondaatje as Filmmaker." *Essays on Canadian Writing* 53 (Summer 1994): 167–85.

Flatley, Jonathan. *Affective Mapping: Melancholia and the Politics of Modernism*. Cambridge: Harvard University Press, 2008.

Flood, Gavin D., and Charles Martin. *The Bhagavad Gita: A New Translation*. New York: Norton, 2015.

Foucault, Michel. "Different Spaces." In *Aesthetics, Method and Epistemology*, vol. 2, edited by James D. Faubio, 175–86. Translated by Robert Hurley, et al. New York: The New Press, 1998.

– *History of Sexuality*. Vol. 1. Translated by Robert Hurley. New York: Vintage, 1990.

– *"Society Must Be Defended": Lectures at the College de France, 1975–1976*. Edited by Mauro Bertani and Alessandro Fontana. Translated by David Macey. New York: Picador, 2003.

Fraser, Russell. "Edwin Muir's Other Eden." *Sewanee Review* 108, no.1 (2000).

Freed, Joanne Lipson. "Invisible Victims, Visible Absences: Imagining

Bibliography 425

Disappearance for an International Audience." *Ariel* 43, no. 2 (2013), 25–44.

Freedman, Adele. "From Gunslingers to Jazz Musicians." *Globe and Mail*, 22 December 1979.

Freud, Sigmund. *Civilization and Its Discontents*. Edited and translated by James Strachey. New York: Norton, 2005.

– *The Ego and the Id*. Edited and translated by James Strachey. New York: Norton, 1990.

– "Mourning and Melancholia." 1917. In *On Murder, Mourning, and Melancholia*, 201–18. Translated by Shaun Whiteside. London: Penguin, 2005.

– "Repression." 1915. In *Standard Edition of the Complete Psychological Works of Sigmund Freud*, vol. 14, edited and translated by James Strachey, 143–58. London: Hogarth, 1957.

Fusco, Serena. "'Black Space Is Time': Intermediality, Narrative, and Community in Michael Ondaatje." *Iperstoria: Testi Letterature Linguaggi* 10 (2017): 146–57.

– "Fading into Unborn Photographs: Narrativizing/Allegorizing the Historical Object in Michael Ondaatje's Fiction." *CosMo: Comparative Studies in Modernism* 14, no. 1 (2019): 107–21.

Gamlin, Gordon. Michael Ondaatje's *In the Skin of a Lion* and the Oral Narrative." *Canadian Literature* 135 (1992): 68–77.

Ganapathy-Doré, Geetha. "Fathoming Private Woes in a Public Story: A Study of Michael Ondaatje's *Anil's Ghost*." *Jouvert* 6, no. 3 (2002): n.p.

– "A Postcolonial Passage to England: Michael Ondaatje's *The Cat's Table*." In *New Soundings in Postcolonial Writing: Critical and Creative Contours*, edited by Janet Wilson and Chris Ringrose, 95–112. Leiden/Boston: Brill/Rodopi, 2016.

Ganz, Shoshannah. "'The Reason for War Is War': Western and Eastern Interrogations of Violence in Michael Ondaatje's *Anil's Ghost*." *East-West Cultural Passage* 20, no. 2 (2020): 94–113.

George, Rosemary Marangoly. *The Politics of Home: Postcolonial Relocations and Twentieth-Century Fiction*. Cambridge: Cambridge University Press, 1996.

Gioia, Ted. *The History of Jazz*. Oxford: Oxford University Press, 2011.

Glazzard, Andrew. *The Case of Sherlock Holmes: Secrets and Lies in Conan Doyle's Detective Fiction*. Edinburgh: Edinburgh University Press, 2018.

Glickman, Susan. "From 'Philoctetes on the Island' to 'Tin Roof': The

Emerging Myth of Michael Ondaatje." In *Spider Blues: Essays on Michael Ondaatje*, edited by Sam Solecki, 70–81. Montreal: Véhicule Press, 1985.

Glissant, Édouard. *Poetics of Relation*. Translated by Betsy Wing. Ann Arbor: University of Michigan Press, 1997.

Goldman, Marlene. "'Powerful Joy': Michael Ondaatje's *The English Patient* and Walter Benjamin's Allegorical Way of Seeing." *University of Toronto Quarterly* 70, no. 4 (2001): 902–22.

– "Representations of Buddhism in Ondaatje's *Anil's Ghost*." *Comparative Literature and Culture* 6, no. 3 (2004): 1–9.

Goldwasser, Orly. *From Icon to Metaphor: Studies in the Semiotics of the Hieroglyphs*. Fribourg, Switzerland: Fribourg University Press, 1995.

Gordon, Avery. *Ghostly Matters: Haunting and the Sociological Imagination*. Minneapolis: University of Minnesota Press, 1997.

Grace, Sherrill. *Landscapes of War and Memory: The Two World Wars in Canadian Literature and the Arts, 1977–2007*. Edmonton: University of Alberta Press, 2014.

Guha, Ranajit. "Chandra's Death." *Subaltern Studies* 5 (1987): 135–65.

Gunesekera, Romesh. *Heaven's Edge*. London: Bloomsbury, 2002.

"Haiku." *Princeton Encyclopedia of Poetry and Poetics*. Edited by Alex Preminger and T.V.F. Brogan, 493–4. Princeton: Princeton University Press, 1993.

Halpé, Aparna. "A Fox's Wedding: Sitting Down with Michael Ondaatje." *South Asian Review* 33, no. 3 (2012): 295–303.

Hand, Seán. *Emmanuel Levinas*. London: Routledge, 2009.

Handke, Peter. *A Sorrow beyond Dreams: A Life Story*. Translated by Ralph Manheim. New York: Farrar, Straus and Giroux, 1974.

Harrison, Dick. *Unnamed Country: The Struggle for Canadian Prairie Fiction*. Edmonton: University of Alberta Press, 1977.

Hass, Robert. *What Light Can Do*. New York: Ecco, 2012.

Heble, Ajay. "Michael Ondaatje and the Problem of History." *Clio* 19, no. 2 (1990): 97–109.

Heighton, Steven. "'Approaching that Perfect Edge': Kinetic Techniques in the Poetry and Fiction of Michael Ondaatje." *Studies in Canadian Literature* 13, no. 2 (1988): 223–43.

Heinze, Eric A. *Waging Humanitarian War: The Ethics, Law, and Politics of Humanitarian Intervention*. New York: SUNY Press, 2009.

Hensher, Philip. "*The Cat's Table* by Michael Ondaatje: Review." *The Telegraph*, 5 September 2011.

Hepburn, Allan. *Intrigue: Espionage and Culture*. New Haven: Yale University Press, 2005.

Bibliography

Herrick, Margaret C.S. "*Katabasis* and the Politics of Grief in Michael Ondaatje's *Anil's Ghost.*" *The Journal of Commonwealth Literature* 51, no. 1 (2016): 35–48.

Hewitson, Justin M. "Mediating Suffering: Buddhist Detachment and Tantric Responsibility in Michael Ondaatje's *Anil's Ghost.*" CLCWeb: *Comparative Literature and Culture* 21, no. 5 (2019): 1–10.

– "Peterson vs. Žižek on the Evolution of Consciousness and Happiness: From Pragmatism to Sarkar's Tantra." In *Pragmatism, Spirituality and Society: New Pathways of Consciousness, Freedom, and Solidarity*, edited by Ananta Kumar Giri, 95–87. Singapore: Springer, 2021.

– "Tantric Metaseity in the *Rig Veda's* 'Creation Hymn'": A Sarkarian Reading and New Translation of X.129." *Concentric: Literary and Cultural Studies* 47, no. 1 (2021): 21–52.

Highway, Tomson. "Oh Little Bear." *The (Post) Mistress: A One-Woman Musical*. Independent Audio-CD of songs, featuring singer Patricia Cano, 2013.

Hilger, Annick. *Not Needing All the Words: Michael Ondaatje's Literature of Silence*. Montreal: McGill-Queen's University Press, 2005.

Hilger, Stephanie M. "Ondaatje's *The English Patient* and Rewriting History." In *Comparative Cultural Studies and Michael Ondaatje's Writing*, edited by Steven Tötösy de Zepetnek, 38–48. West Lafayette: Purdue University Press, 2005.

Hirsch, Marianne. "Marked by Memory: Feminist Reflections on Trauma and Transmission." In *Extremities: Trauma, Testimony and Community*, edited by Nancy K. Miller and Jason Daniel Kougaw, 71–91. Urbana/Chicago: University of Illinois Press, 2002.

Hirsch, Susan F. *In the Moment of Greatest Calamity: Terrorism, Grief, and a Victim's Quest for Justice*. Princeton: Princeton University Press, 2006.

Ho, Chien-Hsing. "The Finger Pointing toward the Moon: A Philosophical Analysis of the Chinese Buddhist Thought of Reference." *Journal of Chinese Philosophy* 35, no. 1 (2008): 159–77.

Hobkirk, Lori. "Villa San Girolamo: The Oasis of Caged Birds." In *Literature, Writing, and the Natural World*, edited by James Guignard and T.P. Murphy, 143–53. Cambridge: Cambridge Scholars Publishing, 2009.

Hochbruck, Wolfgang. "The Intangible Image of Buddy Bolden." In *Image et récit: Littérature(s) et arts visuels du Canada*, edited by Héliane Ventura, Simone Vauthier, and Jean-Michel Lacroix, 177–93. Paris: Presses Sorbonne Nouvelle, 1993.

428   Bibliography

Hoole, Rajan. *Sri Lanka: The Arrogance of Power: Myths, Decadence and Murder.* Jaffna: University Teachers for Human Rights, 2001.

Horowitz, Donald L. *The Deadly Ethnic Riot.* Berkeley: University of California Press, 2003.

Horta, Paulo. "Ondaatje and the Cosmopolitan Desert Explorers: Landscape, Space, and Community in *The English Patient.*" In *Moveable Margins: The Shifting Spaces of Canadian Literature,* edited by Chelva Kanaganaykam, 65–84. Toronto: TSAR Publications, 2006.

Hosseini, Khaled. *The Kite Runner.* New York: Riverhead, 2003.

Howe, Fanny. "Now I Get It." Academy of American Poets Poem-a-Day Series. 27 August 2014. https://poets.org.

Hsu, Shou-Nan. "From Sexual Love to Peace: Endless Care and Respect for Strangers in Michael Ondaatje's *Secular Love.*" *College Literature* 41, no. 4 (2014): 111–28.

Hume, David. "Of curiosity, of the love of truth." In *A Treatise of Human Nature.* 1739. https://davidhume.org.

Hutcheon, Linda. "Canadian Historiographic Metafiction." *Essays on Canadian Writing* 30 (1984–85): 228–38.

– *The Canadian Postmodern: A Study of Contemporary English-Canadian Fiction.* Toronto and Oxford: Oxford University Press, 1988.

– "History and/as Intertext." In *Future Indicative: Literary Theory and Canadian Literature,* edited by John Moss, 169–84. Ottawa: University of Ottawa Press, 1987.

– *A Poetics of Postmodernism: History, Theory, Fiction.* New York and London: Routledge, 1988.

– *The Politics of Postmodernism.* London: Routledge, 1989.

– "The Postmodern Problematizing of History." *English Studies in Canada* 14, no. 4 (1988): 365–82.

– *A Theory of Adaptation.* New York: Routledge, 2006.

Inan, Ilhan. *The Philosophy of Curiosity.* New York: Routledge, 2012.

Ingelbien, Rafael. "A Novelist's Caravaggism: Michael Ondaatje's *In the Skin of a Lion.*" In *The Guises of Canadian Diversity: New European Perspectives / Les Masques de la diversité canadienne: nouvelles perspectives européennes,* edited by S. Jaumain and M. Maufort, 27–37. Amsterdam: Rodopi, 1995.

Ismail, Qadri. *Abiding by Sri Lanka: On Peace, Place, and Postcoloniality.* Minneapolis: University of Minnesota Press, 2005.

– "A Flippant Gesture towards Sri Lanka: A Review of Michael Ondaatje's *Anil's Ghost.*" *Pravada* 6, no. 9 (2000): 24–9.

Jacobs, Karen. "Introduction: Infinite Dialogues." In *Poetics of the*

Bibliography

Iconotext, edited by Karen Jacobs, 1–10. Translated by Laurence Petit. Farnham: Ashgate, 2011.

Jaggi, Maya. "Michael Ondaatje in Conversation with Maya Jaggi." *Wasafiri* 16, no. 32 (2000): 5–11.

– "With Michael Ondaatje (2000)." In *Writing across Worlds: Contemporary Writers Talk*, edited by Susheila Nasta, 250–65. London: Routledge, 2004.

Jameson, Fredric. *Postmodernism, or, The Cultural Logic of Late Capitalism*. Durham: Duke University Press, 2001.

JanMohamed, Abdul R. *The Death-Bound-Subject: Richard Wright's Archaeology of Death*. Durham: Duke University Press, 2005.

Jewinski, Ed. *Michael Ondaatje: Express Yourself Beautifully*. Toronto: ECW Press, 1994.

Joseph, Justy, and Nirmala Menon. "Memory Anchored by Place Attachment and Cognitive Maps in Michael Ondaatje's *Warlight* and *The Cat's Table*." *Rupkatha Journal on Interdisciplinary Studies in Humanities* 12, no. 6 (December 2020): 1–10.

Kamboureli, Smaro. "The Culture of Celebrity and National Pedagogy." *Home-Work: Postcolonialism, Pedagogy, and Canadian Literature*, 35–55. Edited by Cynthia Sugars. Ottawa. University of Ottawa Press, 2004.

Kamboureli, Smaro, and Dean Irvine. "Introduction." In *Editing as Cultural Practice in Canada*, edited by Smaro Kamboureli and Dean Irvine, 1–16. Waterloo: Wilfrid Laurier University Press, 2016.

Kamiya, Gary. "Delirious in a Different Kind of Way: An Interview with Michael Ondaatje." *Salon*, 18 November 1996: n.p.

Kanaganayakam, Chelva. "The Anxiety of Being Postcolonial: Ideology and the Contemporary Postcolonial Novel." *Miscelanea* 28 (2003): 43–54.

Kaplan, Caren. *Questions of Travel*. Durham: Duke University Press, 1996.

Kenaan, Hagi. *The Ethics of Visuality: Levinas and the Contemporary Gaze*. London: I.B. Tauris, 2013.

Kim, Lee-Von. "Scenes of Af/filiation: Family Photographs in Postcolonial Life Writing." *Life Writing* 12, no. 4 (2015): 401–15.

Kipling, Rudyard. *Kim*. New York: Doubleday Page, 1912.

Kirss, Tiina. "Seeing Ghosts: Theorizing Haunting in Literary Texts." In *Haunted Narratives: Life Writing in an Age of Trauma*, edited by Gabriele Rippl, Philipp Schweighauser, Tiina Kirss, Margit Sutrop, and Therese Steffen, 21–44. Toronto: University of Toronto Press, 2018.

Bibliography

Knopf, Dawn Marie, and Michael Ondaatje. "Michael Ondaatje: From Archives to Page." *Columbia: A Journal of Literature and Art* 47 (2010): 76–85.

Koppelman, Charles. *Behind the Seen: How Walter Murch Edited* Cold Mountain. San Francisco: New Riders Books, 2004.

Kranz, David. "*The English Patient*: Critics, Audiences, and the Quality of Fidelity." *Literature/Film Quarterly* 3, no. 2 (2003): 99–110.

Krause, Elizabeth. "Archive of Michael Ondaatje, Author of *The English Patient*, Acquired." https://sites.utexas.edu/ransomcentermagazine/2017/09/25/archive-of-michael-ondaatje-author-of-the-english-patient-acquired/.

Kristeva, Julia. *Powers of Horror: An Essay on Abjection.* Translated by Leon S. Roudiez. New York: Columbia University Press, 1982.

Kurnick, David. *Empty Houses: Theatrical Failure and the Novel.* Princeton: Princeton University Press, 2011.

Küster, Hansjörg. *Kleine Kulturgeschichte der Gewürze: Ein Lexikon von Anis bis Zimt.* Munich: C.H. Beck, 1997.

Lawrence, D.H. *The Letters of D.H. Lawrence.* Vol. 4, June 1921–March 1924. Edited by Warren Roberts, James T. Boulton, and Elizabeth Mansfield. Cambridge: Cambridge University Press, 2002.

Lecker, Robert. "Music in Michael Ondaatje's *Divisadero.*" *The Journal of Commonwealth Literature* 54, no. 2 (2019): 273–91.

LeClair, Tom. "The Sri Lankan Patients." Review of *Anil's Ghost*, by Michael Ondaatje. *Nation*, 19 June 2000: 31.

Levinas, Emmanuel. *Ethics and Infinity: Conversations with Philippe Nemo.* Translated by Richard A. Cohen. Pittsburgh: Duquesne University Press, 1985.

– *Existence and Existents.* Translated by Alphonso Lingis. Pittsburgh: Duquesne University Press, 2001.

– *God, Death and Time.* 1993. Translated by Bettina Bergo. Stanford: Stanford University Press, 2000.

– *Otherwise Than Being: Or beyond Essence.* Translated by Alphonso Lingis. Pittsburgh: Duquesne University Press, 1981.

– "The Servant and Her Master." In *The Levinas Reader*, edited by Seán Hand, 150–9. Translated by Michael Holland. New York: Basil Blackwell, 1989.

– *Time and the Other.* Translated by Richard A. Cohen. Pittsburgh: Duquesne University Press 1987.

– *Totality and Infinity: An Essay on Exteriority.* Translated by Alphonso Lingis. Boston: Martinus Nijhoff Publishers, 1979.

- "The Trace of the Other." In *Deconstruction in Context: Literature and Philosophy*, edited by Mark C. Taylor, 345–59. Translated by Alphonso Lingis. Chicago: University of Chicago Press, 1986.

Li, Yiyun. *Dear Friend, from My Life I Write to You in Your Life.* New York: Random House, 2017.

Lindstrom-Best, Varpu. *The Finns in Canada*. Ottawa: Canadian Historical Association, 1985.

Long-liners Conference on the Canadian Long Poem, York University, Toronto, 29 May to 1 June 1984. *Open Letter* 6, no.2 (Summer-Fall 1985).

Louvel, Liliane. *Poetics of the Iconotext*. Edited by Karen Jacobs. Translated by Laurence Petit. Farnham: Ashgate, 2011.

Lundgren, Jodi. "'Colour Disrobed Itself from the Body': The Racialized Aesthetics of Liberation in Michael Ondaatje's *In the Skin of a Lion*." *Canadian Literature* 190 (2006): 15–29.

Macdonald, Myra. *Representing Women: Myths of Femininity in the Popular Media.* London: Routledge, 1995.

MacLulich, T.D. "Ondaatje's Mechanical Boy: Portrait of the Artist as Photographer." *Mosaic* 14, no. 2 (1981): 107–19.

Malkki, Liisa. "National Geographic. The Rooting of Peoples and the Territorialization of National Identity among Scholars and Refugees." *Cultural Anthropology* 7, no.1 (1992): 24–44.

Manguel, Alberto. *Curiosity*. New Haven: Yale University Press, 2015.

Marais, Mike. "The Time of Hospitality in Samuel Beckett's *Murphy*, Michael Ondaatje's *The English Patient*, and Damon Galgut's *The Good Doctor*." *English Studies in Africa* 58, no. 2 (2015): 15–25.

- "Uncertainty and the Time of the Stranger: Michael Ondaatje's *Warlight*." *Mosaic: A Journal for the Interdisciplinary Study of Literature* 53, no. 1 (2020): 91–106.

Marinkova, Milena. *Michael Ondaatje: Haptic Aesthetics and Micropolitical Writing.* New York: Continuum Books, 2011.

- "'Perceiving [...] in one's own body' the Violence of History, Politics and Writing: *Anil's Ghost* and Witness Writing." *Journal of Commonwealth Literature* 44, no. 3 (2009): 107–25.

Marino, Pierpaolo. "Crossing the Borders of Jazz, Language, and Identity: Michael Ondaatje's *Coming Through Slaughter*." In *(Post)Colonial Passages: Incursions and Excursions across the Literatures and Cultures in English*, edited by Silvia Albertazzi, Francesco Cattani, Rita Monticelli, and Federica Zullo, 218–30. Newcastle Upon Tyne: Cambridge Scholars Publishing, 2018.

Marks, Laura U. *The Skin of the Film: Intercultural Cinema,*

Embodiment, and the Senses. Durham: Duke University Press, 1999.

Marquis, Donald M. *In Search of Buddy Bolden: First Man of Jazz.* Baton Rouge: Louisiana State University Press, 1978.

Marshall, Tom. "Layering: The Shorter Poems of Michael Ondaatje." In *Spider Blues: Essays on Michael Ondaatje*, edited by Sam Solecki, 82–92. Montreal: Véhicule Press, 1985.

Mbembe, Achille. "Life, Sovereignty, and Terror in the Fiction of Amos Tutuola." *Research in African Literatures* 34, no. 4 (2003): 1–26.

– "Necropolitics." *Public Culture* 15, no. 1 (2003): 11–40.

McClennan, Sophia A., and Joseph R. Slaughter. "Introducing Human Rights and Literary Forms; or, The Vehicles and Vocabularies of Human Rights." *Comparative Literary Studies* 46, no. 1 (2009): 1–19.

McDaniel, Craig. "Rethinking Rousseau." *The Midwest Quarterly: Journal of Contemporary Thought* 53, no. 3 (Spring 2012): 215–36.

McGill, Robert. "Michael Ondaatje's *The Collected Works of Billy the Kid* and 1960s America." *Canadian Poetry* 3 (2020): 2–76.

McNary, Dave. "Simon Beaufoy to Adapt 'In the Skin of a Lion' from 'English Patient' Author." *Variety,* June 2017.

McVey, Christopher. "Reclaiming the Past: Michael Ondaatje and the Body of History." *Journal of Modern Literature* 37, no. 2 (Winter 2014): 141–60.

Menand, Louis. "The Aesthete: The Novel and Michael Ondaatje." *The New Yorker,* 4 June 2007: 92–4.

Merton, Thomas. "Message to Poets." In *Selected Essays*, edited by Patrick O'Connell, 172–6. Maryknoll: Orbis Books, 2013.

– *A Search for Solitude: The Journals of Thomas Merton Vol. 3: 1952–1960.* Edited by Lawrence S. Cunningham. San Fransisco: HarperOne, 1997.

Merwin, W.S. "Fact Has Two Faces: An Interview with W.S. Merwin." Interviewed by Ed Folsom and Cary Nelson. In *Conversations with W.S. Merwin*, edited by Michael Wutz and Hal Crimmel, 44–80. Jackson: University Press of Mississippi, 2015.

– "An Interview with W.S. Merwin." Interviewed by Michael Ondaatje, Sam Solecki, and Linda Spalding. In *Conversations with W.S. Merwin*, edited by Michael Wutz and Hal Crimmel, 138–48. Jackson: University Press of Mississippi, 2015.

Metcalf, Allan. *The World in So Many Words: A Country-by-Country Tour of Words That Have Shaped Our Language.* Boston: Houghton Mifflin, 1999.

Mikkonen, Kai. "The 'Narrative is Travel' Metaphor: Between Spatial

Bibliography

Sequence and Open Consequence." *Narrative* 15, no. 3 (2007): 286–305.

Milosz, Czeslaw. *Bells in Winter*. Translated by Czeslaw Milosz and Lillian Vallee. New York: Ecco, 1978.

Mirzoeff, Nikolas. *The Right to Look: A Counterhistory of Visuality*. Durham: Duke University Press, 2011.

Mishra, Vijay. *The Literature of the Indian Diaspora: Theorizing the Diasporic Imaginary*. London: Routledge, 2007.

Morgan, Michael L. *Discovering Levinas*. New York: Cambridge University Press, 2007.

Mufti, Aamir, and Ella Shohat. "Introduction." In *Dangerous Liaisons: Gender, Nation and Postcolonial Perspectives*, edited by Anne McClintock, Aamir Mufti, and Ella Shoat, 1–12. Minneapolis: University of Minnesota Press, 1997.

Mundwiler, Leslie. *Michael Ondaatje: Word, Image, Imagination*. Vancouver: Talonbooks, 1984.

Mutua, Makau. "Savages, Victims, Saviors: The Metaphor of Human Rights." *Harvard International Law Journal* 42, no. 1 (2001): 201–45.

Nasrallah, Dimitri. "What Does Michael Ondaatje Have Left to Say?" Review of *Warlight* by Michael Ondaatje. *The Walrus*, 11 June 2018.

Neumann, Birgit. "Intermedial Negotiations: Postcolonial Literatures." In *Intermediality: Literatures – Image – Sound – Music*, edited by Gabriele Rippl, 512–29. Berlin/New York: De Gruyter, 2015.

Neumann, Birgit, and Gabriele Rippl. *Verbal-Visual Configurations in Postcolonial Literature: Intermedial Aesthetics*. London/New York: Routledge, 2020.

Nixon, Rob. *Slow Violence and the Environmentalism of the Poor*. Cambridge: Harvard University Press, 2011.

Nodelman, Perry M. "The Collected Photographs of Billy the Kid." *Canadian Literature* 87 (1980): 68–78.

Norman, Corrie E. "Religion and Food." In *Encyclopedia of Food and Culture*, edited by Solomon H. Katz and William Woys Weaver, 171–6. New York: Scribner's Sons, 2003.

Norris, Ken. "The Architecture of *Secular Love*: Michael Ondaatje's Journey into the Confessional." *Essays on Canadian Writing* 53 (Spring 1994): 43–50.

Nyman, Jopi. *Displacement, Memory, and Travel in Contemporary Migrant Writing*. Leiden: Brill Rodopi, 2017.

O'Meara, David. "The Company of Thieves: An Interview with Michael

434 Bibliography

Ondaatje." In *Where the Words Come From: Canadian Poets in Conversation*, edited by Tim Bowling, 31–43. Gibbons: Nightwood Editions, 2002.

O'Riley, Michael. *Postcolonial Haunting and Victimization: Assia Djebar's New Novels*. New York: Lang, 2007.

Ondaatje, Michael. "A Conversation with Douglas Barbour and Stephen Scobie." *White Pelican* 1, no. 2 (1971): 19–22.

– "Garcia Marquez and the Bus to Aracataca." In *Figures in a Ground: Canadian Essays in Modern Literature Collected in Honour of Sheila Watson*, edited by Diane Bessai and David Jackel, 19–31. Saskatoon: Western Producer Prairie Books, 1978.

– "How Poems Work." *Globe and Mail*, 18 August 2001, D14.

– "In Search of Happiness." *The Mitre* 70, no. 2 (1962–63): 23.

– "Introduction." *From Ink Lake: Canadian Stories*. Toronto: Lester and Orpen Dennys, 1990. xiii–xviii.

– "More Lost Careers." *Brick* 71 (2003), 57.

– "Mythology in the Poetry of Edwin Muir: A Study of the Making and Using of Mythology in Edwin Muir's Poetry." Master's thesis, Queen's University, 1967.

– "Remembering My Friend Anthony Minghella." *The Guardian*, 23 March 2008.

– "Social Call." *The Mitre* 70, no. 2 (1962–63): 30.

– "We Cannot Rely on Only One Voice." Interview with Tonny Vorm. Posted 16 June 2015. www.youtube.com.

– "The William Dawe Badlands Expedition 1916" (screenplay). *Descant* 14, no. 4 (1983): 51–73.

Ondaatje, Michael, and Teju Cole. Interviewed by Tonny Vorm. Louisiana Literature Sunday, 28 August 2014. www.youtube.com.

Ondaatje, Michael, and Colum McCann. "Without a Map: 'Adventures in the Skin Trade.'" New York Public Library in conjunction with the PEN World Voices festival, 2008. http://colummccann.com.

Ondaatje, Michael, Michael Redhill, Esta Spalding, and Linda Spalding, eds. *Lost Classics*. New York: Anchor Books, 2001.

Ondaatje, Michael, Sam Solecki, and Linda Spalding. "An Interview with W.S. Merwin." *Brick* 62 (1999), 14–19.

Ong, Aihwa. "Experiments with Freedom: Milieus of the Human." *American Literary History* 18, no. 2 (2006): 229–44.

Pallister, David, and Gethin Chamberlain. "Sri Lanka War Toll Near 6,500, UN Report Says." *The Guardian*. Guardian News and Media, 24 April 2009.

Bibliography

Patterson, Orlando. *Slavery and Social Death: A Comparative Study.* Cambridge: Harvard University Press, 1985.

Pennee, Donna Palmateer. "'Something Invisible Finding a Form': Feeling History in Michael Ondaatje's *Coming Through Slaughter.*" *Studies in Canadian Literature/Études en littérature canadienne* 4, no. 2 (2016): 157–76.

Pesch, Josef. "Dropping the Bomb: On Critical and Cinematic Reactions to Michael Ondaatje's *The English Patient.*" In *Reconstructing the Fragments of Michael Ondaatje's Works*, edited by Jean-Michel Lacroix, 229–46. Paris: Presses Sorbonne Nouvelle, 1999.

Petermann, Emily. "Unheard Jazz: Music and History in Michael Ondaatje's *Coming Through Slaughter.*" In *Apropos Canada / À propos du Canada: Fünf Jahre Graduiertentagungen der Kanada-Studien*, edited by Eugen Banauch, Elisabeth Domböck, Anco-Raluco Rodu, Nora Tunkel, and Daniel Winkler, 223–33. Bern: Peter Lang, 2010.

Petroff, Lillian. *Sojourners and Settlers. The Macedonian Community in Toronto to 1940.* Toronto: University of Toronto Press, 1995.

Phu, Thy, and Elspeth H. Brown, eds. *Feeling Photography.* Durham: Duke University Press, 2014.

Pirbhai, Miriam. "South Asian Canadian 'Geographies of Voice': Flagging New Critical Mappings." In *The Oxford Handbook of Canadian Literature*, edited by Cynthia Sugars, 583–601. New York: Oxford University Press, 2015.

Pope, Alexander. "Dog Collars – Brief Poems by Alexander Pope." *Briefpoems*, 17 June 2016.

Proust, Marcel. À *la recherche du temps perdu.* Edited by Jean-Yves Tadié. Bibliothèque de la Pléiade; Paris: Gallimard, 1987–89.

Quint, John. *Epic and Empire: Politics and Generic Form from Virgil to Milton.* Princeton: Princeton University Press, 1993.

Radforth, Ian. *Bushworkers and Bosses: Logging in Northern Ontario, 1900–1980.* Toronto: University of Toronto Press, 1987.

Rae, Ian. *From Cohen to Carson: The Poet's Novel in Canada.* Montreal: McGill-Queen's University Press, 2008.

Rajewsky, Irina O. "Intermediality, Intertextuality, and Remediation: A Literary Perspective on Intermediality." *Intermédialités* 6 (automne 2005): 43–64.

Ramaswamy, Sumathi. "Introduction: The Work of Vision in the Age of European Empires." In *Empire of Vision: A Reader*, edited by Martin Jay and Sumathi Ramaswamy, 1–24. Durham/London: Duke University Press, 2014.

– "Maps, Mother/Goddesses, and Martyrdom in Modern India." In *Empire of Vision: A Reader*, edited by Martin Jay and Sumathi Ramaswamy, 415–49. Durham/London: Duke University Press, 2014.

Rancière, Jacques. *The Politics of Aesthetics: The Distribution of the Sensible*. Translated by Gabriel Rockhill. London/New York: Continuum, 2004.

Ratti, Manav. "Michael Ondaatje's *Anil's Ghost* and the Aestheticization of Human Rights." *Ariel* 35, no. 2 (2004): 121–39.

Ratwatte, Florence. "The Spice of Life: Cinnamon and Ceylon." In *Infolanka*, http://www.infolanka.com/discover/cinnamon (accessed 7 May 2022): 1–7.

Renger, Nicola. "Cartography, Historiography, and Identity in Michael Ondaatje's *The English Patient*." In *Being/s in Transit*, edited by Liselotte Glage, 11–23. Amsterdam: Rodopi, 2000.

Rexroth, Kenneth. "Tu Fu." In *The New Directions Anthology of Classical Chinese Poetry*, edited by Eliot Weinberger, 198–9. New York: New Directions, 2003.

Richie, Donald. *A Tractate on Japanese Aesthetics*. Berkeley: Stone Bridge Press, 2007.

Rilke, R.M. *Duino Elegies*. Translated by Edward Snow. New York: Farrar, Straus, and Giroux, 2000.

– *Letters to a Young Poet*. Translated by Stephen Mitchell. New York: Vintage, 1986.

– *Letters to a Young Poet*. Translated by Reginald Snell. Mineola: Dover, 2002.

Roberts, Gillian. *Prizing Literature: The Celebration and Circulation of National Culture*. Toronto: University of Toronto Press, 2011.

Roochnik, David. *Of Art and Wisdom: Plato's Understanding of Techne*. University Park: Penn State University Press, 1998.

Rooke, Constance. "Dog in a Grey Room: The Happy Ending of *Coming Through Slaughter*." In *Spider Blues: Essays on Michael Ondaatje*, edited by Sam Solecki, 268–92. Montreal: Véhicule Press, 1985. Reprinted in Constance Rooke's *Fear of the Open Heart: Essays on Contemporary Canadian Writing*. Toronto: Coach House Press, 1989, 93–112.

Rose, Al. *Storyville, New Orleans; Being an Authentic, Illustrated Account of the Notorious Red-Light District*. Tuscaloosa: The University of Alabama Press, 1974.

Rose, Charlie, interviewer. "Michael Ondaatje and Anthony Minghella Interview on *The English Patient*. https://charlierose.com/videos/2424.

Bibliography

Roy, Kaushik. *Hinduism and the Ethics of Warfare in South Asia: From Antiquity to the Present.* Cambridge: Cambridge University Press, 2012.

Rushdie, Salman. "Imaginary Homelands." In *Imaginary Homelands: Essays and Criticism, 1981–91,* 9–21. London: Granta, 1991.

Ryan, Marie-Laure, and Jan-Noël Thon, eds. *Storyworlds across Media: toward a Media-Conscious Narratology.* Lincoln: University of Nebraska Press, 2014.

Said, Edward W. *Culture and Imperialism.* London: Chatto and Windus, 1993.

– *On Late Style: Music and Literature against the Grain.* London: Bloomsbury Academic, 2007.

– *Orientalism: Western Conceptions of the Orient.* London: Penguin Books, 1995.

Saint-Amour, Paul K. *Tense Future: Modernism, Total War, Encyclopedic Form.* Oxford: Oxford University Press, 2015.

Salgado, Minoli. *Writing Sri Lanka: Literature, Resistance, and the Politics of Place.* London: Routledge, 2007.

[Sandby, Paul]. *Pug the Painter Following the Example of Messrs Scumble Asphaltum & Varnish. A Satire on Willian Hogarth.* ca. 1754–1757. Graphic Arts Collection. Special Collections, Firestone Library, Princeton University.

Sanghera, Sandeep. "Touching the Language of Citizenship in Ondaatje's *Anil's Ghost.*" In *Comparative Cultural Studies and Ondaatje's Writing,* edited by Steven Tötösy de Zepetnek, 83–91. West Lafayette: Purdue University Press, 2005.

Sarris, Fotios. "*In the Skin of a Lion:* Michael Ondaatje's Tenebristic Narrative." *Essays on Canadian Writing* 44 (Fall 1991): 183–201.

Scafi, Alessandro. *Mapping Paradise: A History of Heaven and Earth.* Chicago: University of Chicago Press, 2006.

Scanlan, Margaret. "*Anil's Ghost* and Terrorism's Time." *Studies in the Novel* 36, no. 3 (2004): 302–17.

Schönfelder, Christa. *Wounds and Words: Childhood and Family Trauma in Romantic and Postmodern Fiction.* Bielefeld: Transcript, 2013.

Schwab, Gabriele. "Words and Moods: The Transference of Literary Knowledge." *Substance* 26, no. 3 (1997): 107–27.

Schwieler, Elias. *Aporias of Translation: Literature, Philosophy, Education.* Scham, Switzerland: Springer, 2022.

– "Reading *The English Patient*: Teaching and Difference." In *Neither East Nor West: Postcolonial Essays on Literature, Culture and Religion,* edited by K.W. Shands, 173–8. Huddinge, Sweden: Södertörn Academic Studies 36, 2008.

Bibliography

Scobie, Stephen. "*Coming Through Slaughter*: Fictional Magnets and Spider's Webbs." *Essays on Canadian Writing* 12 (1978): 5–23.

– "Two Authors in Search of a Character: bpNichol and Michael Ondaatje." In *Spider Blues: Essays on Michael Ondaatje*, edited by Sam Solecki, 185–210. Montreal: Véhicule Press, 1985.

Sedgwick, Eve Kasofsky. *Touching Feeling: Affect, Pedagogy, Performativity*. Durham: Duke University Press, 2002.

Seligman, Craig. "Review of *The English Patient*." *The New Republic*, 15 (1993): 38–41.

Seneviratne, Seni. *Wild Cinnamon and Winter Skin*. Leeds: Peepal Tree, 2007.

Seneviratne, Suharshini. *Exotic Tastes of Sri Lanka*. New York: Hippocrene, 2003.

Shakespeare, William. *Hamlet*. The Folger Shakespeare.

Shou-Nan, Hsu. "Creating a Solid Foundation for Peace: Writing of the Lost Life in Michael Ondaatje's *Handwriting*." *The Journal of Commonwealth Literature* 47, no. 3 (2012): 393–410.

Siddiqi, Yumna. *Anxieties of Empire and the Fiction of Intrigue*. New York: Columbia University Press, 2008.

Sinha, Manoj Kumar. "Hinduism and International Humanitarian Law." *International Review of the Red Cross* 87, no. 858 (2005): 285–94.

Slater, Philip. *Earthwalk*. New York: Anchorbooks/Doubleday, 1974.

Smith, Anna. "*The English Patient* – Is It Time to Revive the Epic Romance?" *Culture* BBC.com, 2021.

Snyder, Gary. "Hsieh's Shoes." In *The New Directions Anthology of Classical Chinese Poetry*, edited by Eliot Weinberger, 201–5. New York: New Directions, 2003.

Solecki, Sam. "An Interview with Michael Ondaatje." In *Spider Blues: Essays on Michael Ondaatje*, 321–32. Montreal: Véhicule Press, 1985.

– "Making and Destroying: *Coming Through Slaughter* and Extremist Art." In *Spider Blues: Essays on Michael Ondaatje*, edited by Sam Solecki, 246–67. Montreal: Véhicule Press, 1985.

– "Nets and Chaos: The Poetry of Michael Ondaatje." *Studies in Canadian Literature* 2, no. 1 (Winter 1977): 36–48.

– *Ragas of Longing: The Poetry of Michael Ondaatje*. Toronto: University of Toronto Press, 2003.

– ed. *Spider Blues: Essays on Michael Ondaatje*. Montreal: Véhicule Press, 1985.

Sontag, Susan. *On Photography*. New York: Delta, 1973.

– *Regarding the Pain of Others*. New York: Picador, 2003.

Sorensen, Eli Park. *Postcolonial Studies and the Literary: Theory,*

Bibliography 439

Interpretation, and the Novel. New York: Palgrave Macmillan, 2010.
Souster, Raymond, ed. *New Wave Canada: The New Explosion in Canadian Poetry.* Toronto: Contact, 1966.
Spalding, Linda. *Daughters of Captain Cook.* Toronto: Lester and Orpen Dennys, 1988.
Spearey, Susan. "Mapping and Masking: The Migrant Experience in Michael Ondaatje's *In the Skin of a Lion.*" *The Journal of Commonwealth Literature* 29, no.2 (1994): 45–60.
Spinks, Lee. *Michael Ondaatje.* Manchester: Manchester University Press, 2009.
Spivak, Gayatri. "Can the Subaltern Speak?" In *Marxism and the Interpretation of Culture,* edited by Cary Nelson and Lawrence Grossberg, 271–314. Champaign: University of Illinois Press, 1988.
– *Critique of Postcolonial Reason: Toward a History of the Vanishing Present.* Cambridge: Harvard University Press, 1999.
– "The Rani of Sirmur: An Essay in Reading the Archives." *History and Theory* 24, no. 3 (1985): 247–72.
– "Righting Wrongs." *South Atlantic Quarterly* 103, nos 2–3 (2004): 523–81.
– "Subaltern Studies: Deconstructing Historiography." In *In Other Worlds: Essays in Cultural Politics,* 197–221. New York: Routledge, 1987.
Staels, Hilde. "A Poetic Encounter with Otherness: The Ethics of Affect in Michael Ondaatje's *Anil's Ghost.*" *University of Toronto Quarterly* 76, no. 3 (2007): 977–89.
Stanton, Katherine. *Cosmopolitan Fictions: Ethics, Politics, and Global Change in the Works of Kazuo Ishiguro, Michael Ondaatje, Jamaica Kincaid, and J. M. Coetzee.* New York: Routledge, 2006.
Stepanova, Maria. *In Memory of Memory: A Romance.* Translated by Sasha Dugdale. Toronto: Book*hug Press, 2021.
Sterba, Christopher M. "'Quién es? Quién es?': Revisiting the Racial Context of the Billy the Kid Legend." *Journal of American Studies* 53, no. 3 (2017): 721–49.
Sternberg, Douglas. "A Firmament in the Midst of Waters: Dimensions of Love in *The English Patient.*" *Literature/Film Quarterly* 24, no. 4 (1998): 255–62.
Stevens, Wallace. *Collected Poetry and Prose.* New York: Penguin, 1997.
Strand, Håvard, Siri Aas Rustad, Håvard Mokleiv Nygård, and Håvard Hegre, "Trends in Armed Conflict, 1946–201." *Prio: Conflict Trends,* 8 (2020): n.p.

440   Bibliography

Strunk, William, and E.B. White. *The Elements of Style*. 3rd ed. New
    York: Macmillan, 1979.
Summers-Bremner, Eluned. "Reading Ondaatje's Poetry." *Comparative
    Literature* 6, no. 3 (2004): 104–14.
Sunder Rajan, Rajeswari. "Death and the Subaltern." In *Can the Subaltern
    Speak? Reflections on the History of an Idea*, edited by Rosalind C.
    Morris, 117–38. New York: Columbia University Press, 2010.
Tambiah, Stanley Jeyaraja. *Sri Lanka: Ethnic Fratricide and the Dismantling
    of Democracy*. Chicago: University of Chicago Press, 1986.
Testa, Bart. "He Did Not Work Here for Long: 'Michael Ondaatje in the
    Cinema." *Essays on Canadian Writing* 53 (Summer 1994): 154–66.
Theodor, Ithamar. *Exploring the Bhagavad Gita: Philosophy Structure
    and Meaning*. Farnham, UK: Ashgate Publishing Group, 2010.
Thomas, Bronwen. "Piecing Together a Mirage: Adapting *The English
    Patient*." In *The Classic Novel from Page to Screen*, edited by Robert
    Giddings and Erica Shen, 197–228. Manchester: Manchester University
    Press, 2000.
– "Post-Apocalyptic War Histories: Michael Ondaatje's *The English
    Patient*." *Ariel* 28, no. 2 (1997): 117–39.
Thompson, Kristin. *Breaking the Glass Armor: Neoformalist Film
    Analysis*. Princeton: Princeton University Press, 1988.
– "The Ordinary Film." In *Breaking the Glass Armor: Neoformalist Film
    Analysis*, 47–9. Princeton: Princeton University Press, 1988.
Todorov, Tzvetan. *The Conquest of America: The Question of the Other*.
    Translated by Richard Howard. Foreword by Anthony Pagden.
    Norman: University of Oklahoma Press, 1999.
Tötösy de Zepetnek, Steven. "Michael Ondaatje's *The English Patient*,
    'History,' and the Other." *Comparative Literature and Culture* 1, no. 4
    (1999): 1–11.
– "Ondaatje's *The English Patient* and Questions of History." In
    Comparative Cultural Studies and Michael Ondaatje's Writing, edited
    by Steven Tötösy de Zepetnek, 115–32. West Lafayette: Purdue
    University Press, 2005.
Trapeze. Directed by Carol Reed. United Artists, 1956.
Truett, Brandon. "Michael Ondaatje, *Warlight*: A Novel" (Review).
    Chicago Review 62, no. 4 (2019): 396–9.
Turner, Brian. "In the Skin of Michael Ondaatje: Giving Voice to Social
    Conscience." *Quill and Quire*, May 1987: 21–2.
UN General Assembly. 1948. *Universal Declaration of Human Rights
    (217 [III] A)*.

Bibliography

Vadde, Aarthi. "National Myth, Transnational Memory: Ondaatje's Archival Method." *NOVEL: A Forum on Fiction* 45, no. 2 (2012): 257–75.

van Manen, Max. "The Call of Pedagogy as the Call of Contact." *Phenomenology and Practice* 5, no. 2 (2012): 8–34.

– *The Tact of Teaching*. Albany: State University of New York Press, 1991.

Verhoeven, W.M. "Playing Hide and Seek in Language: Michael Ondaatje's Historiography of the Self." *American Review of Canadian Studies* 24, no. 1 (1994): 21–38.

Vetter, Lisa Pace. "Liberal Political Inquiries in the Novels of Michael Ondaatje." *Perspectives on Political Science* 34, no. 1 (2005): 27–36.

Volkan, Vamik, and Salman Akhtar. "Immigration, National Identity, and Animals." In *Cultural Zoo: Animals in the Human Mind and Its Sublimation*, edited by Vamik Volkan and Salman Akhtar, 261–71. London: Routledge, 2014.

Wachtel, Eleanor. "An Interview with Michael Ondaatje." *Essays on Canadian Writing* 53 (1994): 250–61.

Walcott, Derek. "The Art of Poetry No. 37." Interview by Edward Hirsch. *The Paris Review* 101 (Winter 1986). www.theparisreview.org.

Watts, Carl. "Ondaatje's Aesthetics of Efficiency: Modernity, Time, and the Body in the Early Ontario Poems." *Canadian Poetry* 70 (Spring/Summer 2012): 77–92.

Webb, Phyllis. "Naked Poems." In *Peacock Blue: The Collected Poems of Phyllis Webb*, edited by John Hulcoop, 147–204. Vancouver: Talonbooks, 2014.

– "Poetics against the Angel of Death." In *Peacock Blue: The Collected Poems of Phyllis Webb*, edited by John Hulcoop, 145. Vancouver: Talonbooks, 2014.

– "Poetics against the Angel of Death." In *The Vision Tree: Selected Poems*, edited with introduction by Sharon Thesen, 60. Vancouver: Talonbooks, 1982.

Weinberger, Eliot. "Introduction." In *The New Directions Anthology of Classical Chinese Poetry*. New Directions, 2003, xvii–xxvii.

Wenzel, Jennifer. "Planet vs. Globe." *English Language Notes: Imaginary Cartographies* 52, no. 1 (1 March 2014): 19–30.

"What Is Brick?" n.d. *Brick*. Accessed 18 April 2022. https://brickmag.com/about.

Williams, Leigh Anne. "Digging up the Past" (Review *Warlight*). *Publisher's Weekly*, 30 April 2018: 30–1.

Woodward, Jenny, "Herbs and Spices." In *Encyclopaedia of Food and Culture*, edited by Solomon H. Katz and William Woys Weaver, 187–95. New York: Charles Scribner's Sons, 2003.

York, Lorraine. *Literary Celebrity in Canada*. Toronto: University of Toronto Press, 2007.

– *The Other Side of Dailiness: Photography in the Works of Alice Munro, Timothy Findley, Michael Ondaatje, and Margaret Laurence*. Toronto: ECW Press, 1988.

– "Prayers for Canadian Daughters: Gender Specificity and the Parental Advice Poem." *Atlantis: Critical Studies in Gender, Culture, and Social Justice* 18, nos 1–2 (1992/93): 60–9.

– *Reluctant Celebrity: Affect and Privilege in Contemporary Stardom*. Cham: Palgrave Macmillan, 2018.

Zacheos, Marilena. "Michael Ondaatje's Sri Lanka in *The Collected Works of Billy the Kid*." *South Asian Review: Sri Lankan Anglophone Literature* 33, no. 3 (2012): 51–69.

Contributors

DI BRANDT's acclaimed poetry titles include *questions i asked my mother, Now You Care,* and *The Sweetest Dance on Earth: New and Selected Poems.* She co-edited, with Barbara Godard, the award-winning critical anthology *Wider Boundaries of Daring: The Modernist Impulse in Women's Poetry.* She teaches Canadian literature at the University of Winnipeg.

MRINALINI CHAKRAVORTY is faculty in the Department of English at the University of Virginia and the author of *In Stereotype: South Asia in the Global Literary Imaginary* (Columbia UP, 2014). She is interested in postcolonial literature and critical theory. She is working on two new books titled *The World Republic of Queer Letters* and *The Novel at the End of the World.*

JOEL DESHAYE is associate professor of Canadian literature at Memorial University. His first book, *The Metaphor of Celebrity* (2013), was substantially on Ondaatje's poetry. He is also the author of *The American Western in Canadian Literature* (2022) and has published widely in national and international journals.

SERENA FUSCO teaches Comparative literature at the University of Naples "L'Orientale." Among her publications: *Incorporations of Chineseness: Hybridity, Bodies, and Chinese American Litera-ture* (2016) and *Confini porosi. Pelle e rappresentazione in quattro narrazioni della modernità* (2018). Her research interests include Chineseness in the transnational space, East/West comparative literature and world literature, Asian American literature, intermediality and photography, and the internationalization of education.

ALLAN HEPBURN is James McGill Professor of Twentieth-Century Literature at McGill University. He has published three monographs and edited seven books, the most recent of which is *Diplomacy and the Modern Novel: France, Britain, and the Mission of Literature*. For Oxford University Press, he co-edits the Mid-Century Studies Series.

JUSTIN M. HEWITSON is associate professor in the Institute of Philosophy of Mind and Cognition at National Yang Ming Chiao Tung University. He researches comparative Indo-Western philosophy/literature. His latest article, "Tantric Metaseity in the *Rig Veda*'s 'Creation Hymn': A Sarkarian Reading and New Translation of X.129," appears in *Concentric: Literary and Cultural Studies*.

PICO IYER is the author of sixteen books translated into twenty-three languages, including *The Lady and the Monk, The Global Soul, The Art of Stillness*, and *A Beginner's Guide to Japan*. His latest is *The Half Known Life: In Search of Paradise*.

ROBERT LECKER is Greenshields Professor of English at McGill University. His books include *Who Was Doris Hedges? The Search for Canada's First Literary Agent*; *Keepers of the Code: English-Canadian Literary Anthologies and the Representation of Nation*; and *Making It Real*. He is the editor of *Canadian Canons: Essays in Literary Value*; *Anthologizing Canadian Literature*; and *Open Country*.

MARTIN LÖSCHNIGG is professor of English and director of the Centre for Canadian Studies at the University of Graz, Austria. His research interests are narratology, autobiography, the literature of war, and Canadian literature. Recent book publications include *The Anglo-Canadian Novel in the Twenty-First Century: Interpretations* (co-edited with Maria Löschnigg, 2019).

JODY MASON is associate professor in the Department of English at Carleton University. Her teaching and research focus

Contributors 445

on literatures and cultures in Canada, settler-colonial studies, print-culture studies, and the sociology of literature.

BIRGIT NEUMANN is chair of Anglophone Literatures and Translation Studies at Heinrich Heine University Düsseldorf. Recent publications include *Verbal-Visual Configurations in Postcolonial Literatures* (2020, with Gabriele Rippl) as well as the edited and co-edited volumes *Anglophone World Literatures* (2017), *Global Literary Histories* (2018), *New Approaches to the Twenty-First-Century Anglophone Novel* (2021), and *Handbook of Anglophone World Literatures* (2021).

IAN RAE is associate professor in the Department of English, French, and Writing at King's University College at Western University. He is the author of *From Cohen to Carson: The Poet's Novel in Canada* (2008), which includes a chapter on Ondaatje, and editor of *George Bowering: Bridges to Elsewhere* (2010).

ULLA RATHEISER is senior scientist for English Literatures and Cultures at the University of Innsbruck. She studied at the Universities of Vienna and Innsbruck and holds a PhD in postcolonial studies. More recently, her research has focused on popular culture, migrant narratives, and the representation of monarchies.

ANTJE M. RAUWERDA is professor of British and postcolonial literatures at Goucher College in Baltimore. Her research focuses on issues of displacement, particularly in relation to third-culture authors. She has a monograph and several articles on the topic, including one considering Ondaatje's *The Cat's Table*.

ELIAS SCHWIELER is associate professor of education at Stockholm University. His most recent publication is *Aporias of Translation: Literature, Philosophy, Education* (2022).

WINFRIED SIEMERLING is University Research Chair and professor of English at the University of Waterloo and an associate of the W.E.B. Du Bois Research Institute at Harvard University. He won the Gabrielle Roy Prize for *The Black Atlantic Reconsidered* (2015; www.blackatlantic.ca; French translation 2022).

446 Contributors

Earlier books include *Canada and Its Americas* (co-edited) and *The New North American Studies* (Routledge, 2005).

KAREN SOLIE's fifth collection of poems, *The Caiplie Caves*, was published in Canada in 2019 and in the US in 2020. She is a lecturer in English and creative writing with the University of St Andrews.

MOEZ SURANI is a writer and artist. He is the author of four poetry collections, including *Operations* (Bookhug, 2016) and *Are the Rivers in Your Poems Real* (Bookhug, 2019). His first novel, *The Legend of Baraffo*, will be published in fall 2023.

BART TESTA is associate professor (teaching) at the Cinema Studies Institute, Innis College, University of Toronto. He has authored two books, *Back and Forth: Early Cinema and the Avant-Garde* (1993) and *Spirit in the Landscape* (1989), and has published journal articles and anthologized essays.

KAI-SU WU is assistant professor in the Department of English at Tamkang University, Taiwan. Dr Wu's recent articles were published by *Concentric: Literary and Cultural Studies*, *Tamkang Review*, and *Review of English and American Literature*. His research interests include critical theory and new literatures in English.

LORRAINE YORK is Distinguished University Professor of English and cultural studies at McMaster University. Her most recent book is *Reluctant Celebrity: Affect and Privilege in Contemporary Stardom* (Palgrave Macmillan), and she is completing a book about reluctance's other – eagerness: *Unseemly: Affect, Gender, New Media, and the Denunciation of Fame Hunger.*

Index

*Note: Abbreviations in parentheses
refer to titles of works.*

Abeysekara, Tissa, 157
Abraham, Nicolas, 341–2, 343, 353n6
acrobat motif, 84–5, 87, 201, 234
affect. *See* emotion
AG. *See Anil's Ghost* (AG)
Agamben, Giorgio, 354n20
Ahmed, Sara, 195–6, 199, 201, 205
"All along the Mazinaw" (S), 87
ambiguity. *See* uncertainty and ambiguity
Ang, Ien, 272
Anil's Ghost (AG): overview, 17–18, 37–8, 167–9, 303–8, 313–15; care and compassion, 342–3, 409, 411n15; civil war, 300, 326–7, 348, 353nn1–2; convergent and divergent plots, 167–9; critical response, 299; disappearances, 165–8, 327, 338–9, 348–50; endings, 301, 308, 312–15, 343–4; human rights projects, 303, 305–8, 340, 347, 353nn3–5, 353n11; metanarrative, 329–31; names, 338–9, 398; narrative fragments, 166, 329–31, 338–40,

342, 408–9; "one victim can speak for many," 306, 340, 347; pedagogical approaches, 408–9, 411n15; prelude, 165, 314–15, 348, 349; publication notes, 187n5; "reason for war was war," 304–6, 316n6, 324, 348; scientific vs imaginative thought, 166, 340, 342–3, 408–9; time shifts, 171, 329; trauma, 37–8, 299–302, 304–6, 313–15, 324, 326–31, 337, 339–43; visuality, 165, 304, 307, 308, 342–3; war's persistence, 324–5, 327, 330–1; writing and editing process, 165–9, 171, 303–4; writing period and style, 35–8, 366–7
—EAST-WEST DIALECTIC: overview, 18, 37, 299–308, 313–15; Buddhist and Tantric influences, 168–9, 299–305, 309, 313–15; detached compassion, 37, 299–302, 304–5, 307–8, 312, 313–15; East-West dialectic, 37, 299–302, 304–5, 311–12, 315; karma (cyclical suffering), 37, 299–302, 305–7, 312–15;

responsibility, 37, 299–302, 304–6, 314–15, 352; trauma, 300, 304–6, 313–15

—LIMINALITY AND GHOSTS: overview, 17–18, 317–31; absence of bodies, 326–7; blurred boundaries of time and life, 317–19, 326; body as story, 327, 329–31; ghostliness and liminality, 17, 317–18, 325–31; mythic underworld, 326–8; trauma, 324, 326–31

—POSTCOLONIAL MELANCHO-LIA: overview, 10, 37–8, 335–54; collective vs. individual memorialization, 10, 37–8, 335, 337, 339–43, 345, 349–52; Freudian psychic crypts, 340–1, 343, 353nn6–8; human rights projects, 38, 336, 338, 340, 343–7, 353n11, 354n14; melancholia, 38, 339–43, 353nn6–7; pietàs, 345–6; postcolonial crypts (deathworlds), 37–8, 326–7, 337, 339–43, 346, 348–52, 353nn6–7; responsibility, 37–8, 314–15, 352; secrets, 342–3, 353nn6–7; stereotypes of civilizational difference, 10, 336–7, 343–52; subalternity, 337, 343–51, 353n3, 354n24; trauma as collective, 37–8, 337, 339–43

animals and creatures: overview, 13, 100, 104, 328; anthropomorphic views, 102–3, 116, 117n12; birds, 32, 102–3, 116, 117n12, 218; close-up images, 54; desert beasts, 274–5; disgust and loathing, 53; domestic familiars, 105, 110–11, 113–17; guides in after-life, 328; human desire to be like other creatures, 102–3, 116; mobility, 263; names, 115–17; as nonhuman otherness, 71, 94–5, 377; paintings and artificiality, 21–2, 25; sexual desire, 100, 104, 107; symbolic role in psyche, 103–5; transformations, 108–10, 112–14, 326, 328; violence as prehuman, 218; writing period and style, 45–6, 48. *See also* dogs

Anubis (Egyptian god), 326, 328

Appiah, Kwame, 348, 354n18

Asad, Talal, 350

Ashcroft, Bill, 125

Atwood, Margaret, 54

autobiography. See *Running in the Family* (RF)

Avison, Margaret, 80

Bachner, Sally, 226n10

Badlands (Kroetsch), 156, 160–1, 173n24, 175, 186n1

Baetens, Jan, 194

Bakhtin, Mikhail, 257

Bal, Mieke, 194, 202

bamboo motif, 65, 89, 145–9, 371

Bandi, Raghu Ram, 186

Banerjee, Mita, 286

Barbour, Douglas, 6, 100, 131, 135–6, 149, 186n1, 329

Barnwell, Ashley, 197

Barry, Michael, 307

Bauman, Zygmunt, 297

"Bearhug" (TTK, CP), 39, 60–1

Beddoes, Julie, 266

Benjamin, Walter, 31, 249, 324, 328, 396

Berger, John, 77, 83, 89, 94, 96–7

Index

Bevington, Stan, 6
Bhabha, Homi, 239
Bhagavad Gita, 302
Bible: cinnamon as spice, 120–1;
Garden of Eden, 119–20, 128n9;
"Song of Solomon," 125–7
Binoche, Juliette, 188n8
"Biography" (*TTK*), 110
"Birch Bark" (*S, CP*), 302
birds. *See* animals and creatures
"Birds for Janet – The Heron"
(*DM*), 83, 102–3
"Birth of Sound" (*TTK, CP*), 105–6
Bishop, Elizabeth, 159, 172n14
Bishop's University, 6, 20
Biskind, Peter, 178–9
Blanchot, Maurice, 283, 329
Blaser, Robin, 141
Bök, Christian, 47, 386
Booker Prize, 7, 34, 174
Bowering, George, 159
Bowers, M.A., 308–9
Boyd, William, 236–7
Brand, Dionne, 90
Brandt, Di, 8, 10, 13, 14, 19, 24,
25, 29–30, 45–76
Braziel, Jana Evans, 272
"Breaking Green" (*TTK*), 57–8, 59
Breitbach, Julia, 225
Brick (journal), 19, 133, 157,
394n16
Brick Reader, The, 157
Bringing Tony Home (Abeysekara),
157
Brittan, Alice, 282, 329–30
*Broken Ark, The (A Book of
Beasts)*, 157–8
Brown, Elspeth H., 195
Bruno, Giuliana, 222
Brushes with Greatness, 158

Bryson, Norman, 242
Buddhist and Tantric influences:
overview, 37, 73, 300–2, 304–6,
313–15; being and non-being,
146–7; communal life, 73; compassion, 37, 299–302, 313–15;
consciousness and mindfulness,
301–2, 314–15; detachment, 37,
301–2, 304–5, 309, 311–15;
dialectic of perspectives, 301–6,
315; enlightenment, 96; iconography and statues, 89–90, 168–
9, 309, 313–15; individual's
responsibility, 304–5, 314–15,
352; karma (cyclical suffering),
37, 299–302, 305–7, 312–15;
meditation gardens, 145–6; myth
of king and corpse, 352; paradise, 120; paradox of retreat,
305; writing period and style, 48
Burcar, Lilijana, 124, 129n35
Burgin, Victor, 195
"Buried" (*HW*), 90–1
"Buried 2" (*HW*), 73–4, 91, 304
"Burning Hills" (*TTK, CP*), 21, 29,
32, 58–9, 80
Bush, Catherine, 160
Butler, Judith, 234–5, 354n27
"Buying the Dog" (*TTK*), 110–11

Canadian Centre for Film, 160,
175
Caravaggio (character across
novels), 219, 220–1, 274
Caravaggio, Michelangelo Merisi
da, 220, 235, 287–9
Carbajal, Alberto Fernández, 282,
290
care and compassion: overview,
377–8; democratization of care,

375, 377–8; detached compassion, 37, 309–15; East-West dialectic, 37, 299–302, 313–15; insufficient caring as crime, 371; intimacy, 36, 367–70, 375–8; limits of identification, 236; pedagogical experiences, 409, 411n15; sentimental values, 375–8. *See also* emotion

Carry on Crime and Punishment (film, Ondaatje), 174, 175

Carson, Anne, 78, 88, 345

Casablanca (film), 139–40, 141, 146–7

Casper, Monica J., 315

Cat's Table, The (CT): overview, 16, 169–71, 228–43, 370–8; *Bildungsroman*, 231–2, 321, 370–2; blurred boundaries, 228–9, 232–3, 235, 237, 243; care and compassion, 371–2; characters as orphans or without family, 36, 371; characters as unknowable, 235–6, 372–3, 376; colonialism, 16, 170, 229–31, 237–40; convergent and divergent plots, 167, 169–71; crimes and misdemeanors, 231, 371–3, 397–8; enchantment response, 367, 370–1, 378; epigraph, 233; intertextuality, 169–70; intimacy, 375–8; marginality and potentials, 233–4; multiple genres, 231–2, 243, 370–1; names, 169, 397–8; power relations, 233–5, 238–40, 375–6; secrets and mysteries, 169–70, 233–4, 235, 370, 375–6; sentimental values, 375–8; storytelling's creative potential, 169–71,

232, 370–1; time shifts, 169–71, 232, 236, 238, 370, 373; trauma, 371–3; writing and editing process, 169–71, 372–3; writing period and style, 35–6, 38, 366–7, 375–8

—INTERMEDIALITY: overview, 16, 228–44; aisthēsis (redirected seeing), 228–30; blurred boundaries, 228–9, 232–3, 235, 237, 242–3; colonialism, 16, 229–31, 237–40; ekphrasis, 232, 238–42; ex-centric modes of seeing, 16, 229–30, 232–7; film (*Four Feathers*), 238–40; frames, 234–5, 241; intermediality, 211–12, 228–30, 232; multiple perspectives, 242–3; orientalism, 237–40; photography, 236–7; poetics of passage, 231–2; position and perspective, 233–4; postcolonial re-visions, 229–30, 237–40; socio-political power of seeing, 229–34; visibility/invisibility, 234–5, 240

celebrity: overview, 22–5; authenticity and the real, 22; L. Cohen as celebrity, 22–5, 28; in detective fiction, 379–80, 382; fame/privacy dichotomy, 226n10; Ondaatje as celebrity, 9, 22–5, 27–9, 34, 72, 382–3; privacy as safety, 381–5, 388–9, 392; public artists, 28; reluctant celebrities, 27–8, 36, 382–3; self-destructiveness, 27–9; troubled relationship with public, 27–8, 382–3; writing period and style, 22–5

Ceylon, as term, 121. *See also* Sri Lanka

Index

Chakravorty, Mrinalini, 10, 18, 37–8, 335–54
Chambers, Iain, 119
characters: overview, 18–19; antagonists and protagonists, 375; authorial detachment, 372–3, 378; chance, 167, 407–10; characters across novels, 219, 220–1, 292; coming-of-age stories, 231–2, 321, 367, 370–2, 374–5; convergent and divergent plots, 166–71; creative process as struggle, 18–21; disappearances, 167–9; enchantment response, 367, 370–1, 378; heterotopic worlds, 398–9; occupations, 11, 218–19, 362, 383; orphans or without family, 36, 39–41, 367–8, 371; otherness, 398–9; outlaws, 34, 366, 371, 375; politicized characters, 36, 268–72, 274, 288–9, 366, 375, 377; self-doubt, 21–2; as unknowable, 235–6, 372–3, 376; verisimilitude, 372–3, 377–8; writing and editing process, 155–6; writing period and style, 35–6, 38, 366–7, 375–8. *See also* names; story and plot
Chez, Keridiana, 101
Chien-Hsing Ho, 96
children and parents: overview, 60–2; child's independence, 55, 87; convergent and divergent plots, 167–8; elegy for Ondaatje's mother, 61; forgiveness for parents, 56, 60; love for children, 39–40, 60–2; orphans or without family, 36, 39–41, 367–8, 371; pyramid motif,

84–5, 198–200, 201, 205; violence against children, 115–17
cinnamon, 120–3, 128n16, 129n21
Cinnamon Peeler: Selected Poems, The (CP): publication notes, 25, 34
—POEMS: "Birth of Sound," 105–6; "Burning Hills," 21, 29, 32, 58–9, 80; "Diverse Causes, The," 81–2; "Elimination Dance (an intermission)," 187n3; "Goodnight, The," 82; "Heron Rex," 28, 32, 83; "King Kong Meets Wallace Stevens," 26, 80; "Late Movies with Skyler," 83, 105; "Letters & Other Worlds," 5, 39, 56, 82–3, 85, 132; "Light," 39, 61–2, 104; "Loop," 104–5, 263; "Philoctetes on the Island," 82, 86; "Uswetakeiyawa," 109–10, 112–13. See also *Secular Love (S)*; *There's a Trick with a Knife I'm Learning to Do (TTK)*
"Cinnamon Peeler, The" (CP): overview, 11, 14, 70, 118–29; biblical analogies, 125–7; colonial criticism, 14, 121, 125, 127–8; conquest of female body, 14, 70–1, 118, 121–8, 129n31; female body as paradisiacal dreamland, 14, 118–28; male gaze, 124–5; power relations, 11, 14; publication notes, 14, 70; return to paradise, 11, 126; Sri Lankan culture, 70, 118, 120–4, 127–8, 128n16; transformation of lovers, 70–1, 122–3, 129n31; woman's consent, 70–1, 124–5, 127–8, 129n31

"Cinnamon Roots" (Seni Seneviratne), 120, 128n16
"Claude Glass" (*S*, CP), 31, 39, 63–4, 85–6, 94, 106–7, 113, 205–6
Clinton Special, The (film, Ondaatje), 156, 163, 174, 176–7
Coach House Press, 6, 157, 159
Cohen, Leonard, 21, 22–5, 28, 132, 261n1
Cohen, Richard, 289
Cole, Teju, 79, 84–5, 88, 93, 97
Coleman, Victor, 6
Collected Works of Billy the Kid, The (CW): overview, 23–5, 40, 49–52, 248–51; awards, 49; Billy as real person, 24, 51, 250–1, 261n4; celebrity, 24–5, 248–9, 381, 382; comic scenes, 49–52; creatures, 50–2, 100, 103, 106–8; critical commentary, 40, 51–2, 191–2 desire for perfection, 24, 40, 248–9; film influences, 186n1; historiographic metafiction, 5, 11–12, 51, 248–51, 261n4; intermediality, 228, 247–8; as long poem, 24, 49, 247, 355; madness, 24, 49–52, 56, 79–80, 103; metafiction, 24; names, 51; narrator/author/Billy relations, 24, 51–2, 247–8; photography, 9, 24, 165, 191–3, 247–51; postmodern aesthetics, 24, 49–50, 97, 193, 247–51, 261n1; publication and adaptation notes, 23–4, 160, 247, 250, 261n1; self-referentiality, 16, 23–4, 35–6, 49–52, 247–8, 366; title, 24, 250; violence, 24–5, 49–51, 66, 79–80, 193, 248–9;

visuality, 49–50, 228; women, 61; writing and editing process, 80, 160, 165; writing and happiness, 40; writing period and style, 23–5, 34, 35–6, 48, 66, 97, 366–7, 375
colonialism: colonial frolic, 354n25; female body as colonized paradise, 14, 124–8, 129n35; "I" and colonized space, 125, 127; intermediality, 228–32; orientalism, 237–40; spectre in civil wars, 326. *See also* postcolonial writing
Coming Through Slaughter (CS): overview, 11–12, 30–3, 64–7, 211–17, 247–61; Bellocq's life, 214–17, 253–4; Bolden's life, 30–1, 64, 212–18, 226n10, 249–52, 262n23; celebrity, 30, 32, 214–15, 226n10, 255, 382, 389; critical commentary, 213; desire for perfection, 30–3, 216–17, 260–1; disappearances, 214; endings, 64, 67, 256–61, 364; fascination as force, 249–51, 261; historiographic metafiction, 5, 11–12, 220, 226n10; intermediality, 211–17, 221; madness, 30–3, 64, 66–7, 215–16, 251–3, 256–7; maps, 257, 395n37; mirror/window/glass motifs, 31, 215–17, 226, 252–5, 260; music and sound, 212–16, 252; narrator/Bolden relationship, 30–2, 64–5, 66–7, 214–17, 226n10, 247, 250–6, 259–61, 262n23; photography, 31, 211–17, 220–1, 247, 254–6; photo of Bolden's band, 31, 192,

214, 220, 249–51, 253–6;
postmodern aesthetics, 192–3;
publication and adaptation notes,
175, 186n1, 247, 261n1, 262n23;
self-referentiality, 10, 30–3, 35–6,
64–5, 214–17, 251–3, 259–61;
story as incomplete, 259–61;
Storyville as place, 214, 217, 251,
253, 395n37; Webb's metafictional search, 214, 254–5, 258–9;
writing and happiness, 30–3;
writing period and style, 25, 30,
35–6, 366–7, 375
compassion. *See* care and
compassion
"Concessions, The" (*S, CP*), 39,
69–71
Confucian philosophy, 88–9, 144,
147–8
Connor, Steven, 241–2
Conrad, Joseph, 232–3, 348
convergent and divergent plots,
166–71. *See also* story and plot;
writing and editing
*Conversations: Walter Murch and
the Art of Editing Film, The* (*TC*):
overview, 12, 15, 156, 162, 178,
187n5, 202–4, 364; atomic
bomb excision in *EP* film,
184–6, 190nn26–7; convergent
and divergent plots, 166–71;
Eastern and Western culture,
203–5; edges of sound, 172n13;
editing the "whole jigsaw," 169;
emotional motion, 202; endings,
163; novels suitable for adaptation, 202–3; publication notes,
178, 187n5. *See also* Murch,
Walter; writing and editing,
connections to filmmaking

Cook, Victoria, 300
Coomaraswamy, Ananda K., 300
"Country Night" (*TTK*), 110–11
CP. See *Cinnamon Peeler: Selected
Poems, The* (*CP*)
creative process. *See* film and film-
making; writing and editing
creatures. *See* animals and
creatures
Creeley, Robert, 84
Cresswell, Tim, 263–4, 266, 272,
277
Critchley, Simon, 296–7
CS. See *Coming Through Slaughter*
(*CS*)
CT. See *Cat's Table, The* (*CT*)
Cummins, Joseph, 197
curiosity and wonder, 77–8, 86–8,
91–2, 160, 360
CW. See *Collected Works of Billy
the Kid, The* (*CW*)
Czíkszentmihályi, Mihàly, 196

D. See *Divisadero* (*D*)
Dafoe, Willem, 187n4, 188n8
Dainty Monsters, The (*DM*):
overview, 25, 159; creatures,
100, 102–3; domestic uncertain-
ties, 80–2; writing period and
style, 25, 52–3
—POEMS: "Birds for Janet – The
Heron," 83, 102–3; "Diverse
Causes, The," 81–2;
"Martinique, The," 25; "Respect
of Landscapes, The," 25
Dämmrich, Ingrid, 123, 125
Dante's *Divine Comedy*, 62–3, 65
Dardenne, Luc, 235
Daughters of Captain Cook
(Spalding), 133

Davenport, Guy, 78
Davey, Frank, 6, 268–9, 270
David with the Head of Goliath
(painting, Caravaggio), 287–9
Davis, Miles, 88
"Death at Kataragama" (HW), 94
Deleuze, Gilles: *Proust and Signs*,
399–402, 405–9; pure thinking,
403; signs, 401–2, 405–9;
texturology, 222
Deleuze, Gilles, and Felix Guattari:
overview, 273–7; non-hierarchical epistemology, 276–7; rhizomatic groups, 267, 273–6, 279n10,
280n27, 281n36; smooth space
(*espace lisse*), 264, 273–6,
280n28, 280n31, 280n34; state
control of nomads, 266, 272,
273; war machine, 273–4,
280n32, 280nn27–8
Derrida, Jacques: art and aesthetics, 12, 84, 87, 94, 283; friends
and enemies, 288–90; hauntology, 239; time and death of
other, 284–6, 290–1, 297;
Western gaze and control, 230.
See also *English Patient, The*
(EP), Derrida and Levinas in
dialogic field
desert: cave as pre-historical, 283–
4, 293–4, 296, 328; nomads,
263, 274–6, 280n30; place without nations and maps, 290, 294,
296, 320–1, 397
Deshaye, Joel, 18, 39, 379–95
detective mysteries, 379–82, 384–6,
391–2
de Zepetnek, Steven Tötösy, 6, 282
diasporic writing: overview, 11,
119; access and expulsion, 119–

20, 127, 128n9; food,
119–20, 122–3, 128n16; melancholic migrant, 196; memory,
120, 122, 197–9; photography,
196–9; place, 395n40; return to
paradise, 11, 119–24, 127–8,
128n16; symbols of return, 119;
tropes of travel, 11, 272. *See also*
postcolonial writing
"Diverse Causes, The" (DM), 81–2
Divisadero (*D*): overview, 224–6,
367–70; awards, 7; characters,
36, 220–1, 362, 367–8; disappearances, 167; enchantment,
367, 370–1, 378; endings, 162,
163–4; illusion of effortlessness,
171–2; intermediality, 211–12,
224–6; intertextuality, 173n33;
intimacy, 36, 367–70, 375–8;
metanarratives, 155–6, 162, 171,
225, 356; mirror/glass motifs,
225, 226; music and sound,
225–6; names, 164, 367;
orphans or without family, 36,
367–8; photography, 224–5;
prelude, 164; repetition of
images, 160, 224–5; scale and
story, 225, 367; secrets and
mysteries, 367–70; segments and
sections, 163–4, 224, 225–6;
sentimental values, 375–8; story
as incomplete, 162, 368–9; time
shifts, 170–1; trauma, 367–9;
verisimilitude, 372–3, 377–8;
writing and editing process, 160,
162, 163–4, 173n33; writing
period and style, 36, 38, 366–7,
375–8
DM. See *Dainty Monsters, The* (DM)
"Dog in San Francisco, A" (*S*), 87

Index

dogs: overview, 13, 100, 104, 328; anthropomorphic limits, 116, 117n12; domestic and untamed, 13, 100–5, 114–17; domestic familiars, 105, 110–11, 113–17; dreams, 110–15; historical dogs, 328; human desire to be like other creatures, 102–3, 116; human longing to escape, 101–2, 110; mad dogs, 108–9, 115–17; mongrel hybridity, 13, 100, 102, 109–10; mythic dogs, 105, 108–10, 112–15, 326, 328; names, 115–17; paradoxical insiders-outsiders, 100, 101–2, 114–15; purebreds and inbreds, 107–8; sexual desire, 100, 104, 107; symbolic role in psyche, 103–5; transformations, 108–10, 112–14, 326, 328; as transient and permanent, 104; as unknowable, 377; writing period and style, 45–6. *See also* animals and creatures
Donne, John, 118, 127
Döring, Tobias, 231
Doyle, Arthur Conan, 379–80, 385, 391
"Do you want to be happy and write?" *See* writing and happiness (Do you want to be happy and write?)
Dragland, Stan, 384, 394n16, 394n23
Dudziak, Mary L., 322–3
Duino Elegies. See *Tin Roof* (S), and Rilke

"Early Morning, Kingston to Gananoque" (TTK), 61

Eastern religions. *See* Buddhist and Tantric influences
Edel, Leon, 364
editing. *See* writing and editing
education. *See* pedagogy; *Warlight* (WL), pedagogical approaches
ekphrasis, 197–8, 200, 224–5, 232, 238–42
Elimination Dance (ED), 97
"Elimination Dance (an intermission)" (CP), 187n3
Elkins, James, 232
emotion: affect, 195–6, 199, 205; affective mapping theory, 131, 136, 138–40; agency of perspective, 236; communal life, 194; critical commentary on poetry, 74; curiosity and wonder, 77–8, 86–8, 91–2, 160, 360; fear, 26, 82–3, 87, 344–5; flow theory, 196; gendered emotion, 68; Indian love poetry (9 sentiments), 73, 92–3; melancholic migrant, 196; pedagogical approaches, 408–9, 411n15; sentimental values, 38–9, 375–8; spiritual power from poetry, 74; truth in feelings, 376–7. See also *Anil's Ghost* (AG), postcolonial melancholia; care and compassion; sentimental fiction
English Patient, The (EP): overview, 16, 174, 221–4, 308–12; ambiguity in identity, 180–1, 286, 397; atomic bomb, 158, 184–6, 190nn26–7, 221–3, 287, 323, 365; Booker Prize, 7, 34, 174; characters across novels, 220–1, 292; convergent and divergent plots, 166–7, 169;

critical commentary, 180, 181–2, 280n30, 282–3, 299; desert cave as pre-historical, 283–4, 293–4, 296, 328; desert nomad, 263, 274–6, 280n30, 294; endings, 185, 224, 287, 365; gardens, 309–10, 319–20; ghosts, 291–2, 325–6, 328–31; Herodotus's *Histories*, 40, 282, 293–4, 321, 330, 399; historiographic metafiction, 5, 11–12, 190n21, 221–2, 362; intermediality, 16, 211–12, 221–4, 287, 289, 320; intimate epic, 158; light and dark (Caravaggism), 200–2, 221, 287, 289; maps motif, 289, 294, 311, 365; metanarratives, 329–31; mirror motif, 286–7, 292; movement and stillness, 163, 200–2, 274; names, 143–4, 397; narrative fragments, 329–31; narrative style, 180–2, 189n16, 329–31; pedagogical approaches, 396, 399–400, 402–3, 410n1; politicized characters, 36–7, 288–90, 366, 377; postcolonial writing, 184–6, 280n30; sections and chapters, 163; story and plot, 179–81; time shifts, 181–3, 189n16, 283–7, 290–2, 324; title, 285; war and violence, 284–5, 289–90, 292–3; war's persistence, 317–18, 322–5, 330–1; wordplay (hana), 143–4; wounds and scars, 223–4, 330; writing and editing process, 158, 163, 204, 319; writing period and style, 9, 35–7, 366–7
—DERRIDA AND LEVINAS IN DIALOGIC FIELD: overview, 12,

17, 36–7, 282–98; alterity, 17, 283, 286–9, 295–7; burial rituals, 291, 293–4; care and love, 285–6, 291–2; desert as place without nations, 290, 294, 296; the face, 12, 17, 285–90; friends and enemies, 288–90; mourning, 283–6, 290–7; nationalism and war, 288–90; otherness, 17, 36–7, 282–5, 286–7, 290; patience, 283–6, 291–3; politicized characters, 36–7, 288–90; responsibility, 284–5; time shifts and death, 283–7, 290–2, 324; war and violence, 284–5, 289–90, 292–3; Western humanism, 282, 284, 290, 296. *See also* Derrida, Jacques; Levinas, Emmanuel
—EAST-WEST DIALECTIC: overview, 17, 37, 299–303, 308–12, 315; detached compassion, 37, 309–13, 315; East-West dialectic, 17, 37, 299–301, 308–15; gardens and statues, 309–10; karma (cyclical suffering), 37, 305, 311–12, 315; Kipling's *Kim*, 300, 312; responsibility, 37, 304–5, 313–15; Sikh spirituality, 301, 311; Tantric influences, 299–302, 312, 315; trauma, 37, 308–11. *See also* Buddhist and Tantric influences
—GHOSTS AND LIMINALITY: overview, 17–18, 317–31; ghosts and liminal motifs, 17, 317–18, 325–6, 328, 330–1; life/death and blurred boundaries, 317–20, 328; metanarratives, 329–31; time and death, 317–19, 324,

328, 330; trauma, 317–18, 325, 329–31; war's persistence, 317–18, 322–5, 330–1

English Patient, The (film, Minghella): overview, 12, 15–16, 174, 177–86; adaptation of novel, 16, 178, 180–6, 189n16, 189n20, 190n21, 204; ambiguity in identity, 180–1, 189n16; atomic bomb excision, 184–6, 190nn26–7; awards, 178; cast, 178, 188n8; classical film form, 16, 179–83, 189n13, 189n16; commentary on dvd, 189n17; convergent and divergent plots, 166–7, 169; critical commentary, 178–9, 182–6, 187n2, 188n12, 190nn26–7; financing, 178–9, 188nn8–11; Minghella as writer and director, 177–9, 188n7, 190n22; Murch as editor, 166, 187n5; Ondaatje's involvement, 12, 15–16, 178, 183–5, 187nn4–5; postcolonial politics, 184–6; production difficulties, 178–9, 188nn8–11; publication of *Conversations*, 178, 187n5; romance film, 179, 181–6, 188n7, 190n22; sounds, 364; story and plot, 179–83, 189n13; time shifts, 181–3, 189n16; Zaentz as producer, 178–9, 188n8, 188n10. *See also* Minghella, Anthony; Murch, Walter

Epic of Gilgamesh, The, 34–5, 264, 269, 275

"Escarpment" (*S*), 112

face: Benjamin's aura in photography, 31, 249, 254–5;

decontextualization of female body, 125; entity without identity, 286; facelessness in colonized body, 125; invocation of responsibility, 286; Levinas's concept, 12, 17, 286; migrant facelessness, 33–4

fame. *See* celebrity

family. *See* children and parents

Farm Show, The (play), 176–7

fathers. *See* children and parents

Favourite Game, The (L. Cohen), 23

fear, 26, 82–3, 87, 344–5. *See also* emotion

females. *See* women

Fernando, Kathleen, 304–5

fiction. *See* novels

Fiennes, Ralph, 188n8

film and filmmaking: overview, 15–16, 179–83; adaptations as new creations, 183, 202–3; classical film form, 16, 179–80, 189n13; documentaries, 177; emotional motion, 202; international film culture, 15, 204–5; narration, 16, 181–2; postcolonial themes, 184–6; realism, 175, 179–80; romance films, 179, 188n7; sound editing, 364; story and plot, 15–16, 160–6, 179–83, 189n13. See also *Conversations: Walter Murch and the Art of Editing Film, The* (TC); *English Patient, The* (film, Minghella); Murch, Walter; writing and editing, connections to filmmaking

—CONNECTIONS TO WRITING AND EDITING: overview, 15–16, 156, 160–6, 204; assembly of

458 Index

whole story, 15–16, 156, 160–2, 166, 169, 204; convergent and divergent plots, 166–71; editing story into existence, 166, 168, 169, 172n13; elliptical scenes, 162, 170; endings, 162–4, 180; motion and stillness, 15, 161–3, 202, 204; preludes, 164–5; repetition, 160–1; scale, 158, 162; sound, 172n13; structure, 156, 160–6, 170–1; time shifts, 170–1, 181–2, 189n16; univocal and multivocal narration, 16, 180–2, 189n16; visuality, 15–16, 162–5; writing process, 158, 160–1, 165–6

film and filmmaking, Ondaatje's: overview, 12, 15–16, 156, 175–7; international film culture, 15–16, 203–5; involvement in *The English Patient*, 12, 15–16, 178, 183–5, 187nn4–5. See also *Conversations: Walter Murch and the Art of Editing Film, The* (TC)

—WORKS: *Badlands* script, 156, 160–1, 173n24, 175; *Carry on Crime and Punishment*, 174, 175; *Clinton Special, The*, 156, 163, 174, 176–7; "Final Days / Father Tongue" (RF), 51; *Love Clinic* script, 175; *Sons of Captain Poetry*, 156, 174, 175–6

Flatley, Jonathan, 131, 136–7, 139

"Flight" (HW), 93

"Flirt and Wallace" (RJ), 115–17

Foucault, Michel: biopower, 354n20; heterotopia, 396, 398–404, 407, 409–10, 410nn1–2

"Four Eyes" (TTK), 106

Four Feathers, The (film and novel), 238–40

Fraser, Russell, 144

Fresco, Robert, 177

Freudian psychic crypts, 341, 343, 353nn6–8

From Ink Lake, 158

Fusco, Serena, 16, 30, 194, 211–27

Gamlin, Gordon, 34–5

Garcia Marquez, Gabriel, 96, 171, 173n36

"Garcia Marquez and the Bus to Aracataca" (Ondaatje), 96, 173n36

gardens: biblical texts, 119–20, 124–7, 319–20; Garden of Eden, 119, 124, 127, 319–20; meditation gardens, 145–6; as paradise, 119–20, 124–7

"'gate in his head, the'" (TTK, CP), 6, 9, 23, 31, 62, 79, 194

"Gentleman Compares His Virtue to a Piece of Jade, A" (HW), 88–9

George, Rosemary Marangoly, 119

ghosts. See *Anil's Ghost* (AG), liminality and ghosts; *English Patient, The* (EP), ghosts and liminality; *Warlight* (WL), ghosts and liminality

Gilgamesh myth, 34–5, 264, 269, 275

Glissant, Édouard, 235

Godfather, The (film), 166

Golden Man Booker Prize, 7

Goldman, Marlene, 324

"Goodnight, The" (TTK, CP), 82

"Great Tree, The" (HW), 95

grief. See *Anil's Ghost* (AG), postcolonial melancholia

Griffiths, Gareth, 125
Guattari, Félix. *See* Deleuze, Gilles, and Felix Guattari

haiku, 144–5, 149
"hana" wordplay and translations, 143–4
Hand, Seán, 283
Handke, Peter, 63, 78
Handwriting (HW): overview, 72–5, 87–98; communal life, 73–5; creatures, 94–5; desire in love poetry, 92, 96; enlightenment, 96–7; handwriting, Ondaatje's mother's, 97; history in practices, 90–2; love for R. Perera (childhood amah), 73, 75, 93–4; nine concerns in Confucian philosophy, 88–9; nine sentiments in Indian love poetry, 73, 92–3; publication notes, 34, 72; silences in, 89–90; Sri Lankan culture, 72–5, 88–98; story as incomplete, 88–9, 95–8; transformation images, 89–90; violence and war, 74, 89–90; writing period and style, 48, 72–3, 97
—POEMS: "To Anuradhapura," 87; "Buried," 90–1; "Buried 2," 73–4, 91, 304; "Death at Kataragama," 94; "Flight," 93; "Gentleman Compares His Virtue to a Piece of Jade, A," 88–9; "Great Tree, The," 95; "House on a Red Cliff," 74–5; "Last Ink," 96–7; "Nine Sentiments, The," 73, 92–3; "Step," 95–6; "Wells," 73, 75, 93–4

happiness and writing. *See* writing and happiness (Do you want to be happy and write?)
haptic aesthetics, 222–3, 241–2
Hass, Robert, 92, 93
Hawaii, 3, 132, 133, 137, 143, 145
Heighton, Steven, 33, 194
Heinze, Eric A., 303
"Henri Rousseau and Friends," 21–2
Hepburn, Allan, 15, 17, 155–73, 393n4
"Her House" (S), 86–7
Hermes figure, 321, 328
Herodotus's *Histories*, 40, 282, 293–4, 321, 330, 399
"Heron Rex" (TTK, CP), 28, 32, 83
Herrick, Margaret, 327
Hewitson, Justin M., 12, 17, 37, 299–316
Highway, Tomson, 61
Hilger, Annick, 6, 302
Hinduism, 300. *See also* Buddhist and Tantric influences
Hine, Lewis, 220, 221
H in the Heart, An, 158
Hiroshima, 303
Hirsch, Susan, 306
historiographic metafiction: overview, 5, 11–12, 212, 248; fascination as force, 248; historical intertexts, 5, 11–12, 248; irony, 265; liminality as force, 248; music, 248; narrative realism, 264; photography, 248, 254–6; rewriting of marginal experience, 264–5; self-referentiality, 5, 248
history: overview, 212; characters' occupations, 11; dimension of

intermediality, 16; history as one of multiple narratives, 212; maps as clues, 389–90; story and history, 402; writing period and style, 45–9

Hobkirk, Lori, 117n12

Hochbruck, Wolfgang, 192

Hogarth, William, on dogs, 101

Holmes, Sherlock, 379–80, 385

Horta, Paulo, 280n30

"House on a Red Cliff" (*HW*), 74–5

Howe, Fanny, 85

Hsu, Shou-Nan, 148, 304

human rights: distrust in international justice, 303, 306–8, 315, 353n4; international projects, 303, 305–8, 353nn3–5, 353n11, 354n14; "one victim can speak for many," 306, 340, 347; victims' needs, 306

Hume, David, 91

Hutcheon, Linda, 5, 184–6, 192, 248, 264, 268

HW. See *Handwriting* (*HW*)

Imagism, 57, 59, 144–5

Inan, Ilhan, 77–8, 87–8

Incognito (Young), 159

Indian traditions. *See* Buddhist and Tantric influences

"Inner Tube" (*S*), 111–12

"Insomnia" (*S*), 110

intermediality: overview, 16, 211–26, 228–30; agency of media, 221; aisthēsis (redirected seeing), 228–30; blurred boundaries, 16, 228–9, 232–3, 235, 237; border blurring of genres, 159; Butler's frames, 234–5; colonialism, 229–30; creases as

media overlap, 211, 221, 224; Deleuze's hieroglyphics, 408–9, 411n12; ex-centric modes of seeing, 16, 229–30, 232–7; forms of, 232; haptic aesthetics, 222, 241–2; historical dimension, 16, 212; illusion of other medium, 211; intermedial continuum/cycle, 225–6; multimedia works, 212; postcolonial re-visions, 229–30, 237–40; remediation and writing, 211, 217, 218, 221, 226n1; sociopolitical power of seeing, 229–30; tactile sensibility, 222–3; theatre as synesthetic, 218, 221; theory, 211–12, 228–30; visuality in, 218, 229–30, 232; Western gaze, 230; writing and editing processes, 159. See also *Cat's Table, The* (*CT*), intermediality; music and sound; paintings and drawings; photography

intertextuality and historiographic metafiction, 5, 11–12, 282. *See also* historiographic metafiction

In the Skin of a Lion (*SL*): overview, 17, 25, 33–6, 218–21; agency, 218, 221, 268; animal skins, 219, 221, 269, 270, 275; characters across novels, 220–1; colour palette, 218–20, 274; convergent and divergent plots, 167–8, 189n18; disappearances, 34, 167–8; endings, 164; epigraph, 97, 275; historical detail, 34–5, 190n21, 265, 269, 271–2, 278n3; historiographic metafiction, 5, 11–12, 264–5; identity, 35, 263, 278; intermediality,

211–12, 218–21; light and dark (Caravaggism), 202, 218–20, 267–8; migrant experience, 33–4, 264–7; movement and subjectivity, 202; movement vs location, 266–8; mythic base (Gilgamesh), 34–5, 264, 269, 275; names, 143–4; politicized characters, 36, 219, 268–72, 274, 371, 377; postmodern aesthetics, 35, 264–6, 272–3, 276; prelude, 164; publication and adaptation notes, 25, 186n1; repetition, 266–7; time shifts, 170–1, 364; title, 34–5, 264; visibility/invisibility, 33–4, 265, 271, 274, 276; visuality, 162–3, 202, 218–21, 274, 364; women as immobile, 35, 202, 277–8; writing and editing process, 162–4, 167–8; writing and happiness, 34; writing period and style, 9, 33–6, 366–7

—NOMADS: overview, 11, 17, 273–8; desert nomad, 274–8, 280n30; fixed vs. fluid identity, 263; migrant as outside officialdom, 264, 265–6; movement vs location, 266, 277; nomadic metaphysics, 35, 263–4, 266–7, 273, 276; obscuring of material history, 11, 35, 264, 266–72, 276–8; postmodern aesthetics, 266, 272–3, 276; power to restrict mobility, 264, 265–6, 272; rhizomatic groups, 267, 273, 276, 279n10, 280n27, 281n36; smooth space (*espace lisse*), 264, 273–5, 280n28, 280n31, 280n34; war machine

(machine de guerre), 273–4, 280n32, 280nn27–8
Irvine, Dean, 157
Iyer, Pico, 7, 11, 12, 15, 18, 355–65

Jaggi, Maya, 160
Jameson, Fredric, 266, 268
Jewinski, Ed, 6, 30
Jungle Book, The (Kipling), 237, 238

Kamboureli, Smaro, 6, 157, 268, 269–70, 271
Kaplan, Caren, 272, 276–7
Kenaan, Hagi, 230
Kim (Kipling), 300, 312
Kim, Lee-Von, 386
"King Kong Meets Wallace Stevens" (*TTK*, *CP*), 26, 80
Kipling, Rudyard, 7, 237–8, 300, 312
Klee, Paul, *Angelus Novus*, 324, 328
Kranz, David L., 179, 187n2, 188n12, 189n16
Kristeva, Julia, 79, 257
Kroetsch, Robert, 156, 160–1, 173n24, 175
Kurnick, David, 393n15

Lacroix, Jean-Michel, 6
Lartigue, Jacques Henri, 236–7
"Last Ink" (*HW*), 96–7
"Late Movies with Skyler" (*TTK*, *CP*), 83, 105
Lecker, Robert, 3–42, 149, 225
Leonard, Elmore, 134
Leonard Cohen (*LC*), 22–5, 28, 132, 261n1

462 Index

Leone, Sergio, 174, 186n1

"Letters & Other Worlds" (CP), 5, 39, 56, 82–3, 85, 132

Letters to a Young Poet (Rilke), 4, 32–3, 85–6. See also *Tin Roof* (S), and Rilke

Levinas, Emmanuel: overview, 12, 16, 17, 36–7, 282–97; alterity, 17, 283, 286–9, 295–7; eros and the feminine, 295–6; ethics of the other, 284–6, 296–7; ex-centric modes of seeing, 16, 232; the face, 12, 17, 285–90; heteronomy, 296–7; imperialism of the same, 235–6; mourning, 283–4, 290–1; otherness, 17, 36–7, 282–5, 287, 290; patience, 283–6, 291–3; responsibility, 284–5; time and death, 283, 290–1; *Totality and Infinity*, 16, 282; "Trace of the Other," 285; war and violence, 284–5, 292–3. See also *English Patient, The* (EP), Derrida and Levinas in dialogic field.

Li, Yiyun, 82, 89

"Light" (TTK, CP), 39, 61–2, 104

liminality, 16–17. See also *Anil's Ghost* (AG), liminality and ghosts; *English Patient, The* (EP), ghosts and liminality; *Warlight* (WL), ghosts and liminality

Lindstrom-Best, Varpu, 271

Long Poem Anthology, The, 130, 158

long poems. See *Collected Works of Billy the Kid, The* (CW); *Coming Through Slaughter* (CS)

"Loop" (TTK, CP), 104–5, 263

Löschnigg, Martin, 17–18, 317–32

Lost Classics, 157

Louvel, Liliane, 242–3

Love Clinic (script, Ondaatje), 175

MacLulich, T.D., 6, 191–2

Manguel, Alberto, 91

Mannur, Anita, 272

man with seven toes, the (tmst): creatures, 100; publication and adaptation notes, 159, 247; violence, 79–80; writing period and style, 34, 52, 79–80, 97

maps motif, 137–8, 143, 289, 294, 319, 365, 389–90, 395n37, 404

Marais, Mike, 114–15, 383, 387–92, 395n32

Marinkova, Milena, 222, 282

Marino, Pierpaolo, 213, 216

Marks, Laura, 242

Marquez, Gabriel Garcia, 96, 171, 173n36

Marquis, Donald, 250–1, 262n23

Marshall, John, 130

"Martinique, The" (DM), 25

Mason, Jody, 11, 17, 35, 263–81

Mbembe, Achille, 348, 354n20, 354n26

McCann, Colum, 83

McClennan, Sophia A., 338, 353n5

McGill, Robert, 52

McVey, Christopher, 101–2, 109, 114–15, 223, 329

melancholia. See *Anil's Ghost* (AG), postcolonial melancholia

memoir. See *Running in the Family* (RF)

Menand, Louis, 7–8

Merton, Thomas, 85, 91, 94

Merwin, W.S., 82, 88, 96, 97, 159

metanarratives, 155–6, 162, 171, 225, 329–31, 356

migrants and migration: audiences for films, 204–5; desire for home, 11; facelessness, 33–4; melancholic migrant, 196; native vs. foreign workers, 263; photography as moving feeling, 205–6; postmodern aesthetics, 266, 272–3, 276; resistance to realism, 35; rewriting of marginal experience, 264; visibility/invisibility, 33–4. *See also* diasporic writing; nomads

Milosz, Czeslow, 94–5, 96

Minghella, Anthony: adaptation of EP novel, 16, 180–6, 189n16, 189n20, 190n21; career, 178–9, 188n7, 190n22; commentary on DVD of EP, 189n17; EP film director and writer, 177–9; Ondaatje's friendship, 178, 187n4, 361. *See also English Patient, The* (film, Minghella)

Miramax, 179, 188n9, 188n11

Mitre, The (student magazine), 20

Morgan, Michael L., 286

mothers. *See* children and parents

motives for writing. *See* writing and happiness (Do you want to be happy and write?)

Mufti, Aamir, 119

Muir, Edwin, 144

Murch, Walter: overview, 161–2, 187n5; adaptations as new creations, 202–3; *Apocalypse Now*, 161–2, 187n5, 363; atomic bomb excision in EP film, 184–6, 190nn26–7; career, 12, 15–16, 161–2, 187n5, 202–4; digital editing, 187n5; editing the "whole jigsaw," 169; emotional

motion, 202–3; Ondaatje's friendship, 161–2, 178, 187n5; *Touch of Evil* restoration, 187n5, 363; unfilmed essential scenes, 162. *See also Conversations: Walter Murch and the Art of Editing Film, The* (TC)

music and sound: overview, 16; edges of sound, 172n13; historiographic metafiction, 5, 248; intermediality, 16, 211–12, 217, 223, 225–6; listening to what can be left out, 88; metaphor for writing, 66, 248; photos and expectations of, 250; *schwer* (difficulty), 322, 379; sonic landscapes, 22, 25. *See also* intermediality

names: overview, 397–8; as broken symbols, 398, 410; gendering, 398; intertextuality, 169; lists of the disappeared, 338–9; maps motif, 137–8, 143, 289, 294, 319, 365, 389–90, 395n37; namelessness, 114–15, 397–8; nicknames, 398, 405; Ondaatje's Dutch name, 199; place names, 143, 294, 398; translations, 367; withholding in preludes, 165; wordplay (hana), 143–4; wordplay (Webb/web), 254, 262n14

Neruda, Pablo, 86

Neumann, Birgit, 16, 228–44

New Wave Canada, 21

Nichol, bp, 6, 158, 175–6

"Nine Sentiments, The" (HW), 73, 92–3

Nixon, Rob, 229

464 Index

Nodelman, Perry, 6, 192–3
nomads: overview, 11, 17, 35, 263–4; immobile female nomads, 35, 202, 277–8; movement vs location, 266, 277–8; nomadic metaphysics, 35, 263–4, 266–7; obscuring of material history, 11, 35, 264, 266–7, 276, 278; postmodern aesthetics, 266, 272–3, 276. *See also* diasporic writing; *In the Skin of a Lion* (*SL*), nomads
nonfiction and memoir. See *Conversations: Walter Murch and the Art of Editing Film, The* (*TC*); *Leonard Cohen* (*LC*); *Running in the Family* (*RF*)
Norris, Ken, 131, 149
novels: overview, 7–9, 23–5, 30–8, 366–7; characters as unknowable, 372–3; convergent and divergent plots, 166–71; critical commentary overview, 6–10; discovery process, 155, 158, 160, 167; endings, 162–4; historiographic metafiction, 5, 11–12, 220–2, 248–51, 264–5; motion and stillness, 162–3; music and sound, 77, 172; preludes, 164–5; stories edited into existence, 165–6, 168, 169, 172n13; structure and patterns, 160–1, 163–4; time shifts, 169–71; visuality, 15–16, 160–5; writing and editing, 15–16, 155–6, 158, 162, 303. *See also* characters; names; story and plot; writing and editing; writing and happiness (Do you want to be happy and write?)

novels, early: overview, 23–5, 30–3, 366–7; critical commentary overview, 6–10; long poems, 23–5, 30–3, 49, 247, 355; personal rebellions, 366; self-referentiality, 9, 35–6; writing and happiness, 40; writing period and style, 23–5, 366–7, 375–8. *See also Collected Works of Billy the Kid, The* (*CW*); *Coming Through Slaughter* (*CS*)
novels, late: overview, 36, 366–7; characters as orphans or without family, 36, 39–41, 367; coming-of-age stories, 367; critical commentary overview, 6–10; liminality, 16; sentimental values, 367; trauma, 36–7, 367; writing period and style, 35–7, 366–7. *See also Cat's Table, The* (*CT*); *Divisadero* (*D*); *Warlight* (*WL*)
novels, middle: overview, 33–8, 366–7; authenticity, 36; communal life, 9, 33, 294; critical commentary overview, 6–10; diasporic writing, 33–4; historical detail, 34–5; liminality, 16; migrant experience, 33–4; moral issues, 34; politicized characters, 35–6; resistance to realism, 35; trauma, 18; writing and happiness, 34, 40; writing period and style, 9, 33–6, 366–7. *See also Anil's Ghost* (*AG*); *English Patient, The* (*EP*); *In the Skin of a Lion* (*SL*)
Nyman, Jopi, 120

"Oh Little Bear" (Highway), 61
Ondaatje, Christopher (Michael's brother), 143, 167

Ondaatje, Enid Doris Gratiaen (Michael's mother), 61, 97, 196–7

Ondaatje, Gillian (Michael's sister), 167

Ondaatje, Griffin (Michael's son), 60–1

Ondaatje, Janet (Michael's sister), 167

Ondaatje, Kim Jones (Michael's first wife), 19, 131

Ondaatje, Mervyn (Michael's father): forgiveness and empathy, 56, 60; postcard-joke, 196–7; troubled legacy, 4–5, 14, 51–2, 56, 67, 71, 132, 263

Ondaatje, Michael: ancestry and heritage, 48, 70, 72–5, 199; archives, 156; awards and recog nition, 7, 34, 72, 174; biogra phy, 6; celebrity, 9, 22–5, 27–9, 34, 72; education, 6, 20, 21, 144, 157; health, 54l; life in Sri Lanka, 33, 51, 72–5, 93–4; mar riage to Kim, 19, 131; marriage to Linda Spalding, 19, 70, 131, 133, 141–2, 157; personal quali ties, 21, 25, 45–9; travels, 143. *See also* Ondaatje, Mervyn (Michael's father); *Running in the Family* (RF); writing and hap piness (Do you want to be happy and write?)

—AS WRITER AND EDITOR: career, 8–10, 174. *See also* nov els; poetry; writing and editing; writing and editing, connections to filmmaking; writing and hap piness (Do you want to be happy and write?)

—EDITOR: overview, 19, 157–60; anthologies, 157–8; *Brick* literary magazine, 19, 133, 157, 394n16; Coach House Press, 6, 157, 159; *Quarry* co-editor, 157

—FILMMAKER. *See* film and filmmaking, Ondaatje's; film and filmmaking, Ondaatje's, works

—NONFICTION AND MEMOIR: commentary on Leonard Cohen, 22–5, 28, 132, 261n1; memoir, 13–14, 16, 71, 84–5, 196–200. See also *Running in the Family* (RF)

—NOVELS. *See* novels; novels, early; novels, late; novels, middle

—POETRY. *See* poetry; poetry, early; poetry, middle and late

"One Art" (Bishop), 159, 172n14

One Hundred Years of Solitude (Garcia Marquez), 171, 173n36

O'Riley, Michael, 326

paintings and drawings: overview, 16, 211–12; artificiality, 21–2, 25; Caravaggio's works, 235, 287, 289; Caravaggism (light and dark), 219–21, 289; medie val tapestry, 241; Rousseau's works, 59; tableaus, 222–3. *See also* intermediality

paradise: overview, 119–20; Abrahamic religions, 119–20, 125–7, 128n9; access and con quest, 118–20, 124–5, 127; diasporic writing, 119–22; Edenic places, 119, 124, 127, 319–20; expulsion from,

119–20, 127, 128n9; female body, 14, 118–28; food, 119–20; loss and return, 120–4, 128n11; Sri Lanka as paradise, 118, 121; walled gardens, 119, 124, 127
parents. *See* children and parents
pedagogy: overview, 40–1, 396–403; care and compassion, 409, 411n15; democratic epistemology, 40, 396–9, 402–3, 410, 410n1, 411n7, 412n17; difference and repetition, 400–2; heterotopia, 396, 398–404, 407, 409–10, 410nn1–2; orientalism, 231, 237, 248, 366, 374; rational vs. imaginative thought, 407–9; responsible knowledge, 402–3; self-discovery, 400–1, 409–10; uncertainty and learning to live, 40–1, 393n13, 397, 400–4, 407–10, 411n4. See also *Warlight* (WL), pedagogical approaches
Perera, Rosalin, 73, 75, 93–4
Personal Fictions, 158
Pesch, Josef, 183–4, 186, 190nn26–7
"Peter" (TTK), 54–6
Petermann, Emily, 213
Petroff, Lillian, 278n3
"Philoctetes on the Island" (TTK, CP), 82, 86
photography: overview, 16, 191–6, 205–6; Benjamin's aura and faces, 31, 249, 254–5; diasporic writing, 197–8; fascination, 249–51; historiographic metafiction, 5, 31, 248, 254–6; intermediality, 16, 31, 211–12, 217, 236–7, 386–7, 390; light and dark, 200,

219–20; metaphor for writing, 248, 254–6; mirror/window/photograph motifs, 216–17; movement and stillness, 191–5, 200–1; for narrative expansion, 217; perspective, 236–7; physical reversals, 250–1; postmodern aesthetics, 49–50, 192–5; presence of absence, 220, 249, 254–6; proximity and distance, 31, 249–50, 254–6; snapshot aesthetic, 237; tableaus, 201–2; theory of moving feeling, 192–5, 201, 205–6; "unborn photographs," 220. See also intermediality
Phu, Thy, 195
Pig Glass, 52, 100
plots, convergent and divergent, 166–71. *See also* story and plot
"Poetics against the Angel of Death" (Webb), 66, 149
poetry: overview, 7–9, 12–15, 18–22, 27, 45–9; authenticity of writing, 4, 22, 36, 40, 84; circulation of solitude, curiosity, and language, 77–8, 83–4; critical commentary overview, 6–10, 47–9, 74; curiosity in writing, 77–8; deep feeling, 74; editorial objectivity, 158–9; evolution of poetics, 48–51; failure of language, 20–1, 25–6, 29; historiographic metafiction, 5, 11–12, 248; punctuation, 159–60; self-doubt, 21–2, 29; self-referentiality, 5, 18–33, 34, 48–9; silences in, 89–90, 148; time and heterogeneity, 90; transformation of scale, 81–2; writing and editing

Index 467

processes, 15–16, 158–60, 172n14; writing and happiness, 3–4; writing period and style, 45–9, 72–5, 97. *See also* writing and editing; writing and happiness (Do you want to be happy and write?)

poetry, early: overview, 23–5, 34, 47–8; celebrity status of artist, 24–5, 27–9, 34; confessional voice, 5; critical commentary overview, 6–10, 47–9; desire for perfection, 28–33; feminism, 89–90; long poems, 23–5, 30–3, 49, 247, 355; multiculturalism, 47–8; mythopoeic aesthetics, 144; postmodern aesthetics, 5, 9, 14–15; publication notes, 25; self-destructiveness, 27–33, 34; self-referentiality, 5, 18–33, 34; shift in representations of women, 61; violence and the macabre, 13, 24–6, 34, 47–8; writing period and style, 45–9. *See also* Collected Works of Billy the Kid, The (CW); Coming Through Slaughter (CS); Dainty Monsters, The (DM); *man with seven toes, the (tmst)*; There's a Trick with a Knife I'm Learning to Do (TTK)

poetry, middle and late: communal and domestic life, 45–9, 73–5; critical commentary overview, 6–10, 47–9; isolated settings, 29, 32–3, 65–6, 85–6, 132; poetic autobiography, 25; publication notes, 34; Sri Lankan culture, 48, 73–5, 88–98; writing period and style, 45–9, 72–5, 97. See

also *Handwriting* (HW); *Running in the Family* (RF); *Secular Love* (S); *Tin Roof* (S); *Tin Roof* (S), and Rilke

"Postcard from Piccadilly Street" (TTK), 106

postcolonial writing: overview, 37–8, 299; Butler's frames, 234–5, 354n27; ex-centric modes of seeing, 16, 229–30, 232–7; excision of atomic bomb from EP film, 184–6, 190nn26–7; gender and power, 240–1; intermediality, 228–30, 237–40; pedagogical approaches, 396, 402–3; postcolonial crypts (death-worlds), 37–8, 326–7, 337, 339–43, 346, 348–52, 353nn6–7; postcolonial pessimism, 348, 354n18; redirected seeing (aisthēsis), 228–30; socio-political power of seeing, 229–30; stereotypes of civilizational difference, 10, 336–7, 343–52; subalternity, 337, 343–51, 353n3, 354n24; trauma, 17–18; visibility/invisibility, 234–5, 240. See also *Anil's Ghost* (AG), postcolonial melancholia; colonialism; diasporic writing; trauma

postmodern aesthetics: overview, 9–10, 192–5; dualities, 193–4; emotion, 193–5; historiographic metafiction, 5, 11–12, 248, 264; history, 212, 266; multimedia, 212; nomads, 266, 272–3, 276; photography, 49–50, 192–5; repetition, 266; self-referentiality, 5, 266; shift from realism, 9, 192,

264; writing period and style, 5, 9, 14–15. See also *Collected Works of Billy the Kid, The* (CW)

"Prayer for My Daughter, A" (Yeats), 55

Proust, Marcel, 120, 128n11, 236–7, 399–402, 405, 407–8

Proust and Signs (Deleuze), 399–402, 405–9

pyramids, human, 84–5, 198–200, 201, 205

Queen's University, 21, 144, 157

"Rabbit as King of the Ghosts, A" (Stevens), 81–2

Radforth, Ian, 269, 271–2, 278n3

Rae, Ian, 4–5, 8, 14–15, 19, 130–51

"Rainy Night Talk" (S), 395n33

Rajewsky, Irina, 211, 226n1

Rancière, Jacques, 92, 230, 240–1

Ratheiser, Ulla, 8, 11, 14, 118–29

Rat Jelly (RJ), 52–3, 100, 132, 159, 257, 263

"Rat Jelly" (TTK), 53

Ratwatte, Florence, 121

Rauwerda, Antje M., 13, 100–17

"Reading *The English Patient*" (Schwieler), 396, 399–400, 402–3, 410n1

Redhill, Michael, 157

religious traditions. *See* Buddhist and Tantric influences

Renger, Nicola, 280n30

"Respect of Landscapes, The" (DM), 25

Rexroth, Kenneth, 148

RF. See *Running in the Family* (RF)

Richie, Donald, 88, 203

Rilke, Rainer Maria, 3–4, 19–20. See also *Tin Roof* (S), and Rilke

"Rock Bottom" (S), 19–21, 67–70, 86–7, 107, 114

Romanticism, 134–6

Rooke, Constance, 256–7

Rousseau, Henri, 21–2, 25, 59

Roy, Kaushik, 301

Running in the Family (RF): overview, 13–14, 16, 70–1, 84–5, 196–200; as autobiography, 16, 25, 33, 62, 64, 70–1, 167, 196–9; colonialism, 199–200, 229–30, 350, 354n25; comic scenes, 71; communal life, 84–5, 198–200, 354n25, 386; convergent and divergent plots, 167; endings, 203; handwriting, Ondaatje's mother's, 97; his father's troubled legacy, 14, 51, 62, 64, 71; historiographic metafiction, 84–5, 88, 261n4, 354n25; human pyramid, 84–5, 198–200, 201; movement and stasis, 84–5, 191, 196–200, 201, 263; parents' postcard-joke, 196–7; partying, 64; photography, 191, 196–200, 354n25, 386; postcolonial literature, 350, 386; postmodern aesthetics, 84–5, 88; prelude, 164–5; publication notes, 14; Sri Lankan culture, 70, 199–200, 350; visuality, 228–30; women, 70–1; writing period and style, 84

—POEMS: "Final Days / Father Tongue," 51; "Women Like You," 70. See also "Cinnamon Peeler, The" (CP)

Rushdie, Salman, 119, 356

S. See Secular Love (S)

Said, Edward, 231, 237, 248, 366, 374, 396

Salgado, Minoli, 395n40

"Sallie Chisum / Last Words on Billy the Kid" (*TTK*), 61

"Saturday" (S), 67

Schmitt, Carl, 288–90, 396

Schönfelder, Christa, 377

Schumann, Robert, 322

Schwab, Gabriele, 299, 305

Schwieler, Elias, 18, 40–1, 396–412

Scobie, Stephen, 6, 51, 186n1, 250

Secular Love (S): overview, 3–5, 14–15, 62–72, 85–7, 130–49; acknowledgments, 143–4; Asian poetics, 65, 132, 142–9; attunement to surroundings, 137–8; bamboo motif, 65, 145–9; community of artists, 137, 139–41, 148–9; confessional voice, 3–5, 14, 19–20, 69, 132; creatures, 63, 65, 85, 100, 113; critical response, 131, 135–6, 149; epigraphs, 63, 134; existential crisis, 32–3, 85–6, 132–3, 137, 142; failure of language, 20–1, 25–6, 29; father's troubled legacy, 64, 65, 71, 85, 132; marital crisis, 4–5, 64, 66–9, 133, 140, 147, 206; muses and models, 66–7, 85–6, 132, 135, 146–7, 149; narrative shifts (1st/3rd person), 4, 86, 135–6, 140; new community life, 69–72; new love, 65, 67, 68–70, 87, 132–5, 141–2, 147; photographic and cinematic images, 106–7, 136–7, 205–6; poetic forms, 4–5, 14–15, 87, 141, 144, 148–9; publication notes, 14, 130–1, 159; river and change, 63, 85, 94, 113; role models and muses, 132, 146–7; self-destructiveness, 26–7, 31–3, 66–7, 85, 86, 131–4, 138–9, 142, 147, 149; self-referentiality, 18–19; solitude, 3–4, 32–3, 65–6, 85–7, 132; structure in movements, 62–3, 65, 67–8, 69–70; title, 67, 87; wind chimes motif, 65, 137, 145; writing and happiness, 3–5, 14, 27, 40; writing period and style, 66, 97, 132, 148–9. *See also* writing and happiness (Do you want to be happy and write?)

—POEMS: "All along the Mazinaw," 87; "Birch Bark," 302; "Claude Glass," 63–4, 85–6, 94, 106–7, 113, 205–6, "Concessions, The," 39, 69–71; "A Dog in San Francisco," 87; "Escarpment," 112; "Her House," 86–7; "Inner Tube," 111–12; "Insomnia," 110; "Rainy Night Talk," 395n33; "Rock Bottom," 19–21, 67–9, 86–7, 107, 114; "To a Sad Daughter," 55, 87; "Saturday," 67; "7 or 8 Things I know about Her / A Stolen Biography," 87; "Skin Boat," 69–72, 87; "(space in which we have dissolved – does it taste of us?, the)," 19–20; "Women Like You," 70. *See also* "Cinnamon Peeler, The" (*CP*); *Tin Roof* (S); *Tin Roof* (S), and Rilke

Sedgwick, Eve Kasofsky, 74

470 Index

Seneviratne, Seni, 120, 128n16

sentimental fiction: overview, 367–78; democratization of care, 375, 377–8; downgrading of domestic, 74; enchantment response, 367, 370–1, 378; incomplete knowledge of others, 376–7; intimacy, 375–8; orphans or without family, 39–41, 367–8; realism and verisimilitude, 372–3, 377–8; secrets and mysteries, 367–70, 374–6; trauma, 367–74, 377–8; truth in feelings, 376–7; writing period and style, 38, 366–7, 375–8

"7 or 8 Things I Know about Her / A Stolen Biography" (S), 87

sewing motif, 313, 329, 330, 402, 405, 406–8, 411n15

sexualized violence, 54–6, 257

Shakespeare, William, 72

Sherlock Holmes, 379–80, 385

Shohat, Ella, 119

Siemerling, Winfried, 8, 11–12, 16, 31, 247–62

"Signature" (TTK), 54

"Skin Boat" (S, CP), 69–72, 87

Skin of a Lion. See In the Skin of a Lion (SL)

Slater, Philip, 68

Slaughter, Joseph R., 338

smell, 70, 120, 122–4, 126–8, 128n16

Snyder, Gary, 147–8

"Social Call," 20

Solecki, Sam, 6, 57, 79, 87, 97, 105, 116, 141–3, 156, 256

Solie, Karen, 7, 8, 13, 26, 77–99

"Song of Solomon" (Bible), 125–7

Sons of Captain Poetry, The (film, Ondaatje), 156, 174, 175–6

Sontag, Susan, 249

Sorensen, Eli Park, 299

"(space in which we have dissolved – does it taste of us?, the)" (S), 19–20

Spalding, Esta, 157

Spalding, Linda (Michael's wife), 19, 131, 133, 141–2, 157

Spearey, Susan, 266–7

Spencer, Stanley, 23

Spicer, Jack, 141

"Spider Blues" (TTK), 27–8, 254

Spinks, Lee, 6, 102–3, 116, 117n12, 320, 323, 325, 381

Spivak, Gayatri, 353n3, 354n24

Sri Lanka: Ceylon as colonial term, 121; cinnamon, 120–3, 128n16, 129n21; civil war (1983–2009), 300, 326–7, 348, 353nn1–2; dogs as magical transformations, 109; Ondaatje's ancestors, 199; as paradise, 121–2; sapphires, 109; Sigiriya Rock, 70; Sinhalese, Tamil, and Sanskrit culture, 70, 73–5, 92–3, 143, 300. See also Buddhist and Tantric influences; Handwriting (HW)

stardom. See celebrity

"Step" (HW), 95–6

Stepanova, Maria, 90

Sterba, Christopher M., 51

Sternberg, Douglas, 189n16

Stevens, Wallace, 5, 26, 80, 81–2, 132

Story, The (TS), 95

story and plot: overview, 160–72, 179–80, 398–401; alternative possibilities, 162, 164, 171; body

Index

471

as story, 168–9, 327, 329–31; chance and luck, 167, 407–9; classical film conventions, 179–80, 189n13; closure, 384, 393n15; convergent and divergent plots, 166–71; disappearances, 167–9; editing into existence, 166, 168–9; expectation and delay, 171; families, 167; heterotopic stories, 399–401; incompleteness and mysteries, 95–6, 162, 164, 259–61, 329, 368–9, 404–7; names as story, 398; narrative fragments, 166, 329, 404–5, 409–10; self-discovery, 400–2; signs as clues, 401–2, 405–7, 409–10; themes, 402. *See also* uncertainty and ambiguity

"Strange Case, The" (*TTK*), 107

style. *See* novels; poetry; writing and editing; writing and editing, connections to filmmaking

subalternity, 337, 343–51, 353n3, 354n24

Summers-Bremner, Eluned, 100

Surani, Moez, 18, 35–6, 38, 39, 366–78

Tacitus's *Annals*, 304, 309

Tantric influences. *See* Buddhist and Tantric influences

TC. See *Conversations: Walter Murch and the Art of Editing Film, The* (TC)

teaching. *See* pedagogy; *Warlight* (WL), pedagogical approaches

Testa, Bart, 12, 15–16, 174–89

Theatre Passe Muraille, 176–7

There's a Trick with a Knife I'm Learning to Do (TTK): overview, 52–61; celebrity, 27–8; comic scenes, 52–3, 106; cover image, 53; creatures, 53–4, 57–9, 104, 106–7, 110–11; desire for perfection, 27; domestic and communal life, 53–61; forgiveness and empathy, 53, 55–6, 60–1; materiality of the world, 54, 57, 59–60; publication notes, 52–3; self-referentiality, 27–8, 53, 56, 58–60; violence, 52–8, 60; women, 53–6, 61; writing and happiness, 27; writing period and style, 52–3, 56–7

—POEMS: "Bearhug," 39, 60–1; "Biography," 110; "Breaking Green," 57–8, 59; "Buying the Dog," 110–11; "Country Night," 110–11; "Early Morning, Kingston to Gananoque," 61; "Four Eyes," 106; "'gate in his head, the,'" 6, 9, 23, 31, 62, 79, 194; "Loop," 104–5, 263; "Peter," 54–6; "Postcard from Piccadilly Street," 106; "Rat Jelly," 53; "Sallie Chisum / Last Words on Billy the Kid," 61; "Signature," 54; "Spider Blues," 27–8, 254; "Strange Case, The," 107; "Walking to Bellrock," 56–7, 78, 111–12; "War Machine," 53, 104; "White Dwarfs," 23, 24, 26–7, 56, 79, 132

Thomas, Kristin Scott, 188n8

Tiffin, Helen, 125

Tin Roof (S): overview, 3–5, 14–15, 65–7, 130–49; affective mapping approach, 131, 136, 138–40; Asian poetics, 65, 132, 142–9; bamboo motif, 65, 145–9; cinematic vantage point, 136–7; community of artists, 137, 139–41, 148–9; confessional voice, 4–5, 19–20; critical response, 131, 135–6; existential crisis, 3–5, 32–3, 86, 132–3, 137, 142; Imagism, 144–5; marital crisis, 4–5, 19, 64, 66–9, 133, 140, 147, 206; publication notes, 14, 130–1; role models and muses, 132, 146–7; Romantic conventions, 135–6; self-destructiveness, 26–7, 31–3, 66–7, 85, 86, 131–4, 138–9, 142, 147, 149; self-referentiality, 18–19; sentimental values, 375; solitude, 32–3, 65–6, 85–6, 132; violence in nature, 133–4; wind chimes motif, 65, 137, 145; wordplay (hana), 143–4; writing and happiness, 3–5, 14, 27, 40. See also *Secular Love* (*S*)

—AND RILKE: overview, 3–4, 19–20, 140–1; community of melancholics, 137, 140–1; confessional voice, 4–5, 19–20; descent into self, 3–4, 19–20; *Duino Elegies*, 3–4, 19–20, 86, 94, 130–1, 140–1; existential question for writers, 19–20, 32–3, 66–7, 86, 132; *Letters to a Young Poet*, 4, 32–3, 85–6; "live by the heart," 65–6, 134–5; Ondaatje's copy of *Duino Elegies*, 19, 131; serial poem, 66, 141; solitude, 32–3, 65–6, 85–6, 132; writing and happiness, 3–4

tmst. See *man with seven toes, the* (*tmst*)

"To Anuradhapura" (*HW*), 87

"To a Sad Daughter" (*S*), 55, 87

"To His Mistress Going to Bed" (Donne), 118, 127

Torok, Maria, 341–2, 343, 353n6

Tötösy de Zepetnek, Steven, 6, 282

touch, 222, 241–2

trauma: overview, 10, 18, 299–301, 377–8; characters as orphans or without family, 36, 39–41; double gesture of past and present, 102; enchantment response, 367, 370–1, 378; ethnocentric blindness, 326–7; intimacy challenges, 36, 367–70, 375–8; pain and beauty, 18; secrets and mysteries, 367–70, 374–6; as spectre of colonialism, 326–7; unassimilated events, 329; verisimilitude, 372–3, 377–8; wildness of traumatized, 373; writing period and style, 35–6, 37–8, 366–7, 375–8. See also *Anil's Ghost* (*AG*), postcolonial melancholia; care and compassion

TS. See *Story, The* (*TS*)

TTK. See *There's a Trick with a Knife I'm Learning to Do* (*TTK*)

Tu Fu (Chinese poet), 144, 147–8

uncertainty and ambiguity: identity of protagonist, 180–2; intermedial aesthetics, 232; nonextraneous detail as key, 7; uncertain of life and clarity of mind, 79; uncertainty and learning to live, 40, 397, 398–404, 407–10, 411n4; Webb/web wordplay, 254, 262n14

University of Hawaii, 143
unrecognizability. See *Warlight*
(WL), unrecognizability
"Uswetakeiyawa" (*TTK*, *CP*),
109–10, 112–13

van Manen, Max, 411n15
Verhoeven, W.M., 299
Vetter, Lisa Pace, 309
violence: and beauty, 18, 22, 25,
26–7; early long poems, 24–5,
49–51, 66, 79–80, 193, 248–9;
early poetry, 13, 24–6, 34, 47–8;
metaphor for creative process,
17; romantic self-consciousness,
20; and seeing, 241–2; sexualized violence, 54–6, 257;
violence in nature, 133–4, 218;
writing period and style, 47–8.
See also trauma; war
visuality: overview, 15–16, 228–30;
aisthēsis (redirected seeing),
228–30; close-ups, 165; colonialism, 229–30; ekphrasis, 200,
232, 238–42; eroticism of seeing,
241; ex-centric modes of seeing,
16, 229–30, 232–7; haptic
aesthetics, 222, 241–2; socio-political power of seeing, 229–33;
visibility/invisibility, 234–5, 240;
writing and editing process,
15–16, 160–6. *See also* film and
filmmaking; intermediality;
writing and editing, connections
to filmmaking
Volkan, Vamik, 103–4

Walcott, Derek, 82
"Walking to Bellrock" (*TTK*, *CP*),
56–7, 78, 111–12

war: overview, 17–18, 300–1;
atomic bomb, 158, 184–6,
190nn26–7, 221–3, 287, 323,
365; Levinas on war and violence, 284–5, 292–3; nationalism, 288–90; pain and beauty,
18; persistence of war, 17–18,
317–19, 321–5, 330–1; "reason
for war was war," 304–6, 316n6,
324, 348; Sri Lankan civil war,
300, 326–7, 348, 353nn1–2; war
machine, 273–4, 280n32,
280nn27–8. *See also Anil's
Ghost* (AG); *English Patient, The*
(EP); *Warlight* (WL)
Warlight (WL): overview, 18,
39–41, 299–301, 312–15, 373–
4; anarchic life, 321–2, 374;
Bildungsroman, 231–2, 325;
chance, 407–9; characters as
unknowable, 376–7; convergent
and divergent plots, 167; crime,
320–1, 373–4, 382, 387, 391,
398; detached compassion, 37,
301, 313–15; detective mystery,
39–41, 379–82, 384–6, 391–2;
disappearances, 168, 319, 383–
4; dogs, 114–15, 313, 321, 328,
377; East-West dialectic, 37,
299–301, 312–15; enchantment
response, 367, 370–1, 378;
endings, 301, 312–13, 380, 383–
5, 406–10; gardens and nature,
312–13, 383–7, 390–1;
incompleteness of story, 405–7;
intermediality, 322, 386–7, 389,
390; intimacy, 375–8; landscapes, 318–21; maps motif,
319, 389–90, 404; metanarratives, 329–31; names, 321, 380,

382, 384, 386, 388, 398, 405; narrative fragments, 329–31, 404–5; photography, 386–7, 390; rational and imaginative thought, 403–4, 407–9; *schwer* (difficulty), 18, 39–41, 322, 379, 383–4, 392, 392n1, 404, 409–10; secrets and mysteries, 312, 320–1, 325, 329–31, 374, 376–7, 379–82; sentimental values, 375–8; sewing motif, 313, 329, 330, 402, 405, 406–8, 411n15; title, 388; trauma, 39–41, 300, 314–15, 380; uncertainties, 40–1, 383–4, 390, 393n13; unreliable narrator, 383; warlight and shadows, 318, 330–1, 377, 388–92, 395n32, 403–4, 409–10; war's persistence, 317–19, 321–5, 330–1; writing and editing process, 10, 157, 167, 318, 329–31, 393n2; writing period and style, 35–41, 366–7, 375–8

—EAST-WEST DIALECTIC: overview, 18, 37, 299–301, 312–15; detached compassion, 37, 301, 313–15; East-West dialectic, 37, 299–301, 312–13; karma (cyclical suffering), 37, 301, 302, 305, 312–13; responsibility, 37, 304, 314–15. *See also* Buddhist and Tantric influences

—GHOSTS AND LIMINALITY: overview, 17–18, 317–31; blurred boundaries, 317–23, 330–1; ghosts and liminal motifs, 17, 317–18, 321, 325, 328; landscapes, 318–21; warlight and shadows, 318, 330–1, 388–92, 395n32; war's persistence, 317–19, 321–3, 325, 330–1

—PEDAGOGICAL APPROACHES: overview, 18, 396–410; chance and luck, 407–9; democratic epistemology, 40, 396–9, 402–3, 410, 410n1, 411n7, 412n17; friends and enemies, 288–90; heterotopia, 396, 398–404, 407, 409–10, 410nn1–2; orientalism, 231, 237, 248, 366, 374; *schwer* (difficult), 397, 399, 409–10; themes and archetypes, 18; uncertainty and learning to live, 40, 397, 398–404, 407–10, 411n4

—UNRECOGNIZABILITY: overview, 379–92; celebrity, 381–2, 385, 388–9, 392; detective mystery, 379–82, 384–6, 391–2; photography, 386–7, 390; privacy and safety, 380–3, 385–92; *schwer* (difficulty), 322, 379, 383–6, 392, 392n1, 409–10; warlight and shadows, 388–9, 395n32

"War Machine" (*TTK*), 53, 104
Watts, Carl, 58
Webb, Phyllis, 66, 149
"Wells" (*HW*), 73, 75, 93–4
Wertheimer, Eric, 315
"When you drive the Queensborough roads at midnight" (*S*), 57
"White Dwarfs" (*TTK*, *CP*), 23, 24, 26–7, 56, 79, 132
"William Dawe Badlands Expedition 1916, The" (script, Ondaatje), 156, 160–1, 173n24

Williams, William Carlos, 144
Wilson, Charlie, 177
Witten, Mark, 30
WL. See *Warlight* (WL)
women: body as paradisiacal
dreamland, 14, 118–28; cover
image of TTK, 53; elegy for
Ondaatje's mother, 61; gendered
emotion, 68; immobile nomadic
women, 35, 202, 277–8; karma
and violence, 305; Levinas's feminine and eros, 295; misrepresentation in early poetry, 61;
nomads and violent lovemaking,
274–5, 278; sexualized violence,
54–6; writing period and style,
47–8, 61
"Women Like You" (RF), 70
wonder and curiosity, 77–8, 86–8,
91–2, 160, 360
writing and editing: overview,
15–17, 18–22, 155–60; curiosity,
77–8, 87–8, 91; descent into self,
3–4, 19–20, 77–8; discovery process, 4, 80, 88, 155, 158, 160;
failure of language, 20–1, 25–6,
29; fear of wordlessness, 26,
82–3, 87; illusion of effortlessness, 171–2; invisibility of process, 155, 157; metaphors for,
17, 155; Ondaatje's sources,
manuscripts, and notebooks, 21,
156; self-construction over
self-expression, 88; as simultaneous processes, 21, 155–6, 158–9,
171; solitude, 77, 82; visuality,
15–16. *See also* novels; poetry;
writing and editing, connections
to filmmaking; writing and

happiness (Do you want to be
happy and write?)
—CONNECTIONS TO FILMMAK-
ING: overview, 15–16, 156, 160–
6, 204; assembly of whole story,
15–16, 156, 160–2, 166, 169,
204; convergent and divergent
plots, 166–71; editing story into
existence, 165–6, 168, 169,
172n13; elliptical scenes, 162,
170; endings, 162–4, 180;
motion and stillness, 15, 161–3,
202, 204; preludes, 164–5;
repetition, 160–1; scale, 158,
162; sound, 172n13; structure,
156, 160–6, 170–1; time shifts,
170–1, 181–2, 189n16; univocal
and multivocal narration, 16,
180–2, 189n16; visuality, 15–16,
162–5; writing process, 158,
160–1, 165–6. *See also*
*Conversations: Walter Murch
and the Art of Editing Film, The*
(TC); film and filmmaking
writing and happiness (Do you
want to be happy and write?):
overview, 3–4, 18–22, 27, 40–1;
authenticity of writing, 4, 22, 36,
40, 84; binary (happy vs
unhappy), 146–7; celebrity status, 22–5, 27–9; L. Cohen's
career, 22–5, 28; descent into
self, 4, 19–20; desire for perfection, 28–33; as existential
question, 3–4, 19–20, 32–3,
66–7, 86, 132; failure of language, 20–1, 25–6, 29; luck,
146–7; Rilke's influence, 3–4,
19–20; self-doubt, 21–2, 25–6,

29; self-referentiality, 18–29. See
also *Tin Roof* (S), and Rilke
Wu, Kai-su, 12, 36–7, 282–98

Yeats, William, 55
York, Lorraine: feminist approach,
47–8; photography as moving
feeling, 31, 191–207; reluctant
celebrities, 28, 33, 36, 382–3,
389
Young, David, 159
"Youth" (Conrad), 232–3

Zacheos, Marilena, 52
Zaentz, Saul, 178–9, 188n8,
188n10